DIVINE COVENANT

Themes in Qurʾānic Studies

Series Editors

Mustafa Shah
School of Oriental and African Studies, University of London
Abdul Hakim al-Matroudi
School of Oriental and African Studies, University of London

This series aims to introduce critical issues in the academic study of The Qur'an and offers a variety of topics essential to providing an historical overview of The Qur'an and the interrelated traditional teachings and beliefs which issue from it.

Published

Muslim Qurʾānic Interpretation Today
Media, Genealogies and Interpretive Communities
Johanna Pink

Philosophical Perspectives on Modern Qur'ānic Exegesis
Key Paradigms and Concepts
Massimo Campanini

The Qur'an and Kerygma
Biblical Receptions of the Muslim Scripture across a Millennium
Jeffrey Einboden

Forthcoming

Prophets and Prophecy in the Qurʾān
Narratives of Divine Intervention in the Story of Humankind
Anthony H. Johns

Sufism and Scripture
A Historical Survey of Approaches to the Qurʾān in the Sufi Tradition
Harith Bin Ramli

DIVINE COVENANT

SCIENCE AND CONCEPTS OF NATURAL LAW IN THE QUR'AN AND ISLAMIC DISCIPLINES

Ulrika Mårtensson

equinox

SHEFFIELD UK BRISTOL CT

Published by Equinox Publishing Ltd.

UK: Office 415, The Workstation, 15 Paternoster Row, Sheffield, South Yorkshire, S1 2BX
USA: ISD, 70 Enterprise Drive, Bristol, CT 06010

www.equinoxpub.com

First published 2022

British Library Cataloguing-in-Publication Data
A catalogue record for this book is available from the British Library.

ISBN-13 978 1 78179 170 7 (hardback)
978 1 78179 171 4 (paperback)
978 1 80050 081 5 (ePDF)
978 1 80050 110 2 (ePub)

Library of Congress Cataloging-in-Publication Data
Names: Mårtensson, Ulrika, author.
Title: Divine covenant: science and concepts of natural law in the Qur'an and Islamic disciplines / Ulrika Mårtensson.
Description: Bristol: Equinox Publishing Ltd, 2022. | Series: Themes in Qur'anic studies | Includes bibliographical references and index. |
Summary: "Divine Covenant explores the Qur'anic concept of divine knowledge through scientific, theoretical paradigms - in particular natural law theory - and their relationship with seven Islamic scholarly disciplines: linguistics, hadith, politics, history, exegesis, jurisprudence, theology. By comparing scholarship within these disciplines with current state-of-the-art, the study shows how the Qur'anic concept of divine Covenant reflects natural law theory, relates to a range of other legal, political, and linguistic Qur'anic concepts, informs the canon's entire literary structure, and has implications for a new, legal theory of 'Islamic origins'"-- Provided by publisher.
Identifiers: LCCN 2021010140 (print) | LCCN 2021010141 (ebook) | ISBN 9781781791707 (hardback) | ISBN 9781781791714 (paperback) | ISBN 9781800500815 (pdf) | ISBN 9781800501102 (epub)
Subjects: LCSH: Islam and science. | Nature--Religious aspects--Islam. | God (Islam)--Qur'anic teaching.
Classification: LCC BP190.5.S3 M365 2021 (print) | LCC BP190.5.S3 (ebook) | DDC 297.2/65--dc23
LC record available at https://lccn.loc.gov/2021010140
LC ebook record available at https://lccn.loc.gov/2021010141

Typeset by S.J.I. Services, New Delhi, India

CONTENTS

Acknowledgements vii

INTRODUCTION 1

CHAPTER 1
THE WRITING OF HISTORY AND THE 'RELIGIOUS OTHER' 11

CHAPTER 2
QUR'ĀNIC THEORY OF CONCEPT? 31

CHAPTER 3
THE QUR'ĀNIC CANON 52

CHAPTER 4
NATURAL LAW THEORY: QUR'ĀNIC COVENANT REVISITED 98

CHAPTER 5
INSTITUTIONAL PRACTICES 120

CHAPTER 6
THE DISCIPLINES AND 'THE SCIENTIFIC QUR'ĀN' 178

CHAPTER 7
MODERN INSTITUTIONAL SHIFTS 289

CHAPTER 8
CONCLUSIONS 318

Bibliography 341

Index 362

ACKNOWLEDGEMENTS

It is perhaps not the most auspicious way to start a book by saying that writing it has been a fantastic learning experience – after all, an author should be expert on the subject. Nevertheless, during the time I have been committed to writing this book, I have gained a whole new education through Mustafa Shah's generosity and guidance, especially regarding the relationship between Arabic linguistics and Qur'an exegesis. If this book has any merits, Mustafa's erudition has contributed greatly to them, and I thank him and Abd al-Hakim al-Matroudi for the opportunity to write this book for *Themes in Qur'anic Studies*.

I also want to thank several other colleagues, for friendship, collaborations, great meetings, discussions and company, and for sharing knowledge, writings, and time. Though this book is far too cursory to do justice to their contributions, I am deeply indebted to Abdulla Galadari, Haifaa Khalafallah, Ahmed Zalaf, Din Muhammad, Angelika Neuwirth, Michael Marx, Nicolai Sinai, George Khalil, Claude Gilliot, Joseph Lowry, Mehmet Akif Koc, Asma Afsaruddin, Fahad Rumi, Sebastian Günther, Mustansir Mir, Michael Pregill, Tor Ivar Østmoe, Gabriel Levy, Massimo Campanini, Haggai Mazuz, Ramon Harvey, Devin Stewart, David Vishanoff, David Thomas, Jørgen Nielsen, Thomas Hoffmann, Johanne Louise Christiansen, Gerd Marie Ådna, Mona Helen Farstad, Bruce Lawrence, Brett Wilson, Rafey Habib, Khalid Saqi, Saeid Edalatnejad, Stefano Bigliardi, Mohammed Fadel, Charles Weller, Anver Emon, Wardah Alkatiri, Marianne Laanatza, Susanne Olsson, Emin Poljarevic, Jenny Berglund, David Thurfjell, Göran Larsson, Torsten Hylén, Håkan Rydving, Einar Thomassen, Abbas Vali, Mohammad Nafissi, Knut Vikør, Mark Sedgwick, Itzchak Weismann, Oddbjørn Leirvik, Abdulhadi Khalaf, Nora Eggen, Amund Bjørsnes, Rania Maktabi, Fahad Qureshi, Zeshan Qureshi, Bushra Ishaq, Tayeb Berghout, Matri Abroud, Abdi Nur Muhammad, Ahmet Karais, Ismail Cuneyt Güzey, Seyed Jamil Naser and Ahl'O Bayt Trondheim, and Jorunn Jasmin Oksvold. Special thanks are also due to the colleagues at SOAS Centre for Islamic Studies, Professor Abdel Haleem, Helen Blatherwick, Marianna Klar, and Ni'ma Burney, who, in addition to the contributions described above, provide me and so many others with the opportunity to present and discuss our work at their biannual Qur'an conferences.

Furthermore, I have received invaluable comments from anonymous reviewers, and Stefano Bisighin, who kindly agreed to read the first draft. His polite assessment – "it seems interesting, but what is it about?" – helped me focus, as did his suggestion of Eric Hobsbawm. Omar Aysha has edited the text and checked translations, so that any remaining infelicitous ones are entirely my own responsibility. My dear partner Lionel Sacks' critical acumen and learning has also provided frequent sanity checks, such as advising strongly, and based on real experience in Physics, that I desist from arguing that the Qur'anic concept of God as light (Q. 24, 35) could prefigure Einstein's theory of relativity …

Yet I dedicate this book to the memory of another partner: The Midnight Snacker. He was a grey cat with a very noble profile and character, who was homeless but found his way to our cat-flap. He (and his loyal brother) moved in, and made it his job to sleep on the desk beside my laptop, in return for food, a warm and safe home, and love. I am so grateful for his efforts and company over many years.

INTRODUCTION

THE DIVINE COVENANT: RELIGION, SCIENCE, AND CONCEPTS OF POLITICS, LAW, AND LANGUAGE IN THE QUR᾿ĀN.

There exist a great number of books about the Qur᾿ān, at all levels, from primers to in-depth specialised studies. Equally, they cover a wide range of topics and methods, including Qur᾿ānic language, rhetoric, composition and canon history; the Qur᾿ān's relationship with other Arabic literary and oral genres; with the Bibles and Jewish and Christian exegetical literatures; with Sharīʿa and the Islamic scholarly disciplines and exegetical literatures; and its modern and contemporary interpretations, concerned with such issues as social and gender justice, human and animals rights, environment, peace, interfaith dialogue, etc. I work within the discipline of Comparative Religion and the History of Religions, and my particular interests concern how, in the current and modern contexts, to understand and conceptualise historical religious terms and writings.

IS THERE SCIENCE IN THE QUR᾿ĀN?

In my view, one of the most fascinating topics in this respect is how we conceptualise the relationship between 'religion' and 'science', hence I have chosen as the leading question to address in this book: *Is there science in the Qur᾿ān*?

From the viewpoint of modern Religious and Qur᾿ānic studies the question may appear misguided, given that the Qur᾿ān constitutes what these disciplines define as a 'religious scripture', 'sacred text', 'canon', or 'revelation'– but not a 'scientific' text. Yet within the Islamic scholarly disciplines, the Qur᾿ān serves distinctly academic functions. As the famous Egyptian jurist and exegete al-Suyūṭī (d. 910/1505) put it in his treatise on the Qur᾿ānic sciences, *al-Itqān fī ʿulūm al-Qur᾿ān*: the Qur᾿ān is the impetus and reference point for the specific disciplines of jurisprudence (*fiqh*), grammar (*naḥw*), and rhetoric (*balāgha*). Moreover, he argued, it contains accounts (*qiṣaṣ*), reports (*akhbār*), paradigmatic examples (*amthāl*), and warnings (*mawā'iẓ*) which remind the analyst of past lessons and in this way lay the foundations for all the sciences (*'ulūm*) and arts (*funūn*) (al-Suyūṭī 2005/1: 4). According to the Oxford Dictionary's contemporary, general definition, 'science' refers to 'The intellectual and practical activity encompassing the systematic study of the structure and behaviour of the physical and natural world through observation and experiment'. This general definition includes 'A particular area of science', for example 'veterinary science', and 'A systematically organized body of knowledge on a particular subject', for example 'the science of criminology'.[1] The definition can apply fairly straightforwardly to the Islamic disciplines of Sharī'a and jurisprudence, statecraft, systematic theology, philosophy, ethics, Prophetic tradition, history, Arabic language and linguistics, etc., all referred to with the Arabic term *'ilm* (plural *'ulūm*). In both early medieval and modern usage, *'ilm* refers to bodies of knowledge gained through systematic studies of, in most cases, the physical and natural world through observation. With this definition, then, the *application* of the Qur'ān within these disciplines is 'scientific'.

It is therefore not surprising that the question whether there is science in the Qur'ān itself has been answered affirmatively by scholars and scientists affiliated with the modern discourse 'Islamization of science', which I will discuss in Chapter 7. Simply put, some of these scholars argue that Qur'ānic statements about the universe, the natural world, and mankind, accord with modern scientific discoveries and thus prove the divine nature of the Qur'ān—for how could it prefigure modern science if it was not the word of the omniscient God?—and the intrinsically scientific nature of the Islamic scholarly tradition. Some of these scholars also understand the Islamic sciences as offering another, spiritual kind of scientific knowledge than the modern 'western' kind considered 'positivist' (Abaza 2002; Stenberg 1996); while others do not perceive any such epistemic conflict (Bigliardi 2014). In either case, these modern scholars and researchers do not operate with a watertight distinction between the Qur'ān as 'religious scripture' and 'science': they perceive them as overlapping. While I too answer the question in the affirmative, my aim is not to prove the divine nature of the Qur'ān through its scientific aspects. It is simply to explore what kind of new understandings of the Qur'ān results from referring its concepts, including that of prophecy, to scientific disciplines and theories. To some extent, the aim involves comparing approaches taken in some of the early and medieval

1 https://en.oxforddictionaries.com/definition/science, accessed 19 June 2018.

Islamic scholarly disciplines with modern research. In this way, the study addresses the long-standing debate within Islamic and Qurʾānic studies over the nature of the Islamic historical and exegetical studies of the Qurʾān and to what extent they offer scientifically valid knowledge. This consideration of the 'scientific' aspects of the Islamic disciplines has implications not only for Qurʾānic studies, but also for understanding what the disciplines' 'religious' dimension refers to. Thus, the study contributes to general theoretical debates about the concept 'religion' within the discipline Religious studies.

ʿilm

The consonant root *ʿ-l-m* from which derives the above-mentioned term *ʿilm*, in modern and medieval idiom 'science', in the Qurʾān refers to the knowledge that God conveys to prophets and messengers, and they to their peoples. In *Knowledge Triumphant: The Concept of Knowledge in Medieval Islam* (1970), Franz Rosenthal counted *ʿilm* and its related verbal forms as among the Qurʾān's most frequently employed roots, and concluded that it occupies a central place in the message: the faith itself is actually equated with *ʿilm* (Rosenthal 2007/1970: 19–30). Since Qurʾānic *ʿilm* refers to the divine knowledge, it occurs only in the singular form. The post-Qurʾānic scholarly disciplines, however, are referred to with the plural form, *ʿulūm*, 'sciences'. These diverse theoretical sciences, with specific sources and methodologies, were afforded 'religious' legitimacy through their connection with Qurʾānic *ʿilm*, especially as developed in Prophetic *ḥadīth*, at the same time as *ʿilm* became a generic term for all knowledge, including the scientific, systematic kind (Rosenthal 2007/1970: 43 *et passim*). Moreover, as Rosenthal shows throughout his study, there is a semantic relationship between *ʿilm* and *ʿamal*, 'action', 'deeds': a scholar must be virtuous in order for the knowledge to be authoritative, and the knowledge should result in good deeds and beneficial courses of action. Similarly in the Mamlūk lexicographer and administrator Ibn Manẓūr's (d. 711/1311) dictionary *Lisān al-ʿArab* ('Tongue (Language) of the Arabs'). According to him, *ʿilm* in the Qurʾān and generally is the opposite of ignorance (*jahl*) and a source of discernment and understanding for its possessor (*al-ʿilm maḥlama lisāḥibihi*). The active participle *ʿālim*, plural *ʿulamāʾ*, 'those possessing knowledge' or the Islamic scholars, are according to Ibn Manẓūr those among God's servants who fear (*yakhshūna*) Him, and who practice what they know. His Qurʾānic reference here is Q. 35 (*al-Fāṭir*), 28:

> And of people, beasts, and cattle, some are also of different hues; in fact, among His servants it is only **those possessing knowledge (*al-ʿulamāʾ*)** who **fear God**, and God is certainly a Mighty One Who Forgives!

A related Qurʾānic adjectival category is *ʿalīm*. One of Ibn Manẓūr's examples is the prophet Joseph, who has knowledge about God's command (*amr*) and Oneness i.e. he knows that God has no likeness, partner, or counterpart.[2] In the Qurʾān itself, the passage Q. 12 (*Yūsuf*), 21–22 describes how God conveyed knowledge to Joseph about how to interpret reports (*aḥādīth*, sing. *ḥadīth*),[3] and how to pass judgement. Interpretation of *ḥadīth* and the giving of legal rulings belong to the Islamic science of jurisprudence (*fiqh*) and legal hermeneutics (*uṣūl al-fiqh*), which implies that the practical, action-related aspect of the knowledge of interpretation refers to law and administration:[4]

> (21) The one from Egypt who bought [Joseph] said to his wife, 'Make his stay dignified, so that perhaps he will benefit us or we may take him as a son!' In this way We gave Joseph a place in the land, to convey to him **knowledge of the interpretation of reports (*linuʿallimahu taʾwīl al-aḥādīth*)**; so God is in charge over his command, though most people **do not have the knowledge** (*lā yaʿlamūna*).
> (22) When he was fully grown, We gave him judgement (*ḥukm*) and **knowledge (*ʿilm*)**, as that is how We reward **those who enact the good (*al-muḥsinīna*)**.

This special kind of interpretive *ʿilm* that God conveys to those who serve Him by doing what is good (*ḥasan*), sometimes occurs together with references to 'prophecy' and 'study' (*d-r-s*), as in Q. 3 (*Āl ʿImrān*), 79:

> It is impossible for a human vessel of the divine word who God has given the writing, the judgement, and the **prophecy** (*al-kitāb wa al-ḥukm wa* ***al-nubuwwa***), to say to the people: 'Be servants of me instead of God!' Rather, [he would say]: 'Be masters by virtue of **the knowledge** of

2 *Lisān al-ʿArab*, online at www.alwaraq.net, entry ʿ-l-m, p. 3997.

3 In Q. 12, both *aḥādīth*, sing. *ḥadīth*, 'reports', and dreams are subject to *taʾwīl*, 'retrieval of original meaning', in the sense of the meaning that was intended by the communicator of a message, including God; for a discussion of definitions of *taʾwīl*, see Mårtensson (2009b: 36–37). Note that dream interpretation or 'conveyance of visions' (*taʿbīr al-ruʾyā*) was a science in its own right, associated first with the Successor and *ḥadīth* scholar Ibn Sīrīn (d. 110/728); see Fahd, 'Ibn Sīrīn', EI2. Hence, this science too refers to the Qurʾān for origins.

4 For a recent study of *uṣūl al-fiqh* as hermeneutics, including useful research surveys, see Vishanoff (2011).

> the divine writing **you have been conveying**, and by virtue of what you have been **studying** (*kūnū rabbāniyyīna bimā kuntum* ***tu'allimūna*** *al-kitāba wa bimā kuntum* ***tadrusūna***)!'

Consequently, the verse Q. 3, 79 connects *'ilm* with prophecy (*al-nubuwwa*), and specifies that the divine knowledge is conveyed through *study* of 'the writing' or 'the scripture' (*al-kitāb*). I will therefore continue to explore prophecy in the Qur'ān in terms of bodies of systematic knowledge, including the practices of 'observation' and, to some extent, 'experimentation', as these are what the Oxford Dictionary defines as 'science'. Following al-Suyūṭī's lead (see above), my thesis is that the Qur'ānic concept of divine *'ilm* refers to the same kind of systematic knowledge as that associated with the systematic disciplines. More precisely, I will argue that the divine *'ilm* communicated to a people through a prophet and messenger, refers to bodies of systematic knowledge based on observation and experiment regarding the terms of social contract, which regulates the 'place' and functions of the sciences in society. Thus, rather than Qur'ānic *'ilm* offering religious legitimacy for sciences, which operate with a different concept of knowledge, as Rosenthal argued, I will argue the case for generic continuity between Qur'ānic and post-Qur'ānic *'ilm*.[5] My analysis focuses on Qur'ānic concepts related topically to the nature of the divine, creation, covenant, and the significance of 'writing' in recording the history of divine communication through prophets and messengers. I will also use the interpretations of these concepts, by scholars working within the Islamic disciplines, and show how their interpretations relate to research on the Qur'ān within modern 'non-Islamic' academic disciplines.

METHODOLOGY

For methodology, I rely on the discourse theory that the French historian of religion Michel de Certeau (d. 1986) developed in his collection of essays entitled *The Writing of History* (*L'Écriture de l'histoire*, 1975). De Certeau's main field as historian of religion was early modern France in the period 1600s to 1800s. His specific interest was to understand how changes in institutional orders in society produced new forms of conceptualising, writing,

5 The science-approach adopted here also diverges from Leyla Ozgur Alhassen's recent rhetorical analysis of God's knowledge, where focus is on the persuasive ethical function (Aristotelian *ethos*) of the distinction between complete divine and limited human knowledge (Alhassen 2015).

and 'practicing' the history of religion. Simply put: before the modern nation-state, it was the Church that produced the authoritative knowledge about religion, and universities were institutionally part of the Church. In the modern nation-states, universities became subordinate to the state and detached from the Church. Consequently, the modern academic study of religion produces a new kind of knowledge about 'religion', shaped by the new institutional order in which 'science' pertains to the university alone and 'religion' becomes 'not-science' and subject matter of new, 'scientific' theories and methods of studying it, distinct from the Church's disciplines. In terms of method, de Certeau's discourse theory implies that texts – here the Qurʾān and those produced within the Islamic disciplines – and their concepts be referred to the social institutions, scholarly disciplines (with theoretical paradigms), and individual scholars, which produce them.

By 'Qurʾānic concepts', I mean 'as recorded in the printed Cairo edition of the Qurʾān from 1924'. It builds on the consonantal script identified with that produced on command by the third Caliph in Medina ʿUthmān b. ʿAffān (r. 23/644–36/656), through a collective effort led by the Prophet's scribe Zayd b. Thābit (d. 45/665). The Cairo edition is based on one of several acknowledged 'readings' (*qirāʾāt*) and vocalisations of the ʿUthmānic script, that from ʿĀṣim via Ḥafṣ. Hence, the Qurʾānic concepts treated in this book follow this specific 'reading', though others exist as well (Dutton 2012).

Preliminarily, I also follow Theodor Nöldeke's chronological organisation of the 114 Qurʾānic *suwar* (sing. *sūra*) into Early, Middle and Late Mecca, and Medina periods. The organisation is based on the trajectory of the Prophet Muḥammad's (570–10/632) mission as described in his Biography (*Sīra*), as well as topical and stylistic criteria. This is what the periodisation looks like:

Early Mecca (48 *sūras*): 96, 74, 111, 106, 108, 104, 107, 102, 105, 92, 90, 94, 93, 97, 86, 91, 80, 68, 87, 95, 103, 85, 73, 101, 99, 82, 81, 53, 84, 100, 79, 77, 78, 88, 89, 75, 83, 69, 51, 52, 56, 70, 55, 112, 109, 113, 114, 1
Middle Mecca (21 *sūras*): 54, 37, 71, 76, 44, 50, 20, 26, 15, 19, 38, 36, 43, 72, 67, 23, 21, 25, 17, 27, 18
Late Mecca (21 *sūras*): 32, 41, 45, 16, 30, 11, 14, 12, 40, 28, 39, 29, 31, 42, 10, 34, 35, 7, 46, 6, 13
Medina (24 *sūras*): 2, 98, 64, 62, 8, 47, 3, 61, 57, 4, 65, 59, 33, 63, 24, 58, 22, 48, 66, 60, 110, 49, 9, 5

In contrast with this historical chronological organisation, the canonised order is largely counter-chronological, with the (generally) long Medina and late Mecca *sūra*s placed in the beginning of the corpus, and the (generally) short and early Mecca *sūra*s towards the end (Sinai 2017: 25–29).

However, and in contradiction of Nöldeke's method, I argue that despite the fact that the *sūra*s pertain to different periods and contexts in the Prophet's life, the Qur᾽ānic canonical corpus does not reflect a diachronic or temporal development of concepts. Instead, I treat the canon as a conceptually coherent 'meta-unit', in which each *sūra* constitutes a sub-topic or 'meso-unit', which in turn has internal 'micro-topics', constituting defined passages of *āyāt* (sing. *āya*), 'signs' or in common parlance 'verses'. Imagine a Russian doll which consists of similar but smaller and smaller dolls encased within the big Mother Doll. The Qur᾽ān can be seen in the same way, as it is organised from longer to shorter *sūra*s, except that each *sūra* has its own individual take on the meta-topic – each doll has its own name, as it were. I will return to this important methodological issue in Chapter 3.

DELIMITATIONS AND OUTLINE

The aim to address the question 'is there science in the Qur᾽ān?' with reference to the Islamic disciplines and their relationship with current research means that the field of enquiry is vast. So vast that exhaustive surveys of scholarship in either sphere are impossible to achieve within the scope of a single monograph. Yet I believe it is important enough to illustrate the current relevance of the Islamic disciplines and scholars to justify a 'selective approach'. I.e., I select for analysis a limited number of disciplines, topics, scholars, and current research debates, organised into seven chapters.

Chapter 1 describes Michel de Certeau's discourse theory and analytical method, which provides the methodology for my study. In brief, his method implies analysing scholarly discourses with reference to the specific societal institutional order and practices of the society in case. I also discuss de Certeau's work with reference to general epistemic debates about scientific knowledge, historiography and modern nation-states, and related debates within Religious studies concerning the concept 'religion'. This refers to the problem I raised above, of how to understand the significance of 'religious' aspects of the Islamic disciplines, such as the concept of the divine, of creation, covenant, prophecy, and divinely mediated 'writing', and how these can be understood in relation to scientific knowledge and observation.

Chapter 2 introduces the meta-concept for this study of Qurʾānic concepts, namely 'concept'. I start by addressing the problem that there are different theories of what a 'concept' is, within both 'western' and Arabic-Islamic discourses on the topic, then I sketch the contours of the main theoretical paradigms I will continue to refer to throughout the study. I also reach a conclusion as to which theories of 'concept' I perceive to be reflected in the Qurʾān itself. At the end of the chapter I return to the Religious studies-debates about 'religion' and refer it to the theories of 'concept' treated here. This approach opens up a new perspective on the debate over whether and how Islamic discourses produce knowledge relevant to current research; I will argue that they are not only sources for information, but offer theoretically informed analysis as well.

In *Chapter 3* I present selected research into the Qurʾānic Arabic language, the canonization process, 'readings', and Qurʾānic composition, including a critical assessment of Nöldeke's chronological theory-discourse and some of its current applications. I then proceed to compare this research with one of the earliest theoretical paradigms developed to explain the same topics, that of the jurist and exegete Muḥammad b. Jarīr al-Ṭabarī (d. 310/923). Al-Ṭabarī's concepts of Qurʾānic Arabic language and of divine 'Covenant' as a compositional structure then forms the base for a model of the Qurʾān's canonical composition and its theoretical foundation, which I develop here. The model, which focuses on the terms of the divine Covenant, then serves as the 'meta-topic', with reference to which I analyse the other selected Qurʾānic concepts at meso- and micro-levels.

Having thus argued for the key role of Covenant as the Qurʾānic organising meta-topic, *Chapter 4* proceeds to analyse the concept with reference to current research, and to other theoretical paradigms than those treated in the previous chapter. Here I show how certain strands within research align with some early and medieval exegetes in conceptualising the Qurʾān in terms of natural law theory. For these exegetes, the practical implication of this kind of theory is a law based on rights. For the aim of this study, this means that in so far as scientific knowledge and observation produced discursively within the Islamic disciplines refer to Qurʾānic knowledge, it includes the practical matter of the law and to what extent it protects rights.

Chapter 5 develops another, closely related aspect of Covenant identified in the preceding chapter, namely its reference to a constitution i.e. the division of power and function between state/ruler and judiciary. Consequently, and in line with de Certeau's approach, in the first part of the chapter I reconstruct a political economy, an administrative institutional order, and a social contract theory as context for the Qurʾānic Covenant, based on current historical research and the Prophet's Biography. The reconstruction highlights the importance of land as the main form of wealth, the organising principle of the political economy and administration, the source of tax income for the state and material sustenance for all people. Hence, Covenant as signifying rights-based law, constitutional rule, and social contract, refers also to the concrete issues of land ownership and land tax. Based on some historical research, I also propose that the Prophet's rule and early Islamic law converged with agricultural developments, and introduced new forms of sharecropping contracts, which granted peasants new property rights to land and protected inheritance. In the second part of the chapter, I proceed from the Prophet's time to sketch the main Islamic societal institutions and historical developments and topics related to constitutional rule, from the early Caliphate to the 900s/1500s. Throughout the chapter, I also analyse Qur'ānic concepts with reference to these topics, following the logic that Qur'ānic knowledge extends into the disciplines.

In *Chapter 6*, I turn to the Islamic disciplines themselves, selecting linguistics, Prophetic tradition (*ḥadīth*), political science (*siyāsa*) and administration (*tadbīr*), history (*ta'rīkh*), exegesis (*tafsīr*), jurisprudence (*fiqh*), and systematic theology (*kalām*). In the first part of the chapter, the aim is to show how the topics and concepts related to constitution and social contract are treated within each discipline, with examples from the early and medieval period. The analysis thus tests al-Suyūṭī's assertion, exploring whether each discipline has corresponding method-related concepts in the Qur'ān, and whether the scholars refer Qur'ānic concepts to topics related to constitution and social contract. In the second part of the chapter, I focus on two scholars from the period 1600–1700, showing how they employ Qur'ānic concepts to develop their critiques of current discourses within the schools of philosophy, theology, and law. They serve here as bridges, connecting the medieval and modern periods.

Finally in *Chapter 7*, I sketch the economic and institutional re-ordering that took place in the context of modern colonial rule and the post-colonial nation-state, its implications for the Islamic scholarly institution and disciplines and the study and use of the Qur'ān, and for constitutional matters. Given the increased international interactions from the colonial period onwards, the perspectives now include the European university context and discourses. I then proceed to analyse institutional practices associated with current academic discourses and contention over what constitutes the 'most scientific' Qur'ānic studies. The analysis includes revisiting both natural law theory (Chapter 4) and the early theological dispute over the Qur'ān's created or un-created nature (Chapter 6).

The *Conclusion* summarizes the results, and discusses them with reference to the applied methodology. Referring the Qur'ānic concepts to the Islamic institutions, disciplines, and scholars has shown the latter consistently using these concepts, to define their specific methodologies and to analyse and deliberate topics related to constitution and social contract i.e. 'Covenant'. The results show the scholars perceive that the Qur'ānic concept of divine knowledge, which prophets convey to their peoples, in their languages, refers to knowledge about state administration. In the Qur'ān itself, this knowledge is conveyed in the form of paradigmatic historical observations of past peoples, which the scholars further concretize and analyse through the parameters of each discipline. The concluding discussion then focuses on the implications of my methodology for Qur'ānic studies and studies of early Islamic history, and for Religious studies debates about the concept 'religion' and its relationship with 'science'.

Chapter 1

THE WRITING OF HISTORY AND THE 'RELIGIOUS OTHER'

> (121) Those to whom We have come with **the writing** and who read it in the right order[1]: they enact security[2] through it. But those who reject security through it: they are the ones who stand to lose!
> (122) O Sons of Israel! Recall and honour My material blessing, with which I blessed you, and that I favoured you above the knowing beings!
>
> Q. 2 (*al-Baqara*), 121–122

> What alliance is there between ***writing*** and ***history***? It was already fundamental to the Judeo-Christian conception of **Scripture**. Whence the role played by religious archaeology within the modern elaboration of historiography, which has transformed the terms and the very nature of this past relation in order to give it the stamp of fabrication, no longer allowing it to seem simply a matter of reading or interpreting. From this standpoint, re-examination of the historiographical operation opens on the one hand onto a political problem (procedures proper to the "making *of* history" refer to a style of "making history") and, on the other, onto the question of the subject (of the body, of enunciative speech), a question repressed in the direction of fiction through the law of a "scientific" writing.
>
> Michel de Certeau (1988: xxvii)

Michel de Certeau (1925–1986) was a French historian of religion and sociological thinker inspired by Marxist and Freudian theory, all the while

1 *yatlūnahu ḥaqqa tilāwatihi*; on *talā* and its sense of 'ordering', and doing (or reading) something in a specific order, see Ibn Manẓūr, Lisān al-ʿarab, www.alwaraq.net, entry *t-l-y*, p. 618.

2 *yuʾminūna*; I follow Ibn Manẓūr's rendering of *ʾāmana* in accordance with the fourth transitive verb declination, as 'inducing' or 'enacting' *ʾamn'* i.e. security; *Lisān al-ʿarab*, entry *ʾ-m-n*, www.alwaraq.net, p. 201. The verb *kafara* in the following sentence is then the opposite, 'to reject security'; for further discussion and references about *ʾāmana*, see "Applying de Certeau and Critical Religious studies" below, p. 29.

affiliated with the Catholic Jesuit order.[3] As the above quote illustrates, his research concerned the relationship between Christianity and modern academia, which he conceptualised as a continuum of textual interpretation and writing. He never wrote on Islamic topics. Yet his analytical model of the discursive production of academic knowledge and its focus on institutional disciplines and practices is generally applicable. I have chosen it because it allows me to direct my enquiry into 'science in the Qur'ān' towards the relationship between institutional practices and discursive knowledge, a relatively understudied area in Qur'ānic studies.

On the French academic scene, de Certeau advanced to the position of Director of studies at École des Hautes Études en Sciences Sociales in Paris. He was closely affiliated with the poststructuralist literary movement and its political counterpart, postmodernism, and engaged enthusiastically with other even more internationally renowned giants, including the philosopher and historian Michel Foucault (d. 1984), the literary critic Jacques Derrida (d. 2004), and the sociologist Pierre Bourdieu (d. 2002).[4] In the 1970s and 1980s, poststructuralism and postmodernism developed as methodological critique of the established ways of reading and writing science, which reflected the positivist assumption that it is possible to "reflect the world without presuppositions, without intruding philosophical and theoretical assumptions into one's work" (Agger 1991: 106). In Ben Agger's view, the critique does not amount to a rejection of empirical facts, or of the scientific aim to understand the truth about a subject matter. Nor does it negate the general Oxford definition of 'science' as systematic, specialised bodies of knowledge, given in

3 His most famous work on history and historiography of religion is the collection of essays *The Writing of History* (1988; French *L'Écriture de l'histoire*, 1975). Sociologically oriented works include *The Practice of Everyday Life* (1984; French *L'Invention du quotidien*. Vol. 1: Arts du faire, 1980) and *Culture in the Plural* (1997, French *La culture au pluriel*, 1974). The last work includes reflections on university pedagogics and public dissemination of research in conditions of mass higher education. De Certeau argues that focus on the methods and practices of producing scientific knowledge and how they shape results is a more engaging and democratic way of teaching and communicating science than simply presenting results, an approach which limits the knowledge of production to scientists.

4 For an overview over the relationship between poststructuralism, postmodernism, and critical theory, and the importance of the early Frankfurt school for their development, see Agger (1991). On de Certeau and his intellectual milieu, including Foucault, Derrida, and Bourdieu, see Ahearne (1995); for his critical engagement with especially Bourdieu, see de Certeau (1984). Compared with Bourdieu, whose theory of 'social capital' emphasises its preserving force, de Certeau's thought is more oriented towards social dynamics and change, and individual agency.

the Introduction chapter above. Rather, the aim is to analyse how scientific knowledge is produced, by drawing attention to the ways in which theory and method serve as tools, which scholars use to shape knowledge about the world.[5] More controversially, many of these thinkers also emphasise the significance of psychoanalysis for knowledge production, seeing psychological mechanisms of 'suppression' and 'othering' reflected in practices of reading and writing, including scientific ones. An illustrative example is Derrida's methodology of de-construction. Writing is not a one-to-one reproduction of a thing existing in the world but the author's construction of that thing by assigning specific meaning to it. Since an author necessarily has complex and often contradictory views and feelings about a topic, meaning is polyvalent, ambiguous, and implicit, forming a range of possible 'sub-texts'. To interpret a text is therefore not a straightforward reproduction of the text's explicit and uniform meaning but the reader's construction of its meaning by drawing out its manifold 'sub-texts'. Critical reading therefore involves de-constructing the author's meaning-making, while simultaneously reflecting upon how one's own reading is engaged in a new construction. Meaning is therefore ultimately indeterminate, even though it is the construct of specific authors and readers (Agger 1991: 112–113).

For the purposes of this book, I focus on de Certeau's historiographical studies, which illustrate the poststructuralist episteme through Marxist and Freudian-inspired reading and writing of Church history and Christian doctrine. It is particularly in the essays collected in *The Writing of History* (1988/1975) that de Certeau developed his discourse theory. His relationship with Marxism is epistemic and theoretical, not ontological and ideological. Thus, he rejected Marxist ideological materialist ontology but used Marxist epistemology to theorise the relationship between knowledge production and institutional practices. By 'ideology', de Certeau meant the reduction of the whole reality of a subject matter under investigation to the selected theory; for example, Marxist reduction of religion to the theory of religion as

5 Agger's assessment of poststructuralism and postmodernism aligns them with the critical realism of the philosopher of science Roy Bhaskar, who has defined two criteria for an adequate account of science: "(i) its capacity to sustain the idea of knowledge as a produced means of production; and (ii) its capacity to sustain the idea of the independent existence and activity of the objects of scientific enquiry" (Bhaskar 2008[1977]: 6). Bhaskar's aim is to offer an alternative to positivism's false claim to objectivity, which includes the fact that science makes real discoveries about how nature and the universe 'work'. In other words, he synthesises the sociology of knowledge episteme, represented famously by Thomas Kuhn in *The Structure of Scientific Revolutions* (1962), with the empirical fact of scientific discoveries, also of 'laws' in nature and the universe.

an expression of alienation (1988: 28–30).[6] Yet theory is also a requirement in any academic study. By 'theory', de Certeau means a set of general principles *independent* of the thing they refer to, but correlated with a *practice* pertaining to an institutional order, which is both a socio-economic mode of production and mode of producing knowledge. Social elites tend to 'ideologise' theory, in the positivist sense of making knowledge seem objective and self-evidently true by masking the practices that produce it. By comparison, theory in the analytical, critical sense brings out the productive, practical relationship between knowledge and an institutional order (1988: 29, 131).

Consequently, de Certeau's aim is to draw analytical attention to the factors involved in the *discursive production* of historical knowledge. 'Discourse' arranges facts according to internal criteria, which determine which events, sources, and methods are considered important and authoritative, and how they should be explained (1988: 119–20). These workings of discourse are not necessarily apparent to the historian, because they constitute the very 'intelligibility' through which the historian makes sense of what (s)he reads (1988: 1–16). Conceptualised in this way, history "vacillates between two poles. On the one hand, it refers to a *practice*, hence to a reality; on the other, it is a closed *discourse*, a text that organizes and concludes a mode of intelligibility" (1988: 21; italics added). In other words, past events and institutional practices are real, but they become known as 'history' only through a discourse, which expresses the institutional practice of the historian.

A discourse in de Certeau's sense can thus be seen as constituted by three factors: institution, discipline, and subject. Firstly, a social *institution* – the university – has a particular place in society's mode of production. European pre-modern institutions of learning and universities were integral to the Church and the monasteries in the monarchic-feudal political economy, while the modern university institutions gain their resources to produce knowledge through their place 'next to' the state, whose needs they serve. Modern academic knowledge is thus an asset, a form of 'capital', which the state invests in to develop society and professionalise the citizens. The discipline of History is particularly instrumental in providing the nation with identity, by tracing and narrating its past, establishing its national archives and significant temporal periods, and identifying its 'others' (1988: 2–6, 26, 45–46, 56–57). The second factor, *discipline*, is thus both a particular scholarly tradition within the academic institution – History, in de Certeau's case – with its sets of theories, concepts, sources, and methods, and the

6 See also Agger on the Frankfurt school's and subsequent postmodernists' critique of 'Marxist positivism' and reductionism (1991: 109–111).

thought-disciplining practices that accompany the former. The concept of 'progress', for example, reflects a historiographical practice of distinguishing between the present and past national society on the one hand, and between one's own and other societies on the other. As such, 'progress' is a mode of intelligibility, which shapes the way in which national history is understood. Finally, the third factor, *subject*, refers to the historian or scholar as a person, affiliated with a particular university and discipline, and with individual interests, experiences, and class and family background, which define how (s)he chooses to place her/himself in relation to institution, discipline, and discourse on a particular subject matter. The historian as subject in this sense shapes the subject matter of the study, so that even if (s)he is writing about a common topic within a discourse, his/her study represents a subjective contribution. For example, de Certeau's description of his schooling in the discipline of history, specifically religious history, and his personal interest in the 'scriptural' relationship between pre-modern religion and modern academia:

> born as a historian within religious history, and formed by the dialect of that discipline, I asked myself what role religious productions and institutions might have had in the organization of the modern 'scriptural' society that has replaced them by transforming them (1988: 14).

All three factors – institution, discipline, and subject – that constitute historical discourse express identity through the distinctions it makes between 'itself' and 'others', in time and place. These identity-forming distinctions turn written discourse into valuable 'capital', which institutions, disciplines and individuals 'invest'. At the subject level, individual scholars' 'investments' are what makes discourses change; i.e. each scholar makes a unique contribution, which moves the direction of the discourse.[7]

Discourse on religion is 'capital' of utmost value for states as well as university disciplines. In the French context, the formation of the modern nation-state and Republic, the Enlightenment, and the modern universities and academic disciplines constitute a new social order, in which the Church has lost its power to produce scientifically authoritative knowledge about religion and its way of ordering society. This authority now pertains to the

7 Similarly, in *The Practice of Everyday Life* (1984), de Certeau conceptualises individual agency in terms of 'tactic', which refers to the individual's subjective choices of how to 'consume' institutional 'strategic' rationalities, policies, goods and services. In part, he developed his approach as a critique of Bourdieu's more static concept of habitus.

state university and the modern discipline of Religious studies. The Church continues to be powerful and to play important social roles, not least as provider of 'Christian morality' and rituals for the citizens, but again, without the scientific authority to define religion and society:

> we witness the breakup of the institutional alliance between Christian *language*, attesting to the tradition of a revealed truth, and the *practices* apportioned to an order of the world. Social life and scientific investigation are slowly exiled from religious allegiance (1988: 149).

Modern French academic study of religion meant conceptualising the subject matter mainly through sociological theories. It is even the case, de Certeau argues, that sociological theory has virtually replaced theology as a reductive, ideological explanation of 'all of religion', with particularly confusing consequences regarding the relationship between religion and science (1988: 147–50).[8] Rather, each scholar must select a theory of 'religion', and acknowledge that another theory would have yielded another analytical result. His critique therefore is not a call to return to theological reductionism, but to analyse the institutional practises involved at the levels of both the studied discourse and the historian's own knowledge production (1988: 21).

EPISTEMIC PLURALISM AND SOCIAL CATEGORISATION OF RELIGION

Like other poststructuralist thinkers, de Certeau examines how discursive practices of constructing identity through differentiation between 'self' and 'other' involve suppression and non-recognition of affinities and continuities. For example, 'Scripture' is constituted of practices – writing, reading, interpretation – which connect pre-modern Jewish and Christian religious traditions with modern disciplines in the Humanities and Social sciences. Yet because modern academia is *institutionally* separate from the Rabbinate and the Church, discourses suppress such real, practical continuities and

8 See also Evans and Evans (2008: 88), addressing American sociology: "we suspect that the field of religion and science is one of the muddiest in all of sociology. The conceptual source of this muddiness lies in the long-running academic assumption that religion and science always conflict and that they conflict over competing truth claims about the world. It is therefore hard for sociologists to analyse the relationship dispassionately because sociology itself was born as a scientific alternative to religion".

instead produce knowledge that establishes and maintains dis-continuity (1988: 4, 14). Theoretical affinities between religion and modern academia are suppressed in the same process. An important case is de Certeau's argument that the theorisation of religion through sociological categories, which characterises modern French Religious studies discourse, followed from earlier developments within Christianity. The medieval Catholic institutions were powerful enough to claim to represent one single Christian social order and one True Teaching, even though the institutions were always facing both internal and external contestation. During the 1600s, however, the Catholic institutional order was irrevocably broken up with the Reformation and the multiplication of Protestant churches affiliated with new polities, as well as new forms of Catholic movements. In the late 1700s, the religio-political diversification was followed by the Enlightenment, the Revolution, the fall of the monarchy, and the founding of the modern Republic. At this point, the Catholic Church's medieval epistemic claim was unsustainable because religious diversity had become an *institutional* reality. In practice, religion increasingly served as the vehicle of identification and signification of different and competing social groups. The institutional change was accompanied by new discursive knowledge about 'religion' *as* a social category, *first* within the religious institutions themselves, and *then* in the modern academic discipline of Religious studies with its sociological theories of religion.

The example shows that religion as practice can be analysed as a *driving force* of social, epistemic, and conceptual change, just as well as a secondary expression or legitimisation of societal changes. De Certeau does not come down prescriptively on either side. His aim is not to 'ideologise' a specific theory and causal analysis but to explore the relationship between institutional practices and theory, in order to show that religious thinkers are perfectly capable of conceptualising 'religion' as a social category, like modern social scientists do (1988: 117–19, and chapters 3–4).[9]

9 Again, see also Evans and Evans (2008:89), on positivist sociology in the American context: "Irrespective of their personal commitments, sociologists took action to remove religion as a contributor to the developing discipline through such tactics as the development of textbooks that described religion as an object of study rather than a source of knowledge (Smith 2003b) and through the active exclusion of religious sociology and its supporters from the field's core institutions (Evans 2009; year modified here, UM). By excluding religion as a source of sociological knowledge, early American sociologists hoped to promote sociology as a respected academic scientific discipline".

OUTLOOK: MARXIST HISTORY AND RELIGIOUS STUDIES

The broader poststructuralist and postmodernist 'critical' movements to which de Certeau belongs of course inspired many other historians, and have also had a major impact on Religious studies. To provide some further context to de Certeau's contributions, I will briefly compare his approach with that of his contemporary colleague, the famous British Marxist historian Eric Hobsbawm (d. 2012), and some prominent critics of the concept 'religion' within Religious studies.

Marxist History

De Certeau's analysis of the significance of the modern nation-state and its institutional order for discursive production of historical knowledge both resembles and differs from the approach Eric Hobsbawm (1983) adopted in his study of nationalism, nation formation, and 'invented tradition' in the late 1800s and early 1900s, with the United Kingdom and the USA as main cases. 'Tradition', Hobsbawm argued, is not a real continuum of ideas and practices but a modern, nationalist construct, made real through ritual performance. Nationalism is a modern ideology tailored for the formation and legitimation of the new nation-state and its institutions. Given the novelty of the nation-state, its legitimacy was construed around the claim that the nation had a long, continuous history. Consequently, nationalism 'invented' the concept 'national tradition' by staking out two pathways reaching back to the past. Firstly, it stretched 'the national heritage' and 'national customs', embodied by new public rituals and mores, back in time. Secondly, it attached the heritage and mores to ideals associated with Ancient high cultures, especially Greece and Rome, which 'the nation' supposedly embodied and carried forth into modern times.[10] Political institutions and academia in particular were provided with such ancient legacies, Hobsbawm observed. Given historical records of public political insistence on the 'stability' of these national traditions and ancient legacies, he concluded that it was the

10 The discourse has earlier forms, however, as a study of German philosophy in the 1700s and 1800s shows. In this context, Kantian philosophers effectuated a shift from a concept of 'universal philosophy', which included African and Asian forms, to one in which philosophy is seen as limited exclusively to that of the ancient Greeks and its continuation in German philosophy. Strikingly, the shift involves the re-definition of German philosophy as 'scientific', and the author shows how new theories about races and civilizations played a decisive role (Park 2013).

real instability attached to the novelty of the nation-states and democratic politics, which explains the perceived need for tradition (1983: 307). Thus, political advocacy of adherence to 'national tradition' and the public mores and rituals through which it was enacted served as a powerful tool to distinguish between 'patriotic' and 'unpatriotic' citizens, and 'strangers', who became seen as agents of instability (1983: 278–280).

Both de Certeau and Hobsbawm, then, analysed how the modern national institutions produced new knowledge about the past, corresponding to new political practices, and how distinctions between 'self' and 'other' are instrumental in this process. However, de Certeau's focus on religion also has a re-constructive aim, whereas Hobsbawm's aim to understand the reasons for 'inventing tradition' is purely analytical. De Certeau's re-construction was not conservative or 'traditionalist'; he had no interest in restoring Catholic theology and doctrine as the hegemonic producer of knowledge about religion. Rather, he sought to introduce into contemporary academic study of religion the awareness that academic theories and practices are also *internal* to religion, and constitute *actual* continuities between religion and modern academia. Yet again, his aim was not to make the modern academic disciplines appear 'old', in the sense of conferring legitimacy on them, like Hobsbawm's nationalist 'invented tradition'. Instead, he wanted to show how modern Religious studies constructed scientific legitimacy by cutting itself *off* from Christian tradition and suppressing continuity. At this point, de Certeau's and Hobsbawm's approaches shed light on two sides of the same practice: the nationalistic elevation of Antiquity as an 'origins' of national politics and academia, which Hobsbawm describes, suppressed the actual long history of Christian thought and its continuation in academic theory and practice, which de Certeau un-earths.

Ironically, the nationalist elevation of Antiquity over Christian tradition also suppressed the fact that the Catholic Church was the real continuator and developer of ancient philosophy in Europe in the medieval period. The example shows how postmodernist and poststructuralist critical theory and 'deconstruction' has produced more accurate knowledge about this period in western intellectual history, including its relations with the Church Fathers, the Eastern Orthodox Churches, and Jewish and Islamic philosophy and theology.[11]

11 See Bernard McGinn, 'Foreword', in the recent volume *Medieval Philosophy: A Multicultural Reader* (2019), edited and introduced by Bruce V. Foltz.

'Religion' in Religious Studies

De Certeau's critique of French Religious studies intersects with debates within Anglo-American Religious studies about the concept 'religion' and its significance as the discipline's premise, that there exist a multitude of 'religions' in the world, past and present. The classical statement on this subject matter is *The Meaning and End of Religion* (1962), by the Canadian Methodist priest and professor of Comparative Religion Wilfred Cantwell Smith. He argues that in the European Christian context it is only with the Renaissance philosopher of Platonism Marsilio Ficino (d. 1499), that 'religion' is seen as referring to a universal category, rather than something specifically Christian, such as the monastic covenant. Ficino's 'religion' had a distinctly Platonic sense; in Cantwell Smith's words: 'a universal instinct in mankind to seek the good, which he [Ficino] argued is to seek the divine; an instinct to which he assigned the name *religio*' (1962: 34). Cantwell Smith's concern is reification. By uncritically applying the concept 'religion', scholars reify and extend a category, whose notions may not aptly describe the specific thing referred to. Instead, he proposes that what is truly universal is the adjective 'religious', which describes the person who has 'faith' i.e. who establishes a bond between himself/herself and God, or whatever the object of faith may be.

As the US-based anthropologist Talal Asad has pointed out in a critique of Cantwell Smith, he ends up proposing simply another essentialist concept of religion, only centred on the personal faith instead of practice and community. In Asad's view, this is problematic, since definitions of 'religion'

> are not mere abstract intellectual exercises. They are embedded in passionate social disputes on which the law of the state pronounces. My problem with universal definitions of religion is that by insisting on an essential singularity, they divert us from asking questions about what the definition includes and what it excludes – how, by whom, for what purpose, and so on. And in what historical context a particular definition of religion makes good sense (Asad 2001: 220).

Asad's anthropological approach to the problem of defining 'religion' is close to de Certeau's approach, since Asad too sheds light on the institutional orders within which academic concepts of religion are 'practiced'. When religion is publicly understood as 'personal faith', it entails problems in understanding and accepting, for example, Muslim practices.

Another important contributor to the debate is Jonathan Z. Smith (d. 2017), American professor of History of Religions. Similar to Cantwell

Smith, he surveyed the history of western concepts of 'religion'. In the article 'Religion, Religions, Religious' (1998), he sketches a conceptual history from Lactantius (d. 320 CE), adviser to the first Christian Roman emperor Constantine, to the Religious studies scholars of his own time. However, where Cantwell Smith focused on temporal and religious differences, J. Z. Smith shows how the concept also depends on the author and discipline. In Catholic terminology, J.Z. Smith finds that 'close and meticulous observance of rituals' is one of the key meanings of the Latin term *religiosus*, which late medieval Catholic scholars and observers extended also to non-Christian practices; whereas Protestants tend to define 'religion' as having to do with virtue, piety, reverence and adoration of God, without ritual connotations (1998: 269–271). From the viewpoint of J.Z. Smith's survey, the Methodist Cantwell Smith's concept of 'religious' as personal faith thus appears specifically Protestant. Jonathan Z. Smith concluded, much like de Certeau did, that since 'religion' is the concept that defines the modern discipline of Religious studies, it cannot be done away with. Rather, each study should critically reflect on its definition and application, since its meaning varies between religions, within one religion, and between scholars within modern Religious studies, depending on sub-discipline (history, sociology, psychology, literary studies, anthropology, etc.) and choice of theory.

Concerning studies of Islam, Talal Asad has repeatedly pointed out the implications of a post-Enlightenment Christian concept of 'religion' as 'belief', understood as a cognitive and moral disposition. Similar to de Certeau, Asad argues that 'belief' as the religious universal corresponds with national organisation of religion as a 'private' matter and 'a perspective' distinct from others e.g. science, aesthetics, law, politics, etc. (Asad 1993: 46–51). This kind of attention to the ways in which Christian concepts govern translations of concepts pertaining to other religions is gaining ground, also beyond the term 'religion'. For example, David Lambert (2016, esp. ch. 4) shows how a Christian concept of 'repentance' as a psychological process of regret, remorse, and penitence for having violated God YHWH's Covenant has dominated English translations of the Old Testament and the Hebrew Bible, distorting the meaning of the Hebrew verb *shûv*. According to Lambert, *shûv* in the Hebrew Bible is not a primarily moral term. Instead, it means to 'return' to the physical place where God YHWH resides and where He can be addressed, as opposed to the places of other gods or oracles. Hence, *shûv* refers semantically to the divine oracle and its physical location. This meaning is lost when the term is translated in psychological terms, as 'repentance'.

As these examples show, critical Religious studies in the postmodernist-poststructuralist sense has stimulated renewed attention to how definitions and use of concepts may vary between scholars within the same religion, between religions and disciplines, over time and context, and between scholars within Religious studies.

APPLYING DE CERTEAU AND CRITICAL RELIGIOUS STUDIES

There are four main ways in which de Certeau's discourse analysis and the Religious studies debates about concepts shape this book.

Firstly and most generally, I follow de Certeau's distinction between ideology and theory and do not reduce the reality of the Qur'ān to the theories that I have selected here to analyse its concepts.

Secondly, I apply de Certeau's method of analysing a discourse and its concepts by referring them to institutional practices, to academic disciplines, and to individual authors. I identify the Qur'ān with the institution of *prophecy* (*nubuwwa*, including messengers, *rusul*) as the medium for divine language-based communication, interpretation, deliberation, and persuasion, and its continuation in the practices of the scholarly institution of 'those possessing knowledge' (*al-ʿulamāʾ*), with its scientific disciplines (*ʿulūm*). The choice to conceptualise prophecy as communicative, interpretive, deliberative, and persuasive practice means that I focus on language and rhetoric, both in the obvious sense that Qur'ānic concepts are expressed in Arabic, and in the 'scientific' sense that Qur'ānic concepts of prophecy refer to language-related theory. Language and rhetoric thus constitute the precondition for communicating the divine knowledge (*ʿilm*). The approach broadly agrees with al-Suyūṭī's brief sketch, where he identifies grammar, rhetoric, and 'law' as the bases of the sciences deriving from the Qur'ān, and the other sciences following from them (see Introduction). However, I develop his analysis by exploring the theoretical paradigms involved.

Thirdly, I will draw on de Certeau's thesis about the significance of religious and epistemic diversity for *religious* concepts of religion as a social category. Relevant to the Islamic context is Joel Kraemer's study of the intellectual environment in the Abbasid capital Baghdad in the 900s, under the rule of the Persian Buyid dynasty (*ca.* 945–1050). In Kraemer's view, the environment represents a humanistic renaissance of ancient Babylonian and Greek philosophy, with the philosophers and scientists in Baghdad taking a 'secular' view of religion. By 'secular', Kraemer means they viewed religion as 'a conventional matrix of social norms and communal behaviour', which is relative in the epistemic sense because it lacked 'the cogency of something absolutely valid and compelling' (1986: 14). While Kraemer connects this secular view of religion with the philosophers and scientists, and the intellectual and religious diversity of Baghdad in the 900s, I extend this claim and transcend the distinction between philosophy and religion. Instead, I will argue that even the Qur'ān describes 'religion' as pertaining to societal groups and institutions, and as subject to rival truth claims. Similar approaches can be seen in the Hebrew Bible and the New Testament, which equally reflect religiously diverse societies (Mårtensson 2020). Here, however, focus is exclusively on the Qur'ān. As we shall see, it consistently frames 'religion' as the property of diverse peoples or groups and emphasises that even though the message is God's and therefore absolutely True, ultimately God cannot persuade them all that it is really He who addresses them, through the prophet or messenger in this case, and in their language. Awareness of competing claims to truth is verbalised in repeated refutations of wrong doctrines, and doctrine, cult, norms, and rules are frequently associated with specific peoples or groups in society. Relevant Qur'ānic concepts here are *dīn* (judicial order, judgement), *milla* (constituency, community), *qawm* (polity), *nās* (some among the people of the polity), and *lisān* (language). I assume here that these refer to the historical reality of, among others, Jewish and Christian communities and polities, which converge with specific religions, creeds, scriptures, and languages.[12] I will analyse these concepts with reference to 'Covenant' as a constitution and a social contract theory, the principles of which the Qur'ān claims are known to *ahl al-kitāb* i.e. Jews and Christians, and even to humanity as a whole; only they do not all recognise this fact. From this viewpoint, the scientific dimensions of Qur'ānic Covenant that I will explore concern the linguistic and rhetorical theory, that God communicates the Covenantal terms to a people through a prophet or messenger, and the political theory related to constitution and social contract. Moreover, I will analyse the non-relative, absolute notion that Covenant applies to all humans from the moment of Creation in terms of natural law theory, a sub-set of legal theory. Finally, I will explore other aspects of Qur'ānic Creation, including the planets, the water, and the 'material blessings', as concepts referring to administration of lands and land tax, and ritual. All this implies that the Qur'ān as 'religious' scripture refers to institutional practices and scientific disciplines related to the management of

12 On Jewish and Christian groups, religions, and languages in 'Late Antiquity' up to the Prophet's time, see Millar (2013).

several peoples and religiously diverse communities. Hence, it is a balancing act between the claim to absolute Truth and the relativist, sociological insight that each group has its own truth (however false it may be).[13]

Fourthly, the problem of translating 'religion' and related concepts. As we shall see, the Qur'ānic meta-concept Covenant describes a contractual relationship between God and man, established at Creation, and which specific peoples then implement (or violate) through history. The Arabic term is *mīthāq*, from the root *w-th-q*, signifying 'firmness', 'reliability' e.g. Q. 7 (*al-A'rāf*), 169, 172. *Mīthāq* sometimes occurs together with *'ahd*, 'contract' in the sense of a political 'compact', and *'aqd*, which connotes 'holding or binding together' two parties in a 'mutual contract'. *'Aqd* is close to one of the meanings of the Latin term *religio*, 'to bind', which can also refer to taking binding monastic vows (J.Z. Smith 1998: 269–270). Yet the Qur'ānic and Islamic concept commonly translated as 'religion' is *dīn*. Already Cantwell Smith argued that Islam presents a unique case in the history of religions. As mentioned, the Qur'ān employs *dīn* as a technical term for *several* different religions, including 'itself'. In the post-Qur'ānic literature, *dīn* occurs also in the plural, *adyān*, applied to Judaism and Christianity as well as other religions. 'Islam' (*islām*) on the other hand denotes the personal, pious attitude of obedience and commitment to submit to and live in accordance with God's commands, which in Cantwell Smith's view is the essential 'religiousness' and therefore *name* of this *dīn* (1962: 80–82; 112). Consequently, Cantwell Smith defined *dīn* as 'used of religion as a generic universal, in both senses: as generalizing personal religiousness or human piety at large, and as generalizing the various systematic religions as ideological or sociological structures' (1962: 82; also 80–82 *et passim*). Moreover, Cantwell Smith recognised that *dīn* has several senses in Arabic, including 'judging, passing judgement, passing sentence', and 'judgement, verdict', which he claimed 'represents an ancient Semitic root'; and 'to conduct oneself, to observe certain practices, to follow traditional usage, to conform' (1962: 102). He emphasised, however, that *dīn* above all refers to systematic religion and the related personal religiousness and piety (1962: 101).[14] The Qur'ānic and Islamic technical term for 'faith' is the noun *īmān* and the active participle *mu'min* of the verb *āmana-yu'minu*, meaning 'to

13 Compared with Kamali (2009), who also treats implications of the Qur'ān and its inclusion of diverse religions, peoples, languages and laws under the divine Covenant with humanity, I thus focus on the science-aspects of diversity.

14 For a further engagement with Cantwell Smith and *dīn* in the context of the Mughal administration of 'religions' as social and legal categories in the Indian context, see Morgenstein Fuerst (2014).

have faith in God's command'. The opposite is *kufr*, active participle *kāfir*, which usually translates as 'infidel' or 'disbeliever'. However, Cantwell Smith argues that *kufr* is not about cognitive denial of the substance of 'belief', but about whether or not one adopts the *attitude* of having faith in God's commands. Consequently, *kāfir* is someone who 'rejects' faith in God's commands (1962: 111–112).

Cantwell Smith also traced conceptual development. *Islām*, which refers to individual religiousness, is relatively rare in the Qur'ān compared with the very frequent *īmān*. However, in post-Qur'ānic literature, *islām* was increasingly often used and 'reified' as synonym for the institutionalised religion. Even more so in modern time, when *islām* served apologetic and defensive purposes against colonial powers and the European label 'Muhammadanism'. Thus, Cantwell Smith found that over time, *īmān* receded in use as *islām* increased (1962: 112–118). More recently, the historian Fred Donner has explored the same issue, though through a slightly different approach. He argues that the Qur'ānic concept *īmān* reflects an ecumenical stage where the community was identified as a union of several groups of monotheist 'believers', and that *muslim* too initially refers to a trans-monotheist attitude of submission to God and the divine rulings. Only later, in Umayyad time, did the boundaries against the other monotheists, notably Jews and Christians, become firm, and *islām* the name of a fully independent religion (Donner 2010: 68–74; 203–204).

In this book, I interpret these concepts as reflecting theory. De Certeau's point, that religious and epistemic diversity entails *religious* concepts of religion as a social category, applies to the Qur'ānic and Islamic concept *dīn*. I will also argue that Covenant and the other contractual terms (*ʿahd* and *ʿaqd*) are the ones that give meaning to *dīn*, *īmān* and *islām*, and that the meaning reflects political theory i.e. concepts of constitution and social contract. A preliminary illustration: Q. 2 (*al-Baqara*), 256, which contains both the noun *dīn*, the verbs *āmana* and *kafara*, and the root *w-th-q* associated with 'firmness' and 'reliability', and the divine Covenant' (*mīthāq*). First Muhammad Abdel Haleem's contemporary translation:

> There is no compulsion in **religion** (***al-dīn***): true guidance has become distinct from error, so whoever **rejects (*yakfur*)** false gods and **believes** in God (***yu'minu*** *bi-Allāh*) has grasped the **firmest** hand-hold (*al-ʿurwa al-****wuthqā***), one that will never break. God is all hearing and all knowing.

To bring out the political-contractual senses of these concepts, we can look at one of Cantwell Smith's sources on *dīn*, the jurist and exegete Muḥammad b.

Jarīr al-Ṭabarī (d. 310/923). In his Qurʾān commentary, al-Ṭabarī gives the following general meanings for *dīn*: recompense and retaliation (*al-jazāʾ wa al-qiṣāṣ*), rule and obedience (*al-sulṭān wa al-ṭāʿa*), humility (*al-tadhallul*), and reckoning (*al-ḥisāb*) (*Jāmiʿ al-bayān*, 1:1, 139). Regarding Q. 2, 256, he begins his exegesis by dating the verse to the Medina period. At this point, the Prophet demanded that the polytheist Arab tribes enter the *dīn* of Islam. 'No compulsion in *dīn*' must therefore refer to Jews, Christians, and Zoroastrians (*mājūs*), who were exempted from entering the Prophet's *dīn*, since they have their own *dīn*s, but obligated to pay the *jizya* tax and accept the legal rule of Islam (*ḥukm al-islām*) (*Jāmiʿ al-bayān*, 3:1, 25). Thus, al-Ṭabarī perceived *ḥukm* as the *legal* part of the Islamic *dīn* that obligates also non-Muslims.[15] By comparison, the later lexicographer Ibn Manẓūr (d. 711/1311) also identifies *al-dīn*, in the determinate form, with *al-islām* and lists the same meanings as al-Ṭabarī, with some additional synonyms: 'a law by which rulings are made' (*dīn yudānu bihi*), 'customary practice' (*ʿāda*), and 'matter' (*shaʾn*),[16] as well as taxes owed and inheritances due i.e. 'material debt'.[17]

These synonyms show that these two scholars perceived law and the practice of giving legal rulings as an integral part of *dīn*, and they understood the Qurʾānic concept *dīn* in the same sense. This is consonant with the fact that e.g. Jewish, Christian, and Zoroastrian (and later 'Hindu') communities under Islamic rule were legal entities in relation to Islamic law, and had their own laws and jurisdiction over their communities' internal affairs. Hence, as Cantwell Smith and Donner have argued, Qurʾānic *islām* can be understood as an attitude associated with *dīn*, which non-Muslims can share, in the legal sense that they should pay their dues, since God commands all people to do so. Consequently, the required acceptance of the Prophet's legal rule does not necessarily indicate that the community was ecumenical, as Donner argues, only that other religious communities were subject to the divine rulings laid down in the Qurʾān. This appears to be the meaning of Q. 5 (*al-Māʾida*), 44–48, a passage which states that some basic legal principles are common to the Torah and Jewish authorities, the Gospel and Christian authorities, and the Qurʾān and the Prophet. Nevertheless, the Prophet has authority to rule over both Jews and Christians:

15 For analysis of al-Ṭabarī's historical treatment of the pre-Islamic Persian kings and their laws with reference to the concept of *dīn*, see Mårtensson (2011: 215–218).

16 *Lisān al- ʿarab*, online at www.alwaraq.net, entry *d-y-n*, p. 1943.

17 *Lisān al- ʿarab*, online at www.alwaraq.net, entry *d-y-n*, p. 1945.

> (44) We have indeed sent down the Torah, in which is guidance and light, and by which the prophets who enacted peace, and the masters and the scribes, judged among those who have turned back, according to what they were made to protect of God's writing and to which they had testified. So do not fear the people, but fear Me, so that you do not trade My signs for a small price! Whoever does not judge by what God has sent down: **those are the rejecters of security (*al-kāfirūna*)**!
> (45) We wrote down for them in it that life is by life, eye is by eye, nose is by nose, ear is by ear, tooth is by tooth, and that injuries is settlement of account. So, whoever accepts compensation in it provides expiation for it (*wa al-jurūḥa qiṣāṣun faman taṣaddaqa bihi fahuwa kaffāratun lahu*). Whoever does not judge according to what God has sent down: **those are the ones who darken right by wrong (*al-ẓālimūna*)**!
> (46) We let follow in their tracks Jesus, son of Mary, confirming what he had before him of the Torah as We gave him the Gospel, in which is guidance and light, confirming what he had before him of the Torah as guidance and admonition for **those who fulfil their obligations (*al-muttaqīna*)**!
> (47) Let the people of the Gospel judge according to what God has sent down in it, as whoever does not judge according to what God has sent down: **those are the ones who rebel (*al-fāsiqūna*)**!
> (48) We have sent down to you the writing with the True Right, confirming the writing that is before it, and superseding it. So judge among them according to what God has sent down, and do not follow their whims so that they divert you from the right that has come to you! To each of you We have opened a path to guidance and a method (*shir'atan wa minhājan*), and had God so wished, He would have made you one nation, but He wanted to test you by what He brought you. So hurry to put forward the good deeds! To God is the return of you all, when He will instruct you about that over which **you used to disagree (*takhtalifūna*)**!

Following this legal and polity-oriented semantic, I interpret *īmān* as connoting both the attitude of holding for true that the message and rulings are from *God* (as distinct from the Prophet's own words), and the corresponding virtue of conveying or enacting security (*amn* and *amāna*) in relation to others in society. The translation is possible, since the form *āmana* is the fourth, transitive verb declination, which can be causative, and since the root *a-m-n* carries the legal sense of trust and security. Ibn Manẓūr's dictionary entry on *a-m-n* stresses that *mu'min* is someone who both holds the Prophet's message for true (*ṣaddaqa*) and acts accordingly, following the *sharī'a* and striving to fulfil the duties towards God by committing his wealth (*māl*) and self (*nafs*). By comparison, *muslim* refers to someone who performs the manifest acts. If he or she also holds the message for true, as *mu'min*, he or she is truly and rightly (*ḥaqqan*) *muslim*, as opposed to only outwardly so.[18] Ibn Manẓūr also gives instructive similitudes, which highlight the material and societal security associated with both *mu'min* and *muslim*. Referring to Prophetic *ḥadīth*, he says:

> In the Prophetic report: "Two rivers are *mu'min*, and two rivers are *kāfir*. As for the two that are *mu'min*, they are the Nile and the Euphrates, while the two that are *kāfir* are the Tigris and the Balkh river. He likened the two to *mu'min*, because they overflow the land and water the crops without any [human] efforts, while he likened the other two to *kāfir* because they do not water or give benefits without great effort and exertion. Consequently, those two come with good and benefit, as *mu'min*s, while the other two come with scarce benefit, as *kāfir*s". And in the Prophetic report: "The fornicator does not fornicate while *mu'min*". It was said: Its meaning is a prohibition although its form is a statement of fact [...], in other words: the *mu'min* must not fornicate, or steal, or drink alcohol, for those acts do not adhere to the *mu'minīna*. It was said: This is a threat aiming at preventing [these acts], as his statement (pbuh): "There is no *īmān* with the one who does not give security (*amāna*), and the *muslim* is the one by whose words and actions the people are kept safe and secure (*salima*)."[19]

Returning to Q. 2, 256 against this background, I would translate it in the following way, to reflect the political order:

18 See *Lisān al-'arab*, www.alwaraq.net entry *'-m-n*, pp. 202–204. Also Rubin (1985: 15) on Q. 6, 82 and 24, 55 regarding the often overlooked sense 'security' that is attached to *'āmana*; and Mårtensson (2008: 378–379), where *'amn* and *'āmana* in the 'security'-sense are also connected with *w-th-q* and *mīthāq* in the political, constitutional sense, applied to Q. 95, 1–8 and 2, 126. By comparison, Eggen (2012), who also points to the senses of 'trust' and 'security' in *'āmana*, retains the standard, intransitive sense 'belief'. See also Berger (1970: 6), referring to Abdul Rauf (1967: 96, 98–99), for a similar interpretation: *īmān* refers to the new communal security and solidarity that the Muslim community offered the Prophet's followers, which replaced tribal solidarity. Thus, 'the problem was association or dissociation, joining or quitting, supporting or rejecting, in an age of socio-political grouping and formation of alliances for the very essential need of survival'.

19 *Lisān al-'arab*, www.alwaraq.net entry *'-m-n*, p. 207.

'Political theory'-translation	Abdel Haleem translation
There can be no force in **the religious part of the judicial order (*al-dīn*)** now that moral rectitude has definitely distinguished itself from wavering! For sure, he who **rejects (*yakfur*)** idolatry and **enacts security through God (*yu'minu bi-Allāh*)** has taken hold of the **firmest** bond (*al-'urwa al-**wuthqā***) that never breaks, as God Hears **Knowing everything (*'alīm*)**!	There is no compulsion in **religion (*al-dīn*)**: true guidance has become distinct from error, so whoever **rejects (*yakfur*)** false gods and **believes** in God (***yu'minu*** *bi-Allāh*) has grasped the **firmest** hand-hold (*al-'urwa al-**wuthqā***), one that will never break. God is all hearing and **all knowing**.

I continue to argue in Chapters 4–6 that Q. 2, 256 and similar verses, which I interpret as reflecting concepts of constitution and social contract, are based on empirical observations systematised into a discourse about God's knowledge of human history, communicated to prophets and messengers. I therefore understand *īmān* in the sense of 'enacting security' through the acceptance of God's communicated knowledge as a *logical conclusion* following from the paradigmatic accounts expounded in the Qur'ān. In other words, *īmān* follows from 'evidence-based and systematic knowledge'. Accordingly, the chronologically first verses that God made descend to the Prophet, Q. 96 (*al-'Alaq*), 1–5, emphasise the importance of learning from the knowledge that God conveys in writing. This is especially clear when the verses are seen in the context of the whole *sūra* 96:

(1) Read, by the Name of your Lord, Who created by distinctions,
(2) Distinguishing mankind out of legal dispute![20]
(3) Read, by your Lord the Most Generous,
(4) Who **conveyed knowledge through the Pen**,
(5) **Conveyed knowledge** upon mankind that they did not have!
(6) But no! Mankind will instead serve idols,
(7) For they see themselves as self-sufficient;
(8) But be sure, you will return to your Lord!
(9) Have you seen he who prevents
(10) A servant when he prays?

20 On *'alaq* and its manifold senses, see entry *'-l-q* in *Lisān al-'arab*, online at www.alwaraq.net. The usual translation is 'clot', like a human embryo in the womb; p. 3988. For the sense of 'legal dispute' (*khuṣūma*), especially concerning (landed) property, see p. 3987, where *'alaq* is connected with rhetorical delivery of arguments and proofs. However, *'alaq* also means 'nourishment' and 'food', e.g. what grows from the fertile land; this sense includes contrasting connotations of scarcity of food and dryness of land (*jaḥd*); p. 3984.

(11) Have you seen whether he was divinely guided?
(12) Or commanded fulfilment of obligations?
(13) Have you seen whether he was lying and withdrawing his loyalty?
(14) Does he not know that God sees?
(15) But no! If he does not cease, We shall blacken his face,
(16) His lying, erring face!
(17) Let him then call for his company:
(18) We shall call for the guards of Hell!
(19) Oh no! Do not obey him, but fall on your knees and draw close!

Chapter 2

QUR'ĀNIC THEORY OF CONCEPT?

This chapter directs the discussion about the concept 'religion', and the thesis that the Qur'ānic concepts related to 'religion' also reflect political theory, towards a new theoretical paradigm: theory of concept. As indicated above, the concepts *dīn*, *īmān*, *islām*, *mīthāq*, and *'ilm*, gain meaning through their internal semantic relationship. The question addressed here, then, is whether the Qur'ān also contains a theory of 'concept', which can be seen as reflected in its use of concepts, and which explains how God can communicate His knowledge to people?

I use the *Stanford Encyclopedia of Philosophy* (SEP) entry 'Concepts' for a selective overview of established theoretical categories within western philosophy (Margolis and Laurence 2014). Scholars working within Philosophy, Psychology, and Linguistics continue to debate and probe these categories in great technical detail. However, the categories surveyed in the SEP entry still stand. The entry therefore suffices for an introduction to theory of concept, which serves as framework for exploring such theory in the Qur'ān. Consequently, I proceed by first describing a theoretical category from SEP, which I then compare with examples from the Qur'ān, referring to the Islamic disciplines for theoretical correspondences.

THE ONTOLOGICAL STATUS OF CONCEPTS: MENTAL OR LANGUAGE-BASED REPRESENTATIONS

The SEP entry 'Concepts' begins with the category 'the ontological status of concepts'. Ontology answers the question of what 'being' is. Applied to concepts, it means asking what the 'concept' *is*. According to Margolis and Laurence (2014), the answers fall into two categories: those who define the nature of concepts as mental representations, or as language-based representations.

The mental representations-category corresponds with the *representational theory of the mind.* Initially, this theory explained concepts as psychological entities. Thought was perceived of as a mind-internal system of representations, in which "Beliefs and desires and other propositional attitudes enter into mental processes as internal symbols". Margolis and Laurence distinguish between this early version of representational theory of the mind, exemplified by Locke (1690) and Hume (1739), according to which concepts are psychological entities ('ideas'), and later, modern versions. The modern versions reject the theory that all concepts are psychological entities and explain them instead as entities in a mind-internal "language of thought" (Fodor 1975).

The second ontological category i.e. language-based representations, is exemplified first by *the abilities view* of concept (Dummett 1993). Here, concept is neither a psychological nor a word-like entity in the mind, but an ability "peculiar to cognitive agents" to make distinctions e.g. between 'cat' and 'non-cat', and on that basis draw inferences about 'cat'. Another approach within this category is the view of concepts as *abstract* objects (i.e. not mental states or representations), specifically *constituents of propositions*. As such,

> concepts mediate between thought and language, on the one hand, and referents, on the other. An expression without a referent ('Pegasus') needn't lack a meaning, since it still has a sense. Similarly, the same referent can be associated with different expressions (e.g., 'Eric Blair' and 'George Orwell') because they convey different senses. Senses are more discriminating than referents. Each sense has a unique perspective on its referent – a unique mode of presentation. Differences in cognitive content trace back to differences in modes of presentation.

As Margolis and Laurence (2014) point out, while there are different possible combinatory theories within both these two ontological categories, the basic distinction between *mind-based* or *language-based* theories of concept remains constant.

In the context of the Arabic and Islamic disciplines, the words that correspond to 'concept' are *ism*, 'name', and *fikra*, 'idea' and 'thought', also in the theoretical sense. Shah (2011) has showed that the Qurʾān contains references to *ism* e.g. Q. 2 (*al-Baqara*), 29–33, which in the schools of systematic theology (*kalām*) in the period 800–1300 were employed as support for competing theories of the origins of language and the relationship between 'names and things', or 'concepts and referents'.[1] As discussed in Chapter 1, 'knowledge' (*ʿilm*) in the Qurʾān refers to knowledge that God conveys to humans. The passage Q. 2, 29–33 defines the substance of the divine *ʿilm* as, firstly, knowledge of everything, including the effects of His creation of

1 Shah (2011: 326–328); other passages adduced in these theological debates are Q. 30, 22, and Q. 14, 4.

human 'deputyship' (*khilāfa*) to govern the lands, and, secondly, knowledge of the names. The passage describes how God conveys knowledge of the names to Adam, who then 'announces' (*anba'a*) them to the angels, similarly to how a prophet (*nabiy*) announces divine messages to his people. Hence, the passage establishes a relationship between human deputised rule on earth, and human concepts:

> (29) [God] is the One Who created for you everything in the land, then attended in the same way to the heaven and layered them into seven levels, so He has **full knowledge** about each individual thing (*wa huwa bikulli shay'in* ***'alīm***)!
> (30) When your Lord said to the angels: 'I will place in the land a deputy (*khalīfa*)!' They said: 'Will You place there one who causes corruption in it and sheds blood, while we sing Your praise and sanctify for You?!' He said: 'But **I know** what **you do not know**! (***a'lamu*** *mā* ***lā ta'lamūna***)'
> (31) He **conveyed to** Adam **knowledge** of all **the names** (*wa* ***'allama*** *Ādam* ***al-asmā'a*** *kullahā*), and then displayed them for the angels, saying: 'Announce to me **the names** of those [things] (*bi'**asmā'i*** *hā'ulā'i*), if you are truthful!'
> (32) They said: 'Glory be to You! We have no **knowledge** (*lā* ***'ilma*** *lanā*) other than what You conveyed to us; You are indeed the One Who **Knows everything** when Judging! (*al-**'alīm*** *al-ḥakīm*)'
> (33) He said: 'O Adam, announce to them **their names** (*bi'**asmā'i-him***)!' When he had announced to them **their names**, He said: 'Did I not say to you that **I know** (***a'lamu***) the unknown in the heavens and on the earth, and that **I know** (***a'lamu***) what you reveal and what you conceal?'

If the passage is compared with the ontological theories of concept described above, it can be seen as conforming to the category of language-based representations. Thus, concepts are abstract constituents of propositions that mediate between thought and language (here: the 'names' God gave Adam knowledge about), and referents (here: the 'things' God created), rather than psychological entities or language internal to the mind. Even before the above-mentioned theological debates in the period 800–1300 (Shah 2011), the linguistically influenced Sunnī exegete Muqātil b. Sulaymān (d. 150/767), who produced the earliest extant complete Qur'ān commentary (*tafsīr*),[2] explained this passage as referring to 'the names of things':

2 On Muqātil's linguistically informed exegesis, see Versteegh (1990; 1993, passim, esp. Ch. 4). On the transmission of his exegesis by some Sunnī exegetes from

> (2, 31) (*He conveyed to Adam knowledge of all the names*): Then God, Most Blessed and High, gathered all the birds and mammals and flying creatures of the earth and conferred upon Adam knowledge of their names, saying: 'O Adam, this is a horse, and this is a mule, and this is a donkey', until He had named for him each mammal and each bird according to its name, (*and then displayed them for the angels*) then He displayed the proprietors of those names (*ahl tilka al-asmā'*) for the angels who were on the earth (Muqātil 2002/1: 98).

Staying with the category of language-based representations, one can push this reading of Q. 2, 31 in the direction of 'ability theory', in the sense that the knowledge that God conveyed to Adam enabled him to make distinctions between the things God had created: 'horse', 'mule', and 'donkey'. The ability to make distinctions through language appears also in another verse, Q. 14 (*Ibrāhīm*), 4, where the verb *yubayyin* of the root *b-y-n* signifies 'conveying clear distinctions'.[3] Note that it is a divine messenger (*rasūl*) who makes the distinctions to his people, in their own language, similarly to how Adam in the creation narrative Q. 2, 29–33 is given the prophetic ability and knowledge that enables him to 'announce' the names of things:

> (4) We have never sent forth a messenger with a message except in the language of his people, so that he can **convey clarifying distinctions** to them (***liyubayyina** lahum*). Then God makes whom He wishes go astray and rightly guides whom He wishes, for He is the Mighty, Who Judges!

According to Muqātil b. Sulaymān, again, this means that God's guidance to His judicial order (*dīn*) can only take place through the languages of the messengers, and in the case of the Qur'ān it is the language of the Messenger of God i.e. the Prophet Muḥammad (2002/2: 397). Hence, Muqātil's perception of concepts can be seen as corresponding with language-based representations.

---

al-Māturīdī (d. 944) onwards and including prominently al-Tha'labī (d. 427/1035–36), see Koc (2008).

3 See Ibn Manẓūr, *Lisān al-'arab*, entry *b-y-n*, www.alwaraq.net. On the root: "In the Arabs' idiom, *al-bayn* has two senses: [it] can be to separate and it can be to bring together" (*al-baynu fī kalām al-'arab 'alā wajhayni: yakūnu al-baynu al-furqata wa yakūnu al-waṣla*). On the verbal noun for the third declination *mubāyana*, to which belongs the adjective *mubīn*, frequently used in the Qur'ān as adjective for its Arabic language: "*al-mubāyana* is to make something separate" (*al-mubāyanatu al-mufāraqatu*); p. 572.

Both the Qur'ānic imagery in Q. 2, 29–33 and Muqātil's exegesis depict God as conveying the concepts in a speech-act, *from* God (speaking subject) *to* Adam (addressed object), just as Adam then conveys the same knowledge to the angels. The imagery is 'anthropomorphic', in the sense that God is described as acting like humans do, speaking and addressing various interlocutors.[4] There are, however, Islamic ontological theories of concept which appear to correspond with the mental representation-theory, and which use different imagery. Following Sajjad Rizvi's entry 'Mulla Sadra' in the *Stanford Encyclopedia of Philosophy* (Rizvi 2009) a case in point might be the Twelver Shīʿī Safavid philosopher Mullā Ṣadrā (d. *c.* 1045/1635–36). Ṣadrā was a major critical developer of the philosopher Ibn Sīnā (d. 428/1037) and his Aristotelianism, using Neoplatonic ontology and epistemology in the form of Suhrawardī's (d. 587/1191) 'Illuminationism'[5] and the 'Light-centred' Sufi cosmology of Ibn al-ʿArabī (d. 638/1240).[6] Ṣadrā assumed that the divine Oneness expressed in the Qur'ān is the beginning of true knowledge, which is philosophical and theoretical. Through another take on the primordial God-to-Adam communication, Ṣadrā in *Risāla fī ḥudūth al-ʿālam* ('Treatise on the coming into being of the world of knowledge') located the beginning of philosophy with Adam. Since Adam was also the first prophet, it follows that prophecy is a mode of philosophy. From Adam, philosophical knowledge was transmitted genealogically through Seth and Hermes, "through the Biblical prophets, Greek philosophers, Indian and Babylonian sages, through to the Prophet Muhammad and then on through the Muslim philosophers and Sufis". In accordance with this chronology, Ṣadrā argued that the ancient Greeks and Romans did not know true philosophy (only rhetoric, epistolary, and poetry) before they were reached by Abraham's prophetic knowledge about divine Oneness, by which the totality of existence both emanates and returns (Rizvi 2009, 'Doing Philosophy'). Ṣadrā's ontology presupposed a unity of all existing things, through the consciousness that they all possess by existing. Reality is the totality of unity of existence, intellect, and soul, beyond the individuality (*shakhṣiyya*) that makes distinct beings possible. Within this scheme, things can be known through the co-existence of consciousness, which allows the intellect to grasp the essence of another being: 'Thus the mind distinguishes

4 On Muqātil and anthropomorphism, see Koc (2008).

5 On Suhrawardī's cognitive and experiential theory of definition and concept, and his critique of Aristotelian 'essentialism' – cf. the 'classical theory of concept' described below – see Ziai (2007/1996: 46–52).

6 Landau (1957); also on Ibn al-ʿArabī's ontology and epistemology, see Little (2007/1987).

an existential meaning of C by which C is not B or anything else negated by it' (cited in Rizvi 2009, 'The Simple existence'; 'The Identity of the Intellect and what is intellected').[7]

In this model, God is not imagined as conveying His knowledge through an act of subject-object verbal communication, but through intellect partaking in His existence: 'His knowledge of all things is a simple knowledge and their presence in Him is a simple reality. Knowledge is only an expression for existence on the condition that it not be mixed with matter' (cited in Rizvi 2009, 'The Simple existence'). Existence itself is simple, while the essences that make individuality are complex. All beings and things are both existence and essence, except God Who is simple and perfect existence. Thus, the Neoplatonic One God is a perfect Unity, hence non-anthropomorphic, as in Q. 112 (*al-Ikhlāṣ*, 'Perfection' or 'Sincerity'):

> (1) Say: 'He is God, One,
> (2) God the Boundless,[8]
> (3) Who did not beget and was not begotten,
> (4) And Who can have no counterpart: One!'

It seems, then, that this concept of God is amenable to Ṣadrā's theory of existential unity through emanation from God as the One, simple existence, and of knowledge as the grasp of another being's essence through intellect. Applied to theory of concept, this ontology and concept of the divine seems to correspond more closely to the mind-based theory than the language-based one, even though it is verbalised as a speech-act: 'Say:'

If the reasoning above is correct, the Qur'ān can be seen as reflecting both these ontological theories of concept. A possible reason might be the Qur'ān's function as reference point for the same *kind* of systematic knowledge as in the disciplines, which had to accommodate both kinds of theories. Tentatively, then, Muqātil b. Sulaymān operated with a language-based theory of concept, while Mullā Ṣadrā followed a mind-based one.

7 See also Salem and Kheradmand (2016). For analysis of Qur'ānic ontology of being along these lines, but with reference to the modern existentialist Martin Heidegger and his hermeneutics of temporal disclosure of truth, see Campanini (2016).

8 *Al-ṣamad* is a difficult word. Ibn Manẓūr argues that applied to men it means a noble lord, who is besought for his favours and who has no one in command above him, or a fighter who battles on without need for food or water; but applied to God as in Q. 112, it refers to God's eternal being, limitless nature, and self-sustaining power as Creator; *Lisān al-ʿarab*, entry *ṣ-m-d*, www.alwaraq.net, p. 3241.

THE STRUCTURE OF CONCEPTS: 'CLASSICAL THEORY' OR 'THEORY THEORY'

After the two basic ontological theories of concept, the authors of the SEP entry turn to theories on the structure of concepts. They start with *the classical theory of concept*, which centres on 'definition':

> a lexical concept *C* has definitional structure in that it is composed of simpler concepts that express necessary and sufficient conditions for falling under *C*. The stock example is the concept BACHELOR, which is traditionally said to have the constituents UNMARRIED and MAN. If the example is taken at face value, the idea is that something falls under BACHELOR if it is an unmarried man and only if it is an unmarried man. According to the classical theory, lexical concepts generally will exhibit this same sort of definitional structure. This includes such philosophically interesting concepts as TRUTH, GOODNESS, FREEDOM, and JUSTICE. (Margolis and Laurence 2014)

Consequently, the definition gives the concept a precise meaning by specifying its constituents: 'bachelor' refers to an unmarried *man*, as distinct from an unmarried *woman*, who is called 'spinster', or a *married* man, who is called a 'husband'. It can however be very difficult to define a concept's constituents, as Margolis and Laurence illustrate through the example 'knowledge'. Traditionally, knowledge was defined as 'justified true belief'. Once this definition was questioned, which happened for the first time in an essay published in 1963, a deluge of new definitions burst forth but without a new consensus forming. One possible explanation, Margolis and Laurence suggest, is that concepts actually lack intrinsic definitional structure and constituents, which challenges 'the classical theory' in a fundamental way.

In the Arabic-Islamic disciplines the common term for definition is *ḥadd*, 'limit' or 'boundary'. According to Muhammad Abdel Haleem, the earliest occurrence of the term *ḥadd* itself is in the Qur'ān, Q. 2 (*al-Baqara*), 229–230 and Q. 65 (*al-Ṭalāq*), 1. In both cases, the topic is divorce, and *ḥadd* occurs in its plural form, *ḥudūd*, God's "restrictive ordinances which should not be transgressed" (Abdel Haleem 1991: 5). Abdel Haleem distinguishes carefully between the Qur'ānic and later legal meaning of *ḥadd*, 'legal ordinance', and *ḥadd* as employed in the disciplines of philosophy (*falsafa*) and systematic theology (*kalām*) from the late 800s onwards. Only in the latter two disciplines does *ḥadd* refer to 'definition' in the technical sense (1991: 6).[9] However, the

9 See Troupeau (1985) for a survey of linguistic writings on *ḥadd*. Troupeau argues that it is with the grammarian and rationalist theologian al-Rummānī (d. 384/994), and

lexicographer Ibn Manẓūr gives more complex meanings for *ḥadd*. According to his sources, *ḥadd* has a simultaneously conceptual and legal sense: it signifies the distinction and demarcation between one thing and another, be it between two concepts, two plots of land, or between what is legally permitted and prohibited. Regarding the Qur'ān, Ibn Manẓūr cites a *ḥadīth*, "Every word has a definition (*ḥadd*), and every definition has a point of departure".[10] For Ibn Manẓūr, the definition *is* also a legal boundary in the sense that the defined concept corresponds to a legal category, which regulates peoples' actions, and this is the case both in the Qur'ān and in later legal contexts.[11] Extrapolating from Ibn Manẓūr, one can translate Q. 2, 229–230 and Q. 65, 1 as follows. Note that in verse 2, 230 the 'knowledge' that God conveys to peoples includes legal topics and rulings, which He makes clearly distinct:

> Q. 2 (*al-Baqara*), 229–230:
>
> (229) Release from marriage contract is two pronouncements. Then either hold on in an acknowledged manner or release in a good manner. It is not lawful for you [men] to take from what you have given [the women], except if you both fear that you cannot uphold **God's defined boundaries (*ḥudūd Allāh*)**. If you fear that **they cannot uphold God's defined boundaries**, then they cause no offense by her ransoming herself. Those are **the boundaries** God has defined so do not transgress them, for those who transgress **God's defined boundaries**, they are the wrongdoers spreading darkness (*al-ẓālimūna*)!
> (230) If he releases her, she shall not be lawful to him after that until she has married another man than him. But if he releases her, they cause no offense if they return to each other and think that they will stand by **God's defined boundaries**. Those are **God's defined boundaries, which He makes clearly distinct (*yubayyinuhā*)** for a people **with knowledge** (*liqawmin **ya'lamūna***)!

---

his treatise *Kitāb al-ḥudūd*, that *ḥadd* is used in the technical sense of 'definition'; in earlier works by other linguists it rather refers to 'categories'. See also Troupeau (1983) for a more detailed study of al-Rummānī's definitions. On the polyvalence of *ḥadd* in the earliest grammatical treatise, *Kitāb Sībawayhi* (d. 180/796), see Iványi (1995); Versteegh (1993: 8).

10 *Lisān al-'arab*, online at www.alwaraq.net, entry *ḥ-d-d*.

11 On the connection between language, linguistics and law as one regulatory system, in the socio-linguistic sense, see Carter (1983); Heck (2002); Ibn Manẓūr established a similar connection, in line with Carter's observation that the grammarians often made these connections explicit, and would have been aware of the theoretical implications of connecting language and power.

Q. 65 (*al-Ṭalāq*), 1:

> (1) O Prophet! When you release women from their contract, release them when they have completed their menstrual period. Calculate the period and fulfil your obligations towards God, your Lord: do not drive them out from their houses and let them not depart unless they have committed a **clearly distinct** sinful act (*fāḥisha* ***mubayyina***)! Those are **God's defined boundaries**, and the one who transgresses **God's defined boundaries** has led himself into the darkness of wrongdoing (*ẓalama nafsahu*), for sure! You are not aware of it, but God may bring about a command after that.

I conclude therefore that even though the Qur'ānic *ḥudūd Allāh* refer to legal restrictive ordinances rather than definitions in the technical sense, the text describes the ordinances as being subject to 'clear distinction', notably in verse 2, 230 and *yubayyinuhā*: 'for which He conveys clear distinctions', referring to *ḥudūd* as the object of conveying clear distinctions. Both in Q. 2, 229–230 and in Q. 65, 1, 'clarity of distinctions' signified by the root *b-y-n* is juxtaposed to the root *ẓ-l-m*, 'darkness', signifying the act of wronging what is right in the legal, ethical, *and* conceptual sense. Thus, it can be argued that the Qur'ān operates with a concept of 'definition' as a crucial part of God's message and rules, although it does not explicitly 'define definition'.

In the history of science, al-Kindī (d. 252/866) was the first philosopher who wrote in Arabic and produced a list of 'definitions and descriptions of the things' (*Kitāb fī ḥudūd al-ashyā' wa rusūmihā*), which included Neoplatonic and Aristotelian concepts.[12] Yet al-Kindī did not define the term *ḥadd* itself. The first philosopher to do so was Ibn Sīnā (d. 428/1037), in *Kitāb al-burhān* ('Treatise on Demonstration'). Here Ibn Sīnā developed Aristotelian categories of things, arguing that a definition (*ḥadd*) must conceptually cover the essential *trait* of the thing referred to, including a range of notions, all of which must however be contained within the scope of the essential trait of the thing (Strobino 2010: 133).[13] Compare with Aristotle's discussion of language and names in the treatise *On Interpretation*:[14]

12 On al-Kindī's treatise on the definitions of things, see e.g. Stern (1959; Klein-Franke (1982); Adamson and Pormann (2012:300 –311).

13 On Ibn Sīnā's concept of 'thing' (*shay'*) and his creative use of Arabic translations of Greek commentaries on Aristotle, see also Wisnovsky (2000).

14 The Complete Works of Aristotle: Revised Oxford Translation, from *De Interpretatione*, p. 25 (16a1:3–8, 19–20, 27–29).

(1) Now spoken sounds are symbols of affections in the soul, and written marks symbols of spoken sounds. And just as written marks are not the same for all men, neither are spoken sounds. But what these are in the first place signs of – affections of the soul – are the same for all; and *what these affections are likenesses of – actual things* – are also the same. (…) Just as some thoughts in the soul are neither true nor false while some are necessarily one or the other, so also with spoken sounds. For falsity and truth have to do with combination and separation. (italics added) (…)

(2) A *name* is a spoken sound significant by convention, without time, none of whose parts is significant in separation. (…) I say 'by convention' because no name is a name naturally but only when it has become a symbol. Even inarticulate noises (of beasts, for instance) do indeed reveal something, yet none of them is a name.

Both Ibn Sīnā's definition of *ḥadd* and Aristotle's understanding of language as signs which gain meaning through specific linguistic conventions, including 'combination and separation', though referring to things with language-independent substances and properties, appear compatible with the classical theory of concept. I.e., the constituents of a concept's definition should capture the properties of the thing it refers to. Below we will return to the question whether Qur'ānic *ḥadd* and the Qur'ān's broader employment of concepts also can be seen as conforming to a classical theory of concept. First, however, I will return to SEP and western critique of the classical theory.

The problem with the classical theory is, as Margolis and Laurence (2014) pointed out, that a concept might not have fixed definitional constituents. One of the solutions to this problem was *the prototype theory* e.g. Wittgenstein's 'family resemblance': a concept does not have a definitional structure but a probabilistic one. Thus, something falls under a concept C if it "satisfies a sufficient number of properties encoded by *C*'s constituents", like a 'family' of definitional constituents. In Margolis' and Laurence's view, this is a psychologically inclined theory, because the placing of a thing under a concept follows from perception grounded in existing common knowledge and conventions. For example, both 'apple' and 'plum' are commonly known to fall under the family-concept 'fruit'. However, the prototype theory eventually runs into the same problem as the classical theory, namely non-agreement as to the constituents of a definition.

Another and more viable solution to the problem of the classical theory is *the theory theory of concept*:

> the view that concepts stand in relation to one another in the same way as the terms of a scientific theory and that categorization is a process that strongly resembles scientific theorizing (…). It's generally assumed, as well, that the terms of a scientific theory are interdefined so that a theoretical term's content is determined by its unique role in the theory in which it occurs. (Margolis and Laurence 2014)

Here, a concept's constituents gain meaning in relation to other concepts within the framework of a *theory*: "A supposition or a system of ideas intended to explain something, especially one based on general principles independent of the thing to be explained." Following from this general definition, 'theory' can also refer to "'a set of principles on which the practice of an activity is based', for example 'a theory of education', and 'an idea used to account for a situation or justify a course of action', for example 'my theory would be that the place has been seriously mismanaged'".[15] In Chapter 1, we have seen the concept 'religion' subjected to critical examination within the discipline of Religious studies, and Michel de Certeau's argument to use theory to define 'religion' in each given study. The implication is that the definitional constituents of 'religion' depend on which theory is selected. For example, Marxist theory defines 'religion' as expressing human alienation, whereas the cultural anthropologist Clifford Geertz defines it as a web of symbols expressing the deep meanings and ethical motivations of a cultural worldview. A theoretician's choice of theory thus depends in part on discipline: Marx was an economic historian, while Geertz was a cultural anthropologist. Yet Geertz took his cue from another economic historian, the sociologist Max Weber. Weber developed a comparative cultural worldview-theory, in which religion functioned as *cause* of historical and economic development, and which he formulated as a critique of Marx's materialist theory of religion as an *effect*.[16] Consequently, a concept's definition depends on both discipline and a scholar's subjective, personal choice of theory, as de Certeau's discourse model implies.

The theory theory of concept appears well established in the Arabic-Islamic context. Early and medieval Muslim scholars routinely defined their technical terms with reference to their respective science (*ʿilm*) and discipline, with its set of theories, methods, subjects, and topics (Abdel

15 Oxford Living Dictionaries, 'theory', https://en.oxforddictionaries.com/definition/theory (accessed 29 June 2017).

16 For an overview of theories and concepts of religions, see Daniel Pals, *Nine Theories of Religion* (2014).

Haleem 1991: 5–6).[17] Abdel Haleem's examples of scholars who wrote on the subject of definition (*ḥadd*) include the philosophers Jābir b. Ḥayyān (d. *c.* 200/815) and the above-mentioned al-Kindī (d. 252/866), who defined concepts referring to physics and metaphysics, and the encyclopaedist and administrator al-Khwārizmī (d. 387/997). In the treatise *Mafātiḥ al-ʿulūm* ('Keys to the Sciences'), al-Khwārizmī showed how the same term (e.g. *rajʿa*) was defined in five different ways in the disciplines linguistics (*lugha*), jurisprudence (*fiqh*), systematic theology (*kalām*), tax administration (*kharāj*), and astronomy. Another case is the theologian Ibn Fūrak (d. 406/1015). Similarly, even though he did not write a treatise on definitions, the above-mentioned jurist and exegete al-Ṭabarī (d. 310/923) was explicitly aware of the rules that discipline poses for a study. He distinguished clearly between jurisprudence, exegesis, history, and *ḥadīth* studies, and provided each of his discipline-specific writings with a methodological introduction, including definitions of the key technical terms (Mårtensson 2009a; 2016; Gilliot 1990). In sum: at least by the 800s scholars within all sciences defined technical terms with reference to the systematic disciplines, and the many competing schools and theoretical paradigms.[18]

With regard to the disciplines Prophetic tradition (*ḥadīth*) and biography (*sīra*), Qurʾān exegesis (*tafsīr*), and jurisprudence (*fiqh*), a case can be made that they evolved in a systematic manner and in written form already from the late 600s (Schoeler 2011[1996], 1992, 1989, 1985). This coincides in time with datings of the earliest extant Qurʾān manuscripts (Déroche 2014), suggesting that the production of the written Qurʾānic codices can be seen as part of the broader development of systematic scientific literature.[19] Such a juncture between the production of Qurʾānic codices and the development of the systematic disciplines might support the argument, that *ʿilm* as a generic term for scientific knowledge corresponds to the Qurʾānic concept of divine *ʿilm*. Within such a framework, *theory theory of concept* could also sup-

17 For earlier studies on the role of definitions and technical terms in the history and philosophy of science, with examples from a range of sciences and philosophy, see contributions to Hourani (1975). These include e.g. Levey (1975), on pharmacology and botany, as an illustration of how the 'religious' disciplines and the other sciences applied the same criteria, in this respect.

18 On the disciplines, see Makdisi (1981; 1990; 1991); Van Ess (1991–1997); Stewart (2013). Stewart in particular argues, based on new analysis of works within jurisprudence, for early dating of the systematic disciplines i.e. at least to the 800s, against Makdisi's dating to the 900s.

19 Specifically on the connection between Qurʾān manuscripts and the disciplines of exegesis and linguistics, see Shah (2003a; 2003b; 2004).

port the idea that the Qur'ān sustains two ontological theories of concept: one language-based, the other mind-based, depending on wider theoretical paradigms. The disciplines philosophy and theology, with their respective schools, are relevant to the examples from Muqātil and Mullā Ṣadrā, since they involve different ways of conceptualising God: 'anthropomorphically', as engaged in a subject-object speech-act and deliberation with Adam and the angels, or as the 'abstract One' in the more Neoplatonic sense. Here I will continue to explore the role of linguistics and law for theoretical paradigms, by focusing on the Qur'ān's *treatment* of concepts.

In a path-breaking study of Qur'ānic concepts, Toshihiko Izutsu (1967) developed a semantic fields-approach, according to which concepts gain meaning from their internal relationships. He coupled the approach to a broader linguistic conceptualisation of the Qur'ān as divine revelation. Thus, he argued that the Qur'ānic term *waḥy*, generally translated as 'revelation', refers to communication of a message, mostly through language. *Waḥy* gains this sense because of its semantic relationship with other concepts, such as *lisān* and *kalām*. In Izutsu's view, these concepts are comparable with the modern linguist Ferdinand de Saussure's (d. 1913) distinction between *langue* ('language' as a spoken idiom, Qur'ānic *lisān*) and *parole* ('discursive speech' in the language in case, Qur'ānic *kalām*). Applying the perspective of theory theory of concept, one could say that the semantic field that includes the concepts *waḥy*, *lisān*, and *kalām* reflects theory pertaining to linguistics. Again, the passage Q. 14 (*Ibrāhīm*), 4–5 shows how *lisān* appears in a context, which describes how divine messengers serve as communicators between God and a people:

> (4) We have never sent forth a **messenger** with a message except in the **language (*lisān*)** of his people, so that he can convey clarifying distinctions to them. Then God makes whom He wishes go astray and rightly guides whom He wishes, for He is the Mighty, Who Judges All!
> (5) Thus, We did indeed send forth Moses with a message through Our signs, so that he could bring his people out of the darkness to the light and honour them with God's glorious deeds; indeed, there are signs in that for every steadfast and thankful person!

In the context of these two verses, there emerge further semantic connections between *lisān* and several other words, observable partly through the Arabic language's consonant roots. Verse 4 mentions 'messenger', *rasūl*, which derives from the root *r-s-l* and refers to someone who God has 'sent out', *arsala*, to communicate His 'message', *risāla*, also formed of the root *r-s-l*. Therefore, the verb *arsala* with God as subject means 'to send out a messenger with a divine message'. These linguistic-communicative senses of the root *r-s-l* appear especially clearly in the context of Q. 14, 4–5, where *rasūl* appears together with *lisān*, 'language', and *yubayyin*, 'he conveys clear distinctions'. To be a messenger sent forth by God thus presupposes the linguistic ability to deliver speech with clear distinctions and terms, in the language and idiom understood by the addressed people. 'Signs', *āyāt*, in verse 5 is another word that signifies communication: God uses His signs to rhetorically persuade the people that it is really He, God, who communicates the message, and not the messenger, who is only the medium. Also *ẓulumāt*, 'dark shades', and 'light', *nūr*, are words that in this context use the physical phenomena of darkness and light to conceptualise in simultaneously linguistic and legal-ethical terms the distinction between what is clear and right *versus* confounded and wrong.[20] Light thus refers semantically to the clarity of God's distinctions and signs, and, by extension, to God's clearly defined legal boundaries, *ḥudūd*, as we saw in Q. 2, 229–230 and Q. 65, 1, cited above. As a concept, *rasūl*, 'messenger', thus includes implicit senses of legal-ethical and linguistic-conceptual clarity that become explicit and evident in the context of the other words, and the Qur'ān itself as a wider context.

The example *rasūl* seems compatible with a theory theory of concept, if we interpret all the related words in the context of Q. 14, 4–5 as reflecting principally linguistic theory, and with implications for defining legal and ethical categories. However, neither the classical nor the theory theory of concept, as described in the SEP entry, have included the factor of 'context', which plays a key role in Arabic linguistics and Qur'ān exegesis. The earliest extant treatise on Arabic language and grammar is *al-Kitāb*, by the Iraqi grammarian Sībawayhi (d. 180/796). To illustrate grammatical and lexical points, Sībawayhi used the Qur'ān, spoken idioms, poetry, and *ḥadīth*, suggesting that he perceived the Qur'ān as exemplifying his theory of language. Contemporary scholars of Arabic linguistics have defined Sībawayhi's theory of language as pragmatist i.e. the meaning of words is not intrinsic to them but equals the message that a speaker intends to communicate to an addressee, in a given *context*, using the language's conventions and grammatical forms (Baalbaki 2007; Carter 2007; Marogy 2010; Versteegh 1997). The theory enjoyed wider support, judging by the fact that contemporaneously with Sībawayhi in the late 700s, a lexicographical and exegetical genre had emerged, *wujūh wa ashbāh wa naẓā'ir*. Its name reflects

20 Cf. Christiansen (2015), who analyses the root *ẓ-l-m* through cognitive theory: 'darkness' as the mental inability to understand the divine revelation.

the theory that a concept with determined meaning (*naẓīr*) can have several *wujūh*, 'aspects' or 'senses', and *ashbāh*, 'synonyms', depending on the context (Shalabī 1980; Rippin 1988; Eggen 2012:62–64; Abdel Haleem 2018). One such work was composed by the above-mentioned exegete Muqātil b. Sulaymān (d. 150/767), author of the earliest extant commentary of the whole Qur'ān. Another, attributed to the North African exegete Yaḥyā b. Sallām (d. 200/815) and compiled in the 900s, illustrates the principle. For example, for the concept *hudā*, 'divine guidance', Ibn Sallām listed the following seventeen senses: *bayān* ('clarifying distinction'), *dīn al-islām* ('the judicial order of Islam'), *īmān* ('faith', or 'enactment of security'), *du'ā* ('supplication'), *ma'rifa* ('experiential knowledge'), *amr* (divine command), *rushd* ('moral rectitude'), *rusul wa kutub* ('messengers and writings'), *al-qur'ān* ('the Qur'ān'), *al-tawrāt* ('the Torah'), *al-tawfīq* ('the attainment'), *lā yahdī* ('He does not guide'), *al-tawḥīd* ('to profess divine Oneness'), *sunna* ('prophetic precedence'), *al-tawba* ('return'), *yusliḥ* ('he restores the good after it was corrupted'), and *ilhām* ('inspiration'). Each sense is brought out through cross-references to other Qur'ānic verses and contexts where it has the same sense, as illustrated by *bayān*, the first aspect of *hudā*:

> Guidance (*hudā*) means to make clarifying distinctions (*bayān*). Thus (God) said in *al-Baqara*, 5: 'Those have received guidance from their Lord', meaning 'they have received clarifying distinctions from their Lord'. In *Luqmān*, 5, He said; 'Those have received guidance', meaning 'clarifying distinctions'. This is supported by His words in *al-Sajda*, 17: 'As for Thamūd, We have guided them', meaning 'We have conveyed clarifying distinctions for them'.[21] And He said in *Hal atā* (*al-Insān*), 3: 'We guided him to the path', meaning 'We made clearly distinct for him the path'. In *Lā uqsim* (*al-Balad*), 10, He said: 'We guided him onto the two highways', meaning 'We made clearly distinct to him'. In *al-A'rāf*, 100, He said: 'Has He not guided' meaning 'Has He not made clear distinctions for' 'those who shall inherit the land'. And in *Tāhā*, 128, He said: 'Did He not guide', meaning 'Did He not make clear distinctions', according to the explanation of Qatāda [b. Di'āma, d. 117/735]. Al-Ḥasan [b. Dīnār *'an* al-Ḥasan al-Baṣrī] said: His speech 'Who measured the capacities and guided rightly' (*al-A'lā*, 3) means 'He distinguished clearly to him the path of right guidance and the path of error'. And in *al-Sajda*, 26, He said: 'Did He not guide them?' meaning 'Did He not convey clear distinctions to them?' And there are many similar cases (Ibn Sallām 1980: 96–97).

21 NB: this is not *al-Sajda* 17 in the printed Cairo edition.

The same context-based theory of conceptual senses has shaped the Arabic discipline of rhetoric (*balāgha*), approx. 'the art of conveying meaning'. In its fully systematized form by the 900s, and as employed by Qur'ān exegetes, *balāgha* conceptualised rhetorical speech as constituted by the three components 'innovation' or 'originality' (*badī'*), 'clarifying distinctions' (*bayān*), and 'forms for conveying meaning' (*ma'ānī*), which in turn are shaped in consideration of context (*ḥāl*, 'condition', and *maqām*, 'standpoint'). Abdel Haleem has argued that the Qur'ān's composition reflects these principles of *balāgha*, which is why some of the medieval exegetes relied on them, and why they should continue to guide analytical studies of the text (Abdel Haleem 2018; 1993).[22] Hence, to the disciplines that can draw on Qur'ānic theory theory of concept, including philosophy, theology, linguistics and law, and the overarching political theory mentioned in Chapter 1, we can add rhetoric and exegeses.

A final example is *ḥadīth*: the discipline that more obviously than any other builds on the context-oriented theory of meaning, and which embodies the Qur'ānic concepts of messenger (*rasūl*) and prophet (*nabī*). As we have seen, Qur'ānic and Islamic theory of prophecy is that it is both an institutional practice – to announce the messenger's divine message – with a long history, going back to Adam as its first model,[23] and the starting point of the scholarly disciplines of 'those possessing knowledge' (*al-'ulamā'*). Hence the famous adage, cited in al-Bukhārī's (d. 256/870) *ḥadīth*-collection *Ṣaḥīḥ*, chapter 10: "It is the possessors of knowledge who are the inheritors of the prophets" (*al-'ulamā' hum warathat al-anbiyā'*). The Qur'ānic reference that al-Bukhārī adduces in support of the statement is Q. 35 (*Fāṭir*), 28, "in fact, among His servants only those possessing knowledge (*al-'ulamā'*) fear God", discussed in the Introduction. From the viewpoint of the scholarly disciplines it is thus obvious that God has presaged them in the Qur'ān, and that their systematic, scientific knowledge (*'ilm*) actually does derive from the divine *'ilm*. The difference, as also discussed in the Introduction, is that where the scholars know only about topics within their disciplines, God represents both the totality of knowledge and the particular knowledge about each thing, as stated in, among other places, Q. 2, 29:

22 Cf. Halldén (2005) for slightly different rendering of the terms associated with *balāgha*, in a comparison with Greek and Roman rhetorical terms, and with emphasis on the significance of rhetoric in the Islamic disciplines.

23 See Ibn Manẓūr, *Lisān al-'arab*, the roots *n-b-y* and *n-b-'*; online at www.alwaraq.net

> He is the One Who created for you everything in the land, then attended in the same way to the heaven and layered them into seven levels, so He has **knowledge** about each individual thing (*wa huwa bikulli shay'in* ***'alīm***)!

In this capacity, God can provide both the general principles and particular rulings pertaining to the disciplines. For example, in Q. 4 (*al-Nisā'*), 11, God explains some general principles for dividing inheritance among family members and concludes with the following statement:

> Your fathers and your sons: you do not know who of them is the most deserving to inherit you as an obligation from God, but certainly God is the Knowing, Who Judges!

As the embodiment of the Prophet's and the Companions' *sunna*, *ḥadīth* plays a special role in forging a textually based transmission-bond between the Prophet as the recipient of the Qur'ān and his scholarly successors. *Ḥadīth* is also the second source of law in jurisprudence, after the Qur'ān itself, which means that they too are subject to exegesis. As we have also seen in the Introduction, interpretation of *ḥadīth* is mentioned in Q. 12 (*Yūsuf*), 21–22, in connection with knowledge and legal judgement:

> (21) The one from Egypt who bought [Joseph] said to his wife, 'Make his stay dignified, so that perhaps he will benefit us or we may take him as a son!' In this way We gave Joseph a place in the land, to convey to him **knowledge of the interpretation of reports (*linu'allimahu ta'wīl al-aḥādīth*)**; so God is in charge over his command, though most people **do not have the knowledge** (*lā ya'**lamūna***).
> (22) When he was fully grown, We gave him **judgement (*ḥukm*)** and **knowledge (*'ilm*)**, as that is how We reward those who promote the good (*al-muḥsinīna*).

It is also striking that the generic form of *ḥadīth*, which places Prophetic statements (with or without a Qur'ānic verse) in given contexts, appears to reflect the same theory of context-dependent meaning that has been attributed to the Qur'ān's use of concepts.

CONCLUDING ANALYSIS

Drawing on Margolis and Laurence (2014) entry 'Concepts', I have argued that the Qur'ān can be seen as containing references to two *ontological theories of concepts – mind-based* or *language-based* – which correspond to two different ways of imagining God: as a speaking, communicating party to an exchange with Adam and the angels, or as the One without any 'formal' likeness. I have also argued that the reason for the presence of these two ontological theories of concept is that at the level of *the structure of concepts*, the Qur'ān reflects a *theory theory of concept*, in which 'prophecy' serves as the broad theoretical paradigm that includes several distinct disciplines with corresponding theories. Each of these must find a reference point in the Qur'ān, following the logic that its *'ilm* is paradigmatic for each discipline (*'ilm*).

In particular, we have seen that the disciplines of linguistics, rhetoric, exegesis, jurisprudence, and *ḥadīth*, share a pragmatist semantic theory of meaning as consisting in a speaker's intended message, when addressing a topic in a given context, and conveying the message through conventional language forms. This semantic theory aligns primarily with the language-based ontological theory of concept, and can be seen as having shaped the organisation of the Qur'ān's concepts, whose internal relationships can then be further analysed with reference to specific discipline. After linguistics, it seems that if any discipline ranks above others regarding the need for the pragmatist semantic theory, it is jurisprudence (*fiqh*), given its objective of deriving guidance and law from the Qur'ān and *ḥadīth*. However, given the legal concern with determining intention and legal categories and distinctions, both mind-based and language-based ontological theory of concepts appear necessary. The former has to do with the relationship between mind and language: how does personal intention relate to words, and can words give access to intention? The latter has more to do with the communicative, conventional, and definitional aspect of language: what is the thing or case at hand? Thus, the discipline of *fiqh* may need both of the ontological theories of concept, as much as theology and philosophy does.

The argument about 'theory theory of concepts' reflected in the Qur'ān's organisation of concepts has implications for how we understand its view of prophecy, and what constitutes the 'context' for this view. As discussed above, the Qur'ān describes messengers and prophets in terms of a language-based, communicative function in a given polity, for a people. Given that the Qur'ānic prophets and messengers include Biblical persons e.g. Adam, Noah, Joseph, Abraham, Moses, the kings David and Solomon, and Jesus, as well as the 'non-Biblical' Hūd, Ṣāliḥ, and Shu'ayb (Tottoli 2002), the Qur'ān implies that *the same theoretical paradigm includes the Bibles*. Substantiating this implication is beyond the scope of this book.[24] Yet it is worth pointing out that when some contemporary scholars discuss the 'scientific validity' of the Islamic disciplines and writings in explaining the Qur'ān, the discussion focuses on whether the Islamic scholars consulted Jewish, Christian, or other non-Islamic materials as contexts for the Qur'ān. For illustration, I have selected a few scholars treating 'the Aramaic context'.[25]

The Arabic language historian Jan Retsö (2010) argues that the Qur'ānic canonical orthographical script represents an early development of the Arabic letters that is closer to Aramaic script than to the subsequent Arabic recitation or reading, which relies on diacritical marks and vowels that are somewhat later than the received orthography. This development, Retsö argues, is reflected in the Qur'ān itself and its self-identification as both *kitāb*, 'writing' or consonantal script, and *qur'ān*, 'reading' of that script. Scientific knowledge about this language development derives from modern research on epigraphic records discovered and analysed through archaeology, modern study of the Semitic languages, and manuscript research. These methods were obviously not available to the early and medieval exegetes, who could only rely on the post-Qur'ānic Arabic alphabet and linguistics. Therefore, Retsö concludes, the exegetical works cannot be used as sources of scientific knowledge about the language history and the development of the Qur'ānic canon. The second example is the historian of early Islam Fred Donner (2011). Inspired by Sidney Griffith, historian of the Oriental Orthodox Churches, and his research into Aramaic Christianity as target of Qur'ānic doctrinal polemics against the Trinity, Donner argues the case for employing the Christian Aramaic biblical and other literature systematically as a context for the Qur'ān, as an alternative to the Arabic-Islamic exegesis and historiography. Donner's student of Middle Eastern literature, Emran El-Badawi (2014), pursues this track in a detailed comparison of Qur'ānic literary and doctrinal motifs with samples from 'the Aramaic Gospel Traditions'. By way of conclusion, El-Badawi proposes a theory of

24 A special issue, which includes investigation of this implication through comparative studies of the Qur'ān, the Hebrew Bible, the New Testament and respective exegetical literatures, is *Journal of Qur'anic Studies*, 22.1 (2020), guest edited by Ulrika Mårtensson and Tor-Ivar Østmoe.

25 There are many other examples, including studies focusing on the Talmud and rabbinical writings as context, for example the recent Galadari (2013) and Graves (2015). For a historical, analytical survey of the significance of scholars' choices of 'context' for Qur'ānic vocabulary, and its implications for debates about Islamic origins, see Shah (2020).

prophecy as *dogmatic re-articulation*, which in the Qurʾānic case reflects engagement with the Aramaic Gospels, among other sources.

Three points can be made here. Firstly, while it is true that the Muslim exegetes did not have access to the kind of sources, methods, and comparative language data that scholars today have at their disposal, they were aware of (in this case) Aramaic Christian contexts for some verses of the Qurʾān.[26] For example, there is an exegetical tradition occurring (at least) in the commentaries of Muqātil b. Sulaymān (d. 150/767), ʿAbd al-Razzāq al-Ṣanʿānī (d. 211/827), and al-Ṭabarī (d. 310/923), which contextualises Q. 19 (*Maryam*), verses 34 and 37. I quote al-Ṣanʿānī's version, to show that some early Muslim exegetes theorised their own religion in terms similar to El-Badawi's 'dogmatic re-articulation', specifically referring to Christian doctrine on Jesus:

> ʿAbd al-Razzāq [al-Sanʿānī] said: I was informed by Maʿmar from Qatāda about [God's] speech (*dhālika ʿĪsā b. Maryam qawla al-ḥaqqi alladhī fīhi yamtarūna*; Q. 19:34), and he said: Banū Isrāʾīl gathered and selected from amongst themselves four groups, each of which appointed a scholar to represent them, and they began disputing about Jesus and his ascension. One scholar said: 'He is God who has descended to earth where He revived those He revived and put to death those He put to death, then He ascended to heaven'; these are the Jacobites. The other three groups retorted: 'That is false!' Then two of them ordered the third to say his view, and he said: 'He is the son of God'; these are the Nestorians. The other two groups retorted: 'That is false!' Then one of them ordered the other to make his case, and he said: 'He is a third of three: God is a god, he is a god, and his mother is a god'; these are the Israelites and they are the kings among the Christians. Then the fourth scholar said: 'That is false! He is the servant of God and His messenger and spirit and word'; these are the Muslims (al-Sanʿānī 1989/2:8).

Inconsistencies in this tradition regarding the creeds and community designations aside: it shows that these exegetes contextualised the Qurʾānic verse about Jesus by referring to Christian disputes about the same topic, including the Aramaic or Syriac language communities (the Jacobites and the Nestorians).

Secondly, the report shows that the fourth 'Muslim' doctrinal position defines Jesus as God's servant, spirit, *messenger* and *word*, emphasising

26 See also Saleh (2008), a study showing how the exegete al-Biqāʿī (d. 885/1480), working in Mamlūk Cairo, produced a commentary where he consistently traced Qurʾānic references to Biblical persons and topics to the Hebrew Bible and the New Testament.

the communicative and language-based function that corresponds to the Qur'ānic theory of prophecy and messengers. This implies that it is the *articulation*-element in 'dogmatic re-articulation' that corresponds to Qur'ānic *language-based theory* of prophecy, into which it includes Jesus. The report therefore offers a *theoretically* grounded doctrine on Jesus, which makes it scientifically relevant.

Thirdly, de Certeau's point that religious doctrine may reflect theory *of* religion, and that it may be of the same kind as theory within modern disciplines. Hence, if there is theoretical continuity between the Qur'ān and the Islamic disciplines, the latter offer important information about the Qur'ān. Moreover, given that both the Qur'ān and the Islamic disciplines assume that Biblical persons share the prophetic ability to communicate the divine message with its clear distinctions, their information may be relevant also for studies of prophets in the Biblical literatures.[27]

27 On this point, see Mårtensson (2020) in Mårtensson and Østmoe (2020).

Chapter 3

THE QURʾĀNIC CANON

In this chapter, I turn to the production of the Qurʾānic canon. I maintain the theoretical approach, but develop it focusing specifically on the significance of language- and rhetoric-theory for the canon's composition. I will also re-introduce Covenant, viewed in relation to language and rhetoric, and as a concept with implications for composition.

The chapter starts with a survey of selected contemporary research on the topics of the Arabic language and Qurʾānic Arabic, canon production and 'readings', and composition or internal organisation of the canon. The survey is followed by examples of how the Islamic scholars treated the same topics. Here al-Ṭabarī (d. 310/923) occupies the centre stage, since he has offered a comprehensive theory of Qurʾānic Arabic language, of prophecy, of the 'canonisation' process, of post-canonical 'readings', and of the principles guiding the composition of the canon.

THE ARABIC LANGUAGE

Starting point is Jan Retsö's studies of the history of the Arabic language and the Qurʾānic Arabic, which provide a long historical perspective stretching back to Antiquity and include a thesis about the religious significance of 'contract'. Both contribute towards a deepened appreciation of the Qurʾānic concept of prophecy as communication of scientific knowledge (*ʿilm*).

Retsö's (2003) approach to the Qurʾānic Arabic language is that it is a specifically religious idiom, which does not correspond neatly with one spoken idiom, and that it plays an important part in the forging of a new kind of united Arab identity. This new identity is the product of the Islamic empire under the Umayyad dynasty. Before Islam, the situation was more complex regarding languages and identities, even though ancient records identify distinct groups of people as Arabs. The earliest record that mentions Arabs as a group dates to the Assyrian Empire in the first millennium BCE, after which time Arabs are mentioned continuously in different kinds of records throughout Antiquity and Late Antiquity. Their main home regions are the

Arabian Peninsula, including its north-western and north-eastern rim i.e. the areas bordering Egypt, Syria, and Iraq. Contrary to the established view, Retsö argues that the Arabs were not predominantly nomads or Bedouin, but mostly settled in oasis villages (*qurā*, sing. *qarya*), farming and raising small cattle, in addition to camel breeding and trading (2003: 580–584). The connection between the Arabs and camels is recorded as far back as 800 BCE. In Retsö's view, the ability to breed and handle the camel gave the Arabs a competitive advantage in trade, since camels made it possible to establish new trade routes through the deserts from south Arabia through western Ḥijāz (2003: 127–128; 191–192). The Arabs also had kingdoms and entered vassal treaties with the imperial states. This is indicated in records of Assyrian kings, including Ashurbanipal (mid-600s BCE), who entered treaties and compacts with Arab kings, which included rights to trade. Breaches of treaties constituted grounds for war (2003: 162–171).

Other sources mentioning the Arabs include Greek ones, and the Bible. In the Hebrew Bible, contexts suggest the information dates to between 700 and 587 BCE, the year of the Babylonian Exile. One famous example is the Genesis story about Josef and 'Ismailite merchants', although these are not explicitly identified as Arab (2003: 171–181; ch. 8). In the New Testament, Acts 2, 11–12 mention Arabic as the language of the people from Arabia (2003: 591). Consequently, Retsö shows the Arabs were members of the same regional history as the peoples who identified with the Hebrew Bible and the New Testament, among numerous other religiously defined groups. In other words, when the Qur'ān identifies with a long history of prophecy, this may reflect ancient historical relations between Arabs and 'Biblical' peoples.

Regarding the Qur'ānic Arabic language, Retsö concludes that it was initially not connected with all peoples inhabiting the Arabian Peninsula and its rim, but specifically with those living in the villages (*qurā*), including in the Ḥijāz. It then becomes the language and identity of those loyal to the Prophet and Islam (2003: ch. 2). As mentioned above (Chapter 2), Retsö argues that the significance of the language for the Qur'ān is attested through its self-identification both as a 'writing' (*kitāb*) and a 'reading' (*qur'ān*), and of these two it is the latter that is 'Arabic' (*'arabī*) (Retsö 2010: 284–288).[1] For example in Q. 12 (*Yūsuf*), 1–2:

(1) *aliflāmrā* Those are the signs of **the writing** that conveys clarifying distinctions (*tilka āyāt* ***al-kitāb*** *al-mubīn*):

1 Cf. Mårtensson (2008: 377–378).

(2) Indeed, We have sent it down as **an Arabic reading (*qur'ānan ʿarabiyyan*)**, so that you might rationally comprehend it!

And Q. 41 (*Fuṣṣilat*), 1–3:

(1) *ḥāmīm*
(2) A sending-down from the Giver of Life, the Continuous Protector of Life:
(3) A **writing** whose signs are expounded as an **Arabic reading** to a people who have knowledge (***kitābun** fuṣṣilat āyātuhu **qur'ānan ʿarabiyyan** liqawmin yaʿlamūna*);

The identification of only the reading as 'Arabic' led Retsö to question that 'Arabic' in the Qur'ān simply refers to the language spoken by the Arabs. Consulting Ibn Manẓūr's *Lisān al-ʿarab*, Retsö concluded that neither ancient nor Qur'ānic references to 'Arab' and 'Arabic' (*ʿ-r-b* and *ʿ-r-b-ī*) refer to one ethnic group with a common genealogy and language. Firstly, *ʿ-r-b* refers to a group of people (*jīl*), to which a person is born or adopted, but which is not a blood-tie. Secondly, it refers to specific practices: 'to clarify', but above all 'to guarantee', 'to give pledges or security', often in commercial contexts, and in political contexts 'to swear oaths' of political allegiance or upon adoption into a tribe. Retsö extrapolates from this that *ʿarab* also could have had the religious meaning "those who have entered into the service of a divinity and remain his slaves or property", referring to Herodotus' (d. *c.* 430–420 BCE) description of pledge-ceremonies among Arabs using the Greek term *pístis*, 'persuasion', 'faith', but also 'pledge', 'guarantee' (2003: 597–598).[2]

Following Retsö, Andrew Marsham pointed out that Herodotus, in his description of Arab pledge ceremonies, claimed that "No nation regards the sanctity of a pledge (*pístis*) more seriously than the Arabs," and that they invoked their gods as witnesses to the terms of the pledge.[3] However, records also show e.g. Assyrian rulers invoking their gods as witnesses to the terms of the vassal oath, who promise to enact the curses specified in

2 Cf. Robert Hoyland, who argues that Arab pledges presupposed kinship as blood ties, based on his reading of the same description by Herodotus of an Arab oath ceremony where the contracting parties mixed blood (2001: 115). Hoyland appears to take the mixing of blood literally, as signifying 'blood ties', whereas e.g. Abd al-Aziz Duri perceived kinship and tribal adoption of new members as based on sharing in the cultivation of the tribal land i.e. a territorial and labour-based concept of kin (1987: 12).

3 Marsham (2009: 24); also Hoyland (2001: 115).

the treaty, should the vassal violate his terms.[4] Entering treaties and pacts and taking gods as witnesses is thus a general practice related both to the vassal contracts and tribal alliances, and to trade and commerce. Whether or not the Arabs took oaths more seriously than others back then, records attest to oath-rituals among them in the 400s BC, and the lexicographer Ibn Manẓūr understood the root *ʿ-r-b* as having to do with clarification, oaths, and pledges of security, in political and commercial contexts.

A complementary perspective is that of Ernst Axel Knauf (2010), from the period 500–600 CE. Like Retsö, Knauf shows the diversity that characterised both Arabic and other surrounding languages. His contribution is to categorise the different kinds of language, distinguishing between language of prestige, of religion, of administration (*lingua franca*), and dialect. During the 500s, 'Early Standard Arabic' (ESA) emerged alongside and gradually replaced Aramaic as *lingua franca* among Pagan, Jewish and Christian Arabs in south-eastern Syria, south-western Iraq, and the Arabian Peninsula. Aramaic was also the language of religion for Jews and Christian Arabs, while the Pagan Arabs had poetic Arabic as their language of both prestige and religion. In the 600s, the Qur'ān becomes the language of both religion and prestige (alongside poetry) among those groups who had adopted first ESA, and subsequently the Standard Arabic (SA), which develops as new *lingua franca* in the 600s; while dialects remained the spoken idioms (Knauf 2010: 245–248).

Retsö and Knauf agree that the Qur'ān is a *religious* Arabic language distinct from the other categories of Arabic (administrative, poetic, and dialect). Moreover, if *qur'ān ʿarabī* reflects the senses that Ibn Manẓūr gave for *ʿ-r-b*, which centre on clarification in the sense of 'clear distinction' (*bayān*) and contractual security (*amn* and *amāna*), the precise meaning of *qur'ān ʿarabī* in Q. 12, 2 and 41, 3 would be 'a reading of divine written signs, which makes clarifying distinctions and ensures contractual security'. Understood in this sense, *qur'ān ʿarabī* does not necessarily imply that the writing represents an earlier stage than the reading, as Retsö argued. It is conceivable that *ʿarabī* also reflects the grammatical term *iʿrāb*, which refers to the nominative, genitive, and accusative desinential inflections that determine the syntax of a sentence. If these inflections are not correctly made, whether in writing or reading, the meaning is highly indeterminate and the opposite of 'clearly distinct' and 'secure'. Hence, *kitāb mubīn* and *qur'ān ʿarabī*

4 Marsham (2009: 25). See also Robin (2015: 118), on a South Arabian pact from around 650 BCE, which includes the following formula: "[W]hen [the ruler] put together an alliance of communes with a god and a patron and a pact and an alliance".

can be seen as two sides of the same coin, rather than signs of temporal development. In either case, the lexical meaning of *ʿ-r-b-ī* merges language (clear distinctions, possibly inflections) and law (contractual security), even making the merger intrinsic to 'Arabic' as adjective for the Qurʾān.

ESTABLISHED SCRIPT AND 'READINGS'

The Islamic reports explaining how the Qurʾān came about state that the Prophet's Companions and scribes memorised and wrote down several collections, more or less complete, already during the Prophet's lifetime, and that they read the Qurʾān in slightly different ways. This was partly because, like all Semitic languages, Arabic consonants can be dotted and vocalised in different ways, depending on how readers understand sentences, grammatically and semantically.[5] Both Sunnī and Shīʿī traditions, which gained currency in the late 600s, attribute the first attempts to establish a whole, uniformly accepted Qurʾān after the Prophet to, respectively, the first two Caliphs Abū Bakr and ʿUmar, or the Prophet's cousin ʿAlī b. Abī Ṭālib (Kara 2018: 186–187).[6] However, with ʿUmar's conquests and expansion of the polity to imperial scale, the different ways of reading the Qurʾān continued in the provinces and even caused conflicts. This motivated the third Caliph ʿUthmān (r. 24/644–36/656) to commission the production of a definitive script (*rasm*). Copies with this script were subsequently distributed in all provinces and the previous collections suppressed, though different readings of the ʿUthmānic script emerged too.

According to the manuscript researcher Francois Déroche, no evidence exists that fundamentally contradicts this version, and production of manuscripts with ʿUthmānic script is firmly evidenced from the second half of the 600s in the time of the Umayyad Caliphate (661–750) onwards (2014: 7; 136ff.).[7] Behnam Sadeghi's study (2010) of a palimpsest from Sanaa in Yemen dating to the second half of the 600s shows that the first text differs from the second layer, which is the ʿUthmānic script. Sadeghi argues that the first text corresponded to one of the early versions from the Prophet's

5 For pedagogical illustrations, see Sinai (2017: 30–32); and Nasser (2013: 8–10), a monograph on 'readings', which also surveys debates within both 'western' and Islamic scholarship.

6 Kara (2018) provides a survey of 'western' and Islamic scholarly debates over the dating of traditions, specifically those reporting on the canonisation process.

7 Déroche (2014) surveys recent manuscript research, including specific details such as orthography, style, and locations.

Companions, and was replaced by the ʿUthmānic version. Both versions must have been in use in the late 600s, given that the manuscript material dates to that period. However, Asma Hilali questions the possibility of ascertaining correspondence of the lower Sanaa text with Companion collections, since she finds it does not match any extant variant readings; hence, she argues, this identification remains a conjecture. Instead, Hilali proposes that both the lower and the upper texts reflect 'variations' of a work in progress, resulting from the text being used in teaching and studying contexts involving continuous exercises in reading and writing (2017: 44–45; 67–71). This kind of scholarly usage of the scripture matches the depiction in Q. 3 (*Āl ʿImrān*), 79:

> It is impossible for a human vessel of the divine word who God has given the writing, the judgement, and the prophecy (*al-kitāb wa al-ḥukm wa al-nubuwwa*), to say to the people: 'Be servants of me instead of God!' Rather, [he would say]: 'Be masters by virtue of the knowledge of **the divine writing** you have been conveying, and by virtue of what **you have been studying** (*kūnū rabbāniyyīna bimā kuntum tuʿallimūna* ***al-kitāb*** *wa bimā kuntum* ***tadrusūna***)!'

Similarly, Nicolai Sinai remarks that recent dating of manuscripts shows ranges between 606 and 652 (Berlin State Library), and 568 and 645 (the Birmingham Qur'ān fragment, Cadbury Research Library), suggesting that extant manuscripts exist from both before and around the time of the ʿUthmānic redaction (2017: 46).[8] In a seminar at the Cadbury Research Library in Birmingham in October 2015, Alba Fedeli, who discovered the Birmingham Qur'ān fragment, presented her conclusion that it was most likely written by one scribe, who may have been copying from a written example, given the nature of corrections made in the script. Fedeli also pointed out that the dating has a margin of +/– 21 years at both ends, making a date up to *ca.* 660 possible. Fiona Brock, specialist in carbon dating methods, pointed out that dates show when the animal(s) used for the parchment lived, not when the script was written, for it is not yet possible to date ink separately from the manuscript surface. This circumstance means that the manuscript could be later than the date-range given for the parchment.[9]

8 Sinai (2017) is a monograph devoted to outlining the most important debates, theories, and methods in several areas of current Qur'ān research, including manuscripts and canon production.

9 See also Shah (2016: 290–292) for a discussion of the earliest manuscripts and their dates.

Details aside, manuscript research supports the Islamic narration about the production of the established script on the following points: Qur'ānic written versions existed before the 'Uthmānic consonantal script was established *ca.* 650; and systematic production of manuscripts following the 'Uthmānic script began from the second half of the 600s onwards. This coincides with the period when both Sunnī and Shī'ī reports on the writing and collection of the Qur'ān up to the 'Uthmānic script gained currency, as Kara (2018) has documented.

However, the research also implies that non-'Uthmānic versions continued to exist. A specific problem concerns the exact relationship between the different readings that preceded the 'Uthmānic script, and the post-'Uthmānic discipline of Qur'ānic 'readings' (*qirā'āt*). Shady Hekmat Nasser (2013) has studied the famous Prophetic *ḥadīth*s, which state that God had sent down the Qur'ān in *sab'at aḥruf*, 'seven modes of recitation' in Nasser's translation, and that the Qur'ān descended through each one of the seven gates of the Garden, or Paradise. The context that the *ḥadīth* on *sab'at aḥruf* addresses is the fact that during the Prophet's time, his Companions were reading Qur'ānic verses in slightly different ways. The Prophet then declared that as long as the Companions had heard a Qur'ānic verse from him, and as long as different readings did not result in contradictory commands or prohibitions i.e. changed the meaning of concepts, they were acceptable, since God had sent down the Qur'ān in *sab'at aḥruf*. As Nasser points out, it has always been debated exactly what *aḥruf* (sing. *ḥarf*) refers to. Al-Suyūṭī (d. 911/1505) claimed it referred to the established 'readings' (*qirā'āt*) of the Qur'ānic script, which thus derive from the Prophet's time. However, the majority of scholars understood *aḥruf* as referring to different dialects and pronunciations among the Arabs at the Prophet's time, which affected their readings of the Qur'ān, but is not the same thing as the post-'Uthmānic readings. Nasser settles for 'modes of recitation', as an approximation, hence 'seven modes of recitation', but otherwise agrees with the majority of the scholars (Nasser 2013: 15–17). He then proceeds to show how analysis of the *ḥadīth*'s transmission gives further insight into the problem of pre- and post-'Uthmānic readings.

The *ḥadīth* about *sab'at aḥruf* was transmitted through several transmission chains. The 'common Successor link' is the two Medinan historians, 'Urwa b. al-Zubayr (d. 95/713) and Ibn Shihāb al-Zuhrī (d. 124/742), while the Companion authorities differ (Nasser 2013: 18–29). One of the Companion authorities is the Prophet's scribe Ubayy b. Ka'b (d. 29/649). According to the biographer Ibn Sa'd (d. 230/845), Ubayy b. Ka'b was one of a group of six Medinan men who collected the Qur'ān during the

Prophet's time or 'compact' (*'ahd*) i.e. during his rule. The group included Zayd b. Thābit, the Prophet's foremost scribe:

> I was told by Muḥammad b. Yazīd al-Wāsiṭī – Ismā'īl b. Abī Khālid – al-Sha'bī: During the rule of the Prophet (pbuh), six persons collected (*jama'a*) the Qur'ān: Ubayy b. Ka'b, Mu'ādh b. Jabal, Abū al-Dardā', Zayd b. Thābit, Sa'd, and Abū Zayd. Mujammi' ['the Collector'; UM] b. Jāriya had already collected the Qur'ān, except two or three *sūra*s, and Ibn Mas'ūd had taken some ninety *sūra*s and acquired knowledge of the rest of the Qur'ān from Mujammi'.[10]

That these first collections were written is indicated by the fact that the Prophet's two scribes Ubayy and Zayd were among the collectors (see also Schoeler 2010). The report thus provides some additional context to the *ḥadīth* about *sab'at aḥruf*, by showing how the collection of the Qur'ān started during the Prophet's rule, although it was read in different modes.

Following the majority of the Islamic scholars, then, the 'Uthmānic script is the divider between the term *aḥruf*, which refers to 'modes of reciting' before this script, while 'readings' (*qirā'āt*) come after. However, there is a difference between the Islamic scholars and Nasser. The former perceived the *ḥadīth* about *sab'at aḥruf* as a historical report about dialectical variants in the Prophet's time, which continued in the earliest written versions and thus motivated the 'Uthmānic script. Nasser argues instead that the *ḥadīth* gained currency in the late 600s and that its purpose was to legitimise the different readings that existed after the 'Uthmānic script, through the report that even the Prophet himself had accepted variant readings (2013: 33–34). Knauf's model of administrative, religious, prestigious and dialectical language appears to support the Islamic scholars' version, in the sense that dialects could have affected the reading of the written Qur'ānic religious language. Similarly, Yasin Dutton has showed how Ibn Mujāhid (d. 324/936) in the treatise 'The Seven: Concerning the Readings' (*al-Sab'a fī al-qirā'āt*), defined seven authoritative post-'Uthmānic readers and readings, perhaps in the image of the seven modes, *sab'at aḥruf*. He identified the readings with the regional cities Mecca, Medina, Damascus, Basra and Kufa, and argued that scholars differ in readings just as they differ in legal interpretations: in both cases there are slight regional variations (Dutton 2012: 4–10).

However, even though *sab'at aḥruf* may have provided a model for Ibn Mujāhid's selection of seven authoritative readings, the number did not impose a universal limitation. Both before and after Ibn Mujāhid exegetes

10 Ibn Sa'd (2001/2: 306); for other variants of this report, see pp. 306–309.

made their own selections of authoritative readers and used a wide range of variant readings. Notably, Ibn Mujāhid's teacher al-Ṭabarī (d. 310/923) operated with twenty or so variants, among which he chose on a case-by-case basis according to the criteria of conformity with the ʿUthmānic script, with *ḥadīth* and exegetical reports, and with his own grammatical and semantic analysis. Since al-Ṭabarī pronounced on which readings he considered correct, and also composed a lost treatise on readings, it appears he sought to construct a standard based on the ʿUthmānic script and a range of readings (Nasser 2013: 39–47).[11] The following example is from his exegesis of Q. 19 (*Maryam*), 34. It shows him disagreeing with the reading of ʿĀsim that the printed Cairo edition follows, which renders the syntactically decisive word (*qawl*) in the accusative inflection (*qawla*):

> (34) That is Jesus, son of Mary, the right statement over which they dispute (*dhālika ʿĪsā b. Maryam qawla al-ḥaqqi alladhī fīhi yamtarūna*)
>
> [al-Ṭabarī:] The readers (*al-qurrāʾ*) have disagreed over how to read that. The majority of readers from Hijaz and Iraq read it as *qawlu al-ḥaqqi*, with (*qawlu*) in nominative inflection, with the meaning I have just described, so that syntactically it follows Jesus as an attribute to him. The matter of its inflection is not, in my view, in accordance with those who claim it is in the nominative as the attribute to Jesus, unless the meaning of 'the statement' (*al-qawl*) becomes 'the word' (*al-kalima*), as we mentioned from Ibrāhīm and his exegesis of that. Thus, it is then correct for it to be an attribute to Jesus. If not, its nominative inflection is, in my view, an implicit pronoun i.e. 'this is the statement of the truth' as the introductory subject, and the predicate leaves the communication about Jesus and his mother [in verse 33] at His statement 'that is Jesus son of Mary' (*dhālika ʿĪsā b. Maryam*). Then the predicate introduces that the truth about what the communities dispute regarding the matter of Jesus is *this* statement by which God has informed His servants about him, and no other. ʿĀsim b. Abī al-Najūd and ʿAbd Allāh b. ʿĀmir read this as adverb as if they intended the infinitive of the verb: 'that is Jesus son of Mary in true statement (*qawlan ḥaqqan*)' (…). Abū Jaʿfar [al-Ṭabarī] said: The correct reading in our view is the nominative inflection, according to the consensus of the readers with [textual] proof (*li ʾijmāʿ al-ḥujja min al-qurrāʾ ʿalayhi*). (1995/9:16, pp. 104–105).

11 See also Mårtensson (2016), on 'readings' in the context of al-Ṭabarī's school of law (*madhhab jarīrī*) and concept of the Qurʾān; for al-Ṭabarī's use of readings in three legal cases, see Shah (2016: 294 et passim).

Similarly, the exegete al-Zamakhsharī (d. 538/1144) freely chose readings, and often rejected some of Ibn Mujāhid's seven (Nasser 2013: 6–7). Eventually, Ibn al Jazarī (d. 833/1429) added another three readings to those of Ibn Mujāhid, producing a total of ten, though he later retracted his assessment. Only with al-Suyūṭī (d. 911/1505) and his definition of Qur'ānic sciences in *al-Itqān fī ʿulūm al-Qur'ān*, the seven or ten readings were defined as the only accepted ones, on the constructed claim that only they had sound transmissions (Nasser 2013: 36).

By comparison, the Shīʿī scholars rejected on principle the *ḥadīth* about *sabʿat aḥruf* and the variant readings, arguing that the Qur'ān only has one *ḥarf* and one reading, since God is One and intended one meaning. When faced with the practical exegetical problem of multiple possible readings, the Shīʿī scholars relied on the Sunnī ones, unless there was a report from one of the infallible Imams, which would trump other alternatives. Otherwise, they now follow one of 'the seven' readings, that of the Kufan ʿĀṣim (d. 127/745) from Ḥafṣ, whose transmission begins with ʿAlī b. Abī Ṭālib (Nasser 2013: 112–115; cf. 31–33). This is the same reading as provides the basis of the 1924 printed Cairo edition (Hilali 2017: 22). In this way, the Cairo edition meets the requirements of both Sunnī and Shīʿī perspectives on readings.

THE COMPOSITION OF THE QUR'ĀN

The result of the process of collecting the Qur'ān and establishing the script is 'the canon' i.e. the specified number of 114 *sūra*s, organised in a particular order. Each *sūra* has a name, which reflects a word or topic treated in it. As mentioned in the Introduction, the apparent principle for composing the canon is that of descending length of *sūra*s and reversal of temporal chronology: after the short opening *sūra* 1 (*al-Fātiḥa*), the longest *sūra*s from Medina and the late and middle Mecca periods are placed before the short ones from the early Mecca period. There is also an immediately apparent difference in generic form: the long *sūra*s consist of narrative accounts and argumentation with reference to historical examples, legal principles and cases, and commands and prohibitions, while many of the short ones are oaths and terse sets of warnings-promises.

Despite this rather evident character of the canon, the topic of Qur'ānic composition is subject to long-standing research debates. I will engage with the compositional model developed first by Theodor Nöldeke, which remains a dominant paradigm.[12] In a nutshell, the 'Nöldeke thesis' is that the Qur'ān evinces substantive development in terms of its ideas because the Prophet's thinking underwent change as the community developed. The thesis constitutes a distinct discourse in de Certeau's sense, with institutional, discipline-specific, and subjective aspects. Theodor Nöldeke (d. 1930) was professor of Semitic languages, including the 'Old Testament' (Hebrew Bible) and the Qur'ān, at the universities of Kiel and Strasbourg. His compositional model has been developed most famously by Angelika Neuwirth, professor of Arabic and Qur'ānic studies at the Free University of Berlin, with background in Semitic languages, and her student Nicolai Sinai, professor of Qur'ānic and Islamic studies at Oxford University's Oriental Institute. Hence, I have selected examples from Nöldeke, Neuwirth, and Sinai to illustrate the 'Nöldeke thesis'- discourse on Qur'ānic composition.

'The Nöldeke Thesis': Substantive Development of Concepts

In western Qur'ānic studies, Nöldeke's *Geschichte des Qorāns* ('The History of the Qur'ān', 1860; 1909–1938) is a landmark study. Here, Nöldeke developed his widely followed chronology over Early, Middle, Late Meccan and Medinan *sūra*s and, to some extent, verses. Nöldeke's method was to critically consult the Islamic exegetes' dating of *sūra*s and verses, which largely follows the outline of the Prophet's Biography (*Sīra*), and combine these with stylistic literary and semantic criteria of what characterized the Prophet's mission in its different stages. Note that he takes for granted that the Qur'ān reflects the Prophet's thought and speech, or authorship, as he addresses shifting contexts:

> By careful observation even the casual reader of the Koran will become increasingly convinced that the passages with passionate diction and ideas must have been promulgated earlier than those with serene, broad

12 Consequently, I will not engage with Andrew Bannister's thesis. Based on theories of the formulaic character of oral narrative literature and the denser, less formulaic character of written poetry and narrative, and quantitative computer analysis of the Qur'ān, he argues that the long, narrative *sūra*s are much more densely formulaic than the short, condensed *sūra*s. Hence, if oral literature is more densely formulaic than written and oral annunciation is assumed to characterise the earliest stages of the Qur'ān, it follows that the long formulaic materials must be considered early and the short, dense late. This challenges 'the Nöldeke thesis', which assumes that the long formulaic *sūra*s reflect a late, written stage of the composition process, as opposed to the shorter, earlier oral *sūra*s (Bannister 2014: chs. 5–6; 276–277).

> content. We realize that Muḥammad moved from the first style to the second gradually rather than instantaneously, and that he displays individual gradations in both.
>
> An important element is the length of the verses. The moving, rhythmic diction of the earlier period, more closely related to the true *saj'*, requires far more pauses than the later style, which gradually moved closer to pure prose. A comparison of two passages with identical subjects – even if they do not originate from entirely different periods – can occasionally suggest the likelihood that one originated earlier than the other. Since Muḥammad often repeats himself explicitly, it is sometimes possible to distinguish the original from the later version. Like all writers [*sic*; UM], Muḥammad's diction in different periods displays preferences of word and phrases that facilitate the establishment of a chronological order. By observing the rhyme, the language in the wider sense, and especially **the context of his ideas**, we can identify the individual parts of which sūras are often made up. Of course, when considering **the context** we must not hastily presume an interpolation whenever a logical connection seems to be lacking. It is a consistent characteristic of the Koranic style that ideas seldom develop calmly, instead jumping from here to there. Yet careful observation easily shows that there is at least an inkling of connection (Nöldeke *et.al.* 2013: 51–52; bold added).

By 'the context of his ideas' is here meant both the external changing circumstances of the Prophet's mission and the community's development from a small group of devout believers into a polity, and contexts internal to the text. This approach does not differ much from the Islamic exegesis. What is specific to Nöldeke's approach is his assumption that *substantive development in the Prophet's thought and wording* can be *chronologically measured* by comparing passages treating the same or similar topics.

Nöldeke's approach has been developed most systematically by Angelika Neuwirth, who premises her method on the assumption that the pre-canonical Qur'ān was an open, universalising, oral-Prophetic dialogue with other faith communities, particularly Jews and Christians, as distinct from the canon, which marks a closed, exclusive, and written religion. This development of the pre-canonical Qur'ān can be traced within the Qur'ānic canon itself, she argues, if attention is paid to signs of the redactional process (2014: 24–26).[13] Thus,

13 For a critique of Neuwirth's development-approach with reference to the concept *kitāb*, see Madigan (2001), who shows that *kitāb* occurs across the canon and all four periods; see also Mårtensson (2008), for further, preliminary examples of *kitāb* related to Covenant and the root *'-m-n*.

> Unlike the canonical codex, the pre-canonical Qur'an must be understood as the documentation of a communication process, as an ensemble of texts which arose from the publicly, or at least audibly, proclaimed recitation (i.e. *qurʾān*) – the Prophet's reading from a celestial template. Not only did the Prophet undergo development as an individual, so too did the debate in his community. There began to emerge, among the audience, a consensus regarding individual messages, so that upon repeated recitation, these messages did not need to be justified or evaluated anew but could rely on the already attained consensus. An example would be the figure of Satan, who is at first depicted as being multi-faceted and ambivalent, but later becomes an unequivocally negative figure. This consensus, once, (*sic*; UM) reached exempted the communicator from needing to rationalise the message to the community. However, as the community kept growing and, in Medina, as the audience occasionally included Jewish listeners, some of the texts for recitation did require later revision. This is why, in many cases, the depiction of episodes from Jewish salvation history was subsequently expanded or revised, generating what is known as the Medinan additions. An example of this is evident in the story of the golden calf in *Sūrat Ṭā Hā* (Q. 20) which adds an interpreting point inspired by Jewish atonement liturgy (…) (Neuwirth 2014: 26).

Neuwirth's example Q. 20 belongs to the Middle Mecca period, and accounts for the story of Moses and God's compact (*ʿahd*) with the Israelites, the golden calf, and God's first contract with Adam. In Neuwirth's view, verses Q. 20, 80–82 consist of a 'Medinan addition' to the otherwise Middle Meccan *sūra*. Here in her translation:

> (80) Children of Israel, We delivered you from your enemy; and We made covenant with you upon the right side of the Mount, and sent down on you manna and quails:
> (81) "Eat of the good things wherewith We have provided you; but exceed not therein, or My anger shall alight on you; and on whomsoever My anger alights, that man is hurled to ruin.
> (82) Yet I am All-forgiving to him who repents and believes, and does righteousness, and at last is guided."

The reason that Neuwirth adduces for the 'Medinan addition'-thesis is that in verse 80, the speaker suddenly addresses the Children of Israel, which must refer to the Jews in the Prophet's audience, and the tone changes from empathy to stern severity. Since there were no Jews in Mecca, which is the context of Q. 20 as a whole, these verses must refer to a Medinan context, where there was a large Jewish community. Hence, the verses were added to

Q. 20 in the canonical redaction process. Neuwirth further supports the argument for a 'Jewish context' by claiming that the verses allude to Ex. 34: 6–7, a passage belonging to the Jewish Day of Atonement liturgy and presumably familiar to the Medinan Jews:[14]

> (6) And the Lord passed by before him, and proclaimed, the Lord, the Lord God, merciful and gracious, longsuffering, and abundant in goodness and truth,
> (7) Keeping mercy for thousands, forgiving iniquity and transgression and sin, and that will by no means clear the guilty; visiting the iniquity of the fathers upon the children, and upon the children's children, unto the third and to the fourth generation.

Alternative 1: balāgha and overarching Covenant

The 'Nöldeke thesis' and discourse is shaped by modern western Bible studies and the text- and source-critical method, which includes a search for repetition, interpolations, and ruptures, assuming that such features are results of editorial activities. As we have seen in Neuwirth's case, the search for interpolations also involves identification of Biblical or Jewish and Christian etymologies and parallels.[15] An alternative discourse related to Islamic Qur'ān exegesis and the rhetorical discipline *balāgha* is represented by Abdel Haleem (1993, 2018). Of *balāgha*'s three sub-disciplines, *ma'ānī*, 'forms for conveying meaning', *bayān*, 'clarifying distinction', and *badī'*, 'innovation', his work on the Qur'ān focuses on *ma'ānī*, in the sense of the various formal aspects of the composition that constitute meaning. Like early and medieval exegetes working within the theoretical paradigm of *balāgha*, Abdel Haleem presupposes that the whole Qur'ān constitutes a semantic unit, reflected in each *sūra*. Furthermore, each *sūra* is a topical unit, with a range of successive topical contexts (*siyāq*) that refer to its main theme. In this way, the Qur'ān can be seen as constituted by three semantic levels: meta-level (overarching meaning), meso-level (*sūra*), and micro-level (contexts within *sūra*s). Viewed from this perspective, shifts of topic within a *sūra* appear as moves from one sub-topic to another, not as ruptures and editorial emendations. Moreover, shifts of topic may converge with changes of speaker position (*iltifāt*) e.g. from second person address to

14 Neuwirth (2014: 310–312).

15 See also Sinai (2017: ch. 4) for a research survey, with some applied analysis of selected *sūra*s and passages.

first and third person accounts. Such changes serve rhetorical aims, to highlight specific points within an account, and move a topic forward. Equally important is the use of the consonant roots for meso-level cross-references and wordplays, and their overlap with rhythm and verse end rhymes. As mentioned in the Introduction, I follow this approach here. In addition, I assume that the Qurʾān's generic identification as divine address and knowledge must be considered for analysis of its composition and language.

For meta-level meaning, I therefore follow Rosalind Ward Gwynne's thesis (2004), that the Covenantal contract is a topic that informs the entire canon, its divine argumentation as well as its examples, promises and threats, and oaths. This sits very well alongside Jan Retsö's Ibn Manẓūr-based understanding of the root *ʿ-r-b-ī* as having to do with contractual security and oaths, and clear distinctions (*bayān*), which relates to *balāgha*, as we have just seen. Considering the divine Covenantal contract and the clarification of its terms as the Qurʾānic meta-concept, rhetorical use of sub-topics and changing speaker position (*iltifāt*) to create topical contexts within *sūra*s and move an account forward, and the use of end-rhymes, the passage Q. 20, 80–82 can be read as fully integrated into its broader context. For example, al-Ṭabarī explained Q. 20, 80–82 with reference to the *internal sūra*-context, which is a divine account of Moses, Pharaoh, and God's compact with the Israelites and His rescuing them. Verses 80 and 81 are God's switch from the preceding third person account about these events to describe how He addressed the Israelites directly, hence the second person address in verses 80–81. Verse 82 changes again to first person speaker position, because it proceeds to make a point of general principle (1995/9: 16, pp. 240–241). Consequently, where Neuwirth's above cited translation assumes that all three verses 80, 81, and 82 are part of the same address, al-Ṭabarī limits the address to verses 80 and 81, on account of the changing speaker positions and slight shift in topic, from a described address to a general point.

To illustrate this alternative approach in more detail, I will cite verses 80–82 in the wider context of verses 72–87. In this longer passage, verses 72–73 pertain to God's third person account of Pharaoh's dialogue with his magicians, who explain to him why they have been persuaded that it is Moses, not Pharaoh, who has God on his side, which makes the magicians 'enactors of security' i.e. advocates of the secure contract with God. In verses 74–76, the speaker position and topic changes into a general statement of the contractual terms between God and two 'clearly distinct' categories of people – 'enactor of offence' (*mujrim*) and 'enactor of security' (*muʾmin*), and their respective outcomes. In verses 77–79, the third person account about Moses resumes, now with a new example, namely Moses' and the Israelites' flight from Pharaoh through the sea. Verses 80–81 turn to second person address to the Israelites, applying the general contractual terms particularly to them, and introducing the covenantal 'promise' (*wa'd*), which, as elsewhere in the Qur'ān, involves 'material sustenance' (*rizq*). Verse 82 changes to first person position and sums up the terms again in a general form, referring back to 'enactors of security' (verses 73 and 75). Verses 83–87 resume the account again, first as God's direct address to Moses and his response, then as a third person account of Moses' exchange with the Israelites, which refers back to the 'promise' (*wa'd*) in verse 80. Viewed from this perspective, then, verses 80–82 do not appear as a new tone or topic but as integral to the progressing account. Here the whole passage 72–87 in my translation, with transcribed key concepts and end-rhymes:

> (72) [The magicians] said [to Pharaoh]: "We cannot prefer you over what came to us of distinctive proofs and over He who formed us! So decide what you will decide: you still only decide over this nearest life **(*al-dunyā*)**!
> (73) We have come to **enact security** through our Lord, so that He will forgive us our mistakes and the magic that you forced upon us, since God is best and most Abiding **(*wa abqā*)**!"
> (74) For him who comes to his Lord as an **enactor of offence (*mujriman*)** is Hell, where he neither dies nor lives **(*yaḥyā*)**,
> (75) while he who comes to Him as an **enactor of security (*mu'minan*)** who has worked for the common good (*qad 'amila al-ṣāliḥāt*): those shall have the highest ranks **(*al-'ulā*)**,
> (76) the gardens of Eden, beneath which the rivers flow, remaining there: that is the reward for him who purifies himself and prospers **(*tazakkā*)**.
> (77) Thus We communicated to Moses: "Set out at night with My servants and strike for them a dry path in the sea, neither fearing to be overtaken nor dreading **(*takhshā*)**!"
> (78) But when Pharaoh followed them with his troops, the waters overwhelmed and drenched them **(*ghashiyahum*)**,
> (79) for Pharaoh led his people astray instead of guiding **(*hadā*)**.
> (80) "O Sons of Israel! We have, then, delivered you from your enemy and **made you a promise (*wā'adnākum*)** on the right side of the Mount, and sent down to you manna and quails **(*salwā*)**:
> (81) Eat of the good things We have provided for **your sustenance (*razaqnākum*)**, but do not exceed in it so that My anger is unleashed upon you, for he upon who My anger is unleashed is certainly ruined **(*hawā*)**!"

> (82) Indeed, I am always forgiving of he who turns back, **enacts security**, works for the common good, and then lets himself be guided ***(ihtadā)***!
> (83) "What made you hurry ahead of your people, O Moses ***(yā Mūsā)***?"
> (84) [Moses] said: "Those are on my tracks, so I hurried towards you, my Lord, so that You would be pleased! ***(litarḍā)***"
> (85) [God] said: "We have indeed tried your people after you left, and the Samaritan led them astray ***(al-Sāmirī)***!"
> (86) So Moses returned to his people, angry and saddened, and said: "O my People! Has not your Lord given you a good **promise** (*alam ya'idkum rabbukum* ***wa'dan*** *ḥasanan*), so that **the compact (*al-'ahdu*)** with you was extended? Or did you want anger from your Lord to be unleashed upon you, and therefore you put **your promise to me** behind you ***(maw'idī)***?"
> (87) They said: "We have not put **our promise to you (*maw'idaka*)** behind us by our own making, but we were made to carry loads of the people's valuables, so we pushed them off, as the Samaritan threw ***(al-Sāmirī)***!"

As we can see, the passage is rife with allusions to Biblical passages: the whole account of Moses and the Israelites and their flight from Egypt parallels the Biblical Exodus narrative. If this holds true for Q. 20 as a Middle Mecca *sūra*, it must mean that the topics are not dependent on the 'other' communities, in the sense that they presuppose direct encounters. Retsö's Antiquity perspective offers an alternative historical-contextual angle. The Qur'ān and the Prophet's community are not blank slates, onto which information derived from other communities gradually accrues. Instead, the Qur'ān may recall ancient Arab traditions about the prophets, with which the Hebrew Bible, the New Testament, and Jewish and Christian exegetical literatures have a longstanding tangential relationship. If this perspective is combined with Qur'ānic *balāgha*, it appears quite arbitrary to single out particular verses as 'editorial additions', based on the assumption that there is substantive change in Qur'ānic ideas.

Alternative 2: Clear distinctions of Contractual Categories

The second alternative reading takes as point of departure Nicolai Sinai, who is continuing to develop the 'Nöldeke theses'. One of several examples of editorial, inserted additions that he adduces is from the Medina *sūra* 3 (*Āl 'Imrān*), verse 7 (possibly extending over verses 7–9). Here I show verses 7–9 in the context of the passage 3, 1–11:

(1) *aliflāmmīm*
(2) God, except for Who there is no god, the Living Who is Long-standing:
(3) He has sent down the writing upon you with the true right, confirming what is in front of Him, when He made the Torah and the Gospel descend
(4) before, as a guidance for the people, just as He made the Forger of Distinctions (*al-furqān*) descend. Indeed, those who have rejected security by God's signs shall have a harsh punishment, for God is a Mighty one with capacity for Vengeance!
(5) Indeed, not a single thing is hidden from God, on the land or in heaven!
(6) It is He Who forms you in the wombs how He wishes: there is no god except Him, the Mighty Who Judges!
(7) It is He Who has sent down to you the writing! Of it there are signs that are unequivocal (*āyāt muḥkamāt*), and they are the source of the writing (*umm al-kitāb*), while others are equivocal (*mutashābihāt*). As for those in whose hearts there is deviation, they follow the equivocal in it, seeking internal strife (*fitna*) and seeking to reach the intended meaning even though no one has knowledge of its intended meaning except God. Those grounded in knowledge say; "We enact security through it: all is from our Lord!" since no one except those with discerning intellects are reminded!
(8) "Lord, do not cause our hearts to deviate after You have guided us, and bestow generously upon us of Your life-protection! You are indeed the Generous Bestower!
(9) Lord, You will certainly be gathering the people for a day which is undoubted, for indeed: God never goes back on a promised appointment (*al-mīʿād*)!"
(10) Indeed, those who rejected security: neither their wealth nor their children shall enrich them from God, as those are the fuel of the fire!
(11) Like the persistence of Pharaoh's family and those before them who deceived by Our signs: God took them by their sins, for God is Harsh in His Punishment!

One of Sinai's arguments for why he thinks verse 7 could be a post-Prophetic addition is that after the Prophet's death, the community found itself faced with ambiguous passages in the Qurʾān but no immediate authority to determine their meaning:

> Thus, Q. 3: 7 can be read as addressing a community in possession of a scriptural corpus that, because of the death of Muhammad, was not felt to admit significant revision and growth anymore, yet nonetheless

> appeared to be characterised by considerable ambiguity. Against this hypothetical background, Q. 3: 7 would provide rudimentary guidance on how to deal with the Qur'ān's seemingly inescapable ambiguity – namely, by discouraging its addressees from pressing scriptural passages that seem enigmatic and obscure and by urging them to concentrate on scripture's readily intelligible core instead (2017: 53).

Here we may recall the above-discussed Prophetic *ḥadīth* on *sab'at aḥruf*, which states that even during the Prophet's time the Companions read the Qur'ān in different ways. The Prophet declared this acceptable, so long as it did not result in contradictory commands and prohibitions. If the *ḥadīth* is seen as conveying information about different readings in the Prophet's time, it could provide a context for Q. 3, 7. The above-mentioned verse Q. 3, 79 about studying the divine writing is another aspect of the same topic in the same *sūra*. As for the passage 3, 1–11, there are topical connections between verse 7 and the preceding verses. The word writing (*kitāb*) in verse 7 refers back to *kitāb* in verse 3. In verse 4, the term *al-furqān*, 'the forger of distinctions', can be seen as referring to the two opposed categories 'those who reject security' (also verse 4, and verse 10) *versus* 'those who enact security' in verse 7. Furthermore, verse 7 defines two other opposed categories: 'those in whose hearts there is deviation' who follow the equivocal in the writing, *versus* 'those grounded in knowledge' who follow the unequivocal. Thus, verse 7 can be seen as fully integrated in the passage's topical context. In terms of meso-level conceptual connections, *al-furqān* in verses 3 and 4 reflect the general Qur'ān practice of *bayān* i.e. making *clear* distinctions between categories, as in *kitāb mubīn*, 'a writing that conveys clear distinctions' (see above, on Arabic language). Read in this light, verse 7 defines two categories related particularly to exegesis and interpretation. I will pursue the issue of making clear distinctions a bit further.

Like Nöldeke and Neuwirth, Sinai develops the thesis of substantial development of ideas in the Qur'ān. Here I have selected his argument, that although the whole Qur'ān swears to the creed of God's Oneness, it only gradually develops into 'monotheism', in the sense of complete exclusivity regarding other faiths:

> To be sure, already the early Qur'anic proclamations emphasise God's power and omniscience to an extent that leaves little conceptual space for other divine or semi-divine beings to play an important religious role. To some extent, then, the emergence of an explicitly monotheistic creed in later strata of the Qur'an may be seen as a natural theological development. Nonetheless, it would not have been doctrinally

> impossible for the Qur'anic proclamations to humour their pagan addressees by conceding the factual existence of a certain number of subordinate deities while rigorously curtailing these deities' functions and autonomous efficacy. This is not, however, what happened, and the line taken by subsequent Qur'anic texts was a frontal renunciation of any divine beings other than Allāh. This monotheistic turn then induced a radical polarisation of the Qur'anic audience into Believers and Unbelievers – a polarisation that would eventually turn violent, as we shall see in the next chapter. It is fascinating that we can pinpoint with some confidence the texts in which this momentous step was first taken (2017: 174)

According to Sinai, the earliest verse that disavows polytheism ('God's daughters') is Q. 53, 19–22, 24–25 (middle of Early Mecca), while God's Oneness is affirmed most likely for the first time in Q. 37, 4 (early Middle Mecca), which Sinai sees as a significant evolutionary step in 'the nascent Qur'anic theology' (Sinai 2017: 174–175, cit. p. 175). Here we can note that Q. 112, from the late Early Mecca period, is not part of Sinai's trajectory, even though it combines the affirmation of divine Oneness with a rejection of divine 'begetting-and-begotten-ness'. The omission of Q. 112 aside: Like Neuwirth, Sinai explains Qur'ānic doctrinal development with reference to the Bible e.g. the creed in Ex. 20, 3 and Deut. 5, 7: 'Hear, O Israel: The Lord our God, the Lord is One'. Hence, he concludes that "The Qur'an's swift progress towards explicit monotheism must therefore have been informed by Biblical precedence", an argument he supports by references to the connection between Abraham and monotheism, also in Q. 37 (2017: 175). On this basis, Sinai finds that the Qur'ānic intrinsic monotheistic divide between Believers and Unbelievers takes a militant turn in the Medinan *sūra*s. Here, militancy becomes "an integral component of the Medinan vision of piety, [...] not just a circumstantially necessary measure of defence", testified to by the fact that Biblical prophets' readiness to fight is adduced as ideal models (2017: 191). This kind of militant piety is in accord with both Biblical and Late Antique monotheistic belligerence, in Sinai's view (2017: 194). Consequently, he reads Q. 9 (*al-Tawba*, 'Return'), 5 as sanctioning full-scale conversion of 'the Unbelievers', and views the subsequent Arab-Islamic conquests as expressions of this "Medinan appropriation of Biblically derived notions of religious militancy" (2017: 195). Q. 9, 5 reads as follows, in Abdel Haleem's translation, modified to suit Sinai's rendering of *al-mushrikūna* as Unbelievers:

> (5) When the [four] forbidden months are over, wherever you encounter **the unbelievers (*al-mushrikīna*)**, kill them, seize them, besiege them, wait for them at every lookout post; but if they turn [to God], maintain the prayer, and pay the prescribed alms, let them go on their way, for God is most forgiving and merciful.

Abdel Haleem instead translates *al-mushrikīna* as 'idolaters' and argues that it here refers to those who break the treaty (2004: 116, note. *c*). Following his cue, I offer an alternative reading of Q. 9, seeing it as the application of Covenantal contract terms to the specific legal case and topic of war, especially of a defensive kind. As Sinai points out, Q. 9 refers to Abraham, the Torah, and the Gospel as written precedent of its principles. However, rather than 'monotheism' as an 'exclusive creed', the key issue appears to be 'exclusive *contract*'. Accordingly, I understand the aim of Q. 9 as 'to establish clear distinctions (*bayān*) between legal and ethical categories of people in the context of war', through references to specific cases. Each case is illustrated through examples, which define the particular terms for each category. Hence, examples and terms for the category *al-mushrikūna* are mapped in relation to a range of specific cases, all related to whether one *in the context of war* fulfils one's contractual obligations and is truthful in entering pacts (*aḥlāf*). *Bayān* thus appears here as a compositional tool, since the cases and categories that are made clearly distinct also structure the *sūra*.

As for the meaning of *al-mushrikūna*, the main problem appears to be their disloyalty in pacts, which makes them obstruct the Qur'ānic community's affairs. In verses 30–31, Jews and Christians are placed in this category. They are not obligated to abandon their creeds, even though they are criticised for them. Rather, they are obligated to contribute to the war by submitting taxes, which they otherwise give to their rabbis and monks. Hence, when *al-mushrikūna* is applied to Jews and Christians, *and* polytheists, it means 'those who take other partners' or 'assign partners to God' so that their loyalties are divided and they do not fulfil their contractual obligations to God and His Messenger. This perspective implies that Q. 9 does not have to be seen as the fruition of a gradually maturing Qur'ānic monotheistic belligerence, but as the establishing of the cases, categories and terms related to contractual obligations in the context of war, which apply to polytheists as well as to other 'monotheists'. In rhetorical terms, this implies that Q. 9 and other *sūra*s treat distinct, sometimes legal topics, which are complementary rather than progressive. For example, the family law-related principles and rulings in Q. 4 (*al-Nisā'*, 'Women') present a different topic and cases than the primarily war-related obligations in Q. 9. This is not to deny developments in the 'external' context. Rather, my argument is that the basic topic of Covenant unites the whole canon, so that even though the *sūra*s treat different related topics at different times, there is substantive consistency from the earliest to the latest parts.

The following survey of the whole Q. 9 illustrates how it establishes cases with reference to which it distinguishes categories, with related examples and terms. Some verses I have cited in full, to highlight the relationship between the categories and 'contract'.

Q. 9, *al-Tawba*, 'Return':

1. Case: 'Exemption':
   "An exemption from God and His Messenger to those among the ones who take other partners with who you have entered contracts (*barā'atun min Allāhi wa rasūlihi ilā alladhīna 'āhadtum min al-mushrikīna*)"
   2. Terms: Four months of safety
   3. Terms: Contract protection
   4. Category: *al-mushrikūna*

5. Case: After the four months other terms for *al-mushrikūna*
   6. Terms
   7. Terms and new category: *al-muttaqīna*
   "How do the ones who take other partners have a compact with God and His Messenger, beyond those with who you entered compact by the sacred place of prostration? So long as they are correct in speech and action[16] in relation to you, be correct in speech and action in relation to them; indeed, God loves those who fulfil their obligations! (*kayfa yakūnu li-l-mushrikīna 'ahdun 'inda Allāhi wa 'inda rasūlihi illā alladhīna 'āhadtum 'inda al-masjid al-ḥarām famā istaqāmū lakum fa-istaqīmū lahum inna Allāha yuḥibbu al-muttaqīna*)

8. Case: If *al-mushrikūna* do not fulfil their obligations and become category *al-fāsiqūna*, 'the rebellious'
   9. Example
   10. Example
   11. Terms

12. Case: Those who break their contracts and insult the judicial order (*dīn*): category *kufr*, 'rejection of security'
   13. Terms and category *al-mu'minūna*, 'enactors of security'
   14. Terms
   15. Terms

16 For this translation of *istaqāma* in the Qur'ān, see below, Chapter 6, on linguistics.

16. Terms

17. Case: Places for prostration to God (*masājid Allāh*), dwelling and prospering there (*ʾamara*), and categories *al-mushrikūna* and *kufr*

18. Terms and category *al-muhtadūna*, 'the divinely guided'

19. Terms and categories *al-muʾminūna*, *al-mujāhidūna fī sabīl Allāh*, 'those who struggle for the duties towards God', and *al-ẓālimūna*, 'those who do wrong'

20. Terms and categories *al-muʾminūna*, *al-mujāhidūna*, *al-muhājirūna*, 'those who leave home', and *al-fāʾizūna*

21. Terms

22. Terms

23. Case: Protective governorship (*walāya*), family, and categories *kufr*, *īmān*, and *al-ẓālimūna*

24. Terms and category *al-fāsiqūna*, 'the rebellious'

25. Example: Battle of Ḥunayn (between Mecca and the city of Ṭā'if)

26. Terms and categories *al-muʾminūna* and *al-kāfirūna*

27. Terms

28. Terms

29. Case: Fighting the People of the divine writing if they resist paying the poll tax (*jizya*), category *ahl al-kitāb*:

"Fight those who have been given the divine writing who do not enact security through God, nor through the furthest day, do not hold sacred what God and His Messengers have prohibited, and do not comply with the true and right judicial order, so that they give the poll tax from their hands, humbly (*qātilū alladhīna lā yuʾminūna bi-Allāh wa lā bi-l-yawm al-ākhar wa lā yuḥarrimūna mā ḥarrama Allāhu wa rasūluhu wa lā yadīnūna dīna al-ḥaqqi min alladhīna ūtū al-kitāba ḥattā yuʿṭū al-jizya ʿan yadin wa hum ṣāghirūna*)"

30. Example of Jews and Christians stating divine fatherhood and sonship, category *ʾifk*, 'false statement'

31. Example of taking rabbis, monks, and the Messiah as lords besides One God, category *al-mushrikūna*

32. Example, category *al-kāfirūna*

33. Terms, category *dīn al-ḥaqq*, 'the true and right judicial order'

34. Terms for rabbis and monks who overtax the people and hoard riches, not contributing their share

35. Terms

36. Case: The correct number of sacred months and calendar, categories *al-mushrikūna* and *al-muttaqīna*

37. Example

38. Case: The obligation to God to break up from the land and struggle

39. Terms

40. Example

41. Terms
42. Example of those who swear loyalty to pacts (*yaḥlifūna*) but deceive, category *al-kādhibūna*, 'the deceptive'
43. Example of categories *ṣādiqūna*, 'the truthful', and *al-kādhibūna*, 'the deceptive'
44. Example of categories *al-muʾminūna*, *al-mujāhidūna*, and *al-muttaqīna*
45. Example of category *al-mutaraddid*, 'the one who vacillates'
46. Example of category *al-qāʿidūna*, 'those who sit back'
47. Example of category *al-ẓālimūna*, 'those who do wrong'
48. Example of category *al-kārihūna*, 'those who are averse'
49. Example of category *al-kāfirūna*, 'those who reject security'
50. Example of category *al-fāriḥūna*, 'those who rejoice over your loss' and turn away from your governorship
51. Example of category *al-muʾminūna*
52. Example of category *al-mutarabbiṣūna*, 'those who wait and see'

53. Case: Accepting monetary contributions from category *al-fāsiqūna*, 'those who rebel'

54. Example of category *al-kārihūna*, 'those who are averse' to spending
55. Example of category *al-kāfirūna*, 'those who reject security'
56. Example of category *al-yafraqūna*, 'those who are afraid'
57. Example, same category

58. Case: Distribution of alms (*ṣadaqa*) and category *al-sākhiṭūna*, 'those who are angry'

59. Example of category *al-rāḍīna*, 'those who are content'
60. Terms

61. Case: Harming the Prophet and category *al-muʾdhūna*, 'those who harm the Prophet'

62. Example of category *al-muʾminūna*, who enter pacts for the sake of God and His Messenger
63. Terms
64. Example of category *al-munāfiqūna*, 'the hypocrites'
65. Example, same category
66. Terms for categories *al-kāfirūna* and *al-mujrimūna*, 'those who commit offense'
67. Example of categories *al-munāfiqūna* and *al-fāsiqūna*, 'those who rebel'
68. Terms
69. Example, historical
70. Example, historical, category *yaẓlimūna anfusahum*, 'those who wrong themselves'
71. Example and terms, category *al-muʾminūna wa al-muʾmināt*
72. Example and terms, category *al-muʾminūna wa al-muʾmināt*

73. Case: Obligating the Prophet to struggle (*jāhada*) against *al-kuffār* and *al-munāfiqūna*
    74. Example and terms
    75. Example
    76. Example of category *al-muʿriḍūna*, 'those who renounce protective governorship'
    77. Example and terms for category *al-munāfiqūna* and *al-kādhibūna*, 'the deceptive' in contracts and pacts
    78. Terms
    79. Example and terms
    80. Terms for *al-fāsiqūna*, 'those who rebel'
81. Case: Obligating the people to fulfil their obligations to God and His Messenger, category *al-mukhallafūna*, 'those who stay behind'
    82. Terms
    83. Terms
    84. Terms and category *al-fāsiqūna*, 'those who rebel'
    85. Terms and category *al-kāfirūna*, 'those who reject security'
    86. Example of category *al-qāʿidūna*, 'those who sit back'
    87. Example
    88. Example of categories *al-mujāhidūna*, *al-muʾminūna* and *al-mufliḥūna*, 'those who induce prosperity'
    89. Terms
    90. Example and terms for categories *al-muʿadhdhirūna*, 'those who seek permission', *al-qāʿidūna*, *al-kādhibūna*, and *al-kāfirūna*
    91. Terms for categories *al-ḍuʿafāʾ*, 'the weak', *al-marḍā*, 'the sick', and *alladhīna lā yajidūna mā yanfiqūna*, 'those who have nothing to spend'
    92. Terms for category 'those for who the Prophet could not provide mounts'
    93. Terms for category *al-mustaʾdhinūna wa hum aghniyāʾ*, 'those who seek exception even though they are rich'
    94. Example and terms
    95. Example and terms
    96. Example and terms
    97. Example of *al-aʿrāb*, 'the nomadic Arabs (?)', and categories *al-kāfirūna* and *al-munāfiqūna* among them
    98. Example, same categories
    99. Example and terms for category *al-muʾminūna*
    100. Example and terms for categories *al-muhājirūna*, 'those who emigrate', and *al-anṣār*, 'those who help to victory'
    101. Example of *al-aʿrāb* and *ahl al-madīna*, 'the people of Medina', and terms for category *al-munāfiqūna* among them
    102. Example and terms of those among them who asked for pardon and did some good deeds

103. Terms
104. Terms
105. Terms
106. Terms

107. Case: Those who take a place for prostration (*masjid*) to cause harm, reject security and promote disunity, but enter the pact, category *al-kādhibūna*, 'those who deceive'

108. Example and terms for categories *al-muttaqīna*, 'those who fulfil their obligations', and *al-muṭṭahhirūna*, 'those who purify themselves'

109. Example of categories *al-muttaqīna*, *al-murtaḍūna*, 'those who are content', and *al-ẓālimūna*, 'those who do wrong'

110. Example of category *al-ẓālimūna*

111. Case: The contract between God and *al-mu'minūna*, its terms, and its written record:

"Indeed, God has bought from the enactors of security their persons and their wealth in return for the Garden, so they shall fight for the obligations towards God, killing and getting killed: a promise from Him with a right in the Torah, the Gospel, and the Qur'ān, and who fulfils his compact better than God? So rejoice over your pledged deal that you have agreed with Him, for that is the magnificent triumph!" (*inna Allāha ishtarā min al-mu'minīna anfusahum wa amwālahum bi'anna lahum al-janna yuqātilūna fī sabīl Allāh fayaqtulūna wa yuqtalūna wa'dan 'alayhi ḥaqqan fī al-tawrā wa al-injīl wa al-qur'ān wa man awfā bi'ahdihi min Allāh fa-istabshirū bibay'ikum alladhī bāya'tum bihi wa dhālika huwa al-fawz al-'aẓīm*)

112. Terms for category *al-mu'minūna*

113. Case: Forgiveness (*istighfār*) for relatives of category *al-mushrikūna*, 'those who assign partners'

114. Example Abraham and his father

115. Case: God's forgiveness and its terms

116. Terms set by God

117. Example *tāba*, 'He returns', categories *al-nabī*, 'the Prophet', *al-muhājirūna*, and *al-anṣār*

118. Example *tāba*, category *alladhīna ḍāqat 'alayhim anfusuhum*, 'those who were in distress'

119. Terms for categories *al-mu'minūna*, *al-muttaqīna*, and *al-ṣādiqūna*, 'those who are truthful'

120. Case: Obligation upon *ahl al-madīna* and *al-a'rāb* not to go back on their pact with the Messenger of God, and terms for category *al-muḥsinūna*, 'those who do good deeds'

121. Terms

122. Case: Some of *al-muʾminūna* should study the principles of the legal order (*yatafaqqahū al-dīn*) to admonish those who return from war

123. Terms for categories *al-muʾminūna* and *al-muttaqīna*

124. Example: a *sūra* sent down with admonition, category *al-muʾminūna*

125. Example: a *sūra* sent down with admonition, category *al-kādfirūna*

126. Example, same category

127. Example: a *sūra* sent down with admonition, category *lā yafqahūna*, 'those who do not analyse the principles of *dīn*'

128. Case: The Messenger from among the people is kind and protects the lives of *al-muʾminūna*

129. Terms for category *tawallaw*, 'those who turn away from protective governorship':
"If they turn away from the protective governorship, say: 'My reckoning is God, there is no god but He: in Him I place my trust, for He is the Lord of the Magnificent Throne!'" (*faʾin tawallaw faqul ḥasbī Allāhu lā ilāha illā huwa ʿalayhi tawakkaltu wa huwa rabb al-ʿarsh al-ʿaẓīm*)

AL-ṬABARĪ'S THEORY OF QURʾĀNIC LANGUAGE, AND COMPOSITION

Within the discipline of *tafsīr*, al-Ṭabarī's Introduction to his commentary, *Jāmiʿ al-bayān ʿan taʾwīl āy al-Qurʾān*, is likely the earliest comprehensive theoretical statement about the Qurʾān. I have therefore selected his theory of Qurʾānic language and composition to develop the case for Covenant as meta-level topic for the Qurʾān and *balāgha* as compositional methodology. The outcome will be a tabular chart over the Qurʾān's topics and their occurrences across the canon.

Qurʾānic Arabic Language: al-Ṭabarī's Theory

Al-Ṭabarī begins his Introduction with an exposition on the *balāgha*-related concept *bayān*, which echoes the first verses of Q. 55 (*al-Raḥmān*):

(1) The Giver of Life (*al-Raḥmān*)
(2) conveyed knowledge of the Reading (*ʿallama al-qurʾān*),
(3) created mankind (*khalaqa al-insān*),

(4) conveyed to them knowledge of **clear distinction** (*'allamahu **al-bayān***)!

Al-Ṭabarī established that *bayān* is one of the greatest blessings that God has conferred upon humans, since it enables them to "convey in a clearly distinct way their innermost subjects, and indicate their personal concerns", through language, "so that they can communicate, get to know each other, and cooperate" (1995/1: 1, 16–17). However, God has created ranks among people according to how well they master *bayān*: while some can never clearly distinguish and communicate their subjective concerns, others can. Among the latter, those who are messengers of God perfect this language-based ability, with the Prophet as their epitome:

> It is thus clear that there is no more clarifying distinction, no more persuasive wise judgement, no higher logic, no nobler discourse, than the clarifying distinctions and logic by which a man challenges a people in a time when they are leading in the art of public oratory and rhetoric (*fī zamān hum fīhi ru'asā' ṣinā'at al-khuṭab wa al-balāgha*), and of the delivering of poetry and elocution, of *saj'* and soothsaying, [and prevails over] every one of their public orators and rhetoricians, poets and the loquacious, and performers of *saj'* and soothsayers. Thus he makes a fool of their sharpest wits, defeats their reasoning, and acquits himself of their judicial order, inviting all of them to follow him, receive and hold him for true, and confirm that he is a messenger to them from their Lord. He informs them that the indication of the truthfulness of his statements and the proof of the reality of his prophecy is the clarifying distinction, the wise judgement, and the distinguishing criterion that he conveys to them in a language like their language, and in a logic corresponding to the meanings in their logic (1995/1: 1, 18).

Al-Ṭabarī thus defines prophecy and messengers generically as a communicative and rhetorical ability, which challenges established forms of speech and reasoning. He then proceeds to explain how, even though God's address through messengers necessarily corresponds to a people's language and logic, God's address is inimitably clearer in conveying distinctions, in logic and in persuasiveness, than any human address, since God is complete in every sense and His creatures always deficient by comparison with Him (1995/1: 1, 18; cf. 13). Referring to Q. 14 (*Ibrāhīm*), 4 for a general statement about God's messengers addressing their people in their own languages, and to Q. 16 (*al-Naḥl*), 64 for a particular application of the topic to the Prophet, al-Ṭabarī concluded the Qur'ān was sent down in Arabic to the Prophet's Arabic speaking people, as stated in Q. 12 (*Yūsuf*), 2 and Q. 26 (*al-Shuʿarāʾ*), 192–195 (1995/1: 1, 19).

He then proceeded to discuss which kind of Arabic this was. 'The Arabs' (*al-ʿarab*), he pointed out, is a collective noun for a people who speak Arabic (*ʿarabī*), but there are several Arabic languages, which differ greatly in terms of *bayān*, logic (*manṭiq*), and discourse (*kalām*) (1995/1: 1, 24). Thus, he defined the hallmark of Qurʾānic Arabic as "conveying clarifying distinctions" and "carrying universals and particulars" i.e. distinguishing general principles and their case-specific implications:

> Since it is the case, that God – Majestic is His honour! – has informed His servants, that He has made the Reading Arabic, and that it was sent down in an **Arabic language that conveys clarifying distinctions (*lisān ʿarabī mubīn*)**, so that then its manifestation **carries particulars and universals** (*thumma kāna ẓāhiruhu* ***muḥtamilan khuṣūṣan wa ʿumūman***), there is no way to knowledge of what God – Elevated is His honour! – meant with His particulars and universals except through the clarifying distinctions of he for who the clarifying distinction was made, namely God's Messenger (1995/1: 1, 24).

One example of how he identified universals and particulars is his exegesis of the Early Meccan oath-*sūra* Q. 90 (*al-Balad*), verse 3. As reflected in its name, the *sūra*'s topic is *al-balad*: an administrative region constituted by cities with surrounding lands, which people should tend and not lay waste (verses 4, 6). Moreover, in the region, people should do good by those in need (verses 13–16). In this context, the categories 'those who enact security' (*alladhīna āmanū*) and 'those who reject security' (*alladhīna kafarū*) in verses 17 and 19 mean doing good by those in need or refusing to do so, respectively:

> (1) *lām ʾalif* I swear an oath by this region and its cities (*lām ʾalif uqsimu bihādhā al-balad*),[17]
> (2) and you are permitted this region (*wa anta ḥillun bihādhā al-balad*):
> (3) By every begetter and what he begets:
> (4) We have in fact created man to toil!
> (5) Does he calculate that no one shall have power over him?
> (6) He says: "I have wasted abundant wealth!"

17 I am here reading the initial letters *lām* and *ʾalif* not as the particle *lā* (for negation or emphasis), but as an example of the category 'isolated letters' (*ḥurūf muqaṭṭaʿa*), which introduce several *sūra*s; as we shall see below, al-Ṭabarī considered these might serve as oaths.

(7) Does he calculate that no one saw him?
(8) Have We not given him two eyes,
(9) a tongue and two lips,
(10) and guided him to the two highways?
(11) Yet he did not brave the rocky pass!
(12) If only you knew what is the rocky pass:
(13) Freeing a slave,
(14) or giving food, on a day of famine,
(15) to an orphan close of kin,
(16) or to a poor man in dire need!
(17) Then, being one of those who enact security, and who obligate each other to perseverance and to the protection of life:
(18) those are the companions of doing good to their people (*ūlā'ika aṣḥāb al-maymana*),
(19) while those who reject security through Our signs, they are the companions of causing problems for their people (*hum aṣḥāb al-mash'ama*),[18]
(20) on who a fire is closing in!

Al-Ṭabarī's starts his explanation of verse 3 by pointing out that it is God Who swears the oath, similar to how Gwynne has argued that the Early Mecca oath-*sūra*s are God's pledges to Covenant (Gwynne 2004: 20–22).[19] He then explains 'By every begetter and what he begets' in terms of the distinction between generals and particulars, arguing that this is a *general* statement:

> God swears an oath by every begetter and what he begets, because God generalised 'every begetter and what he begets'. It is not correct to particularise that except by proof (*ḥujja*), which requires submitting to a report (*khabar*), or to reasoning (*'aql*), and since there is no report that particularizes that, nor any evidence by logic (*burhān*) that requires submitting to its particularization, it is a generalization, as He generalized it (1995/15: 30, 246; cf. 244–245).

18 On the relationship between the roots *y-m-n* and *sh-'-m*, and their reference to how a polity and its people (*qawm*) fare under a leader, see *Lisān al-'arab*, www.alwaraq.net, pp. 2842–2844.

19 By comparison, Bernard Weiss has argued that God does not swear oaths, because unlike humans He cannot be bound by His Covenantal promise (1990: 72–73). As we shall see below and in frequent cases, the Qur'ān actually does depict God as obligated by His promise, hence the oaths can be seen as God's pledges.

Thus, al-Ṭabarī's definition of Qur'ānic Arabic language conceptualises it as a technical discourse, distinguishing between generals and particulars.

Next, al-Ṭabarī proceeded to treat the above-discussed Prophetic *ḥadīth* that the Qur'ān was sent down in *sab'at aḥruf* (1995/1: 1, 24–52). He begins by saying, in line with Retsö's (2003) approach, that the Arabs spoke many more than seven languages, so the 'seven' *aḥruf* do not refer to these. Rather, it is a technical term conveying that the Qur'ān was sent down in 'seven idioms' (*sab'a lughāt*), which are read in 'seven languages' (*sab'at alsin*) (1995/1: 1, 35). He then selects as his preferred transmission of the *ḥadīth* the one by the Prophet's scribe Ubayy b. Ka'b, in which the Prophet says "I am commanded to read the Qur'ān according to seven *aḥruf*, from the seven gates of the Garden". Al-Ṭabarī explains:

> The seven *aḥruf* are, as we have said, the seven languages, and the seven gates of the Garden are the forms conveying meaning (*al-ma'ānī*), which contain command and prohibition (*al-amr wa al-nahy*), instilment of desire and fear (*al-targhīb wa al-tarhīb*), narrative accounts (*al-qiṣaṣ*), and paradigmatic examples (*al-mathal*), which, if a person acts according to them and abides by their defined boundaries, entitles him to the Garden (1995/1: 1, 36).

Since the 'seven languages' and 'forms of meaning' lead to the same goal – the Garden – they preclude disagreement over binding terms: "God sent down His writing in the language of Muḥammad (pbuh) only with one judgement corresponding to all His creatures, not with different judgements concerning them" (1995/1: 1, 37).[20] Hence, the forms of meaning convey a message, which should be enacted, and which obligates people, in a legally binding, contractual sense.

On this basis, and with support from another *ḥadīth*, al-Ṭabarī arrives at a precise definition of *aḥruf*: they are differences in pronounced words (*ikhtilāf alfāẓ*), which can be of orthographic character, or choices between synonyms, like the different 'senses' (*awjuh*) pertaining to a concept with defined meaning (*naẓīr*). For example, 'Come here!' can be said in several different ways, including *halumma* and *ta'ālā* (1995/1: 1, 38–43). Hence, the differences occur within the 'forms conveying meaning' (*ma'ānī*), which al-Ṭabarī lists as seven generic forms:

20 See also his exegesis of Q. 13, 36, where he identifies the divine *kitāb* with *ḥukm 'arabī*, 'a judgement in Arabic'.

> [The Qurʾān] descended in seven forms conveying meaning, which are: commands, prohibitions, promises (*al-waʿd*), threats (*al-waʿīd*), dialectical disputation (*al-jadal*), narrative accounts (*al-qiṣaṣ*), and examples (*al-mathal*) (1995/1: 1, 41).

Thus, al-Ṭabarī lands on a linguistic explanation of *sabʿat aḥruf*: they refer to different words that express different senses of the same concept, within the 'forms conveying meaning' (*maʿānī*). These forms are constitutive of the Prophet's Qurʾān as well as the ʿUthmānic script. The difference is, in al-Ṭabarī's view, that the established script follows one of the seven *aḥruf*, not the others (1995/1: 1, 47). The divine, inimitable rhetoric is preserved in the ʿUthmānic script partly through the abilities of those who led the production. Al-Ṭabarī cited a report from the Prophet's foremost scribe Zayd b. Thābit, who led the work. Zayd reported that the Caliph ʿUthmān appointed Abān b. Saʿīd b. al-ʿĀṣ to assist in the work, for he was "analytically minded and eloquent" (*labīb faṣīḥ*), i.e. capable of preserving the sent-down forms conveying meaning (1995/1: 1, 44).

Al-Ṭabarī's Theory of the 'Cut-off Letter-syllables'

Al-Ṭabarī also tackled one of the long-standing mysteries of the Qurʾān, the *ḥurūf muqaṭṭaʿa*, 'cut-off letter-syllables', which introduce 29 *sūra*s. His main case is Q. 2 (*al-Baqara*), 1–2:

> (1) ***aliflāmmīm***
> (2) That is **the divine writing** in which there is no cause for doubt: guidance for those who fulfil their obligations![21] (*dhālika* ***al-kitābu*** *lā rayba fīhi hudan li-l-muttaqīna*)

Al-Ṭabarī first maps a range of explanations: the syllables are added to *sūra*s after the sending down, or they are integral parts of them; symbolical names of *sūra*s; indicators of some of God's names and attributes, which contain the specific letters in each syllable, and which serve as openings of some *sūra*s; markers of the end of one *sūra* and the beginning of a new one; representations of the letters of the alphabet, which through their various combinations make up the divine writing (*al-kitāb*) referred to in verse 2; symbols

21 Here (as elsewhere) I follow al-Ṭabarī's explanation of *muttaqīna* as those who heed God's commands and prohibitions, and thereby prepare themselves for the final account (1995/1: 1, 148). Hence, 'those who fulfil their obligations', in the contractual sense.

of polysemy i.e. that concepts have several senses; and oaths (*aqsām*, sing. *qasam*) sworn by the divine writing (1995/1: 1, 129–138). The only explanations he refutes are that the syllables are added after the sending-down, because everything in the writing is God's word, and that they could be representations of the letters of the alphabet, which make up the divine writing, because it makes no logical sense in the context and lacks support among exegetical authorities. All the others are acceptable, and he then synthesises them into his own explanation, focusing on polysemy: just as any word can have a range of meanings, for example, *dīn* can mean recompense and account, political power and obedience, humility and reckoning, each of these syllables can mean several things. Had God intended to clearly distinguish only one meaning, He would have done so, or there would have been a sound Prophetic *ḥadīth* defining it. He then continues to argue that because the syllables consist of letter symbols which open some *sūra*s, they can function as initial oaths, sworn by God's names and attributes contained in the divine writing and symbolised by these letters (1995/1: 1, 139–142).[22]

Extrapolating from al-Ṭabarī's perspective on the cut-off letter-syllables, these can be seen as adding more Qur'ānic oaths to the Early Mecca oath-*sūra*s discussed above. If the latter serve generally as God's pledges to Covenant, the letter-syllables function as God's oaths pledged specifically by His writing and its message about Himself. I will return to this issue below, and its implications for Qur'ānic composition.

Al-Ṭabarī on the Composition of the Canon

Al-Ṭabarī's *bayān*-related distinction between general (or universal) and particular statements, and his list of seven 'forms that convey meaning' (*ma'ānī*) in the Qur'ānic Arabic, correspond with two of the three components of *balāgha*. However, he also identified the third component *badī'*, 'innovation' or 'originality', which he related to the Qur'ān's composition (*ta'līf*). Composition, he argued, is the point where the Qur'ān truly 'innovates' compared with both the other prophetic scriptures (the Torah, the Psalter, and the Gospels), and other generic forms of Arabic, notably soothsaying (*kahāna*), poetry (*shi'r*), rhyming prose (*saj'*), rhetoric (*balāgha*), and oratory (*khaṭāba*). None of these can compete with the Qur'ān's

22 I owe thanks to Mehmet Akif Koc for drawing my attention to these aspects of al-Ṭabarī's explanation of the 'cut-off letter-syllables'.

> astonishing grammatical organisation, its extraordinary internal alignments, and its **innovative composition** (*naẓmuhu al-ʿajīb wa raṣfuhu al-gharīb wa **taʾlīfuhu al-badīʿ***) (1995/1: 1, 126).

The innovative character of the composition hinges on Q. 1, entitled 'The Opening' (*al-Fātiḥa*) because of its introductory place in the canon. In al-Ṭabarī's view, Q. 1 defines God's and humans' mutual rights and obligations, which is a topic that suffuses the entire Qurʾān. In other words, it sums up its meta-concept. Q. 1 reads as follows:

> 1. By God's name 'Giver of Life', 'Continuous Protector of Life' (*bi-ism Allāh al-Raḥmān al-Raḥīm*):[23]
> 2. Praise belongs to God, Lord of the knowing beings (*al-ḥamdu li-Allāhi rabb al-ʿālamīn*),
> 3. Giver of Life, Continuous Protector of Life (*al-Raḥmān al-Raḥīm*),
> 4. King of the Day of Judgement (*māliki yawm al-dīn*)!
> 5. You we serve and You we ask for protection (*iyyāka naʿbudu wa iyyāka nastaʿīn*):
> 6. Guide us along the path of correct speech and action (*ihdinā al-ṣirāṭ al-mustaqīm*),[24]
> 7. The path of those on who You **conferred material blessings**, without being angry with them, for they do not stray (*ṣirāṭ alladhīna **anʿamta** ʿalayhim ghayr al-maghḍūbi ʿalayhim wa lā al-ḍāllīn*)!

Al-Fātiḥa, al-Ṭabarī explains, sums up the Covenantal contractual rights and obligations between God and humans, and describes it as a path consisting of correct speech (*qawl*) and action (*ʿamal*) (1995/1: 1, 110, 112). He then expounds the verb 'conferred material blessings' (*anʿamta*) in verse 7 as referring to the material sustenance from God's creation, to which the people have a right:

> What it contains of thanks and glorification and praise of [God] is exhortation for the servants about His magnificence and rule and power, and the magnitude of His kingship, so that they will honour Him for His favours and give thanks to Him for **His material blessings (*naʿmāʾihi*)**.

23 Al-Ṭabarī explains *al-Raḥmān* as referring to God as Creator and Sustainer of all beings, in the general (*ʿāmm*) sense that He provides material sustenance (*rizq*) allowing all humans to live i.e. both *al-muʾminūna* and *al-kāfirūna*, in this world, while *al-Raḥīm* refers to His particular (*khāṣṣ*) and continued protection of *al-muʾminūna* both in this world through His *dīn* and in the hereafter (1995/1: 1, 85–86). I have tried to capture this through my translation 'Giver of Life', 'Continuous Protector of Life'.

24 On *mustaqīm* in this sense, see below, and Chapter 6, on linguistics.

> **They have a right to the surplus of that from Him, and they are entitled to an abundant reward from Him (*fayastaḥiqqū bihi minhu al-mazīd wa yastawjibū ʿalayhi al-thawāb al-jazīl*).** (1995/1: 1, 127).

He then specifies the humans' obligations: to serve only God, obeying His commands and prohibitions, and not rebel against him by serving other gods or rivals (*andād*). Then follows his point concerning composition. Q. 1, *al-Fātiḥa*, is also called *umm al-Qurʾān*, 'the source' or 'front' of the Qurʾān, he argues, because its meaning, with the mutual rights and obligations, is repeated throughout the whole corpus, and constitutes the persuasive proof of the Qurʾān's divine nature:

> That is the meaning of the extensive clarification of the distinctions in *sūrat umm al-qurʾān,* and of what corresponds to it in the other *sūra*s of the Forger of Distinctions (*al-furqān*), and that is the persuasive capacity for just judgement and the comprehensive proof (*wa dhālika al-ḥikma al-bāligha wa al-ḥujja al-kāmila*). (1995/1: 1, 127)

To summarise: The fact that al-Ṭabarī defined the Qurʾānic Arabic language and composition in terms of a theory of language and rhetoric shows that he conceptualised the Qurʾān as simultaneously divine and theoretical. His theory of Qurʾānic Arabic and composition aligns with Abdel Haleem's definition of *balāgha* and its constituent components *bayān*, *maʿānī*, and *badīʿ*. For al-Ṭabarī, *bayān* refers to the distinctions between generals and particulars, while *maʿānī* corresponds with his 'seven forms conveying meaning'. As for *badīʿ*, it refers to the Qurʾān's 'innovative composition', compared with both the Biblical scriptures and Arabic genres of speech. In line with Gwynne's thesis about Covenant as the Qurʾān's overarching concept, but arguably going beyond it through his grounding in *balāgha* and his theory of Qurʾānic Arabic, he defined the principle guiding the composition at meta-level as the Covenantal contractual rights and obligations, defined in Q. 1. Since he argued that these rights and obligations are repeated throughout the whole canon, they can be assumed to be reflected also at the meso-level of *sūra*s, and the micro-level of verse passages.[25]

25 For the same analysis and conclusions, see also Mårtensson (2020).

AL-ṬABARĪ APPLIED: COVENANT AS COMPOSITIONAL PRINCIPLE

Al-Ṭabarī's own applied exegetical method did not involve defining the overall topic or outline of *sūra*s. Instead, he proceeded verse by verse, citing exegetical reports, Prophetic *ḥadīth*, variant readings, and then giving his own, independent grammatical and contextual analysis, often including inter-Qur'ānic references to the same word or phrase in other contexts. As I now proceed to develop his analytical framework and apply it to outline *sūra* composition, I therefore rely on the *balāgha*-based methodology he developed in his Introduction, as follows.

Firstly, bayān: I assume that a concept appears in the form of a general or particular statement, which 'clearly distinguishes' and defines categories of people and the terms that apply to them. *Secondly, ma'ānī*: I also assume that a concept and the distinctions appear in the seven forms conveying meaning i.e. a narrative account (*qiṣṣa*), a dialectical disputation (*jadal*), a paradigmatic example (*mathal*), promise and threat (*wa'd wa wa'īd*), command and prohibition (*amr wa nahy*). *Thirdly, badī'*: I assume that the Covenantal terms set out in Q. 1 are repeated throughout the entire canon, producing the Qur'ānic innovative composition. Hence, distinctions and generic forms all communicate one meaning: the contractual terms. This implies that all terms that apply also to inter-human relations and law derive from the divine-human Covenantal contract defined in Q. 1. One example given above was the outline of Q. 9 (*al-Tawba*). Its cases, categories and terms, which refer to war and loyalty to pacts, are framed in terms of the categories' relationship to the divine Covenant in the sense that those loyal to pacts are also loyal to the terms of Covenant.

Here I will start with the Covenant-*sūra par excellence*, Q. 7 (*al-A'rāf*), which describes the original Covenant between God and Adam's descendants (verse 172). Q. 7 from the Late Mecca period treats the experience-based, historical knowledge of Covenant and its terms, conveyed and confirmed in the divine writing. The point is that the Prophet and Messenger of God now communicates the same written terms that other messengers conveyed before. 'Divine writing' (*kitāb*) can thus be seen as a topic marking shifts between the different sub-topics and examples, and between general statements and particular cases. Many of the category-concepts that occur in Q. 9 occur here too, such as *al-mu'minūna, al-kāfirūna, al-mushrikūna, al-muttaqīna*, etc. Since my aim here is to show the structure related to generals and particulars, I have for the sake of conciseness omitted the category-concepts; however, one could easily plot them into the following model:

1–2: Divine writing sent down for confirmation, warning and reminder of Covenant: general terms

3–10: The Covenant: particular terms for this Messenger

11–25: Adam and Satan: general example & terms of obedience/ prostration and rebellion/refusal to prostrate (as in the prayer)

26–53: Adam's offspring and God's messengers and signs: general terms

52–53: Divine writing conveys knowledge, guidance and protection of life: general example

54–58: God's Creation provides material blessings and sustenance for humanity: general terms

59–64: Noah and his people (*qawm*): particular example

65–72: The messenger Hūd and the people of ʿĀd: particular example

73–79: The messenger Ṣāliḥ and the people of Thamūd: particular example

80–84: Lot and his people: particular example

85–93: The messenger Shuʿayb and the people of Midyan: particular example

94–102: Prophets and messengers sent to afflicted cities to make the people honour their contracts: general example & terms

103–144: Moses, Pharaoh and the Israelites: honouring the Covenant: particular example

145–147: The written tablets convey knowledge, clear exposition of signs: particular example & terms

148–156: Moses, the Israelites and the calf: particular example & terms

157–158: The written promise of this Messenger & Prophet: general terms, compared w. Moses' terms

159–168: The Israelites in the land & the Covenantal terms: particular example

169–171: The Covenant of divine writing with the Israelites: truth & right: particular example & terms

172–174: The Covenant of Creation: Knowledge & testimony: general terms

175–183: Followers of Satan & followers of God, focused on truth/ right & justice: general examples

184–195: Warning of the Hour against taking other partners than God, to the Prophet's people: particular examples & terms

196: Divine writing & God's protective governorship for those who promote the common good: general terms

197–203: Take God not Satan for protective governor, fulfil your obligations, follow His guidance: general examples

204: Listen to the Qur'ān being read and receive protection of life: general terms

205: Remember and honour your Lord: general terms

206: Serve your Lord, praise Him, and prostrate: general terms.

Q. 7 is a largely narrative *sūra*, with generic accounts (*qiṣaṣ*) that include numerous paradigmatic examples (*mathal*) and terms, commands and prohibitions (*amr wa nahy*), promises and threats (*wa'd wa wa'īd*), and long argumentative sequences (*jadal*). By comparison, the Early Mecca *sūra*s treat the same topics, and use the same repertoire of generic forms, but within their shorter, denser forms, hence without the long accounts and argumentative sequences. For example, Q. 75 (*al-Qiyāma*, 'Standing to trial') sets out the same Covenantal terms as in Q. 7 in one compact block of 40 verses, focusing on the terms for the category 'the blameworthy person' (*al-nafs al-lawwāma*) on the Day of the trial:

1: *lām'alif* Divine oath sworn by the divine writing and the Day of standing to trial: general terms

2: *lām'alif* Divine oath by the writing and the blameworthy person (*al-nafs al-lawwāma*): general case

3–6: The blameworthy person questions God's power to bring about the Day: general examples

7–15: The blameworthy person's reactions on the Day, testifying against himself: general examples

16–19: Gathering and reading the reading without changing it, and the obligation to clarify its distinctions: general terms

20–35: The blameworthy person's fate on the Day, and the deeds that got him there: general examples & terms

36–40: God's creative powers that will bring about the Day: general terms

The next *sūra*, Q. 76 (*al-Insān*, 'Mankind'),[26] focuses instead on the category of those who will fare well on the Day of the trial, with only a brief example of the opposite category of wrongdoers towards the last verses. The concept *sabīl*, literally 'path', refers to the sum of humanity's obligations towards God, which they must recall and honour (*dhakara*), while God

26 Gwynne remarks that the Qur'ānic concept *insān*, 'man', was understood by al-Ṭabarī, referring to a report from Ibn 'Abbās, as derived from the root *n-s-y*, 'to forget'. I.e. it is in man's nature to forget and abandon the Covenant unless God makes them recall and remember it; the locus is al-Ṭabarī's exegesis of Q. 20, 115 (Gwynne 2004: 4–5). The argument can be applied to Q. 76 as well.

recalls whether they do so and sends down the Reading (Qur'ān) to remind them. Hence, references to the sum of obligations and the recollection introduce and conclude the *sūra*:

1: Everything man does is **recalled (*madhkūr*)**, at all times: general terms
2–3: God created man & guided him to the sum of obligations (*sabīl*), either grateful or rejecting security: general terms
  4–5: The rejecters of security (*al-kāfirūna*) and the dutiful (*al-abrār*): general terms
6–22: God's servants (*'ibād*) in the Garden: general examples
23: God made the Reading (*al-qur'ān*) descend
  24–28: The Qur'ān's general & particular terms
29: Recollection (*tadhkira*) of the Lord's sum of obligations (*sabīl*)
  30–31: God's power to determine outcomes, and terms for those who do wrong (*al-ẓālimūna*): general

Sūra 87 (*al-A'lā*, 'The Most High') also refers to recollection and honouring (*dhikr*) of the divine obligations through reading. Two opposite categories, those who recollect and those who do not, are given equal treatment, and the *sūra* concludes with a reference to Abraham's and Moses' first written documents (*al-ṣuḥuf al-ūlā*) as verification and confirmation of the terms to be recalled:

1: Glorify God's name 'the Most High' (*al-A'lā*): general term
  2–5: God's material sustenance and power: general terms
6: God makes the recollector and reminder **read so he does not forget**: particular case
  7–9: God's and **the recollector/reminder's** general terms
  10–15: Those who **recollect** and those who do not: general terms
16–17: Those who prefer the nearest life over the furthest away life: particular case
  18–19: Confirmation and verification by Abraham's and Moses' **first written documents**

Similarly, the next *sūra* 88 (*al-Ghāshiya*, 'The Calamity') continues the topic of recollection and now develops it with reference to two other categories: those deserving the fire and those deserving the Garden. Here, the source of authority is a report (*ḥadīth*):

1: The report (*ḥadīth*) on the event of the Calamity: general case
  2–7: The non-nourishing food & drink of those in the fire: general terms

8–16: The drinks & comforts of those in the Garden: general terms
17–20: Creation and its making: general example of God's power
21–23: **The recollector/reminder's** obligation to remind: particular terms
24–26: God's obligation to punish & hold to account: particular terms

The next *sūra*, Q. 89 (*al-Fajr*, 'The Dawn'), begins with a series of oaths (*aqsām*), by the shift between night and day, by ten specific nights (ritually significant and referring to the sanctuary in verse 5), and by odd and even numbers, suggesting 'calculation' as an implicit topic: of the ritual calendar, of lands, and in the final account. References are also made to historical examples, including Pharaoh's idolatry in the city and its surrounding lands (*al-bilād*), a word that connects with the oath that introduces the following *sūra*, Q. 90 (*al-Balad*), mentioned above. Moreover, Q. 89 refers to a legal topic, namely the obligation towards the orphans and the poor with regards to the wealth and sustenance that derives from the land. The categories are those who refuse to comply with these obligations and who will enter Hell, and those who comply and enter the Garden:

1–4: God's oaths by the dawn, by the ten nights, by the even and the odd, and by the night's course: general terms
5: Man should pledge oaths to grant protection by the sanctuary (*ḥijr*):[27] particular term
6–9: Historical examples of mighty idol-worshippers: particular case
10–12: Pharaoh's idolatry & corruption of the city lands (*fasād*): particular case
13: God's punishment of these: particular case
14: God's full overview: general term
15–16: God dignifies man with material sustenance & tests man by diminishing them/man's responses: general terms
17: Man fails to dignify the orphan: particular case
18: Man fails to feed the poor: particular case
19: Man devours the inheritance (land) greedily: particular case
20: Man loves (landed) wealth fervently: particular case
21–24: God devastates the land, brings forth Hell & **makes man recall** & regret: general terms

27 For this interpretation of *ḥijr* as connoting a sanctuary as well as the protection afforded a child or orphan, see *Lisān al-ʿarab*, www.alwaraq.net, root *ḥ-j-r*, p. 1071. This rendering accords well with the topic of protection of the orphans and the poor, in verses 17–18.

25–26: God's punishment & firm binding of man to Covenant (*yūthiqu wathāqahu*): general terms
27–30: The person who is content with God's blessings, serves God, & enters the Garden: general terms

Verses 17–19 of this Early Mecca *sūra* refer to specific legal obligations treated also in e.g. the Medina *sūra* Q. 4 (*al-Nisāʾ*), 2–10. In both *sūra*s the obligations towards the orphans, the poor, and the inheritors, are related to landed wealth and its produce, and they are equated with servitude to God in His capacity as the Creator of all humans (see Q. 4, 1). Consequently, the same topic occurs in both the earliest and the latest *sūra*s. In this case, the *sūra*-specific meso-level *semantic* contexts and *generic forms* combine in Q. 4 to shape the topic into longer argumentation, including sequences of commands and prohibitions, and into short, dense sentences in Q. 89.

Similarly, the even shorter Early Mecca *sūra* 107 (*al-Māʿūn*, 'The Benefaction') also mentions the orphans and the poor, but in the context of defining what it means to deny the reality of God's Judgement:

1: The one who denies the Judgement (*al-dīn*): general term
2: Does not honour the orphan's rights: particular case
3: Does not give food to the poor: particular case
4–5: Prays but without paying heed to the prayer: particular case
6: Dissimulates: particular case
7: Forbids benefaction: particular case

In *sūra* 104 (*al-Humaza*, 'The Backbiter'), the topic of wealth (*māl*) and its righteous use appears again, though in this case with reference only to the 'bad category', identical with the title:

1–3: The Backbiter who amasses and counts his/her wealth: particular case
4–9: God punishes the Backbiter through His fire: particular terms

The last three *sūra*s of the canon – Q. 112, Q. 113 and Q. 114 – break the pattern of general and particular cases and terms, and constitute a distinct section representing the genre command, since all three begin with imperatives. Q. 112 (*al-Ikhlāṣ*) is the famous statement of the creed of the One God, beginning with the imperative "Say: 'He is God, One'", etc. By defining God in this way, Q. 112 introduces Q. 113 and Q. 114. Both of these begin with the same imperative "Say", but then proceed to declare "'I take refuge in the Lord (*qul aʿūdhu bi rabb* ...) of the daybreak (Q. 113)/of the people (Q. 114)'", from harmful evils, envy in the case of Q. 113, and devious thoughts in Q. 114. Hence, if Q. 112 is a statement of the creed, the two closing *sūra*s Q. 113 and Q. 114 invoke the One God as protector against evil, whether envy from others or deceptive thoughts. In this way, the two last *sūra*s in the canon conclude that only God can give protection, as the longer *sūra*s from other periods illustrate through accounts, examples and argumentation.[28] If instead of the canonical order one follows the temporal chronology, then Q. 112, Q. 113 and Q. 114 from the Early Mecca period set a doctrinal paradigm for what follows.

MODELLING QUR'ĀNIC COMPOSITION: CONCLUDING ANALYSIS

Bernard Weiss (1998, 1990) has argued that the concept of Covenant frames the discipline of jurisprudence (*fiqh*) and focuses it around the divine-human mutual obligations and rights, in such a way that the human-to-human laws and ethics constitute derivations of the Covenantal rights and obligations. We have seen an example of how the same mechanism works in the Qur'ān, in the case of Q. 9. Given al-Ṭabarī's theory, that the Covenantal rights and obligations established in Q. 1 are repeated throughout the whole Qur'ān, the Qur'ānic composition appears to set a model for Covenant's function within *fiqh*. This would be logic, given that the Qur'ān serves as the first source and principle for deriving law and guidance within jurisprudence. Hence, the Qur'ānic establishment of the Covenantal terms and distinction of legal-ethical categories, cases, and terms serves the discipline of *fiqh*. The legal-interpretive perspective would also explain the practical function behind the Qur'ānic semantic of context-dependent meaning: the distinct categories are described in different topical and case-related contexts, to show what terms apply to them in each case. This hermeneutics is an integral part of *fiqh* and its key practice of applying principles to new cases, in new contexts. In terms of the structure of concepts and 'the theory theory', it again implies that 'law' is the key discipline that unlocks the theoretical paradigms that shape the Qur'ān's concepts, as well as their use and organisation within the canon.

Compared with 'the Nöldeke-thesis' discourse, which assumes substantive development of ideas, due in part to the Prophet's encounters with Jews and Christians and their literatures, and editorial insertions, this approach

28 E.g. Q. 40, 27; 44, 20; 2, 67; 11, 47; 19, 18; 23, 97–98; 72, 6; 3, 36; 7, 200; 16, 98; 40, 56; 41, 36; and 12, 23, 79.

posits 'contextual variations on the theme of Covenant and derived terms' to explain topical shifts. Consequently, the short Early Mecca *sūra*s are not short because they are early and basic, but because they treat a particular category, case, and terms, in an appropriate condensed form, rather than, as in the longer *sūra*s, rhetorically and logically proving the reality of Covenant through an expanded topical frame and with several cases, categories, and historical exemplary accounts.

Below, I have mapped out my argument in the form of a table, intended to show how Covenant-related topics occur across all four periods: Early, Middle, and Late Mecca, and Medina. The starting-point of al-Ṭabarī's argument is that **Q. 1, *al-Fātiḥa***, establishes the clear distinctions of **Covenantal terms** that from its opening position permeate all periods and all *sūra*s. On this basis, I have constructed four additional topical categories, marked as bold and underlined: **Creed**, **Oath**, **Terms** of the Covenant, and **Divine Writing**, under which I have listed occurrences of these topics according to Nöldeke's chronology. I have also marked as bold and underlined those *sūra*s or verses, which are **the earliest expressions of a topical category**. Under **Creed**, I have added the **protective invocation**, marked in bold. Moreover, I have followed al-Ṭabarī's opinion, that the 'cut-off letter-syllables' that introduce 29 *sūra*s can be seen as oaths, pledged by the divine writing and what it conveys of God's names and attributes. If this view is correct, it considerably increases the number of *sūra*s introduced by oaths, and widens their occurrence from almost exclusively in the Early Mecca period to all periods. Consequently, I have listed the **'cut-off letter-syllable'** *sūra*s in the Oath category, marking them with bold. In some cases, these **'letter-syllables'** are also *technical* oaths (beginning with the oath particle *wa*), in which case I have marked them as bold and underlined.

Covenant: Paradigmatic distinction of terms **1, *al-Fātiḥa***	**Creed**: Covenant with, contract through, & **protection by** the One God, without other partners	**Oath**: Pledge by God's Creative power to sustain and judge, and **by His writing**	**Terms**: God sustains man through Creation's blessings; Man serves God without partners and enacts security; God judges man	**Divine Writing**: Confirms man's knowledge of Covenant & contract with rights/ obligations

Early Mecca	53: 19–28	**74: 30-56**	**111**	**96: 1–5**
	112	92	106	74:31
	113	90	108	97
	114	93	104	80:13
		86	107	68:1, 36–38
		91	102	87:18-19
		68	105	78:29
		95	94	83:7-11, 18-21
		103	80:24-42	69:18-20
		85	87:9-15	52
		81:15	73:8-15	
		53	101	
		84:16	99	
		100	82:6-19	
		79	100	
		77	78:1-3, 37-40	
		89	88:21-26	
		75	83:22-36	
		51	69	
		52	56	
		56:75-78	70:1-10	
			55	
			109	
Middle Mecca	37:35	37	54:50-55	37:157
	44:20	**44**	71:1-4	44:2
	20:14	**50**	76:1-7, 27-31	20:133
	15:96-99	**20**	20:115-127	26:1-2
	19: 1-34, 81,	**26**	26:184-209,	15:1, 4
	91-92	**15**	227	19:12, 78-79
	19:18	**19**	19:93-98	38:28-29
	36:23, 50	**38**	36:1-12	36:12
	43: 57-64, 81	**36**	72:22-28	43:1-4
	72:3	**43**	67:1-15	21:10
	72:6	**27**	23:1-16	17:2,3, 13-14
	67:12		25:58-76	27:1-3
	23:50, 91, 117		17:23-38	18:1-2
	23: 97–98		27:59-69	
	21: 21-29,91			
	17:22, 39, 111			
	27:62-64			
	18:4,15, 110			

Late Mecca	**41:36**	32	32:4-22	32:1-3, 23
	16:22	41	41:5-19	41:1-4
	16:98	45	45:3-15	45:1-2, 16-17
	11:47	30	16:1-9, 90-5	16:89
	14:52	11	30:6-18	30:56
	12:23, 79	14	11:7-11	11:1-2, 6, 17,
	40:27, 56	12	14:31	110
	28:88	40	40:4-14	14:1
	39:4	28	28:54-70	12: 1-2
	31:13	29	39:3-10	40:1-3
	10:68	31	29:52-59	28:1-2, 49-53
	35:3	42	31:4-9	39:1-2, 41
	7:200	10	42:1-13	29:45-50
	13:36	7	10:44-47	31:1-3
		46	34:1-6	42:14-17
		13	35:1-7	34:3
			7: 3, 169-174	35:31-32
			46:31-35	7:169
			6:14-15,	46:1-3, 12, 30
			151-153	6:91-92,
			13:20-25,	154-157
			37-43	13:1
Medina	**2:67**	**2**	2:27, 40-48,	2:1-2, 78-80,
	2:163	**3**	63, 81-84, 93,	89, 101, 174-
	47:19		123-126	177, 282-283
	3:36		64:1-10	98
	3: 47, 59-60, 64		62:1-5	62:2
	4:171-172		8:1-4, 7, 27,	3:3, 7, 23,
	59:22-23		55-56, 72-73	70-75, 81, 199
	22:31		47:1-3	57:16, 25-29
	66:12		3:76-77	4:105
	9:30-31		61:10-12	33:6
	5:72, 75, 116		57:1-7	58:21
			4: 154-162	22:4, 70
			65:8-12	9:111
			59:18-24	5:15, 44, 48
			33:1-8, 70-73	
			63:1-2, 11	
			24:55-56	
			58:5-8, 21-22	
			22:1-7	
			48:10, 29	
			66:8-12	
			60:8-10	
			110	
			49:15	
			9:1-4	
			5:7-14	

The table is not exhaustive, of course. Further sub-topics can be added to the four topics given here, related to the different legal-ethical categories, cases, and terms treated above, with corresponding detailed *sūra* and verse references. This effort is for another monograph. Here, the table only serves to provide initial support for the argument, that a *balāgha*-based approach to Qur'ānic composition, which considers meta-, meso-, and micro-levels, and semantic context, can produce a theoretically grounded and systematically applicable alternative to the 'Nöldeke thesis'.

Chapter 4

NATURAL LAW THEORY: QUR'ĀNIC COVENANT REVISITED

This chapter continues to explore the legal significance of Covenant in the Qur'ān, focusing specifically on natural law theory, which complements the context-oriented semantics in constituting a law-oriented theoretical paradigm. I begin by surveying a selection of contemporary research into Qur'ānic Covenant, including topics of relevance to natural law theory.[1] Next, I proceed to give some 'western' and Islamic definitions and concepts of natural law theory, which I apply to the Qur'ān. I argue that from the viewpoint of jurisprudence (*fiqh*), both Qur'ānic Covenant and the Qur'ān itself acquire functions specific to natural law theory. For illustration and support, I adduce examples from early and medieval scholars within the discipline of exegesis (*tafsīr*).

COVENANT IN CONTEMPORARY RESEARCH

For this survey, I will treat the following aspects of Covenant: as a concept of history; as law and rhetoric; as social contract and political allegiance; and as natural law theory.

Covenant as Concept of History

Within the contemporary discipline of Islamic history, Stephen Humphreys (1989) has argued that the Qur'ānic concept of Covenant (*mīthāq* and *ʿahd*), with Q. 7, 172 as the key verse, is a historical 'myth'. By 'myth' Humphreys means a scriptural term and model, which informed the ways in which the early Muslim historians conceptualised world history and the Prophet's community, so that they wrote history according to the pattern Covenant, Betrayal (of Covenant), and Redemption. Referring to the histories of al-Yaʿqūbī (d.

1 The survey thus does not cover all Covenant research; for a recent and more extensive (though not complete) survey, see O'Connor (2018).

284/897), al-Masʿūdī (d. 345/956), and al-Ṭabarī (d. 310/923), Humphreys argued the historians depicted the Prophet's community as a break with preceding political history, so that Covenant signifies the Islamic terms of loyalty to a ruler: first to the Prophet, then to his successors, the Caliphs. Al-Yaʿqūbī and al-Masʿūdī, who were pro-ʿAlid, deemed the Islamic community had betrayed Covenant when they denied ʿAlī his right to rule, while al-Ṭabarī treated the community as morally intact focusing instead on each ruler's or administrator's moral choices and courses of action.

Another 'mythical' approach to Qurʾānic Covenant is Wadad Kadi's study (2003). Kadi defines Covenant as a mythical vision of human history, which reflects over "man's nature, the nature of sin, and the relationship between God and man" (2003: 333). The reflections centre on God's claim to exclusive worship and man's acceptance of this claim 'by nature' of being God's creature: man has no choice but to agree to the terms of Covenant. Consequently, Kadi perceives Qurʾānic Covenant as enforcing an ethics of obedience and awe of God's powers, which resonates especially with Sufi mystical concepts of human history as the blessings humans incur by obeying God, and the punishments they incur by rebelling. Thus, Kadi argues, attempts by Muslim historians and exegetes to draw the mythical Qurʾānic Covenant into real political history are misguided.

Joseph Lumbard (2015) takes Kadi's approach as point of departure, and then compares the Qurʾānic Covenant with Covenant in the Hebrew Bible and the New Testament. In his view, the Qurʾānic Covenant is unique in its universalism. Where both Bibles refer to Covenant as an argument for their exclusive relationship with God, at the expense of 'others', the Qurʾānic Covenant includes 'the others' by locating itself in Creation (Q. 7, 172).[2] He then takes the argument in a normative direction, suggesting Qurʾānic Covenant should make contemporary Muslims better appreciate the pluralistic approach that the Qurʾān takes to Jews and Christians. In contrast, Andrew O'Connor (2018) has taken issue with Lumbard's analysis, that the universalism of the Qurʾānic Covenant implies a pluralistic and inclusive approach to religious diversity. Rather, O'Connor argues, Qurʾānic Covenant is polemical and draws boundaries, because it has legal implications that subject the other 'Biblical' communities to its terms. However, as we have seen in Chapter 1 with reference to Q. 5, 44–48, the Qurʾānic inclusion of Jews and Christians into a political community ruled by the Prophet implies

2 It appears that Lumbard overlooks the implications of the Hebrew Bible's 'rainbow Covenant' with Noah, where God pledges to sustain all of humanity and all other living beings; Gen. 9.

that inclusion and hierarchical authority are not mutually exclusive but at play simultaneously.

Covenant as Social Contract and Oath of Allegiance

A political theory-related approach to Qur'ānic Covenant focuses on social contract and oaths of allegiance. In a preliminary study, I argued that Covenant in the Qur'ān can be understood in Aristotle's sense of a constitutional principle that defines a political community and guides law-making (Mårtensson 2008). I have also applied Humphrey's pattern Covenant-Betrayal-Redemption in my own studies of al-Ṭabarī's history. However, instead of Humphreys' 'mythical' approach to Covenant, I argued that al-Ṭabarī historicised Qur'anic Covenant as a constitutional principle of 'rule of law' and a model for social contract regulating the relationship between 'ruler and ruled', including rights and obligations referring to land ownership and land tax. Moreover, al-Ṭabarī located Covenant in Creation and then traced its implementation throughout political history in such a way that the Islamic community appears as a continuation of that history, and of its pattern Covenant-Betrayal-Redemption, rather than a break, as Humphreys claimed (Mårtensson 2005, 2009a, 2011). In this context I also highlighted the significance that al-Ṭabarī afforded to both divine and human 'writing' (*kitāb*) for making the terms of any contract transparent and binding, including those of the social contract (Mårtensson 2009a, 2011).

Similarly, in a study of pre-Islamic, Qur'ānic, and Islamic oaths of allegiance to rulers, Andrew Marsham (2009) argues that Qur'ānic Covenant on the one hand bridges pre-Islamic Arab and Islamic concepts of oath and contract, and on the other hand merges them with its own Biblical-prophetic-monotheistic paradigm. However, Marsham does not use the theoretical terms 'constitution' and 'social contract'. Rather, he focuses on information about the oath of allegiance in contexts of succession to the Caliphate.

Marsham's approach to Covenant as a model for oaths of allegiance to Caliphs is structurally similar to how Covenant functions in the institutional context of Sufi 'brotherhoods' (*ṭuruq*, sing. *ṭarīqa*), namely as an oath of allegiance to a *shaykh* in his capacity as protective governor (*walāya*) and transmitter of divine knowledge (see also below, Chapter 5). For example, the study by Radtke, O'Fahey and O'Kane (1996) of the influential early modern Sufi *shaykh* Aḥmad b. Idrīs (d. 1276/1859) and his written instructions regarding novices. The *shaykh* should introduce a novice into his personal, ritual formula or *dhikr*, 'honorific recollection' of God's Covenant, transmitted through the knowledge chains of the *ṭarīqa* and traceable back to the Prophet. Thus, Aḥmad b. Idrīs' *dhikr* recalls and honours the Covenant, and gradually enables the novice to join his spirit with that of the Prophet. The relationship in which the *shaykh* serves as the novice's protective governor is also defined as a compact, mirroring the Covenant between God and Adam's offspring. An illustrative example is Aḥmad b. Idrīs' description of the Khalwatiyya *ṭarīqa*'s compact, where he quotes Q. 16, 91 (Radtke *et. al.* 1996: 154):

> (91) So fulfil the compact with God when you enter into compacts (*wa awfū bi'ahd Allāh idhā 'āhadtum*), and do not break the oaths after you have affirmed them, taking God as legal guardian (*kafīlan*); indeed, God has knowledge of what you do!

These examples show that Qur'ānic Covenant can be seen as reflecting political theory (constitution and social contract), and that it serves as model for political oaths of allegiance with Caliphs as well as oaths of allegiance with Sufi *shaykh*s. Although the latter, as institution, are distinct from the state, they wield considerable socio-economic and political power as local 'middle-men' between the people and their governors and rulers, as we shall see in the next chapter. It is therefore questionable whether Kadi is correct in claiming, as mentioned above, that the Sufi concept of Qur'ānic Covenant is purely theological and mythical, devoid of references to the world of real politics.

Covenant as Law and Rhetoric

Other approaches explore Qur'ānic Covenant in terms of law and rhetoric. An early example is Richard Gramlich's study (1983) of Q. 7, 172, the key verse. After surveying exegesis on this verse pertaining to the different Islamic schools and to different periods, from early to modern time, Gramlich concluded its topic of human recognition of the One God as their Lord at Creation obligates humans in a legal sense, to remember and honour this contract. He also suggested that the verse appears as a natural law-like obligation ('eine naturrechtliche Pflicht'), since it refers to all humans and their capacity to rationally recognize the obligation (1983: 229). Similarly, I have argued that the way in which al-Ṭabarī in his history connected the Qur'ānic Covenant of Creation with a constitutional principle and social contract show that he also perceived Covenant in terms of natural law (Mårtensson 2021; 2016; 2011).

As mentioned in the previous chapter, Bernard Weiss (1998, 1990) has argued that *fiqh* derives the idea that the community members are bound to the whole edifice of ritual, ethical, and legal obligations and rights that constitute Sharīʿa from the principle that Covenant binds humans to rights and obligations in relation to God. Though Weiss does not use the political terms 'social contract' and 'constitution', he points out that Qurʾānic Covenant in Q. 5 (*al-Māʾida*) obligates Jews and Christians, as well as Muslims (1990). Hence, he highlights the connection between the Covenant concept and the Prophet's polity and its laws, which include regulations of relations between Muslims and the other religious communities.[3]

Weiss (1998, 1990) also draws attention to the significance of the divine address (*khiṭāb*) as the means to communicate Covenant and obligate the addressees. Hence, unless a person has been addressed and has understood the message, he or she is not obligated by it. Jurists and theologians therefore argued that God has implanted the ability to recognise God's 'indicators' (*adilla*, sing. *dalīl*) in the human intellect. Along similar lines, Rosalind Ward Gwynne (2004) has compared Qurʾānic Covenant with the Ancient Middle Eastern vassal contracts, which serve as model also for Covenant in the Hebrew Bible (see also Mårtensson 2001/2015), except that in Gwynne's view, the Qurʾānic Covenant is universal, unlike the Hebrew Bible's version (see also Lumbard 2015). Like Weiss, Gwynne highlights the connection between Covenant and the divine speech, arguing that the Qurʾān uses 'Aristotelian-like' syllogistic proof to persuade the addressees of the truth and good of God's Covenant and its terms.

I have taken a similar approach (Mårtensson 2008, 2020). However, I argue that if one compares the Qurʾānic rhetorical proof of Covenant with Aristotelian rhetoric, the closest parallel is not syllogism but *sēmeîon*, 'sign', corresponding to Qurʾānic *āya*. Syllogism is a philosophical, irrefutable demonstration. *Sēmeîon* pertains to the genre of deliberative speech, and refers to a 'fallible demonstration' i.e. it proves a proposition that is refutable even if it is true, unlike the irrefutable syllogism. This has implications for defining the precise nature of the Qurʾānic address on Covenant: in theory it is binding once it reaches someone, but because the 'signs' are 'fallible', in practice not all addressees will be persuaded of its truth. In this context, I also argued (2008) that the Qurʾānic term *ḥaqq*, 'Truth' (and 'Right', see below), reflects the concept of God as One and transcendent, and the ontology and epistemology of realism: the true nature of a 'thing'

3 On Covenant and the Prophet's specific compacts, see Hamidullah (1987); also below, Chapter 5.

is not its 'name' but its language-independent properties and qualities. The opposite epistemology, idealism, establishes a dependency between language and thing, which the Qur'ān rejects because it would imply that God equals the language-based descriptions of Him. In modern western law, this epistemic debate relates to deliberations over the authority of jurists and judges in 'naming' categories, determining intention, and changing laws. I argued, therefore, that the Qur'ānic concept of One God without counterpart connects Covenant with epistemic realism, and legal deliberation and 'proof'. Yet even though the Qur'ānic 'signs' are fallible, the truth that they convey about God's Covenant is still absolute.

Natural Law Theory Approach to Covenant

In what follows, I will develop three of the approaches to Covenant I described above. Firstly, Gramlich's thesis (1983), that Q. 7, 172 is a natural law-like claim that all humans have the innate, rational ability to recognise God's Covenant and its terms. Secondly, Weiss's (1998, 1990) argument that the model of Qur'ānic Covenant extends to *fiqh*, and includes the divine address. Thirdly, my thesis (2008) regarding the legal implications of the term *ḥaqq* and epistemic realism related to Qur'ānic Covenant. Drawing also on a more recent article (Mårtensson 2021), I will develop these approaches by referring them to definitions of natural law theory and to Islamic exegesis, arguing that not only Q. 7, 172 but the Qur'ān itself constitutes a natural law theory within the discipline of jurisprudence.

NATURAL LAW THEORY: 'WESTERN' AND ISLAMIC DEFINITIONS

Now to the question: what is 'natural law theory'? Starting point here is the *Internet Encyclopaedia of Philosophy* and Kenneth Einar Himma's distinction between two forms of natural law theory. The first is *natural law theory of morality*, illustrated by the Catholic Aristotelian scholastic Thomas Aquinas (d. 1274). Aquinas assumed that humans are by nature rational beings, and that it is morally appropriate they should behave in a way that corresponds with their rational 'nature'. Consequently, he posited 'reason' as the first principle of human acts, and the measure and definition of their morality. As Himma puts it, "Aquinas derives the moral law from the nature of human beings". The concept of the divine plays an important part, as well, since Aquinas defined human rational nature as the expression of divine creation and providence. The second form is the *natural law theory of law*. Here the premise is that laws depend for authority "not on some pre-existing human convention, but on the logical relationship in which they stand to moral standards. Otherwise put, some norms are authoritative in virtue of their moral content, even when there is no convention that makes moral merit a criterion of legal validity" (Himma, IEP). In what follows, I focus on the second form, natural law theory of law.

The natural law scholar John Finnis has highlighted that assumptions and definitions of 'reason' and 'normative moral standards' in natural law theory-contexts require a claim to absolute Truth. The moral standard is considered universally valid and justifiable, hence absolutely, not relatively true. In Finnis' words:

> A theory of natural law claims to be able to identify conditions and principles of practical right-mindedness, of good and proper order among persons, and in individual conduct. Unless some such claim is justified, analytical jurisprudence in particular and (at least the major part of) the social sciences in general can have no critically justified criteria for the formation of general concepts, and must be content to be no more than manifestations of the various concepts peculiar to particular peoples and/or to the particular theorists who concern themselves with those people. (2011[1980]: 18)

Accordingly, Finnis (2012) has conceptualized the history of natural law theory as the history of the epistemic claim that a certain moral standard is *true*, as a conscious critique of the relativist episteme. In his potted trajectory of this episteme, Finnis singles out Plato, Aristotle, Thomas Aquinas, and the Universal Declaration of Human Rights (UDHR). For illustration, take the UDHR, promulgated by the United Nations General Assembly in Paris on 10 December 1948:

> *Preamble*:
>
> Whereas *recognition* of the inherent dignity and of the equal and inalienable rights of all members of the human family is the foundation of freedom, justice and peace in the world; (…)
>
> Whereas it is essential, if man is not to be compelled to have recourse, as a last resort, to rebellion against tyranny and oppression, that human rights should be protected by *the rule of law* (my italics) (…).

Article 1:

> All human beings are born free and equal in dignity and rights. They are endowed with reason and conscience and should act towards one another in a spirit of brotherhood.

The Preamble sets up *recognition of the inherent dignity and of the equal and inalienable rights of humans* as the moral standard for the substantive rights that follow in the articles, and *the rule of law* as the practice that protects these rights against tyranny. Article 1 then identifies 'reason' and 'conscience' as something all humans have by nature. Yet it does not identify these as the sources of the recognition of human dignity and rights, or of the requirement of the rule of law for protection against tyranny. In fact, the starting point is the *epistemic claim* that inherent freedom and equality in dignity and rights must be *recognized*, whereupon the ensuing *text* of the Declaration defines these rights and thus constitutes their *authoritative source*. Consequently, the authoritative text of the Declaration does not premise human dignity and rights on reason and conscience, but defines these as coinciding. Similarly, Article 1 starts with the factual claim that all human beings are born free and equal in dignity and rights. The norm, that humans should act towards one another in a spirit of brotherhood, therefore follows from the epistemic claim, not from 'reason'. Equally, the Preamble's identification of 'the rule of law' as the necessary protection of human rights against tyranny and oppression is a statement of fact – again, an epistemic claim. This implies that the claim to absolute Truth on behalf of a moral standard is more important for natural law theory of law than the assumption that the standard derives from 'reason'.

In Finnis's view, the rule of law in the context of the UDHR reflects a constitutional 'social contract', which holds rulers "to their side of a relationship of reciprocity, in which the claims of authority are respected on condition that authority respects the claims of the common good (of which a fundamental component is respect for the equal right of all to respectful consideration)" (Finnis 2011[1980]: 272–273). Following Finnis, then, a constitutional 'social contract' is part of natural law theory, which implies that the latter necessarily plays out within a polity.

Islamic Natural Law Theory

Neither Himma's nor Finnis' definitions of natural law theory state whether such theory can derive from 'divine revelation' i.e. scripture. The situation is different within Islamic studies. The Qur'ān's status as divine revelation, which together with the Prophet's *sunna* constitutes the textual sources for deriving law, has been seen as producing an Islamic social contract theory that precludes natural law theory. Notably, Patricia Crone argued that the Muslim jurists developed a social contract that originated with God, not with human public deliberation, because they conceived of human 'nature' and reason as intrinsically flawed and in need of divine revelation through a prophet. The polity was therefore conceptualised as starting with the Prophet as giver of the divine law. Consequently, the Islamic social contract is not 'man-made' through public deliberation, like those of Thomas Hobbes (d. 1679) and John Locke (d. 1704) and other modern European theorists, and this fact rules out Islamic natural law theory (Crone 2004: 262–272).

Challenging Crone's reasoning, Anver Emon, a scholar of Islamic law, argues the case for Islamic natural law theory. He shifts focus from the Qur'ān and the *sunna* as sources of law to the jurists' hermeneutics, thus allowing the Qur'ān to be seen as any text that the jurists employ to define moral standards for lawmaking. Specifically, he shows how jurists active from the late 300s/900s onwards (though with individual examples also from the 100s/700s) constructed concepts of divine Creation and 'rational human nature'. With reference to these constructs, they defined moral standards for deriving rules and laws. In Emon's words, the jurists thus used divine Creation "as a site where fact and value are fused" (Emon 2010:3) i.e. they justified the moral standard by attributing it to certain 'facts', which they in turn attributed to Creation.

Addressing also the 'common good' aspect of social contract, Emon focuses on the principle *ḥuqūq Allāh wa ḥuqūq al-ʿibād*, 'the rights of God and the rights of the servants', which relates to the concept *maṣlaḥa*, 'common good' or 'public welfare'. Thus, *ḥuqūq Allāh* refers to God's rights to obligate the administration and the jurists to uphold *maṣlaḥa*, while *ḥuqūq al-ʿibād* refers to the individual's rights in relation to the administration and the law (Emon 2004–2005:379–381). Within this common good framework, the jurists developed moral standards in a referential relationship to the Qur'ān, through two distinct methodologies: 'rationalism' or 'Hard Naturalism' (Muʿtazila), and 'positivism' or 'Soft Naturalism' (al-Ghazzālī and the Ashʿarites). 'Hard Naturalists' deduced moral standards, which they then read into Scripture: 'God wants X *because* X is good'. 'Soft Naturalists' instead inductively derived moral standards from Scripture, according to the model 'X is good because *God wants it*'. To illustrate: the 'Soft Naturalist'/'positivist' al-Ghazzālī employed a concept of *maṣlaḥa* as the moral standard for legislation, identifying it with five defined objectives (*maqāṣid*) of the law – the right to protection of religion, life, intellect, lineage and wealth – all of which he derived from the Qur'ānic text (Emon 2004–2005: 366, 378; 2010: 24–37).

Conclusions and Way Ahead

Both of Emon's hermeneutical methodologies align with Himma's definition of natural law theory of law, that law gains its authority through a moral standard, and with Finnis' epistemic claim, since the standard associated with divine Creation is held to be universally justifiable and absolutely true. They also refer to a concept of the common good, according to which God obligates the law and administration to protect the people's rights. Given that the jurists are at liberty to use Creation in order to construct 'facts' for their moral standards, there appears to be enough scope for deliberation to conclude that Scripture does not simply impose a norm upon the law-makers (see also Chapter 5, below). Similarly, contemporary human rights jurists are bound to the UDHR text as well as the several subsequent covenants, which constitute an authoritative textual body that they must relate to, and negotiate in relation to national laws and the public. Tentatively, it therefore seems that Crone's image of 'western man-made social contract equals natural law theory' *versus* 'Islamic revealed social contract negates natural law theory' assumes a wider gap than there actually is between legal practices.

In what follows, I show how the Qur'ānic Covenant establishes an absolutely true and universally justifiable moral standard, with ensuing rights and obligations. I will argue that the deliberation and reciprocity that Finnis associates with a constitutional social contract, is expressed through the reciprocal terms of Covenant, and the fact that God must persuade people of the truth but sometimes fails, given that the 'signs' are fallible; in other words, the people can disagree. This Qur'ānic reciprocity would then reflect the legal principle *ḥuqūq Allāh wa ḥuqūq al-'ibād*, according to which God can hold the administration to protecting the common good, and the people can hold the administration to upholding their rights.

CREATION, TRUTH, AND RIGHT IN THE QUR'ĀN

The verse Q. 7, 172 figures prominently in all studies of Qur'ānic Covenant because it describes its instantiation in the divine act of Creation. This primordial Covenant takes the form of a mutually agreed, reciprocal contract between God and Adam's descendants i.e. humanity:

> (172) And when your Lord took from the sons of Adam, from their backs, their descendants and made them testify against themselves: "Am I not your Lord?" they said: "Certainly, we testify!" so that you cannot say on the Day of Standing to trial: "But we were actually unaware of this!"

This way of locating Covenant in Creation suggests that Emon's observation of jurists employing Creation to 'fuse fact and value' applies also to the Qur'ān itself. Specifically, the verse fuses the absolutely true 'fact' of the Covenantal contract and its terms, and the final account, with the 'value' that humans must uphold Covenant and its practical implications.

Beyond Q. 7, 172, the Qur'ānic epistemic claim for Covenant also refers to the term *ḥaqq*, plural *ḥuqūq*, as in *ḥuqūq Allāh wa ḥuqūq al-ʿibād*. According to Ibn Manẓūr, the opposite to *ḥaqq* is *bāṭil*, 'false' in the sense of 'void' or 'vacuous'. Thus, *ḥaqq* means 'truth' in the sense of a substantive claim. Consequently, *ḥaqq* is also a 'right' or 'rightful claim' that one has in relation to someone.[4] Here, I understand *ḥaqq* to mean that Covenant is a universally justifiable and True Right, which because it is from God is also a kind of meta-right that confers and protects rights in general. An illustrative example is Q. 2 (*al-Baqara*), 176–177. Verse 176 makes a claim to *ḥaqq* on behalf of the writing that God sends down, followed in verse 177 by a list of doctrinal items and a set of specified good deeds and obligations:

> (176) So it is that God has made **the writing** descend **with the true right**, and therefore those who disagree about the divine writing are indeed in far-reaching dissent (*dhālika biʾanna Allāh nazzala* ***al-kitāb bi-l-ḥaqq*** *wa inna alladhīna ikhtalafū fī al-kitāb lafī shiqāq baʿīd*)!
> (177) Righteousness (*al-birr*) is not to turn your faces in the direction of the East and the West, but righteous is rather the one who enacts security through God, the furthest day, the angels, the writings, and the prophets; who gives of the wealth, in spite of his love for it, to his close kin, the orphans, the poor, the wayfarers, and the beggars, and for the freeing of slaves, and who enacts performance of the prayer and pays the community tax (*al-zakāt*). And those who fulfil their contracts that they have entered, and patiently endure privation, affliction, and times of battle: those are the ones who are truthful, and those are the ones who fulfil their obligations!

The problem of persuasion, that God cannot convince all people and make them comply, is intimated in the passage Q. 6 (*al-Anʿām*), 148–153, which is

4 *Lisān al-ʿarab*, online at www.alwaraq.net, entry *ḥ-q-q*, p. 1274.

part of a long account and argument about God's material blessings and the right and wrong human responses. Verse 148 describes how those who take other partners argue their case, and how God therefore afflicted them. Verse 149 continues and says that the affliction is God's persuasive proof, and that it is part of His will that some people are not persuaded. Verse 150 then describes how those who give false testimony and deny God's signs should be treated, after which verses 151 and 152 proceed to list sequences of the right contractual obligations, which secure the welfare of those in need and the common good generally. Verse 153 concludes by stating that the above is God's path of correct speech and action:

> (148) Those who take other partners (*alladhīna ashrakū*) will say: 'If God wished, we would not have taken other partners, nor would our fathers, and we would not have made anything inviolate!' In this way those before them gave the lie, so that they had to taste Our affliction (*ḥattā dhāqū baʾsanā*). Say: 'Do you have any knowledge that you can present to us? Rather, you follow nothing but conjecture and you tell nothing but lies!'
> (149) Say: 'For God has the persuasive proof (*fali-Allāh al-ḥujja al-bāligha*), so had He wished, He would have guided you all!'
> (150) Say: 'Come with your witnesses who can testify that God has made this inviolable (*ḥarrama hādhā*)!' If they testify, do not testify together with them and do not follow those who give the lie to Our signs and those who do not enact security through the End point, for they set up equals to their Lord!'
> (151) Say: 'Come, I will recite what your Lord has made inviolate for you: that you must not make anything partner with Him; goodness towards the parents; that you do not kill your children out of fear of poverty: We provide sustenance for you and for them; that you do not approach indecencies, whether outwardly or inwardly; and that you do not kill a person, which God has made inviolate, except by right. That is what He obligates you, so that you may rationally comprehend it (*laʿallakum taʿqilūna*)!
> (152) And do not approach the orphan's wealth, except for what is best, until he comes of age, and then give full measure and weight equitably! We do not obligate a person except with its capacity, so when you make statements, be just, even if it is a close kin, and fulfil God's compact (*ʿahd Allāh*). That is what He obligates you, so that you may recall and honour it (*laʿallakum tadhakkarūna*)!
> (153) Indeed, this My path is correct in speech and action, so follow it and do not follow the duties that will divert you from the duties to Him! That is what He obligates you to do, so that you may fulfil your obligations (*laʿallakum tattaqūna*)!

In this passage, the divine persuasion is a one-way communication, from God to a people, via a prophet. In other cases, when focus is on the societal implications of the Covenantal terms, a reciprocal communication is described. For example, the early Mecca *sūra* Q. 106 (*Quraysh*) describes the contract between the Prophet's people Quraysh, who have the right and obligation to serve 'the Lord of the House', who in turn provides food and security for Quraysh:

> (1) For Quraysh's contract of protection (*li'īlāf Quraysh*):
> (2) Their contract of protection is the journey of the winter and the summer (*īlāfihim riḥlat al-shitā' wa al-ṣayf*),
> (3) So let them serve the Lord of this House (*falya'budū rabba hādhā al-bayt*),
> (4) Who provided food for them against hunger and secured them against fear (*alladhī aṭ'amahum min jū'in wa āmanahum min khawf*)!

In Q. 14 (*Ibrāhīm*), 35–37, a late Mecca *sūra*, we see Abraham negotiating with God, holding Him to His obligation to feed the people in return for serving Him:

> (35) But Abraham said: "My Lord, make this region with its cities secure and keep me and my sons away from serving the idols!"
> (36) "My Lord, [the idols] have led many people astray, but he who follows me is of me, while the one who disobeys me: surely, You are All-Forgiving, Continuous Protector of life!"
> (37) "Our Lord, I have settled some of my descendants in a valley without crops, by Your Inviolate House, our Lord, so that they can enact standing to the prayer. Then incline the hearts of the people towards them and sustain them of the harvest fruits so that they may become thankful!"

In Q. 2 (*al-Baqara*), 125–126, from Medina, God refers to the contract He has entered with Abraham and his son Ismail, and recalls Abraham's negotiation on behalf of his people:

> (125) When We made the House a meeting place for the people and a secure haven: "Take for yourselves from Abraham's standing place a place for prayer!" We entered a compact (*wa 'ahidnā*) with Abraham and Ismail: "Purify My House for those who circumambulate it, absorbed in worship, and kneeling in prostration!"
> (126) When Abraham said: "My Lord, make this a secure region (*rabbi ij'al hādhā baladan āminan*) and sustain of the harvest fruits those of its inhabitants who enact security through God and the Far-away Day!"

(God) said: "As for those who reject security, I shall materially support them a while (*fa'umatti'uhum qalīlan*), then subject them to the punishment of the fire: a painful outcome!"

In these cases, I read the Qur'ānic Covenant through Finnis' definition of a constitutional social contract as holding rulers "to their side of a relationship of reciprocity, in which the claims of authority are respected on condition that authority respects the claims of the common good (of which a fundamental component is respect for the equal right of all to respectful consideration)" (Finnis 2011[1980]: 272–273; see above). Exceptions are 'those who take other partners' referred to above in the passage Q. 6, 148–152. They are not given 'respectful consideration', because they give false testimony about God's commands and prohibitions. While this is of course true only from within the Qur'ānic Covenant discourse, it is significant that it defines the case in terms of the legal problem of evidence, testimony, and contractual loyalty, in the context of contestation over how to define the common good. In other words, the wrongful actions are cast as a *legal* problem, with negative consequences for the common good. The other examples show that because Abraham has fulfilled his obligations towards God, he can hold God to His side of the reciprocal contract, with the common good at the heart of the negotiation i.e. the food sustenance and security of the region and its people. In Q. 2, 126, God concedes to sustain also those who reject security, if only until the final Trial when they will meet their destiny. In other words, the common good includes those who disagree and dissent.

Three more examples illustrate the deliberative aspect at the level of negotiation between the messenger and his people, and among the people. Q. 29 (*al-'Ankabūt*), 16–18 describes Abraham seeking to persuade the people of the good of God's terms. The legal point here is that the messenger is not responsible if the people reject the message, for God has obligated him only with the persuasion, whereas the response is the people's obligation. Note that the people's Covenantal right to material sustenance (*rizq*) is again at stake:

(16) And Abraham, when he said to his people: 'Serve God and fulfil His obligations: that is good for you, if you have gained the knowledge! (17) Instead you serve, in God's place, idols, creating fabrication (*takhliqūna 'ifkan*). Indeed, those who you serve in God's place do not own the power over sustenance for you (*lā yamlikūna lakum rizqan*). So seek the sustenance from God, and serve Him and give thanks to Him; to Him you will be returned!

> (18) And if you give the lie: for sure, other nations before you have given the lie too, but the messenger is only obligated to the persuasion that makes clear distinctions (*wa mā ʿalā al-rasūl illā al-balāgh al-mubīn*)!'

Consequently, the messenger cannot force the Covenantal obligations on the people. The same point is made in Q. 2 (*al-Baqara*), verses 256 and 272:

> (256) There can be no force in the religious part of the judicial order (*al-dīn*) now that moral rectitude has definitely distinguished itself from wavering! For sure, he who rejects (*yakfur*) serving idols and enacts security through God has taken hold of the firmest bond (*al-ʿurwa al-wuthqā*) that never breaks, as God Hears Knowing everything!
>
> (272) You are not obligated for their being guided, for God guides who He wishes. Whatever you spend of what is good, it is for yourselves. As long as you do not spend except seeking God's countenance, whatever you spend of good will be fulfilled for you, as you are not darkened by wrong (*wa antum lā tuẓlamūna*)!

As for communication among the people, verses Q. 33 (*al-Aḥzāb*), 70–71 command 'those who enact security' to imitate the prophetic speech, in terms of making correct statements coupled with acting for the common good:

> (70) O you who enact security, fulfil your obligations to God and make correct statements when you speak (*wa qūlū qawlan sadīdan*),
> (71) and He will make your actions conducive to the common good and forgive your sins; anyone who obeys God and His messenger has certainly won an immense victory!

Against this background, I conclude tentatively that the Qur'ānic Covenant can be seen as reflecting natural law theory on the following accounts: (1) Covenant is part of divine Creation and thus intrinsic to 'human nature'. (2) Covenant constitutes a claim to 'right' as the absolutely true moral standard, from which derives all other virtues, rights and obligations, and laws. (3) Covenant defines material sustenance as the foundation of the common good. (4) Covenant provides a divine-prophetic model for a reciprocally agreed-upon social contract, and as such, (5) Covenant includes deliberation, in the sense that the people must be rationally persuaded that the contractual terms are beneficent, for individuals and the common good.

Natural Law Theory in the Exegesis of Q. 4, 1

Some of the early and medieval exegetes have made interpretations, which appear to support the thesis. Though there may well be other relevant cases, I have selected six famous exegetes, whose wide recognition implies that their views are 'mainstream'. They are (1) Muqātil b. Sulaymān (d. 150/767), author of the earliest extant complete Qur᾽ān commentary (see also Chapter 2). (2) Al-Ṭabarī (d. 310/923), whose Qur᾽ān commentary was part of his independent *madhhab.* (3) The Twelver Shī'ī theologian, jurist and exegete al-Ṭūsī (d. 460/1067), nick-named *shaykh al-ṭā᾽ifa*, 'Grand scholar of the sect', because of his importance for the formation of Twelver Shī'ī thought. (4) Al-Zamakhsharī (d. 538/1143), a linguist, Mu'tazilī theologian, ethicist, and exegete. (5) Al-Rāzī (d. 606/1209), Ash'arī theologian and Qur᾽ān commentator famous for building his exegesis around systematically derived general and particular statements. (6) The Shāfi'ī jurist and exegete al-Suyūṭī (d. 911/1505), author of the systematic treatise on the Qur᾽ānic sciences, *al-Itqān fī 'ulūm al-qur᾽ān* (see also Introduction).

The selected passage is Q. 4 (*al-Nisā᾽*), 1–2, where verse 1 treats the topic of how God created all humans from the first couple, and verse 2 treats the case of orphans and their rights to property and wealth. The verses can thus be seen as an example of what Anver Emon described as the jurists' use of Creation as a site where 'fact and value' are fused i.e. as the reference point for their moral standards. Q. 4, 1–2 reads:

> (1) O People! Fulfil your obligations towards your Lord, Who created you out of one person and divided from it its spouse, and issued forth from the two of them many men and women! And fulfil your obligations towards God by Who you appeal to one another and invoke kinship relations: indeed, God has been watching over you! (*yā ayyuhā al-nās ittaqū rabbakum alladhī khalaqakum min nafsin wāḥidatin wa khalaqa minhā zawjahā wa baththa minhumā rijālan kathīran wa nisā᾽ wa ittaqū Allāh alladhī tasā᾽alūna bihi wa al-arḥāma inna Allāha kāna 'alaykum raqīban*)
> (2) Give the orphans their properties, without exchanging worthless [lands] for valuable and without devouring their wealth into your wealth: indeed, that would be a great sin! (*wa ātū al-yatāmā amwālahum wa lā tabaddalū al-khabītha bi-l-ṭayyib wa lā ta᾽kulū amwālahum ilā amwālikum innahu kāna ḥūban kabīran*)

Starting with Muqātil: explaining the command *ittaqū rabbakum* ('fulfil your obligations towards your Lord') he paraphrases the phrase in the rhetorical sense that God wants to induce fear of Himself into people (*yukhawwifuhum yaqūlu ukhshū rabbakum*). The created person is Adam, from whose rib God created Eve. Concerning 'God by Who you appeal to one another', Muqātil explained it as the people's practice to invoke God in quests for rights and needs (*al-ḥuqūq wa al-ḥawāʾij*), and 'kinship relations' as that which should be joined together and not severed (2002/1: 355). While Muqātil thus takes for granted that God signifies 'support for rights', he stops short of theorising the significance of divine *Creation* for 'rights' i.e. he does not actually define a moral standard with reference to 'human nature'.

This further step is taken by al-Ṭabarī. Paraphrasing God's intended meaning, he turned the 'fact' that all humans are created by God first out of one person and then out of one father and mother, so that they constitute a universal family, into the 'value' or moral standard that God obligates them to uphold each other's rights as brothers, for the sake of justice and against oppression. He also argued, with an eye to verse 2 and the vulnerable orphans, that God especially obligates the strong to protect the rights of the weak:

> [God], may His honour be exalted, means by His statement (*O People! Fulfil your obligations towards your Lord, Who created you out of one person*): 'Beware, O People, of your Lord so that you do not contravene what He has commanded you to do and what He has prohibited you from, for His punishment will descend upon you and you have no power over it!' Then He, exalted is His honour, described Himself as the One Who uniquely has created all humankind from one individual (*al-mutawaḥḥid bikhalq jamīʿ al-anām min shakhṣ wāḥid*), and He makes His servants understand (*ʿarrafa ʿibādahu*) how the beginning was when He issued that forth from one person (*nafs wāḥida*), making them aware by that, that all of them are descendants of one man and one mother, so that they are from one another, and that the right of some of them over others is the obligation that one brother has to the right of his brother (*wa anna ḥaqqa baʿḍihim ʿalā baʿḍ wājib wujūb ḥaqq al-akh ʿalā akhīhi*), because of their common descent from one father and one mother. What obligates them to guard over each other's right, after the coming together of the descent from the father who is common to them, is like what obligates them of that concerning the closest descent. Through that they feel affection for each other so that they seek justice for each other, and do not oppress each other, so that the strong exerts himself to protect the right of the weak, according to what God has obligated him to do. Therefore He said (*Who created you out of one person*), meaning from Adam (1995/3:4, 296).

Concerning the imperative *ittaqū Allāh*, in the second sentence of verse 1, al-Ṭabarī explains it as meaning that God has come to humans with a contract, and just like with any contract, they are obligated to fulfil its terms; if not, God will punish them (1995/3:4, 298). Thus, with al-Ṭabarī, the closest translation of *ittaqū Allāh* is 'fulfil your obligations towards God', in the contractual-Covenantal sense. The translation is supported by the other exegetes, as well, and is how I translate the verb *ittaqā* throughout this book.

By comparison, al-Ṭūsī starts his exegesis with the word 'appeal to each other' (*tasāʾalūna*) by invoking God, which he explains as meaning 'demand your rights' (*taṭlubūna ḥuqūqakum*) by Him (Vol. 3: 98). He then explains 'fulfil your obligations towards your Lord' as a warning against disobedience towards Him and His commands and prohibitions, and a precaution not to break kinship bonds, by which He gives advice concerning children, women and the weak. Thus, God conveys the knowledge to them that they are all from one person, on the grounds of which He calls them to adhere to His command and His defined legal boundaries concerning their inheritance and who comes after them, and to have empathy with the women and the orphans (Vol. 3: 99). He then expands on this with reference to 'created you from one person', explaining that God refers to the common origin and kinship of all men and women as an argument for them to empathise with, provide security for, and protect each other, and not be arrogant (Vol. 3: 100).

Al-Zamakhsharī identifies two senses for the opening passage. One elliptic, abbreviated sense is that it describes the Creation of man and woman, including their creation from the earth and the creation of Eve from the rib, and the spread of men and women from them. The other is that it is an address to the Prophet's people, stating that they are all from the same mother and father, and are therefore related to each other and to all other nations. He then proceeds to define two different senses of *ittaqū Allāh*. One is general and refers to God's power as Creator, by which He has obligated people so that they should fear the punishment that follows from rejecting Him and neglecting the duty to thank Him. The other is a particular sense, that they should fulfil their obligations to Him with respect to upholding each other's rights and not severe what belongs together (*an yattaqūhu biḥifẓ al-ḥuqūqi baynahum falā yaqṭaʿū mā yajib ʿalā baʿḍihim libaʿḍ*). He concludes that this particular sense is the one that corresponds with the whole *sūra*'s meanings (*wa hādhā al-maʿnā muṭābiq limaʿānī al-sūra*) (2009: 215).

Al-Rāzī starts with an assessment of the whole *sūra*:

> Know that this *sūra* comprises several kinds of obligations (*takālīf*). That is why He, the Exalted, commanded the people in the beginning of

> this *sūra* to empathise with the children, the women, and the orphans, and to show compassion towards them (*al-raʾfa bihim*) and give them their rights and protect their properties. With this meaning, the *sūra* is sealed with His statement (*They ask you for a legal decision. Say: God gives you a decision about collaterals*; 4, 176), and [it is] why He mentioned in the course of this *sūra* other kinds of obligations, namely the command to ritual cleansing, prayer, and fighting those who take other partners (*qitāl al-mushrikīna*). Because these obligations are taxing on the individuals, due to their weight on the characters, it is a given that the *sūra* opens with the legal reason (*al-ʿilla*), which has as its aim to make incumbent the carrying of these hard obligations (1981/9: 163).

He then argues that the command to fulfil the obligations towards God is general to all humanity, but the particular address is to the Arabs, and then to all those obligated (*al-mukallafīna*) by the *sūra* and its rulings, which again apply generally to the right of all knowing beings (*ʿāmm fī ḥaqq jamīʿ al-ʿālamīna*) (1981/9: 164).

The last exegete al-Suyūṭī produced two commentaries: *al-Durr al-manthūr*, where he gives earlier and divergent exegetical reports, and *Tafsīr al-Jalālayn*, which consists in his and his teacher Jalāl al-Dīn al-Maḥallī's interpretations and thus determines one meaning. In *al-Durr al-manthūr*, al-Suyūṭī does not establish a connection between the Creation topic and rights between people, only God's right to having the people fulfil their obligations towards Him (2011/2: 423–425). Here he cites one of al-Ṭabarī's reports on the meaning of *ittaqū Allāh* as 'fulfil your obligations towards God, by Who you enter mutual compacts and contracts (*taʿāhadūna wa taʿāqadūna*)' (2011/2: 423). Implicitly, however, this has to do with protecting rights, since contracts and pacts stipulate both rights and obligations. In *Tafsīr al-Jalālayn* Q. 4, 1 is contextualised as an address to the people of Mecca to fulfil their obligations against God when they invoke Him in legal affairs, particularly to ensure that family relations are not severed. The word 'rights' does not appear here, and the reference to God's creation of the first human couple becomes a model for family ties.

Based on this selection of six early and medieval exegetes, we may conclude that at least from al-Ṭabarī onwards, some exegetes used the topic of Creation in Q. 4, 1 to develop an 'absolutely true' moral standard for law, centred on 'rights'. Their arguments illustrate how exegetes developed the 'right-sense' of the Qurʾānic concept *ḥaqq* in the direction of 'human rights', which they then apply to particular legal topics.[5] However, already

5 See also Mårtensson (2021) on other occurrences of *ḥaqq* in Q. 4, verses 105, 122, 151 and 170–171.

Muqātil, active around the mid-700s, defined God's function in legal invocations as the protection of 'rights' for humans. Also remarkable is the way in which al-Ṭabarī, al-Ṭūsī, and al-Rāzī highlight the importance of empathy (*taʿaṭṭuf*) for protection of rights, and their argument that knowledge about the 'common origin' of mankind promotes this kind of empathy. Their approach is very similar to the UDHR, and the way in which it opens the declaration with a claim regarding the universal brotherhood of all humans.

CONCLUDING ANALYSIS

To read Qurʾānic Covenant as analogous with natural law theory has conceptual implications for the whole canon, assuming that Covenant serves as overarching meta-topic (Chapter 3).

Firstly, the observation of how some of the exegetes argued that God in Q. 4, 1 referred to His Creation of all humans from the first couple to foster the empathy required to support 'human rights'. Regarding Emon's observation of jurists' practice to refer to Creation to fuse 'fact and value', the observation implies that the jurists may, like the exegetes, have conceived of their practice as modelled on the Qurʾān's own 'use' of Creation to make the Covenant into a moral standard.

Secondly, we have seen the reciprocity that Covenant represents reflected elsewhere in the Qurʾān e.g. in the topics of people's right to material sustenance and the problem of rhetorical persuasion. Even though rejection of the obligating message will lead 'the rejecters' to disastrous outcomes in the final account, *as humans* they have the right to sustenance from their Lord. The only point at which it is permissible to kill 'the rejecters' and 'those who take other partners' is when they attack the Qurʾānic polity, as we saw in Chapter 3 with reference to Q. 9.

Thirdly, Covenant as natural law theory would be another Qurʾānic theoretical paradigm, in line with the 'theory theory of concept' as the structural theory of concept reflected in the Qurʾān (see Chapter 2). From this viewpoint, natural law theory would constitute the overarching *legal* theory that informs Covenant as the Qurʾān's meta-level meaning, and which is reflected in its sub-topics and concepts.

Fourthly, the corresponding theory of language and rhetoric would be the intention-, language form-, and context-based semantics of *balāgha*, discussed in Chapters 2 and 3. This natural-law perspective on language- and rhetoric theory re-actualises Jan Retsö's Ibn Manẓūr-based definition of Qurʾānic Arabic (*ʿarabī*) as semantically related to clarity of distinctions (*bayān*) and contractual security (*amn*). The same basic understanding of Qur'ānic *'arabī mubīn* was stated by al-Ṭabarī, who, as we saw in Chapter 3, also argued that the Qur'ānic meaning and composition reflect the Covenantal rights and obligations defined in Q. 1. Here we have seen al-Ṭabarī being possibly the first jurist and exegete to develop a fully-fledged natural law theory of 'human rights' based on Q. 4, 1. It thus appears that he would have perceived natural law theory to be part of the Covenantal meaning extending through the Qur'ān *and its Arabic concepts*.

Fifth, a brief point on intellectual history. John Finnis' potted trajectory of natural law theory, which introduced this chapter, starts with the Greek philosophers Plato and Aristotle in 400–300 BC, passes through the Catholic theologian Thomas Aquinas in the 1200s, and ends with the United Nations' Universal Declaration of Human Rights (UDHR) from 1948. The paradigm thus spans different times, places, religions, and political cultures. Attributing natural law *theory* to the Qur'ān is therefore not far-fetched. Yet in terms of *rights*, there are substantive differences. The UDHR reflects modern liberal principles and posits the inherent freedom of all humans, while the medieval Islamic jurists reckoned with slavery, to take but one example. Nevertheless, a comparison between the terms in al-Ṭabarī's exegesis of Q. 4, 1 and the UDHR brings out some striking parallels, despite the fact that the latter does not refer to God:

al-Ṭabarī, late 800s	**UDHR, 1948**
Exegesis of Q. 4 (al-Nisā'), 1 God means by His speech "*O people, fulfil your obligations towards your Lord Who created you by dividing one person*": (…)	*Preamble*: Whereas recognition of the inherent dignity and of the equal and inalienable rights of **all members of the human family** is the foundation of freedom, **justice** and peace in the world; (…)
He (…) described Himself as the One Who uniquely has created all humankind from one individual, and He makes His servants understand how the beginning was when He issued that forth from one person, making them aware by that, that **all of them are descendants of one man and one mother**, so that they are from one another, and that the **right** of some of them over others is the obligation that one **brother** has to the **right** of his brother, because of their common descent from one father and one mother.	Whereas it is essential, if man is not to be compelled to have recourse, as a last resort, to rebellion against tyranny and **oppression**, that human **rights** should be protected by the rule of law (…).

What obligates them to guard over each other's **right** after the coming together of the descent from the father who is common to them, is like what obligates them of that concerning the closest descent. By that they feel affection for each other so that they seek **justice** for each other, and **do not oppress** each other, and so that the strong exerts himself to protect the **right** of the weak, according to what God has obligated him to do.

Article 1:

All human beings are born free and equal in dignity and rights. They are endowed with reason and conscience and should act towards one another in a spirit of **brotherhood**.

Chapter 5

INSTITUTIONAL PRACTICES

In terms of Michel de Certeau's discourse analysis, a discourse expresses practices related to an institution, a discipline, and an individual scholar. Based on the preceding chapter, Qur'ānic Covenant can thus be seen as a discourse reflecting natural law theory of law, which refers to the discipline of jurisprudence and the institution of the law. However, the research survey in the same chapter showed Covenant has also been defined in terms of political theory, particularly social contract and constitution. Institutionally, political theory refers to the state and its administration, which overlap with the law. Accordingly, as we have also seen, both the UDHR and contemporary natural law-scholars emphasise that protection of legal rights depends on constitutional 'rule of law' and a social contract based on mutual agreement between 'ruler and ruled'. Hence, in this chapter I define the political and legal institutional context for the Qur'ānic Covenant and its assumed natural law theory, historically and with reference to social contract and constitution.

A methodological problem now presents itself. As intimated in the survey of Covenant-related research in the previous chapter, some of the Islamic historical sources of information on the Qur'ān's institutional context were written in accordance with political theories of Covenant. Consequently, these sources present a *theory* of the institutional context of the Qur'ān, in line with de Certeau's argument that discourse necessarily reflects theory, and that historians of religion should pay more analytical attention to religion's function in theoretical development. A theoretical relationship between Qur'ānic Covenant and Islamic historical writing thus appears as the result of the Qur'ān driving the theoretical development that underpins the Islamic disciplines. In this chapter, then, focus is on the political institutions to which these disciplines refer.

The chapter consists of two parts. First, I define the institutional context of the Qur'ān through analysis of the political economy and corresponding theoretical concepts of Covenant as constitution, social contract, and protection of rights. The analysis includes consideration of the Prophet's Biography. Secondly, I sketch institutional and theoretical developments in the period *ca.* 750 to *ca.* 1500, focusing on the constitutional and social contract-related issue of separation of powers between the state and the jurists.

QUR'ĀNIC INSTITUTIONAL CONTEXT

The Agrarian Economy

The world historian Marshal Hodgson has defined the economy of the regions that came under Islamic rule as an 'agrarian citied society'. The mainstay of the economy was agriculture, also for pastoralist nomads, with landed property and land tax the largest source of revenue for the main institutions. These were the state and bureaucracy, the military, and the religious scholarly institution. Cosmopolitan cities with trade, commerce, crafts, and manufacturing were also important parts of the economy, and became increasingly so under Islamic rule (Hodgson 1974/1: 107–108, 301).

Hodgson modelled the historical development of regional institutions by identifying 'three foci of high culture': 'the temple', 'the court', and 'the market'. The temple, with its priests and servants, was the institution around which the cities developed, as it organised the infrastructure required for agriculture, stored agricultural surplus, sent out traders to bring home needed goods, and organised fighting forces to defend its lands. The royal courts and their militaries and bureaucracies developed as a complimentary centre, as the cities grew and the temples became insufficient as 'central commands'.[1] Finally, traders and the market became institutionally independent from both temple and court, though always negotiating access to land and farm produce with both institutions, and depending for profits on the peasants' surplus (Hodgson 1974/1: 107). The 'religious' scholars can thus be understood as a development of the temple institution, which explains why *kharāj* or land tax was a standing topic in Islamic jurisprudence, for the service of the Caliphal administrations (Hodgson 1974/1: 270).

In terms of political economy i.e. the management of economy, government, and law, the political scientist Abbas Vali has defined both the pre-Islamic Sassanid Empire (224–651) and the subsequent Islamic polities in the former Sassanid regions as a 'system of vassalage' with a specific social contract theory. The theory of government defined the dynastic royal ruler as the owner of land in the imperial territory, and as responsible for

1 Similar topics are reflected in the story about Joseph in the Hebrew Bible (Gen. 37, 39–51).

maintaining irrigation and roads, in Marxist terms the basic 'means of production'. The rationale was that the ruler's personal military might was too limited for him to control the whole realm. He therefore relied on regional vassals to raise local armies and secure the provinces for the dynasty, and granted each vassal the right to own and manage a defined land area with its peasant labour force. From the produce of the peasants' labour, the vassal would extract his own living, sustain a local army, and submit tax revenue to the state treasury. Given the limited reach of the ruler's military power, vassals could easily resist submitting their due taxes, sometimes also breaking their compact with the ruler. In such cases, the ruler's legal ownership of all imperial lands allowed him to reclaim land from a rebellious vassal. Vassals who fulfilled their contractual obligations, on the other hand, had ownership and inheritance rights to their land (Vali 1993, ch. 6).

An Agrarian Revolution?

In *Agricultural innovation in the early Islamic world*, Andrew Watson offers the bold thesis that the Islamic state system generated an 'agricultural revolution', documentable in Islamic sources from the period *ca.* 700–1000. The revolution consisted in new fruits and cash crops; extended growth seasons and arable lands; and increased production and wealth. It came about through a combination of factors: new techniques for irrigating and fertilising soils through manure, bones and other biological waste; the use of gardens for introducing and developing new fruits and plants; and the law that secured ownership of land for peasants. This in turn depended on the unification of the entire region from Andalusia in the west to India and China in the east through trade routes, scholarly institutions, law, and administration (Watson 2008/1983: 103–119). However, Watson identifies a decline in agricultural productivity from the late 900s onwards. This could be because of climatic factors and the fragile natural conditions in this semi-arid region. But Watson also points to other factors: the growing power of landlords over peasants, the assignments of lands to military leaders instead of paying them from the state treasury, and the practice of irreversibly assigning lands as *waqf*, 'immobilised property', to institutions, especially the religious scholarly ones, who used them to finance their colleges and charitable funds. Under these circumstances, the 'critical knowledge mass' constituted by the contractual cooperation between state, jurists, landlords, and peasants, and which enabled the early agricultural advances, was broken up, and states could not always restore the conditions for productive agriculture (Watson 2008/1983: 139–146).

According to Stephen Humphreys (1991: 294), research that precedes Watson's study suggests that other sources document new crops and advances in agriculture already in the late 500s. Such a timeframe makes it possible to plot the Qur'ān along a trajectory corresponding with the early stages of the agricultural development. If this is correct, then Watson's argument about the contractual foundation and legal developments that enabled the agricultural revolution may offer an additional perspective on Qur'ānic Covenant and general insistence on fulfilment of contractual terms. Relying on Islamic sources, Watson points out that the city of Mecca, because of the pilgrimage to the Ka'ba Temple and the trade it generated, offered its visitors every kind of fruit (2008/1983: 92). Analogously, it is possible that some of the Qur'ān's garden-imagery, which is usually understood in purely eschatological terms, also have 'inner-worldly' references. For example, Q. 2 (*al-Baqara*), 25, has an eschatological ring to it:

> (25) Carry forth with joy the divine word to those who have promoted security and worked for the common good (*'amilū al-ṣāliḥāt*), that they will have gardens under which rivers flow! Each time they are provided from them fruits (*thamara*) for sustenance, they say: 'This is what we were given for sustenance before!' and they are given what resembles it. There they have spouses who are pure (*muṭahhara*), while they remain there.

On the other hand, Q. 6 (*al-An'ām*), verses 99 and 141, refer to real gardens and varieties of seeds and fruits, which God provides for His servants' sustenance, and from which they must pay their due i.e. tax (verse 141):

> (99) It is He Who sends down from the heavens water, by which we bring forth vegetation of each kind. By it we have brought forth greenery and clustered grains, and from the date palm shoot clusters of dates, low-hanging and near. And gardens of grape vines and olive trees and pomegranates, alike and unlike (each other): Look at their fruits when they bud and ripen; surely, in them are signs for a people who enact security!

> (141) It is He Who brought forth gardens (*jannāt*), trellised and un-trellised, and date palms and crops of various kinds: eat of it! And olive trees and pomegranates, both alike and unlike: eat of His fruits when they are ripe, and pay His due on the day of harvest. But do not be wasteful, for He does not love the wasteful!

Independently of agriculture, Baber Johansen has analysed early Islamic law with reference to the issue of peasants' rights. Based on his studies of Ḥanafī legal documents, Johansen argued that the early Islamic law on land ownership and land tax changed the peasants' pre-Islamic status from serfs whose labour produced tax revenue for the landlord, to owners of their produce with property and inheritance rights to the land they farmed. The crucial change consisted in the introduction of a sharecropping contract (*al-muzāraʿa*). The contract was 'commercial', in the sense that the peasant's labour and produce became his property and commodity (*māl mutaqawwim*), as his part of a mutual contract (*ʿaqd*) with the landlord, who provided the 'credit' of seeds, cattle, and land, and, through the state administration, also maintained waterways and irrigation channels. Given that the peasant was the weaker party in relation to the landlord, this kind of commercial contract protected the peasant's rights as owner of the land he/she worked and the produce of his/her labour. It also gave the peasant access to markets, where he/she could sell his/her produce and maximise income. The spread of the sharecropping contract in the eastern, former Sassanid parts of the Islamic empire effected this change in legal status, and the early Ḥanafī jurists perceived the contract as a means to further social and economic integration of the classes in rural society (Johansen 1988: 56–58; 38–39).[2] However, Johansen also argues that the legal sources reflect a regressive change from the late 900s onwards, at which point the landlords re-entrenched their powers and states expanded tax farming. In this model, landlords could raise the amount of tax they levied on the peasants and take ownership of their labour, produce, and lands if they failed to pay it. Consequently, many peasant land holdings were subsumed into large estates (1988: 80–81). Johansen's observation coincides in time with the decline in agricultural production that Watson noted. Both Johansen and Watson thus point to legal changes and shifts in power as a significant cause for this development, though Watson cautioned that climate change might have been a factor, as well.

Some Qurʾānic verses appear in a new light, if read against this background of rights for peasants. One example is the passage Q. 28 (*al-Qaṣaṣ*), 1–6. Verses 1–3 connect the divine written signs with the true right that God recounts, applied to the case of Pharaoh, the Qurʾānic model-tyrant. Verse 4 describes how Pharaoh weakened the inhabitants in the land, and defines him as belonging to the category *al-mufsidūna*. In legal terminology related

2 Johansen here agrees with an earlier study and thesis (Haque 1977), that the early Islamic legal contract transformed the peasant status from serf to proprietor.

to land tenancy, the term for a 'voidable contract' was *ijāra fāsida*, meaning a contract that is voidable because it does not specify one of four required items: size, quality and location of the plots; how the lands should be used; the duration of the tenancy; and the amount of the rent (Johansen 1988: 34). Such a voidable contract would work to the disadvantage of especially the weaker party i.e. the peasant. Given the topical context of the passage Q. 28, 1–6, with Pharaoh oppressing the weak in the land, I read *al-mufsidūna* in the sense of 'those who enact voidable contract', as a specification of the general sense 'those who cause corruption'. God then opposes this category in verses 5 and 6, where He promises to do good by the weak and make them leaders and inheritors of the land:

> (1) *ṭāsīnmīm*
> (2) Those are the signs of the divine writing that makes clear distinctions:
> (3) We read in correct order upon you from the announcement about Moses and Pharaoh with **the true right (*bi-l-ḥaqq*)**, for a people who enact security:
> (4) Indeed, Pharaoh elevated himself in the land and made its inhabitants factions (*shiya'an*), **reducing a group of them to weakness (*yastaḍ'ifu ṭā'ifatan minhum*)**, slaughtering their sons but letting their women live: He was certainly among those who **enact voidable contracts (*al-mufsidīna*)**!
> (5) We intend to do good by **those who have been weakened in the land** and make them leaders and **make them the inheritors** (*wa nurīdu an namunna 'alā* ***alladhīna ustuḍ'ifū bi-l-arḍ*** *wa naj'lahum a'imma wa* ***naj'lahum al-wārithīna***),
> (6) And give them power in the land, and make Pharaoh and Haman and their armed troops see what they have been fearing!

Through a degree of interpretive force, then, it becomes possible to read the Qur'ān as weighing in on the side of the weak against tyrants who enact voidable contracts. 'Those made weak' here refers to inhabitants (*ahl*) of the land (*al-arḍ*), which is a more general reference than peasants. Nevertheless, because the passage defines God's writing, His messenger Moses, and God's own statement in verses 5 and 6 as strengthening those inhabitants of the land who have been reduced to weakness, including by securing them right to *inherit* i.e. property right, it can include a range of categories. Other examples include Q. 7 (*al-A'rāf*), 75–76, which shows the messenger Ṣāliḥ supporting the weak against 'the self-aggrandising dignitaries' through his divine message, which the weak accept and the dignitaries reject:

> (75) **The dignitaries who were self-aggrandising (*al-malāʾu alladhīna istakbarū*)** among [Ṣāliḥ's] people said to some of **those who had enacted security and been made weak (*alladhīna ustuḍʿifū liman āmana minhum*)**: "Do you know that Ṣāliḥ is sent out with a message from his Lord?" They said: "Indeed, we enact security by the message he has been sent with!"
> (76) The self-aggrandising ones said: "And we definitely reject that by which you enact security!"

In Q. 7, 137, the topic is again about Pharaoh and the Israelites as the paradigmatic case of an enslaved people set free by God giving them land to inherit:

> (137) **We let the people who were made weak inherit (*wa awrathnā al-qawma alladhīna kānū yustaḍʿafūna*)** the eastern and western parts of the land, which We had made blessed; thus your Lord's best word was fulfilled for the Israelites, because of what they had endured, whereas We destroyed the constructions that Pharaoh and his people were making!

In another context, Q. 8 (*al-Anfāl*), 26 treats the same topic in a general sense, referring to the 'the enactors of security' instead of the Israelites. Here the related matter of material sustenance (*rizq*) appears as well, in conjunction with good and nourishing things to eat:

> (26) And remember when you were few and **made weak in the land (*mustaḍʿafūna fī al-arḍ*)**, fearing that the people would snatch you away: then He gave you shelter and aided you with His help to victory and **gave you for material sustenance the good and nourishing things (*razaqakum min al-ṭayyibāt*)**, hoping you will give thanks!

A final example: Q. 4 (*al-Nisāʾ*), 75, which is again addressed to 'the enactors of security', who are encouraged to fight for the protection of the weak, here specified as men, women, and children living in a village (*qarya*) under the oppression of wrongdoers:

> (75) But why do you not fight for the duties towards God and those made weak among men, women and children, who say: "Our Lord, bring us out of this village whose inhabitants are wrongdoers, and give us from Yourself a protective governor, and give us from Yourself a helper to victory!"

To conclude: Recalling de Certeau's argument, that religion can promote developments in theory and institutional practices, in conjunction with Watson's and Johansen's studies, these examples from the Qur'ān can be seen as reflecting new legal theory and new practices within the system of vassalage. This might provide an institutional context for the natural law theory discussed in the previous chapter, and the exegetes' interpretation of Q. 4, 1 as God obligating all humans to empathise with each other so that the strong uphold the rights of the weak. Natural law theory and the extension of rights to weak groups could thus be seen as part of the Qur'ānic Covenant as a new legal-theoretical framework, which applies to a range of particular cases, including peasants' property and inheritance rights.

Covenant as Constitution

In order to show how Qur'ānic Covenant and natural law theory can be seen as referring to a political constitution, I refer to Daniel Elazar's political theory-approach to the Hebrew Bible's Covenant (*berîth*). In his view, Biblical Covenant denotes a constitution, in the sense of "the voluntary establishment of a people and body politic", similar to a love-based marriage contract (Elazar 1998: 29). He then analyses Covenant through Aristotle's model of the three bases of the constitution of any political system (Elazar 1998: 29–30):

> (1) *Moral basis*: The generally accepted ideas about how people should live in the polity, including a concept of justice and other opinions about what is good and right;
> (2) *Socioeconomic basis*: Type of economy, class structure, ethnic composition, and the actual distribution of power;
> (3) *Frame of government*: The institutions and structures of government, including the document(s) that sets out the institutions, establishes their powers and limits them, and indicates who shall govern and how they shall be chosen.

Concerning *the frame of government*, Elazar distinguishes between 'covenant', 'compact', and 'contract'. 'Covenant' always has a moral basis because it refers to natural law theory, and generally posits God as its supervisor and guarantor. In this sense, 'covenant' was used frequently even in early modern British-ruled North America. 'Compact' is functionally identical with covenant and was used interchangeably with it in the early modern Anglo-American contexts until the 1790s. After that point, those political actors who emphasised God's moral authority over requirements of public agreement tended to use the term 'covenant', while the latter increasingly used 'compact' in the sense of a 'secular' social contract. Correspondingly, Elazar perceives 'compact' as predominantly legal rather than ethical (i.e. excluding the natural law-dimension), and preoccupied with the agreement between parties rather than their relationship with a third-party divine supervisor and higher moral authority (Elazar 1998: 31). The third term, 'contract', is distinct from both 'covenant' and 'compact':

> [T]he first two [covenant and compact; UM] are constitutional or public and the last [contract; UM] is private in character. As such, covenantal or compactual obligation is broadly reciprocal. Those bound by one or the other are obligated to respond to each other beyond the letter of the law rather than to limit their obligations to the narrowest contractual requirements. Hence, covenants and compacts are inherently designed to be flexible in certain respects as well as firm in others. As expressions of private law, contracts tend to be interpreted as narrowly as possible so as to limit the obligation of the contracting parties to what is explicitly mandated by the contract itself. Contracts normally contain provisions for unilateral abrogation by one party or another under certain conditions [...]; compacts and covenants generally require mutual consent to be abrogated, designed as they are to be perpetual or of unlimited duration (Elazar 1998: 31).

As for the term '*social* contract', Elazar relates it to Jean-Jacques Rousseau's secular definition, which focuses on the agreement between parties and "even when applied for public purposes, never develops the same level of moral obligation as either covenant or compact" (Elazar 1998: 32). By comparison, D'Agostino, Gaus, and Thrasher (2017) in the *Stanford Encyclopedia of Philosophy* entry 'Contemporary Approaches to the Social Contract' claim that social contract theory goes back at least to Epicurus (d. 270 BCE), although it became particularly important in modern history with Thomas Hobbes, John Locke, Jean-Jacques Rousseau, and Immanuel Kant. In essence, a social contract theory aims to show "that members of some society have reason to endorse and comply with the fundamental social rules, laws, institutions, and/or principles of that society. Put simply, it is concerned with public justification i.e., 'of determining whether or not a given regime is legitimate and therefore worthy of loyalty'".[3]

3 D'Agostino, Fred, Gaus, Gerald and Thrasher, John, "Contemporary Approaches to the Social Contract", *The Stanford Encyclopedia of Philosophy* (Winter 2017 Edition), Edward N. Zalta (ed.), plato.stanford.edu/archives/win2017/entries/

Qur'ānic Covenant as Constitution and Social Contract

I propose that Qur'ānic Covenant can be seen as reflecting *both* a constitution and a social contract, starting with Elazar's categories for constitution. The *moral basis* of constitution can be referred to Qur'ānic Covenant's relationship with natural law theory, discussed in Chapter 4. The *socioeconomic basis* of constitution has been discussed above, with reference to the 'agrarian' society and the system of vassalage, and Watson's and Johansen's studies of agricultural and legal development and its relationship with peasants' property rights. Thus, the Qur'ānic polity assigns legal authority to the institution of 'prophecy', and advocates that the weaker classes in society should enjoy a strengthened legal position. 'Rule by prophecy' relates to *frame of government*. As we have seen, the Qur'ān categorises groups of polity members and gives knowledge and rules for how the prophetic authority should treat these. *'Ilm*, 'knowledge' of the systematic kind, conveyed through God's writing, is thus an important tool for establishing prophetic authority. However, it is also a tool for limiting it. As we have seen in Chapter 4, the Prophet can only convey the divine message but not punish those who reject it – unless they turn against his polity. Fulfilling the terms of compact and individual contracts is part of the legitimacy of prophetic authority, which also binds the Prophet to the divine obligations. Such things as property rights and contracts for land tenure also concern the constitutional level, since they refer to the socioeconomic basis of the constitution. Below we will see further examples of these issues, from the Prophet's Biography.

As for 'social contract', I follow the definition proposed by D'Agostino, Gaus, and Thrasher (2017), who perceive the theory as having an ancient legacy and focusing on reasons for the legitimacy and worthiness of a given regime. This perspective draws rhetorical persuasion into the frame again. We have seen in Chapter 4 how the Qur'ānic Covenant depends on persuasion about the reasons for acknowledging it, and the rules and laws that derive from it. Even though the divine 'signs' that messengers and prophets communicate do not persuade all people, the 'rejecters' still enjoy material support as members of the polity, so long as they do not turn against it. Consequently, the *divine* effort at persuasion that pertains to the Covenant as constitution *functions* as its social contract-aspect, which gives reasons for the legitimacy and worthiness of the rules and laws, and the prophetic

---

contractarianism-contemporary/ . The quote within the citation is to D'Agostino (1996: 23).

authority behind them. In this way, the Qur'ānic social contract incorporates dissent and provides rules for dealing with it.

Against this background, I will give a few more examples from the Qur'ān, to illustrate other aspects of the *moral* and *socioeconomic* basis, and the *frame of government*, including the social contract aspect.

Moral Basis

In addition to the natural law theory-related Qur'ānic claims to a moral standard for the law, a particular virtue is associated with the concept of divine Oneness, the doctrinal foundation for the Qur'ānic Covenant. Q. 112 is the *sūra* that defines God's nature, as discussed in Chapter 2 in relation to ontological theories of concept. Its title is *al-Ikhlāṣ*, which can mean both 'Perfection' in terms of the creed, and 'Sincerity' as a corresponding devotional virtue. It reads:

> Q. 112 (*al-Ikhlāṣ*, 'Perfection', 'Sincerity')
>
> (1) Say: 'He is God, One,
> (2) God the Boundless,
> (3) Who did not beget and was not begotten,
> (4) And Who can have no counterpart: One!'

The emphasis on divine Oneness implies that *ikhlāṣ* here refers to the perfection of the creed, while the sense of 'sincerity' is implicit as the virtue that follows from the creed. In other contexts, the active participle *mukhliṣ* appears in conjunction with conceptualising God. For example, Q. 37 (*al-Ṣāffāt*), 159–160, and here I have spelt out the ethical sense as well:

> (159) Sublime is God, beyond what they attribute (*ṣubḥān Allāh ʿammā yaṣifūna*),
> (160) Except those of God's servants who **perfect the creed in sincerity** (*illā ʿibād Allāh* ***al-mukhliṣīna***)!

Another example is Q. 39 (*al-Zumar*), 1–6. Here the sincere perfection refers to *dīn*, 'judicial order', and a contrasting parallel is made between the 'insincere' legal practice of taking other governors alongside God (verse 3) and the 'imperfect' doctrinal ascription of children to God (verse 4):

> (1) The sending-down of the writing (*tanzīl al-kitāb*) is from God, the Mighty Who Judges Wisely!

(2) Indeed, We have made descend to you the divine writing with the true right (*bi-l-ḥaqq*), so serve God by **perfecting** for Him the judicial order **in sincerity** (***mukhliṣan*** *lahu al-dīn*)!
(3) Is it not to God that the **perfectly sincere** judicial order (*al-dīn al-**khāliṣ***) belongs, while those who took protective governors (*awliyāʾ*) apart from Him [say]: 'We only serve them so that they will bring us closer to God in rank!'? Indeed, God judges between them regarding their disagreement; for sure, God does not guide one who is a liar rejecting security!
(4) Had God wanted to take for Himself a child He would have chosen from what He creates what He wishes: Sublime is He! He is God the One Who Conquers!
(5) He created the heavens and the earth with the true right, wrapping the night round the day and the day round the night, as He laid down the courses for the sun and the moon to each run their defined term: Is He not but the Mighty Who Is Forgiving?
(6) He created you from a single person (*nafs wāḥida*), then out of it He brought forth its mate, and made descend for you of the cattle eight pairs. He is creating you in your mothers' bellies, one creation after another, in three dark shadows: That for you is God, your Lord, to Who belongs the kingdom! There is no god but He, so how can you be diverted?

Thus, according to the Qurʾānic discourse, the fact that God as the guarantor of the constitution is 'perfectly One' and without partner or child corresponds with 'sincerity' as a devotional virtue associated with the moral basis of the constitution and the judicial order deriving from it.

Socioeconomic Basis

The system of vassalage and the agricultural-mercantile economy as the socioeconomic basis of the constitution can be seen as expressed in the same *sūra* passages on the topic of 'food security' that I analysed in terms of the reciprocal social contract in Chapter 4. The passages suggest a semantic connection between 'security' (*amn*), the principal category *muʾmin*, and material sustenance or 'food' from the harvest. Hence, 'food security' is a key obligation upon God and those humans who convey His message, and a social contractual 'reason' for the legitimacy of the constitution and judicial order. For illustration, again, Q. 106 (*Quraysh*):

(1) For Quraysh's contract of protection (*liʾīlāf Quraysh*):

> (2) Their contract of protection is the journey of the winter and the summer (*'īlāfihim riḥlat al-shitā' wa al-ṣayf*),
> (3) So let them serve the Lord of this House (*fa-l-ya'budū rabba hādhā al-bayt*),
> (4) **Who provided food for them against hunger and secured them against fear (*alladhī aṭ'amahum min jū'in wa āmanahum min khawf*)**!

And Q. 14 (*Ibrāhīm*), 35–37, where Abraham appears as the messenger-protagonist who holds God to His obligation to feed the people:

> (35) But Abraham said: "My Lord, **make this region with its cities secure** and keep me and my sons away from serving the idols!"
> (36) "My Lord, [the idols] have led many people astray, but he who follows me is of me, while the one who disobeys me: surely, You are A Forgiving One Who Continuously Protects life!"
> (37) "Our Lord, I have settled some of my descendants in a valley without crops, by Your Inviolate House, our Lord, so that they can enact standing to the prayer. **Then incline the hearts of the people towards them and sustain them of the harvest fruits** so that they may become thankful!"

In Q. 2 (*al-Baqara*), 125–126, God Himself recalls Abraham's negotiation with Him on behalf of his people, adding that He will also materially support the 'rejecters':

> (125) When We made the House a meeting place for the people and a secure haven: "Take for yourselves from Abraham's standing place a place for prayer!" We entered a compact with Abraham and Ismail: "Purify My House for those who circumambulate it, absorbed in worship, and kneeling in prostration!"
> (126) When Abraham said: "**My Lord, make this a secure region** (*rabbi ij'al hādhā baladan āminan*) and **sustain of the harvest fruits** those of its inhabitants who enact security through God and the Far-away Day!" **(God) said: "As for those who reject security, I shall materially support them a while (*fa'umatti'uhum qalīlan*)**, then subject them to the punishment of the fire: a painful outcome!"

There are also specific rules related to the polity's welfare, which concretise the 'perfect sincerity' of the judicial order. For example, the passage Q. 2 (*al-Baqara*), 267–282 expands on economic obligations related to the welfare tax (*zakāt*, lit. 'prosperous' and 'pure' things) and 'alms' (*ṣadaqāt*, lit. 'trust-worthy' things), as well as the ban on usury (*ribā*, lit. 'increase').[4] Thus, verse 267 addresses 'the enactors of security' and refers to the land and its blissful produce, whereupon verse 268 establishes a distinction between poverty, which is associated with Satan's promise, and forgiveness, justice and prosperity, which is God's promise. In practice, prosperity is enacted through the command to spend of one's assets for the common good through the welfare tax and 'alms'. The ban on usury is depicted as part of God's broader aim of allowing the polity to prosper. Note also that usury collected before this ban is considered private property and therefore not subject to confiscation; hence the ban is not retroactive. Finally, verse 282 – the longest verse in the Qurʾān – gives instructions for how to contract a debt in a legitimate manner, through a written document and with witnesses. Given the assumed legal context of strengthening the rights of the weak, these rules on usury and legitimate debt contracting appear intended to protect weak groups in particular (see also verse 280). Thus, the whole passage reads:

> (267) O you who enact security: spend of the good and nourishing things you have acquired and of what We have brought forth for you from the land, but do not turn to the rotten and spend of that, since you yourselves would not take it, except reluctantly: know that God is a Self-Sufficient One Who is Praiseworthy!
> (268) Satan promises you poverty and commands you obscene excesses, while God promises you forgiveness from His side and favour, for God is a Munificent One Who Knows Everything!
> (269) He gives the capacity for just judgement (*al-ḥikma*) to whoever He wishes, and whoever receives the capacity for just judgement has indeed received an abundant good! But no one is reminded (of this), except those with analytical discernment.
> (270) Whatever expense you spend and whatever vow you vow: God has knowledge of them, and the wrongdoers shall have no helpers to victory.
> (271) If you give alms (*al-ṣadaqāt*) publicly, it is commendable, but if you conceal it and give it to the poor it is a greater good for you and will bury some of your bad deeds: God is Informed of what you do!
> (272) You are not obligated to guide them, but God guides who He wishes! Whatever good that you spend will be for your persons if you only spend seeking God's countenance, for whatever good you spend will be recompensed to you, and you will not be wronged!
> (273) For the poor who are detained performing their duties towards God (*fī sabīl Allāh*) and unable to travel in the land: the ignorant take

4 For a detailed study of *ribā*, *zakāt* and *ṣadaqa* as part of the Qurʾānic 'distributive justice', see Harvey (2018: 121–141).

them for rich because of the self-restraint. You will recognise them by their mark: they do not ask the people importunely; whatever good you spend, indeed: God has full Knowledge of it!
(274) Those who spend of their wealth, whether night or day, secretly or publicly, have a reward in store with their Lord, so they shall have no fear, nor shall they grieve.
(275) Those who devour usury do not go about things except in the way of those who Satan disturbed with (his) touch. That is because they state that trade is like usury, whereas God has made trade permissible and usury inviolate. Hence, the one who has received an admonition from his Lord and ceased can keep what he has with him, for his fate is for God [to decide]. But the one who reverts: those are the people of the fire, where they will abide forever!
(276) God obliterates usury but teaches alms, for God does not love any sinful rejecter of security (*kaffār athīm*)!
(277) Indeed, those who have enacted security, acted for the common good (*ʿamilū al-ṣāliḥāt*), performed the prayer, and paid the welfare tax (*al-zakāt*), have a reward in store with their Lord, so they shall have no fear, nor shall they grieve.
(278) O you who have enacted security: fulfil your obligations towards God and forgo what is still due from usury, if you are really enactors of security!
(279) If you fail to do that, beware of war from God and His messenger! But if you return you shall keep your capital, and neither do wrong nor be wronged.
(280) If [the debtor] is in straits, allow him to become at ease. But to remit the debt as alms (*wa an taṣaddaqū*) is better for you, if you have knowledge!
(281) Fulfil your obligations for a day when you will be returned to God, and then each person shall be recompensed for what he has acquired, without them being wronged.
(282) O You who enact security! When you contract a debt (*tadāyantum bidayn*) for a defined period, write it down and let a scribe write it down for you justly. No scribe should refuse to write, according to the knowledge God has conveyed to him! So, let him write while the one who has a right to the debt dictates, and he should fulfil his obligations towards God His Lord and never diminish the debt by anything. If the one who has a right to the debt is feeble-minded or weak or unable to dictate himself, then let his legal guardian dictate justly. Call for witnessing two witnesses of your men; if there are no two men, then one man and two women from among the witnesses you approve of, so that if one of them fails to remember, the other would remind her. The witnesses must not refuse when they are called upon! So do not be adverse to write it down, whether small or large, with its due date. That way of yours is

> more equitable with God, more upright as testimony, and less likely to arouse your doubts. Unless it is a direct transaction between yourselves, when it is not an offence if you do not write it down; but let there be witnesses when you sell to each other. Neither a scribe nor a witness must come to harm, and if you do that it is indeed a transgression on your part! Fulfil your obligations towards God, for God conveys knowledge to you since God has knowledge of every single thing!

Frame of Government

In the long passage above, verse 2, 272 repeats the point related to social contract, that God is obligated by His promise: He will not wrong anyone but will recompense as promised:

> (272) You are not obligated to guide them, but God guides who He wishes! Whatever good that you spend will be for your persons if you only spend seeking God's countenance, for whatever good you spend will be recompensed to you, and **you will not be wronged**!

This establishes the basic principle that even the highest of all authorities – God – is obligated by His promised terms. Since a social contract in the most basic sense regulates the relations between 'ruler and ruled', this principle places the worldly ruler under the law, which is a constitutional principle.

As mentioned several times, the Qur'ānic social contract includes other religions, notably Jews and Christians. Two examples from Q. 3 (*Āl ʿImrān*) illustrate how 'prophecy' provides a common legacy for the communities within the polity. The first example is Q. 3, 64–68. Here Abraham is presented to Jews and Christians as a 'common ancestor', who because he predates the Torah and the Gospel can be considered 'neutral ground' for Jews, Christians and the Prophet's followers. At the same time, there is frustration over the fact that Jews and Christians do not see it the same way:

> (64) Say: "O People of the divine writing! Arise and come to an equitable word between us and you: that we serve no one but God and do not make anything partner with Him (*lā nushrika bihi shay'an*), and do not take each other as lords instead of God!" Should they turn away (*tawallū*), say: "Bear witness that we are enactors of peace (*muslimūna*)!"
> (65) O People of the divine writing! Why do you argue about Abraham when the Torah and the Gospel were not sent down until after him? Will you not be bound by reason (*afalā taʿqilūna*)?

> (66) Here you are: you have argued concerning that about which you have knowledge (*'ilm*), so why do you argue concerning that about which you have no knowledge? God knows and you do not know:
> (67) Abraham was neither a Jew nor a Christian, but a *ḥanīf* and one who enacts peace, since he was not among those who assign other partners!
> (68) Indeed, the people who are most loyal allies of Abraham (*awlā bi'Ibrāhīm*) are those who followed him, and this Prophet and those who have enacted security; and God is the Protective Governor (*walī*) of the enactors of security!

Further on in Q. 3, verse 81 describes how God binds Himself by the Covenant and contract that He enters with all the prophets who preceded the Prophet:

> (81) When God took the Covenant (*mīthāq*) from the prophets: "Now that I have brought you divine writing and capacity for just judgement, and a messenger comes to you confirming what you have, you must enact security through him and support him to victory! Do you affirm this and take upon yourselves My contract (*iṣrī*)?" They said: "We affirm it!" He said: "Bear witness, and I will be a witness together with you!"

In this way, the previous prophets become more than predecessors to the Prophet: they testify to his future mission.

The same strategy of arguing 'common principles' can be seen in Q. 5 (*al-Mā'ida*), the temporally latest *sūra*, and its passages on the relationship between the Prophet's legal authority and 'the people of divine writing', *ahl al-kitāb* (Weiss 1990). Verses 5, 12–14 describe how God has taken the Covenant with both Jews and Christians who, each in their specific way, have then gone on to betray its terms:

> (12) God took the Covenant (*mīthāq*) with the Sons of Israel and We raised among them twelve chieftains. God said: "I am with you! Indeed, if you perform the prayer, give the welfare tax, enact security through My messengers and support them and lend God a good loan, I will certainly bury your bad deeds and let you enter gardens under which waterways flow – but whoever of you rejects security after that has definitely strayed from the path of equity!"
> (13) Because they betrayed their Covenant We cursed them and made their hearts hard, so that they change speech from its established meaning (*yuḥarrifūna al-kalima 'an mawāḍi'ihi*) and forget part of what they were made to honour; thus you will always experience treachery from

> them, but for a few exceptions. Yet pardon them and forgive: indeed, God loves those who do good by others!
> (14) And from those who state "We are Christians!" We took their Covenant, but they forgot part of what they were made to honour. So We stirred up enmity and hatred among them until the Day of Standing to Trial, when God will announce to them what they have been fabricating!

Covenant is thus shown to be something that the Jews and Christians have in common with each other, and with the Qur'ānic polity and Prophet, despite betrayals. Verses 15–19 continue by describing the ways in which the Jews and Christians i.e. 'the people of the divine writing', have erred. From verse 17 is becomes clear that 'rejection of security' (*kufr*) is something both polytheists and Christians are liable to do, the latter through their claim that Jesus the Messiah is God. Note again that they are entitled to stick to their errors, as long as they accept the contract with God's Messenger:

> (15) O People of the divine writing (*yā ahl al-kitāb*)! Our Messenger has now come to you to make clearly distinct for you much of what you have been concealing of the writing, and to forgive a great deal. Indeed, a light and a writing that conveys clear distinctions (*nūr wa kitāb mubīn*) have come to you from God!
> (16) God guides with it those who follow the duties of peace (*subul al-salām*) that please Him, taking them out from the shadows of darkness into the light, by His permission, and guiding them to a path of correct speech and action.
> (17) Those have rejected security who state "God is the Messiah, son of Mary"! Say: "Who owns anything that keeps God from annihilating the Messiah, son of Mary, and his mother, and everyone on the land together? God owns the kingdom of the heavens and the land and what is between them, creating what He wishes, as God continuously governs each thing!"
> (18) The Jews and the Christians have stated: "We are God's sons and His beloved ones!" Say: "Then why does He afflict you for your sins? Instead, you are human bearers of the word among those He has created, forgiving whoever He wishes and afflicting whoever He wishes. God owns the kingdom of the heavens and the land and what is between them, and to Him is the destination!"
> (19) O People of the divine writing! Now Our Messenger has come to you to make clear distinctions for you after a cessation of the messengers, so that you will not be able to say: "No bearer of the good word or warner has come to us!" So now a bearer of the good word and a warner has come to you, as God continuously governs each thing!

Thus, verse 15 addresses Jews and Christians as 'people of the divine writing' because they too have received it, even though they have concealed important parts of it in order to support their erroneous doctrines. The same topic, 'divine writing', is further developed in verses 44–48. Here it is emphasised that it is the commonly recognised source of law across the distinct communities within the polity. Accordingly, there is said to be "guidance and light" (*hudan wa nūr*) in the Torah, the Gospel, and *this* divine writing; the point being that even though it is the last one that conveys the 'True Right' (*al-ḥaqq*) and rules sovereign over the others, the others can judge by their own writings within their own communities. Consequently, 'divine writing' adds to 'rule of law' as constitutional principle, by identifying the *source* of law for the communities in the polity. Note also that verse 45 stipulates a particular shared ruling, namely that injuries should be settled through compensation, by measure of the damage inflicted:

> (44) We have indeed sent down **the Torah, in which is guidance and light,** and by which the prophets who enacted peace, and the masters and the scribes, **judged** among those who have turned back, according to what they were made to protect of God's writing and to which they had testified. So do not fear the people, but fear Me, so that you do not trade My signs for a small price! **Whoever does not judge by what God has sent down: those are the rejecters of security!**
> (45) **We wrote down for them in it** that life is by life, eye is by eye, nose is by nose, ear is by ear, tooth is by tooth, and that injuries is settlement of account. So, whoever accepts compensation in it provides expiation for it. **Whoever does not judge according to what God has sent down: those are the ones who do wrong!**
> (46) We let follow in their tracks Jesus, son of Mary, confirming what he had before him of the Torah as We gave him **the Gospel, in which is guidance and light, confirming what he had before him of the Torah** as guidance and admonition for those who fulfil their obligations!
> (47) Let the people of the Gospel **judge** according to what God has sent down in it, as **whoever does not judge according to what God has sent down: those are the ones who rebel!**
> (48) **We have sent down to you the divine writing with the True Right, confirming the writing that is before it, and superseding it. So judge among them according to what God has sent down,** and do not follow their whims so that they divert you from the right that has come to you! To each of you We have opened a path to guidance and a method, and **had God so wished, He would have made you one nation, but He wanted to test you by what He brought you. So hurry to put forward the good deeds! To God is the return of you**

all, when He will instruct you about that over which you used to disagree!

'Those who enact security' are then commanded not to take Jews or Christians as 'protective governors' (*awliyā'*), in the passage Q. 5, 51–58, meaning they cannot be their political allies or authorities owed loyalty in the political-legal sense.[5] Finally, for the category 'those who go to war' against the Prophet (*al-muḥāribūna*), Q. 5, 33 stipulates a harsh punishment, although these too must be pardoned if they turn back:

> (33) Indeed, the recompense for those who go to war against God and His Messenger and go around spreading voidable contracts in the land is that they be killed or crucified or have their hands and feet cut off on opposite sides, or be exiled from the land. That is a disgrace for them in this nearest life, while in the most distant they have in store a terrible punishment,
> (34) except those who return before you overpower them: know that God a Forgiving One Who Continuously Protects life!

Thus, we have seen how verses in Q. 3 offer Abraham as a 'common ancestor' of a line of prophecy culminating with the Prophet's mission and shared with Jews and Christians, while passages in Q. 5 propose Covenant and divine writing as principles in common between Jews, Christians, and 'the enactors of security'. All three commonalities – prophetic ancestry, constitution, and divine source of law – serve as a strategy for including the two 'other' religious communities into the polity and its constitution. At the social contract level, the same commonalities constitute reasons for the legitimacy of the Prophet's authority. The strategy can also be seen as reflecting natural law theory, which presupposes that the moral standard that authorises the law is universally valid and justifiable. Again, the fact that the Covenant ultimately goes back beyond Abraham to Adam and his descendants (Q. 7, 172) gives it its decisive, universal foundation. Finally, this theoretical universalism translates into an obligation on 'those who enact security' to not only care for next of kin or the rich but to serve the cause of equity and justice, as God obligates them to do; e.g. Q. 4 (*al-Nisā'*), 135:

5 Some translators render *'awliyā'* as 'friends', e.g. Fakhry (2000: 116); Abdel Haleem instead translates the term as 'allies', which brings out the political and legal sense of the term (2005: 73). My own choice, 'protective governor', is motivated by the reference to *walāya* as an institution; see discussion below in this chapter.

> (135) O you who have enacted security! **Be supporters of equity (*kūnū qawwāmīna bi-l-qisṭ*)** as witnesses for God, even if it is against yourselves, your parents or kinsmen: whether rich or poor, God is their foremost Protective Governor. **Do not follow your whims away from doing justice (*falā tattabiʿū al-hawā an taʿdilū*)**, and if you distort or turn away, God is certainly Informed of what you do!

The Prophet's Biography

The moral, socioeconomic, and governmental aspects of Qurʾānic Covenant are reflected in the standardised Biography of the Prophet's life (570–10/632), which is the earliest historical construction of context for the Qurʾān. The collected reports (*akhbār*, sing. *khabar*) that constitute the Biography are attributed to Muḥammad b. Isḥāq (d. 150/767). His family were originally Nestorian Christians from a village in South-Western Iraq near al-Ḥīra, capital of the Arab royal dynasty of Lakhm (late 200s–602), vassals of the Persian Sassanid imperial dynasty (224–31/651). Initially pagan, the Lakhmids converted to Nestorian Christianity in the late 500s. During the Caliphate of the Prophet's first successor Abū Bakr (10/632–13/634), in the course of his wars to maintain the loyalty of the Iraqi Arabs, Ibn Isḥāq's grandfather was taken prisoner and brought to Medina. In Medina, the family became protected adoptees (*mawālī*) of the Prophet's paternal family al-Muṭṭalib and reportedly specialised in the history of the Prophet and the first Caliphs. Ibn Isḥāq himself later moved to Baghdad, capital of the newly ascended Abbasid Caliphal dynasty (133/750–656/1258), where he is said to have tutored the Caliphal heir-apparent al-Mahdī (159/775–169/785) in the Prophet's life and the early Caliphate.[6] Hence, Ibn Isḥāq's reports can be seen as educational material for rulers.

Ibn Isḥāq's reports, which date to the second half of the 600s, were transmitted from the earliest historians from Medina, ʿUrwa b. al-Zubayr (d. 94/712) and his student Ibn Shihāb al-Zuhrī (d. 123/741), who were the first to collect and organise information about the Prophet's life (Khalidi 1994: 30–35; Schoeler 2011/1996; Guillaume 1995: xiv–xvii). Ibn Isḥāq's reports were then collected and edited by the Egyptian historian and genealogist Muḥammad b. Hishām (d. *c.* 213/828) into a manuscript with the title *al-Sīra al-nabawiyya*, approximately 'The Prophetic life trajectory'. Ibn Hishām's edition has become the standardised form of the Prophet's Biography.

6 On Ibn Isḥāq's background, see the Introduction to Alfred Guillaume's translation of Ibn Hishām's edited Biography (Guillaume 1995: xiii–xiv); also Abbott (1957).

However, it is based on one particular transmission of Ibn Isḥāq's reports by his student al-Bakkā'ī, and focuses on the Arabian Peninsula and its surroundings (including Ethiopia) as geographical context for the Prophet's life and mission. Other transmissions of Ibn Isḥāq's material, like the one by Salama b. al-Faḍl used by e.g. al-Ṭabarī, contextualises the Prophet's life in the framework of a universal history starting with Creation and treating also the Biblical prophets and kings, 'Persian' kings, Arab kings, the Prophet's life, and the first four Caliphs.[7] In Tarif Khalidi's view, Ibn Isḥāq's 'universal' material is the first history that develops the Qur'ānic, prophet-centred concept of history, which measured "power and legitimacy against prophetic standards as opposed to their being founded upon communal consensus" (1994: 35). Here I will elaborate on how Ibn Hishām's Biography historicizes the Qur'ānic prophetic standard with reference to Covenant as constitution and social contract.

At the outset, the Biography establishes the Prophet as the continuator and fulfiller of Abraham's prophecy and message about the One God, by tracing his Arab lineage through Abraham and Ismail, back to Adam. Ibn Hishām takes care to point out that the Prophet's lineage included the above-mentioned Arab royal family of Lakhm in al-Ḥīra in south-western Iraq, who were the vassals for the Sassanians and who were also related to a royal dynasty in Yemen (Guillaume 1995: 3–4, 6, 30). Simply put, the following political scenario unfolded just before the Prophet's time. Yemen had been conquered by the Abyssinian ruler of Ethiopia, who marched on towards Mecca with the intent of destroying its temple (*bayt*) named Ka'ba, 'the Cube'. Since the Ka'ba was originally founded by Abraham and his son Ismail, God intervened and stopped the Abyssinian onslaught in its tracks. Eventually the Sassanians replaced the Abyssinians as rulers over Yemen, which coincided in time with the Prophet's life and mission. After the Prophet had gained the allegiances of all tribes and cities on the Peninsula, he dispatched his cousin 'Alī b. Abī Ṭālib to conquer Yemen and incorporate it into the Prophet's polity (Guillaume 1995: 30–34, 678). Thus, Ibn Hishām contextualised the Prophet's mission as part of the local and imperial vies for power, and with the 'Abrahamic' Ka'ba temple in Mecca playing a key role as centre for pilgrimage and trade.

7 Guillaume (1995: xvii); see also Abbott (1957). For a full reconstruction of this material by Ibn Isḥāq gathered from the early 'universal' or world histories, see Newby (1989); though this study is weakened by the fact that the material is put together without (painstaking) analysis of the different transmission chains, and the different ways in which the 'universal' historians employed it.

After the exposé over regional politics, the Biography zooms in on Hijaz and the Prophet's tribe Quraysh in Mecca. Quraysh were merchants, as was the Prophet himself and his family (Guillaume 1995: 34, 79–82). Events before the Prophet's birth and mission centre on Quraysh's custody of the Kaʿba and the pilgrimage. It is described how Abraham and Ismail instituted the pilgrimage ritual and dug the well Zamzam, located within the temple precinct. The narrative accounts how alongside the Kaʿba, the families among Quraysh ran several temples for various gods and their idols, termed *ṭawāghīt*, singular *ṭāghūt*, which had guards and overseers (*sadana wa ḥujjāb*), and to which they "were guided like they were guided to the Kaʿba" (*tuhdī lahā kamā tuhdī li-l-kaʿba*)'.[8] The temples were also sites for legal arbitration and rulings. This had to do with their inviolate status as places where fighting and violence is prohibited; e.g., the following report about the early descendants of Abraham's son Ismail:[9]

> Then God multiplied the offspring of Ismail in Mecca and their uncles from Jurhum were governors of the temple and judges in Mecca (*wulāt al-bayt wa al-ḥukkām bimakka*). The sons of Ismael did not dispute their authority because of their kinship and their awe of the tabooed sanctuary (*al-ḥurma*), lest there should be any conflict or fighting there.

Jurhum were eventually deposed from their governorate over the temple because they mistreated visitors to Mecca who were not of their own tribe, and wrongly appropriated food gifts made to the Kaʿba and its visitors (Guillaume 1995: 46). Such practices would have discouraged trade and commerce, which required that all traders who came to Mecca could go about their business justly and in peace and security. Jurhum's hostility is emphasised in a report, stating that when he was forced to step down he filled in the Zamzam well i.e. he blocked the source of water for pilgrims and the people of Mecca. Symbolically, the report also states that Zamzam was cleansed and re-opened by the Prophet's grandfather ʿAbd al-Muṭṭalib, signalling the equity and fairness associated with his family, the Banū Hāshim (Guillaume 1995: 45).

A significant turn in the narrative describes a development similar to what Hodgson identified as 'the court gaining power over the temple', represented by Quṣayy, the first king (*malik*) of Quraysh. Quṣayy for the first time united all the tribe's families around the Kaʿba. According to the Biography, his authority derived from the people's *recognition* of his rule, and from his

8 Guillaume (1995: 38)/Ibn Hishām (1990/1: 101).

9 Guillaume (1995: 46)/Ibn Hishām (1990/1: 132).

management of the temple and pilgrimage, which included control of the water well and food supplies, and presidency over the public assembly:[10]

> Quṣayy was made governor (*wulliya*) over the temple (*al-bayt*) and took command over Mecca, and brought in his people from their places of residence to Mecca. He assumed kingship (*mulk*) over his people and over Mecca's inhabitants, and they recognised him as king. However, he guaranteed to the Arabs their customary rights (*mā kānū ʿalayhi*) because he himself saw it as a judicial order (*dīn*) which he was not entitled to change. Thus he guaranteed the families of Ṣafwān and ʿAdwān and al-Nasʾa and Murra b. ʿAwf in their customary rights, until Islam came and God thereby put an end to all that. Quṣayy [...] held the gatekeeper function of the temple, the watering from the well, the tax for the food supply, the assembly, and the war banners. He stewarded all the dignitaries of Mecca, and he divided Mecca into quarters between his people so that each of Quraysh's peoples came and settled down in the places of residence that had become theirs.

Ibn Hishām pointed out that collecting the tax for the food supply (*rifāda*) remains the duty of the ruler, to his own time and the Abbasid Caliphate (Guillaume 1995: 56).

After Quṣayy's death, however, the families within Quraysh began to quarrel over the management of the temple, and eventually agreed to divide it between the two large families ʿAbd Manāf (watering, collecting tax for the food supply) and ʿAbd al-Dār (gatekeeping, war standards, assembly). Here Ibn Hishām quotes, on the authority of Ibn Isḥāq, a report from the Prophet, stating that "Whatever pact there was in the period without the divine knowledge, the enacting of peace does not add to it except to strengthen it (*wa mā kāna min ḥilfin fī al-jāhiliyya faʾinna al-islām lam yazidhu illā shiddatan*)" (Guillaume 1995: 57).[11] The statement suggests that treaties and alliances is a good in itself, presumably because they function as a conflict-reducing and just practice. The same approach is taken to the defence-pact that Quraysh concluded among themselves, *Ḥilf al-fuḍūl*, which is described immediately afterwards in the narrative:[12]

> The tribes (*qabāʾil*) of Quraysh decided to make a pact and assembled for that purpose in the house of ʿAbd Allāh b. Judʿān b. ʿAmr b. Kaʿb b. Saʿd b. Taym b. Murra b. Kaʿb b. Luʾayy because of his dignity

10 Guillaume (1995: 52–53)/Ibn Hishām (1990/1: 143–144).
11 Guillaume (1995: 57)/Ibn Hishām (1990/1: 151).
12 Guillaume (1995: 57)/Ibn Hishām (1990/1: 154–155).

> and seniority. Those party to the pact with him were: Banū Hāshim, Banū al-Muṭṭalib, Asad b. ʿAbd al-ʿUzza, Zuhra b. Kilāb, and Taym b. Murra. They entered a reciprocal contract and compact *(fataʿāqadū wa taʿāhadū)* that whenever they find anyone wronged (*maẓlūm*) in Mecca, whether among its inhabitants or anyone else who had entered the city, they must stand up for him against the one who wronged him until the wrong has been righted. Thus Quraysh named that pact 'The Pact of Graciousness' (*Ḥilf al-fuḍūl*).
>
> Muḥammad b. Zayd al-Muhājir b. Qunfudh al-Taymī told me that he heard Ṭalḥa b. ʿAbd Allāh b. ʿAwf al-Zuhrī say: The Messenger of God said, 'I witnessed in the house of ʿAbd Allāh b. Judʿān a pact which I held dearer than any number of fine camels, and if I were called upon it under the enactment of peace I would respond to the call! (*wa law udʿā bihi fī al-islām laʾujibtu*)

Next, the narrative describes a later case during the governorship of the Umayyad Muʿāwiya (18/639–41/661), which illustrates the issues covered by the pact. The commander of Medina at that time was Muʿāwiya's nephew al-Walīd, who had defrauded the Prophet's grandson al-Ḥusayn b. ʿAlī of his right to land property (*māl*) in an area called Dhū al-Marwā. The report describes how the commander al-Walīd abused his powers and refers to al-Ḥusayn's claim to the land as his *ḥaqq*, 'right'. Hence, the pact included protecting property rights. The same report also connects the pact's obligation to defend the right to land with God and His Messenger, and with the latter's 'place of prostration' (*masjid*) i.e. where he prostrated before God. These connotations suggest that the ritual practice of prostrating before God in certain contexts signals one's commitment to the legal practice of upholding rights. Moreover, the 'place of prostration' (*masjid* or mosque in common parlance) in this report has the same function as a public forum, where appeals to justice can be made and tried:[13]

> Al-Walīd had through his power to rule inveighed himself against al-Ḥusayn's right, so al-Ḥusayn said to him: "I compact with God

13 Guillaume (1995: 57–58)/Ibn Hishām (1990/1: 156). For a similar conceptual connection between the inviolate status of place, contract-based rights, and claims-making, see Rubin's observation that the Prophet declared the inner part of Yathrib (Medina) inviolate (*ḥarām*) on a par with Mecca's temple precinct after he had entered the compact with the Arab and Jewish tribes (Rubin 1985: 10). I have also observed how al-Ṭabarī in his History described the Kaʿba temple as continuing to have this function in Caliphal history; e.g. Ibn al-Zubayr pledged a contractual allegiance swearing on God's compact (*ʿahd Allāh*) as represented by the Kaʿba (Mårtensson 2009a: 78, ref. to al-Ṭabarī, History, xviii/Morony: 186).

> that you shall do justice to my right, or else I shall definitely take my sword and take my stand in God's Messenger's place of prostration where I shall call out to the Pact of Graciousness!" (*fakāna al-Walīd taḥāmala ʿalā al-Ḥusayn fī ḥaqqihi – lisulṭānihi – faqāla lahu al-Ḥusayn: aḥlif bi-Allāh litunṣifanī min ḥaqqī aw laʾākhudhanna sayfī thumma laʾaqūmanna fī masjid Rasūl Allāh thumma laʾadʿuwanna biḥilf al-fuḍūl*) ʿAbd Allāh b. al-Zubayr, who was with al-Walīd when al-Ḥusayn said this, said: "And I compact with God that if he calls out to (the Pact), I shall take my sword and I shall take my stand with him until his right is done justice, or we die together!"

The conflict was resolved as others joined in to defend al-Ḥusayn's right, and al-Walīd was forced to comply.

For Quraysh, the right to land involved the above-described obligation to submit a tax to feed the pilgrims at the Kaʿba. In the Biography's narrative, the Prophet's family Hāshim of the ʿAbd Manāf, who were responsible for the watering and feeding, came to be in charge of this because they were among the wealthiest merchants. The ancestral figure Hāshim is described as doing the opposite of the wrong-doing Jurhum, who favoured only his own family and appropriated the food stores. Hāshim instead addressed his people, asking them to collect land produce:[14]

> O tribe of Quraysh! You are God's neighbours and the people of His temple (*ahl baytihi*), and therefore during the pilgrimage season there come to you visitors to God and pilgrims to His temple (*ḥujjāj baythihi*) who are God's guests – and His are the guests most entitled to dignity! So gather for them what you can of food for these days when they have no choice but to stay here, for – by God – had my property been large enough to cover this I would not have obligated you!

Hāshim also instituted two caravan journeys for Quraysh, one in summer and one in winter, and introduced an especially nourishing food, consisting of pieces of bread soaked in broth (*tharīd*), which he fed to the pilgrims who came from outside of Mecca. Thus a poet claimed that his real name was ʿAmr, 'to make prosperous, cause to flourish', but he was called Hāshim because he 'broke' (*hashama*) the bread for the broth stew:[15]

> ʿAmr who broke bread-in-broth for his people,
> A people in Mecca accustomed to hunger,

14 Guillaume (1995: 58)/Ibn Hishām (1990/1: 157).
15 Guillaume (1995: 58)/Ibn Hishām (1990/1: 157).

> For who he established the custom of both the two journeys:
> The caravan of winter and the contractual journey (*riḥlat al-īlāf*).

The poem echoes *sūra* 106 (*Quraysh*), from the earliest Meccan period:

> (1) For Quraysh's contract of protection (*li'īlāf Quraysh*):
> (2) Their contract of protection is the journey of the winter and the summer,
> (3) So let them serve the Lord of this temple (*al-bayt*),
> (4) Who has fed them when they were hungry and secured them against fear (*āmanahum min khawf*)!

To summarise: This section of the Biography establishes that pilgrimage to the 'Abrahamic' Ka'ba temple is a practice that obligates Quraysh to secure food and water for all pilgrims, regardless of origins and background. The obligation has implications for trade as well, since the pilgrimage was a mercantile event with pilgrims engaging in commerce. Hence, the inviolate status of the precinct, as a place for preserving peace, concluding contracts, and making claims to rights. An especially good practice associated with the Ka'ba is the 'Pact of the Gracious', illustrated through the case of defence of property rights *for all*. In terms of governmental practice, the example of Quṣayy states that his authority rested in his recognition by all Quraysh's families, who united under his rule. This mirrors the Qur'ānic Covenantal social contractual principle of reciprocal recognition of terms. Since all these morally and socioeconomically good practices are related to the Ka'ba by virtue of its 'Abrahamic' origins, it is clear that the Biography employs the Ka'ba and the pilgrimage as the connector between good pre-Islamic and Islamic principles, including the natural law-related idea that the needs and rights of *all people* should be protected.

The same principles come to the fore in the sections on the Prophet and his leadership. Concerning Covenant, Weiss (1990) has pointed out that unlike the Hebrew Bible, which narrates a series of distinct Covenantal 'events' e.g. when God gives the law on Mt. Sinai, and later institutes kingship, the Biography does not report on similar events during the Prophet's lifetime. All the treaties and contracts he entered are between humans, which means that it is the Qur'ān itself that is the Covenantal 'event', and which describes *previous* Covenants through its prophetic history (see also Gwynne 2004: 13). Accordingly, the Biography accounts for the beginning of God's sending-out of the Prophet through a reference to Q. 3 (*Āl 'Imrān*), 81, which states that God has taken a Covenant from all the other prophets with the binding terms that they, through their living communities, are obligated to help the Prophet once he is sent out with the final message:[16]

> I was told by Abū Muḥammad ʿAbd al-Malik b. Hishām, from Zayd b. ʿAbd Allāh al-Bakkāʾī, from Muḥammad b. Isḥāq al-Muṭṭalibī[17], who said: 'When Muḥammad the Messenger of God reached the age of forty, God the Most Elevated sent him on a mission (*baʿathahu*) to protect the lives of the knowing beings (*raḥmatan li-l-ʿālamīna*) and to fulfil the transmission of the divine word to the people (*kāffatan li-l-nāsi bashīran*). God the Most Blessed and Elevated had taken the Covenant (*akhadha al-mīthāq*) upon each prophet who He had sent on a mission before him, to enact security through him, and hold him for truthful, and help him to victory over those who opposed him. He took it upon them to convey this obligation to each one who enacted security through them and held them for truthful, and so they conveyed what they were obligated to by right (*mā kāna ʿalayhim min al-ḥaqqi fīhi*). God then said to Muḥammad – God's prayers and peace be upon him and his kin – *Since God has taken the Covenant of the prophets (mīthāq al-nabiyyīna) about what I have brought to you of divine writing and capacity for just judgement, then when a messenger comes to you confirming what you have, you must enact security through him and help him to victory! He said: Do you affirm and take upon yourselves My contract (iṣrī)?* (Q. 3, 81)

A subtle wordplay seems to be at work here, which conveys information about the practices associated with the institution of prophecy. As we saw above in the poem about the Prophet's ancestor Hāshim, the poet claimed that his real name was ʿAmr, 'to make prosperous, cause to flourish', because he prepared nourishing food for the pilgrims from outside Mecca.[18] Q. 3, to which belongs the verse 81 referring to God's Covenant with all the prophets, is named *Āl ʿImrān*, which refers to the prophetic family line. *ʿImrān* is of the same root *ʿ-m-r* as ʿAmr, which suggests that the prophetic legacy as Covenanters with God is to make all people flourish and prosper. Consequently, the subsequent report narrating how the Prophet receives the very first sent-down verses Q. 96 (*al-ʿAlaq*), 1–5, defines the event as 'the same law that came to Moses' i.e. compares the sending-down of the Qurʾān

16 Guillaume (1995: 104)/Ibn Hishām (1990/1: 263–264).

17 I.e. Ibn Isḥāq, whose family were *mawālī* i.e. legally recognised adoptees, of the Prophet's paternal tribe al-Muṭṭalib, hence Ibn Isḥāq's family name al-Muṭṭalibī; see Guillaume (1995: xiii, 65–6).

18 Guillaume (1995: 58)/Ibn Hishām (1990/1: 157).

with the Covenantal law-giving event on Mt. Sinai and establishes it in the prophetic line:[19]

> When it was the night on which God honoured him with his mission and showed mercy on His servants thereby, Gabriel brought him the command of God. "He came to me", said the Messenger of God, "while I was asleep, with a coverlet of brocade whereon was some writing, and said, **'Read! (*iqra'*)'** I said: **'What shall I read (*mā aqra'*)**?' He pressed me with it so tightly that I thought I would die, then he released me and said: **'Read!' (*iqra'*)** I said, '**What shall I read? (*mā aqra'*)**' He pressed me with it again so that I thought I would die, then he released me and said, **'Read! (*iqra'*)'** I said, **'What shall I read? (*mā aqra'*)?'** He pressed me with it a third time so that I thought it was death and said **'Read! (*iqra'*)'** I said, **'What then shall I read? (*mādhā aqra'*)** – and this I said only to deliver myself from him, lest he should do the same to me again. He said:
>
> Read in the name of thy Lord who created,
> Who created man of blood coagulated.
> Read! Thy Lord is the most beneficent,
> Who taught by the pen,
> Taught that which they knew not unto men. (Q. 96, 1–5)
>
> So I read it and, and he departed from me. And I awoke from my sleep, and it was as though these words were written on my heart.

The Prophet then hurried to tell his wife Khadīja about his experience. She in her turn went to see her cousin Waraqa, who was a convert to Christianity and knowledgeable about the Torah and the Gospel. Hearing about the event, he exclaimed:[20]

> 'Holy, Holy! By Him in whose hand is Waraqa's person: if what you say is true, Khadīja, there has come to him the greatest *Nāmūs* who came to Moses before, and he is in fact the prophet of this community! Tell him to stand firm!

Since *Nāmūs* is an Aramaic version of Greek *nomos*, the term here refers to the 'law' that Moses received. Thus, the report defines the first verses God sent down to the Prophet as a Covenant event of the same law-giving

19 Guillaume (1995: 106)/Ibn Hishām (1990/1: 267–269). I here follow Guillaume's poetic rendering of Q. 96, 1–5.

20 Guillaume (1995: 107)/Ibn Hishām (1990/1: 269–270).

character as Moses' reception of the law on Mt. Sinai.[21] Once inaugurated into prophecy in this way, the Prophet becomes one whose divine knowledge causes people to flourish and prosper.

This aspect of prophecy refers also to the Qur'ānic topic of defending the weak. For example, the Biography describes how the Prophet and his Companions faced mounting persecution from the pagan Quraysh, and sought to buy out and free the slaves who had joined their community and therefore were being tortured by their masters. The pagan father of the Prophet's Companion Abū Bakr asked his son why he freed weak slaves (*riqāb ḍiʿāf*) instead of powerful men, who could help defend them? Abū Bakr replied that he was doing so as a duty towards God, and then the report states God sent down verse 5 of the early Mecca oath Q. 92 (*al-Layl*) on account of their exchange; here verses 1–10, for semantic context:[22]

> (1) By the night when it darkens;
> (2) By the day when it lights up;
> (3) By what split between the male and the female:
> (4) For sure, your courses are manifold!
> **(5) As for the one who gives and fulfils his obligation (*fa'ammā man aʿṭā wa ittaqā*),**
> (6) and induces truthfulness by the best (*wa ṣaddaqa bi-l-ḥusnā*),
> (7) We will make things most easy for him
> (8) But as for the one who is mean and self-sufficient,
> (9) and gives the lie by the best (*wa kadhdhaba bi-l-ḥusnā*),
> (10) We will make things most hard for him!

Here, then, the Biography shows that 'giving' is a good deed involving spending money to buy out slaves. Spending for this purpose is a sign of 'inducing truthfulness' (*taṣdīq*, verse 6), which is also a pun on Abū Bakr's honorific name 'al-Ṣiddīq' i.e. he who demonstrates truthfulness by buying out and freeing slaves, as this context shows him doing. Accordingly, the term for 'alms', *ṣadaqa*, derives from the same root (*ṣ-d-q*) (see above, Q. 2, 267–282).

In the course of the Prophet's political career, which the Biography then proceeds to describe, he concludes several contracts, including 'first and

21 See also Mårtensson (2005: 314–315), for al-Ṭabarī's version of the same report, including comparison with the Hebrew Bible and Jeremiah's prophecy about the new 'covenant written in the people's heart'.

22 Guillaume (1995: 144)/Ibn Hishām (1990/1: 346).

second ʿAqaba', and the famous Medina Constitution.[23] First and second ʿAqaba refer to the place named al-ʿAqaba. The background was that the leading members of Quraysh in Mecca were continuing to persecute the Prophet and his Companions. However, twelve men from the neighbouring city Yathrib (Medina) had heard of the Prophet's message. They found it attractive because Yathrib was riven by inter-tribal conflict. At the pilgrimage in the year 621, the men approached the Prophet and invited him to be their ruler. In the First ʿAqaba compact, representatives of these Yathrib tribes pledged allegiance (*bāyaʿū*) to the Prophet. Ibn Hishām cites two reports from Ibn Isḥāq with identical terms:[24]

> To not make anything partner with God; not steal; not commit adultery; not kill our children; not slander our neighbours; and not disobey [the Prophet] in what is known to be right. If you fulfil, the garden is yours (*lakum al-janna*), and if you overrule any of these things your case is for God: if He wishes, He punishes, and if He wishes, He forgives.

When the twelve men returned to Yathrib, the Prophet sent with them a man from his family named Muṣʿab b. ʿUmayr b. Hāshim b. ʿAbd Manāf b. ʿAbd al-Dār b. Quṣayy, and commanded him to "make them read the Qurʾān, and convey to them knowledge about the enacting of peace (*al-islām*), and make them analyse the judicial order (*yufaqqihahum al-dīn*)".[25] In Mecca, however, the Prophet's tribe Quraysh now initiated hostilities towards his new allies, forcing some of them into exile. The increasing aggression required that armed defence be included in the contract, hence the Second ʿAqaba, in the year 622. This compact is described through a reference to Q. 22 (*al-Ḥajj*), 39–41:

> By God's name 'Giver of Life, Continuous Protector of Life': From Abū Muḥammad ʿAbd al-Malik b. Hishām, from Ziyād b. ʿAbd Allāh al-Bakkāʾī, from Muḥammad b. Isḥāq al-Muṭṭalibī: [...]
>
> When Quraysh became insolent towards God Who Rules Mightily and Who is the Majesty and turned back His dignified wish for them, accused His Prophet of lying, and tormented and exiled those who served Him, professed His Oneness, held His prophet to be truthful, and adhered to His judicial order, God gave permission to His Messenger

23 For an exhaustive study of all of the Prophet's treaties and compacts, and their constitutional implications, see Hamidullah (1987).

24 Guillaume (1995: 199)/Ibn Hishām (1990/2: 81).

25 Guillaume (1995: 199)/Ibn Hishām (1990/2: 82).

> to fight (*al-qitāl*) and to seek help against those who wronged them and treated them badly. The first sign that was made to descend regarding His permission of war (*al-ḥarb*), and His making it lawful to shed blood and fight, from what reached me from ʿUrwa b. al-Zubayr and others of those who possess knowledge, is God's statement: *Permission is given to those who were fought and wronged, for God is indeed capable of giving them victory – those who were driven out of their homes without right, merely for stating: 'Our Lord is God!' Had God not repelled some people by others, surely monasteries, churches, synagogues and places for prostration (masājid) where God's Name is frequently honoured would have been demolished. In fact, God will support whoever supports Him, for God is indeed a Strong One With Might – those who, when We empower them in the land, will perform the prayer, give the welfare tax, command what is known to be right and prohibit what is rejected; to God belongs the outcome of all matters.*(Q. 22, 39–41) [...] When God Most Elevated had permitted warfare, and this clan of the Helpers to Victory (*al-anṣār*) had pledged allegiance to him on enacting peace (*al-islām*) and helping to victory him and anyone who followed him and those who enacted peace who had sought refuge with them, the Messenger of God commanded his companions who were among the Migrants (*al-muhājirūna*) from his people, and those who enacted peace who were with him in Mecca, to leave for Medina and migrate there in order to join their brothers among the Helpers to Victory. He said: "God has made for you brothers and houses for you to be safe in!" So they left, group after group, while the Messenger of God stayed behind in Mecca waiting for his Lord to give him permission to leave Mecca and migrate to Medina.[26]

In the same year, 622, the Prophet migrated from Mecca to Yathrib, which then assumes the name Medina, 'the City'.

Once settled in Medina, the Prophet began delivering public addresses (*khuṭba*). Two of his speeches recorded in the Biography conclude with the phrase: "Love each other through God's spirit among yourselves, for God is indeed angered when His compact (*ʿahduhu*) is broken; may peace be upon you (*al-salām ʿalaykum*)!"[27] Directly afterwards follows the narrative about the written contract (*kitāb*) that the Prophet entered with his Migrant followers from Mecca (*al-muhājirūna*), the Helpers to Victory (*al-anṣār*) from Medina, and some of the Jewish tribes of Medina (*al-yahūd*). The contracting parties have equal rights and obligations, including protection of *dīn*, life, and property, and mutual defence against one's enemies, stipulated

26 Guillaume (1995: 212–213)/Ibn Hishām (1990/2: 108–109).

27 Guillaume (1995: 231)/Ibn Hishām (1990/2: 143).

in the written document. As such, they are all part of one *umma*, or 'political community'.[28] These are the opening paragraphs:[29]

> The Messenger of God wrote a document (*wa kataba rasūl Allāh kitāban*) between the Migrants (*al-muhājirūna*) and the Helpers to Victory (*al-anṣār*), in which he made a friendly agreement with the Jews and entered a contract with them, confirming them with regards to their judicial order and their property. He laid down conditions for them, and took upon himself the [same] conditions:
>
> In God's Name "The Giver of Life, The Continuous Protector of Life": This is a written document from Muḥammad the Prophet between the enactors of security and the enactors of peace from Quraysh and Yathrib and those who followed them and stood by them and struggled with them. They are one political community among the people (*innahum ummatun wāḥidatun min dūn al-nās*).

The document emphasises the mutual solidarity within the polity against attacks from the outside, also and perhaps especially with reference to the Jews. It is stressed that although the Jews and the enactors of security are one political community, they each have their own *dīn*:[30]

> The Jews shall spend together with the enactors of security so long as they are at war. The Jews of Banū ʿAwf are a political community (*umma*) with the enactors of security, with the Jews having their judicial order and the enactors of peace having their judicial order (*li-l-yahūd dīnuhum wa li-l-muslimīna dīnuhum*) (…).

28 For the full report about the contract, Guillaume (1995: 231–235)/Ibn Hishām (1990/2: 143–148). Note Uri Rubin's important point that the Jews included in this contract were those who agreed to join it and who lived within the city, and not those powerful Jewish tribes with territories surrounding Medina. These latter rejected the Prophet's terms, which led to armed conflict; hence the contract had a territorial foundation (Rubin 1985: 5–12).

29 Guillaume (1995: 231–232)/Ibn Hishām (1990/2: 143).

30 Guillaume (1995: 232–233)/Ibn Hishām (1990/2: 144). See also Rubin on the point that the Jews' inclusion in the Prophet's *umma* does not mean that they have to give up their own *dīn* i.e. their own religion/judicial order, but rather that they are full members of the political community, enjoying legal 'security' (*amn*) with the other *muʾminūna* (1985: 12–17). For a recent study of this contract as 'the Medina Constitution', see Arjomand (2009), which includes a survey of previous research on the topic, including Hamidullah's early studies of its constitutional aspects and his argument that this is the earliest written constitution recorded in political history, preceding e.g. the Magna Carta by several centuries (1937; 1968).

In many ways, this compact resembles the pre-Islamic *ḥilf al-fuḍūl*, except that it also includes non-Qurayshite and Jewish tribes. On the inclusion of the Jews, the Prophet's document (*kitāb*) reflects the constitutional and social contractual sense that the divine *kitāb* takes in the above discussed Q. 5 (*al-Māʾida*), 44–48 namely as a shared constitutional principle and source of law, through which Jews and Christians are included in the political community.

As for the Prophet's political relationship with Christians, there is a long report about how he concluded a compact with the community of the city Najrān, who sent a large delegation to Medina, including their political representative and their bishop. The report states that they belonged to the Byzantine i.e. Roman Orthodox or Melkite creed on the Trinity. It then details at some length how God in Q. 3 (*Āl ʿImrān*) refutes the Trinitarian doctrine and proves that Jesus is a prophet. The Christian delegation persisted in its doctrine, of course, but promised not to curse the Prophet or obstruct his rule, and concluded a pact of friendly relations. The Prophet also sent a deputy from his side who would decide between them in disputes concerning their wealth and land properties (*amwāl*).[31]

Concluding Analysis

According to Ibn Hishām's edition of the Prophet's Biography, the 'Covenant-event' is the first sending-down of the Qurʾān, with its principles for constitutional rule and social contract. These principles then guide the Prophet's contractual pacts with various groups. In terms of governmental frame, the Biography describes the institution of Abrahamic prophecy as related to reciprocal social contract, where political leaders are legitimate when recognised by the people and when adhering to the agreed-upon terms of rule. Significantly, legitimacy also involves rights-focus over kinship and social rank, and the obligation of all members of the polity to support the weak in terms of protecting their rights as well as distributing food and wealth (through tax) to the benefit of all. These practices reflect the constitutional 'rule of law'-principle, as well. It seems, therefore, that Ibn Hishām's editorial aim was to provide a historical, institutional context for the Qurʾān, to concretise its constitutional and social contract-related principles and their practical implications.

31 Guillaume (1995: 270–277)/Ibn Hishām (1990/2: 215–226).

INSTITUTIONAL DEVELOPMENT: THE DYNASTIC CALIPHATE

The second part of this chapter sketches institutional developments in the dynastic Caliphate up to around 900/1500, focusing on the constitutional issues of 'separation of powers' and legal diversity and disagreement. Specifically, I will explore how the Prophet, who in the Biography is portrayed as uniting in his own person both the sovereign rule and the law-making function, served as the ideal for the scholarly institution that legitimised its law-making authority as subjecting the ruler to the law. My argument is that this kind of constitutional 'separation of powers' is already implicit in the Qur'ānic concept of prophecy as the communication of divine knowledge, which gives the law to rulers and makes them rule equitably. In other words, the Qur'ānic discourse reflects upon the same issues that were continuously debated within the Islamic institutions, through the constitutional theory that pertains to the Qur'ānic concept of prophecy.

Separation of Powers: A Historical Trajectory

In modern political theory, democratic constitutional rule requires 'separation of powers' between legislative (deliberative and law-making), executive (government), and judiciary (applying the law, courts) authorities. The aim is 'rule of law', or the submission of government to the law, achieved through the checks and balances of power between the three institutional authorities. Commonly, the Prophet is seen as embodying all three powers, a model continued by the first four Companion Caliphs in Medina, while a gradual separation of powers follows during the dynastic Quraysh caliphates: the Umayyads of the Sufyān and Marwān families (661–750), and the Abbasids of the Prophet's family Hāshim (750–1258), in tandem with the emerging institution of the legal scholars (*fuqahā'*), resulting in a separation of powers around the late 800s. At this point, the scholars were the lawmakers, not the Caliphs (Feldman 2008; Heck 2004; Watt 2007/1963). In what follows I will discuss possible modifications to this trajectory.

The dating of developments is complicated, considering the historical sources may reflect *theory* on the matter. Joseph Lowry (2008) has argued that the separation of powers between state and legal scholars was a reality already with the establishment of the Abbasid Caliphate in 133/750. Yet there were critics of this model. For example, the Abbasid administrator and scribe Ibn al-Muqaffa' (d. *c.* 139/757), who drew theoretical inspiration from the pre-Islamic Sassanian legacy, defined the Caliph as having law-making authority on specific topics (see Chapter 6, below). Lowry's point is that Ibn al-Muqaffaʿ's writings are not testimony to an early stage of Caliphal law-making authority, as argued by Heck (2004), but express his own political *theory*, that it was necessary to centralise law-making around the Caliph to counteract the increasingly numerous and diverse schools of hermeneutical methodology (*madhāhib*) and attain uniformity and predictability in legislation. Consequently, Ibn al-Muqaffaʿ was responding critically to 'separation of powers' and legal diversity as an institutional reality.

The legal scholars who, following Lowry (2008), constituted the legislative and judiciary authority that was effectively separate from the Caliph as the executive power at least by 750, self-identified as the inheritors of the prophets' divine knowledge. In the Abbasid Caliphate, one of the powers vested in the scholars as institution was their simultaneously knowledge-based and socially approved authority to confer or withhold recognition of a caliph appointed within the dynastic succession (Feldman 2008; Kamali 2016). Effectively, it was this scholarly power, which subjected the Caliph to 'the rule of law'.[32] Furthermore, the scholars' institutional independence in relation to the Caliph depended on their access to landed property and tax revenue (Feldman 2008: 27–35, 101). Contestation of their power came from different quarters. By the early 800s, the *shuʿūbiyya*-movement was in full swing among the literati and scribes at the Abbasid court in Baghdad. *Shuʿūbiyya* derives from *shaʿb*, a word that according to Ibn Manẓūr's *Lisān al-ʿarab* refers to groups of people, either in the sense of 'a unified and peaceful group' or 'a fragmenting and confrontational group', depending on the standpoint of the person using the word.[33] This movement aimed to reclaim prestige and positions for the Persians and their cultural and political legacy; after all, they had ruled over the heartlands of the Abbasid Caliphate until 640, when the Arabs led by the second Medina Caliph ʿUmar b. al-Khaṭṭāb gained control over the Sassanid fertile agricultural lands.[34] The historian Marshall Hodgson analysed the *shuʿūbiyya*-movement in terms

32 Two recent special journal issues on the topic 'New Conversations in Islamic and Christian Political Thought', are *The Muslim World*, 106 (2), April 2016 (Part I). On separation of powers, rule of law and political legitimacy according to the dominant Sunni legal system, see especially the contributions by Fadel (2016) and Kamali (2016). The second part of the special issue is published in *Studies in Christian Ethics*, 29 (2), May 2016 (Part II). The contribution by Heck (2016) treats the political theory of al-Māwardī (d. 450/1058) with reference to the rule of law and political legitimacy.

33 Entry *sh-ʿ-b*, online at www.alwaraq.net, p. 2958.

34 Al-Ṭabarī, History, vol. V/Bosworth.

of the tug-of-war between the royal absolutism associated with the Persian legacy, and the more egalitarian and pietistic legacy of the legal scholars, particularly those associated with the emerging *Ahl al-ḥadīth* i.e. those who claimed the *ḥadīth*-based legacy of the Arab Prophet with its connections to the pre-Islamic Arab culture. Hodgson saw the movement's logic reflected in the Caliph Hārūn al-Rashīd's (r. 170/786–190/806) decision to divide the imperial realm between his two sons, al-Amīn who descended from an Arab mother and enjoyed support by the majority in Baghdad, and al-Maʾmūn who had a Persian mother and support in the Persian-dominated region of Khurāsān (Hodgson 1974/I: 461–478). Al-Maʾmūn eventually had his brother al-Amīn killed and became sole ruler (r. 198/813–218/833), avoiding a division of the empire. Constitutionally significant, however, was al-Maʾmūn's attempt to appoint his own successor from outside of the Abbasid succession line, namely ʿAlī "al-Riḍā", grandson of the sixth Alid *imam* Jaʿfar al-Ṣādiq (d. 148/765). Faced with resistance from both the population and the legal scholars of Baghdad, al-Maʾmūn reverted to Abbasid succession. Later, in the year 218/833, al-Maʾmūn imposed the doctrine of the 'createdness of the Qur'ān', *khalq al-Qurʾān*, as a state doctrine, and launched an inquisition (*al-miḥna*, 'the test') against over forty legal scholars, judges and administrators who adhered to the doctrine that the Qurʾān is God's own, uncreated word (*kalām*). Some of them were affiliated with the *Ahl al-ḥadīth*, who claimed this doctrine as the Prophet's *sunna*. Al-Maʾmūn's inquisition meant that the Caliph took control over the Qurʾān and its meanings, and the promulgation of doctrine, rather than leaving that to the legal scholars, for who the Qurʾān served as the divine source of the law (Nawas 1996:698; Cooperson 2000). Eventually, in the year 233/847, the inquisition was abolished and the separation of powers entrenched.

It is possible to detect deliberation over these issues in some reports, collected at this time, which show a kind of division of functions at work already during the Prophet's rule. The biographer Ibn Saʿd (d. 230/845), who lived and worked in Baghdad, reported that the four Companion Caliphs Abū Bakr, ʿUmar, ʿUthmān, and ʿAlī used to give legal rulings under the Prophet's rule (*kāna yuftī al-nās fī zaman Rasūl Allāh*; *kāna yuftūna ʿalā ʿahd Rasūl Allāh*), because they had the required knowledge (*ʿilm*) (2001/2: 289–293). Another Companion who gave rulings during the Prophet's time based on *ʿilm* was Muʿādh b. Jabal (2001/2: 299–302). After the Prophet passed away, reports show the first Caliph Abū Bakr consulting with a group of Companions including ʿUmar, ʿUthmān, and ʿAlī, as well as Muʿādh b. Jabal, ʿAbd al-Raḥmān b. ʿAwf, Ubayy b. Kaʿb, and the Prophet's scribe Zayd b. Thābit; the latter two were also expert readers of the Qurʾān (*qurrāʾ*).

These men also gave rulings to the people, and when the Caliphate passed on to ʿUmar, the practice continued (2001/2: 302). Other reports add names to the list, such as Abū Mūsa al-Ashʿarī and the Qurʾān reader ʿAbd Allāh b. Masʿūd, showing the continued knowledge transmission (2001/2: 303ff.). Concerning Abū Mūsa al-Ashʿarī, the Companion Qatāda reported that he had the required knowledge about what qualifies a person to judge and give rulings:

> Abū Mūsa (al-Ashʿarī) said: "It is not appropriate for the judge to pass judgement unless what is right appears as clearly distinct to him as the night distinguishes itself from the day! (*ḥattā yatabayyana lahu al-ḥaqq kamā yatabayyanu al-layl min al-nahār*)" This reached ʿUmar, who said: "Abū Mūsa is truthful!" (2001/2: 298)

The chronicle then proceeds to list those who learned the whole Qurʾān during the Prophet's time, and eventually describes the production of the Qurʾānic script, involving some of the same Companions, notably Muʿādh b. Jabal, ʿUthmān, Zayd b. Thābit and Ubayy b. Kaʿb, among others (2001/2: 306ff.). It is also described how Zayd b. Thābit served as judge and teacher of the permitted and prohibited, and of the Qurʾān, to the people appointed to govern the regions under the Caliphates of ʿUmar, ʿUthmān, and ʿAlī, and that he was succeeded in this role by Ibn ʿAbbās (2001/2: 309–312).

These reports, then, depict the leadership of the community as consisting already under the Prophet of two institutions: the ruler and those who give rulings to the people. The reports can be seen as reflecting deliberations over constitutional issues in the biographer Ibn Saʿd's context i.e. early 200s/800s. However, since there are no 'simple origins' in social history, they can also be seen as describing a historical reality of institutional complexity. Viewed from this perspective, the theory reflected in Ibn Saʿd's reports could reflect institutional realities before, during, and after the Prophet. The perspective would add to the explanation why the Prophet served so well as model for the scholarly authority as lawmakers: already during his time the transmission of his knowledge to the Companions had begun, so that the administration of the law was delegated to those qualified to give rulings and teach the Qurʾān. This division continued during the Companion Caliphs, as the reports show.

To return to the Abbasid context: One way of seeing the constitutional separation of powers is that it enabled 'the rule of law' even though politics developed in a way that reduced Abbasid rule to symbolical legitimacy (Feldman 2008: 34–44). With the ascent of the Persian Buyids (945–1050), who hailed from the Daylam region near the Caspian Sea, non-Arab dynasties established themselves alongside the Abbasids as *de facto* rulers, due to their military strength and command over provinces and revenue. This political development relates to increased religious-legal diversity at the government level. In their home region of Daylam, the Buyids affiliated with Zaydī Shīʿa. The Zaydī school transmitted its divine knowledge through the ʿAlid descendent Zayd b. ʿAlī b. al-Ḥusayn b. ʿAlī b. Abī Ṭālib (d. 122/740), who like his grandfather al-Ḥusayn had rebelled against Umayyad rule because its governor had wronged his rights to allowance and property. Once the Buyids established their rule over Baghdad, however, they sponsored instead Twelver Shīʿa i.e. the knowledge transmission through Jaʿfar al-Ṣādiq (d. 148/765), sixth *imam* and descendent from ʿAlī b. Abī Ṭālib and al-Ḥusayn. By Buyid times, the Twelver school tended to postpone the goal of fully just and legitimate rule to the eschatological return of the twelfth and last *imam* in the line from ʿAlī b. Abī Ṭālib and al-Ḥusayn, Muḥammad al-Mahdī, 'the divinely guided', believed to have become 'occult' (*ghāʾib*) in 264/878).[35] The Buyids were in their turn deposed by the Turkic Saljuq dynasty, which took control over Baghdad and established themselves as commanders and sultans alongside the Abbasids in 447/1055. The Saljuq dynasty affiliated instead with what at this stage constituted 'Sunnī Islam' i.e. knowledge transmitted through the dominant schools of law named after the respective eponym founders of their methodologies (*madhāhib*): Ḥanafī (Abū Ḥanīfa, d. 150/767), Shāfiʿī (al-Shāfiʿī, d. 205/820), Mālikī (Mālik b. Anas, d. 179/795), and Ḥanbalī (Aḥmad b. Ḥanbal, d. 241/855). While Twelver Shīʿa continued as a school in Abbasid Iraq even after the demise of the Buyid dynasty, nominally recognising Sunnī political hegemony, militant resistance was taken up by the Ismaʿīlī Shīʿa. These included groups following the knowledge transmission through Jaʿfar al-Ṣādiq's son Ismaʿīl (d. 138/755) over that of his other son Mūsā (d. 183/799), whose transmission is followed in the Twelver school. The Fatimid dynasty (297/909–567/1171), which declared itself a Caliphate and founded Cairo (*al-Qāhira*) as their new capital, represented the Ismaʿīlī school. The Fatimids ruled large parts of North Africa and Syria and rivalled both the Sunnī Abbasid-Saljuq alliance and the Sunnī Umayyad Caliphate eventually established in al-Andalus, with Córdoba as capital (317/929–422/1031). As we will see below, the Fatimid Caliph's legitimacy was premised on him serving as lawmaker; hence, he merged within his authority both the legislative and executive functions.

35 On the branches of the Shīʿa and the Buyids, see e.g. Kraemer (1986: 39–43, 65–72).

In political terms, then, 'Sunnī' refers to the recognition of the Abbasids, the Umayyads, and the first four Companion Caliphs of Medina, while 'Shīʿa' (broadly speaking) refers to the claim that the ʿAlīd descendants are the legitimate rulers, even though Sunnī rule was nominally recognised, and *vice-versa*: even though Sunnī rulers claimed the Caliphate, they recognised the special status of the ʿAlīds as the Prophet's closest kin within the Hāshim family of Quraysh, if not as rulers. Hence, the pre-Islamic pattern of tribal and family allegiances with ruling dynasties continued within the Islamic institutional system of vassalage and government. The Arab identity of the Prophet is transmitted not only through dynastic identity, but more lastingly and consistently through the Arabic language of the Qurʾān and *ḥadīth*, and the role of Arabic as the scholarly, administrative, and literary *lingua franca*. However, in the eastern parts of the empire especially, Persian also developed as an additional language of literature and administration, sponsored by governors and rulers.

With the Mongol invasion of Baghdad and abolishment of the Abbasid Caliphate in 656/1258, at which time the Fatimid and Umayyad Caliphates of Cairo and Córdoba had also fallen, surviving members of the Abbasid family fled to the Sunnī Mamlūk dynasty (648/1250–923/1517) ruling Egypt and Syria, and took up residence in Cairo. Thus the Abbasids conferred Sunnī Caliphal legitimacy on the Mamlūks, and subsequently on the Turkic Osman tribe or 'Ottomans' (ca. 1300–1922/24) when they conquered Egypt in 1517 and incorporated into their empire most of North Africa, as well as Anatolia, Syria, Iraq, and the Ḥijāz (with Mecca and Medina). Famously, the Ottomans defeated the remaining Byzantine Empire and conquered its capital Constantinople in 857/1453, making it their own glorious seat of power, named Istanbul. Under the Ottomans, the Ḥanafī school of law became the official one, and both Persian and the new literary and administrative Osmanli language developed complementary to Arabic.

Mirroring the Ottoman-Sunnī assertion, in the 1500s Twelver Shīʿa established at the state level as the official school of the Safavid dynasty, which ruled over roughly the same area as today's Iran until 1148/1736. On the Indian sub-continent, Muslim conquests of the region Sind began in the 700s. By the 600s/1200s Muslim dynastic rule was established in the northern regions, known as the Delhi sultanates after their capital. By the 900s/1500s, a new dynasty ascended, the Mughal Sultanate (932/1526–1273/1857), gaining hegemony over most of the sub-continent's territory. The Mughal dynasty's official school was the same as that of the Ottomans, namely the Ḥanafī school, but Twelver and Ismaʿīlī Shīʿa polities were also represented on the sub-continent. Since the Mughals ruled over a population which was majority ‘Hindu’ i.e. followers of the several Vedic schools of philosophy, law, ethics, and ritual, and included Jain, Buddhist and Sikh communities, the Islamic legal and feudal system incorporated rights and obligations for these ‘non-Abrahamic and non-monotheistic’ peoples in the same way as it did with Jews, Christians, and Zoroastrians elsewhere. The Mughal language of learning and administration was initially Persian, with Urdu developing as a new idiom.

However, the Ottoman and Mughal Empires signal a shift in the distribution of law-making authority. As Samy Ayoub’s recent study of Ottoman law shows, collections of Ḥanafī legal treatises and pronouncements on guidance (*fatāwā*) show scholars from the 1600s onwards granting the Sultan a new authority to regulate legal issues, and including sultanic orders in their legal manuals. The legal topics concerned such matters as the Sultan’s right to dispose over public land property, conditions for establishing and managing endowments (*awqāf*), and supervision over judges. In Ayoub’s words, “[t]he result was a new paradigm of legal reasoning in which Ḥanafī legal doctrine was opened up to allow sultanic edicts and orders to influence legal discourse” (Ayoub 2020: 93). The process can be seen as reaching full fruition with the production of a fully codified law (*Mecelle*, Arabic *majalla*) in 1293/1876 (Ayoub 2020: Ch. 4). In the Moghul context, Sultan Akbar (r. 963/1556–1013/1605) represented a shift, where he claimed the double authority as Caliph and supreme *mujtahid*, who could adjudicate disagreements among the legal scholars, and issue new laws on any topic. For example, Akbar abolished the *jizya* tax on non-Muslims, and ceased funding of pilgrimage to Mecca (Pirbhai 2009: 76–81). This transfer of law-making authority to the ruler can be seen as marking the end of the medieval and beginning of the early modern period, and I will return to it below, in Chapter 7.

Taking a step back in time, one can see that alongside the scholarly institutions that accompanied the ruling dynasties, merchants and mercantile trade routes continued to function as important conveyors of Islam, just as it did at its ‘origins’ as described in the Prophet’s Biography. It was through trade routes conveying merchants and scholars and connecting North Africa, West Asia and the Indian sub-continent, that Islamic institutions from the 900s onwards established in West, East and sub-Saharan Africa, and the South-East Asian lands of Indonesia, Malaysia, and the Philippines. In China, Muslim merchants founded mosques and tombs for Sufi shaykhs in Canton as early as the 700s (Lapidus 1988: 432; also Part II). This phenomenon, Sufism, brings us to another important institution with implications for the relationship between state and scholars, namely *walāya*.

Institutionalised walāya

Walāya is the verbal noun for the term *walī*, plural *awliyāʾ*. In studies of Sufism, *walāya* is often rendered as 'sainthood' and 'closeness' (*qurba*), in terms of both familial and spiritual kinship and 'friendship'. However, its precise meaning is subject to debate, since it also connotes overlapping epistemic and societal authority.[36] The earliest systematic treatise on *walāya* dates to the late 800s and is attributed to al-Ḥakīm al-Tirmidhī (d. probably between 907 and 912), a Ḥanafī scholar from Khurasan who influenced such important scholars as al-Ghazzālī (d. 505/1111) and Ibn al-ʿArabī (d. 638/1240). In a detailed study of al-Tirmidhī's treatise, Palmer Aijub points out that *walāya* refers to the institution of clientage and patronage (*walāʾ*), which mediated "social relationships of dependence between Arab rulers and non-Arab subjects up into the early Abbasid period" (Aijub 2015: 14). In fact, *walī* and *walāya* mirror the Arabic word for 'governor' of a province (*wālī*) and the office of provincial governorship (*wilāya*). Hence, the root *w-l-y* connotes 'to be close to power, authority' or 'to hold power, govern, be in charge of some office', also when it applies to the 'religious' institution.[37] In al-Tirmidhī's thought, *walāya* is conceptualised in relation to the institution of the scholars, *al-ʿulamāʾ*. The *awliyāʾ* are the highest in the ranks of the *ʿulamāʾ*, because they have immediate, experiential knowledge of God (*maʿrifa*). This knowledge, which goes beyond the systematic *ʿilm* and scriptural interpretation, is the capacity to pass just judgement (*ḥikma*) that comes from being enlightened by the light (*al-nūr*) that emanates from God Himself.[38] This is the same kind of knowledge that the Shīʿī scholars claim for the *imams*, and thereby for their own status as transmitters of the *imams*' divine knowledge, making it exclusive to their particular kinship-and spiritual affinity-based knowledge-transmission. In other words, the Shīʿī scholars attributed to the *imams* the status of *awliyāʾ* or 'protective governors'

36 For a recent survey of definitions, see Aijub (2015: 2–9).

37 Aijub (2015: 55), ref. to Patricia Crone, 'Mawlā', EI2.

38 Aijub (2015 passim) follows the standard translation of *ḥikma* as 'wisdom' and the adjective *ḥakīm* as 'wise', though he points out that al-Ḥakīm al-Tirmidhī's Ḥanafī legal methodology, which allowed the jurist to use his concept of 'the good' in deriving law (*istiḥsān*), may well be decisive for his concepts of *ḥikma* and *ḥakīm*, in the sense that the scholar who possesses *ḥikma* is the one qualified to employ *istiḥsān* (2015: 98; cf. 120 on the *ḥakīm* as the one who can reconcile contradictions between the Qurʾān and *ḥadīth*, in the sense of *uṣūl al-fiqh*). I choose to stress the sense of 'passing judgement' that pertains to the root *ḥ-k-m*, according to Ibn Manẓūr, who defines *ḥikma* as the noun for passing judgement based on *ʿilm*, the knowledge that God has sent down; *Lisān al-ʿarab* (www.alwaraq.net), entry *ḥ-k-m*, p. 1288.

whose access to the divine knowledge was transmitted to the scholars as their 'clients' (*mawālī*, sing. *mawlā*).[39] Al-Ḥakīm al-Tirmidhī instead developed his *walāya*-system as a Sunnī counterpart, where the *awliyā*''s knowledge was independent of family genealogy and thus theoretically accessible to all scholars, through spiritual affinity (Aijub 2015: 39, 66).

Referring back to Chapter 2 and the two ontological theories of concept discussed there – mind-based and language-based – I suggested the ontology developed by the Twelver Shīʿī philosopher Mullā Ṣadra, via Ibn Sīnā and Ibn al-ʿArabī (who drew on al-Tirmidhī, as mentioned) might be congruent with the mind-based theory of concept. Given the ontology behind *maʿrifa* i.e. enlightening the scholar's intellect with the divine light, it is possible to view the institutions of the Shīʿī *imams* and of Sunnī *walāya* as representing the mind-based ontological theory of concept. *Walāya* thus seems to reflect the notion that the language-based theory of concept represents the basic interpretive work of the 'regular' *ʿulamāʾ*, whereas the mind-based theory operates at a higher level of experience-based insight.

In Chapter 2 I also suggested that Q. 112 can be seen as a Qurʾānic reference point for the Neoplatonic concept of the divine that accompanies Mullā Ṣadra's mind-based theory of concept. However, there are other verses, which appear as references to the exegetical and ritual practices related to *walāya*. Most prominently, the notion that God guides through His light is expressed in Q. 24 (*al-Nūr*), 34–37.[40] In this passage, those favoured by the divine light are identified as those who take the time from their commercial activities to recall and honour God by mentioning and honouring (*dhakara*) His name, and perform their ritual and community obligations, including paying the welfare tax:

> (34) We have indeed sent down to you signs conveying clear distinctions, a paradigmatic example (*mathal*) from those who have gone before you, and an exhortation to those who fulfil their obligations:
> (35) God is the Light of the heavens and the earth. The example (*mathal*) of His Light is like a niche in which there is a lamp, the lamp is in a glass, the glass is like a glittering star, kindled from a blessed olive tree neither of the East nor the West. Its oil will almost shine even though no fire has touched it: Light is upon light as God guides to His Light who

39 Aijub (2015: 4), ref. to Dakake (2007: 30).

40 See also Q. 7, 157; 24, 40; and 39, 22. Karamustafa (2007: x), on the scarcely researched but important Sufi-Shīʿī convergence over *walāya* as an exegetical strategy of 'interiorising approaches' to attaining the Qurʾān's meanings. On the function of the first and sixth Shīʿī Imams ʿAlī b. Abī Ṭālib (d. 41/661) and Jaʿfar al-Ṣādiq (d. 148/765) in Sufi traditions of Qurʾān exegesis, see Sands (2006: 12–13, 25–26, 33, 61–62, 82).

> He wishes, and God gives the examples to the people since God has knowledge of every single thing!
> (36) There are houses which God allowed to be raised, in which His Name is honourably mentioned (*yudhkar fīhā ismuhu*), and in which praise for Him is offered morning and evening,
> (37) by men who trade or commerce cannot distract from mentioning and honouring God (*dhikr Allāh*), performing the prayer, and giving the community tax (*al-zakāt*), fearing a day when the intellecting hearts and the discerning sights will turn upon themselves (*yakhāfūna yawman tataqallabu fīhi al-qulūb wa al-abṣār*),
> (38) so that God may reward them for the best of what they have done and increase them of His bounty, for God sustains (*yarzuq*) who He wishes without counting!

Verses 36 and 37 thus serve as reference points for the Sufi ritual practice of *dhikr* i.e. the rhythmic and repeated mentioning of 'Allāh' and other devotional formula. Similarly Q. 39 (*al-Zumar*), 22 connects recollection and honouring (*dhikr*) of God with His light:

> (22) What about the one whose bosom God has exposed for the enactment of peace so that he is upon light from his Lord (*a-faman sharaḥa Allāhu ṣadrahu li-l-islām fahuwa ʿalā nūrin min rabbihi*)? Woe to those whose hearts are too hard for recalling and honouring God (*dhikr Allāh*), they are in clearly distinct error!

The aspect of *walāya* that refers to governorship is also identifiable in the Qur'ān, in passages where God appears as the supreme Protecting Governor. For example, Q. 42 (*al-Shūrā*), 6–11, where the topic of the divine governorship is related to the practical issue of legal disagreement (*ikhtilāf*), which can be settled by referring the matter to God's judgement (verse 10):

> (6) Those who have taken apart from Him **protecting governors (*awliyā'*)**, God oversees them and you are not a legal guardian for them (*mā anta ʿalayhim biwakīl*)!
> (7) And thus We communicated to you an Arabic reading (*awḥaynā ilayka qur'ānan ʿarabiyyan*) for you to warn the Mother of the Villages and those in its surroundings, and warn about the Day of Gathering: there is no doubt that on it a group will be in the garden and a group will be in the blazing flame!
> (8) Had God wished, He would have made them one single polity. Instead He admits who He wishes into His life-protection (*raḥmatihi*), while the wrongdoers have no **protecting governor** or helper to victory (*wa al-ẓālimūna mā lahum min* ***waliyyin*** *wa lā naṣīr*) –

> (9) Or have they taken apart from Him **protecting governors (*awliyā'*)**? It is God Who is **the protecting governor (*al-waliyyu*)** as He revives what is dead because He has power over every single thing!
> (10) Whatever thing about which you are **in legal disagreement (*wa mā ikhtalaftum fīhi*)**, its judgement is unto God. That, you see, is God my Lord, on Who I rely for legal guardianship and to Who I turn,
> (11) Shaper of the heavens and the earth! (…)

Imagery associated with the socioeconomic vassalage system also figures in Qur'ānic references to *walāya*. It is possible to detect such a topical link also in the background of al-Tirmidhī, the theoriser of *walāya*: he was a landowner from a wealthy patrician family of the governorate of Khurasan (Aijub 2015: 36). Two Qur'ānic passages serve as examples: Q. 18 (*Ahl al-kahf*), 44 and Q. 7 (*al-A'rāf*), 3–10. The verse 18, 44 appears in a context treating God's requirement of loyalty i.e. that He must not be shared with other partners, and His reward for loyalty in the form of sustenance from farmlands and victory against adversaries. Two categories of people are defined. The first has been given two gardens with vines, and he starts to brag to his companion that he has more wealth and more offspring than he (verses 32–34), to the point that he 'wrongs himself' (*ẓalama nafsahu*) by saying that his assets will never perish, that he does not believe in the approaching hour (of judgement), and that if he is returned to his Lord he will find an even better place (verses 35–36). His companion, who represents the second category, admonishes him to make no one partner with God, and to praise his Lord God, Who creates everything and Who may turn fortunes around so that he is given an even better garden (*janna*) while his companion's lands are hit by a thunderbolt and laid waste (verses 37–41). Of course, the wrongdoer's crops were destroyed:

> (42) Then his crop was destroyed, and he started to wring his hands over what he had spent on it, while it had fallen down upon its trellises, saying: 'If only I had not made a single one partner with my Lord! (*laytanī lam ushrik birabbī aḥadan*)
> (43) And he had no contingent to help him to victory, nor could he help himself (*wa lam takun lahu fi'a yanṣurūnahu wa mā kāna muntaṣiran*):
> (44) There, you see, **the protective governorship** belongs to God the Truly Rightful (*hunālika* ***al-walāya*** *li-Llāh al-ḥaqq*): He is the Best in rewarding and the Best in requiting!

In this scenario, the wrong (*ẓulm*) consists in 'making someone else partner with God' (*ashraka*), in the context of land grants and harvests. The following verses 45–50 state explicitly that the particular examples from 'this nearest life' serve to drive home the general principle about the loyalty required by the divine Covenant (Q. 7, 172), alluded to in verse 48:

> (45) Forge for them the example (*mathal*) of the nearest life (*al-ḥayāt al-dunyā*): like water that We send down from heaven, with which the vegetation of the land immerses, then becomes straw which the wind dries, for God is the One Who has power over every single thing!
> (46) Wealth and descendants are the fleeting adornment of the nearest life, but the lasting works for the common good (*al-bāqiyāt al-ṣāliḥāt*) are best with your Lord in terms of reward, and a best expectation,
> (47) for the Day when We shall make the mountains move and you shall see the land uncovered as We gather them all, having left no one among them unattended,
> (48) and they will be paraded before your Lord in rows: 'You have indeed come to Us like when We created you the first time, even though you claimed that We would not fix an appointed time for you!'
> (49) The divine writing will be laid down (*wa wuḍiʿa al-kitāb*) and you will see the offenders apprehensive of what is in it, saying: 'Woe upon us! What is it with this writing? It has left nothing unattended, small or large, but enumerates them!' And they will find what they did present, for your Lord does not wrong a single one! (*wa lā yuẓlimu rabbuka aḥadan*).
> (50) As when We said to the angels: 'Prostrate before Adam!' and they prostrated, except Iblīs. He was one of the Jinn, so he rebelled against the command of his Lord (*fafasaqa ʿan amri rabbihi*); will you really take him and his offspring as **protecting governors** instead of Me (***awliyā'a*** *min dūnī*), when they are your enemies? Evil is the exchange for those who do wrong!

The second example, Q. 7 (*al-Aʿrāf*), 3–10, sets out the Covenant terms: the people should take no other lords besides God, and they know through the messengers that God will hold them to account for this, while God is obligated to sustain people through the land:

> (3) Follow what has been sent down to you from your Lord and **do not take other protective governors (*awliyā'*) apart from Him**; but how seldom you let yourselves be reminded!
> (4) How many a town have We made perish, as Our tribulation reached it at night or when they were resting,
> (5) And their only call when Our tribulation reached them was to say: "We have indeed been doing wrong!" (*innā kunnā ẓālimīna*)
> (6) Therefore We shall question those to who a message was sent, and We shall question those sent out with the message (*al-mursalīna*),

(7) and We will be recounting to them with knowledge (*bi ʿilmin*), for We were not absent.
(8) On that day the weighing is the true right (*al-ḥaqq*): those whose scales are heavy, they are the ones who promote prosperity (*al-mufliḥūna*),[41]
(9) while those whose scales are light, they are the ones who lost their selves on account of their darkening Our signs through wrongdoing (*kānū bi ʾāyātinā yaẓlimūna*),
(10) even though We have indeed established you firmly **in the land and given you of it means of livelihood (*maʿāyish*)**; but seldom do you give thanks!

Another topical context in which *walāya* occurs is war. For example, Q. 8 (*al-Anfāl*), 70–75 stipulates terms for the related categories. The addressee here is the Prophet, who can offer protective governorship to those loyal to him, according to the Covenantal model of loyalty:

(70) O Prophet! Say to those captives who you hold: "If God has knowledge of any good in your intellecting hearts, He will bring you better than what was taken from you and forgive you, for God is an All-Forgiving One Who Continuously Protects life!"
(71) But if they seek to betray you, they have first betrayed God so He subdued them; God is an All-knowing One Who Passes Judgement!
(72) Indeed, those who have enacted security and emigrated and struggled (*jāhadū*) by means of their wealth and lives for the sake of meeting the duties God has laid down (*fī sabīl Allāh*), and those who gave refuge and help to victory, those are each other's **protective governors (*awliyā'a*)**. But those who have enacted security but did not emigrate, you owe them no **protective governorship (*walāya*)** until they emigrate. Should they seek your help to victory on the basis of the judicial order (*al-dīn*), you are obligated to help them, except against a people with who you have a firm covenant (*mīthāq*); God has full overview of your actions!

41 The word *al-mufliḥūna* is derived from the root *f-l-ḥ*, which carries the meanings of 'obtainment', 'being in a state of lasting blessings', and 'agriculture' i.e. tilling the land. Here it occurs in the transitive fourth declination and as active participle, suggesting 'those who promote attainment of blessings'. See *Lisān al-ʿarab* (online at www.alwaraq.net), pp. 4468–4469. However, considering that verse 10 refers to the land and the means of livelihood derived from it as a semantic context for the positive and negative categories in verses 8 and 9, I understand 'attainment of blessings' as referring also to the material livelihood from the land, and therefore translate *al-mufliḥūna* as 'those who promote prosperity'.

(73) As for those who rejected security (*kafarū*), they are each other's **protective governors (*awliyā'a*)**. Unless you enact this, there will be civil war in the land and great corruption!
(74) As for those who enacted security, emigrated, and struggled for the sake of meeting the duties God has laid down, and those who gave refuge and helped to victory, they are the enactors of security, with true right (*ḥaqqan*), and to them belong forgiveness and dignified sustenance (*rizq karīm*)!
(75) As for those who enacted security after a while and emigrated and struggled with you, those are part of you. But the next of kin are **more** each other's **protective governors** in God's writing (*wa ūlū al-arḥām baʿḍuhum* ***awlā*** *bibaʿḍin fī kitāb Allāh*); God does indeed have knowledge about every single thing!

Based on these examples, the Qurʾānic term *walī/awliyā'* appears related to governorship as defined by the Covenantal terms of loyalty to God. In the societal context, it implicates the scholars in several functions: as landowners in their own right; as transmitters of both the systematic (*ʿilm*) *and* the experience-based (*maʿrifa*) knowledge of God; and as legislators for regional governors and the Caliphal administration.

By the 500s/1100s, scholarly *walāya* was integral to the *ṭuruq*, sing. *ṭarīqa*, a 'trodden path' of transmitted knowledge and ascetic practices, including the *dhikr* ritual. From this time onwards, *ṭuruq* could be found in all Islamic polities and, as mentioned, contributed to the spread of Islam. Each *ṭarīqa* has its own genealogy and transmission of its specific experience-based knowledge and *dhikr* formula, which distinguishes it from the other *ṭuruq*. It is this stage of universal institutionalisation that is meant when the term 'Sufism' is used. Following the logic, that *walāya* in its earliest formulation accompanied the institution of the *ʿulamāʾ*, we can see that the Sufi *ṭuruq* overlapped with the *madhāhib*, since many legal scholars were affiliated with a *ṭarīqa*. In the same way, through affiliation and loyalty, the *ṭuruq* overlapped also with the court, the market, and the various professional guilds.[42]

This stage of universal institutionalisation of *ṭuruq* as the specifically Sufi form of *walāya* is signified in the Sunnī sphere by al-Ghazzālī's (d. 505/1111) leadership of the Niẓāmiyya college in Baghdad under the Saljuq dynasty. Al-Ghazzālī formally incorporated Sufism as the discipline *taṣawwuf*, 'to become *ṣūfī*', into the Sunnī education for legal scholars,

42 See again Aijub (2015: 13), with further references to Anjum (2006); Malamud (1994); Ohlander (2008); Blain (2012).

alongside jurisprudence (*fiqh*) and systematic theology (*kalām*). In his *magnum opus*, *Iḥyāʾ ʿulūm al-dīn*, 'Revival of the sciences of the judicial order', al-Ghazzālī argued that without the Sufi experiential knowledge of God and enlightenment by the divine Light, the sciences were merely human constructs supporting various quests for power. The concept 'revival' (*iḥyāʾ*) in the title says something about his concept of the divine enlightenment as what keeps the systematic scientific knowledge (*ʿilm*) 'alive'. Similarly, Ibn al-ʿArabī (d. 638/1240), whose Neoplatonic cosmology aimed at connecting the scholar's intellect with the One God, is known by the honorific Muḥyī al-Dīn, 'Reviver of the judicial order'. His works gained favour with members of the Ayyūbid dynasty (1176–ca. 1250) in Syria and Anatolia, where they became particularly influential, later playing an important part within the Ottoman educational system.[43] In fact, when the Moghul Sultan Akbar appointed himself as supreme *mujtahid* and law-interpreter, as mentioned above, he apparently drew on Ibn al-ʿArabī's cosmology and theory of direct intellectual enlightenment by the divine light to legitimise his lawmaking authority despite his lack of legal education (Pirbhai 2009: 81–83). Whether the same idea lay behind the Ottoman Sultans' new law-making authority, also discussed above, is not clear, although Ibn al-ʿArabī's works were influential in Ottoman education. In any case, the 'revival' associated with the *walī*'s experience-based divine knowledge has a reference in the Qurʾān, which states that God is the *walī* with the power to 'revive what is dead'; e.g., Q. 42 (*al-Shūrā*), 9:

> (9) Or have they taken apart from Him **protecting governors (*awliyāʾ*)**? It is God Who is **the protecting governor (*al-waliyyu*)** for He **revives** what is dead (***yuḥyī*** *al-mawtā*) because He has power over every single thing!

Rule of Law and the Challenge of Legal Disagreement

As we have just seen in the case of Q. 42 (*al-Shūrā*), 6–11, the Qurʾān portrays divine *walāya* as a solution to the problem of legal disagreement (*ikhtilāf*). In this final section of the chapter, I will discuss this problem with reference to 'the rule of law' and its procedural aspects. According to the political scientist Jeremy Waldron (2016), formal procedure is an important component of the rule of law, underpinning the institutional separation of powers and an independent judiciary:

43 Ateş (2012), 'Ibn al-ʿArabī', Encyclopaedia of Islam, Second Edition.

> The Rule of Law comprises a number of principles of a formal and procedural character, addressing the way in which a community is governed. The formal principles concern the generality, clarity, publicity, stability, and prospectivity of the norms that govern a society.

Legal disagreement can constitute a challenge for formal procedure. In the above sketch of institutional separation of powers in the dynastic Caliphates and the Sultanates up to the 1600s, we saw how the Abbasid Caliph al-Maʾmūn attempted in the 830s first to introduce an ʿAlid heir to the Caliphate, then to enforce the state doctrine of 'the createdness of the Qurʾān'. While the two moves may have been unrelated, they can also be seen as attempts to deal with legal disagreement. The doctrinal imposition and inquisition involved unifying the jurists and judges around the doctrine, under the Caliphal authority, and against competing legal methodologies such as that offered by *Ahl al-ḥadīth*. In some cases Shīʿī *walāya* discourages legal diversity. Shīʿī political theory unifies political and religious-legislative powers in the ideal model of the *imam*. As mentioned above, the theory was implemented in the Ismāʿīlī Fāṭimid Caliphate (296/909–567/1171). The first Fāṭimid Caliph al-Mahdī (r. 296/909–322/934) identified as the Imam, unifying in his own person the powers of ruler, doctrinal authority, and lawmaker. The model consciously challenged the Abbasid division of power. According to al-Qāḍī al-Nuʿmān (d. 363/974), chief judge for al-Mahdī and main theoretician of Fāṭimid rule, the Abbasid separation of powers reduced the Caliphate to sheer power brokering and the law to the jurists' subjective inclinations and divergent opinions, lacking grounding in either God's *kitāb* or the Prophet's sayings. Consequently, the Abbasid Caliphate no longer enacted the divinely guided just rule that legitimized the institution (al-Qāḍī al-Nuʿmān/Stewart 2017: 9–15). Al-Mahdī's rise to power thus signified the return of Caliphal legitimacy, with al-Mahdī ruling by the divine writing (*kitāb*), the speech of the Prophet, and the rulings of the *imams*, referred to by the Qurʾānic term 'those in command' (*ūlū al-amr*; Q. 4, 59, 83) (al-Qāḍī al-Nuʿmān/Stewart 2017: 11–12, 16–21). In this way, al-Qāḍī al-Nuʿmān depicted the Sunnī diversity of methodologies and rulings as a form of tyranny, where the jurists do not rule by the law but make it up.

One could see al-Qāḍī al-Nuʿmān's theory as a move to strengthen the procedures required for the rule of law by reducing legal diversity and disagreement. However, by concentrating powers in the ruler, the theory limits deliberative freedom among jurists, which others perceived as problematic. The movement *Ikhwān al-Ṣafā*, 'Brethren of Purity', was active around 900–1000 in the intellectual borderlands between political philosophy, ethics and law. According to Ian Netton, they used terminology highly similar to that of Ismāʿīlīs, but rejected the Ismāʿīlī political theory precisely on account of diversity. *Ikhwān al-Ṣafā* praised both legal and religious diversity, declaring the disagreement of the legal scholars 'life-protecting' (*ikhtilāf al-ʿulamāʾ raḥma*), and the doctrinal divergences between scholars of all religions and sects (*ahl al-diyānāt*) the essence of the capability for just judgement (*ḥikma*). Diversity and contestation spur the scholarly minds to seek more knowledge and gain greater intellectual achievements, they argued (Netton 2007/1980: 6).[44]

Given that the Qurʾān describes legal disagreement as something negative, to be overcome by referring matters to God's judgement as *walī*, I will explore some passages with an eye towards topics related to procedure and separation of powers. One of the formal principles Waldron identified with rule of law is 'clarity', as well as generality, publicity, stability and prospectivity of norms. We have already seen in Chapter 3 how al-Ṭabarī associated 'clear distinction' (*bayān*) both with Qurʾānic Arabic language and composition, reflecting the terms of Covenant. *Bayān* can thus be seen as a procedural term, related to clarifying and making Covenant and legal terms publicly known, for the sake of stability and prospectivity. The distribution of power is such that the Prophet is subject to the law that comes from God; this follows from for example Q. 20 (*Ṭāhā*), 1–8 and 113–114:

> (1) *Ṭāhā*
> (2) We have not sent down upon you the reading to distress you (*mā anzalnā ʿalayka al-qurʾān litashqā*),
> (3) Only as an honouring recollection to the one who fears (*yakhshā*)
> (4) A sending-down from the One Who created the land and the high heavens:
> (5) It is the Giver of Life Who rules equitably upon the Throne (*al-Raḥmān ʿalā al-ʿarsh istawā*),
> (6) To Who belongs what is in the heavens and in the land, and what is between the two, and what is under the ground!
> (7) You may be speaking loudly, but He has knowledge of the secret and what is even more hidden:

44 Netton (2007/1980) disagrees with the dominant view that Ikhwān al-Ṣafā were Ismāʿīlī, since their positive appraisal of diversity and allegiance to each other under the sole leadership of Intellect (*ʿaql*) challenges the Ismāʿīlī theory of the Imām as sole source of legal and religious guidance; see also Netton (1996: 27–41). Cf. Baffioni (2000) for preliminary arguments that their key terms can be seen as aligning with both general Shīʿī and Ismāʿīlī concepts of the Imāms; however, this brief study does not address the specific issue of legal disagreement.

> (8) God except for Who there is no other god Who has the best beautiful names (*al-asmāʾ al-ḥusnā*)!
>
> (113) In this way We have made it descend as an Arabic reading in which We diversified the warning so that they may fulfil their obligations, or it induces them to an honouring recollection.
> (114) Since God, the King Who is the True Right, is Exalted, do not hasten with the reading before its communication to you is completed, and say: "My Lord, increase me in knowledge!"

Thus, God makes His terms publicly known, and it is emphasised that He also knows everything because He is the Creator Who rules in equity from His position above on the Throne, which gives Him the supreme overview of human affairs. The Prophet *receives* the reading from above, and therefore he must take care to understand it properly by asking God for more knowledge. In terms of understanding the message, the Prophet appears to be in the same hermeneutical position as the scholars.[45] In terms of the rule of law, the Prophet receives the reading and its legal contents from God, which subjects him to the law. This too can be seen as reflecting the scholars' position as recipients of the Qurʾān.

'Clear distinctions' is then the norm for the prophetic public announcement of the message, as in the frequently cited Q. 14 (*Ibrāhīm*), 4–5:

> (4) We have never sent forth a messenger with a message that is not in the language of his people, so that he can **convey clarifying distinctions** to them (***liyubayyina*** *lahum*). Then God makes whom He wishes go astray and rightly guides whom He wishes, for He is the Mighty, Who Passes Judgement!
> (5) Thus, We did indeed send forth Moses with a message through Our signs, so that he could bring his people out of the darkness to **the light** (*min al-ẓulumāt ilā* ***al-nūr***) and honour them with God's glorious deeds; indeed, there are signs in that for every steadfast and thankful person!

The legal sense of the light and clear distinctions is brought out in e.g. Q. 4 (*al-Nisāʾ*), 163–166 and 174–176. The passages adduce the previous prophets as evidence that this is no arbitrary rulemaking but something stable, publicly known, and prospective i.e. the terms are laid out clearly and their implications are predictable:

45 See also Mårtensson (2008: 406–407), on the epistemic aspects of understanding God's intended meaning in this passage.

(163) We have communicated to you like we communicated to Noah and the prophets after him, as We communicated to Abraham, Ismail, Isaac, Jacob and the Tribes, Jesus, Job, Jonah, Aron and Solomon, and We gave David a written genealogical record (*zabūran*);[46]
(164) And messengers whose examples We have already accounted for you (*qaṣaṣnāhum ʿalayka*), and messengers whose examples We have not accounted for you, as God spoke directly to Moses;
(165) Messengers who carried forth the divine good word and warnings so that the people would not have any valid argument (*ḥujja*) against God after the messengers; God is the Mighty Who Passes Judgement!
(166) Yet God testifies by what He has sent down to you that He sent it down with His knowledge (*bi ʿilmihi*). And the angels testify, but God suffices as witness! (...)

(174) O People! Evidence (*burhān*) has come to you from your Lord as We sent down to you a light that enables clear distinctions (*nūran mubīnan*)!
(175) As for those who enact security through God and hold fast to Him, He will let them enter life protection from Him and bounty as He guides them to Himself along a path of correct speech and action (*ṣirāṭan mustaqīman*).
(176) They ask you for a legal decision (*yastaftūnaka*). Say: God gives you a decision about collaterals:[47] if a man has died leaving no offspring but he has a sister, she shall have right to one-half of what he leaves, and he inherits her if she does not have an offspring. If there are two sisters, they shall have two thirds of what he leaves. If there are siblings, both men and women, the male shall have the equivalent of the share of two females. God conveys clarifying distinctions for you so that you do not go astray, for God has knowledge of every single thing!

These passages depict evidence (*burhān*), argument leading to authoritative proof (*ḥujja*), and clarity of distinctions as the hallmark of the divine legal rulings.

Finally, the principle of divine 'writing' (*kitāb*) further supports the publicity, stability and prospectivity of norms, since the Qurʾān frequently connects writing with knowledge about terms. For example, the passage Q. 7 (*al-Aʿrāf*), 168–174 starts by locating the peoples in their assigned lands, and then proceeds to argue that the Covenant is embodied in divine writing so

46 This translation of *zabūr* is discussed below in Chapter 6, "History (*taʾrīkh*)".

47 For the translation of *kalāla* as 'collateral' i.e. a person having the same ancestor as another but through a different line (Oxford Dictionaries Online), see Cilardo (2005: 83).

that all humans can know its terms, and that these were established already at Creation:

> (168) We assigned to them grants of land and made them into nations (*wa qaṭṭaʿnāhum fī al-arḍ umaman*), some of them working for the common good, and some otherwise. We tried them with good things and bad, so that they might return,
> (169) But there succeeded them successors who inherited the divine writing (*warithū al-kitāb*) yet took the vanity of this nearest existence, saying: "We shall be forgiven!" And were similar vanity to come their way, they would take it. Has not the firm Covenant of the divine writing – and they studied what is in it – been taken upon them, that they should not state upon God except what is right (*a-lam yuʾkhadh ʿalayhim mīthāq al-kitāb an lā yaqūlū ʿalā Allāh illā al-ḥaqq*)? The furthest abode is better for those who fulfil their obligations; will they not be bound by reason?
> (170) As for those who hold fast to the divine writing (*yumsikūna bi-l-kitāb*) and perform the prayer: indeed, We do not restrain the reward of those who promote the common good (*al-muṣliḥīna*)!
> (171) When We shook the mountain over them as if it was a canopy, and they thought it would come down with them: hold on firmly to what I have brought you and honour its contents; perhaps you will fulfil your obligations!
> (172) When your Lord took from the backs of Adam's children their offspring and made them bear witness to themselves: "Am I not your Lord?" They said: "Certainly, we testify!" So that you cannot say on the Day of Standing [to trial]: "But we were unaware of this!"
> (173) Or say: "But our fathers used to assign partners before, and we are their offspring: will you make us perish on account of what the promoters of false vacuity did?"
> (174) In this way We expound the signs in detail (*wa kadhālika nufaṣṣil al-āyāt*); perhaps they may return!

It is thus possible to identify a Qurʾānic concern with the traits, which Waldron (2016) defines as the procedural aspects of the rule of law. 'Generality', in the sense that Covenant applies to all peoples who received a messenger. 'Clear distinction' of its terms as expounded in the message. 'Publicity' in that the messengers publicly address the peoples. 'Stability' in that the terms are established and recognised as valid since Creation. Finally, 'prospectivity' in that what constitutes the terms and the consequences of upholding or violating them is recorded in the divine writing.

Given this assumed concern with the procedural aspects of legislative, executive, and judiciary authority, it is logical that God worries about legal disagreement. For example, Q. 42 (*al-Shūrā*), 12–15 and 21 give a deterring example of what the Qur᾿ānic polity should avoid:

> (12) To [God] belongs the storage magazines of the heavens and the land, and He expands the sustenance to who He wishes, and He measures, for indeed, He has knowledge of every single thing!
> (13) He has set you on the path of divine guidance (*shara῾a lakum*) in the judicial order (*dīn*) with which He appointed Noah, and which We have communicated to you, and with which We appointed Abraham and Moses and Jesus: "Perform the judicial order and do not split up internally within it!" That to which you invite those who assign others as partners is greater than them! God elects to Himself for abundant bounty whoever He wishes and guides to Himself whoever He appoints!
> (14) They only split up internally after the knowledge had come to them, out of wrongful excesses among themselves. If it was not for a word preceding from your Lord to a defined term, judgement would have been passed between them. Indeed, those who were given the divine writing as inheritance after them are in disquieting doubt from [the wrongful excesses]!
> (15) Therefore, announce the invitation and be correct in speech and action (*istaqim*) as you were commanded, and do not follow their inclinations but say: 'I enact security through whatever writing God has sent down, as I have been commanded to do justice between you! God is our Lord and your Lord, we have our actions and you have your actions, and there is no argument between us and you: God brings us together for towards Him is the destination!' (…)
> (21) Or do they have partners who set them upon a path of guidance of a judicial order for which God did not grant permission? If it was not for the word that expounds the details (*wa lawlā kalimat al-faṣl*), judgement would have been passed between them, and indeed, those who darken right by doing wrong own a painful punishment!

Q. 45 (*al-Jāthiya*), 17–18, treats the same topic of problematic dissent through the technical, legal term *ikhtilāf*:

> (17) We came to them with clarifying distinctions pertaining to the command, and **they did not disagree (*famā ikhtalafū*)** until the knowledge (*al-῾ilm*) came to them, because of wrongful excesses amongst themselves. Indeed, your Lord shall judge between them on the Day of Standing to trial regarding **that over which they used to disagree**!
> (18) Then We set you upon a path of divine guidance pertaining to the command (*sharī῾a min al-amr*), so follow it and do not follow the inclinations of those who do not have knowledge (*lā ya῾lamūna*)!

Q. 5 (*al-Mā'ida*), 48, discusses disagreement through another legal technical term, *minhāj*, 'method' within *fiqh*:

> (48) We have sent down to you the divine writing with the True Right (*bi-l-ḥaqq*), confirming that of the writings that is before it and superseding it. So judge between them according to what God has sent down, and do not follow their inclinations that divert you from the right that has come to you! To each of you We have introduced a path of divine guidance and **a method** (*shir'atan wa* ***minhājan***), and had God so wished, He would have made you one nation, but He tests you regarding what He brought you. So hurry to put forward the good deeds! To God is the return of you all, when He will announce to you regarding **that which you used to disagree upon** (*fayunbi'ukum* ***bimā kuntum fīhi takhtalifūna***)!

A closely related practice is interpretation. Q. 3, 7 discusses the problem of disagreement and dissent in terms of different interpretative strategies:

> (7) It is He Who has sent down to you the writing! Of it there are signs that are unequivocal (*āyāt muḥkamāt*), and they are the source of the writing (*umm al-kitāb*), while others are equivocal (*mutashābihāt*). As for those in whose hearts there is deviation, they follow the equivocal in it, seeking internal strife (*fitna*) and seeking to reach the intended meaning even though no one has knowledge of its intended meaning except God. Those grounded in knowledge say: "We enact security through it: all is from our Lord!", since no one except those with discerning intellects are reminded!

Thus, the Qur'ānic discourse describes conflicting interpretation and legal disagreement as practices that undermine the generality, clarity, stability, and predictability associated with God's message about Covenant and its terms. It appears therefore that Qur'ānic criticism of legal disagreement can be understood as referring to the same constitutional principles as the verses that emphasise the procedural aspects of the rule of law.

CONCLUDING ANALYSIS

In this chapter, I have analysed Qur'ānic Covenant through political theory, concluding that it can be seen as reflecting both a constitution and a social contract. I also traced these topics in the Prophet's Biography. There they are given concrete form in reports about the Arabian legacy of 'Abrahamic prophecy' related to the Kaʿba, which protects the legal and material (sustenance) rights of all people, and especially the weak. The Prophet is described as reviving this legacy through the compacts connected with the constitution of his polity. I then charted the institutional development in the period ca. 100/700 to ca. 900/1500, focusing on the constitutional issue of 'separation of powers' and the rule of law. It appears that the Islamic polities at least since the Umayyad dynasty (41/661–133/750) operated with an institutional separation of power between the state and the legal scholars, the latter being the lawmakers. However, the fact that historians such as Ibn Saʿd reported that a division of labour was at play already during the Prophet's rule, with his delegation of judicial authority to Companions, suggests that institutional complexity was a reality at the 'origins' of the Islamic polity. These reports, as well as the Prophet's Biography, actualises de Certeau's point, that historical discourse *theorises* facts referring to an institutional order. Consequently, the early historians can be seen as treating the Prophet's rule in terms of the political and legal institutions, whose legacies span both his time and their own.

Accordingly, the post-600s diversity of schools of law, and dynastic rivalry, combined to make separation of powers and legal diversity a point of contention. Simply put, Sunnī polities formally recognised legal diversity in the form of the four main schools of law, whereas Shīʿī theory considered only its own school to be legitimate. In addition, some Shīʿī political theory tended to unite powers in the ruler, whether ideally (Twelvers) or actually (Ismāʿīlīs). The institution of *walāya* is particularly interesting when viewed from this perspective. Its function is to legitimise 'protective governorship' as the transmission of divine, *experience*-based knowledge – a kind of super-authorisation of scholarly knowledge, which also relates to the mind-based theory of concept. In the context of the Sufi brotherhoods or *ṭuruq*, with their diverse knowledge transmissions, *walāya* encouraged diversification in practice, despite its theoretical claim to connect with the singular divine knowledge.

The argument that the Qurʾān contains the concepts, which define the institutions and their practices, implies that the Qurʾānic discourse is historically accurate when it says these are long-standing political and legal challenges related to the ancient institution of prophecy. Furthermore, the Qurʾānic insistence on the good of the procedural aspects related to its discourse on Covenant suggests the discourse theorises these challenges in a way that speaks to both the institutional separation of powers that the Islamic polities grappled with, and legal diversity. The Qurʾān criticises legal diversity from the perspective of a rule of law-constitution where the

Prophet and thereby the Qur'ānic message itself prefigures the institution of legal scholars. There is also a simultaneously moral and socioeconomic aspect to this criticism, namely the Qur'ānic command to protect the rights of the weak. Watson's (2008/1983) and Johansen's (1988) studies of agricultural and legal change in early Islam suggest that the Qur'ān could have effectuated a change of legal status for peasants by granting property rights. Consequently, the problem of legal disagreement may also refer to rights for the weak, which could be an additional reason why the Qur'ān insists that disagreement with its norms is a negative thing. I will return to this issue in the next chapter, in the context of *fiqh*.

Chapter 6

THE DISCIPLINES AND 'THE SCIENTIFIC QUR'ĀN'

This chapter outlines the ways in which seven of the scholarly disciplines produced systematic knowledge (*ʿilm*) with reference to Qur'ānic concepts. The topics related to Qur'ānic Covenant as constitution and social contract remain central, but here I address in a more consistent manner 'the science question': to what extent can Qur'ānic concepts, as employed within the disciplines, be seen as referring to observation and empirical data?

The survey begins with a sketch of the internal relationship between the sciences, and then treats each of the seven selected disciplines: Linguistics; Prophetic tradition (*ḥadīth*); Political science (*siyāsa*) and administration (*tadbīr*); History (*ta'rīkh*); Qur'ān exegesis (*tafsīr*); Jurisprudence (*fiqh*) and legal hermeneutics (*uṣūl al-fiqh*); and Systematic theology (*kalām*). In a second part of the chapter, I focus on two scholars from the late medieval-early modern period, to illustrate how the disciplines can overlap in the works of an individual scholar, and how certain topics continued to be relevant.

THE DISCIPLINES' INTERNAL RELATIONSHIP

Scholarly disciplines based on written documentation and transmissions in the Arabic language, can be traced to the late 600s, which coincides in time with systematic production of Qur'ān manuscripts by scribes (Déroche 2014). There is thus a temporal relationship between the earliest Qur'ān manuscripts and the disciplines. In Chapters 2, 3, 4, and 5, I have argued that Qur'ānic concepts can be seen as reflecting theories of concept, language and rhetoric, natural law, constitution and social contract, because the Qur'ān is 'organically' part of the scholarly disciplines and their systematic knowledge. In the case of these theories, the corresponding disciplines are philosophy, linguistics and rhetoric, law, and political science. These disciplines can overlap, because theoretical paradigms transcend disciplinary boundaries, and because disciplines produce knowledge addressing common societal and scholarly concerns. For example, the concept 'clarity of distinctions' (*bayān*) can refer to formal and procedural aspects of the rule of law, as discussed in the previous chapter, just as it serves as a key concept in the rhetorical discipline *balāgha*, as shown in Chapter 3, and as a legal hermeneutical concept, as we shall see in this chapter.

Another approach to the relationship between the sciences is that of the philosopher and political scientist al-Fārābī (d. 339/950–51). Charles Butterworth has analysed al-Fārābī's synthesis of Plato and Aristotle within the framework of his political theory, which includes the role of science. For al-Fārābī, the aim of government and the sciences is to make the city prosperous and improve the citizens' lives so that they can attain happiness. In this context, al-Fārābī reflected on the relationship between the political theories of the Ancients Plato and Aristotle, and the Islamic revealed, prophetic law. He argued that lawgiving is the main tool for human happiness, which is a philosophical concern. Consequently, law is ultimately a philosophical inquiry, also when given by a prophet (Butterworth 2008: 474–476). He therefore concluded that prophetic religious language expresses philosophical and theoretical truths, but conveyed through images which can persuade the majority, who are not trained philosophers, about the good of the law:[1]

> These things are philosophy when they are in the soul of the lawgiver. And when they are in the souls of the multitude, they are religion. For when the lawgiver knows these things, they are evident to him through certain insight, whereas what is established in the souls of the multitude is through an image and persuasion.

From al-Fārābī's viewpoint, then, the images and rhetorical persuasion that characterise Qur'ānic language forms, can be seen as 'religious' expressions of the philosophical-theoretical truth that the divine Covenant and law are conducive to prosperity and happiness.

In line with this approach, al-Fārābī made an Aristotle-inspired classification of the scientific disciplines in the treatise *Iḥṣā' al-'ulūm* ('Enumeration of the sciences'), starting with linguistics:[2]

1 Butterworth (2008: 477), ref. to al-Fārābī, *Taḥṣīl al-sa'āda* ('Attainment of Happiness'), p. 44, lines 2–13.

2 Cf. Kraemer (1986: 9), ref. to al-Fārābī, *Iḥṣā' al-'ulūm*, ed. Angel González Palencia (1953), pp. 7–9. I have modified Kraemer's list of six sciences (linguistics, logic, mathematics, physics, metaphysics, and politics), based on al-Fārābī's itemisation into five disciplines and his explanations of their internal relationships. For an overview of other categorisations and lists of the sciences in the encyclopaedic genre, with particular reference to Aristotle, see Peters (1968: 104–120).

1. Linguistics (*ʿilm al-lisān*), including grammar, syntax, writing, reading, and poetics (*al-ashʿār*).
2. Logic (*ʿilm al-manṭiq*), including the application of the rules of language in reasoning, argumentation, and demonstration. While language rules are specific to a nation's language, logic proceeds to use language to identify trans-national and trans-linguistic, rational truths. Here, al-Fārābī distinguishes between *khaṭāba* as the rhetorical art of persuasion (*iqnāʿ*), which can convey rational truths pertaining to topics of enquiry but can also be on any topic and be devoid of rational demonstration, and *jadal* or dialectical argumentation, which proceeds from defined topics (*mawāḍiʿ*) under investigation and aims at the demonstration of rational truths about these.
3. The sciences of higher education (*ʿulūm al-taʿālīm*), including mathematics (*ʿadad*), mechanics (*handasa*), optics (*manāẓir*), astronomy (*ʿilm al-nujūm al-taʿlīmī*), music (*mūsīqā*), and physics (*ʿilm al-athqāl* i.e. weight and gravity, and *ʿilm al-ḥayl* i.e. force).
4. The natural science (*al-ʿilm al-ṭabīʿī*), including metaphysics or the divine science (*al-ʿilm al-ilāhī*). Natural science is the study of the forms and substances of existing things and beings, complex or uniform, man-made or naturally existing, while the divine science is the study of being, of first principles (*mabādiʾ*) of sciences and beings, and of Being without form and end, the One by which all other existing beings and things proceed, namely God.
5. The political science (*al-ʿilm al-madanī*), including jurisprudence (*ʿilm al-fiqh*) and systematic theology (*ʿilm al-kalām*). Political science involves the study of human society, desires, and happiness, and royal rule and state administration, including virtue ethics and laws (*qawānīn*), and the possibility of virtuous rule (*faḍl*) as distinct from rule based on power and experience. Jurisprudence is the art of deriving the divine guidance (*sharīʿa*) by defining principles (*uṣūl*) for views and social interactions in the polity (*madīna*), through which one thing after another can be derived; while theology is the support and triumph of views and actions and the falsification of their opposites, through dialectical reasoning.

As we can see, al-Fārābī placed the disciplines of *fiqh* and *kalām* under political science, serving the prosperity and happiness of citizens, and he placed metaphysical enquiry into God under natural science. Since natural science is concerned with the beings and things that are studied also in higher education, and since God is considered the One through which everything else exists, the empirical higher education sciences point ahead to the natural sciences rather than separate themselves from them.

In what follows, I adopt al-Fārābī's view of the sciences as tools for government to make the city prosper and the citizens happy, and his theory of prophetic-religious language. However, apart from starting with linguistics, my selection and arrangement of disciplines does not follow his list. This is because my aim is not to map the relationship between the sciences, as such, but to discuss some of their concepts and theories with reference to Covenant as constitution and social contract. I will not treat logic, the sciences of higher education, and the natural science as disciplines, only as topics occurring within the other disciplines. I have also included Prophetic *ḥadīth*, history, and Qur'ān exegesis. Consequently, my selection is: (1) Linguistics; (2) *ḥadīth*; (3) Political science (*siyāsa*) and administration (*tadbīr*); (4) History (*ta'rīkh*); (5) Qur'ān exegesis (*tafsīr*); (6) Jurisprudence (*fiqh*) and legal hermeneutics (*uṣūl al-fiqh*); and (7) Theology (*kalām*).

LINGUISTICS

Linguistics appears a logical choice for first discipline, since language is a precondition for scientific investigation and conceptualisation. Since I have already touched upon the discipline's early overlap with Qur'ān manuscript production and exegesis from the late 600s onwards in Chapters 2 and 3, I limit the discussion here to Sībawayhi's (d. 180/796) treatise *al-Kitāb*, the earliest extant grammar of the Arabic language, mentioned in the same chapters. Furthermore, I will focus exclusively on one concept: *mustaqīm*.

Mustaqīm is the active participle of *istaqāma*, 'to be upright', 'to be straight', with verbal noun *istiqāma*. In Sībawayhi's linguistics, *mustaqīm* refers to correct semantic and syntactic construal of phrases. Since Sībawayhi also worked within jurisprudence, Michael Carter has perceived his use of *mustaqīm* as related to law and the pragmatist aim to define legal categories and references. Kees Versteegh, on the other hand, rather stresses the term's reference to grammatical logic i.e. what makes logical sense.[3] In a recent study, Amal Marogy explores both the logical and the pragmatist aspects, arguing that *mustaqīm* is a key term for Sībawayhi's grammar because it encapsulates his theory of language as communication of *intended meaning*. Hence, "[b]y *mustaqīm*, Sībawayhi broadly means that the utterance should be meaningful to the listener and should successfully convey the intended information, otherwise the speech becomes *muḥāl*, 'nonsensical and unviable'" (Marogy 2010: 49). For illustration, I provide Sībawayhi's initial

3 See Versteegh (1993: 34–35), with refs. to Carter (1972: 83–84, 87ff.).

exposition of *mustaqīm*. He does not give a concise definition but shows what he means by it through concrete examples. Both the logical and the listener or usage-oriented aspects are prominent, in the sense that meaning and syntax should align in the best possible way, making the message logically consistent and clear to the listener.

The section *al-istiqāma min al-kalām wa al-iḥāla* appears at the beginning of the treatise and treats the topic of correct (*mustaqīm*) and impossible (*muḥāl*) semantic and syntactic construal of correspondence between words. The correct construal can be 'good' (*ḥasan*), 'deceptive' (*kadhib*), and 'unpleasant' (*qabīḥ*). An example of 'good correct construal' (*al-mustaqīm al-ḥasan*) is: 'I came to you yesterday and I will come to you tomorrow', where the meaning corresponds logically with the syntax i.e. the tenses of the verbs and the adverbs align logically. An impossible construal is one where there is no such correspondence, for example: 'I came to you tomorrow' or 'I will come to you yesterday', where the verb tense does not correspond with the adverb. An example of 'deceptive correct construal' (*al-mustaqīm al-kadhib*) is 'I carried the mountains' or 'I drank the water of the ocean', where the syntax is correct but the meaning is deceptive: no one can carry the mountains or drink all the water in the ocean. An example of 'impossible deceptive construal' is one where the syntax is also wrong, as in 'I will drink the water of the ocean yesterday'. Finally, 'unpleasant correct construal' (*al-mustaqīm al-qabīḥ*) is when a word is in a syntactically awkward place, for example: 'Zayd I have seen' or 'so that may come to you Zayd', instead of the good and correct 'I have seen Zayd' and 'so that Zayd may come to you' (Sībawayhi 1988/1: 25–26).[4] Even in the case of poetry and poetic license (*mā yaḥtamilu al-shiʿr*) words can only be used to signify their possible ranges of meanings, within the limits of the syntactically possible (Sībawayhi 1988/1: 26ff.).

In other contexts, Sībawayhi makes it clear that the listener's understanding is the aim that underpins his grammar, in line with Marogy's analysis. For example, his discussion of ellipsis or omission of a word. This is done when the listener is assumed to know who or what is meant, so that explicit utterance of a specific word becomes semantically superfluous: "you will use ellipsis when you can assume that the addressee already knows who you intend" (*annaka innamā tuḍmir ḥīna turā anna al-muḥaddath qad ʿarafa man taʿnī*) (Sībawayhi 1988/2: 11). Similarly, he declares that if the speaker is speaking about a man and wants to clearly distinguish (*yubayyin*) who he means for the addressee, he adds a qualifier (*ṣifa*) for distinction,

4 See also Versteegh (1993: 34) for a list of these categories.

for example, adding his name: "Zayd", or "the tall one", if there are several Zayds (Sībawayhi 1988/2: 12). Thus, the logical, the semantic, and the syntactic converge with the speaker's aim of conveying to the listener the intended meaning.

Although Sībawayhi frequently adduces Qur'ānic examples of syntax or words, as mentioned in Chapter 2, he never explicitly identifies his grammatical terms with Qur'ānic terms. Not even *mustaqīm*, which famously occurs in Q. 1 (*al-Fātiḥa*), verse 6:

> 1. By God's name 'Giver of Life', 'Continuous Protector of Life' (*bi-ism Allāh al-Raḥmān al-Raḥīm*):
> 2. Praise belongs to God, Lord of the knowing beings (*al-ḥamdu li-Allāhi rabb al-'ālamīn*),
> 3. Giver of Life, Continuous Protector of Life (*al-Raḥmān al-Raḥīm*),
> 4. King of the Day of Judgement (*māliki yawm al-dīn*)!
> 5. You we serve and You we ask for protection (*iyyāka na'bud wa iyyāka nasta'īn*):
> 6. Guide us along **the path of correct speech and action** (*ihdinā* ***al-ṣirāṭ al-mustaqīm***),
> 7. The path of those on who You conferred material blessings, without being angry with them, for they do not stray (*ṣirāṭ alladhīna an'amta 'alayhim ghayr al-maghḍūbi 'alayhim wa lā al-ḍāllīn*)!

Sībawayhi refers to the term *al-ṣirāṭ al-mustaqīm* once, and then not to Q. 1, 6 but Q. 42 (*al-Shūrā*), 52–53:

> (52) In this way We communicated to you a spirit by Our command. You were not aware of what the divine writing is, nor of what enactment of security is, but We made it a light by which We guide whoever We wish among Our servants. Indeed, you will guide to **a correct path (*ṣirāṭin mustaqīmin*)**,
> (53) **The path of God (*ṣirāṭi Allāh*)**, to Who belongs what is in the heavens and what is on the land: is it not to God that all matters lead?

He does not go into the meaning of *mustaqīm* in this Qur'ān context, which he seems to take for granted. Instead, he refers to the verses to illustrate case agreement between verse 52, '*ṣirāṭin mustaqīmin*' in genitive inflection, and its qualifying '*ṣirāṭi Allāh*' in verse 53, which must also be in the genitive case (Sībawayhi 1988/2: 14). This is what the grammatical technical term *i'rāb* refers to: to make syntactically correct vowel inflections

However, as we saw in Chapter 3, al-Ṭabarī explained *al-ṣirāṭ al-mustaqīm* in Q. 1, 6 as referring to the sum of the Covenantal terms, which humans should fulfil through speech (*qawl*) and action (*ʿamal*) (1995/1: 1, 110). Although al-Ṭabarī did not explicitly define *mustaqīm* as a grammatical term, he did understand it as 'correctness', as the following quote shows: "God qualified [this path of speech and action] by **correctness**, because it is attainment of what is right and does not contain faults" (*wa innamā waṣafahu Allāh bi-l-**istiqāma** liʾannahu ṣawāb lā khaṭaʾ fīhi*) (1995/1: 1, 112). Combining al-Ṭabarī and Sībawayhi thus makes it possible to see *al-ṣirāṭ al-mustaqīm* in Q. 1, 6 as referring to correct Arabic speech in the grammatical and semantic sense, and the deeds that turn the speech into action, which is the pragmatist and legal-ethical aim.

Viewed from the perspective of al-Fārābī's theory of prophetic religious language as conveying philosophical-theoretical truth through images, 'the correct *path'* can be seen as an image conveying the linguistic theory that the Qurʾānic guidance is grammatically correct speech that defines specific categories and courses of action. In this way, one can see the opening Qurʾānic *sūra* as introducing the canonical corpus by invoking a linguistic term, just as al-Fārābī began his list of sciences with linguistics: language is the medium for communicating both divine and scholarly *ʿilm*.

PROPHETIC *ḤADĪTH*

The beginnings of the discipline of *ḥadīth* or reports from the Prophet is traceable to the late 600s–early 100s/700s, if discipline is understood as the existence of a written genre, albeit one that was fragmentary and based on notes from lectures.[5] Gregor Schoeler has singled out as representing this early stage of *ḥadīth* the 'Successor' (*tābiʿ*) ʿUrwa b. al-Zubayr (d. *c.* 94/712) from Medina. ʿUrwa was the son of one of the Prophet's cousins and nephew of the Prophet's wife ʿĀʾisha bint Abī Bakr (d. 59/678), who is one of his authoritative sources. He was biographer of the Prophet and one of Ibn Isḥāq's main sources (see Chapter 5), and *ḥadīth* collector. His *ḥadīth*, which are said to have been written, featured the transmission chain (*isnād*) and treated topics of legal and ritual nature, for example 'divorce' (*ṭalāq*), including 'divorce initiated by the wife' (*khulʿ*), and 'pilgrimage' (*ḥajj*). Consequently, they represent the distinct *ḥadīth* methodology and generic form of 'topic', which characterise the later compilations dating to the second half of the 100s/700s. These are considerably expanded and organise topical *ḥadīth* into chapters, in the genre *muṣannafāt*. The Medinan

5 For a brief state of the art on the emergence of written collections, see Claude Gilliot's introduction to Schoeler (1997), pp. 423–424; see also Schoeler (2010: 201–202).

legal scholar Mālik b. Anas' (d. 179/795) collection *al-Muwaṭṭa'*, and the compilations of Aḥmad b. Ḥanbal's (d. 241/855) students al-Bukhārī (d. 256/870) and Muslim (d. 262/875), are examples of this genre (Schoeler 2010: 202–203).

Schoeler (2010) has also argued that the early production of written *ḥadīth* compilations replicates the production of written Qur'ān manuscripts, though at a slightly later stage. Thus, just as the Qur'ān emerged through the collection of written partial collections, resulting in around 650 in the full codex form, *ḥadīth* emerged from partial collections into the fuller compilations evident from the late 700s. Given that, as we saw in Chapter 3, the earliest Qur'ān codices date to the late 600s, the beginning of *ḥadīth* as a discipline thus coincides in time with the more widespread 'publication' of Qur'ān manuscripts (see also Schoeler 1997).[6] Considering the topics of 'Urwa's early *ḥadīth*s, they appear to systematize and develop the practical implications of Qur'ānic principles and rulings.[7] Accordingly, the form in which Mālik b. Anas' (d. 179/795) *ḥadīth* collection *al-Muwaṭṭa'* was transmitted in several versions by his students is as a work in jurisprudence (*fiqh*) (Schoeler 2010: 203); it is even the earliest full treatise in jurisprudence.[8]

As for the Shī'ī branch, the Twelvers began the process of collecting *ḥadīth* slightly later than the emergence of the first full compilations in the proto-Sunnī sphere, in the two centuries following the 'occultation' (*ghayba*) of the twelfth Imam in 260/873-4. This coincided politically with Persian Buyid rule in Baghdad and the eastern parts of the Abbasid Caliphate (945–1050), under which Twelver Shī'a enjoyed official sponsoring. The most authoritative are 'the four written collections' (*al-kutub al-arba'a*), attributed to three legal scholars: al-Kulaynī (d. 329/940-1) and his *al-Kāfī fī 'ilm al-dīn*, Ibn Bābawayh al-Qummī's (d. 380/991) *Man lā yaḥḍuruhu al-faqīh*, and al-Ṭūsī's (d. 460/1067) *Tahdhīb al-aḥkām* and *al-Istibṣār fīmā ukhtulifa fīhi min al-akhbār*. These consist of reports from the Imams in the Twelver genealogy, on doctrinal, legal and ritual topics, which were current across 'sectarian' divides (Newman 2000).

6 Schoeler (2010b) has also used these findings to critique John Wansbrough's thesis (1977), that the Qur'ān and the Prophetic tradition emerge together and simultaneously, and turn into written corpora first in the 200s/800s.

7 For example, 'divorce' is treated in Q. 2 (*al-Baqara*), 227–232, 236–237, 241; Q. 4 (*al-Nisā'*), 20–21, 35; Q. 33 (*al-Aḥzāb*), 28–29, 37, 49, 52; Q. 58 (*al-Mujādila*), 1–4; Q. 65 (*al-Ṭalāq*), 1–7; and Q. 66 (*al-Taḥrīm*), 5.

8 For a discussion of the transmission of *al-Muwaṭṭa'*, and a survey of critical debates about dating, see the Introduction to Mohammad Fadel's and Connell Monette's new English translation (2019).

Similarly on the Sunnī side a process of consolidation and authorisation was taking place, which has been described in terms of the 'canonization' of especially al-Bukhārī's and Muslim's collections. Jonathan Brown (2011) has argued that among the numerous *ḥadīth* collections circulating in the 200s/800s and 300s/900s, none was considered more authoritative than others. Such a ranking process began only in the 400s/1000s and 500s/1100s, when the Turkish Saljuqs had taken over rule in Baghdad and consolidated Sunnī law and theology, and leading jurists working primarily within the Shāfʿī school of law and Ashʿarī theology focused particularly on al-Bukhārī's and Muslim's collections. Eventually, this led to their 'canonisation' as the two most authoritative Sunnī collections, followed by Abū Dāwūd (d. 276/889), al-Tirmidhī (d. 279/892), al-Nasāʾī (d. 303/915), and Ibn Māja (d. 274/887). Together, these make up the Sunnī 'six written collections' (*al-kutub al-sitta*), complemented by Mālik's *al-Muwaṭṭaʾ* and Aḥmad b. Ḥanbal's *Musnad*, and some others.

Brown does not think that Twelver Shīʿism played any significant role as 'opposed others' for the formation of a Sunnī *ḥadīth* canon (2011: 372–374). Nevertheless, the Sunnī canonization follows after the production of the Shīʿī compilations from the Imams under Buyid rule during the 900s and early 1000s. Hence, one can imagine a mutual process within the two main branches. An interesting detail in this respect is that both the Sunnī six and the Shīʿī four authoritative collections contain some hundred so-called *ḥadīth qudsī*, 'sacred *ḥadīth*', which transmit extra-Qurʾānic *divine* sayings through the Prophet (or other prophets) or the Imams. Both Sunnī and Shīʿī *ḥadīth* collections thus also transmit the divine knowledge that defines scholarly *walāya*. From the 600s/1200s, these *ḥadīth qudsī* exist also as separate collections.[9] Again, this coincides with institutional developments, since we are now in the period when *walāya* established on a universal scale in the form of *ṭuruq* and their knowledge transmissions, as discussed in Chapter 5.

For illustration, I have selected a few *ḥadīth* on the topic of Covenant and its terms, starting with the Sunnī collections. In al-Bukhārī's book on God's Oneness (*Kitāb al-tawḥīd*), Chapter 1, 'The Prophet (pbuh) invites his community to declare God's Oneness', we find the following *ḥadīth* on God's and the servants' mutual rights:

> Muḥammad b. Bashshār – Ghundar – Shuʿba – Abū Ḥaṣīn, and al-Ashʿath b. Sulaym – al-Aswad b. Hilāl – Muʿādh b. Jabal, who said: "The Prophet (pbuh) said: 'O Muʿādh! Do you know what God's right (*ḥaqq*) from His servants is?' I said: 'God and His Messenger have the

9 See entry by William Graham, "Ḥadīth qudsī", *Encyclopaedia of Islam*, 3rd ed.

> most knowledge!' He said: 'That they serve Him and do not assign anything as partner to Him! Do you know what their right from Him is?' I said: 'God and His Messenger have the most knowledge!' He said: 'That He does not punish them!'"

God's obligation to provide sustenance to all, including the rejecters, appears in the same book, Chapter 3, 'Indeed, God is the One Who Provides Sustenance, Owner of Power, The Strong'. This particular *ḥadīth* reflects the point about correct speech as well: one should not say wrong things about God, even though He provides sustenance also for those who do so, as we have seen several examples of from the Qur'ān:

> ʿAbdān – Abū Ḥamza – al-Aʿmash – Saʿīd b. Jubayr – Abū ʿAbd al-Raḥmān al-Sulamī – Abū Mūsā al-Ashʿarī, who said: "The Prophet (pbuh) said: 'No one is more forbearing with words that he hears than God: they ascribe children to Him, yet He bestows on them good health and material sustenance!'"

Similarly, Chapter 24, 'Some faces on that Day shall be [gazing], gazing towards their Lord', contains a prayer, in which the Covenantal terms are listed:

> Thābit b. Muḥammad – Sufyān – Ibn Jurayj – Sulaymān al-Aḥwal – Ṭāwūs – Ibn ʿAbbās, who said: "Whenever the Prophet (pbuh) offered his Tahajjud prayer at night, he would say: 'O God, our Lord! The praise belongs to You: You are the Maintainer of the heavens and the land! The praise belongs to You: You are the Lord of the heavens and the land and what is in them! The praise belongs to You: You are the Light of the heavens and the land and what is in them! You are the True Right (*al-ḥaqq*), Your speech is True Right, Your promise is True Right, Your encounter is True Right, the garden is True Right, the fire is True Right, and the hour is True Right! O God, for You I have enacted peace, by You I have enacted security, in You as legal guardian I have put my trust (*tawakkaltu*), for You I have disputed, and by You I have given rulings: So forgive me for what I have committed and for what I will commit, and what I have done in secret and in public, and for the things You have more knowledge of than I do: there is no god but You!'"

An example of a *ḥadīth qudsī* from al-Bukhārī's collection, also the Book on God's Oneness, is the following, where the Covenantal mutual relationship between God and humans is described as a communicative one where God responds to the calls from each individual servant, and adds to them. Note the special genre, in which the Prophet reports sayings from God:

> ʿUmar b. Ḥafṣ – his father – al-Aʿmash – Abū Ṣāliḥ – Abū Hurayra, who said: "The Prophet (pbuh) said: 'God, Exalted is He, says: "I am by My servant's thought of Me, and I am with him when he recalls and honours Me. When he honours Me within himself, I honour him within Myself, and if he honours Me in a gathering of people, I honour him in a better group. If he draws closer to Me by a fraction, I draw closer to him by a cubit; and if he draws closer to Me by a cubit, I draw closer to him by two arms-widths; and if he comes to Me walking, I come to him running!"

In the same chapter, a connection between keeping the terms of God's Covenant and fulfilling oaths and contracts with people is established. This *ḥadīth* also implicitly alludes to the prayer in Q. 1, 7, to not be among those with who God is angry (*ghayr al-maghḍūb ʿalayhim*), by specifying what it is that makes God angry, namely to appropriate wealth through deceptive oaths (*yamīn kādhib*). The point being, that 'deceptive speech' has concrete, legal implications. An explicit reference to the Qurʾān concludes the report, specifically Q. 3 (*Āl ʿImrān*), 77:

> Al-Ḥumaydī – Sufyān – ʿAbd al-Malik b. Aʿyan, and Jāmiʿ b. Abī Rāshid – Abū Wāʾil – ʿAbd Allāh [b. ʿAbbās], who said: "God's Messenger (pbuh) said: 'When he who takes for himself as fief the landed property of a Muslim person through a deceptive oath (*biyamīn kādhib*) meets God, He will be angry (*ghaḍbān*) with him!' ʿAbd Allāh said: 'Then God's Messenger (pbuh) read its corresponding confirmation from God's writing, Majestic is His Honour: "Indeed, those who purchase through God's contract and their oaths for a small price shall have no share in the furthest existence, nor will God speak to them" (Q. 3, 77).

In the Book on Blood Money (*kitāb al-diyāt*) in al-Tirmidhī's collection, the following report establishes the same obligating relationship between God's contract and human contracts:

> Muḥammad b. Bashshār – Maʿdī b. Sulaymān – Ibn ʿAjlān – his father – Abū Hurayra – the Prophet (pbuh), who said: "Whoever kills a person who has entered a contract with protection from God and a protection from His Messenger has certainly violated God's protection, so he shall not get to smell the fragrance of the Garden, even though its fragrance can be sensed from the distance of seventy autumns!"

Another example is from al-Nasāʾī's collection, the Book on the Ethics of Judges (*kitāb adab al-qāḍī*). Here, the Prophet serves as the model for judges on how to rule in cases where there is no evidence, only assertions backed by oaths:

> ʿAlī b. Saʿīd b. Masrūq – Yaḥyā b. Abī Zāʾida – Nāfiʿ b. ʿUmar – Ibn Abī Mulayka, who said: "There were two maids in the city of al-Ṭāʾif who used to do leatherwork. One of them came out with her hand bleeding and claiming that her companion had injured her, but the other one denied it. I wrote to Ibn ʿAbbās about it, and he wrote back: 'God's Messenger (pbuh) has ruled that the person against who the claim is made should take an oath, for if people were to be given what they claimed they would make claims for the property and blood of others. So invite her and recite to her this sign: "Indeed, those who purchase through God's contract and their oaths for a small price shall have no share in the furthest existence" (Q. 3, 77), until the sign is completed'. So I invited her and recited to her, and she acknowledged that. That pleased him.

Finally, Covenant as the contract with God and the social contract with His Messenger is stated in Ibn Māja's collection, the chapter on tribulations (*al-balāʾ*):

> Maḥmūd b. Khālid al-Dimashqī – Sulaymān b. ʿAbd al-Raḥmān Abū Ayyūb – Ibn Abī Mālik – his father – ʿAṭāʾ b. Abī Rabāḥ – ʿAbd Allāh b. ʿUmar, who said: "God's Messenger (pbuh) approached us and said: 'O Migrants! Five things may afflict you, which I seek refuge from God that you will not have to experience: Immorality never appears among a people to the extent that they commit it openly without plagues and diseases unknown to their predecessors afflict them. They do not cheat on weights and scales without being stricken with famine, severe calamity, and brutal rulers. They do not withhold the welfare tax on their landed property without rain being withheld from the sky, and were it not for the cattle, no rain would fall on them. They do not break their contract with God and the contract with His Messenger without God enabling their enemies to overpower them and take some of what they possess. Unless their leaders pass judgement by God's writing and do the good according to what God has sent down, God will make them fight each other.

This list of prohibited acts and their consequences draws on the Qurʾānic historical, paradigmatic examples. While it can be seen as simply a list of threatening deterrents from unwanted behaviour, the connections between specific practices and outcomes are interesting considering the issue of 'empirical observation'. Arguably, illicit sexual relations may contribute to spreading disease, and cheating on market rules may cause weak groups to starve and rebel, disrupting agricultural production and encouraging tyrannical rule. While holding back rainfall is clearly beyond human capacity, all the other acts and consequences are fully explicable through 'normal' societal cause and effect. In other words, while the consequences are depicted in 'image-language' as God punishing the people, most of them are also observable outcomes following from certain actions.

Examples of the topic of property rights to land appear in al-Bukhārī's Book on the Beginning of Creation (*kitāb bad' al-khalq*), in the second chapter entitled "What has been said about Seven Earths". The title refers to Q. 65 (*al-Ṭalāq*), 12: "God is the one Who has created seven distinct heavens and their likes of the land, with the command descending between them so that you may know that God is in full control over every single thing, and that God envelops each thing with knowledge". Three versions of a *ḥadīth* explain the "seven earths" implied in the verse with reference to the punishment for unjust acquisition of land, which is then one of the things about which God has full knowledge:

> ʿAlī b. ʿAbd Allāh – Ibn ʿUlayya – ʿAlī b. al-Mubārak – Yaḥyā b. Abī Kathīr – Muḥammad b. Ibrahīm b. al-Ḥārith – Abū Salama b. ʿAbd al-Raḥmān [who narrated that] there was a dispute between him and some people about land, so he went to ʿĀʾisha and told her about it. She said: "O Abū Salama, stay on your side of the land [boundary] (*ijtanib al-arḍ*), for indeed, God's Messenger (pbuh) has said: 'May anyone who wrongly appropriates even an inch be enveloped by seven earths! (*man ẓalama qīda shibrin ṭuwwiqahu min sabʿi arḍīna*)"

> Bishr b. Muḥammad – ʿAbd Allāh – Mūsā b. ʿUqba – Sālim – his father, who said: "The Prophet (pbuh) said: 'Anyone who takes anything from the land without right will on the Day of Standing to Trial be made to sink through seven earths! (*man akhadha shayʾan min al-arḍ bighayri ḥaqqin khusifa bihi yawm al-qiyāma ilā sabʿi arḍīna*)"

> ʿUbayd b. Ismāʿīl – Abū Usāma – Hishām – his father – Saʿīd b. Zayd b. ʿAmr b. Nufayl [who narrated] that Arwā had taken a dispute with him to Marwān over a right she claimed he had withheld from her. Saʿīd said: "How could I withhold anything from her right? I testify that I myself heard God's Messenger (pbuh) say: 'Anyone who takes anything of the land wrongfully shall on the Day of Standing to Trial be enveloped by seven earths! (*man akhadha shayʾan min al-arḍ ẓulman faʾinnahu yuṭawwaquhu yawm al-qiyāma min sabʿi arḍīna*)"

In al-Bukhārī's Book on Knowledge (*kitāb al-'ilm*) the topic of land appears in reports about the proper management of its produce:

> Al-Ḥumaydī – Sufyān – Ismā'īl b. Abī Khālid, in another version than the one al-Zuhrī reported to us – Qays b. Abī Ḥāzim – 'Abd Allāh b. Mas'ūd, who said: "The Prophet (pbuh) said: 'Do not desire to be like anyone except in two cases: A man who God has given landed property and who is made to govern over its spending for what is right (*fasulliṭa 'alā halakatihi fī al-ḥaqq*); and a man who God has given capacity for just judgement (*al-ḥikma*) and who judges by it and conveys knowledge about it!'"

Also related to land are the books on topics such as sharecropping (*muzāra'a*), which meant that a farmer rented land and paid the landlord a share of the harvest. The cases and conditions related to this topic reflect a complex legal issue, which I cannot go into here. Yet in al-Bukhārī's Book on Sharecropping several reports agree that the Prophet prohibited this practice for Muslims, even though some Companions unknowingly of the prohibition had continued it. Instead, the Prophet insisted that lands be farmed by those who own them, or else given to those who can farm them; in both cases, the peasants become the owners. For example:

> Sulaymān b. Ḥarb – Ḥammād – Ayyūb – Nāfi', that Ibn 'Umar used to rent his farms in the time of Abū Bakr, 'Umar, 'Uthmān, and in the early days of Mu'āwiya. Then he was told the narration of Rāfi' b. Khadīj that the Prophet (pbuh) had forbidden the renting of farmlands (*nahā 'an kirā' al-mazāri'*). Ibn 'Umar went to Rāfi' and I accompanied him. He asked Rāfi', who replied that the Prophet (pbuh) had forbidden the renting of farmlands. Ibn 'Umar said, "You know that we used to rent our farmlands in the lifetime of God's Messenger (pbuh) for the yield of the banks of the water streams and for a certain amount of figs".

A final report on this topic relates to Retsö's (2003) theses, that the Arabs were predominantly farmers, settled in villages. The following incident is reported in al-Bukhārī's Book on Sharecropping:

> Muḥammad b. Sinān – Fulayḥ – Hilāl – 'Abd Allāh b. Muḥammad – Abū 'Āmir, and Fulayḥ – Hilāl b. 'Alī – 'Aṭā' b. Yasār – Abū Hurayra, who said: "Once the Prophet (pbuh) was giving an account, while a bedouin (*rajul min ahl al-bādiya*) was sitting with him: 'One of the inhabitants of the Garden will ask his Lord to allow him to cultivate the land, and He will say to him: 'Are you not in what you desired?' He will say: 'I am, but I love cultivating the land!' The Prophet (pbuh)

continued: 'When the man sows the seeds and the plants grow up and get ripe, ready for reaping and the harvest piles up as hills, God will say to him: 'O son of Adam! Here you are, nothing (else) satisfies you!' On that, the bedouin (*al-aʿrābī*) said: 'The man must be either from Quraysh or an Anṣārī, for they are friends of farming, whereas we are not friends of farming!' Then the Prophet (pbuh) laughed."

For a brief comparison, we can look at the Twelver Shīʿī al-Kulaynī's *al-Kāfī*. Whereas the Sunnī collections tend to cover the topic in the book and section at hand by giving series of short *ḥadīth* treating various aspects of it, al-Kulaynī merges reports into longer topical treatises in a discursive, narrative form. He also introduces the collection with an opening address (*khuṭbat al-kitāb*). The Prophet's legacy is God's writing, al-Kulaynī explains, and the Imam discourses logically on behalf of God about the writing (*yanṭiq al-imām ʿan Allāh fī al-kitāb*), guiding the servants so that they fulfil their obligation to obey God and the Imam's protective governorship (*walāya*). In this way, the Imam ensures the completion of the judicial order and its enlightenment by God's light so that true right and justice are preserved (al-Kulaynī 1961/1: 4). With the end of the succession of Imams, 'those possessing knowledge' (*al-ʿulamāʾ*) preserve their knowledge. These are further qualified as 'the people of sound veracity and peace' (*ahl al-ṣiḥḥa wa al-salāma*), who therefore have the authority to issue commands and prohibitions, and to obligate the people through them (*taklīf*) (al-Kulaynī 1961/1: 5). Al-Kulaynī then refers to the Qurʾānic Covenant as the contractual obligation upon *ahl al-ṣiḥḥa wa al-salāma* to guide the servants according to God's writing, citing Q. 7 (*al-Aʿrāf*), 169 (al-Kulaynī 1961/1: 6):

> (169) Has not the Covenant of the divine writing been taken from them, that they must not state upon God except what is right?

In this context, the reference reflects a social contract, since the legal scholars ruled the Twelver Shīʿī community during the Imam's occultation. The social-contract issues of due consideration and deliberation are expressed as the scholars' obligation to truth and right (*ḥaqq*), to give proof (*ḥujja*) for their statements, and to respond to the community's questions (al-Kulaynī 1961/1: 6). Accordingly, the collection includes a section with chapters on visits to the tombs of the Prophet and the Imams or the sanctuaries with their relics (*abwāb al-ziyārāt*), which for this community complement the pilgrimage to the Kaʿba and visit to Medina (al-Kulaynī 1961/4).

An illustrative example is the first report in the Book on God's Oneness (*kitāb al-tawḥīd*) and the metaphysical topic of God's origination of the world. The report, which is very long, describes how an Egyptian *zindīq* ('heretic', possibly pagan philosopher or proponent of ontological dualism) gets word of the knowledge of ʿAlī's son al-Ḥusayn who resided in Medina. The *zindīq* travels to Medina, but learns upon arrival that al-Ḥusayn has gone to Mecca. He then sets off to Mecca, and finds al-Ḥusayn in a group of companions circumambulating the Kaʿba. In this setting, by the Kaʿba, al-Ḥusayn engages the *zindīq* in a question-and-answer session, which makes the latter see that the One God must logically be the Originator of the heavens and the land and all that is in them. He exclaims that no one else has engaged with him in this way before – a testimony to the scholarly obligation to convey knowledge and proof (al-Kulaynī 1961/1: 72–76).

Reason is at the forefront also in the book with the telling title On Intellect and Ignorance (*kitāb al-ʿaql wa al-jahl*). In this final example, ʿAlī voices the argument that intellect and *dīn* are one and the same, and the rational proof is that *dīn* produces *amn*, 'security', without which life is not worth living:

> Muḥammad b. Yaḥyā (…) said: "The Commander of Those Who Enact Security said: 'Anyone whose disposition to do good makes him side with me, I shall because of it forbear and forgive what was lost besides it, though I shall never forgive the loss of intellect or judicial order because departing from the judicial order is departing from security (*liʾanna mufāraqat al-dīn mufāraqat al-amn*). Since there is no pleasure to life with fear, the loss of intellect is the loss of life and is only analogous with the dead.

To summarise: the discipline of *ḥadīth* can be seen as simultaneously systematizing the Qurʾānic knowledge and expanding it, by relating it to a range of topics. While these do not always refer to a specific Qurʾānic verse, many of them retain a referential relationship with the Qurʾān. The examples selected here show how Covenant with the One God is conceptualised as a contract with mutual rights and obligations, which also expands into the obligation to fulfil other contracts and oaths, including loyalty to the Prophet, the Imams, and the scholars, *because of the common good that their legal authority enacts*. Hence, the examples show that the social contract-aspect of Covenant is evident also in *ḥadīth*. The scientific issue of observation-based knowledge is another way in which *ḥadīth* refer to Qurʾānic topics; for example, the list of specific actions and their consequences, which draws on Qurʾānic narratives of historical peoples and their experiences. Similarly, the last example from al-Kulaynī's collection reasons with reference to known facts about life without security. Finally, as for al-Fārābī's theory of prophetic language, *ḥadīth* certainly concretise theoretical matters, by locating them in events and narrations about community affairs and deliberations, conveyed in image-rich language.

POLITICAL SCIENCE (*SIYĀSA*) AND ADMINISTRATION (*TADBĪR*)

The third selected discipline is political science and administration. I begin this section with three examples of political theory related to constitutional separation of powers and social contract, and then continue with a discussion about the relationship between administration and science.

Separation of Powers and Social Contract

Among the earliest political theoretical writings are those by the scribe Ibn al-Muqaffaʿ (d. *ca.* 140/757), mentioned in Chapter 5 in connection with separation of powers and the theory of the Caliph as lawmaker. Ibn al-Muqaffaʿ construed his theory as a genealogical continuity with the pre-Islamic Sassanid imperial administration and its legacy of *ḥikma* i.e. capacity for just judgement. In the treatise *Kalīla wa Dimna*, which is a narration through fables and dialoguing animals, Ibn al-Muqaffaʿ singles out the famous Sassanid Shah Khusraw Anūshirwān (r. 531–579), who reportedly had acquired *ḥikma* from 'the kings of India' (*mulūk al-Hind*) and the advice (*naṣīḥa*) that they in turn got from a Brahmin philosopher (*faylasūf*). At the behest of the Indian king, this philosopher wrote down his advice, the substance of which Ibn al-Muqaffaʿ says is conveyed in *Kalīla wa Dimna*. In actual terms, *Kalīla wa Dimna* was the fruit of Ibn al-Muqaffaʿs translation into Arabic of a Pahlavi translation of the Sanskrit treatise *Panchatantra*.[10] Presumably, the political context was significant. During Ibn al-Muqaffaʿs career the Hashimite Abbasids, with their support in the eastern, former Sassanid regions of the Caliphal realm, had emerged as claimants to the

10 See the collection of Ibn al-Muqaffaʿs writings, *ʾĀthār Ibn al-Muqaffaʿ* (1989), including e.g. *Kalīla wa Dimna*, *al-ʾAdab al-kabīr*, *al-ʾAdab al- ṣaghīr*, *Risāla fī al-ṣaḥāba*, and *al-Durra al-yatīma*; for *Kalīla wa Dimna*, pp. 3–244. I will refer to it as Ibn al-Muqaffaʿ (1989). On the translation, Hermansen (2013: 341, n. 2).

Caliphate against the Syria-based Umayyads, and Muslim commanders had made inroads into Sind in western India. Thus, Ibn al-Muqaffaʿ incorporated what he perceived to be important administrative knowledge pertaining to these regions into his political theory.

Kalīla wa Dimna has an interesting relationship with the Qurʾān. It reflects the theory that the king is prone to becoming a tyrant 'idol' (*ṭāghī*), who oppresses the people unless he gains access to *ḥikma*, through advice (*naṣīḥa*) from philosophers and scholars (*ʿulamāʾ*). The latter group are obligated to provide the advice no matter the considerable risks involved, for the king regularly abuses his unlimited powers whenever annoyed. Since the scholars must give advice for the sake of the good (*ṣalāḥ*) of the people, they should do so by making the ruler see the truth himself. For this purpose, they can use paradigmatic accounts (*qiṣaṣ*) and examples (*amthāl*), and offer the king trustworthy friendship without harping on about his abuses, lest he let anger and embarrassment block him from taking the good path of action. *Kalīla wa Dimna* is thus defined as a writing (*kitāb*), which offers its advice through 'the languages of animals and birds', to illustrate the general principles pertaining to *ḥikma* and its arts and sources (Ibn al-Muqaffaʿ 1989: 3). Though Ibn al-Muqaffaʿ does not compare *Kalīla wa Dimna* with the Qurʾān, the same advice method is reflected in verses about the prophet-king David – who is also associated with birds. Through an example, God makes David see that he is guilty of having his companion Uriya killed out of desire for his only wife Bat-Sheva, even though David himself was already married; then God forgives his transgression once he sees it himself:

Q. 38 (*Ṣād*), 17–26:

(17) Bear patiently what they say and **recall with honour (*udhkur*)** Our servant David, the one with support: he was indeed one who returns!
(18) We have subjected the mountains together with him, to glorify at sunset and daybreak,
(19) And **the birds** were called upon: each one returning to him!
(20) We strengthened [David's] kingdom by giving him **the capacity for just judgement** and the ability to make distinctions in public speeches (*ātaynāhu* ***al-ḥikma*** *wa faṣl al-khiṭāb*):
(21) Has the announcement reached you of the adversaries when they scaled the walls of the sanctuary?
(22) When they entered and came upon David, he was afraid of them. They said: 'Do not fear! We are two adversaries, one of us having abused the other, so judge between us by what is right (*bi-l-ḥaqq*), and do not transgress but guide us to the equitable path (*sawāʾ al-ṣirāṭ*):

> (23) So, here is my brother, who has ninety-nine ewes while I have only one. He said: "Let me be its guardian!" and he overcame me through the argumentation (*fī al-khiṭāb*).'
> (24) [David] said: 'He has wronged you by asking for your ewe in addition to his ewes! Indeed, many companions have abused one another, except those who have come to enact security and work for the common good, but how few they are!' It occurred to David that We had tried him, so he asked his Lord for forgiveness and fell down on his knees and returned.
> (25) So We forgave him that, and indeed, he has a close relationship with Us and a good shelter!
> (26) O David, We have made you a vicegerent (*khalīfa*) on the land, so judge between the people by the true right and do not follow your urges, for they will lead you astray from the duties towards God (*sabīl Allāh*); indeed, those who lead astray from the duties towards God will have a harsh punishment for having forgotten the Day of the Account (*yawm al-ḥisāb*)!

This advice perspective on the Qur'ān suggests that Ibn al-Muqaffaʿ could have drawn on Qur'ānic concepts related to *ḥikma* when he wrote *Kalīla wa Dimna*.

In other Qur'ānic contexts, *ḥikma* is invoked rhetorically, as a reason for accepting the message and its practical implications; e.g. Q. 43 (*al-Zukhruf*), 63, where it is presented as a solution to legal disagreement:

> (63) When Jesus brought the clear distinctions (*al-bayyināt*), he said: 'I have come to you with **the capacity for just judgement (*al-ḥikma*)** to make clearly distinct for you (*li'ubayyina lakum*) some of what you disagree about, so fulfil your obligations towards God and comply!'

The use of examples and parables, also seen in the David-example above as the recommended form of advice for testy rulers, occurs frequently across the Qur'ān. Q. 2 (*al-Baqara*), 26–27 illustrates the function of examples:

> (26) Indeed, God does not shy away from forging an **example** (*an yaḍriba* ***mathal***) even by something as small as a gnat, or larger: those who have come to enact security know that it is the true right from their Lord, but those who have rejected security say: 'What does God want with this?' An **example** by which He leads many astray, just as He leads many right, though He does not lead anyone astray by it except the rebellious ones,
> (27) those who break God's compact (*ʿahd Allāh*) after it has been firmly covenanted (*baʿda mīthāqihi*), and break apart what God has

> commanded to be joined, and promote voidable contracts in the land (*wa yufsidūna fī al-arḍ*): it is those who are the losers!

In Ibn al-Muqaffaʿ's *oeuvre*, the constitutional topic of separation of powers is treated in *Risāla fī al-ṣaḥāba*, 'Treatise on the Companions', which refers to the Caliphate and the companions of the Caliph i.e. his advisers (Ibn al-Muqaffaʿ 1989: 309–323). As mentioned, Lowry (2008) emphasises the *theoretical* nature of Ibn al-Muqaffaʿ's *Risāla fī al-ṣaḥāba*, as an argument for Caliphal law-making authority. This involved delineating between two categories of laws. Firstly, the laws and rules established in the scriptural sources, on which the ruler has no legal discretion, namely the ritual obligations, the *ḥalāl-ḥarām* rules, and 'the defined limits' (*ḥudūd*).[11] Secondly, topics where the ruler has sole discretion and authority, namely (1) military strategy; (2) collection and distribution of war spoils; (3) appointment and removal of officials; (4) legal interpretation for cases without precedent; (5) implementation of limits and rulings according to the divine writing and the *sunna* (*imḍāʾ al-ḥudūd wa al-aḥkām ʿalā al-kitāb wa al-sunna*) i.e. applying the source-based limits and rulings to new cases; (6) declaring war and concluding truces; and (7) accepting and disbursing property on behalf of the Muslims.

Within this structure, management of the land tax appears the main reason Ibn al-Muqaffaʿ advocated for Caliphal lawmaking authority. The argument runs as follows. God has invested the Caliph in his function as *amīr al-muʾminīna*, 'the Commander of the enactors of security', with the authority to command (*amr*). No one but he has the authority to implement the defined limits (*ḥudūd*) and the rulings in the divine writing (*kitāb*) and the *sunna*, to fight the enemy, and to take booty and distribute it among the Muslims. Since his authority is from God, the Commander's rule is just and clement, and the subjects or 'the flock' (*al-raʿiyya*) are obligated to obey him. However, the Commander does not have the authority to command anything counter to God's obligations, and should he do so, the subjects have the right to disobey him (Ibn al-Muqaffaʿ 1989: 312–313). It is also absolutely necessary, for the good of the people (*ṣalāḥ*), that the Commander be in charge of the land tax and pay the military, for if the military is in charge of taxation they will extort the people (Ibn al-Muqaffaʿ 1989: 314). The Commander must develop a documented, transparent system for the land tax, staffed with men educated to implement it (Ibn al-Muqaffaʿ 1989:

11 Here I have translated *ḥudūd* as 'defined limits', instead of Lowry's 'penal laws'; for the complete list with commentary, see Lowry (2008: 31–33, 38).

321–322). When delivering this advice, Ibn al-Muqaffaʿ uses the same verb *dhakara*, ‘mention, remember, recall, honour’ something, as is used in the Qurʾānic David-example, Q. 38, 17: ‘(…) recall with honour Our servant David’, although in the context of ‘reminding’ the Commander:

> Among that of which the Commander of the enactors of security is **honourably reminded** is the command of the land and the land tax (*mimmā* ***yudhkaru*** *bihi amīr al-muʾminīna amr al-arḍ wa al-kharāj*). Indeed, the most weighty of that and the greatest in importance, the most significant for provisions, and the closest in terms of peril is if that which is between his plains and his mountains does not have an explanation (*laysa lahā tafsīr*) of the dams and the villages, and the tax collectors do not have a command to adhere to, according to which they can make calculations, and by which they can relate to the rulers over the people of the land after they have grown attached to it through cultivating it and hoping it will favourably return the work of their hands (Ibn al-Muqaffaʿ 1989: 321).

Another Qurʾānic concept that Ibn al-Muqaffaʿ employs with reference to the land tax is the derivatives of *ṣ-l-ḥ*, which he uses in the sense of ‘the common good’ i.e. what benefits all the people. The following passage shows Ibn al-Muqaffaʿ premising ‘the common good’ upon the scholars’ divine knowledge, God being the power that transcends special interests:

> We have gained a knowledge, which is not mixed with any doubt: that no general public (*ʿāmma*) ever becomes inclined to promote the common good (*lam tuṣliḥ*) from within themselves, nor has the common good ever come to them, except from the direction of their specialists (*khāṣṣatihim*); and that no specialists ever become inclined to the common good from within themselves, nor has the common good ever come to them, except from the direction of their leader (*imāmihim*). That is because a number of people are in a state of weakness and lack of knowledge, and they cannot by themselves manage legal opinion, since they do not convey knowledge and cannot bring matters forward. But when God makes among them specialists from among the people of the judicial order and the rational [sciences; *al-ʿuqūl*] who see to them and listen to them, then their specialists will pay attention to the matters of the general public and approach them with commitment, advice, and persistence. It is a force that God made that, as a common good for their whole society (*lijamāʿatihim*), as a motivation for those inclined to the common good among the specialists, and as an increase of the blessings God thereby has given them, and a persuasive message towards attaining the good in its totality (*balāghan ilā al-khayri kullihi*). And

> the specialists' need for the leader through who God makes them promote the common good is like the general public's need for their specialists, and more than that. For through the leader God ensures their benefit, as he restrains their impeachers, and ensures their consensus in opinion and discourse, and clearly distinguishes for the general public their standing, and provides for them proofs and support in statements against anyone who makes acquisitions for himself from what constitutes their right (Ibn al-Muqaffa' 1989: 323).

There are several Qur'ānic instances where the root *ṣ-l-ḥ* appears to have a similar sense of 'common good', in contexts related to gardens and the upholding of right e.g. Q. 85 (*al-Burūj*), 11:

> (11) Indeed, those who have enacted security and **acted for the common good (*'amilū al-ṣāliḥāt*)** shall have **gardens** under which rivers flow: that is the great obtainment!

In Q. 103 (*al-'Aṣr*), 1–3, the connection is between *ṣ-l-ḥ* and right:

> (1) By the afternoon time (*wa al-'aṣr*):
> (2) Mankind is indeed in a state of loss,
> (3) Except those who have enacted security, **acted for the common good (*'amilū al-ṣāliḥāt*)**, obligate each other with **the true right (*bi-l-ḥaqq*)**, and obligate each other with steadfastness!

In Q. 4 (*al-Nisā'*), 113–114, *ṣ-l-ḥ* appears in connection with *ḥikma* and the knowledge that enables just judgement, which in turn promotes both individual good deeds and the common good:

> (113) If it were not for God's favour towards you and His life-protection, a group of them would have resolved to lead you astray; but they lead no one astray except themselves, and they do not harm you in any way. God has sent down to you the writing and **the capacity for just judgement (*al-ḥikma*)** and conveyed to you **knowledge** about that which you did not know, for God's favour towards you has been great!
> (114) There is nothing good (*khayr*) in much of their secret conversation, except in the case of those who command giving the alms, and doing good deeds, and **promoting the common good among the people (*iṣlāḥ bayna al-nās*)**. Whoever does that seeking to please God, We will grant him a vast reward!

In contexts related to land and the land tax, *ṣ-l-ḥ* sometimes occurs together with its opposite *f-s-d* e.g. *mufsid*, plural *mufsidūna*. As discussed in Chapter

5, in legal terminology related to sharecropping contracts *ijāra fāsida* is a contract that is 'voidable' because one of four items is not specified: size, quality and location of the plots; how the lands should be used; the duration of the tenancy; and the amount of the rent (Johansen 1988: 34). For example, in Q. 7, 56 and 85, and Q. 2, 27, the verb *afsada* has land as its objective, suggesting that the meaning 'promote voidable contracts' can be seen as a practice that is opposed to the common good. Thus, Q. 7, 56 and 85, and Q. 2, 27:

> (56) And **do not promote voidable contracts in the land after it is made to promote the common good (*wa lā tufsidū fī al-arḍ ba'da iṣlāḥihā*)**, but call on [God] in fear and hope: indeed, God's life-protection is close to those who do good (*al-muḥsinīna*)!
>
> (85) And to Midian [We sent] their brother Shu'ayb. He said: 'O my people! Serve God, you have no other god than He! A clear distinction has now come to you from your Lord, so fulfil the measure and the weight, and do not reduce for the people their things, and **do not promote voidable contracts in the land after it is made to promote the common good (*wa lā tufsidū fī al-arḍ ba'da iṣlāḥihā*)**! That is good for you, if you are enactors of security.
>
> (27) Those who break God's compact (*'ahd Allāh*) after it has been firmly covenanted (*ba'da mīthāqihi*), and break apart what God has commanded to be joined, and **promote voidable contracts in the land (*wa yufsidūna fī al-arḍ*)**: it is those who are the losers!

If we view Ibn al-Muqaffa''s advice and concept of the people's welfare and the common good from this perspective, his works can be seen as discourses that apply Qur'ānic concepts in the production of administrative knowledge and political theory. Furthermore, by tracing this knowledge to historical legacies of imperial administration, he grounded Qur'ānic concepts in 'observation' i.e. empirical experiences of above all the management of the land tax.

In this respect, one can compare Ibn al-Muqaffa' with al-Fārābī (d. 339/951), who worked during Abbasid rule just before Buyid ascendance in 945. In the treatise *Iḥṣā' al-'ulūm*, mentioned above, al-Fārābī states that political science (*al-'ilm al-madanī*) is based on observation (*mushāhada*) and experience (*tajriba*), like medicine (*al-ṭibb*). The role of political philosophy (*al-falsafa al-madaniyya*) is to examine the legacies (*sunan*) of kingdoms, and on that basis provide both the universal laws (*al-qawānīn al-kulliyya*) and the particular descriptions of each case (al-Fārābī 1953:

39). Regarding constitutional principles, Muhsin Mahdi has pointed out that al-Fārābī's Plato- and Aristotle-inspired theory of the virtuous political community (*al-madīna al-fāḍila*) presupposes the practical separation of powers between the Caliph and the legal scholars. However, in order for the city to flourish the ruler must have *ḥikma*, either in person or through the legal scholars, who must in turn master philosophy i.e. the knowledge of universals without which practical, particular knowledge is impossible (Mahdi 2001:166–167). The source of *ḥikma* is the divine communication, *waḥy*, through prophecy, which conveys practically useful knowledge, which people cannot gain through their own reasoning and experiences. Al-Fārābī identifies this divine knowledge with *al-milal* i.e. the religious communities, whose 'founders' received and transmitted the divine knowledge and duties (*sabīl*), which is the practical, useful expression of the same kind of knowledge of universals that philosophers can gain – i.e. *ḥikma*. People often object to this kind of knowledge because it challenges what they already know, al-Fārābī argued, but through edifying education (*ta'dīb*), they can acquire the habit of seeking and accepting the truth of the unknown when it confronts them (al-Fārābī 1953: 41–42). A similar sentiment is expressed throughout the Qur'ān and its examples of resistance against the prophets and messengers, for example in Q. 12 (*Yūsuf*), 108–111:

> (108) Say: 'This is the sum of my duties (*hādhā sabīlī*): I invite to God based on overview (*'alā baṣīratin*), I and those who follow me, for, praise be to God, I am not among those who assign partners!'
> (109) We only sent forth as messengers before you men from the inhabitants of the villages to who We communicated (*rijālan min ahl al-qurā nūḥī ilayhim*). Did they not travel in the land and see what the outcome was for those who came before them? Surely, the abode of the furthest end is better for those who fulfil their obligations; will you not be bound by reasoning?
> (110) When the messengers despaired thinking that they had been lied to, Our help to victory reached them and We saved those We wanted to, while the criminal people could not avert Our affliction!
> (111) Indeed, in these accounts about them (*qiṣaṣihim*) there is a transmitted lesson to those with discerning intellects! It is not an invented report but verification of what came before it, and a detailed exposition of each thing, and guidance and life-protection for a people who enact security!

In *Majmū' fī al-siyāsa* ('Collected writings on statecraft'), under the rubric *al-nubuwwāt*, 'matters of prophecy', al-Fārābī also connected prophecy with *ṣ-l-ḥ*, 'the common good'. He explains that prophets are those who are more capable than others of receiving the divine communication and who, based on this power and understanding, can "open the path to guidance for the rulings and the method-ways that invite to the common good for the creatures" (*tashrīʿ al-aḥkām wa nahj al-subul al-dāʿiya ilā ṣalāḥ al-khalq*) (al-Fārābī, *Majmūʿ*: 13). This complements his model of prophetic language as aiming at persuading the people of the good of the law, through images and rhetoric, as discussed above. However, it should be noted that his Plato- and Aristotle-inspired focus on the city's prosperity and the happiness of the citizens is very much in line with the principles and concepts in the Prophet's Biography, as discussed in Chapter 5.

One century later, in the overlap between the Buyids and the Saljuqs, the famous Shāfiʿī jurist and political scientist al-Māwardī (d. 450/1058) developed his theory of legitimate leadership (*imāma*) in the treatise *al-Aḥkām al-sulṭāniyya*, 'The Rulings on Governmental Power'. He defined political leadership as the succession to prophecy (*khilāfat al-nubuwwa*) tasked with protecting the judicial order and administrating the polity's affairs, and constituted through a mutual contract (*ʿaqd*) with the political community (*al-umma*) (al-Māwardī 2006: 15). Addressing the question of whether *imāma* follows from rational deduction (*ʿaql*) or is a divinely revealed principle (*sharʿ*), he argued the latter referring to Q. 4 (*al-Nisāʾ*), 59:

> (59) O you who have come to enact security! Obey God and obey the Messenger and those foremost in command among you! (*yā ayyuhā alladhīna āmanū uṭīʿū Allāh wa uṭīʿū al-nabī wa ūlī al-amr minkum*)

Hence, the reference to 'those foremost in command among you' provides a Qurʾānic model for the Caliph as successor to the Messenger of God. He supports his interpretation with a *ḥadīth*, which states that the people are obligated to obey those governors who apply the true right i.e. who rule by the divine law, but not the licentious governors since their bad rule affects the people negatively (al-Māwardī 2006: 16):

> Hishām b. ʿUrwa – Abū Ṣāliḥ – Abū Hurayra, who said that God's Messenger (pbuh) said: "After me protective governors will govern you, and since the righteous (*al-barr*) will govern you through his righteousness while the licentious will govern you through his licentiousness, you must listen to them and obey in everything that corresponds with the true right (*al-ḥaqq*). If they do good things it affects them and you, and if they do bad things it affects you but is upon them." (*faʾin aḥsanū falakum wa lahum wa in asāʾū falakum wa ʿalayhim*)

The *ḥadīth* can be seen as defining a social contract, where the ruled have the right to not obey a ruler who violates the law. However, it does not say that the ruled can *depose* a bad ruler; rather, it seems they should simply not follow his commands.

As for the issue of separation of powers, al-Māwardī defines one of his seven conditions for a Caliph that, in addition to descent from Quraysh, he has the knowledge required to make independent interpretation (*ijtihād*) i.e. function as lawmaker (2006: 19). The majority of legal scholars and theologians agree, he concludes, that the Caliph is chosen by the body called *ahl al-ʿaqd wa al-ḥall*, 'the people who give and dissolve contract'. The precedent is the body of Companions who elected the first Caliphs in Medina, which in al-Māwardī's discourse applies to the collective of legal scholars, and their authority to grant or withhold their legitimization of a dynastic successor (2006: 21–28). Hence, only the scholars can de-legitimize a Caliph, not the public. To support the case for collective legitimization of the Caliph and election of incumbents through fixed conditions, al-Māwardī argued that *imāma* is one of the general rights defined within the relationship between God's right and the rights of the human beings (*al-imāma min al-ḥuqūq al-ʿāmma al-mushtaraka bayna ḥaqq Allāh taʿālā wa ḥuqūq al-ādamiyyīna*) (2006: 28). This should be seen in relation to al-Māwardī's definition of *imāma* as the protection of the judicial order i.e. of the rule of law required to protect rights. At this point in the discourse, he refers to the Qur'ānic term *ʿahd* as the technical term for a Caliph's legitimate rule. In other words, *ʿaqd* is the mutual contract conferred by the scholars, which grants the Caliph his *ʿahd*, or compact, which in turn makes him the *divinely* sanctioned protector of the judicial order (2006: 32ff.). As the incumbent of *ʿahd*, a Caliph has the right to appoint his successor and the members of the scholarly body. The precedence is the first Caliphs, specifically ʿUmar, who chose the members of the council (*shūrā*) that elected his successor; the argument being, that the constituents (*al-shaʿb*) were split into factions over the issue so that a consensus could only be reached through deliberation in the council (2006: 33–35). Other adduced precedents are the Umayyad Caliph Sulaymān b. ʿAbd al-Malik's appointment of ʿUmar b. ʿAbd al-ʿAzīz, and the Abbasid Caliph Hārūn al-Rashīd's designation of three of his sons as successors, all of which were considered legitimate (2006: 36–37).

It appears, then, that although al-Māwardī recognised the body of legal scholars as an autonomous institution authorised to grant or withhold the contract on behalf of the people, he gave the Caliph the authority to select the scholars assigned with the task, and he aligned with Ibn al-Muqaffaʿ's theory that the Caliph must have the capacity and authority to make law.

Consequently, he defined the following ten responsibilities for the office (2006: 40–41):

1. Protect the judicial order and know its sources and principles;
2. Arbitrate between conflicting rulings;
3. Maintain law and order, and safety of roads, as protection of people's livelihood;
4. Implement God's legal boundaries so that the people's rights to security and life-protection are protected;
5. Defend the imperial borders;
6. Secure recognition of Islam and include the rejecters in compacts of protection (*dhimma*);
7. Raise taxes on conquered lands assigned for the common good (*fay'*) and for alms, according to the divine guidance in scripture and through independent interpretation, and without fear;
8. Determine stipends and manage state finances;
9. Secure the responsibilities and landed properties that he delegated to his trustees and advisers;
10. Supervise the affairs and the administration to protect the community, and not delegate this to others, for as God said in Q. 38 (*Ṣād*), 26:

> (26) O David! We have made you a successor (*khalīfa*) in the land, so judge between the people by the true right and do not follow your urges, for they will lead you astray from the duties towards God!

To the last point and the verse Q. 38, 26, al-Māwardī remarks it shows that God obligates the Caliph personally to ensure that justice prevails, so this obligation cannot be delegated.

Administration and Science

Proceeding now to administration, a suitable starting point is the land tax, which we have just seen motivated Ibn al-Muqaffaʿ's argument for Caliphal lawmaking, and played a prominent part in al-Māwardī's list of Caliphal obligations.

The land tax was an important impetus for scientific development. Managing it involved setting the tax rates for specific lands and crops, and collecting and redistributing the revenue.[12] These activities required cadas-

12 On *kharāj*-theory in early legal writings, see Løkkegaard (1950); Ben Shemesh (1958; 1965; 1969). For a detailed study of the different administrative policies on collecting and redistributing *kharāj* in the Abbasid administration, see Sourdel (1959; 1960).

tral surveys, defining types of lands, and measuring their extent and the boundaries of properties. Such surveys thus involved both spatial measuring and the legal drawing of boundaries between neighbouring plots and proprietors, which required the specialist skills of scientists, administrators, and legal scholars. Among the sciences, geography, astronomy, and mathematics were involved since the land surveys entailed measuring heights and cavities, among other things. Accordingly, George Saliba shows that the Caliphal land registry (*dīwān*) and administration of the lands, the land tax, and the infrastructure (roads, irrigation channels), generated translations and the production of scientific literature generally in the Arabic language (Saliba 2007: Ch. 2). The beginnings of translating these sciences and their further development in Arabic writings dates to the late 600s, but the process began already with the Arab conquests of the Sassanian lands in the first half of the 600s, when the second Caliph ʿUmar b. al-Khaṭṭāb instituted the *dīwān* at the conquest of Iraq *c.* 19/640 (Saliba 2007: 33, 54).[13] A later example of a geographical work drawing on such knowledge is *Kitāb al-masālik wa al-mamālik* ('The Treatise on Routes and Realms'), composed around 870 by the Abbasid administrator Ibn Khorradādhbih.[14]

Through the focus on practices related to the land tax and the state administration, Saliba revises the dominant historical discourse, which treats science history in terms of ideas while neglecting institutional and material dimensions. The dominant discourse on science in Islamic contexts assumes that science and philosophy began when the Abbasid Caliphs in the 200s/800s initiated sponsoring of translations of Greek and other ancient texts i.e. when the Arab Muslims became 'exposed' to Greek rationality and philosophy, transmitted through the Sassanid Persian and/or Syriac Christian traditions. This Islamic 'rationalism' is then identified as the intellectual factor that enabled the sciences to develop, and seen as embodied especially by the Muʿtazilite school of theology, as opposed to the supposedly anti-rationalist 'traditionalists'. In this way, scientific progress appears dependent on the particular rationalism associated with Muʿtazilite theology (Saliba

13 See also Duri (2011) on tax and political institutions from the Prophet onwards.

14 For a detailed study of Ibn Khorradādhbih, see Zadeh (2011). On the crucial importance of land administration and taxation, and hence the maintenance of roads, as the rationale for the production of geographical works, see Heck (2002). According to Karen Pinto (2016:10), Heck by his emphasis on these material concerns corrects dominant explanations of the geographical works as originating within the ʾ*adab* literary culture, as travel literature written for the sake of general edification. For anyone interested in Islamic cartography, including its artistic expressions and visualisations of the world, Pinto (2016) is a rich resource.

2007:52).[15] However, as Saliba shows, the mathematics, astronomy, physics, and geography associated with cadastral surveys and land tax administration did not depend on any specific theological school. Institutionally, these sciences depended on the state administration and the scribal office (*kitāba*), which ranked under the *wazīr* or 'minister of the interior'. For illustration, Saliba cites the treatise *Adab al-kātib* ('Ethics for the Scribe') by Ibn Qutayba (d. 276/889), who specifies the kind of knowledge a scribe must possess. Note that he equates this knowledge with that embodied in the Persian imperial administration, here referred to as *al-aʿjam*, i.e. there is a continuation from Sassanid to Islamic administration:

> He must – in addition to our books – investigate matters relating to land surveying, so that he would know the right-angled triangle, the acute, and the obtuse-angled triangle; the vertical plumb lines (*masāqiṭ al-aḥjār*), the various squares (sic), the arcs and the curves, and the vertical lines. His knowledge should be tested on the land and not in books, for the one who reports is not like the eyewitness. And the non-Arabs (*aʿjam*) used to say: 'whoever was not an expert in matters relating to water distribution (*ijrāʾ mijāh*), the digging of trenches for drinking water, the covering of ditches, and the succession of days in terms of length increase and decrease, the revolution of the sun, the rising of the stars, the conditions of the moon when it becomes a crescent as well as its other conditions, and the control of weights, and the surface measurement of the triangle, the square, and the polygons, the erection of arches and bridges as well as water lifting devices and the norias [waterwheels; UM] by the waterside, and the conditions of

15 Kraemer (1986), referred to above, Chapter 1, would be an example of this kind of idea-focused approach. King (2004: xvi) offers another critical appraisal of incorrect yet still persistent assessments of Islamic history of science as mere application and transmission of the Ancient and Greek heritage, rather than as innovative scientific discoveries; King's own research field is astronomy. Also important are Irmeli Perho's studies of 'traditionalist' i.e. Ḥanbalī, methodology, which in idea-focused studies is seen as the cause of scientific decline. Perho (1995) shows how Ḥanbalī scholars in Damascus under Mamlūk rule (8th/14th c.) 'acculturated' the existing Graeco-Islamic medicine into the Islamic frame through Prophetic tradition, which indicates that 'traditionalist' scholars were not averse to science of 'non-Islamic' origins but employed their specific method in order to 'Islamise' it. The 'traditionalists' were scientific in their approach to medicine since they accepted causality i.e. the causal relationship between a drug and the cure of a disease, whereas their opponents, including 'rationalist' theologians, did not accept general causality and saw God as the cause of each disease or recovery. While the 'traditionalists' used the same Graeco-Islamic medicine as the philosophers, their specific approach was to include it into the Prophetic framework.

> the artisans and the details of calculations, he would be defective in his craft.[16]

Scribes are also the professional group who wrote down the Prophet's Qur'ānic statements during his lifetime, and produced the canonical manuscripts (Chapter 3 above). Numerous Qur'ānic passages describe God's creative acts through images that echo the scientific knowledge that scribes should possess and apply; e.g. Q. 13 (*al-Ra'd*), 1–4:

> (1) *aliflāmmīmrā* Those are the signs of the divine writing: what has been sent down to you from your Lord is the true right (*al-ḥaqq*), but most of the people do not enact security!
> (2) God is the one Who raised the heavens without pillars visible to you, then He ruled equitably over the Throne, making the sun and moon subservient, each one running for a defined term (*li'ajlin musammā*). He administrates the command (*yudabbir al-amr*) and distinguishes the signs (*yufaṣṣil al-āyāt*) so that you will be certain of meeting your Lord!
> (3) It is He Who spread out the land and made therein firm mountains and flowing waters, Who of each kind of fruit made two pairs, and Who causes the night to cover the day: indeed, in that there are signs for a people who reflect!
> (4) And in the land there are assigned plots adjoining each other, and gardens of vines, tillage and palm trees, from one or different roots, irrigated by one and the same water, and yet We favour some of them over others in produce: surely, in that there are signs for a people who use their reason!

Another passage, Q. 6 (*al-An'ām*), 95–99 connects God's creation of the edible vegetation with His origination of the light of day, the sun and the moon for calculation, and the stars for navigation, and with His creation of humans, who could not live without the other blessings:

> (95) Indeed, God is the one Who cleaves the seed and the kernel, bringing out what lives from what is dead, and what is dead from what lives: *that* is God for you! So how did you become perverted?

16 Saliba (2007:55), quote from Ibn Qutayba (1996:12–13). On the land tax and the scribal administration as analysed by Qudāma b. Ja'far (d. 337/948), see Heck (2002). Bennison largely agrees with Saliba's emphasis on the administration for scientific progress, though her focus is more on the intellectual aspects and during Abbasid time (2009, especially Ch. 5).

> (96) Cleaver of the dawn, He made the night for rest, and the sun and the moon **for calculation (*ḥusbānan*)**: *that* is the ordering of the Mighty **Who Possesses Full Knowledge** (*al-ʿazīz* ***al-ʿalīm***),
> (97) He Who made for you the stars so that you may be guided by them in the darknesses of the plains and the sea; We have certainly distinguished the individual signs for a people **with knowledge** (*laqad faṣṣalnā al-āyāt liqawmin* ***yaʿlamūna***)!
> (98) And it is He Who issued you forth from one person, then [made] places to dwell and to shelter: We have certainly distinguished the individual signs for a people **who analyse (*yafqahūna*)**!
> (99) And it is He Who has sent down from the sky water, by which we brought forth vegetation of every kind, from which we brought forth greenery and clusters of grain. And from the date palms' shoots come clusters of dates, within reach. And gardens of grapes and olives and pomegranates, alike and unlike: look at their fruits when they grow and ripen; surely, in that there are signs for a people who enact security!

These two passages, Q. 13, 1–4 and Q. 6, 95–99 are particularly interesting if read with reference to Watson's study (2008/1983) of agricultural innovation in the early Islamic period, mentioned in Chapter 5. As we saw, Watson argued that the production of new fruits and cash-crops, the extended growth seasons and arable lands, and the increase in crops and wealth, depended on new techniques for irrigation and fertilisation of soils, through manure, bones and other biological waste, on ownership rights for peasants, and on the use of gardens (Watson 2008/1983: 103–119). The Qurʾānic images of waterways, gardens, adjoining plots, seeds, kernels, growth/life and decay/death, and the light without which none of these sources of sustenance and life would exist, makes it possible to see God's Creation not only as reflecting Covenant as a model for mutual rights and obligation, but also as *images* reflecting both scribal knowledge and agriculture.

Moreover, the calculation of time is an important scientific practice related to scribal duties, such as calendar dates for tax collection, as well as to the ritual practice of the religion, including the daily prayers. David King has showed that the need to calculate the prayer times and the time spans between them played an important role both in astronomy, where calculations relied on mathematical methods and tables, and in the works of the legal scholars, who used shadows as measurements. King adduces several Qurʾānic verses, which mention prayer times: Q. 20, 130; Q. 52, 48; Q. 30, 17–18; Q. 11, 114; Q. 17, 78–79; and Q. 2, 238 (King 2004: 544). This perspective offers a new aspect on the Qurʾānic concept *ḥisāb*, which usually refers to the Day when God will finally settle 'the accounts' of whether one has fulfilled the Covenantal obligations, or not. Since God is served also through prayer on the right time, one might say that Covenant requires the scientific calculation of time. The passage Q. 13 (*al-Raʿd*), 16–22 illustrates the point. Verses 16–17 describe God's creative acts, referring to land, water, and artisanship, and the distinction between the true, right, and useful, and the false, useless, and vacuous. Verses 18–19 admonish through a reference to 'bad calculation' (*sūʾa al-ḥisāb*), land and time. Verse 20 reminds of Covenant, and in verse 21, *sūʾa al-ḥisāb* reappears. With a stretch of imagination, it seems that in this verse, it points ahead to verse 22, which mentions the obligation of prayer:

> (16) Say: 'Who is the Lord of the heavens and the land?' Say: 'God!' Say: 'Have you then taken, besides Him, protective governors who have no power to benefit or harm even themselves?' Say: 'Are the blind and the seeing equal? Or are the dark shades or the light equal? Or have they made for God partners who created the likeness of His creation, so that it appeared to them as the creation?' Say: 'God is the Creator of every single thing, for He is the One Who Subjects!'
> (17) He sends down water from the heaven so that the waterways flow according to their measures. The torrent carries along swelling foam, similar to the foam that comes out of that which they melt on the fire when they produce ornaments or tools. In this way, God forges the true right and the useless vacuity (*al-ḥaqq wa al-bāṭil*): the foam is cast away, but what benefits the people remains in the land! In this way, God forges the examples!
> (18) To those who respond to their Lord belong the best, while those who do not respond to Him, if they had all that is in the land, plus its equal, they would use it to ransom themselves! Those have **a bad calculation (*sūʾ al-ḥisāb*)**, and their abode is Hell; what a miserable resting place!
> (19) Is he who has knowledge that what was sent down to you from your Lord is the true right like he who is blind? Indeed, only those with firm intellects will recall and honour,
> (20) Those who fulfil God's compact (*biʿahd Allāh*) and do not violate the firm Covenant (*mīthāq*),
> (21) Those who join together what God has commanded to be joined, fear their Lord and dread **the bad calculation (*sūʾ al-ḥisāb*)**;
> (22) And those who are steadfast, seeking the countenance of their Lord, and **perform the prayer**, spend of the provisions We have given them, secretly and publicly, and counter evil with good: to those belong the most blissful abode!

Indeed, our al-Ṭabarī perceived a semantic relationship between Covenantal obligations and prayer *on time* in verse 22: "[God] states: Perform the obligatory prayer within its defined limits **on its times** (*addū al-ṣalāt al-mafrūḍa biḥudūdihā **fī awqātihā***)" (1995/8:13, 184).

To summarise: theoretical works within the discipline of *siyāsa* treat, among other things, constitutional separation of powers and social contract, and show how these relate to such practical administrative matters as the land tax and the scientific efforts that its management requires. Indeed, the land tax, and its redistribution, is one of the material premises for the flourishing and prosperity of the city and the citizens' happiness, a key concern for al-Fārābī. Hence, it indicates that the justice and rule of law that justifies the Caliphate refers to the collection and redistribution of the land tax as the common good. For Ibn al-Muqaffaʿ and al-Māwardī, who argued for Caliphal law-making power and supervision over the administration, control over the land tax management emerges as an important concern. Ibn al-Muqaffaʿ in particular stressed that this kind of administrative knowledge requires a combination of observation, experience, and philosophy, transmitted also from polities brought under Islamic rule, notably the Sassanid Empire and Indian kingdoms; similarly, Ibn Qutayba identified scribal administration with the Sassanid legacy. This way of discursively including 'ancient civilizations' differs from the modern western nationalistic practice of identifying with ancient Greece and Rome (see Chapter 1), since the civilizations in case are physically part of the Islamic realm. Hence, the aim appears scientific, to improve administration, and political, seeking legitimacy from peoples under Islamic rule, who are now members of the Islamic polity and will hopefully see it as a continuation of their own legacies. As for the evident *siyāsa*-specific knowledge about the Qurʾān, it concerns its concept *ḥikma*, 'capacity for just judgement', as guarantor for just rule and advice for rulers (e.g. Q. 38), and its reference to authorities after or beside the Prophet (Q. 4, 59). However, I have also argued that connections between common good and land are reflected in several verses, along with scientific practices related to the scribal administrative institution, notably land surveys, and the calculation of prayer times, can be seen as reflected in some Qurʾānic imagery.

HISTORY (*TAʾRĪKH*)

The discipline of history also reflects the concerns of the state administration, and therefore, like political writings, includes histories of pre-Islamic polities and advice for rulers. Thus, at the time when all disciplines were reaching mature forms i.e. the 200s/800s, history included several genres, some of which continued pre-Islamic forms of writing history and recording data.[17] However, the discipline began long before that. In his survey of Islamic historiography, Franz Rosenthal dates the earliest *written* historical material to the second half of the 600s, "if not before" (1968: 129–132) i.e. when Qur'ān manuscripts were publicised and *ḥadīth* transmission began.

As we have seen in Chapter 5, the Prophet's Biography or *Sīra* builds on such early material. However, not all history focused exclusively on the Prophet. While Ibn Hishām's *Sīra* and edition of Ibn Isḥāq's material focused on the Prophet's life in the Arabian Peninsula, another major transmission from Ibn Isḥāq, which e.g. al-Ṭabarī used, plotted the Prophet's life and mission in the context of 'universal history', beginning with Creation and then proceeding through the prophetic and royal histories of the Israelites, the Persians, the Romans, and the Arabs, and then continuing after the Prophet's life with the Companion Caliphs (Newby 1989). Other histories virtually ignored the Prophet. Al-Dīnawarī's (d. *ca.* 282/895) *Akhbār al-ṭiwāl*, 'The Long Narratives', synchronised pre-Islamic Biblical, Persian, and Arab history, and treated early Islamic history through the Caliphal reigns and with focus on Persia, passing over the Prophet "in complete silence" (Rosenthal 1968: 133). Tarif Khalidi has explained such diverse approaches in terms of institutional affiliations. For the *'ulamā'* the Prophet is the obvious nexus of the history of prophecy and the divine knowledge (*'ilm*), while the scribal administrators at the courts produced their own historical literature, *adab*, which treated a wider range of topics, administrative as well as ethically edifying, entertaining as well as fact-gathering, and temporally open-ended (1994: 85; Ch. 3).

By the mid-300s/900s, history included both the *'ulamā'*- and the scribal fields of interest, and the genres of local and city histories; geography and travel writings; dynastic and royal history and biographies (*siyar*); histories of professional and other classes of people and generations (*ṭabaqāt*); genealogical history (*ansāb*); and 'universal' or 'world history' (Rosenthal 1968: 87–98, 106–110). One example, which Rosenthal adduces from an encyclopaedia of the sciences from the mid-300s/900s, defines history as a required discipline for administrators and a major component of *ḥikma*, including the following topics. (1) Events of far-reaching consequence (earthquakes, deluges, famines, epidemics). (2) The succession of dynasties and rulers

17 For introductory historiographical surveys of early genres and historians, see e.g. Duri (1960/1983); Rosenthal (1968); Khalidi (1994); Robinson (2003).

according to their climes and lengths of rule. (3) Creation, Resurrection, and the physical and intellectual conditions of past generations, a material so remote and extensive that only God knows it all – with reference to Q. 14 (*Ibrāhīm*), 9:

> (9) Has not the announcement (*naba'*) reached you about those who preceded you – the people of Noah, of 'Ād and Thamūd, and those who came after them, who no one has knowledge about except God?

This material, furthermore, is acceptable only when based upon written sources or trustworthy information. (4) The Prophet's Biography, for information on his political and military activities. (5) The Companion Caliphs, their conquests, administration, and revolts against them. (6) The transition of power from the Umayyads to the Abbasids, illustrative of dynastic and temporal change. (7) Pre-Islamic Bedouin history and poetry. (8) Persian royal books and biographies, including the Sassanid Covenant of Ardashīr, the speeches of Khusraw Anūshirwān, etc., which are informative for political affairs and the administration of justice. (9) Events and deeds connected with the individual rulers; and (10) The histories of noblemen, scholars, scribes, poets, rhetoricians, religious men, and other moral 'types' (Rosenthal 1968: 35–36).

The measure of time was of course decisive for history. By the 200s/800s, the technical term for the discipline of history was *ta'rīkh*, 'date' or 'era', and the corresponding form was annalistic. Its practical importance is illustrated by al-Ṭabarī's (d. 310/923) universal 'History of the Messengers and the Kings' (*Ta'rīkh al-rusul wa al-mulūk*). It includes all the ten above topics, treated with reference to the Qur'ānic prophet-focused historical paradigm, with the aim of finding empirical knowledge about past experiences that can improve administration, land tax management, and justice in his present time (Mårtensson 2005; 2011). Setting out to write this history, al-Ṭabarī had to deal with the fact that for the period before Islam and the Hijrī calendar, which starts in the year 622 CE, each polity, dynasty, and religion had its own calendar. He therefore chose to write pre-Islamic history dynasty by dynasty and ruler by ruler, using the Persian king lists as basic structure because these were the longest and most continuous ones available. The term for this time measure according to the rule of a king is *zamān* (HT1/Rosenthal: 171, 184–186, 318–320). Into this temporal structure, al-Ṭabarī wove reported information about the Israelite prophets and kings, the Arab kings, and some about the Byzantines. From the Prophet onwards, he used the Hijrī calendar as a 'universal Islamic' time measure and consequently switched to the annalistic form, narrating history year by year, which is the *ta'rīkh* form proper. Papyrus using the Hijrī calendar has been found with dates to the year 22, in the Caliphate of 'Umar b. al-Khaṭṭāb (13/634–23/644), who is accredited with instituting the calendar (Rosenthal 1968: 13).

The term *ta'rīkh* is not mentioned in the Qur'ān, but has been identified in South Arabian inscriptions related to royal dynasties in Yemen (Duri 1960/1983: 14–15). Franz Rosenthal has traced the South Arabian etymology of *ta'rīkh* as related to 'moon' and 'fixed way'. He argues:

> A literal translation of *ta'rīkh* would then be 'lunation', that is, 'the indication of the (month and) day of the month through observation of the moon.' The transition of meaning from 'lunation' to 'date' and 'era' may, in this case, be reconstructed hypothetically as resulting from the use of the word for the indication of the day and the month in documents ('date'), with the next step being the widening of its meaning to indicate the most important date in the documents of a well-organized, permanent administration, the year of the 'era'. (Rosenthal 1968: 13; 12–13)

This proposed etymology can be seen as echoing the Qur'ānic topic of the moon and the sun as measures. For example, Q. 6 (*al-An'ām*), 96: "[God is] the Cleaver of the dawn, having made the night for rest and the sun and the moon for calculation (*ḥusbānan*)". And Q. 13 (*al-Ra'd*), 2: "God is the one Who raised the heavens without pillars visible to you, then He ruled equitably upon the Throne, making the sun and moon subservient, each one running a defined term". Thus, the Qur'ānic references to the moon and the sun, and to time measures, may refer not only to administration and ritual but also to historical time and the practice of writing history. This is also how al-Ṭabarī as historian perceived such verses; for example, he declared that Q. 36 (*Yā Sīn*), 37–40 and similar references to God's creation of the sun and the moon mean that day and night can be used by humans to measure time, in his case: historical time (HT1/Rosenthal: 186).

Yemen played an important part also for the historical practice of dating and writing genealogical records, *zubur* (sing. *zabūr*), pertaining to some families and clans. Abd al-Aziz Duri shows that the historian al-Hamdānī (d. ca. 334/945) referred to *zubur* as ancient written records, which Yemenite families and tribes possessed and employed to document their origins (1960/1983: 15). Such documented genealogical records secured a family's and tribe's right to land. This aspect of *zabūr* can perhaps be gleaned from the Qur'ān, where *zabūr* does occur, unlike *ta'rīkh*. The Qur'ānic word *zabūr* refers to a scripture, which is mostly associated with David. Since David in the Hebrew Bible is associated with the Psalms, the Qur'ānic term *zabūr* is normally translated as 'the Psalms', or 'David's scripture': Q. 54: 43, 52; Q. 35: 25; Q. 26: 196; Q. 23: 52–53; Q. 21: 105; Q. 17: 55; Q. 16: 44: Q. 4: 163; and Q. 3: 184. However, Qur'ānic *zabūr* also occurs in the plural *zubur*, and sometimes in conjunction with *arḍ*, 'earth' or 'land'. Given that David in the Hebrew Bible is the king who starts the Judean royal genealogy, and with it the Covenantal right to the promised land of Kanaan, Qur'ānic *zabūr* can be seen as referring to a written genealogical record, which documents a right to land. I have selected passages from Q. 21 (*al-Anbiyā'*), Q. 17 (*al-Isrā'*), Q. 23 (*al-Mu'minūna*), and Q. 26 (*al-Shu'arā'*) as examples.

Q. 21 (*al-Anbiyā'*) refers to *zabūr* (v. 105) in the context of describing the day when God will fulfil His rightful and true promise (*al-wa'd al-ḥaqq*, v. 97), taking the good from those who did wrong, who will languish in *jahannam* (Hell), and giving it to His servants (v. 98–103). Here verses 104–105 in my translation:

> (104) the day when We will fold the heaven like a sealed scroll of writings! As We initiated the first creative act, We will return it: this is a promise We have made and which We certainly effect, (*kamā bada'nā awwala khalqin nu'īduhu wa'dan 'alaynā innā kunnā fā'ilīna*)
> (105) as We have written **in the genealogical record**, after the honouring reminder, that **the land is the inheritance** of My servants who promote the common good! (*wa laqad katabnā fī* ***al-zabūr*** *min ba'd al-dhikr anna* ***al-arḍ yarithuhā*** *'ibādiya al-ṣāliḥūna*)

The standard translation of verse 105 would be: 'For We have written in the Psalms (…)'.

The second example, Q. 17 (*al-Isrā'*), 55, is preceded by a long list of commands to protect life and do justice, redistribute wealth to those entitled and in need, and serve God alone (v. 22–48). Against this background, God, the Creator, avers to punish those who stray and call upon others than God and reward His servants (v. 49–52). Verses 53–55 continue by describing what the Prophet can do to prepare the servants:

> (53) Say to My servants to state that which is the best (*wa qul li'ibādī yaqūlū allatī hiya aḥsanu*) – though indeed, Satan sows dissension between them, as Satan is indeed a clearly distinct enemy of humans!
> (54) Your God has the most knowledge about you. If He wishes, He protects your life, but if He wishes, He causes you pain! But We have sent you with a message to them, not to be their legal guardian (*rabbukum*

> *aʿlamu bikum in yashāʾ yarḥamukum aw in yashāʾ yuʿadhdhibukum wa mā arsalnāka ʿalayhim wakīlan*).
> (55) And your Lord has the most knowledge about those in the heavens and in **the land**! Therefore We have in fact favoured some of the prophets over the others: We brought David **a genealogical record (*zabūran*)**.

The standard translation of verse 55 is 'We gave to David Psalms (or the Book of Psalms)'.

The third case, Q. 23 (*al-Muʾminūna*), 53, refers to the problem of divisions in a context mentioning writings, good food, landed property (*māl*), and offspring (v 49–56). Here *zabūr* appears in the plural, *zubur*, and in connection with the verb *taqaṭṭaʿa*, which derives from the same root (*q-ṭ-ʿ*) as the term for land fief, *iqṭāʿ*:

> (49) We have in fact given Moses the divine writing (*al-kitāb*), so that they would be guided,
> (50) And We made Mary's son and his mother a sign when We gave them shelter on an inhabited hillside with water springs.
> (51) O Messengers! Eat of the good foods and work for the common good (*kulū al-ṭayyibāt wa aʿmilū al-ṣāliḥāt*)! Indeed, I have full knowledge of what you do!
> (52) Indeed, this your polity is one polity, and I am your Lord, so fulfil your obligations towards Me! (*inna hādhihi ummatukum umma wāḥida wa anā rabbukum fa-ittaqūnī*)
> (53) Thus, they divided up their command into fiefs **according to genealogical records**, each faction rejoicing at what they had; (*fataqaṭṭaʿū amrahum baynahum* ***zuburan*** *kull ḥizb bimā ladayhim fariḥūna*)
> (54) So leave them in their exuberance for a while!
> (55) Do they reckon that, through the property and offspring (*māl wa banīn*) We extended to them,
> (56) We are hastening to them the good things (*al-khayrāt*)? No, they do not perceive!

Other, standard translations of verse 53 render *zubur* as divisions according to 'sect' e.g. Abdel Haleem (2004): "This community of yours is one – and I am your Lord: be mindful of Me – but they have split their community into **sects**, each rejoicing in their own". Others emphasise the scriptural foundation of sectarian divides e.g. *The Study Qurʾān*: "And truly this community of yours is one community, and I am your Lord, so reverence Me. But they made their affair to be founded upon different scriptures, each party exulting in what it had" (see also Droge 2013).

The fourth and last example is Q. 26 (*al-Shuʿarāʾ*), 192–197. Here, the plural *zubur* appears in connection with the Arabic language and 'those who have knowledge among the Israelites':

> (192) Indeed, it is the sending-down of the Lord of the knowing beings (*wa innahu latanzīlu rabb al-ʿālamīn*),
> (193) which the Secure Spirit brought down
> (194) upon your intellect, so that you would become one of the warners,
> (195) in a language that is Arabic and that conveys clarifying distinctions!
> (196) Indeed, it is in **the genealogical records** of those who came first (*wa innahu lafī **zubur** al-awwalīna*),
> (197) so is it not a sign for them that those who have knowledge among the Israelites know about it?

Of course, it may make the most common sense to translate *zabūr* (singular) as the Psalms, since this is the scripture, which the Qurʾān connects with David. However, the implications of 'land' were noted by al-Ṭabarī, who in his History described how our first example Q. 21 (*al-Anbiyāʾ*), 105 was referred to in the context of the Muslims' battles against the Sassanians, in the fertile lands of Iraq. Al-Ṭabarī cited a written report (from al-Sarī–Shuʿayb–Sayf b. ʿUmar–Muḥammad, Ṭalḥa, and Ziyād) about a public speech delivered by the Caliph ʿUmar's commander Saʿd b. Abī Waqqāṣ to his troops, preparing them for battle. In the speech Q. 21, 105 appears together with the identification of the addressees as the nobles of the Arab tribes (*qabāʾil*, sing. *qabīla*):

> God is indeed the True Right, Who has no partner in His dominion and Whose statement does not go unfulfilled! God, may His praise be mighty, has stated: *as We have written **in the genealogical record**, after the honouring reminder, that **the land is the inheritance** of My servants who promote the common good!* (Q. 21, 105) **This is indeed your inheritance and your Lord's promise (*mawʿūd rabbikum*), and He has permitted you to take possession of it** since three pilgrimages ago (*thalāthi ḥijajin*), so that you could get food from it, eat from it, kill its people, collect taxes from them, and imprison them, until this day, by virtue of the damage that the Companions of the Battles had inflicted upon them. Now this group [of them] has advanced to you! You are the nobles and notables of the Arabs, the elect of each tribe, and the might of those following behind you, and if you renounce in the nearest and seek the furthest, God will bring together for you the nearest and the furthest without that bringing anyone closer to his appointed time. But

if you lose courage and become weak and feeble, you will expire and your furthest will perish! (HT 12/Friedmann 1992: 84–85; mod.)

Abrahamic Prophecy and Food Security: Version 2

The topic of God's promise of land brings us back to Covenant, which served as the paradigm that several of the early historians, including al-Ṭabarī, employed to define where the *umma* took a right or wrong turn (Humphreys 1989; see Chapter 4). Here I will focus on the significance of the system of vassalage and 'food security' for this historical discourse, represented by al-Ṭabarī and his *Ta'rīkh al-rusul wa al-mulūk*. In Chapter 5 we have seen how Ibn Hishām's Biography provided the Prophet with the Abrahamic genealogy and connection with the Ka'ba, which in practical terms meant unifying the tribes through pacts and providing security and food for all in the city, including pilgrims and merchants from abroad. Al-Ṭabarī expanded on this topic within a historical outline that actualises his natural law theory, discussed in Chapter 4. Simply put, he began his history with God's Creation, then traced political history through Persians, Israelites, Byzantines, and Arabs, to the Prophet and after him the Caliphate until the year 302/915, and focusing on the institutions of 'kingship' and 'prophecy'.

First and foremost, al-Ṭabarī described God's Creation of the world in six days, including several versions of reports on the Covenant between God and Adam's future descendants described in Q. 7, 172 (HT1/Rosenthal: 304–307). The first of Adam's offspring who God gave prophecy was Idrīs (Enoch), who introduced writing to humans and exerted himself to serve God, al-Ṭabarī reported (HT1/Rosenthal: 343). He then traced the beginning of political history to the mythical Persian king Ôshahanj or, as he was also called, 'Fêsh-dâd', 'The First to Judge in Justice'. Al-Ṭabarī explains that he established places for prostration (*masājid*), and taught humans everything they needed to develop civilization: mining for minerals, production of iron, agriculture, watering, etc. He was recognised as ruler by his people, and he established the constitutional principle of social contract by writing a Covenant document (*mīthāq*) with mutual terms with which he bound the rebel Iblīs and his troops (HT1/Rosenthal: 341–342). Covenant, as translated into social contract, is thus defined here as the foundation of all political history; as such, it is a principle and practice intrinsic to humans as political beings and can be seen as reflecting the universality associated with natural law theory.

Further into the history, where al-Ṭabarī narrates reports on Abraham, the topic of 'food security' becomes connected with his prophetic genealogy. Compared with Ibn Hishām's Biography, which treats Abraham only with reference to Mecca and the Kaʿba, al-Ṭabarī's discourse locates Abraham first in Mesopotamia, his 'Biblical' land of origins. His reports describe how God decided to try (*ibtalā*) Abraham, referring to Q. 2 (*al-Baqara*), 124: "When God tried Abraham with words, which he fulfilled". But al-Ṭabarī also supplied additional material on what the trial involved. First, he cited two reports from the Prophet, which explain that the trial was the obligation to pray at specific times (HT 2/Brinner 1987: 104). Then he described how Abraham secured food for the people in situations when they depended on tyrannical kings. The institutional practices associated with servitude of the One God as opposed to servitude of a tyrant here become clear. Kings store grain and food in the city. The tyrant is the king who aggrandises himself by not accepting God as His Lord, and who denies food to the people unless they declare him their lord:

> When God had come to know Abraham's perseverance through all the trials He put him through, and his performance of all the ritual obligations (*farāʾiḍ*) He made incumbent upon him, and his preference of obedience to Him over everything else, He took him as a friend (*khalīl*), and made him leader (*imām*) of those of His created beings (*khalqihi*) who came after him. He chose him (*iṣṭafāhu*) as messenger to His created beings and appointed for his descendants' prophecy, writing, and message, and He singled them out with sent-down divine writings and persuasive just judgements (*kutub munzala wa al-ḥikam al-bāligha*). He made among them scholars, leaders, chiefs and nobles, so that whenever one appointed among them passed away he was succeeded by a noble one, and their honour was remembered for the coming generations. All the nations would take [Abraham] as their governor and praise him, and speak of his excellence as an honour to him by God in the nearest world, while the esteem which God has stored up for him in the yet-to-come is more splendid than anyone can describe.
>
> Let us now return to the account of the enemy of God and of Abraham, who refused to enact security through what Abraham had brought him from God and who rejected Abraham's counsel out of ignorance and error about God's indulgence with him: Nimrod b. Kush b. Kanaan b. Ham b. Noah. (…) God was forbearing with him and did not hasten to punish him for his rejection of security through Him and for his attempt to burn His friend Abraham for calling upon him (Nimrod) to enact security only through God and abandon his gods and idols. (…) The proofs of Himself which God advanced to Nimrod and the examples

> he showed him only made Nimrod persist in his transgression. (HT 2/Brinner 1987: 104–105; mod.) (…)
>
> It was reported to me from al-Ḥasan b. Yaḥyā – ʿAbd al-Razzāq (al-Ṣanʿānī) - Maʿmar (b. Rāshid) – Zayd b. Aslam, that the first oppressor (*jabbār*) in the land was Nimrod. People used to go out and go to him seeking food (*ṭaʿām*), and Abraham went out seeking with those who sought. When people passed by [Nimrod] he would ask them, 'Who is your lord?' They would say, 'You!' Until Abraham passed by him, and he said, 'Who is your lord?' Abraham answered, *'My Lord is He Who gives life and causes death!' He said, 'I give life and cause death!' Abraham said, 'God brings the sun from the east: now you try causing it to rise from the west!' Thus was the one who rejects security defeated'.* (Q. 2, *al-Baqara*, 258) [Nimrod] dismissed [Abraham] without food. Abraham went back to his family. On the way he passed a dust-coloured sand dune and said to himself, 'Let me take some of this and bring it to my family, to make them feel better when I come to them!' So he took some of it to bring to his family. He put his baggage down and slept. His wife arose, went to his baggage and opened it, and found there the best food anyone had ever seen. So she prepared some of it and presented it to him. To his knowledge the family had no food, so he asked, 'From where does this come?' She answered, 'From the food you brought!' So he knew that God had provided sustenance for him (*razaqahu*), and he praised God. (HT 2/Brinner 1987: 106; mod.)

Hence, Abraham is the prophet whose mission establishes that tyrannical idolatry is connected with a king's requirement to be served as a god, which in practice means that he disposes over food stores. Serving the king as god thus means enslavement by the king, in return for food, as opposed to servitude of God, which equals personal freedom and food security through the welfare and redistribution measures related to the law.

As the main source of revenue for states and landlords, the land tax occupies an important place in al-Ṭabarī's history, just as it does in works on *siyāsa*. He described how the Persian king Manūshihr institutionalised the system of vassalage as a contract with mutually agreed terms between the king and the tax-paying people. The terms are defined in a speech attributed to Manūshihr, and addressed to his administrators and governors. The speech invokes God as the Creator and Provider of material blessings, then applies the model relationship between Creator and created being to the roles of the one who is owed and the one who owes, which translates into the king's right to tax revenue and military service, and the people's right to sustenance from land grants and produce. Thus, the speech connects *khalq*, 'creation', with *rizq*, 'sustenance', through *kharāj*, 'land tax', and *ʿahd*, 'compact' securing the mutual rights (*ḥaqq*) and obligations (*ḥaqq ʿalā*):

> O People! Just as **creation belongs to the Creator (*al-khalq li'l-khāliq*)**, thanks belongs to the Provider of material blessings, peaceful surrender belongs to the All-powerful, and what is is inevitable, **there is none weaker than a created being (*makhlūq*)**, whether he seeks or is sought, **none stronger than a creator (*khāliq*)**, none more powerful than the one who holds in his hand what he seeks, and none more powerless than he who is in the hand of the one who seeks him. Indeed, reflection is light, carelessness is darkness, and ignorance is error! Because the first is followed by the last, by the inevitable attachment of the last to the first, and thus there have passed before us principles (*uṣūl*) of which we are the derivatives (*furūʿ*), since what derivative could be without its principle! Since God Almighty and Splendid gave us the kingdom the praise belongs to Him, and we ask Him to inspire us with the divine guidance, trustworthiness and certainty. For **the king has a right in relation to the people of the kingdom and the people of his kingdom have a right in relation to him (*wa inna li-l-malik ʿalā ahl mamlakatihi ḥaqqan wa liʾahl mamlakatihi ʿalayhi ḥaqqan*)**. The right of the king in relation to the people of his kingdom is that they obey him, counsel him, and fight his enemy, while their right in relation to the king is that he provides them with their sustenance when it is due, for they have recourse to nothing else since that is their trade. The ruled (*raʿiyya*) have the right in relation to the king that he sees to them, treats them in a friendly manner, and does not burden them with more (tax) than they can bear, so that if a disaster befalls them from the heavens or the land that diminishes its returns he reduces the land tax in proportion with the loss. If a calamity ruins them, he should give them what they need to rebuild themselves, and then for a year or two only take from them a proportion that does not harm them. Command of the army is for the king like the wings of a bird: it is the wings of the king, and when a feather is lost from the wings, it is a loss to him; likewise with the king: he depends on his wings and his feathers. Moreover, the king must possess three qualities: first, he must be trustworthy and never lie; he must be munificent and not miserly; and he must control himself when angered, for he is empowered when his hand is stretched out and the land tax is coming to him. He must not appropriate for himself what the army and the ruled are entitled to, and he must be generous with pardoning for there is none more long-lasting king than he who pardons or one more quick to perish than he who punishes. Moreover, a man who errs in pardoning and pardons is better than one who errs in punishing. (…) Know that this kingship stands only through moral and verbal correctness (*istiqāma*; cf. Q.1, 6, *ṣirāṭ al-mustaqīm*), obedience

> in good, suppression of the enemy, fortification of the frontiers, justice towards the ruled, and fairness towards the wronged! Your treatment is within yourselves, for the remedy in which there is no ailment is moral and verbal correctness (*istiqāma*; cf. Q.1, 6) and commanding the good and prohibiting the bad (*al-amr bi-l-khayr wa al-nahy ʿan al-sharr*), and there is no strength except through God. Look after the ruled, for they are your source of food and drink, and when you act justly towards them they desire cultivation, which will increase your land tax and manifest itself in the increase of your sustenance (*ziyādat arzāqikum*). But if you wrong the ruled they will abandon cultivation and leave most of the land idle, which will reduce your land tax and manifest itself as a deficit in your sustenance (*naqṣ arzāqikum*). **Enter reciprocally into a compact (*taʿāhadū*) of just treatment with the ruled!** (HT 3/Brinner 1991: 25–27; mod.)

At a later point in the history, where al-Ṭabarī treats the Persian Sassanid kings, he cites reports about a major cadastral survey (*masḥ al-arḍ*), initiated by Shah Qubādh (r. 488–496 and 498–531) and implemented by his successor Khusraw Anūshirwān (r. 531–579). The purpose of the survey was to reform the land tax in a way that allowed the Shah to centralise control over the vassals and create a new kind of troops under the state control and on its payroll (HT 5/Bosworth 1999: 255–256; Rubin 1995). According to the reports, Khusrāw's tax reform assigned a new authority to written documentation (*kitāb*) of the survey and the tax rates on crops and lands, copies of which were kept with the Shah's administration, with the tax collectors, and with the regional judges. The judges were also to ensure that tax collectors did not charge the peasants additional sums, and to consider any extraordinary circumstances affecting the crops and making it harder for them to pay the fixed rates (HT 5/Bosworth 1999: 261). The tax was also levied only on specified crops and lands, to secure reasonable sustenance for the peasants (HT 5/Bosworth 1999: 258).

These reports about the cadastral survey and land tax are significant in al-Ṭabarī's historical discourse because he stated that when the Caliph ʿUmar conquered the Sassanid lands, with the rich farmlands of Iraq, he instituted the same tax system, including the measures to protect the peasants' livelihood (HT 5/Bosworth 1999: 260–261).[18] As the Caliph whose conquests transformed the city-state of Medina into a fully-fledged empire,

18 Also the early Ḥanafī jurist Abū Yūsuf (d. 182/798) attributed this tax system to ʿUmar b. al-Khaṭṭāb (Ben-Shemesh 1969: 103–104). See also Ibn Manẓūr, who cites a report from ʿUmar, 'Fulfil your obligations towards God regarding the peasants (*ittaqū Allāha fī al-fallāḥīna*); *Lisān al-ʿarab* (www.alwaraq.net), p. 4469. For the thesis that

ʿUmar occupies a large space in al-Ṭabarī's history, second in quantity only to the Prophet. Al-Ṭabarī cited a speech where ʿUmar actualises the importance of correct (*mustaqīm*) speech and actions (see the speech above), in this case providing a definition of 'justice' in the context of the conquests:

> Al-Sarī wrote to me, from Shuʿayb – Sayf (b. ʿUmar) – Muḥammad and Ṭalḥa and Sahl – al-Qāsim: ʿUmar accompanied [the troops] from Ṣirār to al-Aʿwaṣ, then he stood up amongst the people and addressed them (*khaṭīban*): 'Indeed, God Most High has made paradigmatic examples (*amthāl*) for you and nuanced for you the speech (*ṣarrafa lakum al-qawl*) so that the hearts may be revived by it, for the intellecting hearts are dead in their bosoms until God revives them. Let anyone who has knowledge about a thing benefit from it. Indeed, justice has its signal-banners (*amārāt*) and heralds (*tabāshīr*). As for the signal-banners: diffidence, generosity, modesty, and gentleness. As for the heralds: protection of life (*raḥma*). God has made for every issue a gate and provided for each gate a key. The gate of justice is to take things into consideration, and its key is renunciation (*zuhd*). Taking things into consideration is to honour death by remembering the dead, and to prepare oneself for it by the deeds one puts forth. Renunciation is to take what is rightly owed from those who owe it and to give what is rightly due to those who have a right to it. Do not grant favour to anyone in this matter, and content yourself with what suffices for you; a person who is not satisfied with what suffices for living, nothing will make him rich. Indeed, I am between you and God, and no one is between me and Him. God has in fact obligated me to prevent petitions from reaching Him, so direct your complaints to us. Whoever is not able to do this, let him hand the complaint over to someone who can bring it to us; we shall willingly take his rightful due for him (HT 12/Friedmann 1992: 11–12; mod.).

ʿUmar also figures in al-Ṭabarī's history in connection with the topic of separation of powers. Consider the following report about ʿUmar and the Abbasid ancestor ʿAbdallāh b. ʿAbbās (d. 68/687), who like ʿAlī b. Abī Ṭālib, the ancestor of the Alids, was a cousin of the Prophet though through another uncle. ʿUmar takes Ibn ʿAbbās to task for the Abbasid family seeking to join 'prophecy and caliphate':

> ʿUmar (b. al-Khaṭṭāb) – ʿAlī (b. Abī Ṭālib) – Abū al-Walīd al-Makkī – one of the sons of Ṭalḥa – Ibn ʿAbbās: I went with ʿUmar on one of his

---

al-Ṭabarī used this model of land tax management to analyse conditions for successful and failed imperial administration, see Mårtensson (2005; 2009a; 2011).

journeys. (…) ['Umar] said: 'I ask God's forgiveness, Ibn 'Abbās, but what kept 'Alī from coming with us?' I said: 'I don't know?' He said: 'O Ibn 'Abbās, your father is the uncle of God's Messenger (pbuh), and you are his cousin, so what kept your people from you?' I said: 'I don't know?' He said: 'But I know! They resented having you govern them!' I said: 'Why, when we are good for them?' He said: 'May God forgive me: they resented that you should unite in yourselves the prophecy and the caliphate, which would bring about self-aggrandizement! If you say, 'Abū Bakr did that!' then no, by God, but Abū Bakr did his best under the circumstances. Recite to me what Zubayr, the poet of poets, composed:

'When Qays b. 'Aylān hasten to a goal of royal glory, the one who reaches it first is made the ruler'.

I read it out to him as the dawn broke, and he said: 'Read 'The Event'! (Q. 56, *al-Wāqi'a*) I read it, then he dismounted and prayed, and read 'The Event'. (HT 14/Smith 1994: 135–136; mod.)

Thus, 'Umar accuses Ibn 'Abbās' family i.e. the Abbasid dynasty, for merging prophecy and caliphate and says this was why they were not elected to succeed the Prophet, an honour that instead went first to Abū Bakr and then to 'Umar himself. 'Merging prophecy and caliphate' refers to the two institutions of the state and the law. The Qur'ānic *sūra* 56 (*al-Wāqi'a*) is about the Companions of Blessings (*aṣḥāb al-maymana*) and of the Right (*aṣḥāb al-yamīn*), who will enter the luscious gardens, and the Companions of Calamity (*aṣḥāb al-mash'ama*) and of the Left (*aṣḥāb al-shimāl*), who will taste misfortunes. The latter, instead of swearing their oaths (*qasam*) by God's creative powers, gain their sustenance (*rizq*) by giving a lie to the reading (*al-qur'ān*) and divine writing (*kitāb*) that is sent-down from the Lord of the knowing beings (*tanzīl min rabb al-'ālamīna*) (verses 75–82).

Read in this way, al-Ṭabarī's inclusion of the report which refers to Q. 56 in his historical discourse can also be understood as expressing his view of events that occurred in the Abbasid Caliphate. Above, I mentioned the Caliph al-Ma'mūn's failed attempt in the year 201/816 to appoint the 'Alid descendent al-Riḍā for his successor, thus breaking the Abbasid dynastic succession as well as bypassing the approval of the legal scholars. Al-Ṭabarī's History is one of the sources of information about al-Ma'mūn's politics, which involve the nature of the Qur'ān.[19] In the year 218/833, al-Ma'mūn imposed

19 For an overview of the sources, see K. V. Zettersteen, 'al-Ma'mūn', Encyclopaedia of Islam, First edition (1913–1936).

the doctrine *khalq al-Qur'ān*, 'the createdness of the Qur'ān', associated with the theological school Mu'tazila, as a state doctrine. He also launched the only inquisition recorded in Islamic history (*al-miḥna*, 'the test') against over forty legal scholars, judges, and administrators who opposed the doctrine and defended the doctrine of the Qur'ān as God's uncreated Word, propounded by *Ahl al-ḥadīth* (Nawas 1996; Cooperson 2000).

By the time of al-Ma'mūn's reign, doctrinal debates about the Qur'ān's nature were decisive for the drawing of boundaries between schools within the disciplines of theology and legal hermeneutics. Simply put, the Mu'tazila argued for the doctrine of *khalq al-Qur'ān* ('the created Qur'ān') primarily on the grounds of creed. They interpreted the Qur'ānic doctrine of God's Oneness and absolute incomparability with anything created in the sense that if God is One and cannot take any material form, the Qur'ān cannot be a physical and temporal extension of Himself in the form of His Word but must be created (Shah 2011: 316–317; Vasalou 2009). The Mu'tazila also developed a particular theory of language. Language is a human institution and communicative activity in time and place, and meanings of words are established conventions. Hence, to the extent that the Qur'ān is constituted as language, it is 'created'. Michael Carter has seen a connection between this theory of language, and the Mu'tazila's initial method of deriving the law from the Qur'ān through subjective reasoning. This view, Carter argues, was particularly amenable to Twelver Shī'ism because it legitimised the doctrine of continuous Qur'ānic revelation to the Shī'ite Imams as custodians of its meanings, which dovetailed both with al-Ma'mūn's appointment of an 'Alid successor in the Twelver line, *and* his later imposition of *khalq al-Qur'ān* as state doctrine (Carter 1983:68). Mu'tazila's opponents *Ahl al-ḥadīth* argued that the Qur'ān is indeed God's own Word, which is uncreated since it is part of His essence. The Prophet sealed the revelation, and the text should be read through the scholars' contextualisation with the aid of *ḥadīth*, which also constituted a source of law alongside the Qur'ān (Carter 1983:68; Shah 2011:317). The theory of language propounded by *Ahl al-ḥadīth* as well as the later Ash'arite theological school was that language was something that God had implanted in humans with creation, along with the meaning of words (to put it simply). By implication, the fact that God spoke in a human language does not entail infringement or 'externalisation' of the divine essence (Shah 2011: 315).

Mustafa Shah however warns against assuming a perfect correspondence between the two competing doctrines on the Qur'ān and the two theories of language, since there are examples of e.g. Mu'tazilites who adhered to the theory of divine origins of language at the same time as they upheld the doctrine of *khalq al-Qur'ān* (Shah 2011:325, 333). Instead, Shah identifies as the dividing issue the relationship between meanings of words and divinely commanded, binding obligations. If the meaning of words is laid down by God in the Qur'ān and its extension in *ḥadīth*, the command remains valid through time, whereas if meaning is subject to human convention it can change, and with it the understanding of the command (Shah 2011:334). Aspects of both Carter's and Shah's arguments appear to be supported by al-Ṭabarī's historical reports about al-Ma'mūn's inquisition, which show the Caliph interpreting the Qur'ān to support his doctrine and his own authority to define its meanings. Al-Ṭabarī cited excerpts from the Caliph's letter to Isḥāq b. Ibrāhīm, the official charged with summoning judges and legal scholars to the inquisition. The excerpts show the Caliph arguing, first, that God has appointed the caliphs as the people's legal and religious authority and guide; secondly, that the Qur'ān itself supports the doctrine that it is created; and thirdly, that those who do not adopt this doctrine are unfit for public office:

> That which God has a right to expect from His representatives (*khulafā'*, Caliphs) in His land and from those entrusted by Him with authority over His servants, upon whom He has been pleased to lay the setting up of His judicial order (*iqāmat dīnihi*) and upon whom He has laid the burden of caring for His creatures, the putting into effect of His judgement and His precedence (*ḥukmihi wa sunanihi*), and the conscious imitation of His justice among His creation, is that they should exert themselves earnestly for God; render Him sincere service in that which He has asked them to keep safe and has laid upon them; make Him known through that favour of knowledge (*'ilm*) which He has entrusted to them and the experience (*ma'rifa*) which He has placed within them; guide back to Him the one who has turned aside from Him and bring back the one who has turned his back from His command; trace out for their subjects the way of salvation for them; draw their attention to the limits of their faith and the way to their heavenly success and protection from sin; and reveal to them those of their affairs which are hidden from them and those which are dubious and obscure by means of what will remove doubt from them and bring back illumination and clear distinctions (*al-bayyina*) to them all. (HT 32/Bosworth 1987: 205–206; mod.)
>
> Among the things which the Commander of Those who enact security has clearly distinguished through his reflection and ascended to through his thinking, so that its great danger has become clearly manifest to him, as well as the seriousness of the corruption and harm that will rebound on the judicial order (*al-dīn*), are the statements that the

enactors of peace are passing around among themselves about the Reading (*al-Qur'ān*), which God has made as an example (*imām*) for them and an enduring legacy of the Messenger of God, His chosen one, Muḥammad. There is confusion regarding it for many of them, to the point that it appeared good to them and attractive to their intellects that it is not created. They thereby lay themselves open to the risk of rejecting God's creative act by which He is distinguished from His creatures (*khalq Allāh alladhī bāna bihi 'an khalqihi*) and remains apart in His splendour in the bringing forth of all the things through His capacity for just judgement (*ḥikmatihi*) and their being originated through His power to measure (*qudratihi*), and in His priority in time over them by reason of His primordial existence, whose beginning cannot be attained and whose extent cannot be comprehended. Everything apart from Him is a creature from His creative act (*khalqan min khalqihi*) and an event that He brought about (*ḥadathan huwa al-muḥdith lahu*). [They hold this erroneous view about the uncreatedness of the Reading] even though the Reading itself speaks about [God's creative act], sets forth its proof and decisively confutes all difference of opinion about it. [These people] talk just like the Christians when they claim that Jesus son of Mary was not created, because he was the Word of God. But God says, *Indeed, We have made it an Arabic Reading* (Q. 42, 2–3), meaning, 'We have created it', just as He also says, *And He made from him his spouse, that he might dwell with her* (Q. 7, 189). He also says, *We have made the night a garment and have made the daylight as a means of sustenance* (Q. 78, 10), and, *We have made every living thing from water* (Q. 21, 30–31). Thus God places the Reading and these created things, which He mentions with the indications of the act of making, on an equal footing, and He gives the information that He alone is the one who made it, saying, *Indeed, it is a glorious Reading on a preserved tablet* (Q. 85, 21–22). (HT 32/Bosworth 1987: 206–207; mod.) (…)

By their statements concerning the Reading, these ignorant people have enlarged the breach in their judicial order (*dīnihim*) and the uncertainty in their trust, making the way easy for the enemies of the enactment of peace (*al-islām*). They have confessed to changing [the Reading] and heresy against their own hearts; they have made known and described God's creative act and His actions by that attribute that is for God alone, and compared Him with it, whereas it is only His creation that can be compared. The Commander of the Faithful does not consider the person who makes this statement to have any share in the judicial order, nor any part in the enactment of security and the certainty. Nor does he regard any of them permissible for an office of confidence like that of trusted depository, person in good legal standing, legal witness, person veracious in speech or report, or one involving the exercise of any aspect of

> authority over the subjects. Moreover, even if any of them is outwardly known for his equitable behaviour and is recognised for his straightforwardness, as one who pursues a just course among the subjects, nevertheless, the branches must be traced back to their roots and must be classified among the categories of praise or blame according to those roots. A man who is ignorant in the matter of his judicial order regarding that which God has commanded him about His divine Oneness, is even more sunk in ignorance in regard to other things, more blind in finding right guidance concerning other matters and more erring from the right road. (HT 32/Bosworth 1987: 208–209; mod.)

Among the scholars who were associated with *ahl al-ḥadīth* and singled out for inquisition was Aḥmad b. Ḥanbal (d. 241/855), whose collection of *ḥadīth*, legal method, and theology on the uncreated nature of the Qur'ān, eventually became constituents of the Ḥanbalī *madhhab*. The Caliph's inquisitioner Isḥāq b. Ibrāhīm interrogated him:

> 'What is your view concerning the Qur'ān?' Aḥmad replied: 'It is the word of God'. Isḥāq said: 'Is it created?' Aḥmad retorted: 'It is the word of God; I cannot add any more to these words'. (HT 32/Bosworth 1987: 212)

Isḥāq b. Ibrāhīm then asked him about physical descriptions of God in the Qur'ān:

> 'What do His words "He is the Hearing One With Insight" (Q. 42 (*al-Shūrā*, 11) mean?' Aḥmad replied: 'He is as He qualified Himself (*huwa kamā waṣafa nafsahu*)!' [Isḥāq b. Ibrāhīm] said: 'But what does it mean?' He replied: 'I do not know: He is as He qualified Himself'. (HT 32/Bosworth 1987: 213; mod.)

If Aḥmad b. Ḥanbal typifies the theology rejected by the Caliph, there was also an administrative logic to the inquisition. As the Caliph's above-cited instructions to Isḥāq b. Ibrāhīm convey, those who propounded the wrong doctrine were deemed unfit to serve in the judiciary and administration. John Nawas (1996) has argued the inquisition was motivated by the fact that *ahl al-ḥadīth* had become an increasingly autonomous movement among the scholars, which the Caliph sought to quell for political reasons. Al-Ṭabarī sheds further historical light on the Caliph's motivations. Two years before the inquisition, in 216/831, al-Ma'mūn initiated raids into Christian Byzantine territory, with ensuing military confrontation. Eventually he decided to erect defence fortifications inside enemy territory (HT 32/Bosworth 1987:

184–197). For this purpose, the Caliph in the year 833 i.e. the same year as the inquisition, required a vast troop and revenue levy on the provinces and Baghdad itself. He appointed as revenue-raiser over Baghdad and Iraq the same Isḥāq b. Ibrāhīm who led the inquisition, summoning the judges and officials, and testing them as to their adherence to the doctrine of the created Qur'ān (HT 32/Bosworth 1987: 198f.). This context of war campaigns and extraordinary tax levies for the inquisition suggests al-Ma'mūn may have used the doctrinal 'test' as an excuse to fire not just anyone who rejected his doctrine, but also those officials and judges who opposed his troop and tax levy, which the Caliph now accuses of unduly hoarding tax revenue (HT 32/Bosworth 1987: 214–222). The coincidence between the inquisition and the war against Christian Byzantium appears supported by the Caliph's comparisons between the doctrine of the uncreated Qur'ān and Christianity: "[These people] talk just like the Christians when they claim that Jesus son of Mary was not created, because he was the Word of God" (above, p. 225). In a similar, war-rhetorical vein, the Caliph also accused his opponents of "making the way easy for the enemies of the enactment of peace (*al-islām*)" (above, p. 226), who at the time were the Christian Byzantines.[20]

This historical treatment of the doctrinal dispute over the Qur'ān's createdness or uncreatedness and the context of war and land tax helps bring out the complex senses pertaining to the Qur'ānic concept *khalq*. It seems to refer to the connection between the material Creation of which people live and the power to define meaning, through speech. Therefore, speech must be correct (*mustaqīm*) also in the sense that it 'creates' beneficial conditions. For example, Q. 16 (*al-Naḥl*) conveys a semantic relationship between the writing and the life-giving water, both of which are sent down by God in His capacity as Creator. The water is the precondition for the creatures that produce the edibles – 'the milk and the honey'. The writing contractually obligates God to sustain men through creation, and the people to share sustenance gained from the land with those who need it, and to thereby enact security and peace:

> (64) We have only **sent down upon you the divine writing (*anzalnā 'alayka al-kitāb*)** so that you may convey to them clear distinctions regarding that which they disagree about, and as a guidance and protection of life (*raḥma*) for a people who enact security (*liqawmin yu'minūna*).

20 See also Mårtensson (2009a: 137–139).

(65) **God sends down water from the heavens (*wa Allāh anzala min al-samā'i mā'an*)** and revives thereby the land after its death; indeed, in that is a sign for a people who listen!
(66) Indeed, there is **a transmitted message (*'ibratan*)** to you in the cattle: We give you to drink from what is in their bellies between the bowels and the blood, pure milk palatable to those who drink it!
(67) And from the fruits of palm trees and vines you get wine and good sustenance; indeed, in that is a sign for a people who use their reason!
(68) Your Lord **communicated (*awḥā*)** to the bees: 'Take the mountains for houses, and the trees and what they construct!
(69) Then eat from all the fruits and follow your Lord's commands humbly!' From their bellies comes out syrup of different hues in which is healing for men; indeed, in that is a sign for a people who reflect!
(70) **God has created you (*wa Allāh khalaqakum*)**, then He causes you to die. Among you are those who will be returned to the worst age so that after having had knowledge they will not have knowledge of anything; indeed, God has full knowledge and power!
(71) **God has favoured some of you over others with sustenance (*al-rizq*)**, but what about those favoured who do not return their sustenance to those [slaves] who their right hand possesses so that they be equal therein: are they denying God's **blessing**?
(…)
(73) **They serve apart from God what does not own a thing of sustenance (*rizq*)** for them from the heavens and the land, nor can they!
(…)
(81) God has made (*ja'ala*) for you from what **He created (*khalaqa*)** shades from the sun, and from the mountains places of shelter, and He has made for you garments to shield you from the heat, and coats of mail to shield you from injury. In this way He has completed His **blessing** upon you, so that **you may enact peace (*la'allakum tuslimūna*)**.
(82) If they make themselves governors (*in tawallaw*), your obligation is only to **convey the message that makes clear distinctions (*'alayka al-balāgh al-mubīn*)**!
(83) They have experienced (*ya'rifūna*) God's **blessing** but then deny it, for most of them are rejecters of security (*aktharuhum al-kāfirūna*)!
(84) On the day when We dispatch from each nation a witness, then those who reject security shall not be granted leave or return;
(85) When those who do wrong see that the punishment shall not be lightened for them and that they shall not be reprieved;
(86) When those who made partners see their partners and say: 'Our Lord, these are our partners who we used to call upon besides You!' but these return to them the statement (*fa'alqaw ilayhim al-qawla*): 'You are indeed liars!'

(87) and when they return to God on that day **the peace** (*wa alqaw ilā Allāh yawma'idhin al-salama*), that which they used to fabricate shall err away from them.
(88) Those who rejected security and divert from the duties towards God (*sabīl Allāh*): We will increase punishment on top of the punishment for their promoting corruption (*yufsidūna*)!
(89) On the day when We dispatch in each nation a witness against them from among themselves, We will bring you as a witness against these, for **We have sent down upon you the writing (*anzalnā 'alayka al-kitāba*)** as a clear distinction for everything, as a guide and protection of life and a good word **to those who enact peace (*li-l-muslimīna*).**
(90) God commands justice, the good, and the giving to kindred, and He forbids indecency, the reprehensible, and aggression: He admonished you so that you may recall and honour!
(91) So fulfil the contract with God when you enter into compacts (*wa awfū bi'ahd Allāh idhā 'āhadtum*), and do not break the oaths after you have affirmed them, taking God as legal guardian (*kafīlan*); indeed, God has knowledge of what you do!

The Historicity of the Qur'ān and al-Ṭabarī's History

To conclude I will briefly discuss the historical validity of e.g. al-Ṭabarī's history, in particular the way he located the origins of Abrahamic prophecy in ancient Mesopotamia and related it to 'food security', which as we have seen in Chapters 3 and 4 is also closely related to the Qur'ānic concept *mu'min* and the terms of Covenant. As we also saw in Chapter 3, Retsö's (2003) 'long history' of the Arabs defines them as agriculturalists and merchants with vassal- and commercial contracts with imperial rulers, and living at the crossroads of the Greek, Roman, Egyptian, Hebrew, Mesopotamian, Persian, and Indian societies and cultures. This has implications for how we understand the Qur'ānic references to a Covenant-history of Abrahamic prophecy, shared with Jews and Christians and known but forgotten by Arab polytheists. Even though the Qur'ānic *scripture* is 'later' than the Bibles and some Jewish and Christian literatures,[21] the Qur'ān *reminds* its addressees of this history. Given that Retsö's records show the Arabs entering vassal treaties already with the Assyrian kings in the 800s B.C.E., they could have had their own ancient history of Covenant, alongside the Hebrews and eventually the Christians.

21 See however Lowin (2006) on Islamic topical contributions to some rabbinical *midrash*, and the 'openness' of the Babylonian Talmud into Islamic times.

We can then re-consider al-Ṭabarī's historical contextualization of Q. 2 (*al-Baqara*), 258, in Mesopotamia and Abraham's negotiations with the self-deifying tyrant king Nimrod to secure food for his people. In the Hebrew Bible and rabbinical literature, King Nimrod is connected with both southern Iraq (Mesopotamia) and the northern royal cities of Nineveh and Nimrud (former Kalhu) of the neo-Assyrian and then Babylonian Empires, and he appears like a personification of Assyrian and Babylonian empire and cities (van der Toorn and van der Horst 1990). Royal friezes from the *city* Nimrud depict kings surrounded by winged attendant 'angels', often grouped around a tree.[22] Shari Lowin (2006) has mapped and compared common topics associated with Abraham in Jewish and Islamic sources, and the 'food-negotiation'-topic is not among them. One of al-Ṭabarī's main sources for the history of ancient Iraq was Hishām b. al-Kalbī (d. 204/819), from the southern Iraqi city al-Ḥīra, capital of the Lakhmids, the pre-Islamic Arab vassal kings of the Sassanid Empire. He specialised in Iraqi Arab history, including information about ancient time.[23] Yet the report on Abraham's 'food-negotiation' was transmitted by Zayd b. Aslam (Medina, d. 136/753), Maʿmar b. Rāshid (d. 153/770, Basra, southern Iraq, student of al-Zuhrī, Medina), ʿAbd al-Razzāq al-Ṣanʿānī (d. 211/827, Yemen), and al-Ḥasan b. Yaḥyā (d. 263/877). It is therefore possible that al-Ṭabarī reported a specific Arab Abraham-tradition, which relates royal self-deification and 'idolatry' to the conditions for food distribution, a topic that the Qur'ān also raises in relation to Abraham in several *sūra*s (see Chapters 3 and 4 above).

This makes sense also with reference to the studies by Johansen (1988) and Watson (2008/1983), discussed in Chapter 5, that early Islamic 'divine law' gave ownership rights to peasants, raising them from the status of serfs to proprietors and commercial agents. From this perspective, a king who claims servitude to himself keeps the people in serfdom, in contrast to servitude of God in exchange for rights. Consequently, both al-Ṭabarī's history and the Qur'ānic Abraham-account can be seen as transmitting historical knowledge, which is specific to the Arab peoples' histories but general to the vassal system, and therefore serves to clarify the Qur'ānic legal innovation.

22 On the royal city of Nimrud, see Collins (2018); Brereton (2018); Edgeworth Reade (2018).

23 On Ibn al-Kalbī and al-Ṭabarī's sources for Assyrian and Babylonian history, see Retsö (2003: 473–476 et passim).

QUR'ĀN EXEGESIS (*TAFSĪR*)

The next, fifth discipline is Qur'ān exegesis or *tafsīr*, 'explanation' of the Qur'ān's meaning. As discussed in Chapters 2 and 3, the beginnings of exegesis can be seen as coinciding with both the production of Qur'ān manuscripts and the development of linguistics in the late 600s.[24] Reports by the Prophet's cousin, the Companion ʿAbd Allāh b. ʿAbbās (d. 67/687), play a key role as representative of this early stage. Kees Versteegh, who has studied the co-development of linguistics and exegesis, perceives Ibn ʿAbbās as a figurehead for *tafsīr*, due to his proximity to the Prophet. Because Ibn ʿAbbās' reports reflect several, sometimes contradictory, exegetical strands, Versteegh concludes that he cannot himself be the source of all these reports, but the exegetical methodologies attributed to him may well date to his lifetime i.e. the second half of the 600s (Versteegh 1990: 236–238).[25] In other words, it is historically viable to date the beginnings of exegesis to Ibn ʿAbbās' time.

Some contemporary scholars have conceptualised *tafsīr* primarily as a literary genre, represented by the commentaries on the whole Qur'ān (Calder 1993; Bauer 2013). Others have argued that *tafsīr* should rather be seen as a distinct discipline, since these commentaries are informed by theories of language and interpretation (hermeneutics), which overlap with legal hermeneutics (*uṣūl al-fiqh*) and theology (*kalām*), and to some extent, ontology and epistemology in the philosophical sense (Mårtensson 2009b; 2016; Pink & Görke 2014). There are also several different literary genres within *tafsīr*, so the discipline is not limited to the commentaries of the whole Qur'ān (Shah 2013a; Pink & Görke 2014).

Nevertheless, the examples I have selected for illustration belong to commentaries of the whole Qur'ān, which are composed by seven well-known

24 References in Chapter 2 for this convergence are Shah (2003a; 2003b; 2004).

25 For the same assessment of Ibn ʿAbbās' reports, see Goldfeld (1981; 1988). Rippin (1994), by contrast, thought it impossible to trace any substance associated with Ibn ʿAbbās to his lifetime; rather, Ibn ʿAbbās should be seen as a mythologised persona, which exegetes from the third/ninth and fourth/tenth centuries onwards employed to legitimise various points. Gilliot (1985) is in agreement with Rippin's approach. However, Gilliot (2013: 312, note 3) revises his previous scepticism due to Gregor Schoeler's research into early written sources, and continuities between Islamic scholarly practices and Late Antiquity. Note also that the biographer Ibn Saʿd (d. 230/845) reported that Ibn ʿAbbās carried forth the knowledge about the Qur'ān and about how to give rulings based on it, that the Prophet's scribe Zayd b. Thābit had in his capacity as compiler of the established Qur'ānic script (Ibn Saʿd 2001/2, 312; cf. 310–311). On Zayd and the established script, see also Chapter 3, above.

exegetes from the earliest period to the 1500s (see also Chapter 4, on Q. 4, 1). The aim is not to analyse the exegetes' methodologies but to show how they treated verses that can be seen as related to constitution and social contract. Yet the pragmatist and rhetorical premise that a speaker's intended message addresses a topic with reference to a specific context, discussed in Chapters 2 and 3, informed the commentaries in two basic ways. Firstly, the exegetes pay attention both to a verse's context within a *sūra* and occurrences of a concept in other *sūra*s i.e. the micro/meso-levels of meaning. Secondly, they adduce external context for verses, primarily through references to Prophetic or other historical reports.

The first selected exegete is Muqātil b. Sulaymān (d. 150/767), author of the earliest extant commentary of the whole Qur'ān, titled simply *Tafsīr*. Muqātil was a tradition-expert and jurist who hailed from Khurasan but lived and worked in the Iraqi city Basra. Versteegh has traced Muqātil's methodology and use of linguistic terms to Ibn ʿAbbās' exegetical reports transmitted by scholars from the Iraqi city Kufa. Thus, Muqātil followed Ibn ʿAbbās' basic method, explaining words and phrases with reference to a specific context (Versteegh 1990: 214–215). Furthermore, Muqātil is famous for introducing most *sūra*s with his own summary of their aim (*hadaf* or *maqṣūd*, 'objective'), which he used as a guide for his exegesis (Versteegh 1990: 210–213; 1993: 130).[26] Thus, he understood a *sūra* as a topical unit, which constitutes a semantic context for its verses. He also stated that the Qur'ān contains general and particular statements i.e. what is particular (*khāṣṣ*) for 'the enactors of peace' (*al-muslimūna*) and 'those who assign partners' (*al-mushrikūna*), and what is general (*ʿāmm*) for all people (Muqātil 2002/1: 27).

The second exegete is ʿAbd al-Razzāq al-Ṣanʿānī (d. 211/827). He hailed from Ṣanʿā in Yemen, from a family of scholars; his father specialised in Prophetic tradition. His *Tafsīr* covers the whole Qur'ān, but he did not treat all the verses. Instead, he selected specific words and phrases that required explanation. Even though he may have conceived of *sūra*s as topical units, this is not explicit in his method. He relied almost exclusively on exegetical reports from his teacher, the Prophetic biographer Maʿmar b. Rāshid (d. 153/770), who transmitted from the Successor Qatāda (d. 117/735), then various Companions.

26 Mir (1993) identifies the earliest explicitly stated view of *sūra*s as units with the medieval exegetes al-Zarkashī (d. 794/1391) and al-Suyūṭī (d. 911/1505), and shows how this developed into a consistent methodology with modern exegetes. To Mir's trajectory, one should add Muqātil.

The third selected exegete is our al-Ṭabarī and his commentary *Jāmiʿ al-bayān ʿan taʾwīl āy al-Qurʾān*. His conceptualisation of the Qur'ān's composition as reflecting the terms of Covenant, and constructed around general and particular statements, has already been treated in Chapter 3. Al-Ṭabarī also frequently referred to Ibn ʿAbbās' reports, as well as those in al-Ṣanʿānī's commentary, among many others (Horst 1952). Moreover, al-Ṭabarī defined *sūra* as derived from *sūr*, 'wall', meaning an elevated location, which is walled off from its surroundings, like a city: *al-sūra (....) al-manzila min manāzil al-irtifāʿ wa min dhālika suwar al-madīna summiya bidhālika al-ḥāʾiṭ alladhī yaḥwīhā li-irtifāʿihi ʿalā mā yaḥwīhi.*[27] Even though he thus defined *sūra* as a unit, he did not begin his commentary by describing the aim of each *sūra*, as Muqātil did. Instead, he explained verse by verse, and phrase by phrase, contextualising each one in terms of a specific topic. A good illustration is the passage Q. 6 (*al-Anʿām*), 95–97, which I cited above, in the section on *siyāsa*:

> (95) Indeed, God is the Cleaver of the seed and the kernel, bringing out what lives from what is dead, and what is dead from what lives: *that* is God for you! So how did you become perverted?
> (96) Originator of the dawn, He made the night for rest and the sun and the moon **for calculation (*ḥusbānan*)**: *that* is the ordering of the Mighty Who Possesses Knowledge,
> (97) He Who made for you the stars so that you may be guided by them in the darknesses of the plains and the sea; We have certainly distinguished the signs for a people who possess knowledge!

Explaining the word *ḥusbān*, 'calculation', in verse 96, al-Ṭabarī starts by citing reports from earlier exegetes. Some said it means that the sun and the moon run according to fixed, calculated times, corresponding to day and night; others said it means they are lights. Al-Ṭabarī favoured the first option, because the internal context i.e. verses 95 and 97, implies that God calculated the times for the sun and the moon for the benefit of Creation, just as He brings out edible vegetation for His creatures, and provides the stars for their guidance. Guidance therefore refers to both physical orientation in the land, and correct understanding of the divine message so as not to go astray morally and serve others than God (1995/5:7, 370–373). However, al-Ṭabarī also argued that since God addressed the Qurʾān to the Prophet, and he was the most capable of understanding and conveying the message,

27 Al-Ṭabarī (1995/1:1, 71; see also p. 69, on the long Medina *sūra*s as topical units).

sound Prophetic reports are the decisive authority on meaning (1995/1:1, 18–24).

The other four exegetes display the same basic method, though with individual profiles, as we shall see. They are the Twelver Shīʿī theologian, jurist, and exegete al-Ṭūsī (d. 460/1067) and his *al-Tibyān fī tafsīr al-Qurʾān*; al-Zamakhsharī (d. 538/1143), who was a linguist, Muʿtazilī theologian, ethicist, and exegete, and his commentary *Al-Kashshāf ʿan ḥaqāʾiq al-tanzīl wa ʿuyūn al-aqāwīl fī wujūh al-taʾwīl*; al-Rāzī (d. 606/1209), Ashʿarī theologian and Qurʾān exegete famous for building his commentary *Mafātīḥ al-ghayb* around systematically derived topical issues (*masāʾil*) with related general and particular statements; and the Shāfiʿī jurist al-Suyūṭī (d. 911/1505). As mentioned in Chapter 4, al-Suyūṭī authored two commentaries: *al-Durr al-manthūr fī al-tafsīr al-maʾthūr*, where he gives earlier and diverse exegetical reports with different interpretations, and *Tafsīr al-Jalālayn*, which consists of his and his teacher Jalāl al-Dīn al-Maḥallī's definition of one meaning for the Qurʾān. I will refer to both.

Q. 16 (*AL-NAḤL*), 91 (LATE MECCA)

For the first example, I have selected Q. 16 (*al-Naḥl*), 91, which refers to God's *ʿahd*, 'compact':

> (91) So fulfil the compact with God when you enter into compacts (*wa awfū biʿahd Allāh idhā ʿāhadtum*), and do not break the oaths after you have affirmed them, taking God as legal guardian (*kafīlan*); indeed, God has knowledge of what you do!

Muqātil explains the first part of the verse as God saying that one should not go back on oaths after they have been affirmed, and the second part as meaning that God is a witness to the fulfilment of compact (Muqātil 2002/2: 484). Thus, he interpreted it as a general command. ʿAbd al-Razzāq al-Ṣanʿānī, our second exegete, only explains specific words and this verse is unfortunately not among them. Al-Ṭabarī explained that the verse is about God obligating people to fulfil their compact with Him in particular, and in general to fulfil their oaths and not go back on them, unless their terms are such that God forbids them. He added that although some have argued that the verse addresses the oath of allegiance (*bayʿa*) to the Prophet, at a time when the Muslims were in the minority and their adversaries in the majority, and the Muslims therefore might change their minds, there is no firm report evidence for that interpretation (al-Ṭabarī 1995/8:14, 215–216). Al-Ṭūsī joins the verse 91 with the preceding verse 90, which commands justice and promoting the good (*iḥsān*), including what concerns the Prophet's family. He then explains verse 91 as the general obligation to fulfil compacts when their terms are good (*ḥasan*) and when God is invoked as guarantor; but he adds that some have said that the oath of allegiance to the Prophet may have been a specific context (al-Ṭūsī, vol. 6: 418–420). Al-Zamakhsharī explained 'the compact with God' in specific terms, as the oath of allegiance (*bayʿa*) to the Prophet, cross-referencing to Q. 48 (*al-Fatḥ*), 10, "Indeed, those who swear allegiance to you swear allegiance to God, and God's hand is upon your hands". Thus, he explained the second part of the verse too as referring to the oath of allegiance to the Prophet, which should not be broken after having been affirmed, meaning that it was taken 'in the name of God', which makes God its legal guardian (al-Zamakhsharī 2009: 582). Al-Rāzī, who consistently broke down verses into topical issues and sequences of universals and particulars, agrees with al-Zamakhsharī's approach and explanation, that the general principle is that one should fulfil one's compact, particularly the oath of allegiance to the Prophet. Al-Rāzī then elaborates on God's general command regarding all kinds of oaths and contracts, explaining that that is what is meant by God's statement that He knows what people do: i.e. whether they fulfil their compacts and oaths, or not (al-Rāzī 1981/20: 108–109). Finally, al-Suyūṭī in *al-Durr al-manthūr* lists what earlier exegetes have concluded, and attributes to al-Ṭabarī (among others) the reported view that the first part of the verse could refer to the oath of allegiance to the Prophet, when the Muslims were in the minority, and that the second half addresses the general issue of fulfilling oaths taking God as witness and guarantor. Al-Suyūṭī then concludes it is not possible to determine the exact context (2011/5: 161). Accordingly, in *Tafsīr al-Jalālayn* the defined meaning is that this is a general command to fulfil the terms of contracts when one has invoked God in one's oaths and pledges (2003: 277).

In sum: the exegetes converge around the concept of God as the ultimate guarantor of compact and oaths, provided the terms do not expressly violate His commands. This includes pre-Islamic pacts (*aḥlāf*, sing. *ḥilf*), which can be maintained. They also use the term *kafara* in this context as referring to those who go back on oaths i.e. 'reject compact'. Al-Ṭabarī, al-Ṭūsī, and al-Suyūṭī are evidence-oriented: without reports that the verse actually refers to the Prophet's oath of allegiance, this cannot be concluded with certainty, although that oath would theoretically fall under the general command. Al-Zamakhsharī instead bypasses external contextual evidence in favour of intra-Qurʾānic support for this interpretation, and al-Rāzī follows his lead.

Q. 3 (*ĀL 'IMRĀN*), 79 (MEDINA)

> (79) It is impossible that any human vessel of the divine word who God has given the writing, the judgement, and the prophecy, would say to the people: "Be servants to me instead of to God!" Rather, [he would say]: "Be **masters** by virtue of the knowledge of the divine writing that you have been conveying, and by virtue of what you have been studying! (*kūnū* ***rabbāniyyīna*** *bimā kuntum tu'allimūna al-kitāba wa bimā kuntum tadrusūna*)"

Q. 3, 79 describes God giving the writing and the ruling to prophets, who convey the knowledge to the people, who study the divine writing. The knowledge implies that they are obligated to *serve* only God, not human authorities. The key word I have selected here is *rabbāniyyūn*. Muqātil set out by saying that the 'human vessel of the divine word' refers to Jesus, son of Mary, and the writing is the Torah and the Gospel, and the people are the Israelites. Referring to the context of doctrinal polemics against serving human or angel authorities instead of God, which is mentioned in the next verse 3, 80, he defines *rabbāniyyūn* as those who devote their servitude to God (Muqātil 2002/1: 286). By comparison, al-Ṣan'ānī begins by stating that God with the divine writing has obligated *ahl al-kitāb* to confirm the Prophet. In this way he directed the meaning of *rabbāniyyūn* towards a specifically Islamic context, explaining it as referring to 'discerning ones with knowledge' (*ḥulamā' 'ulamā'*) i.e. the scholars (al-Ṣan'ānī 1989/1: 125; also p. 124). This Islamic context is fully developed by al-Ṭabarī, who explained *rabbāniyyūn* with reference to the scholars and the discipline of *fiqh*, particularly those among them who represent *ḥikma* and defend the common good and equity for the people, in the spheres of the judicial order (*dīn*) and the material or 'nearest' world (*dunyā*). In his exposition, al-Ṭabarī includes a quote from the early exegete Mujāhid (d. 104/722), who argued that representing the people's welfare means that the scholars oversee the state administration. This view of the scholars' responsibility goes against al-Māwardī's view, discussed above, that the Caliph must himself oversee the administration. It thus appears that al-Ṭabarī via Mujāhid asserted the autonomy of the scholars as the judiciary that checks the state administration:

> [By 'masters' (*rabbāniyyīn*) is meant] the scholar of jurisprudence (*fiqh*) and just judgement (*ḥikma*), who is among those who promote the common good (*al-muṣliḥīna*), and manage the people's affairs by teaching them the good (*al-khayr*) and inviting them to that which is their common good (*maṣlaḥatihim*). [This kind of scholar] is one who

> judges justly (*ḥakīm*) and fulfils his duties towards God, and is the governor who governs the people's affairs according to the method of those among the promoters of the common good who promote equity (*al-muqsiṭūna min al-muṣliḥīna*) (…). Thus, the 'masters' are the support of the people in jurisprudence, scholarship, and matters of the judicial order and the material nearest life (*al-dīn wa al-dunyā*). (…) Mujāhid said: They are above the scholars (*wa hum fawqa al-aḥbār*), because the scholars are the men with knowledge (*al-ʿulamāʾ*), whereas the master combines knowledge and jurisprudence so as to oversee politics and administration and represent the affairs of the ruled so that their common good is furthered in their nearest life and their judicial order. (al-Ṭabarī 1995/3:3, 444–445)

Al-Ṭūsī contextualises the verse with reference to a group of Jews, who asked if the Prophet required them to serve him, like the Christians serve the Messiah i.e. Jesus. He then explains *rabbāniyyūn* as those scholars who convey knowledge to the people, and relates that some have said it means judges who administrate the people's affairs to ensure the common good under the governorate (*mudabbirī amr al-nās fī al-wilāya bi-l-iṣlāḥ*). He also proposes the meaning that conveying knowledge of this kind, which benefits the people, is what entitles someone to the honorary epithet *ʿālim*, on account of his sincerity (*ikhlāṣ*) (al-Ṭūsī, vol. 2, 511–512). Thus, al-Ṭūsī aligns broadly with the explanation by al-Ṭabarī/Mujāhid. Al-Zamakhsharī starts by contextualising the verse with reference to the Prophet's meeting with Christian dignitaries from Najran, who asked if they should serve him, which the Prophet of course rejected. He then explains *rabbāniyyūn* as referring to the legislators (*al-shāriʿ*) among the scholars (2009: 179). Al-Rāzī similarly defines the context as the Christians' deification and servitude of Jesus, resulting from their having changed the letters of the scripture, and lands on a definition of *rabbāniyyūn* as a term occurring in Hebrew, Syriac, and Arabic, which refers to governors and scholars who use their knowledge to teach the people good things; thus, it is a cross-communal term (1981/8: 120–123). Al-Suyūṭī in *al-Durr al-manthūr* contextualises the verse with reference to the report about a delegation of Christians (and Jews, he adds) from Najran to the Prophet, and the Prophet's rejection of servitude to himself. He then explains *rabbāniyyūn* as referring to the scholars of jurisprudence, who serve as governors for the people. Though he refers to al-Ṭabarī's report from Mujāhid, he does not mention the issue that the scholars should oversee the state administration, which is contained in al-Ṭabarī's own Mujāhid report (al-Suyūṭī 2011/2: 250–251). In *Tafsīr al-Jalālayn* the context is said to be the Christian delegation from Najran and their servitude to Jesus, or some Muslims who wanted to prostrate before the Prophet, while *rabbāni-yyūn* refers to the scholars who practice their understanding of *sharīʿa*; the issue of overseeing the administration is not mentioned here (2003: 60).

In sum: with the exception of Muqātil, these exegetes refer *rabbāniyyūn* to the institution of the scholars and the law, as representing the people's welfare and the common good. Al-Ṭabarī/Mujāhid stand out for making explicit the constitutional topic of 'the rule of law', by defining *rabbāni-yyūn* as those who, on account of their concern for the people's welfare, the common good, and equity, have the authority to also supervise the state administration. We thus find al-Ṭabarī on the opposite side of the political theorist al-Māwardī on this topic.

Q. 4 (*AL-NISĀʾ*), 58–60 (MEDINA)

This passage includes the verse 4, 59 discussed above under political theory, where al-Māwardī explained it as referring to the Caliphate, as the succession to the Prophet's legal authority:

> (58) Indeed, God commands you (*inna Allāh yaʾmurukum*) to return trusts to their owners and, when you judge between the people, that you judge justly; what God exhorts you to do is certainly a blessing! Indeed, God is a Hearing One Who Oversees!
> (59) O you who have come to enact security! Obey God and obey God's Messenger and those in command among you (*ūlī al-amr minkum*), so that if you dispute over a matter, refer it to God and the Messenger. If you enact security through God and the Furthest Day, that is best and the best reference in interpretation (*dhālika khayrun wa aḥsanu taʾwīlan*)!
> (60) Have you not seen those who claim they have enacted security through what was sent down to you and what was sent down before you? They want to take their judgement to the idol (*ṭāghūt*) even though they have been commanded to reject it (*yakfurū bihi*), for Satan wants to lead them far astray!

Compared with al-Māwardī's straightforward political explanation of verse 59, the exegetes bring out the complexities. Muqātil refers verse 58 and 'return trusts' to the Prophet who, having conquered Mecca, took the keys to the Kaʿba from its guardian ʿUthmān b. Ṭalḥa, but then returned them to him. Regarding verse 59, he explained that 'those in command among you' refers to the Prophet's military commander Khālid b. al-Walīd, while 'refer it to God and the Messenger' means the Qur'ān and the Prophet's *sunna* i.e.

the two sources of the law. The 'idol' in verse 60 refers to a specific Jewish soothsayer-oracle, Muqātil argues (2002/1: 381–385). Al-Ṣanʿānī only treats verse 59 and the words 'refer it to God and the Messenger', which he too explains as referring to the Qurʾān and the Prophet's *sunna* (1989/1: 167).

Al-Ṭabarī considers two interpretations of verse 58. One says the verse is God's general address (*khiṭāb*) to rulers, that they must protect the people's property and rights; and another that it addresses the episode with the Prophet, the keys, and ʿUthmān b. Ṭalḥa. Al-Ṭabarī concludes the first is the correct interpretation, but that the episode with the Prophet is also possible, as it would fall under the general command to rulers to rule justly (1995/4:5, 200–203). Verse 59 he explains as meaning that one should obey God and the Prophet as His Messenger while he was alive, and after his death one follows first the Qurʾān, and if it contains no guidance, then the *sunna*. 'Those in command' are defined in a Prophetic tradition as the commanders and governors, so he rejects an alternative interpretation that it refers to the scholars. Muslims are obligated to obey those in command, but only if they rule justly according to the Qurʾān and the *sunna*, and according to *maṣlaḥa li ʿāmmat al-raʿiyya*, 'the common good for the ruled' (1995/4:5, 208; 203–208). The idol (*ṭāghūt*) in verse 60 refers to those who people magnify, and whose rulings they follow instead of God's rulings through His Prophet; though he cites reports about the Jewish oracle, he does not validate this reference since it is not a Prophetic report (1995/4:5, 210–214).

Al-Ṭūsī gives two general meanings for verse 58: that one should always return a thing one has been entrusted with; and, addressed to the leader-commanders, that they should peacefully transfer the command to those who come after them, perform all the ritual obligations, and return to the people all the alms and booty they have a right to. The context that occasioned the sending-down of the verse is the tradition about the Prophet and the keys to the Kaʿba (al-Ṭūsī, vol. 3, 234). Regarding verse 59, al-Ṭūsī explains that 'obey God and His Messenger' means to adhere to their commands and prohibitions, which after the Prophet's death are represented by his *sunna*. 'Those in command' has been interpreted in two ways by other exegetes: the commanders or the scholars, al-Ṭūsī says. He rejects both and states that it must refer to the Imams of the Prophet's family (*al-aʾimma min āl Muḥammad*), since obedience is stated in absolute terms and God and the Prophet are without sin (*maʿṣūm*) and just, and therefore can command absolute obedience of in their commands and prohibitions. Since neither the commanders nor the scholars meet this requirement, it must refer to the Imams. Consequently, he explains 'refer it to God and His Messenger' as including 'and to the Imams who are without sin' (*al-a'imma al-ma'ṣūmīna*) (al-Ṭūsī, vol. 3, 235–237).

Al-Zamakhsharī explains verse 58 as a general address (*khiṭāb 'āmm*), sent down because of the episode with the Prophet and the keys of the Temple. He also refers to the interpretation that the address concerns the governors (*al-wulāt*) and their obligation to rule justly; and to the reading that 'trust' depends on the declaration of divine Oneness (*al-amānatu 'alā al-tawḥīd*) i.e. the commitment to returning trusts is guaranteed through the creed. Verse 59 he explains as referring to the commanders and rulers, based on the Prophetic tradition, and like al-Ṭabarī he emphasises that God only commands obedience to them if they rule justly and uphold rights, in accordance with God's Qur'ān and the Prophet's *sunna*, which cannot possibly mean that obedience is due also to unjust rulers. He mentions the interpretation that 'those in command' refers to the scholars as an alternative. Regarding verse 60, he follows the others (2009: 242).

Al-Rāzī explains that God's general objective of verse 58 is to command the return of trusts under all circumstances, also to non-believers, which he then contextualises through the same narrative about the Prophet and the keys to the Temple. He then breaks the topic down into a huge number of general and particular issues! Concerning verse 59, al-Rāzī argues that, on account of the just rule that God commands for those in authority, He also commands the people to obey those in authority. These must be the scholars, since the commanders and governors are as a rule not just, and it is the scholars who have the authority to 'dissolve and bind' (*al-ḥall wa al-'aqd*) i.e. declare a ruler legitimate or not, as discussed above (1981/10: 149–150).[28] He concludes by saying that most of the issues pertaining to legal hermeneutics (*uṣūl al-fiqh*) can be deduced from this verse, and that it took him a mere two hours – i.e. it was a piece of cake – to produce the hugely long exposition of general and particular issues that then follows (1981/10: 157). Verse 60 he explains like the other exegetes.

In *al-Durr al-manthūr* al-Suyūṭī too contextualises verse 58 through the report about the Prophet and the keys, citing e.g. al-Ṭabarī's commentary to the effect that the Prophet gave the right to the custody of the Ka'ba's keys to 'Uthmān b. Ṭalḥa's family, Banū Ṭalḥa. He concludes that the verse was addressed to commanders in general, but then proceeds to cite other reports that establish a semantic and ethical relationship between *īmān* and the word

28 Other 'pre-modern' Sunnī exegetes who took the same position as al-Rāzī are al-Sarakhsī (d. 1106), al-Mināwī (d. 1662), and al-'Umarī (d. 1803); see Hatina (2010: 458). For modern cases, see Chapter 7.

for 'trust', *amāna*. Similarly to al-Zamakhsharī's reasoning, though taking the etymological approach, al-Suyūṭī then argues that anyone who has *īmān* also has *amāna*, which is enacted in the legal sense of returning trusts (unless the trustee is manifestly untrustworthy), and in the ritual sense of performing the prayers, the fast, and the ritual purification (al-Suyūṭī 2011/2: 570–573). For verse 59, al-Suyūṭī starts with several reports stating 'those in command' refers to the commanders, as per the Prophetic tradition. Then he refers to another sequence of reports stating it refers to the scholars. He appears to come down on the side of those who argue it refers to commanders, who should be obeyed unless they divert from God's *kitāb* and the Prophet's *sunna* (al-Suyūṭī 2011/2: 573–579). Verse 60 al-Suyūṭī considered part of the passage verses 60–63, and he contextualised it with reference to the Jewish tribes of Medina and their judges in the pre-Islamic period, giving several examples of how they did not judge justly and behaved arrogantly. The word 'idol' (*ṭāghūt*) thus, in his view, refers to the Jewish judges. However, he also cites a general interpretation from Mujāhid, that 'idols' are satans in human form, from whom people seek judgement because they are in command over them; i.e., instead of seeking judgement based on objective justice (al-Suyūṭī 2011/2: 582; 580–582). In *Tafsīr al-Jalālayn* verse 58 is defined as addressing the incident with the Kaʿba's keys, but in the form of a general command to rule justly and protect rights, conveyed through the plural form ("God commands you", plural). Verse 59 is explained as referring to the authority of God and His writing and the Prophet and his *sunna*. 'Those in authority' are the governors, obeyed if their command aligns with God and His Messenger. It is then added that following God/His writing and the Prophet/his *sunna* is the safeguard against disputes and opinion-based statements (*al-qawl bi-l-raʾy*), i.e. a legal hermeneutical point is made here. For verse 60 the interpretation of 'idol' aligns with that in *al-Durr al-manthūr* (2003: 87–88)

In sum: all the exegetes approached the passage 4, 58–60 as having to do with 'rule of law'-related matters. Regarding the crucial verse 59, the Twelver Shīʿī al-Ṭūsī predictably stands out for defining the Shīʿī Imams as the referent for 'those in command'. Among the Sunnīs, al-Rāzī argues forcefully that 'those in command' refers to the scholars' authority 'to dissolve and bind' loyalty to commanders and rulers because the latter tend not to be just, while the other exegetes opt for the commanders and governors as referents. In this particular case, then, al-Rāzī is the one who explicitly reads the issue of separation of powers into his exegesis. Although all the other exegetes agree that the commanders must be just and comply with God and His Messenger in order to command obedience, al-Ṭabarī stands out for making the principle of the common good of the ruled a criterion for obedience – the same principle that he identified as the hallmark of 'the master scholars' in his exegesis of Q. 3, 79. However, because he assigned final exegetical authority to sound Prophetic reports, and there is a Prophetic report that 'those in authority' refers to the governors in Q. 4, 59, his methodology prevented him from arguing that it can refer to the scholars in this case.

Conclusions

These few and summarily described examples show the exegetes apply perspectives related to constitutional principles and social contractual reasons for authority in their explanations of the selected Qur'ānic passages and concepts. Hence, the exegetes align in their *topical-theoretical* understanding of these verses with the political science approach. Yet their exegetical *methods* bring out the complexity involved in determining meaning, because they consider both general and particular statements, internal and external contexts, evidence, and alternative interpretations. Overall, these exegetes depict their own scholarly institution's authority as consisting in the capacity for just judgement, equity and upholding the common good. It would be easy to see this simply as an expression of self-interest e.g. al-Rāzī's argument that since the governors are patently unjust, the scholars must be the ones in command after the Prophet (Q. 4, 59). However, it could also reflect al-Rāzī's empirical observations of governors. By comparison, al-Ṭabarī illustrates another use of empirical data: he could not use *this* verse to assert scholarly authority over the administration because of Prophetic evidence that it referred to commanders.

Finally, all these exegetes consider the distinction between generals and particulars intrinsic to the Qur'ān, which supports al-Ṭabarī's analysis discussed in Chapter 3 (see also Harvey 2020). Al-Rāzī, the virtuoso of such distinctions, assumes that these stem from the text itself while he himself is merely deriving further, implicit applications. Thus, the exegetes assumed that meaning depends on which of the two categories a term or phrase is seen as pertaining to, and distinguishing between them is part of defining semantic context.

FIQH

The Covenantal Dimension

The next discipline *fiqh*, 'jurisprudence', and *uṣūl al-fiqh*, 'legal hermeneutics', is intrinsically connected with *tafsīr*, given that interpretation of the Qurʾān is central in 'lawmaking'. Many of Ibn ʿAbbās' exegetical reports therefore contain rulings and guidance of the kind produced within *fiqh*. Considering also that *ḥadīth* emerged as part of the process of deriving further guidance and law from the Qurʾān, one can date the beginning of *fiqh* to the same time as *ḥadīth* and *tafsīr* began i.e. the late 600s.

Topically, *fiqh* is concerned with both the ritual service and obligations to God, and legal, ethical, and administrative matters. In contrast with *ḥadīth* and *tafsīr*, but like the science of language, it is listed in al-Fārābī's 'Enumeration of the sciences'. He placed *fiqh* under political science (*ʿilm al-madanī*), because he perceived the law as the main tool for the political aim to make the city prosper and enable the citizens' happiness. Accordingly, *fiqh* relates to the theoretical topics of constitution and social contract pertaining to Covenant. I therefore start this brief exposition with Bernard Weiss' analysis that Covenant and the rights and obligations that derive from it serve as the model for *fiqh*, which expounds further sets of rights, obligations, and divine guidance through exegesis (see also Chapter 4 above).

Weiss highlights the importance that the legal scholars attribute to the Qurʾān's function as the obligating speech (*khiṭāb*) that God as speaker (*mukhāṭib*) addresses to the human addressee (*mukhāṭab*): "The *mukhāṭib–mukhāṭab* relationship on which all Muslim jurisprudential thought turns thus presupposes the terms of the covenant discussed in the Qurʾānic commentaries" (Weiss 1998: 34; also 31–34). In this divine-human contractual relationship, the Prophet serves as the communicator, who also, through his *sunna*, carries the obligating divine address further:

> The initial covenantal moment, when the divine sovereignty and human subordination are recognized as the fundamental terms of the covenant, does not entail a prophetic intermediary. But subsequent to this moment the covenantal addressor-addressee relationship continues thanks to the faithful conveying of God's words to humans by the Prophet. In this continuing phase of the relationship the law unfolds (Weiss 1998: 35).

In the section on *siyāsa* above, we saw how Q. 38 (*Ṣād*), 20 and 23 attributed the 'obligating address' (*khiṭāb*) as a capacity that God conferred on David to strengthen his kingdom, and which he abused when he wronged the shepherd. Related forms occur in other contexts as well, including Q. 23 (*al-Mu'minūna*), 26–30, where it refers to Noah, who has been rejected by his people. In verse 27, God commands Noah not to try to address a binding *khiṭāb* to Him regarding those who have done wrong, since He will not change His command regarding them:

> (26) [Noah] said: 'My Lord, help me prevail over their denial!'
> (27) So We communicated (*awḥaynā*) to him: 'Make the Ark under Our eyes and according to Our communication (*waḥyinā*). When Our command comes and the oven boils over, conduct into it a couple of every kind, and your kin, except those against who the statement has already come. **Do not direct an obligating address to Me (*wa lā tukhāṭibnī*) regarding those who have done wrong**, for they will certainly drown!'
> (28) When you have fairly shared your places upon the Ark, you and those who are with you, say: "Praise be to God Who has saved us from the people who wrong the right!"
> (29) And say: "My Lord, bring me down in a blessed landing place, as You are the best of those who bring down!"'
> (30) Indeed, in that are signs of how We have been testing [people]!

Similarly, in Q. 78 (*al-Nabā'*), 35–40, *khiṭāb* occurs in the same sense, as an obligating address that the humans cannot direct to God, unless they are among those given permission to do so because they speak rightly. The context is the Day of judgement, when only those who have made correct statements are allowed to speak in their defence:

> (35) On it, they will not hear idle talk or denials,
> (36) as a reward from your Lord, a calculated gift;
> (37) Lord of the heavens and the land and what is between them, the Giver of Life to Who they are not capable of directing **an obligating address** (*lā yamlikūna minhu* ***khiṭāban***)!
> (38) The Day when the spirit and the angels shall stand in line none shall speak except those who the Giver of Life has granted permission and **who have spoken rightly (*wa qāla ṣawāban*)**!
> (39) That is the Day of the True Right (*al-yawm al-ḥaqq*), and he who wishes takes to his Lord and returns.
> (40) Indeed, We have warned you of an imminent punishment on the Day when a man sees what his hands have brought forth and the rejecter says: 'O, how I wish I was soil of the earth!'

In order to be binding, the Covenantal address must be properly understood by the addressee. Our al-Ṭabarī, who also wrote on *fiqh*, expanded on this point in the Introduction to his commentary on the Qur'ān:

> Indeed, if the addressee and recipient of the message (*al-mukhāṭab wa al-mursal ilayhi*) does not understand the message addressed to him, his state before the address and the arrival of the message and after it is the same, as the address will not have benefitted him in the least. (…) And God, Mighty in Honour, is High Above addressing an obligating speech and sending a message that does not benefit the addressee and recipient of the message (1995/1:1, 18–19).

The key to understanding the obligating speech and message is God's Messenger, who, as al-Ṭabarī pointed out, is the addressee who communicates the particularities and generalities of God's Covenant to his people:

> We have no way to knowledge of what God, Elevated is His honour, meant by His particulars and generalities except through the clarifying distinctions of he for who the Qur᾽ān's clarifications were made, namely God's Messenger (*lam yakun lanā sabīlan ilā al-ʿilm bimā ʿanā Allāhu taʿālā dhikruhu min khuṣūṣihi wa ʿumūmihi illā bibayān man juʿila ilayhi bayān al-Qur᾽ān wa huwa rasūl Allāh*) (1995/1:1, 24).

Al-Ṭabarī's approach of course has a theoretical reference point in the famous verse Q.14 (*Ibrāhīm*), 4, discussed in Chapters 2 and 4 above:

> (4) We have never sent forth a messenger with a message that is not in the language of his people, so that he can make clarifying distinctions to them (*liyubayyina lahum*).

The Hermeneutical and Linguistic Dimensions

The above shows *fiqh* may derive from the Qur᾽ān's identity as God's address that obligates people to the Covenant. The addressees' understanding of the message therefore becomes a key concern, both because they will stand to account for their actions based on its terms and because they should benefit and prosper from the message, and help others prosper too. Consequently, Kevin Reinhart has pointed out that *fiqh* means 'disciplined understanding' of the subject matter *sharīʿa*; another way of putting it would be 'analytical understanding'. The root *sh-r-ʿ* does not refer to the act of giving legal rulings (*ḥakama*) but to the 'opening a path to divine guidance'. Metaphorically, *sharīʿa* signifies 'the riverbank from which animals can reach the water and drink', and the path they beat as they repeatedly go to drink. In the Qur᾽ān the metaphor applies to God's breaking open a path into the world through His sent-down scripture, which therefore constitutes 'an access to His realm'. The concept of *sharīʿa* thus defines the divine guidance as leading humans along a path, which they repeatedly walk (Reinhart 1983:188). Within *fiqh*, *sharīʿa* is developed into two categories: *ʿibādāt* or 'servitude to God', defined as the testimony to God's Oneness; the prayer; the fast; the pilgrimage, and the welfare tax; and *muʿāmalāt* or 'interactions' between people, including ethical categories; ritual purity rules; permitted and prohibited food and drink; family law; civil law; and criminal law. In this way, *sharīʿa* is the totality of the divine guidance.

The root *sh-r-ʿ* occurs in a few places in the Qur'ān, including Q. 42 (*al-Shūrā*), 13 and 21. In verse 13, God is the subject:

> (13) **He has set you on the path of guidance (*sharaʿa* *lakum*)**, of the judicial order (*dīn*) with which He appointed Noah, and which We have communicated to you, and with which We appointed Abraham and Moses and Jesus: 'Establish the judicial order and do not engage in internal strife (*lā tatafarraqū*) within it!' That to which you invite those who take other partners is bigger than these! God elects to Himself who He wishes and guides to Himself who He wishes.

In verse 21, the subjects are humans, specifically the partners that people take together with God. The case shows that although only God's path of guidance is the right one, humans can try to assume the same function.

> (21) Or do they have partners (*shurakāʾ*) **who set them on a path of guidance (*sharaʿū lahum*)** of a judicial order, which God has not permitted? If it was not for the word that makes distinctions, judgement between them would have been passed, and indeed, those who do wrong shall have a painful punishment!

The term *fiqh* has Qurʾānic foundation too: the root *f-q-h* occurs in 20 verses, mostly in the form of the verb *faqiha*, and sometimes as a synonym to *ʿaqala*, to rationally 'comprehend' or 'grasp' God's message and guidance.[29] However, in the late Medina *sūra* Q. 9, verses 122 and 127, the verb appears to takes on a technical sense, related to understanding the judicial order and Qurʾānic *sūra*s, which is the aim of *fiqh* as a discipline:

> (122) The enactors of security do not all go forth [to war], so why not have a company from each group go forth and **learn to understand in an analytical way** the judicial order (***liyatafaqqahū*** *fī al-dīn*), so that

29 Q. 17, 44; Q. 11, 91; Q. 20, 28; Q. 4, 78; Q. 6, 25, 65, 98; Q. 7, 179; Q. 8, 65; Q. 9, 81, 87, 122, 127; Q. 18, 93; Q. 48, 15; Q. 59, 13; Q. 63, 3, 7; Q. 17, 46; and Q. 18, 57.

> they can admonish their people when they return: perhaps they will pay heed!
>
> (127) Whenever a *sūra* is made to descend, they look at each other: "Does anyone see you?" Then they turn away: May God turn their intellects, for they are a people **who do not understand analytically**! (*naẓara baʿḍuhum ilā baʿḍin hal yarākum min aḥadin thumma inṣarafū ṣarafa Allāhu qulūbahum biʾannahum qawmun* ***lā yafqahūna***).[30]

Another important technical term related to *fiqh* is *ikhtilāf*, 'scholarly disagreement' on points of law and ritual. In Chapter 5, I discussed the constitutional challenge that legal disagreement may pose. Within Sunnī *fiqh*, however, *ikhtilāf* filled an important deliberative function, and special written works were devoted to surveying agreement and disagreement on given topics. According to Joseph Schacht, *ikhtilāf* pertains to the process that gave rise to diverse schools of law (*madhāhib*), and occurs in this sense in writings attributed to Abū Ḥanīfa (d. 150/767), patronym of the Ḥanafī *madhhab*. Thus, Schacht argues, *ikhtilāf* was accepted when referring to disagreements between schools of law, but not internally to a school. With the consolidation of *uṣūl al-fiqh* or legal hermeneutics, from al-Shāfiʿī (d. 205/820) onwards, the concept of *ijmāʿ*, 'consensus', fostered both coherence and acceptance of a degree of disagreement on innocuous issues. For example, the Qurʾān commands prayer as part of the people's Covenantal obligations, so the scholars in *fiqh* discuss how exactly the prayer should be performed. While there can be no disagreement about the obligation of prayer, it is acceptable to disagree on the details of the performance. Equally, disagreement on issues not stated in scripture is tolerated.[31]

Ikhtilāf also refers to a literary genre. Here too, al-Ṭabarī made an important contribution through his extensive but largely non-extant *Kitāb*

30 I have translated this verse in the literal sense. However, several of the words relate to terms also used in technical senses within *fiqh*, notably *naẓara*, which can mean 'analyse', 'discern' a meaning; *yarā* from *raʾā*, which can mean 'to have a legal opinion'; and *ṣarafa*, which in the second verb form *ṣarrafa* can mean to 'inflect' a word, 'conjugate' a verb, or 'decline' a noun. It seems to me that the verse is making a pun, by using several words that have both ordinary and *fiqh*-related meanings, in addition to the verb *lā yafqahūna*.

31 Schacht, 'Ikhtilāf', in Encyclopaedia of Islam, Second Edition. Consulted online on 07 October 2018 dx.doi.org/10.1163/1573-3912_islam_SIM_3515. The entry surveys *ikhtilāf* from the earliest works into modern time. On accepted and not accepted disagreement, see also Belhaj (2015), who engages critically with Bauer (2011) and his thesis that *ikhtilāf* expresses a generally high degree of tolerance of ambiguity.

ikhtilāf al-fuqahā' ('Disagreement among the Jurists'), where he maps and analyses agreement and disagreement among eight leading jurists from the 700s and 800s, including Abū Ḥanīfa and al-Shāfiʿī. The analysis served as a first step in the process of developing his own legal hermeneutics and methodology, *al-madhhab al-jarīrī*.[32] The extant text of *Ikhtilāf al-fuqahā'* is preserved in two editions, whose contents give a good view over some disputed topics at the time. The first edition by Friedrich Kern (1902) contains the topical treatises (*kutub*) *al-Mudabbar*, 'Contract for manumission of a slave after his owner's death'; *al-Salam*, 'Advance payment'; *al-Muzāraʿa wa al-musāqā*, 'Sharecropping and irrigation'; *al-Ghaṣb*, 'Usurpation of property'; and *al-Ḍamān wa al-kafāla wa al-ḥawāla*, 'Guarantee, surety, and money transfer' (al-Ṭabarī 1999). The second edition by Joseph Schacht (1933) includes the treatises *al-Jihād*, 'War as divine obligation';[33] *al-Jizya*, 'Tax' (poll tax and land tax); *Aḥkām al-muḥāribīna*, 'Rulings on enemy combatants'; *al-Zakāt*, 'Community tax'; *Qaṭʿ al-sāriq*, 'Amputation on robbers'; and *al-Janā'iz*, 'Funerals' (al-Ṭabarī 1933). In addition, there exists an unpublished manuscript, treating the topic *al-Nikāḥ*, 'Marriage contract' (Stewart 2016: 142).

Ikhtilāf in a sense that appears close to how the term functioned within *fiqh* has a reference in Q. 45 (*al-Jāthiya*), 17–18, where it occurs together with *sharīʿa* and *ʿilm*:

> (17) We came to them with clarifying distinctions of the command, and **they did not disagree (*famā ikhtalafū*)** until **the knowledge (*al-ʿilm*)** came to them, and then because of wrongful excesses amongst themselves. Indeed, your Lord shall judge between them on the Day of Standing to trial regarding that over which they used to **disagree (*yakhtalifūna*)**!
> (18) Then We set you upon a **path of guidance** of the command (***sharīʿa*** *min al-amr*), so follow it and do not follow the fancies of **those who do not have knowledge (*lā yaʿlamūna*)**!

In Q. 5 (*al-Mā'ida*), 48, *sh-r-ʿ* and *ikhtilāf* appear together with *minhāj*, 'method' or 'procedure', which is yet another technical term within *fiqh*. The context of this verse refers to the Torah and the Gospels, and the Jewish

32 On al-Ṭabarī's *Ikhtilāf al-fuqahā'* see Rosenthal (1989: 101); Gilliot (1990: 41–46); on his *madhhab*, see Rosenthal (1989: 63–66); Gilliot (1990: 39–41); Stewart (2004; 2013; 2016); Mårtensson (2016).

33 *Kitāb al-Jihād* has been translated into English, by Yasir S. Ibrahim, *Al-Ṭabarī's Book of Jihād: A Translation from the Original Arabic, With Introduction, Commentary, and Notes*.

and Christian communities, each of who rule by their own writing, even as *this* writing is now the valid one for the Qur᾽ān's addressees:

> (48) We have sent down to you the writing with the True Right (*bi-l-ḥaqq*), confirming that of the writings that is before it and superseding it. So judge between them according to what God has sent down, and do not follow their fancies that divert you from the true right that has come to you! To each of you We have opened up **a path of guidance and a method (*shir῾atan wa minhājan*)**, and had God so wished, He would have made you one nation, but He wanted to test you by what He brought you. So hurry to put forward the good deeds! To God is the return of you all, when He will instruct you about that which you used to **disagree upon (*takhtalifūna*)**!

Method or *minhāj* is related to *uṣūl al-fiqh*, the hermeneutical side of *fiqh* that contributed to defining the schools of law or *madhāhib*, sing. *madhhab*. *Madhhab* literally means 'a way to proceed', in the sense of interpretive method for deriving law from the Qur᾽ān and *ḥadīth*. This sense emerges from David Vishanoff's analysis of the *madhāhib* as competing hermeneutical methodologies, focusing on "how legal theorists imagine the relationships between text, author, reader, and law" (Vishanoff 2011:9). A key Qur᾽ānic verse that preoccupied the legal scholars during the late 600s and the 700s is Q. 3 (*Āl ῾Imrān*), 7, a verse in which the writing that constitutes the Qur᾽ān is divided into two categories of signs: *āyāt muḥkamāt* and *āyāt mutashābihāt* (see also Chapter 3, above). At first, the scholars tended to interpret the two categories substantively, as referring to verses that were generally valid, as distinct from those that were abrogated by later verses, or rulings versus allegories, or rulings versus repeated narratives about the prophets. By the early 800s, Mu῾tazilite scholars began interpreting the verses in a linguistic-hermeneutical sense, suggesting that *muḥkamāt* means verses with one meaning only i.e. unequivocal or unambiguous, while *mutashābihāt* are linguistically polyvalent i.e. equivocal or ambiguous (Vishanoff 2011:17).[34] Understood in this way, *āyāt* ***mutashābihāt*** would correspond to the exegetical-linguistic genre of *wujūh wa* ***ashbāh*** mentioned in Chapter 2 (above), which treats the Qur᾽ānic concepts' different senses and aspects of meaning in different contexts. Thus, Q. 3, 7 can be translated as referring to linguistically informed hermeneutics:

34 For studies of these two concepts in terms of the Qur᾽ān's 'self-referentiality', see e.g. Wild (2003); studies of other forms of Qur᾽ānic self-references include contributions to Wild (2006); also Madigan (2001); Boisliveau (2014).

> (7) It is He Who has sent down to you the writing! Of it there are signs that are unequivocal (*āyāt muḥkamāt*), and they are the source of the writing (*umm al-kitāb*), while others are equivocal (*mutashābihāt*). As for those in whose hearts there is deviation, they follow the equivocal in it, seeking internal strife (*fitna*) and seeking to reach the intended meaning even though no one has knowledge of its intended meaning except God. Those grounded in knowledge say; "We enact security through it: all is from our Lord!" since no one except those with discerning intellects are reminded!

Understood along these lines, Q. 3, 7 served as a reference point also for the legal hermeneutics developed in the late 700s and early 800s by Muḥammad b. Idrīs al-Shāfiʿī (d. 204/820) in his treatise *al-Risāla*, 'the Divine Message'. Addressing a context where there were several rival methods for deriving guidance from the Qur'ān, and written Prophetic *ḥadīth* had emerged as a second source alongside the Qur'ān, al-Shāfiʿī sought to establish consistency of the divine guidance across the two written sources. This was a hermeneutical and linguistic challenge, since there are ambiguities within both sources. Al-Shāfiʿī's solution was to turn polysemy into a hermeneutical asset i.e. the fact that the same concept can take on different senses in different contexts. On that basis, he developed a methodology around *bayān*, 'clear distinctions'. In practice, *bayān* meant distinguishing categories and meaning in a way that harmonised Qur'ānic verses and *ḥadīth* with reference to legal, doctrinal, ritual, and ethical topics. Nevertheless, al-Shāfiʿī defined the Qur'ān as God's message (*risāla*) as the divine source of the whole law. He argued that *bayān* clearly distinguished the guidance that was implicit in the Qur'ān, so that it could be claimed that all guidance was based on the divine, sent-down message, to which there were corresponding and explanatory *ḥadīth* (Vishanoff 2011: 34–61). Consequently, al-Shāfiʿī located both the whole divine guidance *and* the methodology of *bayān* in the Qur'ān, as testified to by its derivations of the root *b-y-n*, for example in the above cited Q.14 (*Ibrāhīm*), 4.

Viewed from Vishanoff's perspective, then, al-Shāfiʿī's *bayān* methodology is one of the earliest consistent hermeneutics of *uṣūl al-fiqh* developed from the linguistic theory of the Arabic language's polysemy. In Vishanoff's view, the *madhāhib* that by the 900s had taken the shape of the Sunnī schools of law – Ḥanafī, Mālikī, Shāfiʿī, Ḥanbalī, plus al-Ṭabarī's short-lived *madhhab jarīrī*, and the Ẓāhirī one – were hermeneutical responses to al-Shāfiʿī's *bayān* methodology. Differences concerned both how the jurists weighed the Qur'ān and the *ḥadīth* relative to each other, as mentioned, and how they negotiated the jurists' interpretations and analogical reasoning (*qiyās*) relative to both 'text' and consensus within the school (*ijmāʿ*). The Twelver and Ismāʿīlī Shīʿī schools deliberated the same issues, though referring to their particular traditions and consensus based on their Imams.

THE SYSTEMATIC DIMENSION AND THE COMMON GOOD-PRINCIPLE

The period from 1000 onwards represents a development towards systematic use of logic in formal and substantive legal reasoning. Felicitas Opwis has described the development such that although early jurists employed logic too, the political context from the second half of the 900s onwards with competing Sunnī and Shīʿī dynasties, challenged scholars in new ways. Their aim was to strengthen the universal legitimacy and applicability of the law through new methods, especially the 'common good'-principle *maṣlaḥa*. Because this development required a high level of legal expertise, the principle preserved the law as the scholars' domain, protected against arbitrary political interests and rivalry; in other words, the move aimed to secure the separation of powers (Opwis 2010: 340–341; ref. Hallaq 1984: 685–686; 1987: 67). To this picture, one may add Baber Johansen's study of Ḥanafī legal works (1988). In this period, he argues, the landlords were becoming increasingly autonomous in relation to the state and the jurists had to find ways to adjust the law. Moreover, Sufi brotherhoods and lodges were expanding, and although many affiliates were legal scholars, brotherhoods competed with the schools of law for royal patronage and land, as discussed in Chapter 5. In addition, Jewish and Christian communities continued to be important members of the Islamic polities. This period coincides with the Crusades in Syria (1095–1291) and the gradually advancing Christian Reconquista in Andalusia, which may have added impetus to the need to legitimise the law in terms of 'the common good' i.e. principles agreed also across religious boundaries.

The legal development drew on new formulations in philosophy and linguistics. The philosopher Ibn Sīnā (d. 428/1037) and his Aristotle-inspired theory of 'definition', mentioned in Chapter 2, made important contributions. Similarly, al-Rāghib al-Iṣfahānī (d. c. early 400/1000), who worked in Iṣfahān under the Būyid dynasty (934–1055), integrated Platonic ontology and epistemology, and Aristotelian ethics and categories, into Shāfiʿī *fiqh*. He influenced several famous scholars, including the exegetes and jurists al-Rāzī (d. 605/1209) and al-Ghazzālī (d. 505/1111). Moreover, al-Rāghib introduced a new kind of dictionary. In his lexicon over Qurʾānic 'exceptional words' (*gharīb*), entitled *al-Mufradāt fī gharīb al-Qur'ān*, he arranged words alphabetically according to consonant roots (Rippin 1988). This lexicographical method enabled him to produce universal and context-independent meanings in Qur'ānic terms, to facilitate connecting them with general objectives pertaining to *sharī'a* (al-Mar'ashlī 1988: 52; Mohamed 1995). Such methodologies paved the way for systematic use of the principle *maṣlaḥa*, 'the common good'. Here, I will trace the development with reference primarily to Felicitas Opwis (2010) account of how *maṣlaḥa* emerged as a legal tool in the period 800–1400, across the boundaries of *madhhab*.

Opwis identifies the earliest use of 'public welfare' as a lawmaking principle (*istiṣlāḥ*) in Ibn al-Muqaffa''s (d. c. 139/757) *Risāla fī al-ṣaḥāba*. As we saw above in the section on *siyāsa*, Ibn al-Muqaffa' argued that the ruler, faced with a diverse law, should create a unified law canon by considering the people's *ṣalāḥ*, 'welfare' or 'common good', applied to existing law derived from *sunna* and *qiyās* ('analogy'). Here, *sunna* means the precedence of previous rulers and jurists, not the Prophet's *sunna*, and the authority to judge what constitutes the people's welfare is the ruler's prerogative (Opwis 2010: 14–15). We also saw that Ibn al-Muqaffa' identified the administration of the land tax as the principal concern for the 'common good'. Yet he did not represent a systematic application of this principle through the sources and methods of *uṣūl al-fiqh*, which is the legal scholars' domain.

Our al-Ṭabarī (d. 310/923), who was both exegete and jurist, may represent a transition in this respect. As we saw above, concerning exegesis on Q. 3, 79, al-Ṭabarī and Mujāhid (d. 104/722) defined the *legal* scholars as protectors of the people's *maṣlaḥa*. Al-Ṭabarī also made the point that the scholars' protection of *maṣlaḥa* concerns both the judicial order and the final Judgement (*dīn*) and this material life (*dunyā*). In Opwis' account, the significant shift occurs with the polymath al-Khwārizmī (d. after 387/997), who defined the term *istiṣlāḥ*, 'the jurist's individual application of *maṣlaḥa*', as pertaining to *uṣūl al-fiqh*. However, the jurists disagreed over what *maṣlaḥa* referred to. The Mu'tazilī theologian and Ḥanafī jurist al-Jaṣṣāṣ (d. 370/981) defined *maṣlaḥa* not as a law-making principle but as welfare in the hereafter, resulting from a person's intention to comply with God's guidance and commands. While the aim of God's guidance is *maṣlaḥa*, there is no way for any human scholar to ascertain that their understanding of a specific legal ruling or religious command leads to *maṣlaḥa* (Opwis 2010: 24–26). As Opwis shows, al-Jaṣṣāṣ was contradicted on this point by the later Ash'arīs al-Juwaynī (d. 478/1085), *imām* of Mecca and Medina, and his student al-Ghazzālī (d. 505/1111) of Baghdad. Both al-Juwaynī and al-Ghazzālī defined *maṣlaḥa* in terms of ascertainable welfare in the here and now, including subjecting the rulers to the law. They also developed *maṣlaḥa* into a mechanism for law-finding beyond the textual rulings but with the texts as reference points, and within the parameter of *qiyās*, or 'reasoning by analogy'. Al-Ghazzālī, furthermore, produced the final formalization of *maṣlaḥa* as law-finding tool in the sense it has today, by defining five objectives (*maqāṣid*) of the law, which corresponded with the preconditions for human existence and therefore the people's welfare in this life: protection of life (*nafs*), religion as part of the judicial order (*dīn*), intellect (*ʿaql*), progeny (*nasl*), and wealth and property (*māl*). Moreover, al-Ghazzālī argued that these objectives are affirmed by all religions (Opwis 2010: Ch. 1 and 2).[35] Again, al-Ṭabarī/Mujāhid appear as an earlier instance, since they too argued that *maṣlaḥa* refers to the people's welfare also in this life, and that it requires the scholars' supervision of the state administration. Jurists' debates over the scope and terms of *maṣlaḥa* may thus have been going on at least since the 700s, in parallel with the developing *madhāhib*.[36]

To return to Opwis' account: The Cairene Mālikī jurist al-Qarāfī (d. 684/1285) proceeded beyond al-Ghazzālī, defining the *maqāṣid* as 'universals' (*kulliyāt*), and expanding *maṣlaḥa* beyond the five objectives into a set of legal precepts (*qawāʿid*). For example, to find out the meaning of 'protecting *dīn*', he introduced the precept of 'averting harm' as a concrete means of identifying welfare, with the result that e.g. rituals causing harm to self or others could be ruled as against welfare (Opwis 2010: Ch. 3). Similarly, the great Ḥanbalī scholar Ibn Taymiyya (d. 729/1328) of Damascus widened *maṣlaḥa* beyond the five objectives, though he limited its sources to the Qurʾān and the Prophetic *sunna*. He defined the jurists' duty to find the universal welfare principles in the divinely guided texts through the expert scholars' independent interpretation (*ijtihād*). His main guiding precepts were need and averting harm, and anything not explicitly prohibited in the texts is allowed if it promotes *maṣlaḥa*. However, he did not allow for changing rulings defined in the texts. Yet his student, the Ḥanbalī jurist al-Ṭūfī (d. 763/1361) of Cairo, developed a *maṣlaḥa* concept and method that allowed precisely that (Opwis 2010: Ch. 4).

Opwis' last example is the Andalusian Mālikī jurist al-Shāṭibī (d. 790/1388) of Granada, for who *maṣlaḥa* equals God's intention with the entire guidance of the Qurʾān, and thus constitutes the true meaning of each

35 The same rights are upheld by Islamic law in relation to the non-Muslim religious communities and their members.

36 For this view (though without reference to al-Ṭabarī), see Bin Sattam (2015), who also argues the debate is traceable to the Companions.

ruling ever reached, even though rulings may change to address new circumstances. In this way, al-Shāṭibī made *maṣlaḥa* a truly universal source of the law, covering all human activities, also future ones. *Maṣlaḥa* is ascertained through universal legal indicators, detached from but still discernible within the textual sources. These include needs (*ḥājiyyāt*), necessities (*ḍarūriyyāt*), and improvements (*taḥsīniyyāt*), which overlap with the classical five objectives of the law, and which are common to all religious communities (Opwis 2010: 252–253). Al-Shāṭibī also included analysis of the Qur'ān's composition in his theory of *maṣlaḥa*, focusing on the relationship between universals and particulars. Thus, he distinguished between Mecca and Medina *sūra*s, arguing that Meccan ones lay down the universal five objectives, whereas the Medina ones develop the particulars that derive from them. In relation to the *sunna*, the Qur'ān constitutes the sum (*jāmi'*) of all universals, while sound *ḥadīth* either expand on these or add new cases, which are however congruent with the Qur'ān (Opwis 2010: 295–298).

Al-Ghazzālī's and al-Shāṭibī's point, that the objectives of the law are universal because they both have references in the Qur'ān *and* are common to all religions, is in fact reflected in the passage Q. 5 (*al-Mā'ida*), 44–48. It argues that although *this* divine writing (*kitāb*) supersedes the preceding ones, they all lay open God's path to guidance and His rulings. Hence, the Jewish and Christian communities can continue to judge by their scriptures: it is substantially the same law as that based on the Qur'ān. Note how, at the end of each verse, ethical categories are defined in relation to the general principle of whether one judges by the light of God's writing, or not, and these categories include the Jews and the Christians:

> (44) We have indeed sent down the Torah, in which is guidance and light, and by which the prophets who promoted peace, and the masters and the scribes, judged among those who have turned back, according to what they were made to protect of God's writing and to which they had testified. So do not fear the people, but fear Me, so that you do not trade My signs for a small price! Whoever does not judge by what God has sent down: **those are the rejecters of security (*al-kāfirūna*)**!
> (45) We wrote down for them in it that life is by life, eye is by eye, nose is by nose, ear is by ear, tooth is by tooth, and that injuries is settlement of account. So, whoever accepts compensation in it provides expiation for it (*wa al-jurūḥa qiṣāṣun faman taṣaddaqa bihi fahuwa kaffāratun lahu*). Whoever does not judge according to what God has sent down: **those are the ones who darken right by wrong (*al-ẓālimūna*)**!
> (46) We let follow in their tracks Jesus, son of Mary, confirming what he had before him of the Torah as We gave him the Gospel, in which

is guidance and light, confirming what he had before him of the Torah as guidance and admonition for **those who fulfil their obligations (*al-muttaqīna*)**!
(47) Let the people of the Gospel judge according to what God has sent down in it, as whoever does not judge according to what God has sent down: **those are the ones who rebel (*al-fāsiqūna*)**!
(48) We have sent down to you the writing with the True Right, confirming the writing that is before it, and superseding it. So judge among them according to what God has sent down, and do not follow their whims so that they divert you from the right that has come to you! To each of you We have opened a path to guidance and a method (*shirʿatan wa minhājan*), and had God so wished, He would have made you one nation, but He wanted to test you by what He brought you. So hurry to put forward the good deeds! To God is the return of you all, when He will instruct you about that over which **you used to disagree (*takhtalifūna*)**!

Regarding Shīʿī law, Asma Afsaruddin (2013) has argued that *maṣlaḥa* in the pragmatic sense of considering the common good over special interests guided the Shīʿī traditions from the Imams and their scholars up to the mid-900s (Buyid time). Within Twelver Shīʿa after the 900s, however, the jurists did not follow the same path as the Sunnīs in developing systematic methods for applying *maṣlaḥa*. Yet it is possible that Shīʿī thought indirectly contributed to Sunnī use of *maṣlaḥa*, through Sufism. The first Shīʿī Imam ʿAlī b. Abī Ṭālib often serves as the first link in the transmission chains of the divine knowledge in the Sufi *ṭuruq*. At the ontological level, as discussed above in Chapters 2 and 5, this connection is expressed in the fact that both Sufi and Shīʿī concepts of *walāya* appear to draw on Neoplatonic 'mind-based' theories of concept. This might explain Opwis' observation, that Sufi methodologies contributed to the systematic development of *maṣlaḥa* by providing ways to access God's own intended *maṣlaḥa*. Accessing God's intention coincides with what Opwis sees as the jurists' efforts to merge the early, predominantly formal legal reasoning, with moral-substantive legal reasoning, where attaining God's ethical intention becomes part of defining the *maṣlaḥa* (Opwis 2010: 343).[37] Consequently, al-Ghazzālī integrated Sufism (*taṣawwuf*) as a discipline into the Sunnī education, as expressed in his *Iḥyāʾ ʿulūm al-dīn* ('Bringing to life the sciences of the judicial order') and *al-Munqidh min al-ḍalāl* ('The Deliverer from Erring'). He also wrote

37 For more general studies of Sufi exegesis aiming at connecting with the divine mind, see Böwering (1980) and (2003: 352, 355–356); in the latter study, comparisons are made with Shīʿī exegesis attributed to Jaʿfar al-Ṣādiq.

two legal statements on the conditions for setting up a permanent land endowment (*waqf*) for a Sufi lodge, reflecting the circumstance that increasing numbers of members of the political and societal elites wanted to do so (Karamustafa 2007: 126–127).

Ibn Taymiyya, who as we have seen also contributed to *maṣlaḥa* theory, is a more complex case. He was strongly critical of the Sufi Neoplatonism of Ibn al-ʿArabī (d. 638/1240) and his treatise *al-Futūḥāt al-makkiyya* ('The Meccan Disclosures'), but himself wrote the commentary *Sharḥ futūḥ al-ghayb* on the treatise *Futūḥ al-ghayb* ('Disclosures of the Unknown') by the Ḥanbalī founder of the Sufi Qādiriyya *ṭarīqa*, ʿAbd al-Qādir al-Jīlānī (d. 561/1166). Ibn Taymiyya rejected Ibn al-ʿArabī's idea of existential unity of Creator and creatures, and the corresponding claim that the personal self can become one with the divine self-disclosure, but he maintained the idea that scholars could know God's intention and will (*irāda*) through His address (*khiṭāb*). On this basis, he confronted the Sufi concept of *walāya*, 'protective governorship', as initially defined by al-Tirmidhī and transmitted by, among others, Ibn al-ʿArabī (see Chapter 5 above).[38] The treatise *al-Furqān bayna awliyāʾ al-Raḥmān wa awliyāʾ al-Shayṭān*, 'The Forger of Distinctions between al-Raḥmān's protective governors and Satan's protective governors', is devoted to this task. Against the Sufi claim that only a spiritual elite could attain *walāya* status, Ibn Taymiyya argued that those who follow the Prophet's *sunna* as the embodied creed of divine Oneness without human equivalents, so that they perfectly fulfil the defined obligations (*ittaqā*), are protective governors of God. Hierarchies between governors thus correspond to degrees of fulfilling the obligations. Hence, the Prophet's *sunna* is 'the Forger of Distinctions' (*al-furqān*) that distinguishes between governors on behalf of God, and governors on behalf of Satan. The Prophet, Ibn Taymiyya emphasises, was not simply a king ruling his people as their political leader, or a community leader like the Jews and the Christians, or a bringer of the external law but not the internal realities, as some Sufis claim: no, the Prophet and his *sunna* is the one and *only* path that leads to God, the Creator (Ibn Taymiyya 1982: 6, 10–11; also Sarrio 2011: 278–279).

38 For a survey of research on Ibn Taymiyya's critique of Ibn al-ʿArabī, see Sarrio (2011: 276), ref. to Knysh (1999); Haque (1966); Michel (1983); Hoover (2006); Michot (2007). The topic is also treated throughout Sarrio (2011). However, Ibn Taymiyya's ontological critique should not detract attention from the close relationship between early Sufism in Bagdad, especially the transmission chain from al-Junayd (d. 298/910), and early Ḥanbalī scholars, based on the shared ascetic ethos and the rejection of opinion-based reasoning beyond the scriptural texts; see Karamustafa (2007: 22–23).

Further qualifying the nature of the Prophet's governorship, Ibn Taymiyya establishes that his chief virtue is his commitment to serve God, as defined in the sent-down written guidance. To illustrate this virtue, Ibn Taymiyya distinguishes between two ethical levels among Qur'ānic prophets, which correspond to two ethical levels among governors. Firstly, the Prophet-King (*nabī malik*), like David, Solomon, and Joseph, who is obligated to follow God's commands and prohibitions but is free to dispose of his governorship and property as he sees fit, giving or withholding to whoever he wishes, without incurring sin. Secondly, the Messenger-Servant (*rasūl ʿabd*), like Abraham, Moses, and Jesus. God let the Prophet choose if he wanted to be a Prophet-King or a Messenger-Servant, and he chose the latter. Consequently, he voluntarily chose to make all his actions into servitude of God and His rules in the Qur'ān. In terms of landed property and wealth, he cannot give it to or take it from whoever he wishes, but he is obligated to distribute it according to the rules in the Qur'ān (1982: 16–17; Sarrio 2011: 279–280). Ibn Taymiyya framed this distinction and ethical hierarchy as a legal objective (*maqṣūd*) related to the protection of wealth and property (*māl*), which had support also in the other schools of law i.e. not only the Ḥanbalī one (1982: 17). Hence, at least in Ibn Taymiyya's view, protecting ownership rights of land were an issue at stake in the context of universally recognised legal objectives. It appears his concern was with rulers favouring some governors over others, possibly Sufi brotherhoods over the legal institution, given the treatise's topic.

Governorship relates to 'obedience'. Those who claim the status of God's protective governors claim they should be obeyed because they are addressed by God (*mukhāṭab*, *muḥaddath*). However, Ibn Taymiyya argues, only the Prophet was directly addressed by God and can rightfully demand obedience. Anyone claiming to speak for God must therefore prove his claim with reference to the Qur'ān and the *sunna*. If he can provide no such evidence, he cannot claim obedience. Ibn Taymiyya supports the argument with reference to the second Caliph ʿUmar b. al-Khaṭṭāb, who was in fact addressed by God on several occasions but still had to prove his case to the other Companions:

> Therefore ʿUmar, may God be pleased with him, used to take counsel from the Companions, may God be pleased with them, and deliberate with them on an equal footing (*yushāwiru al-ṣaḥāba wa yunāẓiruhum*), and return to them with some matters and contest with them over things. He and they would adduce as evidence against each other the divine writing (*al-kitāb*) and the *sunna*, by means of which he prevailed over them in his contestation, not by saying to them: 'I am spoken to and

> have received inspiration and have been addressed (*anā muḥaddath mulham mukhāṭab*), so you are obliged to accept from me and not contradict me!'
>
> Thus, anyone who claims – or whose companions claim on his behalf – that he is God's protective governor and that he is addressed, and that his followers must accept everything he says without contradicting him, and surrender themselves to him, without consideration of the divine writing and the *sunna*, both he and they are wrong, and this is the like of those who lead the people astray. For 'Umar b. al-Khaṭṭāb, may God be pleased with him, who is more virtuous than they are, when he was the Commander of the enactors of security, the promoters of peace used to contest his statements with him, and both he and they relied on the divine writing and the *sunna*! Therefore, the political community's predecessors and leaders (*salaf al-umma wa a'immatuhā*) agree that each one takes or leaves a statement unless it is from the Messenger of God, peace be upon him (1982: 30–31).

A Qur'ānic reference to 'Umar's practice of deliberative counsel (*shūrā*) is the *sūra* with the same name, Q. 42 (*al-Shūrā*), verse 38:

> (38) And those who respond to their Lord and perform the prayer, who treat their affairs through counsel among themselves and spend of the sustenance We have provided for them, (…)

Ibn Taymiyya's polemics thus shows how the concept of the divine guidance constituting an obligating address (*khiṭāb*) became a bone of contention between legal scholars and some Sufis (Sarrio 2011: 281). However, the issue of rule of law is also implicated. As in his other, more famous treatise, *al-Siyāsa al-shar'iyya*, 'The divinely guided political science', Ibn Taymiyya is making a strong case that the Prophetic *sunna* subjects the ruler to the law and to deliberation (*shūrā*). This comes with an inclination towards the language- and capability-based theory of concept over the mind-based alternative. Accordingly, he distinguishes between a set of Qur'ānic terms for God's actions: intention (*irāda*), command (*amr*), decree (*qaḍā'*), permission (*idhn*), prohibition (*taḥrīm*), mission (*ba'th*), sending out with a message (*irsāl*), discursive speech (*kalām*), and making (*ja'l*). Regarding these, he then distinguishes between two levels: the level of calling into being (*kawnī*) and the level of judicial order (*dīnī*). The *kawnī* level is God's sphere of action, which does not obligate people and thus cannot make anyone a protective governor on behalf of God, whereas the *dīnī* level is the level of obligations, the fulfilment of which (*ittiqā'*) can make one a protective governor. Yet, since God's intention (*irāda*) and will (*mashī'a*) with Creation is that all His creatures should fulfil their obligations, His intention and will incorporates them even though they cannot participate in His other actions (1982: 60ff.). This does not amount to accessing God's mind, only to understanding the discourse of His message, with which He sent forth His Messenger.

Consequently, for Ibn Taymiyya, it is through reading and reciting the Qur'ān that the servant comes close to God and understands and effectuates His intention and will. Above all, His will includes the legal objective of protecting life (*nafs*), which is signified by God's name *al-Raḥmān*, 'The Giver of life'. He explains this through exegesis of Q. 76 (*al-Insān*, 'Mankind'), 5–6. The verses belong to the passage 5–10, which reads:

> (5) Indeed, the pious shall drink of a cup with a mixture of relieving camphor (*inna al-abrāra yashrabūna min ka'sin kāna mizājuhā kāfūran*),
> (6) a spring which God's servants make gush forth abundantly as they drink from it (*'aynan yashrabu bihā 'ibād Allāh yufajjirūnahā tafjīran*),
> (7) fulfilling their vows in fear of a day whose woes are rampant,
> (8) and giving food, despite their love of it, to the poor, the orphan, and the captive:
> (9) 'We feed you solely seeking God's countenance, without wanting from you any recompense or gratitude!'
> (10) 'Indeed, we fear from our Lord a dark and dreadful day!'

Ibn Taymiyya explains that the spring in verse 6 must refer to the Qur'ān, because drinking is here put in terms of 'drinking *by*' i.e. the preposition is *bi-*, instead of *min*, 'of', which is the normal preposition used for 'drink of' something liquid, as in verse 5. Therefore, verse 6 should be understood as saying that God's servants recite from the Qur'ān, thereby making the good deeds, which it obligates the servants, abound or 'gush forth', as described in verses 7 and 8. He then refers to Prophetic *ḥadīth* to expound the meaning further:

> God's servants are the ones who are made to come close and who are mentioned in this *sūra*, and thus it is that the reward is in the nature of good deeds or bad deeds, as the Prophet (pbuh) stated: 'Whoever relieves (*naffasa*) an enactor of security from some of the hardship of this nearest existence, God will relieve him of some of the hardship of the Day of Standing to trial. Whoever makes things easier for a poor person, God will make it easier for him in the nearest and furthest existence, for God helps the servant as much as the servant helps his brother. Whoever is on a path seeking to gain knowledge, God will facilitate

> by it his path to the Garden. Whenever a group of people convene in one of God's temples (*bayt min buyūt Allāh*) reciting God's writing and studying it together, the Presence descends upon them (*nazalat ʿalayhim al-sakīna*), the life-protection envelops them (*ghashiyathum al-raḥma*), and the angels surround them, and God honours them to those who are with Him. Whoever is slow in his deeds, He does not hasten with his portions.' Muslim reported this in his *Ṣaḥīḥ*. And he stated (pbuh): 'Those who protect life, the Giver of life will protect them (*al-rāḥimūna yarḥamuhum al-Raḥmān*): Protect the lives of those on the land, and those who are in the heavens will protect you!' [The *ḥadīth* compiler] al-Tirmidhī stated: this is a sound *ḥadīth*. And in the other sound *ḥadīth* found in the *Sunan* compilations: 'God, may He be Exalted, states: I am the Giver of Life Who created the life-protecting relationships and tears them apart, as a concept of My Name (*isman min ismī*), so whoever established these relations, I establish a relationship with him, and whoever breaks them, I cut him off.' And he stated: 'Whoever establishes life-protecting relationships, God establishes a life-protecting relationship with him, and whoever breaks them, God will break His relationship with him.' And there are many other examples (1982: 15).

Based on this reading, the Qur'ānic concept of God as *al-Raḥmān* can be understood as a reference point for the first of *sharīʿa*'s legal objectives, to protect the lives of fellow humans, through specific good deeds, including providing them with food.[39] This shows how Ibn Taymiyya perceived the moral-substantive aspect of *maṣlaḥa*, which consists in identifying God's intentions, as conveyed in the Qur'ān's commands and prohibitions.

SYSTEMATIC THEOLOGY (*KALĀM*)

The last example of discipline is *kalām*, 'discursive speech', referring to systematic theology. According to al-Fārābī's list over the sciences, *kalām* belongs together with *fiqh* to political science, and has to do with defending principles and making them triumph. Hence, it shares topics as well as

39 See also the later Ḥanafī and Naqshbandī Sufi scholar Shāh Walī Allāh of Delhi (d. 1176/1762), who argued concerning *raḥma* as God's attribute: "[T]he meaning of 'Mercy' (*al-raḥma*) is the bestowing blessings, not sentimentality of the heart or gentleness. It is necessary to use the words which metaphorically refer to the King's domination of his city for indicating His domination over all existent things, since there is no more apt expression for this concept"; transl. Hermansen (2013: 190). More on Shāh Walī Allāh follows below.

essential logical and demonstrative skills with *fiqh*, but specialises in the latter sphere. An example of political implications of *kalām* relate to the Qurʾānic concept of God's Oneness, which is intrinsic to Covenant, with its constitutional and social contract implications. It is therefore accurate to say that systematic theology starts in the Qurʾān, and we will see below how theologians employed its discourse on divine Oneness.

As a discipline, *kalām* depends heavily on philosophy. Already in its early stages in the 100s/700s, its topics overlap with metaphysics, ontology, and epistemology (Wisnovsky 2004). This is clear from al-Khwārizmī's treatise of the sciences and their concepts, *Mafātīḥ al-ʿulūm*, from the late 300s/900s. Al-Khwārizmī introduced the section on *kalām* with a list of all the many different Islamic schools and positions, including the minutest ones, followed by lists of 'prophetic' Christian and Jewish schools and main positions, as well as various 'polytheist' and non-prophetic belief systems. This is yet another example of how Muslim scholars connected the Islamic sciences with the hugely diverse intellectual legacies of the lands and peoples under Islamic rule.[40] As for the specifically Islamic topics, al-Khwārizmī defined those that the theologians (*al-mutakallimūna*) had been dealing with up to his own time as *uṣūl al-dīn*, 'the principles of the judicial order'. In chapter seven of the section *kalām*, entitled 'On the principles of the judicial order that the theologians discourse about', he argued that all theological debate is about the following principles:

> Firstly: Statements on the origination of bodies and the refutation of the school of *dahriyya*, who declare the eternity of time (*al-dahr*), and the evidence that the world has an originator, who is God, may He be Exalted. And the refutation of the dualism of the Zoroastrians (*al-mājūs*) and the Zanādiqa; of the trinitarianism of the Christians and others who

40 See also Goodman (1992:13–14), on continuation of topics: "[the] same reasoning Proclus employed, and Simplicius and others after him, detached from any inference about the eternity of the sensory world, had for centuries been used to discover that God's word or wisdom, the Christ in Christian theology, the Torah in Jewish theology, was eternal, an attribute or hypostasis of God, mediating the act of temporal creation by serving as the pattern or paradigm of nature and the basis of nature's intelligibility. Such Platonic and Philonic notions penetrate the Qur'an and Qur'anic thinking in much the way that they penetrate the Hebrew wisdom literature and Apocrypha, with their references to the pre-eternity of Wisdom, or the opening lines of the Gospel of John, where the identifying of God's word or wisdom with God Himself is presented as a solution to the problem of creation, the emergence of the temporal from the Timeless. In Islam the locus is taken by the pre-eternal Qur'an, God's word and wisdom, identified with His command to nature, the creative imperative BE!, by which the world was called into existence."

state there are several makers (*kathrat al-ṣāniʿīna*), that He is not like the things; and the refutation of the Jews and others of those who liken (God to creation; *al-mushabbiha*), that He does not have a body.

Many of those Muslims who liken (God to creation), state that He has body – but God is Exalted high above what they state, since He, Almighty, is knowing, in power, and alive, by His essence (*bidhātihi*). The majority state, except the Muʿtazila, that He is knowing through knowledge, and alive through life, and in power through power, and that these attributes are co-eternal together with Him.

And the discourse on the vision (of God) and the rebuttal or affirmation of it; if His will is originated or co-eternal; if His discourse (*kalām*) is created or un-created; if the servants' actions are created and originated by God or by the servants; if obedience precedes the action or is simultaneous with it; if God, may He be Exalted, wills the bad actions or not; if the one who dies having committed grave rebellion and not returned will remain forever in the Fire, or if it is possible that God, may He be Exalted, mercifully saves him and foregoes him and lets him enter the Garden. The Muʿtazila state that those who commit grave rebellion (*kabāʾir al-fisāq*) is neither an enactor of security nor a rejecter, but it is an in-between state. Others state that the people are either an enactor of security or a rejecter, declaring that intercession does not apply to the rebellious (*al-fāsiqīna*). Others state that it does apply to them, and that it is for rebellion above other things.

The evidence for prophecy is a refutation of the Brahmins and others who invalidate prophecy and the evidence of the prophecy of Muḥammad, God bless him and grant him peace.

And statements about leadership (*al-imāma*) and who is qualified for it and not qualified.

Note how the last topic, about the qualifications of political leadership, is included among the theological and metaphysical principles.

Several of these theological principles have references in the Qur'ān, as we shall see. Indeed, the above-mentioned jurist al-Shāṭibī held that all of *uṣūl al-dīn* is contained in the late Meccan *sūra* Q. 6 (*al-Anʿām*), together with the basic tenets of the creed (*al-ʿaqāʾid*), and he considered Q. 2 (*al-Baqara*) to constitute particular treatments of the general principles set out in Q. 6.[41] For example, Q. 2, 285 enumerates the following tenets of the creed: God, His angels, His writings, and His messengers – among who no distinction is made. Q. 4 (*al-Nisāʾ*), 136 offers a complemented version: God, His angels, His writings, His messengers, and the Furthest Day (*al-yawm al-ākhir*).

41 Opwis (2010: 296), ref. to al-Shāṭibī, *Al-Muwāfaqāt*, 3: 406–407.

Regarding the relationship between *kalām* and *fiqh*, Bernard Weiss has elucidated that the aim of *fiqh* – to gain substantive knowledge of the divine guidance, *sharīʿa* – is not attainable without prior knowledge about God's self and being. Weiss' prime statement on this topic is a quote from the Shāfiʿī jurist Sayf al-Dīn al-Āmidī (d. 631/1233):[42]

> As for the science of theological discourse (*ʿilm al-kalām*), it establishes the knowledge [required] for constructing indicators of rulings, which are beneficent and lead along a path of guidance (*sharʿan*) to recognition of God and His attributes (*ṣifāt*), of the truthfulness of His Messenger in what he brought, and of other matters, which can only be recognised through the knowledge of theological discourse.

Thus, the answer to the theological question of how God is in relation to Creation determines how one defines His guidance, with the commands and prohibitions that the people are obligated to enact. Viewed in this way, *kalām* takes on a foundational role for *fiqh*.

DISPUTATION AND PROOF

Kalām and *fiqh* share the basic methods of *jadal*, 'disputation' or the dialectical positing of thesis and anti-thesis in order to develop a point, and *munāẓara*, 'debate'. The earliest writings on the topic of rules for disputation for jurists are attributed to our administrator Ibn al-Muqaffaʿ i.e. the first half of the 100s/700s, while works by theologians on *jadal* are recorded from the 200s/800s.[43] However, there are Qurʾānic references to *jadal*, 'disputation' (Van Ess 2017/1991: 62–64). Q. 58 is entitled *al-Mujādila*, referring to a woman who disputes with the Prophet about her husband, making a legal case described in the first verse of the *sūra*. Another example, which

42 Weiss (2010:33), ref. to al-Āmidī, *Kitāb al-Iḥkām fī uṣūl al-aḥkām*, vol. 1, p. 9. I have modified Weiss' translation, which reads: "[T]he knowledge that the indicators of the divine categorizations of human acts are indeed indicators of those categorizations, that they constitute a revelation from God, presupposes a knowledge of God's existence and attributes and a knowledge that the Apostle of God is truthful with respect to his claim to be a bearer of divine revelation and other matters [*ghayr dhālik*] that are known only through theology".

43 For an overview, see Wagner, E., 'Munāẓara', Encyclopaedia of Islam, Second Edition. Edited by: P. Bearman, Th. Bianquis, C.E. Bosworth, E. van Donzel, W.P. Heinrichs. Consulted online on 15 October 2018 dx.doi.org/10.1163/1573-3912_islam_SIM_5507

refers to debates with Jews and Christians or 'the people of divine writing' (*ahl al-kitāb*), is Q. 29 (*'Ankabūt*, 'Spiders'), 46:

> (46) **Do not engage** the people of divine writing **in disputation** except by that which is best [and most correct][44] (***lā tujādilū*** *ahl al-kitāb illā bi-llatī hiya aḥsan*); unless it is those of them who have done wrong (*alladhīna ẓalamū*). Say: "We enact security through that which has been sent down to us and sent down to you, that our God and your God is One, and we enact peace for Him!"

In other cases, the Qur'ān refers to its divine message as *ḥujja*, 'proof', from the same root *ḥ-j-j* as 'pilgrimage' to God's Temple, *ḥajj*. I have selected examples from Q. 42 and Q. 6. Q. 42 is entitled 'Counsel' (*al-Shūrā*), and verse 15 occurs in a context explaining how the message God communicated to Noah, Abraham, Moses, and Jesus is the same as the Qur'ānic message, though the peoples have disagreed over it (verses 13 and 14). Verse 15, which addresses the Prophet, includes the command *istaqim*. As we have seen in the section on Sībawayhi's linguistics, *istiqāma* refers to 'correct speech', which led e.g. al-Ṭabarī to argue that the Qur'ānic *ṣirāṭ mustaqīm* is a path of correct speech and action, since God's speech is guidance. I follow his concept here; hence, Q. 42, 15:

> (15) Therefore, announce the invitation and **be correct in speech and action (*istaqim*)**, as you have been commanded, and do not follow their whims but say: 'I have enacted security by whatever writing God has sent down, and I have been commanded to do justice among you! God is our Lord and your Lord. We have our actions and you have your actions. There can be no decisive **proof (*ḥujja*)** between us and you. God will gather us together, as to Him is the destination!'

Q. 6 (*al-An'ām*), verses 80, 83 and 149–153 occur in contexts illustrating how the peoples have disputed with the previous messengers, and what one can learn from that. Verses 73–81 are about Abraham and describe how God created the heavens and the land, and therefore is the only One deserving of worship, while Abraham's family and people served the stars, the moon and the sun. Verse 80 uses the verb *ḥājja*, 'seek to prove through disputation':

44 Given the semantic context of discursive disputation, it is possible that 'by that which is most good' (*bi-llatī hiya aḥsan*) here has a grammatical-linguistic sense, as in Sībawayhi's term *mustaqīm ḥasan*, 'correct and good'. Hence, I have added [and most correct].

> (80) [Abraham's] people **disputed with him to prove themselves**. He said: '**Are you disputing with me to prove yourselves** over God (*wa* ***ḥājjahu*** *qawmuhu qāla* ***a-tuḥājjūnī*** *fī Allāh*), when He has guided me and I do not fear what you assign as partners to Him, except a thing my Lord wishes! My Lord encompasses each thing in knowledge: will you not recall and honour yourselves?'

Verse 83 then changes speaker position to God, and raises the particular case of Abraham and his people to the general statement, that God has the decisive proof and gives it to His messengers:

> (83) That is **Our proof (*ḥujjatunā*)** which We gave to Abraham against his people. We raise in degrees whoever We wish; indeed, your Lord is One Who Judges With Full knowledge!

Verses 149–153 illustrate how the proof also relates to God's rhetorical 'signs' and leads to commands (in this case an equivalent to the Hebrew Bible's 'ten commandments'):

> (149) Say: 'To God belongs **the persuasive proof (*al-ḥujja al-bāligha*)**, so had He wished He would have guided you all!'
> (150) Say: 'Come with your witnesses to testify that God has made this inviolate!' If they testify, do not bear witness together with them, and do not follow the whims of those who give a lie to **Our signs (*āyātinā*)** and who do not enact security through the furthest end, for they set up equals with their Lord.
> (151) Say: 'Come, I will recite what your Lord has made inviolate for you: that you do not assign to Him anything as partner; that you do good by your parents; that you do not kill your children for fear of poverty for We provide sustenance for you and for them; that you do not approach indecencies whether openly or secretly; and that you do not kill the person, which God has made inviolable, except by right: that is what He obligates you to do, so that you may rationally comprehend!'
> (152) 'And do not close in on the wealth of the orphan, unless it is for what is best, until he comes of age, and give full measure and weigh equitably! We do not obligate a person except with what is within his limits. And when you make statements, be just, even if it is against someone close in kin – and God's contract, fulfil it! That is what He assigns to you, so that you may be reminded!'
> (153) Indeed, this My path is correct in speech and action (*wa anna hādhā ṣirāṭī mustaqīman*): follow it and do not follow the duties that will set you off from your duties to Him: that is what He obligates you to do, so that you may fulfil your obligations!

Al-Ṭabarī is an example of a legal scholar who, in the same vein as these verses, defined the Qur'ānic signs (*āyāt*; verse 150 above) as vehicles for God's persuasive proof (*al-ḥujja al-bāligha*), and which are conveyed through narrative accounts (*qiṣaṣ*) (1995/1:1, 13–14, 18–19). His approach suggests that the Qur'ānic *qiṣaṣ*-accounts are demonstrative in nature, defining and proving the nature of God as a way to understanding His commandments. Both *kalām* and *fiqh* thus draw on this function of the accounts.[45]

DIVINE ONENESS

The concept of God that above all others constitutes the Qur'ānic Covenant is that He is One, without partner or counterpart. Consequently, as we have seen in al-Khwārizmī's definition of *uṣūl al-dīn*, God's Oneness is foundational for *kalām*, both externally in relation to other communities and internally between competing schools.

Externally, the Qur'ānic rejection of 'sharing' God with other partners (*shirk*) applies to both polytheist 'idolatry' and the Christian Trinitarian creed, which presupposes that God is simultaneously Father, Son, and Holy Spirit, and that as Son, He takes the form of the human person Jesus. The early Mecca *sūra* Q. 112, named *al-Ikhlāṣ*, 'Perfection' or 'Sincerity', succinctly states the canonical creed:[46]

> (1) Say: 'He is God, One,
> (2) God the Boundless,
> (3) Who did not beget and was not begotten,
> (4) And Who can have no counterpart: One!'

In fact, the whole Qur'ān argues for the rational nature of this creed, which is premised on the incapability of anything or anyone but God the Creator to sustain people. Hence, He can have no partners in Covenant. For example, the late Mecca Q. 6 (*al-An'ām*) and the passage 135–141 shows that the doctrinal topic of 'partners' relates to sustenance, and the legal-administrative matter of tax-shares of agricultural produce:

45 See also below on Shāh Walī Allāh's treatise *al-Ḥujja al-bāligha*, which subsumes *kalām* and *fiqh* under the divine *ḥujja*; Hermansen (2013).

46 As discussed in Chapter 3 (above), Nicolai Sinai argues instead that the canon evinces a gradual 'transition to explicit monotheism' (2017: 174–176), though without considering Q. 112.

(135) Say: 'O my people! Do what you are capable of, for I certainly do! You shall come to know who will have a good abode; indeed, the wrongdoers do not cause prosperity!
(136) They apportioned to God a share of the harvest and cattle He created, saying, 'This is for God', as they declare, 'This is for our partners'. And while that which is for their partners does not reach God, that which is for God will reach their partners: evil is what they rule!
(137) In the same way, their partners have made it appeal to many of those who take partners to kill their children, in order to ruin them and confound them in their judicial order. But had God wished, they would not have done this, so leave them and what they fabricate!
(138) They said: 'These cattle and harvests are taboo, and no one can eat them except those we wish' – so they claim! And there are cattle whose backs are inviolate, and cattle over which they do not mention God's Name,[47] fabricating lies about Him while He will reward them by what they have been fabricating! (...)
(140) Those have certainly lost who kill their children in folly and without knowledge, and who make inviolate the sustenance that God has provided for them, fabricating lies about God; they have certainly gone astray, since they were not guided!
(141) It is He Who brought forth gardens, with and without trellises, and palms and crops of diverse fruits, and olives and pomegranates, with and without parallels: eat of His harvest fruits when He brings them to fruition, and bring His due right (*ḥaqqahu*) on the day of harvest; and do not be wasteful, for God certainly does not love the wasteful!

The topic of the nature of Jesus also appears frequently, especially in Q. 19 (*Maryam*) and Q. 21 (*al-Anbiyāʾ*) from the middle Mecca period, and Q. 3 (*Āl ʿImrān*), from Medina.[48] The examples here are from Q. 19, verses 27–30, and Q. 3, verses 64–68. Starting with Q. 19: verses 27–30 define Jesus' nature with reference to *kitāb*, 'divine writing', arguing that he is a prophet and messenger to a specific polity. In verse 27, Mary, who has just given birth to Jesus, brings him to her people (*qawm*), 'carrying him' (*taḥmi-*

47 Abdel Haleem translation: 'some animals they exempt from labour' i.e. from carrying burdens on their backs, 'and some over which they do not pronounce God's name [during slaughter]'.

48 For a survey of the many, also Arabic, studies of Q. 19, which is the *sūra* with the fullest account of 'Jesus family' and his birth, see Toorawa (2011), which includes an amazing end-rhyming English translation! Cf. Ozgur Alhassen (2016) on further lexical details related especially to the root *r-ḥ-m* ('mercy' and 'kinship') and God's name *al-Raḥmān*. For a PhD thesis on the topic of Jesus and Mary in the Qurʾān, and especially Mary's connection with concepts of purity and abundance (*zakā*), and virtue and bodily comportment, see Farstad (2012).

luhu). This may be a pun: in linguistics terminology, 'carry' (*ḥamala*) means 'carry meaning', referring to definitions of categories.[49] Since the context has to do with 'defining Jesus as a prophet', one can read verse 27 as playing with the notion that Mary 'defined Jesus' to her people. The theological topic is perhaps also emphasised through the verb *kallama* in verse 29, of the same root as *kalām*, theological 'discourse':

> (27) So she brought him to her people**, carrying him** (***taḥmiluhu***). They said: 'O Mary, you have certainly come to a strange thing!
> (28) Sister of Aaron, your father was not an evil man and your mother was not unchaste!'
> (29) Whereupon she indicated towards him, and they said: 'How can we **engage in discourse** (*kayfa* ***nukallim***) someone who is still an infant in the cradle?'
> (30) [Jesus] said: 'Indeed, I am a servant of God, Who has given me the writing (*kitāb*) and made me a prophet!'

In Q. 3 (*Āl ʿImrān*), verses 42–60 demonstrate that Jesus is a fully human prophet, created by God's command. The selected passage 64–68 addresses 'the people of the divine writing', challenging them not to share God with any other partners. A distinction is made, between the category of those who share God with other partners, and the category of those who enact peace, like Abraham:

> (64) Say: 'O People of the Divine Writing! Arise and come to an equitable word between us and you: that we serve no one but God, and do not make anything partner with Him (*lā nushrika bihi shayʾan*), and do not take each other as lords instead of God!' Should they turn away (*tawallū*), say: 'Bear witness that we are **enactors of peace** (***muslimūna***)!'
> (65) O People of the Divine Writing! Why do you **dispute to prove yourselves** (***tuḥājjū***) about Abraham when the Torah and the Gospel were not sent down until after him? Will you not be bound by reason (*afalā taʿqilūna*)?
> (66) Here you are: you have argued concerning that about which you have knowledge (*ʿilm*), so why do you argue concerning that about which you have no knowledge? God knows and you do not know:
> (67) Abraham was neither a Jew nor a Christian, but a *ḥanīf* and **one who enacts peace** (***muslim***), since he was not among those who take other partners!

49 See Versteegh (1993: 24–25), referring to Ibn al-Muqaffaʿ, al-Kindī, and al-Fārābī.

> (68) Indeed, the people who are **the foremost governors** to Abraham (***awlā*** *bi'Ibrāhīm*) are those who followed him, and this Prophet and those who enacted security; and God is **the protective Governor** (***walī***) of the enactors of security!

Also significant are the references to *walāya* in verse 68. Thus, the recognition that God is One, in the manner that Abraham knew God, means to enter into a compact of governorship with the Prophet. The same invitation is extended to the polytheists of Quraysh, addressed in many other verses, including Q. 38, 4–7; Q. 36, 74–75; and Q. 34, 41–44. Hence, knowledge (*ʿilm*) about God's Oneness corresponds with the Covenantal compact ethics that obligates Jews and Christians as well as polytheists, namely to enter it and uphold its terms. The Jews and Christians, however, are addressed in special terms, since they already received sent-down divine writings.[50]

Polemics against the Christian Trinitarian creed played an important part in *kalām*, and theological debates with Christians continued in Umayyad and early Abbasid time, often sponsored by the Caliphs (van Ess 2017/1991: 13; 60–64). The political interest is not surprising, given that the main imperial rival, Byzantium, had Christianity as the state religion. As we saw above in the section on history, the Caliph al-Ma'mūn charged judges and governors who presented obstacles to his war against Byzantium with pro-Christian leanings, expressed in their erroneous doctrine of the uncreated Qur'ān, which the Caliph equated with the doctrine of Jesus as God's uncreated Word.[51]

50 Gerald Hawting (1994) has argued, that the Qur'ānic root *sh-r-k* and its derivatives means 'associate' and refers primarily to the other monotheistic religions, especially Christianity and the Trinity, and that it is through the later Biography of the Prophet, and the exegetical literature, that *shirk* has been made to refer to 'polytheism' or 'idolatry'. His thesis is that the Muslim scholars sought to isolate the Qur'ān and Islam from the historical monotheistic setting and emphasise the divine nature of the revelation by constructing a polytheistic setting. Fred Donner (2010) pursues a similar line of argumentation, that the Qur'ānic community consisted of monotheist 'believers' without a firm new identity, and that this identity (Islam) was formed under the Umayyads together with the more systematic production of the canon itself; see also Hawting (2000). However, both Hawting and Donner overlook the contractual aspects of *sh-r-k*, that to share God with other partners means to break the contract, a charge which the Qur'ān levels at Christians, Jews, and polytheists, although in some contexts one group is singled out, subject to the topic at hand.

51 On the relationships, also commercial, intellectual and diplomatic, between the Caliphate and Byzantium, and the correspondences between legal and doctrinal topics and debates across the imperial boundaries, see Jokisch (2007).

Within *kalām*, the topic of divine Oneness was treated as *metaphysics* or the exploration of God's existence, *ontology* or being, and *epistemology* or how to gain knowledge about God through His attributes or qualities (*ṣifāt*). Wisnovsky has identified the Ḥanafī jurist and theologian al-Māturīdī (d. 333/944) and his *Kitāb al-tawḥīd*, 'Treatise on the profession of divine Oneness', as a starting point and template for subsequent Sunnī treatises and textbooks. *Kitāb al-tawḥīd* begins with God's existence, followed by His Oneness and attributes (Wisnovsky 2004:66). David Thomas has argued that even though al-Māturīdī took the Christian Trinity as his point of departure, his aim was not polemics against actual Christians. Rather, he referred to the Trinity to probe the meaning of God's Oneness and prove the cogency and authority of the Islamic creed. For this purpose, he mobilised Qur'ānic polemics showing the Trinity as an inherently irrational creed, as well as formal logic and argumentation (Thomas 2007/1997:73). Like in Q. 3 (*Āl ʿImrān*), 64–68, al-Māturīdī introduced *walāya* into his refutation of divine 'begetting of children' (*bunuwwa*): begetting children requires similarity of kind (*jins*), and since God and man are of different kinds there can be no such relationship between man and God. However, there can be friendship (*khulaʾ*), affection (*maḥabba*), and protective governorship (*walāya*) between different kinds i.e. between God and man. Al-Māturīdī concludes: "it is not similarly possible with children, as there can be no power except through God" (*lā yajūz mithluhu fī al-banīn wa lā quwwata illā bi-Allāh*), suggesting that if God is thought to beget children, He cannot be the Supreme Protective Governor i.e. the assumption of kinship would reduce God's power (Thomas 2007/1997: 82). Consequently, the metaphysical concept of God's Oneness overlaps with the Covenantal compact of loyalty to God as the Protective Governor and model for political social contract.

In the period from 400/1000 onwards, when jurisprudence was systematized and universalised through philosophy and logic, the interdependence between philosophy and *kalām* deepened as well (Wisnovsky 2004; 2003). This is when al-Māturīdī's *Kitāb al-tawḥīd* gained wider currency as a template for further development of philosophical categories and terms. Al-Juwaynī (d. 478/1085) and al-Ghazzālī (d. 505/1111), both of whom represent Ashʿarī *kalām* and Shāfiʿī *fiqh*, are two examples among dozens of other scholars who were part of this trend, which spanned both *fiqh* and *kalām*. The development coincides with when Brown (2011) finds the *ḥadīth* collections of al-Bukhārī and Muslim gained canonical status, as mentioned above. Because this period sees a widening of the application of philosophy within *kalām* and *fiqh*, Wisnovsky challenges the previously common discourse in Islamic studies, that philosophy became obsolete within Sunnī *kalām* after al-Ghazzālī, because he denied that reasoning could gain any further knowledge about God than the divine self-disclosure in the Qur'ān. Rather, Wisnovsky shows, when al-Ghazzālī attacked the philosophers' metaphysical and epistemic reasoning concerning knowledge about God, he did so through "assiduous incorporation of basic metaphysical ideas into central doctrines of Sunnī *kalām*" (Wisnovsky 2004:65).

More precisely, al-Ghazzālī, and the other Ashʿarī theologians, directed their dialectical reasoning towards two opponents: the philosophers and the Muʿtazila. Against the philosophers, the Ashʿarī aim was to prove the eternity of God and His origination of the temporally limited, material Creation (*al-khalq*) over the philosopher's eternal universe. Against the Muʿtazila, the aim was to prove the eternity of all of God's attributes or qualities (*ṣifāt*) as parts of His essence or self (*dhāt*) over the Muʿtazilī distinction between God's 'qualities of the self' (*ṣifāt al-dhāt*) and 'qualities of the act' (*ṣifāt al-fiʿl*). This distinction follows from the Muʿtazilī version of God's Oneness (*tawḥīd*), where God's self is radically other than material creation. Examples of qualities of the self are God's power, life, and knowledge, which are not separate entities but parts of God's self, without reference to creation. In contrast, qualities of the act, such as God's provisions for humans (*rizq*), do refer to creation (Wisnovsky 2004:68–71). This Muʿtazilī metaphysics and epistemology included their doctrine of *khalq al-Qur'ān*, 'the Qur'ān's createdness': God *made* His word in the form of a human language, voiced by the Prophet in his address to a specific people in time and space. Hence, the Qur'ān is part of God's act, not of God's self.

Some of these terms have references in the Qur'ān, notably God's qualities. One instance is Q. 37 (*al-Ṣāffāt*), 159–160. The verses belong to a context treating the topic that God's being is other than what those who attribute a child to Him claim. The verb 'they attribute' in verse 159 is the same root *w-ṣ-f* as in the term for qualities, *ṣifāt*. Note also that verse 160 refers to the name of Q. 112, *al-Ikhlāṣ*, 'Sincerity', by stating that those servants who do not attribute a child to God also enact perfect sincerity:

> (159) Glorious is God, beyond what **they attribute** (*ṣubḥān Allāh ʿammā* ***yaṣifūna***),
> (160) except God's servants who **enact perfect sincerity** (*illā ʿibād Allāh* ***al-mukhliṣīna***)!

We may refer this matter back to al-Ṭabarī's historical report about the Caliph al-Maʾmūn, who compared the doctrine of the uncreated Qur'ān with the Christian doctrine that Christ is the divine Word incarnate, showing the continuous political significance of the topic:

> [They hold this erroneous view about the uncreated the Qur'ān] even though the Qur'ān itself speaks about God's creative power, sets forth its proof and decisively confutes all difference of opinion about it. [These people] talk just like the Christians when they claim that Jesus son of Mary was not created, because he was the Word of God. (HT 32/ Bosworth 1987: 206–207; mod.)

TWO SCHOLARS AT THE THRESHOLD OF THE MODERN ERA

This second part of the chapter is a continuation of the section on *kalām*. It shows how the concept of God's Oneness intersects with topics from other disciplines, in the works of two scholars from the early modern period: the Twelver Shī'ī Neoplatonist philosopher Mullā Ṣadrā (d. 1050/1640) from Shiraz and the Naqshbandī Sufi and Ḥanafī scholar Shāh Walī Allāh (d. 1176/1762) from Delhi.

Mullā Ṣadrā

Mullā Ṣadrā lived and worked under the Safavid dynasty (1501–1736). After initial, revolutionary use of Ismā'īlī propaganda about the appearance of the Imam in the here and now, the Safavids switched to the eschatologically 'moderate' Twelver Shī'ism, making the Ja'farī *madhhab* the official doctrine and law of their empire, which corresponded roughly to the territory of today's Iran. In Chapter 2, I referred to Mullā Ṣadrā as an example of a Neoplatonic mind-based ontological theory of concept, with Q. 112 as reference. Here I will illustrate how his ontology plays out in conceptualising the Qur'ān and God's 'persuasive proof'.

The institutional, political context for Mullā Ṣadrā's work was one where the Sunnī Ottoman Caliphate rivalled the Safavids in the west, and the Sunnī Mughal Empire in the Indian subcontinent in the east. Society in the Safavid Empire included Sufi brotherhoods and Sunnī schools present before the official Safavid turn towards Twelver Shī'a. Both the state and Twelver institutions viewed these groups with suspicion, as potential allies of the rival powers. Considering this state of affairs, James Morris (1981: 18–20) has analysed Mullā Ṣadrā's Neoplatonism as an effort to carve out a school of his own amongst competitors, and a corresponding pragmatic effort to 'transcend' conflict-laden boundaries, in the minds of scholars and in society. To this end, he mobilised the metaphysical and ontological theory that all beings and things co-exist in a unity of existence, emanating by the transcendent One God. Compared with the above-discussed Sunnī systematisers of *maṣlaḥa*, who addressed several rival power centres and institutions when developing the objectives of the law and the common good as universalising and legitimising tools, Mullā Ṣadrā faced one assertive political centre supporting one specific school of law and developed as a universalising and legitimising tool his Neoplatonic ontology and epistemology through interpretations of the Qur'ān, the Prophetic *sunna* as transmitted through Sufi traditions, and the traditions of the Shī'ī Imams.

In the essay *Risāla fī al-ḥudūth* ('Treatise on Origination'), Mullā Ṣadrā initially defines his metaphysics as improvement upon formulations by Plato and Aristotle, by integrating these into the divine knowledge that proceeds from God's 'illuminating' (*ishrāqī*) Light, channelled through the Prophet whose light (*al-nūr al-muḥammadī*) includes all other prophets and the Imams. Mullā Ṣadrā's aim was to demonstrate that this metaphysics enables 'the people of true right and certainty' (*ahl al-ḥaqq wa al-yaqīn*), who are also 'the protective governors grounded in knowledge' (*al-awliyā' al-rāsikhūna*), to attain the divine insights that constitute the path of scientific knowledge and action (*al-'ilm wa al-'amal*). The path involves:

> purifying the internal from the vacuous, making the heart perfectly sincere by freeing it from preoccupations, edifying the moral dispositions against vice, stripping the thoughts from habitual temptations, and extinguishing hatred and delusion from the soul, so that they arrive at the highest council (the angels; UM) and behold the ultimate happiness and witness the divine presence and obtain the eternal grace. This is the path of all the prophets and those sent with the divine message, and the sum of duties pertaining to the capacity for just judgement and pronouncement of divine Oneness (*ṭarīqat jamī' al-anbiyā' wa al-mursalīna wa sabīl al-ḥikma wa al-tawḥīd*) (Mullā Ṣadrā 1958: 18).

Hence, the path leading to certain knowledge about God corresponds to a moral discipline of perfecting thoughts and emotions, and it is the same path for prophets and messengers as it is for anyone aiming at just judgement i.e. scholars and administrators, as well.

As the One, God is the Originator and totality of existence. However, as pure Being without form (Q. 112), God necessarily 'transcends' time and all other beings, whose individual (*shakhṣī*) existences are predicated on time (*zamān*), form (*ṣūra*), body (*jism*), and movement (*ḥaraka*). As Mullā Ṣadrā explains with reference to Q. 2, 117, Q. 3, 47, and Q. 19, 35, God originates things through His verbal command (*amr*): '"Be!" And it comes into being (*kun fayakūn*)' (Mullā Ṣadrā 1958: 103). This is God's highest command (*amruhu al-a'lā*) and 'the greatest spirit' (*al-rūḥ al-a'ẓam*), which corresponds to the 'knowledge sphere' of God's kingdom and divinity (*'ālam malkūtihi wa ilāhiyyatihi*)' (Mullā Ṣadrā 1958: 108). The word *'ālam* derives from the same root *'-l-m* as *'ilm*, 'knowledge' of the systematic kind. Hence, *'ālam* refers to a 'knowledge sphere', in this case the knowledge of concepts pertaining to God's kingdom and divinity. God's highest command, the spirit, is an act in the image of speech, Mullā Ṣadrā explains, referring to the first Shī'ī Imam 'Alī b. Abī Ṭālib:

> The spirit is an angel which brings together and comprises many angels, which are soldiers (*junūd*) for the Lord, may He be Exalted, as He indicated by His statement: 'No one has knowledge about the soldiers of the Lord except He (Q. 74, 31)', as He has co-essential existence of many intellectual essences. From the Commander of the enactors of security ['Alī b. Abī Ṭālib], peace be upon him, who stated: 'The spirit is one of the angels, which has 70.000 senses (*wujūh*), and each sense has 70.000 languages (*lisān*), and each language has 70.000 idioms (*lugha*), and it glorifies God with all those languages. Of each glorification is created an angel, which flies with the angels towards the Day of Standing to trial', immersing themselves in the essence of divine duty (*mustaghriqatan fī al-huwiyya al-wājibiyya al-ilāhiyya*).
>
> The relationship of the spirit, as being God's command, to Him is like the relationship of the command to the commander from where he issues the command, and the relationship of the discourse to the theologian from where he discourses. (…) But the knowledge sphere of His creation (*'ālam khalqihi*), which is everything that has moulded form, measure, and expanse as bodies and embodied things, their essences originate in degrees of existence whose material realities separate them from His power. (…) And He commands and creates in eternity, but His command is eternal while His creation originates – as I have come to understand it – and therefore He stated in His great writing: 'And God's command was made to act (*wa kāna amr Allāh maf'ūlan*)!' (Q. 4, 47; Q. 33, 37) (Mullā Ṣadrā 1958: 108–109).

In the treatise *Ḥikmat al-'arsh*, 'The Capacity for just judgement pertaining to the Throne' i.e. God's construction[52] over which He rules, Mullā Ṣadrā

52 The verb *'arasha* means to erect a trellis or lattice for grape vines to climb on. As a noun, *'arsh* refers to 'throne'. However, in the Qur'ānic context, where God's creative blessings involve gardens and vines, it is tempting (though probably wrong) to understand *'arsh* in the sense of a construction on which Creation grows, in the image of a trellis. God then rules from above His constructed *'arsh*.

treats the topic of the Qurʾān's nature. Rejecting both the Ashʿarite doctrine that it is one of God's uncreated qualities, and the Muʿtazilite doctrine that it is a created act in the form of speech, Mullā Ṣadrā distinguishes between the Qurʾān as the uncreated divine speech and command, and the *kitāb*, the written text, which is part of material creation:[53]

> God's 'Speech' is an expression for His establishment of Perfect Words and *the sending down of unequivocal Signs [-They are the source of the writing-] and others which are equivocal* (Q. 3, 7), in the clothing of words and expressions. Hence His Speech is 'Qur'ān' (that is, 'joining,' or the noetic Unity of Being) from one point of view and 'Furqān' (that is, 'separating', manifest reality) from another point of view. (As Qur'ān, or the inner noetic reality of Being and the source of the writing), God's Speech is different from the 'Writing', because the 'Writing' belongs to the world of (manifest) Creation: *You (Muḥammad) did not recite any writing before This, nor did you write one with your right hand, for else those who would oppose (you) might have doubted (your purely divine inspiration)* (Q. 29, 48). For His Speech belongs to the World of the Command (that is, the noetic modality of Being), and its dwelling is the hearts and bosoms (of mankind), as in His saying: *The Faithful Spirit brought it down upon your heart, with God's permission* (Q. 26, 183–184; Q. 97, 4), and His saying: *Indeed, it is clear Signs in the bosoms of those who have been given knowledge* (Q. 29, 49). The 'Writing' (of manifest, contingent beings) can be perceived by everyone: *And We wrote down for him (Moses) upon the tablets the counsel to be drawn from everything* (Q. 7, 145)· But God's Speech (that is, noetic Being) is *[a hidden Writing] that can only be touched by those purified* (Q. 56, 78–79) from the pollution of the world of man's mortal (animal) nature.

Hence, the divine Qurʾān is accessible only through the intellect, located in the heart, which means that it 'transcends' the written text embodied as scripture, even though the written text is the reference point.

Mullā Ṣadrā also wrote a Qurʾān commentary, arranged around selected topics for which he adduces relevant verses. In this work, he explains the concept 'sending down' (*inzāl*). The angel hears God's speech and sees the corresponding forms. The forms are stable, while the message-substance emanates downwards through the knowledge spheres and through a (Neoplatonic) process of negation, while the intellecting self (*nafs*) ascends upwards, towards the highest reality of intellect (Mullā Ṣadrā 1998/2:

53 I am here relying on Morris' English translation of the Arabic original, slightly modified; Morris (1981: 110–111).

149–150). In a commentary on Q. 5 (*al-Mā'ida*), 67, he introduces the Prophet into this picture:

> [God] said, may He be Exalted: 'O Messenger, convey the message that has been sent down to you! (*yā ayyuhā al-rasūl balligh mā unzila ilayka*; Q. 5, 67)', meaning: 'Emanate upon the hearts of My servants of what We have emanated upon your heart, and convey to them the knowledge that We have conveyed to you!' But this emanation and conveyed knowledge, even though it is general and comprehensive, and this guidance and wise judgement, even though it is complete and full, only those persons will benefit from it who are safeguarded from the diseases of evading the just judgement, rejecting security, and tyranny, and the hearts that are innocent of the evils of envy and tyranny; as He stated: 'Except for those who come to God with a safeguarded heart [containing the intellect]' (*qalb salīm*; Q. 26, 89). As for the personal selves who are hard, stubborn and rebellious, who reject God's blessings, they are not imprinted with the capacity for just judgement and the Qur'ān, but rather they are imprinted by the opposite of what the people of peace and enactment of security are imprinted with (Mullā Ṣadrā 1998/7: 119).

Similarly, Mullā Ṣadrā explains that God as the Maker of things 'began with the intellect and completed with the intellecting'. He asks the reader to contemplate the secret reality of Q. 3 (*Āl 'Imrān*), 79 and the word *rabbāniyyīn*, 'masters'. The Sunnī and Shī'ī exegetes discussed above under *tafsīr* explained *rabbāniyyīn* as referring to the scholars (with or without the authority to oversee the state and protect the common good). Mullā Ṣadrā instead defines the word as referring to the illuminated, who have more insight into the true reality than others, and who should teach the others, for the trustworthy will mirror each other (Mullā Ṣadrā 1998/5: 366–367). Correspondingly, he explains the concept 'sustenance' (*rizq*) as what nourishes and increases an individual's essence, corporeally and spiritually. The essence of the human being is the intellect and its nourishment is the theoretical sciences. Without them, the intellect weakens and dies. Mullā Ṣadrā then applies this sense of semantic and scientific sustenance (*al-rizq al-ma'nāwī al-'ilmī*) to Q. 20 (*Ṭāhā*), 131: "Your Lord's sustenance is better and more lasting" (Mullā Ṣadrā 1998/2: 140).

Regarding 'God's proof' (*ḥujja*), Mullā Ṣadrā mentions it in his commentary on Q. 36 (*Yāsīn*), 17: "We are only obligated to convey the message that makes clarifying distinctions" (*al-balāgh al-mubīn*). Here, he conceptualises the proof as a two-fold process of external message and internal intellectual grasping, which opens up paths of guidance both outside and inside the intellecting self:

> By this statement He directed the argumentation to them, (…) that the duty of reflection is an intellectual command, and each intellecting being gains knowledge by himself according to the intellectual natural disposition that God has given him, and the basic nature (*fiṭra*) in which people are formed. God's proof is over His creatures, and the judge between Him and them is that to thank the Provider of blessings is a duty, because in neglecting it is the risk of a bad outcome, while in doing it is security and peace (*al-amn wa al-salāma*). The intellecting being does not choose risk over security, nor does he prefer to bring upon himself harm rather than the certainty of peace. (…) [God] sent the messengers to them from the outside, after He had given them intellect from the inside, so that the messengers would awaken their intellects from the sleep of oblivion and the slumber of ignorance and imitation (*taqlīd*); therefore it is said: 'The intellect is a path to guidance (*sharʿ*) from within, and the path of guidance is intellect from outside'. If God had not made the intellects emanate internally, they would not have been guided and could not have benefitted from the sending-out of the Messenger. Thus, the meaning is: 'He only obliges us to effectuate the message and to convey the rulings'.
>
> And it has been said that its meaning is: It is not our duty to carry you to the enactment of security, for we do not have the capacity to do so, because enacting security is a gift attained through God, may He be Exalted, making it emanate upon the heart [containing the intellect], which cannot be attained through enforcement and power, like He stated, may He be Exalted: 'There can be no enforcement in the judicial order (Q. 2, 256)' (Mullā Ṣadrā 1998/6: 53–54).

Mullā Ṣadrā's Neoplatonic lens thus allows him to conceptualise the Qurʾān as an emanation descending through the knowledge-spheres that are at once metaphysical, and physically located inside the heart, which is the container (*qalb*) of the intellect. The decisive obligation is to understand reality, by attaining the simultaneously external/descending and internal/ascending knowledge, which can only come from the voluntary pursuit and teaching of philosophical thought. In Chapter 4 above, we saw how Sunnī and Shīʿī jurists commented on the Creation-verse Q. 4 (*al-Nisāʾ*), 1 and emphasised that the 'common descent' of all humans from Adam obligates them to empathise with each other so that the strong protect the rights of the weak. These jurists can be seen as working with a language-based ontological theory of concept. Mullā Ṣadrā, applying a mind-based theory of concept, arrives at a 'common origins' through his Neoplatonic metaphysics of unity of existence and 'common descent' in the emanatory sense.

Shāh Walī Allāh

Shāh Walī Allāh (d. 1176/1762) descended from a scholarly family affiliated with the Naqshbandī Sufi brotherhood and the Ḥanafī school of law, and residing in Delhi, capital of the Mughal Empire (1526–1858). Like Mullā Ṣadrā, his scholarship engages the political vicissitudes of his time. In his case, these included advances on Delhi by Hindu rulers, Sikh insurgencies, invasion by the Persian Qajar dynasty's forces (successors to the Safavids), rising Afghan power, and rivalries between Sunnī and Shīʿa factions at the Mughal court and in society (Hermansen 2013: xxviii–xxix). Moreover, the British and French were making incursions from the coasts, with Kolkata (Calcutta) in west Bengal coming under the control of the British East India Company in 1696. Though the Mughal rulers initially granted the Company control over lands and their tax revenue, the British in the course of the 1700s gained control of larger and larger parts of the sub-continent. Hence, this period represents the beginning of British colonial rule in India, fully established in 1858.

Shāh Walī Allāh had read the writings of Ibn Taymiyya (Hermansen 2013: xxx), who aimed at making the Prophet's *sunna* the sole 'protective governorship' (*walāya*), and stripping Sufi institutional governorship of its claim to personal, divine knowledge beyond the textual sources. Shāh Walī Allāh's family adhered to a branch of the Naqshbandī brotherhood called *mujaddidiyya*, 'renewing'. The epithet *mujaddid* is traditionally ascribed to original thinkers, including al-Ghazzālī and in the Indian context Shaykh Aḥmad Sirhindī (d. 1033/1624), who is seen as initiating Naqshbandiyya-*mujaddidiyya*. Its renewal consists in two main points. Firstly, rejecting the idea of ontological co-existence between God and humans and the Sufi claim to realization of this state. Secondly, replacing the Sufi *walī*s as mediators of divine knowledge and blessings with the Prophet, and reducing the role of the Sufi *shaykh* to guiding individuals towards spiritual encounters with the Prophet and realization of his *sunna*. Hence, this path aims at continuously 'renewing' the community, by putting its members in touch with the Prophet and his knowledge.[54] Shāh Walī Allāh, who is considered a major developer of this path, sought to unite Indian Muslims based on the Prophet's *sunna*,

54 On the origins of the Naqshbandiyya-*mujaddidiyya* and its decisive intellectual and political influence during the whole period between the 1100s/1700s and the

which he expounded by combining his Naqshbandiyya-*mujaddidiyya* Sufi metaphysics with *fiqh* in the treatise *Ḥujjat Allāh al-bāligha*, 'God's Persuasive Proof'.

The title refers to Q. 6 (*al-Anʿām*), 149, "Say: To God belongs the persuasive proof, so had He wished, He would have guided you all!" Shāh Walī Allāh takes God's persuasive proof to refer to "the motives underlying religious obligation and requital and the inner dimensions of God's laws granted by this mercy and guidance" (Hermansen 2013: 9; also 60). In this sense, the proof indicates and makes known the beneficial 'common good' principles or *maṣlaḥa*, which equal God's intent with His guidance and laws. Like most of the legal scholars discussed above under *fiqh*, he defined *maṣlaḥa* as encompassing both this life and the hereafter, not only the latter:

> It may be thought that the rulings of the divine laws do not encompass any aspect of the beneficial purposes (*maṣāliḥ*) and that there is no relationship between human actions and that which God makes a requital for them, and that being obligated by the divine laws is like the case of a master who wants to test the obedience of his servant, so he orders him to lift a stone or to touch a tree – something which has no use to it besides being a test, so that when he obeys or disobeys, he is requited for his action. This is a false idea which is refuted by the practice of the Prophet, may the peace and blessings of God be upon him, and the consensus of the generations whose goodness (*khayr*) has been attested. (…) The Prophet, may the peace and blessings of God be upon him, said: "Indeed, actions are judged according to the intentions", and God, may He be Exalted, said: "[The sacrificial animals'] flesh and blood will not reach God, but your fulfilling your obligations will reach Him" (Q. 22, 37). (Hermansen 2013: 11)

He then proceeded to define the intentions behind the obligatory service to God: the prayer, the welfare tax, the fast, and the pilgrimage. Since there is disagreement among the scholars and Sufis, he sees it as his duty to re-define the divine intentions, with reference to the Qurʾān and the Prophet's *sunna*. In doing so, he developed his own version of a Neoplatonic scheme of emanation, for which he drew on al-Ghazzālī's metaphysics (Hermansen 2013: 47, n. 18).

In two dream visions, cited below, Shāh Walī Allāh prepares for this daunting task by connecting with the Prophet's spirit, which cloaks him like a robe. This alludes to the Prophet's own mantle (*al-burda*), which signifies

1300s/1900s, including the formation of the modern Islamic schools under British colonial rule, see Metcalf (1982), Buehler (1997), and Alam (2004).

his authority. In Shīʿī traditions, the Prophet passes his mantle on to ʿAlī and his family as a sign of their succession to his leadership, while in Sufi contexts it is replicated in the *walī*'s mantle, which his *shaykh* gives him as a sign of the covenant of the *ṭarīqa* in case. In this dream, then, Shāh Walī Allāh receives the Prophet's mantle as a sign of his scholarly and Sufi authority, within the Naqshbandiyya-*mujaddidiyya*, to expound God's persuasive proof. In a second dream, where he is in Mecca, he meets the second and third Shīʿī Imams, who suggest it is 'almost as if' he is writing with the Prophet's own pen. The Imams are often part of Sufi knowledge transmission-chains (*silsila*), and here they may serve the purpose of adding Shīʿī legitimacy to Shāh Walī Allāh's quest for Muslim unity in Moghul India:

> While I was sitting one day after the afternoon prayer with my concentration turned to God, suddenly there appeared the spirit of the Prophet, may the peace and blessings of God be upon him, which covered me from above with something which appeared to be a robe thrown over me. It was inspired in my heart at that spiritual event that this was a sign of the manner of expounding religion. At this I found in my bosom a light which does not cease to expand every minute. Then my Lord inspired me, after a time, of what He had written for me with the exalted Pen, that someday I would undertake this important matter, and that "the land would be illuminated with the light of its Lord" (Q. 39, 69) and that the rays of light would be reflected at the time of sunset, and that the divine law of Muḥammad would shine forth in this age by being presented in long and loose-fitting robes of demonstrative proof. After that I saw the two Imāms, al-Ḥasan and al-Ḥusayn, may God be pleased with them, in a dream, while I was in Mecca, in which it was as if they gave me a pen, and said: "This is the pen of our grandfather, the Messenger of God,[55] may the peace and blessings of God be upon him." (Hermansen 2013: 7; mod.)

The treatise itself consists of seven 'investigations', in Hermansen's translation: The Causes of Religious Obligations and Requitals; The Manner of Requital during Life and after Death; Human Felicity; Piety and Sin; The Regulation of Religion; and The Derivation of the Sharīʿa Laws from the Reports of the Prophet. Thus, it constitutes a comprehensive, introductory guide, which explains in concrete terms what it means that there are connections between God the Originator, the different knowledge-spheres, and the

55 It seems a bit unusual to claim that the Prophet possessed a pen, given that he could not read or write.

human beings. In the first investigation (chs. 1–13), under the heading 'The Knowledge Sphere[56] of Images', Shāh Walī Allāh describes how around God upon the Throne is the highest council of angels (Q. 37, 8; Q. 38, 69), who intermediate between God and humans by causing good impulses in the bosoms of the latter. The lights of the most excellent angels constitute the Spirit, which Shāh Walī Allāh describes through the same tradition as Mullā Ṣadrā. The Spirit contains countless semantic senses and languages, and as such is the extension of the highest council, through the Sacred Enclave (*ḥaẓīrat al-quds*), which communicates with prophets and inspires the hearts of their people so that they are prepared to follow them. In the heart of the Prophet, the Sacred Enclave represents "branches of knowledge which will make the people righteous and guide them, either by revelation, dreams, or a voice from the Unseen (*al-ghayb*)". Below these are a lower council of souls, which also inspire other humans, and animals; etc. (Hermansen 2013: 46–47; mod.) Following al-Ghazzālī, Shāh Walī Allāh then describes the Qur'ān as the sum of all God's decrees for all Creation and the totality of its duration, which are engraved on the Tablet (*al-lawḥ*) with an engraving unlike any material one, just as the Tablet is not of any comparable material. The relationship between the Tablet and the Qur'ān is like that between the Qur'ān and the heart:

> [T]he fixing of the determined things on the Tablet [is] analogous to the words and letter of the Qur'ān in the brain and the heart of the one who has memorized it. These words are written on his heart as if he were reading them off, looking at them. If you were to examine his brain piece by piece you would not find a single letter of this script. In this fashion you must understand the engraving of the Preserved Tablet with everything which God, may He be Exalted, has decreed and determined (Hermansen 2013: 83; mod.)

Also in the first investigation, under the heading 'How religious obligation is derived from what is divinely commanded', Shāh Walī Allāh explains how God's persuasive proof relates to the sciences, and from there to the obligations. He uses examples from nature and human societies for illustration, creating the impression that his arguments (which resemble Aristotelian concepts of forms) are universally recognizable because they align with the proof that belongs to the Creator of everything that exists:

56 Hermansen has 'world' instead of 'knowledge sphere' for *'ālam*, but I choose the latter for the sake of consistence with the discussion of Mullā Ṣadrā's concept, above.

> You should know that God has signs (*āyāt*) in His Creation which guide the one who considers them to the fact that God has the persuasive proof in His imposing on man the obligations of the divine laws.
>
> Look at the trees, their leaves, their blossoms, and their fruit and at all their characteristics, visual, gustatory, or otherwise. He made for every species leaves in a particular form, blossoms with a particular colour, and fruits with a particular taste. Due to these things it can be known that this individual is from such and such a species. All of these follow the specific form and are bound up with it, coming from where the specific form comes. God, may He be Exalted, decreed, for example, that this material would be a date palm, involving His specifying command that its fruit should be a certain type and its leaves a certain type. (…) Then look at the types of animals, you will find that every species has a form and a natural constitution, just as is found among trees. (Hermansen 2013: 60; mod.).

What distinguishes humans from animals is "rationality, understanding speech, and the derivation of acquired sciences from the ordering of axiomatic principles or from experience, induction, and intuition". Hence, the sciences based on systematic knowledge (*ʿulūm*), which are the ones that prophets are inspired with, are recognizable as beneficent by all humans:

> [A]ll peoples have coinciding ideas on the principles of [the refinement of the self and the subjugation of regions under their control], even the inhabitants of the remote mountain heights. This is due to nothing other than a secret arising from the basis of the specific form, and this secret is that the disposition of man requires that his intellect dominate his heart and that his heart dominate his lower self (Hermansen 2013: 61; mod.).

This approach is in line with *siyāsa*, which, as we have seen, assumed that certain political and administrative issues are universal, and that God's knowledge offers a historical, empirically grounded overview over these.

The third investigation in the treatise (chs. 18–28) is devoted to 'the supports of civilization' i.e. statecraft and its *maṣlaḥa* principles. These include the land tax, regarding which he argues it is essential for peace that the ruler does not allow governors to overtax neither peasants nor professional groups, since this will drive them to destitution and rebellion (Hermansen 2013: 131). Shāh Walī Allāh introduces this investigation by describing a language-based theory of concepts, saying that it is through their various languages that humans can express their thoughts, interact, and create 'the supports of civilization' i.e. agriculture, institutions, and sciences, including statecraft (Hermansen 2013: 119).[57] He also points out that the Qur'ān laid out the basic scientific principles for all this:

> God, may He be Exalted, blessed His servants in His Great Writing by inspiring the branches of this first stage of civilization with His knowledge that the imposition of the religious-judicial obligations in the Qur'ān extends to all types of people, and that only this level of the first stage of civilization encompasses all of them, and God has the most knowledge (Hermansen 2013: 120; mod.).

Like all the other jurists, Shāh Walī Allāh sees the Qur'ān and the law as laying down principles for including non-Muslims in the polity, though they have different specific rules than Muslims. He expounds on this constitutional topic in the sixth investigation, with reference to Q. 42 (*al-Shūrā*), 13:

> (13) [God] has set you on the path of guidance (*shara'a lakum*), of the judicial order (*dīn*) with which He appointed Noah, and which We have communicated to you, and with which We appointed Abraham and Moses and Jesus: "Perform the judicial order and do not engage in internal strife (*lā tatafarraqū*) within it!"

Commenting on this verse, through references to the early exegetes Mujāhid and Ibn 'Abbās, Shāh Walī Allāh argues that "the basis of the judicial order (*dīn*) is one, upon which the prophets, may peace be upon them, agree, and (…) any variations are in the divine laws and the methods (*manāhij*)" (Hermansen 2013: 257; mod.; also 258–259). Thus, *dīn* here refers to the constitutional level where there is agreement on basic principles, as distinct from the community-specific rules, laws, and rituals.

In line with his own aim to re-invigorate *maṣlaḥa*, Shāh Walī Allāh defined prophets as sent out by God "to bring the people out of the darkness into the light", in the sense of bringing back *maṣlaḥa* after it had been corrupted or abandoned. Since each time, people, and context is unique, the specific rules and rituals necessarily differ and change, for it is essential that each people can recognise in the divine rules things which they have prior knowledge about (Hermansen 2013: 261; ch. 57, ch. 64). Thus, God sent out the Prophet because the Sassanids and the Byzantines over-indulged in luxury and had become corrupt, and because they ruled over the whole

57 See also al-Ṭabarī (1995/1: 1, 16–17).

known world, including parts of India, it was not possible to institute the common good under their rule:

> Therefore God decreed the end of their power, and the Prophet, may the peace and blessings of God be upon him, informed that Khusraw would be destroyed and there would be no Khusraw after him, and that Caesar would be destroyed, and that there would be no Caesar after him. The true right was revealed refuting the vacuous all over the earth, through the triumph over the vacuity of the Arabs by the Prophet and his Companions and the triumph over the vacuity of these two kingdoms by the Arabs, and the triumph over the rest of the countries by these two, as God has the persuasive proof! (Hermansen 2013: 343; mod.)

To maintain the common good after the Prophet, the Caliphate was instituted, and its leaders (Imams) obligated to publicly manifest the Islamic rituals that distinguish this *dīn* from others (circumcision, places for prostration, call to prayer, the Friday prayer, and other assemblies). However, the Imam will not be able to maintain power through force, which causes people to rebel. Instead, people must be persuaded to understand the beneficial principles, so that they voluntarily support the Imam's rule:

> Therefore, [the Imam] must confirm by proofs which are demonstrative or rhetorical, and which benefit the mind of the common person that these other judicial orders must not be followed (…). He must prove this in public and explain the justifications for the rightful judicial order in that it is easy and tolerant, that its limits are clearly distinguished so that reason recognizes their value, and that it is as clear as day, that its practices will be more beneficial for the common people, and that it is most similar to what remains among them from the behaviour of the preceding prophets, may peace be upon them, and other things like this, as God has the most knowledge. (Hermansen 2013: 345; mod.)

Here Shāh Walī Allāh makes the Qur'ānic divine rhetorical proof a model for a reciprocal social contract, which offers reasons for the legitimacy of rule, and thus obligates the Imam to prove the justification of his rule and law, to Muslims and to the public at large. Furthermore, Shāh Walī Allāh treated the institution of the Caliphate, which at least the Moghul sultan Akbar had claimed to represent (see Chapter 5, above). Shāh Walī Allāh conceptualised it as the ruling institution that ensures all provincial kings (*mulūk*, sing. *malik*) in the realm rule by the law, that they do not try to acquire each other's lands and wealth, and do not allow plunder and brigandage which ruins the people; hence, peace and security depends on the just Caliphate (Hermansen 2013: 137–139).

We can compare Shāh Walī Allāh with Mullā Ṣadrā, who employed his Neoplatonic and Sufi paradigms to expound on philosophical topics, through which he conceptualised the Qur'ān and God's persuasive proof. For him, God's proof is the security that follows from thanking him for sustenance, which is ultimately of an intellectual nature, like existence. Shāh Walī Allāh applied his version of the same paradigms for the broader, multi-disciplinary purpose of explaining why metaphysics and theology concerning God's nature and attributes matters for practical things i.e. ritual obligations, ethics, statecraft, and law. In doing so, he also provides an analysis of the connections between these levels and topics within the Qur'ān, since he argued that they are all contained within God's persuasive proof.

CONCLUDING ANALYSIS

In this long chapter, I have sketched the disciplines of linguistics, *ḥadīth*, political science and administration, history, Qur'ān exegesis, jurisprudence, and systematic theology, focusing on both their Qur'ānic conceptual references and their conceptualisations of the Qur'ān, as well as their institutional contexts. The main question was how Covenant and its constitutional and social contract-related theories is conceptualised within the different disciplines, and I find that the meaning that scholars derive from related Qur'ānic concepts align with (a) discipline, (b) 'school' and theoretical paradigm, and (c) individual aims. Thus, Covenant is understood across the disciplines as referring to a compact with constitutional and social-contractual implications, whose exact definitions depend on factors a, b, and c. The bottom line is, that unless the terms of Covenant are correctly understood, the law will not promote security, prosperity and equity. The correct understanding then requires the scientific knowledge of language, Prophetic *sunna*, statecraft and administration, historical legacies and lessons, Qur'ān exegesis, jurisprudence, and theology.

The analysis, that the Qur'ānic concepts refer to knowledge of the same kind that the disciplines systematically developed, has implications for how we perceive the early and medieval scholars' discursive knowledge about the Qur'ān. If their knowledge is an extension of the Qur'ānic concepts, then it is *scientifically accurate knowledge* about the Qur'ān. They perceived the Qur'ān as conveying *empirically grounded and systematically developed* knowledge about historical peoples, rulers, and prophets, which defines the principles and actions that promote or obstruct prosperity and the common good. These principles and actions converge around the positive category 'enacting security' (*īmān*), 'perfecting sincerity' (*ikhlāṣ*), and 'clear distinction' (*bayān*), and the negative 'rejecting security' (*kufr*), 'taking other partners' (*shirk*), and 'darkness/wrongdoing' (*ẓulm*). More conceptual categories can be plotted under these opposites. The point is that if one follows the scholars in understanding Covenant as referring to political rule, it becomes possible to see the positive category as associated with rule of law, rights-based law, documentation, and reciprocity, and the negative with the opposites: tyranny, arbitrariness, 'might is right', and unilateral enforcement. Consequently, these conceptual categories have practical implications for administrations and peoples. It therefore appears that although the Qur'ānic address (*khiṭāb*) obligates everyone, it highlights the responsibilities resting on lawmakers and people in authority, including landlords, i.e. those whose power to implement the rulings and guidance affects others' livelihoods.

Put in Michel de Certeau's terms: there is discursive continuity between the Qur'ān and the Islamic disciplines, because they are part of the same institutional order. In this order, what we call 'religion' reflects the idea that God is the overseer and guarantor of the constitutional compact, and giver of the law to prophets. Hence, the notion of 'divine law' expresses the idea that no one is above the law as embodied in the Qur'ān, whether ruler, jurist, or common person. Viewed from this perspective, modern discourses on 'religion' as *primarily* personal faith, morality, and spirituality, do indeed, as de Certeau argued, reflect a modern institutional separation between 'religion' and the other societal functions 'politics', 'law', and 'science'.

Consequently, and pushing de Certeau's point about religion and scientific innovation: if the Qur'ān and the Islamic disciplines are seen as reflecting such paradigms as theory of concept, semantics, and rhetoric, natural law theory, and political theory and legal hermeneutics, real *theoretical* continuities appear between the Qur'ān, the Islamic disciplines, and modern disciplines. I have argued in Chapters 4 and 5 that the decisive theoretical innovation that is associated with Qur'ānic Covenant is natural law theory, expressed as rights-based law, also for the peasants and 'weak groups'. Having now treated the seven selected disciplines as well, I would add that natural law theory aligns with the Qur'ānic and scholarly Arabic language and its insistence on 'clear distinctions' and contractual categories, which are important not only for scholarly pursuits but also for the procedural and formal aspects of the rule of law and a constitutional social contract. Within this context, the natural law paradigm adds an important dimension to the explanation of why political scientists and historians incorporated non-Arab peoples and administrative legacies into the Islamic law and administration, namely to show that the latter is founded upon universally valid principles and known 'facts'. Since these peoples and legacies, including the non-Islamic religions, were part of the realms of the Islamic polities, the paradigm of natural law theory thus expresses institutional practices related to a diverse polity, where prosperity and happiness are not considered limited to one group only.

Chapter 7

MODERN INSTITUTIONAL SHIFTS

The pre-modern, dynastic Islamic empires included ethnically, linguistically, and religiously diverse peoples and groups, by legitimising the statecraft and the law in terms of *ḥikma* i.e. capacity for just judgement, which was considered *universally valid* because it conveyed the divine and 'truly general' knowledge (*ʿilm*) of the experiences of historical peoples, rulers, and prophets. This Islamic 'universalistic' use of historical legacies differs from modern nationalism. Universalism is a discursive strategy that recognises diversity but argues for common principles, in line with natural law theory, whereas nationalism is an argument for the unity and particularity of the nation and the civilization with which it identifies. Consequently, as I discussed in Chapter 1 with reference to Eric Hobsbawm's analysis of western nationalism, nationalistic identification of the national civilization with for example ancient Rome or Greece excluded other nations and civilizations from that legacy, including the Islamic one, even though the latter made systematic use of e.g. Greek philosophy, as we have seen.[1] Put in Michel de Certeau's terms, it is thus clear that a common discursive strategy – 'ancient roots' – can have different forms expressing different institutional orders and practices.

The nationalist paradigm has shaped modern western academic theory about culture, civilizations, and religion, since the academic disciplines in the modern national universities reflect the nation-state institutional order and its legitimising discourses.[2] As de Certeau pointed out, this circumstance has significantly shaped modern academic knowledge about 'religion', through an ideologically motivated discursive relegation of knowledge associated with religious institutions and disciplines to the sphere of 'not science'. Moreover, there is a strong normative dimension to such discourses e.g. 'religion' is 'not science', or 'not law', etc., means 'religion' *must not be* 'science', or 'law', but rather must comply with how science and national

1 This is one of the key points of Edward Said's *Orientalism* (1978).

2 For analysis of the Romantic paradigms and concepts that shaped nationalist historical discourses on cultural essences and 'vital spirits', see also Al-Azmeh (2007: 3–26).

law defines religion. Yet modern science claims to be objective, based on observation and empirical data: in de Certeau's terms, academic normativity is thus implicit and not theorised, and therefore works in ideological ways. In this chapter, I will map the modern institutional shifts that took place in the Islamic context, and the emergence of Qur'ānic studies in the west, and then proceed to analyse the production of knowledge about the Qur'ān within new, modern disciplines. Focus will be on what is considered to constitute 'scientific' approaches to the Qur'ān, and discursive continuity and change.

THE NATION-STATE

In the Islamic polities, modern nationalism as ideology and social movement emerged 'naturally' at popular, intellectual, and political levels, and transcended the various religious identities and legacies in the regions. Yet the political *institution* of the nation-state was established in connection with colonial rule from the early 1800s onwards.[3] The Mughal Empire ended with the formal establishment of British rule over India (1858). In the Ottoman realm, the province of Algeria had come under the French colonial rule already by 1838. In the Ottoman heartlands of Anatolia, a Turkish nationalist movement instituted the modern Republic of Turkey in 1923, and the Caliphate was formally abolished in 1924. By that time, Arab and other nationalist movements had challenged Ottoman rule, and most of the Ottoman provinces in North Africa and the Fertile Crescent had come under British, French, and Italian rule in the aftermath of the First World War (1914–1918). The Iranian realm remained un-colonized but subject to heavy Russian-Soviet, British, and eventually American imperial domination, politically and economically. From 1962, the year when Algeria finally liberated itself from French rule after an extremely costly war, in terms of casualties and economic destruction at the hands of the French, the sovereign nation-state is the political institution of all the Islamic countries, as elsewhere in the modern world.

3 For definitions and distinctions between 'nation', 'ethnicity', 'nationalism', and 'nation-state', see Smith (2003). Simply put, 'ethnicity' refers to a perceived genealogical relationship, including language, history and culture; 'nation' involves also a territory and public culture, including laws and political myths and memories, and can incorporate several ethnic groups; 'nationalism' is the ideology of 'the people' and advocates its unity, freedom, and sovereignty; while the 'nation-state' is the national political institution.

Political scientists and scholars of Islamic law have drawn different conclusions about the nature of the institutional changes. Noah Feldman (2008) has schematically described a shift from a pre-modern imperial constitutional order of rule of law, where the rulers depended on tax revenue for income to the treasury and the legal scholars had the power to confer or withdraw legitimacy from the ruler, to an authoritarian state, with a rentier-like economy, where all powers are concentrated to the ruler and the state, and the judiciary serve as functionaries of the state.[4] In Feldman's view, the process of concentration of powers in the state began in the Ottoman Empire in the 1800s as a consequence of modernisation programmes, and culminated in the post-colonial nation-states:

> In the absence of either the scholars to interpret the law or a popularly elected legislature to enact it, the law came to be conceived simply as the command of the sovereign. Judges trained in the new, state-issued law generally understood their position in much the same way that modern European judges applying their own legal codes did: they saw themselves as faithful servants of the state. Unlike the contemporary European state, though, the late nineteenth-century Ottoman state was not itself a differentiated entity in the sense of incorporating popular and monarchic institutions. The state was, in effect, the executive – and nothing more. With the executive as the source of law, and the judges charged with applying the law conceived as servants of the executive, the state became a totalizing sovereign entity such as never existed before in Islamic history (2008: 78–79).

Others, such as Sami Zubaida (2003), rather argue that the modern change was not so uniform or clear-cut, since rulers have functioned as lawmakers and legal scholars served the state administration also in pre-modern contexts, and since the legal scholars were actually engaged in the production of modern national law codes, and in many cases continue to have legislative functions; moreover, there are considerable differences between countries.[5] Samy Ayoub (2020) aligns with this kind of approach, showing how

4 According to Feldman, the exception is the Kingdom of Saudi Arabia, which is the only case of a modern monarchic constitution that maintains the pre-modern separation of power between the state and the legal scholars, although the non-elected nature of the body of legal scholars means the monarchy is not a constitutional one in the modern democratic sense (2008: 92–102).

5 See also Sultany (2017), which focuses on the contemporary Arab Spring and its contexts and aftermaths, but also provides cases from the Ottoman centre and Arab provinces in the turn of century 1800–1900 (Chapters 1–2).

Ottoman Ḥanafī legal scholars gradually, since the 1600s, included Sultanic rulings in their legal treatises, thus paving the way for the modern law-code of the late 1800s (see Chapter 5, above). Chapters 5 and 6 have also shown that while the majority of the selected early and medieval Sunnī jurists rallied around the *theory* of constitutional separation of powers, some political theorists rather argued for expanded law-making and supervisorial powers for the Caliph, a theory that e.g. the Fatimid Ismāʿīlī Caliphs and legal scholars adopted, as well. Hence, contestation over this issue has a long legacy, extending into contemporary research.

Moreover, in the 1800s, the land tax continued to play a crucial part, in ways that shed more light on why the state may have needed to control legislation. In Egypt, which was one of the most important provinces in terms of revenue for the central Ottoman state, the management of the land tax was among the factors that enabled colonial domination and rule. During the late 1800s, land was concentrated into large estates, including land given as an 'immobilised' grant (*waqf*) for the scholarly institution, with a corresponding weakening of the peasant tenants' ownership rights. Large estates strengthened the power of landlords, who could negotiate new and stronger ownership rights, and retain tax from the Ottoman provincial administration, whose tax revenues were diminished (Cuno 1980). Since the administration sought to invest in modernisation programmes, they took loans from European banks. Due to default on debts, Britain was able to establish colonial rule in Egypt in 1882, co-opting the Ottoman provincial administration for this purpose (Tuncer 2015: Ch. 3; also Cromer 1908). Though the central Ottoman state managed to keep control over Anatolia until 1923, it too was indebted to European banks.

Political change was also coupled to the gradual establishment of modern educational institutions at basic and higher levels. From now on, the Islamic scholarly institution's and the Sufi brotherhoods' authority as the principal providers of divine knowledge was challenged by new thinkers with new discourses on Islam, publicised through modern print media and organisations. One of the most well-known was the program for pan-Islamic unity and modern progress, propounded by the Iranian Twelver Shīʿī scholar, journalist, and cosmopolitan political activist Jamāl al-Dīn al-Afghānī (d. 1315/1897) and his friend, the Egyptian Sunnī scholar Muḥammad ʿAbduh (d. 1323/1905), later chancellor of al-Azhar university in Cairo. From a temporary base in Paris, they published during the year 1884 the magazine *al-ʿUrwa al-wuthqā*, 'The Most Reliable Handle', referring to Q. 2 (*al-Baqara*), 256:

> (256) There can be no force in the religious part of the judicial order! Since moral rectitude has become distinct from wavering, the one who rejects the idols and enacts security through God has indeed taken hold of the most reliable handle that has no rupture, for God is One Who Hears Knowing All!

To withstand the colonial onslaught, with its political, economic, and cultural effects on Islamic societies, al-Afghānī and ʿAbduh urged Muslims to unite across sectarian and school boundaries, along lines similar to Shāh Walī Allāh's vision a century earlier. In their view, the established schools and disciplines were conservative and obscurantist, and concerned with defending their positions instead of tackling the serious challenges that the rulers and peoples faced. Hence, the scholarly institution constituted obstacles to the political and scientific progress that Muslims had to embrace in order to regain sovereignty over their lands. The method they advocated was to return to the sources of Islam – the Qurʾān and the Prophet's *sunna* – and read them anew, to revive Islam's progressive and vital spirit, which had inspired the scientific and institutional advances of the early centuries. Al-Afghānī travelled widely in the Iranian Qajar Empire, the Mughal Empire, the Ottoman Empire, Russia, France, and the United Kingdom, seeking to further this cause.[6]

Equally important was the discourse on the necessity to revive the Caliphate as unifying Islamic institution, in some form, and reinvigorate *sharīʿa* as public law. Shāh Walī Allāh can be seen as an early representative of the argument, which after him became popularised in the Moghul Empire and later in the Indian resistance against British rule, as well as in the course of the late 1800s in the Arab countries.

In 1926, al-Azhar University organised The Cairo Congress for the purpose of deliberating the issue, and what new forms the Caliphate might take (Ihsanoglu 2010: 15–16). One of the most famous activists was the Syrian Sunnī scholar and journalist Rashīd Riḍā (d. 1354/1935), who moved to Cairo to connect with al-Afghānī and ʿAbduh. Riḍā focused on reviving the Islam of the first generations, 'the precursors who worked for the common good' (*al-salaf al-ṣāliḥ*), and therefore his discourse has been labelled

6 On al-Afghānī's thought and politics, including his relationship with ʿAbduh, and his international connections, see the collection of essays in Chaghatai (2005). For contextualisation of al-Afghānī's thought and activism with reference to national Romanticism, see Al-Azmeh (2007: 19–23).

salafiyya, or 'Salafism'.[7] After al-Afghānī's death, Riḍā and ʿAbduh together launched in 1897 the magazine *al-Manār*, 'The Lighthouse', which eventually became Riḍā's own project for publishing and disseminating his ideas, including a good deal of Qurʾān exegesis.

Central to Riḍā's discourse on *sharīʿa* was the well-established concept of *maṣlaḥa*, which he gave a new form, *maṣlaḥa ʿāmma*, communicated to the public through his magazine. In this way, he opened up the jurists' specialist definitions of *maṣlaḥa* to public deliberation among the emerging professional classes, in the context of anti-colonial resistance and nationalism. Indeed, Riḍā conceptualised journalism as the new Islamic social contract, arguing that it was the modern public medium for teaching and communicating the divine, obligating address (*khiṭāb*), and negotiating power between the rulers and the ruled. Thus, he saw his journalistic work as complementing that of the legal scholars in their function of reforming and codifying the law and developing the doctrine, and he invited their public critique on his thoughts, for improvement (Hamzah 2013: 100–108, 116–117).

The publicisation of Islamic topics to an increasingly literate public meant that although the Islamic scholarly institution and disciplines continued, other professional classes became capable to produce interpretations. As a result, the scholarly institution and the Sufi brotherhoods were now complemented by new membership-based organisations, reflecting the general development of modern associations. The famous organisation *Jamāʿat al-Ikhwān al-Muslimīn*, or The Muslim Brotherhood, was founded in 1928 by the Egyptian public school teacher Ḥasan al-Bannā (d. 1369/1949). Al-Bannā, who was initially member of a Sufi brotherhood (al-Ḥasafiyya), became engaged in politics and Riḍā's *salafiyya* project. His aim was to counter the abolition of the Caliphate in 1924 and recreate Islamic unity from the grassroots upwards, on a country-by-country basis. Similar to how Sufi brotherhoods function, al-Bannā's Muslim Brotherhood drew members from all classes of Egyptian society, including the rural population, though with a strong presence of the new urban professional groups at the higher organisational ranks. On this basis, al-Bannā formulated a comprehensive (*shāmil*) program for infusing Islamic principles into all societal institutions, by educating individual members and the public in the meanings and practical purposes of *sharīʿa* (Lia 1998; Mitchell 1969). For similar reasons,

7 On the 'reformist' Syrian Salafī group in Damascus in the period 1885–1914, see Commins (1986); on the Syrian Salafīs and their inspiration, through the Naqshbandī brotherhood, from Shāh Walī Allāh and his *mujaddidiyya*-branch, see Weismann (2001: 270ff.).

the Indian journalist Abū Aʿlā Mawdūdī (d. 1399/1979), who was from a Sufi family with distinguished scholars, founded in 1941 the organisation *Jamāʿat-ī Islāmī*. With the creation of Pakistan in 1947, the year of Indian independence from British rule, Mawdūdī settled there. In the Pakistani context, *Jamāʿat-ī Islāmī* has played a key role in the post-1979 Islamisation of the national law. Similarly, in the Egyptian context, the Muslim Brotherhood played a part in getting the clause that *sharīʿa* is the main source of the law included into the national constitution, in 1972.

Given the colonial and post-colonial context, 'the West' occupies an important place in virtually all Islamic discourses. Without hostility, both the Muslim Brotherhood and the Jamāʿat-ī Islāmī define Islam as clearly distinct from western thought and civilisation, in terms of the ideologies and actual practices their thinkers observed, though there can be overlaps on principles. For instance, Ḥasan al-Bannā rejected socialism and nationalism, because they are founded on the idea of conflict of interest, between social classes and between nations and peoples. Islam means solidarity and co-operation between all Muslims, for the benefit of all, while nationalism seeks benefit only for its people, and thus pits one Muslim nation against another, sapping their strength while the colonial enemy triumphs (al-Bannā 1977: 16–17).[8] At the societal level, Islam is a comprehensive order with specific forms of legitimate authority, and methods for electing political leadership through counsel (*shūrā*) and holding it to account concerning how

8 See also Goldberg (1986) on labour organisations in Egypt 1930–1952. The study includes a section (pp. 105–116) on al-Bannā's approach. Instead of Marxist analysis of class struggle and concept of 'workers' as an international class and movement, al-Bannā's Islamic discourse framed exploitation of Egyptian workers in terms of colonial oppressive rule and its encouragement of the essentially individual vice of *ẓulm*, Goldberg argues. However, as I have argued here, Islamic discourses on ethical categories can be seen as referring to institutional practices, i.e. the ethical categories that define individual virtue and vice can have 'structural', practical societal implications; it is not clear to me that this possibility has been examined and found untenable in Goldberg's study. See also Berger (1970), on the numerous religious (mainly Muslim and Christian) and other charities that provided welfare and educational services to people around the mid-1960s. Regarding the Islamic charities, Berger emphasises the continued significance of Qurʾānic and Islamic principles. However, Berger perceives 'Islam' as principally oriented towards societal, voluntary welfare provisions, as opposed to state-centered programs of President Nasser's socialist kind, which in principle supports Goldberg's analysis of al-Bannā's discourse in the preceding period. Nevertheless, since we have seen in Chapter 5 above that the state administration was held responsible for just redistribution of revenue, the idea that the state is responsible for public welfare is certainly not antithetical to medieval political theory. Thus, it is possible that Berger (1970) reflects the Cold War context and anti-socialist discourse.

well it represents all groups' interests and manages the welfare of all (Lia 1998). Correspondingly, within the organisation, members of the Muslim Brotherhood pledged an oath of allegiance to Ḥasan al-Bannā as leader, conditioned on his knowledge of the Qurʾān, its interpretation, the Prophet's *sunna*, the other Islamic disciplines, and their beneficial implementation. He also wrote treatises on these subjects, including *Maqāṣid al-Qurʾān al-karīm* ('The Objectives of the Dignified Qurʾān') and *al-ʿAqāʾid* ('The Doctrines'), where he employed the creed of divine Oneness in the same way as the medieval scholars did, namely to derive principles for individual, social and legal ethics, administration, and lawmaking (Mårtensson 2015).

In economic terms, al-Bannā's discourse and that of the Muslim Brotherhood after him is not in conflict with the interests of the rather wealthy classes, including landowners. Because of its proximity to the latter group, the organisation did not resist landowners' and developers' attempts since the late 1970s to push the state to abolish the land reform launched in 1966 by the second and socialist President of independent Egypt, Gamal Abd al-Nasser (r. 1956–1970), which strengthened peasants' right to tenancy (Springborg 1991: 242, 248). Instead, the organisation has taken up a mildly social democratic stand, advocating strong public welfare and 'ethical capitalism', to counter the combined effects of urbanization, neo-liberal reforms, and elite clientelism. Thus, Abu-Odeh (2009) has argued that in Egyptian politics the Muslim Brotherhood offers a 'parallel Islamic track' and 'Islamic commonwealth-ism', which is funded and managed by wealthier members and Islamic charities, and attracts also groups excluded from the state elites. In order to finance its public outreach, the Muslim Brotherhood organisation in the period 1970–1981 became increasingly integrated into the modern economy and the state institutions, drawing in funding from both private businesses and the public sector. For example, one substantial source of income was commercial advertising in print media outlets associated with the organisation and its cause (Rock-Singer and Brooke 2018).

The point here is not to analyse Muslim Brotherhood policy but to highlight that within institutional change, there were discursive continuities with the medieval Islamic disciplines and topics, which include taking up positions regarding land ownership, tax, redistribution, and the common good. Such continuities are easily obscured by the epithet 'Islamism', often applied to these organisations and their 'lay' members. 'Islamism' implies that their organisation-specific views of Islam as a program in the political sense is new: it is a modern ideology, hence Islam-*ism*. It is of course true that the modern continuations of the scholarly institution and disciplines are distinct from these modern organisations, even though individual scholars may be members or supporters of the organisations. Consequently, 'Islamist' advocacy for *sharīʿa* and 'Islamization of society' is not a call for return to a pre-modern institutional order. Rather, it is a call for government, legislation, and society as a whole to be infused with 'Islamic values' or principles, in a context where 'lay' people and the public have as much say on what these are as the scholars have (Feldman 2008: 107–115). For example, Ḥasan al-Bannā rejected political parties because they were tools of power for the Egyptian elites who collaborated with the British, excluding the majority of the people from having their voices and interests heard (Lia 1998: 203–207). Since the 1990s, however, Muslim Brotherhood thinkers have responded to public political developments and defined Islamic values and principles in constitutional democratic terms, now recognising political parties as legitimate. The theory is then, that the people as a voting body "accept responsibility for implementing what God has commanded", and a "democratically elected legislature should draft and pass laws that incorporate the content of Islamic law". If Islamic law does not provide answers, the legislature can "use its discretion to adopt laws infused by Islamic values" (Feldman 2008: 119). Nevertheless, the concern with the common good, understood as including both material-societal and personal-eschatological dimensions, is certainly a continuity between the pre-modern scholarly disciplines and modern organisations, such as the Muslim Brotherhood.

As Meir Hatina has pointed out, both Sunnī legal scholars and the Muslim Brothers represent continuity with the Sunnī legacy of separation of powers, since neither party claims authority over the state. An exception was the early writings in the 1930s by the Syrian legal scholar Shaykh Muṣṭafā al-Sibāʿī (d. 1384/1964), who founded the Syrian branch of the Muslim Brotherhood in 1946. In this early phase, al-Sibāʿī advocated that the legal scholars should have governing authority, since they have the knowledge of the law required for just government – similar to al-Rāzī's argument in the 1200s. However, in the course of the 1950s, the Syrian Muslim Brotherhood entered public politics and formed a party. Al-Sibāʿī accordingly modified his views and redefined the role of Islamic law as "to colour the state with a spiritual, moral hue so that the regulations and laws will be carried out under the impetus of a deep, spiritual force" (Hatina (2010: 468; 463–468).

In Iran, on the other hand, the legal scholars have actually assumed governing power. Initially, modern Iran was a continuation of the monarchy of the Safavid and Qajar dynasties into the Pahlavi dynasty (r. 1925–1979), with Twelver Shīʿism as the official school of law. In response to the Qajar Shahs' arbitrary concessions on trade and raw materials to Russia and Britain and the need to curb the Shah's powers, and as an expression of broader popular demands for political participation, a constitutional movement broke out 1905–1911. It aimed to transform the monarchy into a constitutional one with an elected parliament. The movement was partly successful, though the Pahlavi Shahs asserted control over the parliament. Moreover, the Iranian state became increasingly indebted to Britain and, after 1945, to the USA. This was the case even after the discovery of oil, which came under the ownership of a British-American oil company. In 1951, Iran's first elected Prime Minister, Mohammad Mossadegh, attempted to nationalise Iranian oil, only to be ousted in 1953 by a British-American orchestrated coup, which reinforced the Shah's powers over parliament. In the period late 1960s-early 1970s, the Shah pushed through a land reform, which all the leading Islamic scholars opposed since it affected lands held by the scholarly institution, and infringed on the property rights of landowners protected by *sharīʿa*. One of the scholars who fronted opposition to the land reform and to the Shah's rule generally was Ayatollah Khomeini (d. 1410/1989), who in the same period composed the essays that make up the constitutional theory *velāyat-e faqīh*, 'Governorate of the Jurist'. Due to several factors, including popular resentment of the Shah's repressive rule, American dominance over the Shah, poverty, the Soviet invasion of Afghanistan (1978), and Ayatollah Khomeini's ability to mobilise popular support for the idea that Islamic rule would both solve all Iran's problems and represent an authentic political system, a revolution took place in late 1978.[9] The Shah fled the country and in 1400/1979 the Islamic Republic of Iran was established.

Velāyat-e faqīh is unique in Islamic history. For authorisation, Khomeini cited a *ḥadīth* from al-Kulaynī's collection: *al-fuqahāʾ umanāʾ al-rusul*, "the legal scholars are the trustees of the prophets", which he interpreted as saying that the legal scholars should not only derive law but implement it, like the prophets i.e. have executive authority (Hatina 2010: 457). Consequently, the supreme head of state is a legal scholar, elected by a Council of Experts consisting of distinguished legal scholars (not unlike how a Catholic Pope and Head of the Vatican State is elected by the College of Cardinals). In addition, there is a popularly elected parliament and President, and a Guardian Council, composed of both Islamic legal scholars and civil law experts, since the law includes many areas not covered by 'traditional' *sharīʿa*. The Islamic character of the national law is ensured through the Guardian Council, which

9 The earliest English language reference work on the Iranian revolution, which also treats the foreign economic and political direct interventions during the Qajar (1785–1925) and the Pahlavi (1925–1979) dynasties, is Keddie (1981). On the specific issue of land reform, see Bakhash (1989).

also vets candidates for parliament and presidency. In 1988, the constitution was complemented by a Committee for Discerning the Benefit (*maṣlaḥa*) of the System, which advises the Supreme Leader and resolves conflicts between the Guardian Council and parliament. The reason behind it was that in the wake of the revolution in 1978, many peasants had seized the lands they were cultivating from the landlords, who resided in the cities. The legal ownership of these lands had to be resolved. Since the Islamic Republic was ideologically committed to protect the rights and interests of the poor, the legal scholars' pre-revolution resistance to changes in land ownership could not prevail. Famously, in the Iranian context, the social justice-norm that the Islamic Republic upheld is referred to Q. 28 (*al-Qaṣaṣ*), 5–6:

> (5) We intend to favour **those who have been weakened in the land (*alladhīna 'ustuḍ'ifū fī al-arḍ*)** and make them leaders and make them the inheritors,
> (6) And give them powers in the land, and make Pharaoh and Haman and their armed troops see what they have been fearing!

We have seen above in Chapter 5 how this passage could be read as reflecting changes in the peasants' legal status, as early Islamic law testifies to. In the Iranian context, the verses were given new revolutionary meaning by reference to the famous anti-colonial book, *The Wretched of the Earth* (1961; *Les damnés de la terre*), written by the Martinique author Frantz Fanon. Hence, Ayatollah Khomeini in 1988 instituted the Committee for Discerning the Benefit (*maṣlaḥa*) of the System to negotiate consensus between parties regarding the specific issue of land ownership (Bakhash 1989; also Hooglund 2009). The mandate was later widened to include any divisive issue, to the effect that the constitution of the Islamic Republic represents a return to the early Twelver Shī'ī pragmatism that the best interest of the community should be considered, through the jurists' rule (Afsaruddin 2013: 25–30).

To sum up: In Sunnī contexts, the nation-state model integrated the Islamic legal scholars as functionaries of the state law, in nationally specific ways with varying degrees of legislative authority. The 'Islamist' organisations run parallel to both the state and the scholars, advocating society-wide commitment to *sharī'a* and Qur'ānic principles, and drawing into an Islamic discourse and practices many people otherwise excluded from state and scholarly elites. In the Iranian, Twelver Shī'ī context, modernity produced the Islamic Republic, in which the legal scholars are the highest representatives of the state and the law. Here too, the ambition has been to 'Islamise' society, including regulations of public mores, rituals and dress codes as signs of sincerity and security; as in Q. 24 (*al-Nūr*), 30–31:

> (30) Say to the male enactors of security to lower their gaze and guard their private parts: that is purer for them; indeed, God is informed of what they do!
> (31) Say to the female enactors of security to lower their gaze and guard their private parts and not show their adornment (*zīnatahunna*), except what manifests itself. Let them drape their veils over their bosoms and not show their adornment except to their husbands, their fathers, their husbands' fathers, their sons, the sons of their husbands, their brothers, the sons of their brothers, the sons of their sisters, their women, their slaves, the male attendants who do not have sexual desire, or children who have not been exposed to women's sexual parts. Also, they should not stamp their feet so that the adornment they have concealed becomes known. And return to God, all of you, O enactors of security, so that you may come to promote prosperity (*laʿallakum tufliḥūna*)!

At the international level, all the nation-states which identify as Islamic in some way have created the intergovernmental organisation named The Organisation of the Islamic Conference (OIC). Founded in 1969 in Rabat, the OIC can be seen as providing a replacement for the Caliphate, i.e. an institution where representatives of each member state convene and act on the basis of common concerns as Muslims. The member states retain their membership in and commitments to the UN, including its human rights covenants. In 1990 the OIC adopted its own Cairo Declaration of Human Rights in Islam. It has some significant limits compared with the UDHR, including the right of the prophets not to be subject to defamation, but illustrates how the member states conceptualise the Qurʾān, the Prophet's *sunna*, and Islamic law, as foundations for human dignity, rights-based law and universally valid principles (Ihsanoglu 2010). Human rights with its natural law theory is thus another example of continuity from early and medieval into modern time.

THE QURʾĀN AND MODERN DISCIPLINES

The modern diversification of educational institutions and academic disciplines corresponds with the increasingly diversified economy and closer international connections. This meant that the Qurʾān is being studied in public universities and their disciplines, both in Muslim majority countries and elsewhere, including western countries. The study of Islam and the Qurʾān through British and American colonial and post-colonial scholarly discourses is the topic of Edward Said's famous *Orientalism* (1978). His critique is directed towards discourses that, in the western nationalistic spirit, presuppose essential differences between Islamic and Western civilizations, and which prove their point by amassing overwhelming amounts of 'unassailable facts'. However, there were other western discourses as well, which suggest that the Qurʾān and Islamic thought may have played an important role in the development of social contract theory in Europe, as we shall see here.

Studies of the Qurʾān in Europe began in the context of Christian theological polemics. In 1143 during the Crusades and the Spanish Reconquista, the Englishman Robert of Ketton produced the first Latin translation, on behalf of the Benedictine Abbott of Cluny (France). This remained the main translation until new ones in French and Latin were made in the 1600s (Irwin 2006: 26).[10] At this time, it was the Protestant 'return to Scripture' and its original languages that generated a broader interest in translation. Chairs in Hebrew, sometimes with Arabic as a second 'Semitic language', were established in Britain at Oxford and Cambridge universities, and in the Netherlands at Leiden. The first professor of Arabic at Oxford University was Edward Pococke (d. 1691). His translations of Arabic works appear to have inspired John Locke's empiricism, so influential in modern British philosophy and political theory (Irwin 2006: 93–97). Denise Spellberg has pointed out that Locke himself took classes in Hebrew and Arabic, and that he was a close friend of both Pococke and his son, who translated into Latin the treatise *Ḥayy ibn Yaqẓān* by the Andalusian scholar Ibn Ṭufayl (d. 581/1185).[11] The translation was widely publicised, and Locke and others perceived it as a remarkable synthesis of 'reason and revelation' and a statement of natural philosophy. Once translated into English, it also inspired Daniel Defoe and his novel *Robinson Crusoe* (1719), and then made its way into some Puritan circles in North America (Spellberg 2013: 65–66).

Locke's interest in Islamic thought also had to do with his friendship with Henry Stubbe (d. 1676), with who he took Arabic classes. Though Stubbe erroneously assumed that the Prophet wrote the Qurʾān, he praised

10 But see Bennison (2009: 210), on a revision of an alternative to Ketton's translation from the early 1400s; ref. to Burman (1998). Apparently, Ketton employed Arabic exegetical works for his own, in Bennison's words, 'exuberant' rendering of the Qurʾān. For a survey of Qurʾān translations up to the present, see Elmarsafy (2020).

11 According to Bennison, again, in the 1600s Arabic became one of the required languages for all higher degree students at Oxford (2009: 213).

the Prophet and Islam for their rationality and remarkable tolerance of Christianity and other religions. Drawing on Pococke's Latin translations, Stubbe in 1671 wrote a defence of Islam entitled *An Account of the Rise and Progress of Mahometanism: with the Life of Mahomet and a Vindication of him and his Religion from the Calumnies of the Christians*. Though the treatise was never published, due to its inflammatory potential in the Christian milieu of the time, Stubbe's work influenced Locke in his development of a social contract theory based on religious tolerance, in *A Letter Concerning Toleration* (1689) (Spellberg 2013: 66–69).

One arguably influential translation of the Qur'ān was that by George Sale (d. 1736), English solicitor and autodidact scholar of Semitic languages. Based on a Latin translation, Sale produced an annotated English version, intending to do justice to the ideas and virtues of the Prophet and Islam. It was later translated into French (Irwin 2006: 120–121). In France, Ziad Elmarsafy shows, Voltaire had begun working on a universal history, in the Enlightenment spirit. He was initially suspicious towards Islam and the Ottoman Empire, but after studying a French version of Sale's Qur'ān translation, he undertook to write a historically sound explanation of the Qur'ān, the Prophet, and Islam, correcting the dominant and overwhelmingly hostile Christian discourse. Elmarsafy argues that Voltaire, through the process of understanding the Qur'ān, came to identify with the Prophet as a man striving to introduce a rational approach to the divine and to society, against the grain of established prejudice. Based on his new insights into the roles that Moses and the Abrahamic concept of divine Oneness play in the Qur'ān, and into the Qur'ānic legal material, Voltaire concluded that the Muslim countries were not ruled by an 'Oriental despot', as the dominant discourses would have it. Rather, they were ruled by 'the Book', and since 'the Book' contained many laws, the Muslim sovereigns were effectively subject to the law – precisely what Voltaire wished for the French people (Elmarsafy 2009: 90; Ch. 4).

These political and theoretical understandings of the Qur'ān and the Islamic disciplines show that when the Qur'ān began to be translated and studied within European academic disciplines, it was drawn into the competing discourses about the best direction of European politics, much like the scholars within the Islamic disciplines used it to argue for one policy or another. Thus, there is a real historical possibility that the Qur'ān and Islamic disciplines have contributed towards shaping European political theory in a tolerant direction, through the Enlightenment's social contract-oriented thought, which recognised the necessity of founding modern civil rights on religious diversity.[12]

As for the contemporary period i.e. 1900s–2000s, European Qur'ānic studies has branched out from departments for Semitic languages and Faculties of Theology to Religious and Islamic studies, where the Qur'ān is conceptualised as the Scripture and canon of Islam, comparable with the Hebrew and Christian Bibles and often analysed with Bible studies methods (see Chapter 3). It is also being analysed through the theories and methods pertaining to the modern disciplines of Literature especially, and to some extent Philosophy, Politics, and so on. Yet as European Protestant-majority countries are currently establishing Chairs and programs in Islamic theology at university faculties of Christian theology, studies of the Qur'ān are making their way back into Christian theology contexts, though with the new aim to produce normative Islamic discourses for European Muslims within the orders of European nation-states.[13]

The increasing internationalization of academia from the colonial period onwards means that the study of the Qur'ān within modern disciplines has been developing simultaneously within the West and in Islamic countries. This was evident in British ruled Egypt, among other places. In the midst of the movement for national independence, the Muslim Brotherhood's founder Ḥasan al-Bannā (d. 1369/1949) analysed the implications of modern disciplines as applied to the Qur'ān in his treatise *Maqāṣid al-Qur'ān al-karīm*, 'The Objectives of the Dignified Qur'ān'. He starts with a definition of the Qur'ān:

> God made it descend upon His Prophet, may God bless him and grant him peace, in order for the enactors of security to recite it, so that their bosom would be laid open by this recitation and their hearts and intellects become enlightened, and through it bestow God's reward on the Day of Standing to trial! No one comes even close to the words of God Most High. Then, it was to be the constitution of their life and the order of their society (*dustūra ḥayātihim wa niẓāma mujtama'i-him*), drawing for them the courses to the felicitous life in this nearest,

12 On the general point, that western Islamic studies scholars analyse Islam in terms of both the political theory and the current western policy debates in which they are engaged, see Sadowsky (1997). Kamali (2009: 46) also argues the case for Qur'ānic and Islamic contributions to Enlightenment ideals, though based on other studies than the ones I have referred to here.

13 For a recent special issue discussing Islamic theology in (mainly) the context of the Scandinavian countries, see Leirvik and Flaskerud (2018), and specifically on the Qur'ān in the same issue, Hoffmann (2018).

> material existence, and the courses to success and safety in the furthest abode [citations of Q. 16, 97 and Q. 20, 124]. Thus, the objective of the Qurʾān is not only recitation and the seeking of blessings, although it is truly blessed. Rather, its greatest blessing is in pondering it carefully and understanding its meanings and objectives, and then realizing them through actions that are equally judicial and of the nearest world. The one who does not do this but contents himself with the recitation alone, without contemplation or action, should fear that the promise applies to him, which al-Bukhārī transmitted from Ḥudhayfa, may God be pleased with him: "O Readers of the Qurʾān! Be correct in speech and action, for then you will have proceeded by far, but if you took right and left, you will have strayed by far!" (1981: 6)

He then describes how *tafsīr* developed historically in relation to the various Islamic disciplines, showing how the exegetes chose different methods and topics, pushing interpretation in new directions according to individual preferences as well as the intellectual and political developments of each historical period (1981: 10–13).

Addressing his contemporary Egyptian context, al-Bannā alerts his readers to 'points where interpreters slip' (*mazāliq al-mufassirīna*). 'Slipping' is the result of insufficient mastery of the Islamic sciences related to *sharīʿa*, the Arabic language, and *dīn*, which prevents one from understanding the topics, meanings, and lessons that the Qurʾān conveys. The worst example is the Orientalists (*al-mustashriqūna*) i.e. western scholars studying Islam. Given their deficient qualifications, even the sincere among them consistently draw the wrong conclusions, let alone the adversarial ones. Despite this fact, the Orientalists' knowledge transmission is pervasive, with followers also among Muslim researchers within the new disciplines of History and Literature studies. One example is Dr. Ṭāhā Ḥusayn (d. 1393/1973). In al-Bannā's view, Ṭāhā Ḥusayn enraged some members of the Muslim public by rejecting the reality of the prophets and messengers and miraculous events accounted for in the Qurʾān and the Bibles, arguing there is no historical evidence for them. Ṭāhā Ḥusayn's 'slippage', al-Bannā explains, is that the Qurʾān is not history in the technical scientific sense. It does not aim to identify the exact times, places, and personalities of the prophets, but to provide guidance, using the prophets as examples of general issues with societal implications.[14] Consequently, for Muslims the reality of the prophets and messengers is a higher Truth, which cannot be questioned without negating

14 On this specific point, al-Bannā aligns with Muḥammad ʿAbduh and other Egyptian modernists, including Ṭāhā Ḥusayn; see Abu Zayd (2003: 19–20, 26–27).

the Qurʾān's function as divine guidance. In al-Bannā's view, Ṭāhā Ḥusayn could have avoided clashing with the people and creating an opposition between Islam and modern science, had he taken the humbler approach that not all of reality is ever fully known and research may yet uncover new facts, as the sciences have done throughout history (1981: 13–17). A second example is Muḥammad Aḥmad Khalafallāh's (d. 1412/1991) PhD dissertation 'The Narrative Art in the Dignified Qurʾān' (*al-Fann al-qaṣaṣī fī al-Qurʾān al-karīm*), submitted in 1947 to the Department of Arabic Language and Literature within the Faculty of Arts at King Fuʾād I University in Cairo.[15] Khalafallāh argued that the Qurʾān should be analysed in terms of comparative literature and mythology. Hence, the narratives about the prophets were mythical stories known by the Arabs at the time, and which were employed as literary devices, to convey specific messages. Al-Bannā criticises this thesis for reducing the Qurʾān to literature, to the exclusion of anything else, because this again means negating the Truth-claim connected with the divine guidance and its societal implications. Instead, al-Bannā argues, the author could have depicted the literary aspect as one of several aspects of the Qurʾān, and as one way of studying it (1981: 17–18). Finally, he addresses the so-called scientific interpretation, which seeks to align Qurʾānic references to nature and the cosmos with findings of modern natural sciences, as in Ṭanṭāwī Jawharī's (d. 1359/1940) *al-Jawāhir fī tafsīr al-Qurʾān*.[16] In this case too, al-Bannā uses his definition of the Qurʾān as divine guidance as a corrective measure. Since it was not intended to serve as a scientific text, its references to nature and the cosmos aim to make people reflect on their status as creatures in relation to God the Creator, and the benefits that nature and cosmos provide for humans (1981: 18–19).

Al-Bannā's critique of Ṭāhā Ḥusayn and Khalafallāh for reducing the Qurʾān respectively to history and literature, and claiming that these methods are the scientifically sound way to understand it, is comparable with Michel de Certeau's critique of social scientific, 'ideological' reduction of religion to a social phenomenon (Chapter 1, above). Al-Bannā defined the Qurʾān as divine guidance for the improvement of individuals and society, and therefore True in the ontological and epistemic sense. Yet he showed, through his trajectory of *tafsīr*, that within this belief-paradigm, the Qurʾān has been studied and analysed in several ways, depending on the exegete's discipline and choice of method and topic. He thus took a non-reductive approach. It is also possible that the paradigm of natural law theory adds a

15 On Khalafallāh's dissertation seen in a historical light, see Abu Zayd (2003).

16 For a monograph devoted to Ṭanṭāwī Jawharī's *tafsīr*, see Daneshgar (2017).

dimension to his analysis that the Qur᾿ān's historical references must be held *True* in the absolute sense, even though the Qur᾿ān is not a scientific treatise. If the Qur᾿ān is conceptualised as a human-authored as opposed to divinely-created text, its truth claim becomes relative and loses its function as divine moral standard for the law. Viewed from this natural law perspective, al-Bannā's critique can be seen as 'theoretically correct', in the sense that reducing the Qur᾿ān to a particular historical and human phenomenon risks undermining its *generic* function as divine guidance, also in law-making contexts. A comparable case would be critics of human rights who reduce the Universal Declaration of Human Rights to a statement of western liberal principles, thus relativising its truth claim and rendering its moral standard void.

THE QUR᾿ĀN AS ACADEMIC 'BOUNDARY OBJECT'

Since al-Bannā's time, debates over the divinity of the Qur᾿ān and what constitutes properly 'scientific' approaches in Qur᾿ānic studies are a distinct topic within international academic discourse. To some extent, this has to do with the broader modern, discursive relegation of 'religion' to a new and limited function, as 'not science'. Evans and Evans (2008) and Evans (2009) have studied this development with reference to changing practices and discourses within American sociology in the late 1800s and early 1900s. Initially, leading American sociologists collaborated with Christian communities who, like the sociologists, were engaged in various social reform and outreach programmes. Gradually, however, sociologists began drawing a boundary between sociology as 'science' and religion as 'not science'. The authors' point is that the boundary-drawing did not reflect any changes in attitudes to science among members of the Christian communities. Instead, it was motivated by the sociologists' perceived need to enhance their scientific credibility in the eyes of particular public audiences and readerships, and their conclusion that distancing themselves from religious communities would advance this goal. Thus, it was the sociologists' perceptions of the intended audiences' views of religion that determined the boundary. Furthermore, the boundary was accompanied by an epistemic shift within the sociological discourse, from 'Baconian' empiricism and inclusion of the knowledge coming from the religious communities, to Positivist exclusive claims to scientific knowledge. The case illustrates how a discipline-dependent discourse (sociology) reflects institutional practices (from cooperation to non-cooperation with religious communities due to new 'partnerships').

Boundary drawing involves 'boundary objects': specific things that communicate information meaningful to the concerned parties – the academics, the intended readership, and religious communities – and thus create both bridges and divides between them. Examples of boundary objects are museums, and the leading American journals of sociology, which during the first half of the 1900s began excluding knowledge produced by Christian communities previously included in sociological research (Evans and Evans 2008: 16–19). From this perspective, one can see academic discourses as making 'the Qur'ān' into a boundary-object, in the sense that some methodological approaches to it are deemed 'scientific' and others not. Applied to al-Bannā's case, the scholars who studied the Qur'ān within modern History and Literature studies can be seen as addressing an audience of Egyptian and international academia, and drawing a boundary against the Islamic disciplines and their approaches to the Qur'ān. Al-Bannā instead defends the scientific status of the Islamic disciplines, by contextualising them in terms of intellectual history in the same basic way as he treated the modern studies, and arguing for continued harmony between faith and science in the modern context, addressing the Muslim community in Egypt and in the Arabic speaking countries.

This fault-line is perpetuated in some forms of contemporary Qur'ānic studies, where the science-boundary intersects with academics' political visions and projects, and selections of historical precedence. Naṣr Ḥāmid Abū Zayd (d. 1431/2010) is a famous Egyptian scholar who was based at Cairo University's Department of Arabic Language and Literature, and who identified closely with Khalafallāh's literary approach to the Qur'ān (Abu Zayd 2003). Abu Zayd also belongs to an international group of scholars, including the Algerian-French thinker Mohamed Arkoun, who argue that the continued vitality of Islamic thought, and democratic and gender egalitarian development in Islamic countries, requires departing from *some* Islamic scholarly traditions. Simply put, these scholars conceptualise the Qur'ān as the Prophet's *experience* of the divine communication, which necessarily differs from contemporary experiences of the same divinity. Thus, the Qur'ān is seen as expressing the divine in terms of a historical, human experience, and the Islamic scholarly disciplines generally do not recognise this fact (Dransfeldt 2015). Therefore, they argue that scientific study of the Qur'ān means investigating it as a historical text (Abu Zayd 2004a: 54–55).[17]

17 For studies of a wider range of modern and contemporary interpreters of the Qur'ān, including Sunnī and Shī'ī, 'Islamist', revolutionary, social justice, anti-colonial, anti-racist, and gender-oriented interpretations, see Taji-Farouki (2004) and Campanini (2011). On literary interpretations, see for example Boullata (2000).

Abu Zayd also addresses the chastisement that Khalafallāh, and eventually he himself as his follower, underwent at the hands of both the established Islamic scholars in Egypt and 'Islamists' i.e. the Muslim Brotherhood as well as more radical, militant factions. Khalafallāh's dissertation from 1947 was never accepted and he was barred from teaching the Qur'ān. Abu Zayd was severely punished by the Egyptian state authorities, who in 1995 acquiesced to a ruling from the *sharīʿa* court that he had reneged from Islam. Since such a ruling amounts to withdrawing the law's protection of a person's life, wealth, and marriage to a Muslim wife, Abu Zayd and his wife moved to the Netherlands. European colleagues helped him establish there and created for him the Ibn Rushd Chair of Humanism and Islam at Utrecht University.

According to Abu Zayd's own analysis, the controversy is a continuation of the doctrinal disputes since the 800s over the created or uncreated nature of the Qur'ān. Abu Zayd himself aligns with the Muʿtazila's doctrine of the 'created Qur'ān' (*khalq al-Qur'ān*): the Qur'ān is not God's Word in the sense of an extension of His essence, but a creative act in time and space (see Chapter 6 above, on *kalām*). Merging modern German hermeneutics *à la* Gadamer, the Japanese scholar Toshihiko Izutsu's (1964) linguistic understanding of *waḥy*, Muʿtazila's doctrine of *khalq al-Qur'ān*, and the literary-linguistic approach to the Qur'ān represented by al-Jurjānī (d. 471/1078), Abu Zayd argues that the Qur'ān's constitution as *language* makes it as much a human as a divine communication, just as Jesus is both the divine word and human at the same time (Abu Zayd 2004a: 55–56; 2003; 1990; 1992; also Sukidi 2009: 186–87). The present-day form of the Islamic disciplines is, however, incompatible with academic approaches, he argues. Upholding the doctrine of the uncreated Qur'ān, the Islamic scholars and their 'lay' supporters identify the canonical written text (*kitāb*) with the divine word and therefore insist on a literal understanding of the Qur'ān, contextualising its verses only with reference to *ḥadīth*. By comparison, from Abu Zayd's 'neo-Muʿtazilite' perspective, the text has no fixed literal meaning but must be interpreted with reference to changing contexts (2003: 34–40).

Abu Zayd's 'neo-Muʿtazilite' claim can also be viewed against the background of western Islamic studies discourse on the topic 'Islam and science', which accredits the Muʿtazila with the rationalist approach that enabled philosophy and science to flourish in the early Abbasid Caliphate. As discussed in Chapter 6, George Saliba argues that this discourse is flawed and biased, since philosophy and science in the Arabic-Islamic context continued Sassanid statecraft and is manifest already in the Umayyad Caliphate

(661–750). The discourse also overlooks the fact, Saliba points out, that the Caliph al-Maʾmūn's enforcement of Muʿtazila's doctrine as state creed entailed repression of the intellectual freedom of those who believed in the uncreated Qurʾān, which is hardly a scientific ideal. Moreover, philosophy and science were sponsored just as much if not more by later Caliphs and rulers who did not subscribe to Muʿtazilite doctrine (Saliba 2007: Ch. 1–2).[18] Nevertheless, the discourse on the scientific virtues of Muʿtazila and of 'humanising' approaches to the Qurʾān remains attractive and appears related to the project of establishing Islamic theology at European universities within Christian Faculties of theology, as mentioned above. In an early critique, Shabbir Akhtar (1991) drew attention to the Christian interfaith scholar Kenneth Cragg's (1984[1999]) claim, that Muslims must rethink their concept of the Qurʾān as the divine Word become *written text*, mediated through the passive Prophet. If Muslims would recognise that the Prophet Muḥammad was the divinely inspired but actively engaged speaker of the Qurʾān, which then can be assumed to express *his* experience, including encounters with Jews and Christians, they could view the text as historically bounded and thus open to reinterpretation in dialogue with other faiths. In Akhtar's view, Cragg's argument expresses Christian polemics, since Muslim scholars have always made new interpretations of the Qurʾān with reference to changing contexts, without having to renege on the belief that it is the divine speech and sent-down divine *kitāb*. To return to Abu Zayd, his effort to integrate Qurʾānic studies into the Humanities through his Ibn Rushd Chair of Humanism and Islam entailed close cooperation with Christian colleagues involved in the project of Islamic theology for western Muslims. Some of them argue, like Abu Zayd, that the doctrine of the uncreated, divine Qurʾān obstructs progress by producing literal readings which preserve Islamic law and putting the Qurʾān in the service of the state or other political, i.e. 'Islamist', agendas. Instead, the 'oral Qurʾān' represents continuous dialogical openness, also towards those of other faiths, which is the desired progressive attitude (Van Ess 1996; Madigan 2001: 191).[19]

18 See also Kamali (2009: 41–42), on the inquisition's suppression of scholars' freedom of expression and thus its anomalous character in Islamic history.

19 See also Abu Zayd (2004a), 'Introduction', on the dialogue with European colleagues in order to penetrate behind the written Qurʾānic text and 'open up' its oral, dynamic essence; cf. interview with Mohamed Arkoun in Benmakhlouf (1995), about how societal, political and scientific progress in North Africa requires sociologisation and historisation of the Qurʾān, as well as replacing nationalistic stereotypes with social scientific modes of understanding society. Also, the Berlin-based project Corpus Coranicum statement: "Die heute in der innerislamischen Koranforschung oft gestellte Frage nach

Hence, the discourse on 'the oral and created Qur'ān for western Islamic theology' can be seen as drawing a boundary that is simultaneously scientific and political, against 'the written and uncreated Qur'ān' considered wedded to Islam's legal and political history. Of course, this is no different to how the pre-modern Islamic disciplines link together political science and theology, as shown in Chapter 6. My point here is merely to draw attention to the continuous discursive conflation between politics and theology, and its normative definitions of what constitutes 'scientific Qur'ānic studies' in western universities.

Precisely because of the project to establish western Islamic theology, one would anticipate more academic interest in the Qur'ān's and Islamic political-philosophical theory related to rule of law, social contract and religious tolerance, and their significance for foundational European thinkers like Locke and Voltaire, as discussed above. During the 1990s and 2000s, however, European social policy became increasingly dominated by a discourse that 'culturalises' national civic values, to the effect that ethnic and religious minorities have been considered as having different *political* values than the national majorities simply by virtue of different ethnicity or religion (Stolcke 1995; Verkaaik 2010). Yet recent quantitative surveys show that European Muslims' political values correspond with the averages among the majority populations, though Muslim respondents are slightly more supportive of democracy and the national political and justice systems, and attribute more positive significance to their religion than the national averages (Jackson and Doerschler 2012). Comparative research into political and legal theoretical history is contributing new knowledge, which combined with quantitative research, can be employed to test the thesis that religious, ethnic, and cultural differences do not necessarily entail different civic and political values, since the latter differ also within religious-culturally defined sections of populations. Indeed, one could ask: given that contemporary European Muslims report both strong commitment to their religion *and* to

der für die ersten Hörer intendierten Aussage des Korans kann damit einer Antwort näher gebracht werden. Dieses gerade von den „Neudenkern" geforderte Wissen um die historische Bedeutung der einzelnen Korantexte ist wichtig, da es die gegenwärtig in fundamentalistischen Kreisen grassierende Dichotomie zwischen Koran und Bibel infrage stellt. Der oft missbräuchlich eingesetzten Lektüre des Textes als einer nur im wörllichen Sinn zu verstehenden Aussage, wie sie von den modernen Kommentaren nahegelegt wird, kann ein hermeneutisch differenzierteres Modell entgegen gehalten werden, das den Koran als einen weitgehend typologisch und allegorisch arbeitenden Text erkennbar macht"; "Über das Project", "Was ist der Nutzen?", https://corpuscoranicum.de/about/, accessed 10.12 2018.

democratic political and justice systems, is it because they associate these political values with Islam?[20] And, given that European Muslims have backgrounds in a vast number of Islamic countries, and are more or less closely affiliated with the whole range of Islamic schools, brotherhoods, modern organisations, and individual thinkers, is it necessary or desirable to enforce a specific doctrine in western Islamic theology departments? Or should such departments reflect the real intellectual *diversity* among Muslim Europeans, which itself, as I have argued here, relates to the scientific character and potential of the Islamic disciplines? Finally, how ought Qurʾān researchers, who for personal reasons are normatively committed in one way or another, achieve transparency of theory and method and avoid problematic ideological reduction?

'ISLAMIZATION OF SCIENCE' AND 'SCIENTIFICATION OF ISLAM'

Another approach to the Islamic disciplines is the academic discourse and initiative of 'Islamization of science' (Stenberg 1996) or, more loosely defined, 'Islamization of knowledge' (Abaza 2002). The initiative started officially in Mecca in 1977, and is represented in the west especially in American academia, through its founding scholars Seyyed Hossein Nasr and Ismail Raji al-Faruqi (d. 1407/1986) (Abaza 2002; Stenberg 1996). During the 1980s and 1990s, the initiative was institutionalised as the International Islamic University, with branches in Islamabad (Pakistan) and Kuala Lumpur (Malaysia); the International Institute of Islamic Thought (IIIT), founded in 1981 in Washington, DC (the USA) and with offices in e.g. Pakistan and Egypt; and the Association of Muslim Social Scientists in Cologne (Germany). The IIIT and the Association of Muslim Social Scientists publish the *American Journal of Islamic Social Sciences* (Abaza 2002: 24; Hanafi 2016: 47–48).

The Islamization of knowledge-discourse puts forward Islamic disciplines as alternatives to perceived deficiencies in 'western' science: positivism, materialism, moral nihilism, individualism, and denial of spiritual reality. By contrast, 'Islamic knowledge' is spiritual, holistic, and family-community oriented, and thus provides the key to beneficent scientific and societal development in Islamic countries, and happiness among western Muslims

20 A preliminary but statistically reliable study of Norwegian Muslims' political values and views of Islam indicates this kind of association among an overwhelming majority of the respondents (Ishaq 2017).

(Nasr 1993). Holism and spirituality have to do with the fact that, as in the pre-modern Islamic disciplines, the Islamization of knowledge-discourse posits divine Oneness as the first principle, which all sciences related to metaphysics, nature and society derive from. Consequently, 'Islamic knowledge' is conceptualised as reflecting different aspects of the same One divine reality (Bigliardi 2014: 17–25). Nuances among the scholars in this respect depend on which ontology they follow. For example, Seyyed Hossein Nasr teaches a modern 'perennialist' interpretation of illuminationist Sufism and Mullā Ṣadrā; al-Attas pursues another Sufi tradition; while al-Faruqi focuses on *fiqh* (Abaza 2002; also Dzilo 2012; Stenberg 1996).[21]

The sociologist Mona Abaza has argued that this discursive rejection of 'western science' may express these scholars' strategic quest for recognition within western and American academia, which itself propagated discourses on cultural essentialism, especially intensely after the Soviet Union's fall in 1989 and the loss of credibility for Marxist theory and leftist forms of nationalism. There may also be other reasons for some Muslim scholars working within American academia to criticize positivist epistemology, for as we have just seen, American sociological discourse used positivism to exclude religious communities from active participation in research programs, as opposed to serving only as objects of research (Evans and Evans 2008; Evans 2009). Hence, the concept of 'Islamic knowledge' can be understood as reflecting both western academic discourses on Islam, and global politics; at both levels, Americanization and Islamization intersect (Abaza 2002: 8–11, 79; also Al-Azmeh 2007).

Although the associated scholars' objective is to make the Islamic disciplines relevant in contemporary academia, they are not always primarily trained in these disciplines. In this respect and through some individuals, the 'Islamization of knowledge' discourse overlaps with the organisations of the Muslim Brotherhood and Jamāʿat-ī Islāmī. There is also a certain connection between the discourse and nation-states, which identify as Islamic in a 'heightened' sense e.g. Pakistan, Saudi Arabia, the Islamic Republic of Iran, and Malaysia. In these countries, the initiative's educational programs compete both with the established Islamic disciplines and with 'secular' academia. In Abaza's view, their aim is to create opportunities for graduates with a particular kind of modern knowledge about Islam, in the west as well as in Islamic countries (Abaza 2002: 33).

21 See also Sedgwick (2004) on the modern 'perennialist' discourse, including Seyyed Hossein Nasr; and Sedgwick (2017) on the Neoplatonic ontology and epistemology of 'perennialism' and its medieval and late Antique genealogies.

One example is Sayyid Muhammad Syeed's article 'Islamization of Linguistics' (1986), published in the affiliated *American Journal of Islamic Social Sciences*. Syeed argues that both pre-modern religious scriptural cultures and early modern linguistics elevated respectively their sacred or national language as superior in sophistication to other languages. Later linguists have discarded such hierarchical views, since research shows that all languages are complex enough to enable all peoples to express and develop the concepts and distinctions that they need. Syeed then proceeds to argue that the Qur'ān can be seen as reflecting a similar theory of language, because it does not describe its Arabic language as superior to other languages. Rather, the Qur'ān defines *all* languages as having a divine origin in God's imparting of 'the names of things' to Adam. When God then wishes to address a people, He uses that people's language; e.g. Q. 14 (*Ibrāhīm*), 4:

> (4) We have never sent forth a messenger with a message that is not in the language of his people, so that he can convey clarifying distinctions to them.

Hence, Syeed argues, the Qur'ān does not elevate Arabic as superior to other languages, it just happens to be the language that God used to address the final Messenger, whose people spoke Arabic. Similarly, Q. 30 (*al-Rūm*), 22 shows that God's creation involved distinguishing between humans through their different languages and colours, which are all equal – only 'knowledge' stands out as a distinguishing factor, but one which is accessible to all language groups:

> (22) And among His signs is the separation between the heavens and the land, and the differences in your languages and your colours: indeed, there are signs in that for those who possess knowledge!

Therefore, Syeed argues, all Muslim peoples should be assisted in strengthening their mother tongue languages to achieve full literacy, something which has been impaired in some countries for historical and political reasons, and then learn Arabic for the purpose of studying the Qur'ān and Islam.

The verses Syeed adduced were discussed in Chapters 2 and 3 above, with reference to theories of concepts and Arabic-Islamic linguistics, showing that the early exegetes also perceived them as having theoretical implications. My point here is not to determine whether Syeed's analysis is sound but to illustrate his method. It aligns closely with that of the renowned scholar Toshihiko Izutsu (1964), who on the basis of his de Saussure-approach reached similar conclusions, that Qur'ānic concepts of language can be seen as compatible with modern linguistic theory. Viewed from this perspective, Islamization of knowledge-related studies correspond well with modern 'mainstream' Qur'ānic and Islamic studies.

On the social sciences side, Sari Hanafi, professor of the Social sciences at the American University of Beirut, has addressed the question of whether the Islamization of knowledge-initiative has made any substantial contributions to research. He starts with the observation, that the initiative's aim to align Islamic and scientific thought in order to further social development is compatible with the aim of modern social sciences. Yet their resolve to conduct *Islamic* social science research has failed because it is misconstrued. These scholars, Hanafi argues, fail to acknowledge that current social sciences comprise a range of *empirical* disciplines with advanced and nuanced epistemology, and that they themselves have reduced social science to philosophy of society, renamed '*Islamic* philosophy of society'. 'Islamic' here boils down to 'rejecting western positivism'. But since contemporary sociologists in the west have moved far beyond old school positivism, the rejection is redundant. Consequently, while social science researchers apply analytical categories developed for particular research problems and social contexts, 'Islamic philosophy of society' revolves around fixed categories and sources derived from the Islamic disciplines, and therefore has only produced normative ethical studies and ontological reflections of no practical societal consequences (Hanafi 2016: 45–46, 55–56).

On the other hand, Hanafi also sees potential in the Islamic disciplines. For example, linguistic analysis of the Qur'ān can operate separately from normative doctrinal-religious analysis, in a scientifically sound manner. Hence, the linguistic discipline, and its exegetical applications, is worth further research, because of its historical interest and potential in current Qur'ānic studies and Arabic linguistics (Hanafi 2016: 60). This is not least the case since language and concepts are important critical tools, useful for the development of the social sciences in Arab countries. This leads Hanafi over to Ismail Raji al-Faruqi's focus on *fiqh*. *Fiqh*, Hanafi argues, is the Islamic discipline *par excellence* that uses language to produce 'guiding' knowledge in all fields e.g. law, government, ethics, social conduct, ritual, etc. Especially if scholars adopt the method of *maqāṣid* (see Chapter 6 above), modern research results can be employed in *fiqh*. Thus, the potential lies not so much in 'Islamizing knowledge' (*aslamat al-ʿilm*) as in 'sciencifying Islam' (*ʿalmanat al-islām*), which requires recognising the social sciences' empirical nature. If this approach is adopted, Islamic disciplines can start to make substantial contributions towards scientific, societal, and political development (Hanafi 2016: 52–53, 57–59, 62–64).[22]

Within the natural sciences, Stefano Bigliardi has identified a current, new discourse, which relates to 'Islamisation of knowledge', although it is not institutionally affiliated with that initiative. In Bigliardi's view, Mohammad Basil Altaie (Quantum Physics, Jordan), Mehdi Golshani (Theoretical Physics, Iran), Bruno Abd al-Haqq Guiderdoni (Astrophysics, France), and Nidhal Guessoum (Astrophysics, UAE, Sharjah), represent 'the new generation' thinkers on natural science and Islam. Compared with earlier predecessors, who would fall prey to al-Bannā's criticism of exegetes who read modern science discoveries into the Qurʾān, the 'new generation' are experienced scientists who follow the rules of their disciplines and then proceed to build bridges to the Qurʾān and Islamic sciences (Bigliardi 2014: 160–62).[23]

For example, Mohammad Basil Altaie views the 'Islamization of knowledge' scholars as having an important goal but inadequate specialization. He maintains the absolute integrity and freedom of scientific research relative to Qurʾānic and Islamic principles, and acknowledges real conflicts between science and Islam as religion. Thus, he explores compatibilities by first treating both the scientific data and the Islamic sources separately, and in methodologically consistent ways (Bigliardi 2014: 71–102). He himself has taken a special interest in systematic theology (*kalām*), both the Muʿtazilite and the Ashʿarite schools. He stresses that while Muʿtazila is the school commonly considered compatible with philosophy and science, Ashʿarite thinkers like al-Ghazzālī (d. 505/1111) are even more interesting for natural scientists, because they grappled rationally with the *empirical* problem of knowledge and evidence of the divine.[24] Within this framework, Altaie finds the Ashʿarite doctrine on the Qurʾān as God's uncreated word logical i.e. as the empirical starting point for knowledge about God (Bigliardi 2014: 74–75). In his view, the salient difference between Muʿtazila and Ashʿarism rather concerns natural philosophy, and the conflict between free will or acquisition of pre-determined acts, including the peculiar Ashʿarī atomistic theory of causality (Bigliardi 2014: 74). Similarly to his colleague Nidhal Guessoum, Altaie emphasises that, after patronage and funding, the exis-

22 A similar approach was advocated by Zaki Badawi (d. 1427/2006), Azhar-educated scholar of Islam and founder of the British Muslim College, and student of Psychology at London University; see Badawi (1982), a dictionary of technical terms of the social sciences in Arabic, English and French.

23 See also Bigliardi (2014) for bibliographies of these authors' publications in English.

24 On al-Ghazzālī's empiricism, see also Mårtensson (2009b).

tence of many competing sciences and schools, and the freedom of thought and critical investigation, were key factors contributing towards the flourishing of sciences in the early and medieval Islamic societies (Bigliardi 2014: 86–87, 163–64). Applied to the European context, his point supports the argument for diversity over the political temptation to enforce doctrinal unity.

SUMMARY

This chapter has given some examples of what the colonial rule and the post-colonial nation-states implied institutionally, in terms of the emergence of national universities and modern disciplines, as well as the modern Islamic or 'Islamist' organisations. It has also sketched how, from the early modern period onwards, translations and studies of the Qur'ān began in Europe. On this international stage, the Qur'ān and the Islamic literatures appear to have inspired British and French political philosophers in the direction of empiricism, social contract with tolerance of religious diversity, and the rule of law i.e. Enlightenment thought. Modern discourses thus bring together scholars of Muslim and non-Muslim backgrounds in the west, as well as scholars from Islamic and western countries. As the case of Egypt illustrates, confrontations between some Egyptian scholars within modern History and Literature studies, and 'traditional' Islamic scholars and 'Islamists' over what constitutes sound academic analysis of the Qur'ān, from the outset engaged Orientalist discourses. The core issue of this confrontation continues in a new form, tangential to current projects to establish western and European Islamic theology in connection with Faculties of Christian theology, and to foster progress regarding Muslims' concepts of the Qur'ān. Specifically, influential scholars have argued in a normative way that the doctrine of the uncreated, divine Qur'ān is incompatible with scientific approaches to the text, and with certain societal goals related to the European nation-state institution and its practices.

The multi-disciplinary 'Islamization of knowledge' initiative is another normative discourse, some of whose proponents presuppose that 'western' science is harmful due to its grounding in positivism, materialism, and individualism, whereas the Islamic disciplines are beneficial because of their holistic spiritual, idealist, and collectivist frame. Acknowledging the sociological relevance of engaging with Islamic institutions for scientific and societal progress, the social scientist Sari Hanafi argued that if 'Islamization of knowledge' turns into an *empirically* grounded 'sciencification of Islam', linguistics and *fiqh* could contribute to both academic and social development. Similarly emphasising the need for empirical grounding of science, as well as the scientific benefits of theoretical diversity, some researchers within the natural sciences – here Physics – find that all historical Islamic schools can be of scientific interest.

The latter approach suggests that when it comes to potential for scientific and societal advances, no Islamic school should be rejected out of hand. This speaks to Ḥasan al-Bannā's and Michel de Certeau's point, that ideological reduction is scientifically problematic. As George Saliba (2007) also showed, there is no evidence that the *doctrine* of the uncreated, divine Qurʾān obstructed scientific and social progress. Other factors might be more decisive. Moreover, if the deliberations and dialectical argumentation generated by opposing theories are good for theoretical progress, then this doctrine has played and continues to play a progressive role. Historically, it was also related to resistance against the Caliph al-Maʾmūn's attempt to impose state doctrine by force. Whatever the individual scholars' motivations might have been in the 200s/800s, the result was that they insisted on their right to freedom of belief and conscience. If such freedoms are the goal of those who construct western Islamic theology, then the legacy of this doctrine must be seen as an asset. Even more so if dialogue with Christianity is seen as a vital component of such Islamic theology. According to al-Ṭabarī's historical reports about the Caliph al-Maʾmūn's inquisition, discussed in Chapter 6, the Caliph accused believers in the uncreated, divine Qurʾān of mirroring the Christian belief in Jesus as the divine Word.

Chapter 8

CONCLUSIONS

This book aimed to answer the question 'Is there science in the Qur'ān?' by analysing Qur'ānic concepts with reference to seven Islamic scholarly disciplines, and related theoretical paradigms. The approach shows, quite predictably, that scholars working within these disciplines perceived Qur'ānic concepts as referring to their sciences. By drawing in current research, I have argued that these scholars provide *scientifically relevant* knowledge about said concepts. In this final chapter, the aim is to summarise the results and draw conclusions. I have therefore divided it into two parts. First, a summary of each chapter, with the main results. Secondly, reflections over the results and their implications for methodology in Qur'ānic studies.

SUMMARY

Introduction

Given that the Qur'ān generically constitutes a 'religious scripture' and not a scientific treatise, answering the leading question requires a definition of 'science' applicable to this case. In the *Introduction*, I therefore gave the Oxford Dictionary's basic definition of science as the "intellectual and practical activity encompassing the systematic study of the structure and behaviour of the physical and natural world through observation and experiment", within distinct sciences and disciplines. I then proceeded to argue that the Islamic scholarly disciplines developed through the use of Qur'ānic concepts, in such a way that the former were direct continuations of the latter, representing the same kind of systematic, observation-based knowledge (*'ilm*). Hence, I set out with a tentative definition of the Islamic disciplines as sources of scientifically valid knowledge about Qur'ānic concepts, and not as later developments representing paradigms that differ substantially from the Qur'ān's meanings, as has been claimed. Consequently, I hypothesised that exploring the Qur'ān's concepts through a selection of seven main disciplines and certain theoretical paradigms will produce new knowledge of the latter's meaning and historical references. As a particular focus for the analysis, I selected the concept Covenant and its legal and political dimensions, which have implications for the kind of knowledge produced in the Qur'ān and the disciplines.

Chapter 1

In *Chapter 1*, I develop the methodology for the study, namely Michel de Certeau's discourse analysis and its implications for conceptualising the relationship between 'religion' and 'science'. The starting point is de Certeau's post-structuralist critique of modern, discursive separation between 'religion' and 'science', and his counter-thesis that religion can function as driving force in theoretical, scientific development. In de Certeau's view, modern academic discourse on 'religion' reflects the institutional order of the nation-state, where religion/Church is separate from science/University, as opposed to medieval orders where Church and scholarship were one. According to modern discourse, then, 'religion' cannot theorise itself as a societal phenomenon, and therefore cannot offer scientifically relevant analysis of society, either. Yet de Certeau finds that Christian sources from the post-Reformation period show precisely that theologians conceptualised religion in social terms, which he argues relates to new forms of religious diversity and prefigures the later social scientific concepts of religion; hence, religion can serve as a force in theoretical development. On this basis, I assume preliminarily that the Qur'ān could have been a force in theoretical development. I also elaborate de Certeau's methodology, to analyse discourse with reference to institutional practices, scholarly disciplines, and scholars' individual positions. Approaching the Qur'ān and the Islamic disciplines as discourses, I analyse Qur'ānic concepts with reference to an institutional framework related to prophecy, and the seven disciplines: the Arabic language, with linguistics and rhetoric, Prophetic *ḥadīth*, political science, history, Qur'ān exegesis, jurisprudence, and systematic theology.

For further analytical perspectives, I then contextualised de Certeau's critique of modern academic discourse on religion with reference to the historian Eric Hobsbawm's analysis of modern western nationalism, and debates about the concept 'religion' within the discipline of Religious studies. Hobsbawm shows how nationalistic ideology constructed legitimacy for the new nation-state through a double move: on the one hand, by claiming long historical legacies for 'the nation', reaching back even to temporally and geographically distant Roman and Greek Antiquity, and on the other hand, by emphasising its cultural particularity and superiority. Within Religious studies, critics have argued that its key concept 'religion' has particular Christian meanings, which cannot automatically be assumed to apply universally, in other cultures, times, and places. The Qur'ān and Islamic scholars have then gained special attention among these critics, since these conceptualise 'religion' (*dīn*) as a social and legal category, with diverse forms, and identify Islam as such a universal category. I show how this has implications for translation of Qur'ānic concepts related to Covenant as a divine-human contract, with *dīn* and *īmān* as key cases. Hence, *dīn*, normally 'religion', refers to a 'judicial order', with religious aspects such as faith in God and ritual divine service, while *īmān*, normally 'belief', 'faith', refers to the enactment of security (*amn*) in societal-political and contractual terms. I then show, preliminarily, how Qur'ānic passages establish a common legal legacy, shared between its own community and those of Jews and Christians. This suggests that the Qur'ān establishes its community by *connecting* it with historical legacies of other communities existing in the same time and place. The practice is the opposite of how Hobsbawm showed nationalistic discourse works, which I assume indicates that the Qur'ānic concept *dīn* refers to institutional, administrative practices that seek to include the 'other' communities into its own polity. In other words, the Qur'ānic 'religious' concepts can be seen as having senses, which point in the direction of political theory and law.

Chapter 2

In *Chapter 2*, I provided definitions and theories of 'concept', the key term in this book, and explained their implications for the argument about the scientifically relevant knowledge provided through the Islamic disciplines. My procedure here is to adduce western philosophical definitions of ontological and structural theories of concept, and then compare them with examples from the Qur'ān and the Islamic disciplines. Thus, ontological theory of concept addresses the question of what concept is: a psychological phenomenon of the mind, as in a mind-based theory of concept, or a language-based and communicative capability to name things, as in capability-based theory. I argued that the Qur'ān can be seen as corresponding overall with the capability-based theory of concept, but that its creed of divine Oneness (Q. 112) can serve as a reference point also for the mind-based theory of concept. The structural theory of concept explains how concepts acquire meaning through definition. According to classical theory of concept, a definition covers properties pertaining to a thing, while theory theory of concept holds that concepts gain meaning through their relationship with a theoretical paradigm, within which several concepts also refer to each other. I concluded that the theory theory best captures how Qur'ānic concepts relate to each other i.e. by referring to theoretical paradigms pertaining to the disciplines.

Against this background, I return to the issue of whether the Islamic disciplines provide scientifically relevant knowledge about the Qur'ān. For example, some scholars argue that consideration of Christian Syriac-Aramaic sources offers more historically valid information about the Qur'ān's concepts than the 'late' Muslim exegetes and historians. I counter by showing how the Qur'ānic concept of prophecy as a language-based capability to persuade people rhetorically, can be seen as reflected in an exegetical report about various Christian factions and their disputes over the nature of Jesus, and the doctrinal definition of Islam with respect to this topic. In other words, I find a theoretical agreement between the Qur'ān and the exegetical report, which I take as saying something equally scientifically valid about the Qur'ān and its context of doctrinal polemics as the Syriac sources. Consequently, I proceed in the other chapters on the assumption that the Qur'ān reflects a theory theory of concept, and that its concepts therefore constitute connections between it and the theoretical paradigms of the disciplines.

Chapter 3

In *Chapter 3*, I develop the approach with reference to the semantic paradigm related to early Arabic linguistics and rhetoric, which I also, relying on the exegete al-Ṭabarī (d. 310/923), apply in analysis of Qur'ānic Arabic language and canonical composition. I begin by surveying research into Qur'ānic Arabic language, including linguistics and rhetoric, and the production of the Qur'ānic canon in the second half of the 600s. I then develop Jan Retsö's thesis (2003) that ancient records dating back to the 800s BCE show Arab peoples settled mainly in farming villages, and concluding political compacts and treaties, and trade agreements, with imperial rulers. Retsö's records include references to Arabs in the Hebrew Bible and the New Testament. This implies, I argue, that Arabs could have shared an ancient regional legacy of prophecy and Covenant with the 'Biblical' polities. Following the medieval lexicographer Ibn Manẓūr, Retsö also shows the Qur'ānic word *'arabī*, 'Arabic', carries the senses of clear distinction (*bayān*) and contractual security (*amn*). I take this as referring to Covenant as a contract with clearly distinct terms, which contribute towards societal-political and eschatological security, suggesting that the concept of Covenant is reflected in the Qur᾽ān's self-identification as 'Arabic'.

Next, I show that the discipline of Arabic linguistics can be traced to the late 600s, making it contemporary with the period when the established Qur᾽ānic script and canonical order is disseminated. The relevant linguistic paradigm is Sībawayhi's semantic theory of 'meaning' as the combination of a speaker's intended message when addressing a given topic in a given context, and choice of language forms appropriate to the addressee's comprehension. This semantics corresponds with the rhetorical and exegetical sub-discipline of *balāgha*, which has implications for Qur᾽ānic composition. Notably, Abdel Haleem (1993, 2018) argues Qur᾽ānic composition reflects *balāgha* and its concepts *ma῾ānī*, *bayān*, and *badī῾*, and that the canon constitutes a semantic unit, with reference to which *sūra*s and verse-passages constitute specific sub-topics. For over-arching meaning, Gwynne (2004) has argued that Covenant structures the divine, rhetorical argumentation across the Qur᾽ān. On this basis, I turned to 'the Nöldeke thesis' that the Qur᾽ānic canon reflects a gradual development of concepts, reflecting the Prophet's developing thought and interactions with various groups, as well as a redaction process with breaks and additions. I counter, showing how what has been seen as topical breaks can equally be seen as an integral part of a progressing topic, if attention is paid to the semantic context and other rhetorical tools associated with *balāgha*. This approach implies that concepts do not develop semantically from the beginning to the end of the canon, but take on specific meaning within given topical contexts, where they refer to other, interrelated concepts.

Against this background, I elaborated on the apparently earliest complex and consistent theory of Qur᾽ānic Arabic language and composition, that of the exegete al-Ṭabarī. Qur᾽ānic written Arabic, he argued, conveys clearly distinct particular and general statements. Using the terms of *balāgha*, he then defined the Qur᾽ān's overarching meaning and composition as conveying the Covenantal terms between God and humans. In his view, Q. 1 (*al-Fātiḥa*) establishes these terms, which are then repeated throughout the canon in the form of general and particular statements pertaining to topically defined cases. In this way, al-Ṭabarī argued, the Qur᾽ān conveys God's persuasive proof about the True Right (*ḥaqq*) that constitutes Covenant and its terms: God sustains humans through the material blessings of Creation, and they serve only Him and take no other partners. Consequently, Covenant provides the meta-semantics of the canon, to which all other topics and general-particular statements refer.

Finally, I applied al-Ṭabarī's theory to the analysis of the structures of some *sūra*s and passages, which I then developed into a table illustrating the Qur'ān's composition through topics related to Covenant. Preliminarily, the results suggest that the Covenantal terms occur across the canon, and that they define legal and ethical cases, terms, and conceptual categories, which constitute topically defined contexts. The exegete al-Ṭabarī thus agrees with Abdel Haleem that semantic concepts related to *balāgha* structure the Qur'ān, and with Gwynne (2004) that Covenant structures its divine argumentation. Yet he moves beyond them by showing how the Covenantal terms subsume in Q. 1, and from there repeat through the canon, and also by identifying the distinction between general and particular statements.

Chapter 4

Chapter 4 continues to analyse the Qur'ānic concept of Covenant, applying the legal paradigm of natural law theory. An initial research survey shows Qur'ānic Covenant has been analysed in terms of theology, political compact and oaths of allegiance, law, and, in a preliminary study by Richard Gramlich (1983), in terms of a 'natural law-like obligation'. I then develop the natural law aspect. Based on some western definitions of natural law theory, I conclude it entails the premise that law depends for its authority on a moral standard, considered 'absolutely true'. A case in point is the Universal Declaration of Human Rights (1948), which includes the claim that human rights require protection by the rule of law against tyranny. I then treat definitions of natural law theory in Islamic contexts, including Anver Emon's (2004–2005, 2010) studies of how Muslim jurists referred to divine Creation to define 'facts' that justify the moral standards from which they then derive legal principles and rulings.

Subsequently I apply these definitions to interpretations of Q. 4 (*al-Nisā'*), 1 on God's Creation of the first man and woman, and humanity from them. The selected exegetes represent Sunnī and Twelver Shī'ī schools, and span the period 100/700 to 900/1500. Again, al-Ṭabarī appears important, since he develops a theory of 'human rights' from Q. 4, 1, which is then followed by some of the later selected exegetes. Because God has created all humans from Adam and Eve, al-Ṭabarī argued, they are a universal brotherhood and God has obligated them to protect each other's rights (*ḥuqūq*, sing. *ḥaqq*), so that justice prevails over tyranny – and God especially obligates the strong to protect the rights of the weak. The fact that the other exegetes after al-Ṭabarī aligned with this approach suggests they too perceived Q. 4, 1 as establishing a moral standard for the law – 'rights protection' – motivated by the 'fact' that God created all humans from one father and mother (Adam and Eve), and endowed them with rights.

Since *ḥaqq* is not mentioned in Q. 4, 1 itself, I then proceed to examine this concept in other Qur'ānic contexts. I conclude that when attributed to God's message and writing, *ḥaqq* takes on the sense of 'true right'. In this way, it can be seen as what makes the Qur'ān itself into the 'absolutely true' moral standard for the law, in its role as its first source. In addition to theory of concept and semantic theory, which pertain to philosophy and linguistics (with rhetoric) respectively, natural law theory can thus be seen as another Qur'ānic theoretical paradigm, related to jurisprudence.

Finally, and referring back to my de Certeau-inspired thesis that the 'religious' Qur'ān might represent theoretical, 'scientific' advances, I suggest that the exegetes' focus on 'rights', especially for the weak, imply that a Qur'ānic natural law theory justifying a rights-based law could be central components of innovative theory. This legal theory also relates to linguistics and rhetoric, and the overarching concept Covenant, in the sense that the Covenantal rights and obligations must be clearly distinguished and persuasive, so that people can understand, accept and implement them. And again, I find that the early and medieval exegetes' interpretations of Q. 4, 1 provide knowledge about the Qur'ānic concept of Creation, which identifies its theoretical reference to natural law, and its practical implications for rights-based law.

Chapter 5

Chapter 5 proceeds to treat the political aspects of Qur'ānic Covenant, identified in the initial research survey in Chapter 4. Specifically, I analyse Covenant in terms of a constitution and a social contract theory, which refer to an institutional order and practices, and outline their continuation in Islamic political history.

To begin with, I describe the region's 'agrarian' economy, with the state, the religious-priestly-scholarly institution or 'temple', and the market as three distinct institutions. To this economy belongs a system of vassalage, where the imperial ruler is theoretically the legal owner of all lands in the realm, who grants lands to regional governors and landlords in return for land tax revenue and military protection of the realm. In this context, I introduce Andrew Watson's (2008/1983) study of agricultural advancements in the period around the rise of Islam and into the 900s, and his argument that Islamic law and peasants' property rights were crucial factors in this development, along with farming techniques, such as the creation of gardens, irrigation, and fertilisation. The thesis is particularly interesting considering Retsö's (2003) conclusion that the Arabs were primarily farmers. In support of Watson's thesis, I adduce Baber Johansen's (1988) argument that early Islamic law granted ownership rights to peasants, turning this group's legal status from serfdom to proprietors. Though I cannot investigate the matter further, these studies appear to gain significance when seen in relation to natural law theory and support for 'right', also for 'weak' groups, which would include the peasants.

Against this background, I develop a model of Qur'ānic Covenant as constitution and social contract, drawing primarily on Elazar (1998) and his model of Covenant as a constitution with a *socio-economic base*, a *moral base*, and a *governmental frame*, which I illustrate with examples from Qur'ānic passages. *The socio-economic base*, then, is the 'agrarian' economy and system of vassalage, in which the vassal treaty of compact was since ancient time seen as protected and monitored by a deity. Hence, the frequent Qur'ānic depiction of gardens, fruits, seeds, animals, and water for irrigation, as the material sustenance God provides for humans, and of human duty to pay their due tax and contribute to the common good. *The moral base* refers to natural law theory and the moral standard of God's 'true right' (*ḥaqq*). At the human level, the moral base is concretised through the ethical concepts of 'perfect sincerity' (*ikhlāṣ*) in word and deed, which results from confessing the creed of divine Oneness, and 'enacting security' (*īmān*), which is service to God by fulfilling contractual terms (*taqwā*), including equitable distribution of food and wealth, and protection of all rights. Finally, *the governmental frame* refers to the constitutional principle of 'the rule of divine law', and the social contract-principle that God gives reasons for Covenant as well as for why people should enter into a compact with the Prophet. Reasons provided for the social contract are that the divine law protects and benefits the common good for all people, including the weak and those of 'other' religions. This social contract has a pronounced deliberative dimension, expressed as the fact that people often reject God's reasons, but that God nevertheless secures their material sustenance here and now, and defers their punishment to the Day of judgement.

Next, I turn to Ibn Hishām's standard edition of the Prophet's Biography, showing how this source concretises the institutions and practices that Qur'ānic Covenant and related concepts refer to. The main institutions are tribal confederations and compacts, where rulers' legitimacy consists in the people's recognition of their just rule, and the Kaʿba 'temple', which is centre for both pilgrimage and trade i.e. the market. The Biography establishes a continuity between the Prophet and the Qurayshite Arabs' 'Abrahamic-prophetic' practices of providing security for the traders and pilgrims coming to the Kaʿba, in terms of food supplies and peace, and pacts for mutual defence against aggression of any kind, including protection of property rights and defending the rights of weak groups. Eventually, the Prophet's compacts include also 'other religions'. Consequently, the contractual security senses related to Qurʾānic 'Arabic' and the possible antiquity of Arab prophecy, discussed in Chapter 3, can be seen as reflected in the Biography's identification of what constitutes the 'Abrahamic prophetic' legacy of the Arabs. I therefore conclude that ancient Arab legacies of prophecy are reflected in the Biography's contextualisation of the Prophet and the Qurʾān, and its construction of political-contractual continuity.

I then sketch the historical development of the main Islamic institutions, from the early Caliphate to the 900s/1500s, focusing on the issue of constitutional separation of powers. Current scholarship largely portrays a development from a state of 'united powers' in the Prophet and the Companion Caliphs, which then gradually develops into separation between the state as the executive authority and the legal scholars as legislative and judiciary authority. Disagreement concerns when the separation occurred: in the late 100s/700s or in the 200s/800s-early 300s/900s. Lowry (2008) argues that the early sources from the 700s already reflect theory on separation of powers, which complicates assumptions of development from one stage to another. Adopting this approach, I show that reports from Ibn Saʿd (d. 230/845), who chronicled the transmission of knowledge through the generations, describe a diversification of authority and functions already during the rule of the Prophet and the Companion Caliphs. Some Companions with knowledge read and taught the Qurʾān to the administrators and people in the regions, and gave rulings and judged based on it. I argue that these reports can be seen as theorising institutional practices during the Prophet's and the Companion Caliphs' time, in a way that reflects practices associated with the diversified institutional order I described in the first part of the chapter.

The Islamic institutions, whose development I then sketch to the 900s/1500s are the Qurayshite Caliphate and the other forms of dynastic political rule (the Shīʿī Imamate and the Sultanate), the legal scholars, 'protective governorship' (*walāya*), and the Sufi brotherhoods, focusing on how they relate to the transmission of Qurʾānic divine knowledge (*ʿilm*). The sketch shows that contestation over separation of powers, and thus over the terms of the social contract, is constant throughout political history, and subject in part to rival dynastic claims to legitimate rule. Compared with the agricultural advances of the early period, the late 300s/900s appear to represent a downturn, and a weakening of peasants' property rights as landlords solidified their power. Although I have not been able to investigate exactly how, it is clear that distribution of land and land tax are important issues in contestation over lawmaking authority. The 900s/1500s signal a turning point, after which Ottoman and Mughal rulers obtain legitimacy for increased lawmaking authority on their part.

In this way, the chapter shows Qur'ānic concepts can be seen as referring to constitution and social contract, how the Prophet's Biography defines an institutional order and the practical issues that these Qur'ānic concepts refer to, and how the constitutional and social contract-related issues of separation of powers and lawmaking authority continue to be contested in political history. This method i.e. reading the Qur'ān, the Biography, and Islamic political history with reference to each other, on the assumption of basic institutional and discursive continuity, brings out new senses of Qur'ānic concepts, which also add to our understanding of the Qur'ān's continued relevance as a source for the scholarly disciplines.

Chapter 6

Chapter 6 refers Covenant and the constitution and social contract-related issues to the seven selected disciplines: linguistics, Prophetic *ḥadīth*, political science and administration, history, Qur'ān exegesis, jurisprudence, and systematic theology. The aim is to show how each discipline's technical terms relate to the Qur'ān, what kind of systematic knowledge each discipline produces, and how that knowledge relates to Covenant and the constitution and social contract-related issues.

The starting point is al-Fārābī's (d. 339/950) treatise 'Enumeration of the sciences', which I follow selectively. He listed language and grammar as the first science that lays the conceptual foundation for all the others, and I therefore start my exposition with linguistics. I include also his theory of prophetic language, that it conveys general, theoretical truths through images and rhetorical persuasion, so that the public can understand how the law promotes prosperity and happiness. Here I expand his theory somewhat, to analyse how Qur'ānic imagery can be seen as reflecting theoretical paradigms pertaining to several disciplines. Against this background I trace the beginnings of Arabic linguistics to the late 600s, when dissemination of the established Qurʾānic script was under way, along with exegesis and the derivation of rulings and guidance from it. I then focus specifically on Sībawayhi's term *mustaqīm*, which refers to speech that is 'correct' i.e. clearly and logically conveys a speaker's intended message through correct grammar and forms appropriate for the addressee and context. In this sense, I argue, the term corresponds with the Qurʾānic image of 'the correct path', *al-ṣirāṭ al-mustaqīm*, in Q. 1, 6. Similarly, al-Ṭabarī argued that *al-ṣirāṭ al-mustaqīm* refers to the Qurʾān as constituting the path of correct speech *and* actions, both of which comply with the terms of Covenant and their general and particular applications. I therefore conclude Q. 1, 6 refers to language as the foundation for the correct forms of speech and action that constitute the rest of the Qurʾān.

The second discipline, *ḥadīth*, shows the Prophet speaking and acting in accordance with the divine guidance. Like linguistics, its beginning has also been dated to the late 600s. I then sketch how Sunnī, Shīʿī and Sufi collections formed in the course of the period 200s/800s to 500/1100s, alongside the fluctuations of ruling dynasties legitimised by the Abbasid Caliphate. Finally, I give examples of topics related to Covenant, land management, separation of powers and reasons for social contract from the collections. Importantly, the *ḥadīth* also provide information on the empirical, observation-based aspect of the Qurʾānic divine knowledge. The case in point lists specific socially unwanted practices, which undermine the common good and societal security, and shows how God has previously punished these practices in ways that correspond with real disasters. Since most of the divine 'punishments' correspond with things that humans can control, the report conveys observations of what undermines the common good. In this way, the list summarises Qurʾānic accounts about peoples who rejected their prophets' divine guidance, and explains them in social contract-related terms of the common good.

The third discipline, political science (*siyāsa*) and administration (*tadbīr*), is devoted to theoretical topics related to constitution and social contract, and the practical implications of the divine knowledge. I begin by exploring three political theories. First, the scribe Ibn al-Muqaffaʿ (d. 138/756), attributed the earliest theoretical writings. He framed administrative knowledge as connected with the legacies of the Sassanid Empire and India, and by implicitly using Qurʾānic topics and terms related to the common good he made the Qurʾān's divine knowledge appear as conveying the same *ḥikma*, 'wisdom' or rather 'capacity for just judgement', as these administrative legacies. In this way, Ibn al-Muqaffaʿ created a 'universal' framework for including into the administration both pre-Islamic and non-Muslim legacies, represented by peoples living within the Islamic polities. His method opens an important perspective on the observation-based nature of Qurʾānic knowledge: it can be seen as reflecting historical imperial legacies, which he connected with the 'Abrahamic-Arab' prophetic legacy. Secondly, I describe al-Fārābī's philosophical theory of 'the virtuous political community', where the law serves as the tool to make the city prosper and promote the people's happiness. He assumed a division of powers between the ruler and the jurists, but premised the virtue of the order on *ḥikma*, embodied ideally in both ruler and jurists, or conveyed to the ruler through the jurists. The third example, al-Māwardī (d. 450/1058), is closer to Ibn al-Muqaffaʿ, since he assigned to the ruler the authority to make law and supervise the administration. For both thinkers, ensuring that the land tax and land distribution are justly managed is an important reason for this. Al-Māwardī also uses several Qurʾānic terms related to Covenant in his theory of legitimate political leadership and the terms of the social contract, which he frames as 'the rights of the human beings' (*ḥuqūq al-ādamiyyīn*) to a just ruler, obligated to a defined set of responsibilities. The ruler is then elected by the legal scholars, who have the power to grant or withhold legitimacy, on behalf of the people. Despite different theories of separation of powers, the three theorists agree that the law must serve the common good, as the people's welfare. The case of al-Māwardī also shows how the concept of 'human rights' was used within political science with reference to the ruler's 'rule by divine law', and his authority to derive new laws and supervise the administration. By comparison, Chapter 4 showed how exegetes interpreting Q. 4, 1 referred to 'human rights' as the law's moral standard, in the natural law theory-sense. In both cases, however, it is by virtue of being God's creatures that humans have their intrinsic rights, which illustrates how Qurʾānic images of Creation and Covenant can reflect both political theory and the legal natural law theory.

I then turn to the administration and the practical sciences. Following Saliba (2007), I show that it was the state administration and not least the land tax management that drove scientific progress, illustrated by the knowledge that a scribe should master in the period of the Umayyad Caliphate (661–750), though the knowledge itself is transmitted from pre-Islamic legacies, e.g. the Sassanid empire. This knowledge can be seen as reflected in Qurʾānic concepts and topics related to land, gardens, types of fruits and seeds, water canals and irrigation, and tax – all of which may reflect 'the agricultural advances-thesis' – as well as to weights and measures, account keeping, and time calculation. Consequently, the administration continues pre-Islamic practices, even though the earliest extant theoretical writings are later.

The fourth discipline History (*taʾrīkh*), literally 'annalistic dating', which dates to the late 600s, provides more perspectives on the practical-empirical implications of divine knowledge. I start by outlining the development of the historical time measures and genres. Here, I pay special attention to the South Arabian term *zabūr* (pl. *zubur*), which refers to written genealogies documenting tribal land ownership. *Zabūr* occurs in the Qurʾān mainly with reference to the prophet-king David's writing. Since it is said to contain the divine promise to inherit the land, I argue that the Qurʾānic term *zabūr* refers specifically to written genealogy confirming ownership and inheritance right to land, as another example of Qurʾānic references to legal and administrative issues related to land management in the 'agrarian' economy and system of vassalage.

I then turn to al-Ṭabarī, here in his role as historian of 'universal political history', and his historicization of Qurʾānic natural law theory. According to his discourse, God established Covenant with all Adam's future descendants at Creation, then its constitutional and social contractual implications were institutionalised at the inception of human political rule with the ancient Persian royal dynasties, complemented by Idrīs' prophecy i.e. the divinely conveyed art of writing. Al-Ṭabarī's universal history-discourse provides more information on the land tax and its practical implications, and on practices related to 'Abrahamic' prophecy, than what Ibn Hishām reported on in the Prophet's Biography. Specifically, al-Ṭabarī reported that in Abraham's home-region Iraq, the tyrant king Nimrod would store grains and food, which he gave to people on condition they serve him as their lord. Abraham refused, since he only served God as his Lord, and consequently did not receive food. God then rewarded him for his steadfastness, miraculously providing the needed food. This is the same topic of food security that the Biography associated with just management of the 'Abrahamic' Kaʿba, and the pilgrimage and trade associated with it, except that al-Ṭabarī's report shows it was a general, regional issue connected with state power. Abraham's prophetic commitment to serve only God thus corresponds to the practice of giving food to all people, unconditionally. The report, moreover, appears to have no correspondence in Jewish traditions about Abraham. Tentatively, this suggests it could reflect specific Arab legacies of prophecy. I then show how the topic of food security is reflected in several Qurʾānic passages from different periods, where it is also connected with both Quraysh and Abraham. Since al-Ṭabarī in his Qurʾān commentary argued that the Covenantal terms repeated throughout the Qurʾān obligate God to sustain people materially, as

I showed in Chapter 3, we can here see how he used his historical discourse to illustrate what this means in concrete terms.

A final point concerns al-Ṭabarī's historical reports on the Abbasid Caliph al-Maʾmūn, which show his Inquisition enforcing the doctrine of 'the created Qurʾān' was related to the Caliph's war campaign against the Christian Byzantines. The Caliph accused those who propounded the doctrine of the uncreated Qurʾān of aiding and abetting the enemy, for it resembled the Christian creed that Jesus is God's own Word. Al-Ṭabarī's reports suggest that the Qurʾān's own claims to divine identity have constitutional implications. It is by virtue of being *divine* that the writing subjects everyone to its rule and its moral standard, and in this case the Caliph asserted over the dissenting scholars his definition of in what way it is divine, in the context of war. I conclude, therefore, that the discipline of history provides further examples of the practical issues that Qurʾānic concepts related to political and legal theory refer to.

The next, fifth discipline is Qurʾān exegesis or *tafsīr*, which overlaps especially with linguistics and *ḥadīth*, and dates to the late 600s and the dissemination and teaching of the Qurʾān. Here I selected seven major exegetes from the period 100/700 to 900/1500, most of whom I referred to in Chapter 4. The aim here is to see how they interpreted Qurʾānic verses related to contractual obligations, constitutional separation of powers, and authority. In Chapter 3, I showed that al-Ṭabarī defined the distinction between general and particular statements as basic to Qurʾānic Arabic. All these exegetes perceived this distinction integral to the Qurʾānic text, though they differed somewhat in their applications. I conclude therefore that this distinction really is a structure that governed the composition of verses. Concerning the theoretical points, most of them agreed that God obligates people to obey God (represented by the Qurʾān), the Prophet (represented by the *sunna*), and governors, provided they rule justly by God's law. Al-Rāzī stands out for arguing that governors never rule justly, so only the legal scholars can justifiably claim obedience. Al-Ṭabarī and his early authority Mujāhid (d. 103/722) stand out on another topic, namely the claim that those legal scholars who know the common good, and apply it for the purpose of social equity and the people's material and eschatological welfare, should supervise the state administration. Compared with the political scientists, two of who argued that the ruler has law-making authority, these exegetes interpreted the Qurʾān rather in support of the theory, that it is the legal scholars who have this authority.

The sixth discipline is jurisprudence or *fiqh*, and its methodology *uṣūl al-fiqh*. Given its intrinsic relationship with linguistics, *ḥadīth*, and *tafsīr*, its beginnings can also be dated to the late 600s. According to al-Fārābī's list of the sciences, *fiqh* sorts under political science because the law is the principal tool for promoting prosperity and happiness among the city's inhabitants. Against that background, I outline the development of the discipline with reference to the institutional history I sketched in Chapter 5, including the constitution- and social contract-related issues, and show concepts related to *fiqh* which occur in the Qur'ān. The starting point is Weiss' (1990, 1998) analysis, that the Qur'ānic Covenant, with its mutual rights and obligations between God and humans, is the model for *sharīʿa*. The mechanism that obligates humans to both Covenant and the law is the divine *speech*: once reached by it, the addressee is obligated by the terms it conveys. This topic is of course central to the Qur'ān. Consequently, I show how this contract- and language-based relationship between Qur'ānic Covenant and *fiqh* relates to semantic theory in early legal hermeneutics, to the constitutional challenges related to legal disagreement, and to the systematic development and application of the common good (*maṣlaḥa*) and the Qur'ān-based objectives (*maqāṣid*) of *sharīʿa* from the late 300s/900s onwards. It is the latter topic that I summarise here.

According to Opwis (2010), the political scientist Ibn al-Muqaffaʿ (d. 138/756) represents an early phase where some jurists refer to the common good as a lawmaking principle, but the practice was not generally acknowledged and formalised. Al-Ṭabarī (d. 310/923)/Mujāhid (d. 103/722) who in the context of exegesis defined some jurists as considering *maṣlaḥa* in their legislation, thus reflect this emerging methodology. Given al-Ṭabarī's reference to the Qur'ān (Q. 3, 79) for his concept of *maṣlaḥa*, I adduce further examples of Qur'ānic terms and topics, which can be seen as referring to the common good. In several cases, the topics refer to land, which was also the context for the political scientists' references to the common good, as we have seen.

The systematic phase coincides with increasing use of the 'universalising' disciplines of philosophy and logic within *fiqh*. Accordingly, Opwis argues *maṣlaḥa* and *maqāṣid* served as strategies to universalise the law and legal methodology in contexts of rival political centres and diverse schools of law. Though a Muʿtazilite scholar defined *maṣlaḥa* as referring only to the individual's moral good and benefit in the final, eschatological account, the majority agreed that it referred to both 'this life' and 'the hereafter'. Leading in this respect was the famous Shāfiʿī jurist and Ashʿarī theologian al-Ghazzālī (d. 505/1111), the first to define a set of objectives representing the common good, namely the right to legal protection of life, religion/judicial order, wealth, intellect, and lineage. Furthermore, Opwis shows he and other outstanding jurists argued all religions recognised these objectives i.e. also Jews, Christians and other non-Muslim members of the polity. Sufi hermeneutics played an important part, Opwis noted, since it offers a method for attaining God's own intention with the law. With my terminology, this would be because Sufi *walāya* represents a mind-based ontological theory of concept, which allows the jurist-exegete to attain God's intention, beyond the text. I illustrate this point with reference to Ibn Taymiyya (d. 728/1328), who ranks among the important developers of *maqāṣid* and himself followed a particular Sufi path. Yet he criticised some Sufi theory of *walāya* precisely for its claim to access the divine intention through a personal, divine address 'within', as it were. God's obligating address, Ibn Taymiyya argued, is the Qur'ān. Everything in it and its continuation in the Prophet's *sunna* is binding, but everything else is human, non-binding knowledge. He expands this into a political argument, that even the Caliph ʿUmar b. al-Khaṭṭāb, who *was* in fact addressed by God, as recorded in reports, could not command the Companions to obey him. He could only persuade them to do so if he could prove his case with reference to the Qur'ān and the *sunna*. Consequently, no obedience is owed to *walī*s who claim God has addressed them, unless they can prove their cases. The argument relates to the social contractual requirement to give the ruled 'reason' to accept the rule and the law, and frames the requirement as a critique of mind-based ontological theory of concept.

By way of conclusions, I find that key concepts related to *fiqh* occur in the Qur'ān, including ones related to the common good and the divine, obligating address with its social contractual aspect that God gives 'reasons' for why Covenant is good and should be kept. From this perspective, one can see the systematic development of *maṣlaḥa* and *maqāṣid* as a strategy to give new 'reasons' for the social contract, in changing contexts. Finally, since the *maqāṣid* define a set of universally valid objectives, which embody rights, they can also be seen as related to natural law theory, with its Qur'ānic references.

The seventh and last discipline is systematic theology, *kalām*, which like *fiqh* draws on philosophy, logic, and rhetoric. I show how *kalām* relates to Qur'ānic Covenant, focusing on the concept of rhetorical proof, the creed of divine Oneness, and the doctrinal debate about the nature of the Qur'ān. According to al-Fārābī's list of the sciences, *kalām* belongs together with *fiqh* under political science, and aims to defend principles and make them triumph. Technical terms referring to this function e.g. argumentation and proof, occur in the Qur'ān. Weiss (2010), however, shows *kalām* is the prerequisite for *fiqh* because it defines God's nature and attributes, without which it is impossible to develop the divine guidance i.e. *sharīʿa*. I then show how this function of *kalām* too relates to Qur'ānic contexts, which mention God's attributes, and connect professing the creed of God's Oneness with specific virtues, rituals and other practices. In fact, this creed is the very foundation of Covenant and its basic term that humans recognise only the One God as their Lord and take no other partners than Him. Several Qur'ānic passages show that 'sharing God with other partners' (*shirk*) can take several forms: serving other deities or human authorities as supreme governors, or professing the Christian Trinity. In this way, the doctrine of divine Oneness implies the virtue and practice of contractual loyalty. Accordingly, the Ḥanafī jurist and theologian al-Māturīdī (d. 333/944), in his influential 'Treatise on the declaration of divine Oneness', argued that ascription of children to God presupposes kinship between God and humans, which is logically impossible since God and man are different kinds. Consequently, the only possible human relationship with God, which does not require similarity of kind, is that they serve Him as their supreme 'Protective Governor' (*walī*). Ascribing children to God would mean that He shared His role as supreme Protective Governor, which is impossible because it would reduce His sovereign power. In this way, al-Māturīdī illustrates how the Qur'ānic doctrine of divine Oneness refers to contractual loyalty in the Covenantal sense. I then turn to the period 400/1000 onwards, focusing on the Qur'ān's nature and what divided the Mu'tazilī and Ash'arī schools regarding this doctrinal topic. Since the Mu'tazila were unable to identify God's *self* with anything in material creation, they defined the Qur'ān as His *act* of speaking to the Prophet, in the human language of his people. The Ash'arīs instead argued the Qur'ān is part of God's self, as His word. This depended on their argument against philosophers, that only God is eternal while the universe is His creation and temporally limited, as the Qur'ān frequently points out. If the Qur'ān was not part of God but of creation, it would not be eternally or perhaps even universally valid.

I then concluded the survey with two thinkers from the late medieval-early modern period, and their concepts of God's Oneness and His 'persuasive proof': the Twelver Shī'ī Neoplatonic philosopher Mullā Ṣadrā (d. *c.* 1045/1635–36) from Shiraz in the Safavid Empire, and the Ḥanafī jurist and Naqshbandī-*mujaddidī* Sufi Shāh Walī Allāh (d. 1176/1762) from Delhi in the Moghul Sultanate. Mullā Ṣadrā staked out a philosophical school of his own, intended to transcend sect- and school-based rivalries. Thus, he developed an ontology and epistemology of 'common descent' of all existing beings by God the One Being, Who is Unbounded existence. The human task is to 'ascend' back to God, through intellectual grasping of this reality and of God's proof. The proof gives reason for the obligation to thank Him, and is arrived at through a path of divine guidance (*sharīʿa*) that opens up 'externally' to the intellect through prophetic message, and 'internally' to it through a process of dialectical negations, ending with the non-describable One Being (as in Q. 112). In line with this Neoplatonic scheme, Mullā Ṣadrā also conceptualises God's sustenance of humans as the nourishment that comes from the capacity for scholarly, philosophical knowledge (*ʿilm*), with which God has endowed humans.

With a similar aim, Shāh Walī Allāh in the treatise 'God's Persuasive Proof' sought to develop a synthesis between Naqshbandī 'renewing' (*mujaddidī*), Prophet-centred Sufism, *kalām* and *fiqh*, as a framework that could unite the Islamic sects, schools, and brotherhoods, in a time when the Moghul Empire was struggling to keep the territory under central control. According to Shāh Walī Allāh, who had studied Ibn Taymiyya's writings, God created all beings through His command 'Be!' However, he did not see them as 'descending' by God in Mullā Ṣadrā's more radically Neoplatonic sense. God's persuasive proof then makes known the beneficial 'common good' principles (*maṣlaḥa*), which concern both this life and the hereafter. Although these principles equal God's intent with His guidance and obligating laws, His intent is known not through personal divine address but through the Qurʾān, and through spiritual encounters with the Prophet. Similar to Ibn Taymiyya, Shāh Walī Allāh makes God's proof a model for the legitimate ruler, who must publicly prove to the people that his rule is just and beneficial. Hence, his concept of God's proof has immediate social contractual implications, which are not as apparent in Mullā Ṣadrā's case. Despite their differences, however, both Mullā Ṣadrā and Shāh Walī Allāh, like the exegetes described above, operate with the natural law-like theory, that divine Creation equals 'common human descent' – a 'fact' which underpins the law's moral standard.

As with the other disciplines, then, I conclude that key terms and concepts related to *kalām* appear in the Qurʾān, and that the theologians' works bring out both theoretical aspects of the Qurʾānic concepts and their practical implications. In particular, the concept of divine Oneness and its implications for Covenantal contractual loyalty, and the divine proof as a model for social contractual 'reasons' to accept political rule.

Chapter 7

In *Chapter 7* I proceed to the modern period, tracing institutional and constitutional changes in Islamic polities related to the nation-state, with its modern universities and disciplines, and the 'internationalisation' of Qur'ānic studies. Put in simple terms, in most cases the states assume legislative authority and lead the production of modern law codes, with varying degrees of involving the Islamic legal scholars and *sharīʿa*. Current scholarship is divided on the extent to which this generalised model represents continuity or break with the pre-modern institutional orders. While some see it as a drastic change, others point out that the legal scholars were always involved with state administration, and that legal scholars in the Ottoman realm were increasingly recognising the Sultans as lawmakers from 1000/1600 onwards. Although my surveys in Chapters 5 and 6 are far from exhaustive, they do show that the scholars debated this issue since the early days of the Caliphate. Though I have mainly shown theoretical expressions of the debate, the continuous deliberations and examples from Ismāʿīlī Shīʿī, Ottoman and Moghul contexts suggest practices varied. In any case, the social contractual requirement for rulers to give 'reasons' for the legitimacy of their rule, in terms of the common good, justice, and prosperity, remained a critical theoretical ideal. I then show how modern Islamic organisations led by 'lay' professionals, such as the Muslim Brotherhood, can be seen as drawing on this legacy of legitimate rule, seeking on the one hand to give *sharīʿa* more prominent role in national law, and on the other hand to mobilise the people through mass-education about Islamic values and principles, and eventually through political parties. In this context, modern associations and media becomes a crucial institutional means for conveying the divine address to the public.

Having outlined continuities and changes in this way, I turn to the exceptional case of the Islamic Republic of Iran, with a legal scholar in the function of head of state, or Supreme Leader, and a constitution, which combines modern presidency and parliament with a law based on both *sharīʿa* and modern civil law. I also show how a Shīʿī *ḥadīth* served as legitimation for elevating legal scholars to head of state, and how Qur'ānic verses about securing the rights for 'those made weak in the land' legitimised granting new, extended property rights to peasants. Though this is a modern interpretation and application, the possibility that the Qur'ānic verses may have referred to similar issues in the Qur'ān's own context turns the contemporary case into an indicator of how Islamic discourses may offer valid information about the Qur'ān's concepts.

I then turn to modern scholarly disciplines and discourses in the context of 'internationalised' Qur'ānic studies. Tracing European translations of the Qur'ān from the medieval into the modern period, I show how early modern political philosophers developing social contract theory e.g. John

Locke and Voltaire, found the Qur'ān and the literature about the Prophet to be useful models for religious tolerance and the rule of law i.e. legal and political innovation in European contexts. Against this background I return to de Certeau and the modern institutional and discursive distinction between 'religion' and 'science'. Within Qur'ānic studies, this kind of discourse has tended to single out the pre-modern school Muʿtazila as more 'scientific' and academically relevant than those who profess the Qur'ān is God's uncreated word, in written form. Some Qur'ānic studies scholars with Christian backgrounds have even claimed that belief in this doctrine is 'fundamentalist' and undesirable, because it prevents Muslims from developing new norms and doctrine. I refer this specific discourse to the European and western project to develop academic Islamic theology, although similar arguments have been made also in Islamic countries, as I discuss with reference to Egypt. Here I show how the Muslim Brotherhood's founder Ḥasan al-Bannā argued against scholars within modern History and Literature studies, who defined Qur'ānic accounts about prophets as culturally specific, human myths and narratives. This reduction of the Qur'ān to categories of modern disciplines, al-Bannā argues, misses the point that the Qur'ān does not tell about prophets simply to narrate a story, or prove the historical details of each prophet in a scientific sense, but to provide divine guidance. As such, its accounts of prophets must be held true, otherwise they cease to function as guidance. I argue that al-Bannā's concept of the Qur'ān is analytically relevant, as it captures its use of prophets to convey knowledge about beneficial and harmful social practices, and can be seen as reflecting the natural law-related epistemic claim for absolute Truth for the Qur'ān as the law's moral standard. Finally, I return to the present, giving examples of how scholars outside of Qur'ānic studies, notably in the Social and Natural sciences, have argued that several Islamic disciplines and theological schools (including the Ashʿarī one), can be made relevant to societal and scientific challenges today.

REFLECTIONS

My approach can be seen as 'de-constructive', in the sense that I have sought to draw out 'sub-texts' through references to theoretical paradigms, which I assume relate to both the Islamic disciplines and scholarly discourses, and the Qur'ān as their conceptual source, and western disciplines and discourses about Islamic disciplines and the Qur'ān. Applying this method, I have made the case for using the Islamic discourses as sources of scientific knowledge about the Qur'ān and its concepts. If one follows research dating the disciplines' beginnings to the late 600s, when the Qur'ānic established script was 'publicised', one can see them as historical extensions of the Qur'ānic discourse, rather than as 'later' attempts, from hindsight, to make sense of this scripture, which is the source to which they all 'must' refer, for 'confessional' reasons. I therefore contend that the Islamic discourses provide the *most* scientifically relevant knowledge about the Qur'ān, not the least. This is also because the Islamic disciplines reflect discursive continuity with the socio-economic and political institutional practices that the Qur'ān refers to, while modern Qur'ānic studies represent an institutional 'break'. I do not mean by this that Islamic societies and disciplines were static before the modern period. The point is that modern universities and disciplines are institutionally separate from the Islamic ones, and some scholars consciously distinguish themselves from the Islamic discourses. Consequently, when they turn to the latter and select items for study and inspiration, they assess them in terms of compatibility with the scientific principles of their own, modern disciplines. Notably, the long-standing topic of the Qur'ān's divine nature becomes subject to new deliberations, where schools considered to have grappled with the issue in ways that historicise and 'humanise' the scripture are seen as offering the scientifically promising pathways for Qur'ānic studies.

The idea that the Prophet, conceived as a divinely inspired person, developed *his* thought gradually, through the community's evolution and encounters with e.g. Jews and Christians, appears both in 'the Nöldeke thesis'-discourse and among other scholars engaged in the project of western Qur'ānic studies and Islamic theology, as we have seen (Chapters 3 and 7). The Nöldeke-thesis discourse, represented by scholars at some of Europe's most prestigious universities, aligns with Islamic exegesis in making 'external context' decisive for dating and understanding *sūra*s and verses. However, it breaks with the exegetes selected here over internal context, and the knowledge issue. The exegetes understood the Qur'ān as conveying *God's* full knowledge of each individual thing, past, present and future. They also concluded that the divine knowledge takes the form of general and particular statements regarding a range of different cases and topical contexts, which structure the Qur'ānic text. Consequently, whether one perceives the Qur'ān as reflecting a *human* individual's and community's evolving thought or the categories of *divine* knowledge has immediate consequences for how one analyses the text and its concepts. Even though the claim that the Qur'ān is divine is definitely 'religious', I contend that because the Islamic scholars perceived 'the divine' as referring to scientific knowledge and societal issues, taking this claim into analytical consideration may open up new paths for research into both internal and external contexts and concepts.

Paradoxically, the normative appeal in e.g. European contexts of viewing the Qur'ān as reflecting the Prophet's and his community's evolving thought through dialogue with Jews and Christians is itself a connection with the Islamic disciplines, which are normative too. Scholars have always used the Qur'ān to derive new guidance and laws in new contexts, for the benefit of individuals and society. Yet the *diversity* of Islamic disciplines, schools, and individual scholars' opinions mitigates normativity, since it is clear to everyone concerned that there are competing norms, doctrines, definitions and theories at play, which is a precondition for scientific analysis. As Sari al-Hanafi argued (Chapter 7), modern social sciences' aim to contribute to societal development is an objective they share with *fiqh*. One can thus see the disciplines that feed into *fiqh* e.g. linguistics, *ḥadīth*, political science, history, exegesis, and systematic theology, in the light of modern social science. Such a perspective adds Islamic material to Michel de Certeau's argument, that 'religious' theoretical paradigms prefigure modern social science, and that it was the diversity of religions and polities that in the European context stimulated religious thinkers to conceptualise religion as a social category. Again, this was the premise of the Qur'ān and the Islamic disciplines.

Diversity, then, benefits science but poses a problem for normativity in general and for nationalistic discourse in particular, which strives to implement the norm of 'national unity', stability and cohesion. Confining science to national university departments and disciplines can aid such purposes. Yet I find it especially vexing that scholars affiliated with those parts of the Islamic legacy that are considered problematic today because of e.g. the doctrine of the uncreated Qur'ān, can be seen historically as operating with natural law theory, and endorsing rule of law and a social contract theory requiring rulers to give reasons and gain recognition from the people. Though these principles did not have the same practical implications in their medieval contexts as in a modern, liberal democracy, the principles themselves and their theoretical paradigms nevertheless connect with constitutional concepts of the rule of law, and human rights. Given the positive interest early modern European political thinkers associated with social contract theory and the Enlightenment took in Islamic thought, it appears it is the slightly later and still enduring paradigms associated with nationalism and 'national sciences' that put an end to pursuits of political theory 'from outside' of the nation and the civilization it identifies with.[1] Consequently, principles of the rule of law, social contract, and eventually human rights, only become constructed as 'western' in nationalist discourses, as distinct from the somewhat earlier, more public law- and natural rights-oriented ones, where these principles' Islamic 'origins' is acknowledged. The analysis in this preliminary study suggests that the latter discourses were onto something 'real', i.e. the practices that concerned early modern European political thinkers overlapped with those that concerned the Islamic scholars when they used the Qur'ān; in de Certeau's words: "There exists a historicity of history, implying the movement which links an interpretive practice to a social praxis" (1988: 21).

1 See reference to Park (2013) in Chapter 1, the section on Hobsbawn and nationalist discourse.

BIBLIOGRAPHY

PRIMARY SOURCES

al-Āmidī, Sayf al-Dīn. (1914) *Kitāb al-Iḥkām fī uṣūl al-aḥkām*. 4 vols. Cairo: Dār al-Kutub al-Khidīwiyya.

Aristotle. (1984) *The Complete Works of Aristotle: The Revised Oxford Translation*. Ed. Jonathan Barnes. 2 vols. Volume 1. Bollingen Series LXXI.2. Princeton University Press. www.doi.org/10.1515/9781400835843

al-Ashʿarī, Abū al-Ḥasan ʿAlī b. Ismāʿīl. (1980) Ed. Ritter, Helmut. *Maqālāt al-islāmiyyīna wa ikhtilāf al-muṣallīna*. Wiesbaden: Franz Steiner Verlag.

al-Bannā, Ḥasan. (1977) *al-Rasāʾil al-thalātha: Daʿwatunā; Ilā ayyi shayʾ nadʿū al-nās; Naḥw al-nūr*. Cairo: Dār al-Ṭibāʿa wa al-nashr al-Islāmiyya.

— (1981) *Maqāṣid al-Qurʾān al-karīm*. Tunis: Dār Bū Slāma li-l-Ṭibāʿa wa al-Nashr wa al-Tawzīʿ.

al-Bukhārī (1987) *Ṣaḥīḥ*. 9 vols. Beirut: Dār al-Qalam.

al-Fārābī, Abū Naṣr Muḥammad. (1953) *Iḥṣāʾ al-ʿulūm*. Ángel González Palencia (ed.). 2nd edition. Madrid.

— *Majmūʿ fī al-siyāsa*. Ed. Fuʾād ʿAbd al-Munʿim Aḥmad. Alexandria: Muʾassasat Shabāb al-Jāmiʿa.

— *Kitāb taḥṣīl al-saʿāda*. (1926) Hyderabad: Maṭbaʿat Majlis Dāʾirat al-Maʿārif al-ʿUthmāniyya.

Hermansen, Marcia K. (2013) *Shāh Walī Allāh of Delhi's Ḥujjat Allāh al-Bāligha: The Conclusive Argument from God*. Translated by M. K. Hermansen. New Delhi: Kitab Bhavan.

Ibn Hishām, Muḥammad. (1990) *al-Sīra al-nabawiyya li-Ibn Hishām*. 4 vols. Ed. ʿUmar ʿAbd al-Salām Tadmurī. Beirut: Dār al-Kitāb al-ʿArabī.

Ibn Khordadhbih, ʿUbayd Allāh b. ʿAbd Allāh. (1889) *Kitāb al-mamālik wa al-masālik wa yalīhi nabdh min Kitāb al-kharāj wa ṣanʿat al-kātib li-Abī al-Faraj Qudāma b. Jaʿfar al-kātib al-Baghdādī*. Leiden: Brill.

Ibn al-Muqaffaʿ. (1989) *Āthār Ibn al-Muqaffaʿ*. Beirut: Dār Al-kutub al-ʿIlmiyya.

Ibn Qutayba. (1996) *Adab al-kātib*. Ed. Muḥammad al-Dālī. Beirut, 2nd ed.

Ibn Saʿd, Muḥammad. (2001) *Kitāb al-ṭabaqāt al-kabīr*. Ed. ʿAlī Muḥammad ʿUmar. 11 vols. Cairo: Maktabat al-Khānjī.

Ibn Sallām, Yaḥyā. (1980) Ed. Shalabī, Hind. *al-Taṣārīf litafsīr al-Qurʾān mimmā ishtabahat asmāʾuhu wa taṣarrafat maʿānīhi*. Tunis: al-Sharika al-Tūnisiyya li'l-tawzīʿ.

Ibn Taymiyya, Aḥmad Taqī al-Dīn. (1982) *Al-Furqān bayna awliyā' al-Raḥmān wa awliyā' al-Shayṭān*. Riyadh: Maktabat al-Ma'ārif.

Kennedy, George A. (2007) *Aristotle: On Rhetoric – A Theory of Civic Discourse*. Translated by George A. Kennedy. Oxford: Oxford University Press.

al-Kulaynī, Muḥammad b. Ya'qūb b. Isḥāq. (1961) *al-Kāfī*. 8 vols. Tehran: Maktabat al-Ṣaddūq.

Morris, James Winston. (1981) *The Wisdom of the Throne: An Introduction to the Philosophy of Mulla Sadra*. English translation of *Ḥikmat al-'arsh*. Princeton, N.J.: Princeton University Press.

Mullā Ṣadrā, Ṣadr al-Dīn Muḥammad al-Shīrāzī. (1958) *Risāla fī al-ḥudūth (ḥudūth al-'ālam)*. Ed. Sayyid Ḥusayn Mūsāwiyān. Tehran: Ṣadrā Islamic Philosophy Research Institute.

— (1998) *Tafsīr al-Qur'ān al-karīm*. 8 vols. Beirut: Dār al-Ta'āruf li'l-maṭbū'āt.

Muqātil b. Sulaymān. (2002). *Tafsīr*. Ed. 'Abd Allāh Maḥmūd Shaḥāta. 5 vols. Beirut: Mu'assasat al-Ta'rīkh al-'Arabī.

al-Qāḍī al-Nu'mān/Stewart. (2017) *Disagreements of the Jurists: A Manual of Islamic Legal Theory*. Translated by Devin Stewart. New York: New York University Press. https://doi.org/10.2307/j.ctt1pwt9dx

al-Rāzī, Muḥammad Fakhr al-Dīn. (1981) *Mafātīḥ al-ghayb*. 33 vols. Beirut: Dār al-Fikr.

al-Ṣan'ānī, 'Abd al-Razzāq. (1989) *Tafsīr al-Qur'ān*, ed. M. M. Muḥammad. 3 vols. Riyadh: Maktabat al-Rushd.

al-Shāṭibī, Ibrāhīm b. Mūsā. (n.d.) *Al-Muwāfaqāt fī usūl al-sharī'a*. 4 vols. Ed. 'Abdallāh Darāz. Cairo: Dār al-Fikr al-'Arabī.

Sībawayhi. (1982 (vol. 4); 1988 (vols. 1–3); 1996 (vol. 5)) *al-Kitāb*. Ed. 'Abd al-Salām Muḥammad Hārūn. 5 vols. Cairo: Maktabat al-Khānjī.

al-Suyūṭī, Jalāl al-Dīn 'Abd al-Raḥmān. (2011) *al-Durr al-manthūr fī al-tafsīr al-ma'thūr*. 8 vols. Beirut: Dār al-Fikr.

— (2005) *al-Itqān fī 'ulūm al-Qur'ān*. 7 vols. Ed. Markaz al-Dirāsāt al-Qur'āniyya. Riyadh: Wizārat al-Shu'ūn al-Islāmiyya wa al-Da'wa wa al-Irshād al-Sa'ūdiyya.

— and Jalāl al-Dīn al-Maḥallī. (2003) *Tafsīr al-Jalālayn al-muyassar*. Ed. Fakhr al-Dīn Qabāwa. Beirut: Maktabat Lubnān Nāshirūna.

al-Ṭabarī, Muḥammad b. Jarīr. (1995) *Jāmi' al-bayān 'an ta'wīl āy al-Qur'ān*. Ed. Ṣidqī Ḥamīd al-'Aṭṭār. 15 vols. Beirut: Dār al-Fikr.

— (1997) *Tārīkh al-Ṭabarī*. 6 vols. Beirut: Dār al-Kutub al-'Ilmiyya.

— (1999) *Ikhtilāf al-fuqahā'*, ed. Friedrich Kern. Beirut: Dār al-Kutub al-'Ilmiyya.

— (1933) *Das Konstantinopler Fragment des Kitāb Ikhtilāf al-Fuqahā' des Abū Ja'far Muḥammad b. Jarīr aṭ-Ṭabarī*, ed. Joseph Schacht. Leiden: Brill.

— (2007) Yasir S. Ibrahim. *Al-Ṭabarī's Book of Jihād: A Translation from the Original Arabic, With Introduction, Commentary, and Notes*. Lewiston, NY: The Edwin Mellen Press.

The History of al-Tabari. Ed. Ehsan Yar-Shater. 40 vols. Albany: State University of New York Press.

HT1: Rosenthal, Franz (1989). *General Introduction and From the Creation to the Flood.*
HT 2: Brinner, William M. (1987) *Prophets and Patriarchs.*
HT 14: Smith, Rex G. (1994) *The Conquest of Iran.*
HT 32: Bosworth, C. E. (1987) *The Reunification of the 'Abbāsid Caliphate.*
al-Ṭūsī, Muḥammad b. al-Ḥasan. *Al-Tibyān fī tafsīr al-Qur'ān.* 10 vols. Beirut: Dār Iḥyā' al-Turāth al-'Arabī.
al-Zamakhsharī, Maḥmūd b. 'Umar. (2009) *Al-Kashshāf 'an ḥaqā'iq al-tanzīl wa 'uyūn al-aqāwīl fī wujūh al-ta'wīl.* Beirut: Dār al-Ma'rifa.

SECONDARY SOURCES

Abaza, Mona. (2002) *Debates on Islam and Knowledge in Malaysia and Egypt: Shifting Worlds.* London: Routledge.
Abdel Haleem, Muhammad. (2018) 'The Role of Context in Interpreting and Translating the Qur'an', *Journal of Qur'anic Studies*, 20:1, pp. 47–66. www.doi.org/10.3366/jqs.2018.0320
— (2004) *The Qur'an: A new translation by M. A. S. Abdel Haleem.* Oxford: Oxford University Press.
— (1993) 'Context and internal relationships: keys to qur'anic exegesis. A study of *Sūrat al-Raḥmān*', in Hawting, Gerald R. and Shareef, Abdul-Kader A. (eds.) *Approaches to the Qur'ān.* London: Routledge, pp. 71–98.
— (1991) 'Early Islamic Theological and Juristic Terminology: *Kitāb al-ḥudūd fī al-uṣūl*, by Ibn Fūrak'. *Bulletin of the School of Oriental and African Studies*, 54:1, pp. 5–41. www.doi.org/10.1017/S0041977X00009587
Abbott, Nabia. (1957) *Studies in Arabic Literary Papyri. 1: Historical Texts.* Chicago: The Oriental Institute Publications.
Abdul Rauf, Muhammad. (1967) 'Some Notes on the Qur'anic Use of the Terms Islām and Imān'. *The Muslim World*, 57, pp. 94–102.
Abu-Odeh, Lama. (2009) 'On Law and the Transition to Market: The Case of Egypt'. *Emory International Law Review.* 23, pp. 351–381.
Abu Zayd, Nasr Hamid (2004a) with Esther R. Nelson. *Voice of an Exile: Reflections on Islam.* Westport, CT: Praeger Publishers.
— (2004b) *Rethinking the Qur'ân: Towards a Humanistic Hermeneutics.* Amsterdam: SWP Publishers.
— (2003) 'The Dilemma of the Literary Approach to the Qur'an'. *Alif: Journal of Comparative Poetics*, 23: Literature and the Sacred, pp. 8–47. www.doi.org/10.2307/1350075
— (1992) *Naqd al-khiṭāb al-dīnī.* Cairo: Dār Ṣinā'a li'l-Nashr.
— (1990) *Mafhūm al-naṣṣ: Dirāsa fī 'ulūm al-Qur'ān.* Beirut: al-Markaz al-thaqāfī al-'arabī.
Adamson, Peter and Bormann, Peter E. (2012) *The Philosophical Works of al-Kindī.* Karachi: Oxford University Press.

Afsaruddin, Asma. (2013) '*Maslaha* as a Political Concept'. In Boroujerdi, Mehrzad (ed.). *Mirror for the Muslim Prince: Islam and the Theory of Statecraft*. New York: Syracuse University Press, pp. 16–44.
Agger, Ben. (1991) 'Critical Theory, Poststructuralism, Postmodernism: Their Sociological Relevance'. *Annual Review of Sociology*, 17, pp. 105–131. www.doi.org/10.1146/annurev.so.17.080191.000541
Ahearne, Jeremy. (1995) *Interpretation and its Other*. Cambridge: Polity Press.
Aijub, Palmer. (2015) *The Social and Theoretical Dimensions of Sainthood in Early Islam: Al-Tirmidhī's Gnoseology and the Foundations of Ṣūfī Social Praxis*. PhD Thesis, Near Eastern Studies, University of Michigan.
Alam, Muzaffar. (2004) *The Languages of Political Islam: India 1200–1800*. Chicago: The University of Chicago Press.
Alhassen, Leyla Ozgur. (2015) '"You Were Not There": The Creation of Humility and Knowledge in Qur'anic Stories: A Narratological and Rhetorical Analysis'. *Comparative Islamic Studies*, 11(1), pp. 65–94. www.doi.org/10.1558/cis.28486
— (2016) 'A Structural Analysis of *Sūrat Maryam*, Verses 1–58'. *Journal of Qur'anic Studies*. 18:1, pp. 92–116. www.doi.org/10.3366/jqs.2016.0223
Ali, Mohamed M. Yunis. (2000) *Medieval Islamic Pragmatics: Sunnī Legal Theorists' Models of Textual Communication*. Richmond: Curzon.
Anjum, Tanvir. (2006) 'Sufism in History and its Relationship with Power'. *Islamic Studies*, 45 (2), pp. 221–268.
Arjomand, Saïd Amir. (2009) 'The Constitution of Medina: A Sociolegal Interpretation of Muhammad's Acts of Foundation of the *Umma*'. *International Journal of Middle East Studies*, 41, pp. 555–575. www.doi.org/10.1017/S0020743809990067
Asad, Talal. (2001) 'Reading a Modern Classic: W.C. Smith's "The Meaning and End of Religion"'. *History of Religions*, Vol. 40:3, pp. 205–222. www.doi.org/10.1086/463633
— (1993) *Genealogies of Religion: Discipline and Reasons of Power in Christianity and Islam*. Baltimore: Johns Hopkins University Press.
Ayoub, Samy A. (2020) *Law, Empire, and the Sultan: Ottoman Imperial Authority and Late Ḥanafī Jurisprudence*. Oxford: Oxford University Press. www.doi.org/10.1093/oso/9780190092924.001.0001
al-Azmeh, Aziz. (2007) *The Times of History: Universal Topics in Islamic Historiography*. Budapest: Central European University Press.
Baalbaki, Ramzi. (2007) 'Inside the Speaker's Mind: Speaker's Awareness as Arbiter of Usage in Arab Grammatical Theory'. Ditters, Everhard and Motzki, Harald. Eds. *Approaches to Arabic Linguistics*. Leiden: Brill, pp. 3–23.
Baffioni, Carmela. (2000) 'Different Conceptions of Religious Practice, Piety, and God-Man Relations in the Epistles of the Ikhwān al-Ṣafā''. *Al-Qantara*, 21:2, pp. 381–386. www.doi.org/10.3989/alqantara.2000.v21.i2.432
Bakhash, Shaul. (1989) 'The Politics of Land, Law, and Social Justice in Iran'. *Middle East Journal*. 43:2, pp. 186–201.

Bannister, Andrew G. (2014) *An Oral-Formulaic Study of the Qur'an*. Lanham: Lexington Books.

Bauer, Karen. (2013). 'Introduction'. In Bauer, Karen. Ed. *Aims, Methods and Contexts of Qur'anic Exegesis (2nd/8th – 9th/15th C.)*. Oxford: Oxford University Press/The Institute of Ismaili Studies, pp.1–16.

Bauer, Thomas. (2011) *Die Kultur der Ambiguität: Eine andere Geschichte des Islams*. Berlin: Verlag der Weltreligionen.

Belhaj, Abdessamad. (2015) '*Al-Risāla* (attributed to al-Šāfiʿī) and the Question of Vagueness in Islamic Legal Hermeneutics'. *Comparative Islamic Studies*, 11.1, pp. 95–107. www.doi.org/10.1558/cis.20372

Benmakhlouf, Ali. (1995) 'Entretien: Mohamed Arkoun. Penser le statut de donné révélé en islam'. *Prologues* (*Muqaddima: nashrat al-kitāb ḥawla al-maghrib al-ʿarabī*), 4, pp. 5–13.

Bennison, Amira K. (2009) *The Great Caliphs: The Golden Age of the 'Abbasid Empire*. New Haven: Yale University Press. www.doi.org/10.5040/9780755696918

Ben-Shemesh, Aharon. (1958) *Taxation in Islam. Volume I: Yaḥyā b. Ādam's Kitāb al-Kharāj*. Leiden: Brill.

— (1965) *Taxation in Islam. Volume II: Qudāma b. Jaʿfar's Kitāb al-Kharāj, Part 7, and Excerpts from Abū Yūsuf's Kitāb al-Kharāj*. Leiden: Brill.

— (1969) *Taxation in Islam. Volume III: Abū Yūsuf's Kitāb al-Kharāj*. Leiden: Brill.

Berger, Morroe. (1970) *Islam in Egypt Today: Social and Political Aspects of Popular Religion*. Cambridge: Cambridge University Press.

Bhaskar, Roy. (2008[1977]) *A Realist Theory of Science*. London: Routledge.

Bigliardi, Stefano. (2014) *Islam and the Quest for Modern Science. Conversations with Adnan Oktar, Mehdi Golshani, Mohammed Basil Altaie, Zaghloul El-Naggar, Bruno Guiderdoni and Nidhal Guessoum*. Istanbul: Swedish Research Institute.

Bin Sattam, Abdul Aziz. (2015) *Sharīʿa and the Concept of Benefit: The Use and Function of Maṣlaḥa in Islamic Jurisprudence*. London: I.B. Tauris. www.doi.org/10.5040/9780755608874

Blain, Auer. (2012) 'Intersections between Sufism and Power, Narrating the Shaykhs and Sultans of Northern India, 1200–1400', in Curry, John J. and Ohlander, Eric S. Eds. *Sufism and Society: Arrangements of the mystical in the Muslim world, 1200–1800*. Hoboken: Taylor & Francis. pp. 17–33.

Boisliveau, Anne-Sylvie. (2014) *Le Coran par lui-même. Vocabulaire et argumentation du discours coranique autoréférentiel*. Leiden: Brill. www.doi.org/10.1163/9789004259706

Boullata, Issa. (2000) Ed. *Literary Structures of Religious Meaning in the Qurʾān*. Richmond: Curzon.

Brereton, Gareth. (2018) 'The Neo-Assyrian Empire'. In Brereton, Gareth. Ed. *I am Ashurbanipal, king of the world, king of Assyria*. London: Thames & Hudson Ltd., pp. 100–117.

Brown, Jonathan. (2011) *The Canonization of al-Bukhārī and Muslim: The Formation and Function of the Sunnī Ḥadīth Canon*. Leiden: Brill.

Buehler, Arthur. (1997) 'Currents of Sufism in Nineteenth- and Twentieth Century Indo-Pakistan: An Overview'. *The Muslim World*, vol. 87, issue 3/4, pp. 299–314. www.doi.org/10.1111/j.1478-1913.1997.tb03641.x

Burman, Thomas. (1998) 'Tafsīr and translation: traditional Arabic Qur'ān exegesis and the Latin Qur'āns of Robert of Ketton and Mark of Toledo'. *Speculum*, 73:3, pp. 703–732.

Butterworth, Charles. (2008) 'What Might We Learn From al-Fārābī About Plato and Aristotle With Respect to Lawgiving?' *Mélanges de l'Université Saint-Joseph*, pp. 471–489.

Böwering, Gerhard. (1980) *The mystical vision of existence in classical Islam: the Qur'ānic hermeneutics of the Ṣūfī Sahl at-Tustarī (d. 283/896)*. Berlin: De Gruyter.

— (2003) 'The Scriptural "Senses" in Medieval Ṣūfī Qur'ān Exegeis', in McAuliffe, Jane, Walfish, Barry D., and Goering, Joseph W. Eds. *With Reverence for the Word: Medieval Scriptural Exegesis in Judaism, Christianity and Islam*. Oxford: Oxford University Press, pp. 346–365. www.doi.org/10.1093/acprof:oso/9780195137279.003.0023

Calder, Norman. (1993) '*Tafsīr* from Ṭabarī to Ibn Kathīr: Problems in the description of a genre, illustrated with reference to the story of Abraham', in Hawting, Gerald R. and Shareef, Abdul-Kader A. Eds. *Approaches to the Qur'ān*. London: Routledge, pp. 101–140.

Campanini, Massimo. (2016) *Philosophical Perspectives on Modern Qur'ānic Exegesis*. Shah, Mustafa and al-Matroudi, Abdul Hakim. Eds. Themes in Qur'ānic Studies. Sheffield: Equinox.

— (2011) *The Qur'an: Modern Muslim Interpretations*. London: Routledge.

Cantwell Smith, Wilfred. (1962) *The Meaning and End of Religion*. New York: The Macmillan Company.

Carter, Michael. (2007) 'Pragmatics and Contractual Language in Early Arabic Grammar and Legal Theory', in Ditters, Everhard, and Motzki, Harald. Eds. *Approaches to Arabic Linguistics*. Leiden: Brill, pp. 25–44. www.doi.org/10.1163/ej.9789004160156.i-762.13

— (1983) 'Language control as people control in medieval Islam'. *Al-Abḥath*, 31, pp. 76–84.

— (1972) 'Les origines de la grammaire arabe'. *Revue des études islamiques*, 40, pp. 69–97.

de Certeau, Michel. (1988) *The Writing of History*. Translated by Tom Conley. New York: Columbia University Press. [French original (1975) *L'Écriture de l'histoire*. Paris: Gallimard]

— (1984) *The Practice of Everyday Life*. Berkeley: University of California Press. [French original (1980) *L'Invention du quotidian. Vol. 1: Arts de faire*. Paris: Union générale d'éditions.]

— (1997) *Culture in the Plural*. Minneapolis: University of Minnesota Press. [French original (1974) *La culture au pluriel*. Paris: Union générale d'éditions.]

Chaghatai, M. Ikram. (2005) Ed. *Jamāl al-Dīn al-Afghānī: An Apostle of Islamic Resurgence*. Lahore: Sang-e-Meel Publications.

Christiansen, Johanne Louise. (2015) 'The Dark Koran: A Semantic Analysis of the Koranic Darknesses (*ẓulumāt*) and their Metaphorical Usage'. *Arabica*. 62:2/3, pp. 185–233. www.doi.org/10.1163/15700585-12341352

Cilardo, Agostino. (2005) *The Qur'ānic Term Kalāla. Studies in Arabic Language and Poetry, Ḥadīth, Tafsīr, and Fiqh: Notes on the Origins of Islamic Law*. Edinburgh: Edinburgh University Press.

Collins, Paul. (2018) 'Life at Court'. In Brereton, Gareth. Ed.. *I am Ashurbanipal, king of the world, king of Assyria*. London: Thames & Hudson Ltd., pp. 34–51.

Commins, David. (1986) 'Religious Reformers and Arabists in Damascus, 1885–1914'. *International Journal of Middle East Studies*, 18, pp. 405–425. www.doi.org/10.1017/S0020743800030762

Cooperson, Michael. (2000) *Classical Arabic Biography: The Heirs of the Prophets in the Age of al-Ma'mūn*. Cambridge: Cambridge University Press. www.doi.org/10.1017/CBO9780511497469

Cragg, Kenneth. (1984) *Muhammad and the Christian: a question of response*. London: Darton, Longman and Todd. [(1999) Oxford: Oneworld]

Cromer, Evelyn Baring. (1908) *Modern Egypt, by the Earl of Cromer*. 2 vols. (Vol. 2). London: Macmillan & Co.

Cuno, Kenneth M. (1980) 'The Origins of Private Ownership of Land in Egypt: A Reappraisal'. *International Journal of Middle East Studies*. 12, pp. 245–275. www.doi.org/10.1017/S0020743800026301

D'Agostino, Fred. (1996) *Free Public Reason: Making It Up As We Go Along*. New York: Oxford University Press.

Dakake, Maria Massi. (2007) *The Charismatic Community: Shī'ite Identity in Early Islam*. Albany: State University of New York Press.

Daneshgar, Majid. (2017) *Ṭanṭāwī Jawharī and the Qur'an: tafsir and social concerns in the twentieth century*. London: Routledge.

Donner, Fred M. (2011) 'The historian, the believer, and the Qurān', in Reynolds, Gabriel Said. Ed. *New perspectives on the Qur'ān: The Qur'ān in its historical context 2*. London: Routledge, pp. 25–37.

— (2010) *Muhammad and the Believers: At the Origins of Islam*. Cambridge, Mass.: The Belknap Press.

Dransfeldt, Tina. (2015) 'Transcending Institutionalized Islām, Approaching Diversity: 'Abdelmajīd Sharfī's Conception of a Qur'ānic Ethics of Liberation'. *Tidsskrift for islamforskning/Journal of Islamic Research*, 9:1, pp. 58–78. www.doi.org/10.7146/tifo.v9i1.25345

Duri, Abd al-Aziz. (1960/1983) *The Rise of Historical Writing Among the Arabs*. Edited and Translated by Lawrence I. Conrad. Introduction by Fred M. Donner. Princeton: Princeton University Press.

— (1987) *The Historical Formation of the Arab Nation: A Study in Identity and Consciousness*. London: Routledge.

— (2011) *Early Islamic Institutions: Administration and Taxation from the Caliphate to the Umayyads and ʿAbbāsids*. London: I.B. Tauris.

Dutton, Yasin. (2012) 'Orality, Literacy and the "Seven Aḥruf" Ḥadīth'. *Journal of Islamic Studies*, 23:1, pp. 1–49. www.doi.org/10.1093/jis/etr092

Dzilo, Hasan. (2012) 'The concept of "Islamization of knowledge" and its philosophical implications'. *Islam and Christian–Muslim Relations*, 23:3, pp. 247–256. www.doi.org/10.1080/09596410.2012.676779

Edgeworth Reade, Julian. (2018) 'The Assyrian Royal Hunt'. In Brereton, Gareth. Ed. *I am Ashurbanipal, king of the world, king of Assyria*. London: Thames & Hudson Ltd., pp. 52–79.

Eggen, Nora S. (2011) 'Conceptions of Trust in the Qur'an'. *Journal of Qur'anic Studies*, 13.2, pp. 56–85. www.doi.org/10.3366/jqs.2011.0020

Elazar, Daniel. (1998) *Covenant & Polity in Biblical Israel: Biblical Foundations & Jewish Expressions*. Volume 1 of the Covenant Tradition in Politics. New Brunswick, N.J.: Transaction Publishers.

El-Badawi, Emran I. (2014) *The Qurān and the Aramaic Gospel Traditions*. London: Routledge. www.doi.org/10.4324/9781315855981

Elmarsafy, Ziad. (2009) *The Enlightenment Qur'an: The Politics of Translation and the Construction of Islam*. Oxford: Oneworld.

— (2020) 'Translations of the Qur'an: Western Languages'. Shah, Mustafa and Abdel Haleem, Muhammad. Eds. *The Oxford Handbook of Qur'anic Studies*. Oxford: Oxford University Press, pp. 541–551.

Evans, John H. and Evans, Michael S. (2008) 'Religion and Science: Beyond the Epistemological Conflict Narrative'. *The Annual Review of Sociology*, 34, pp. 87–105. www.doi.org/10.1146/annurev.soc.34.040507.134702

Evans, Michael S. (2009) 'Defining the public, defining sociology: hybrid science-public relations and boundary-work in early American sociology.' *Public Understanding of Science*, 18, pp. 5–22. www.doi.org/10.1177/0963662506071283

Fadel, Mohammad. (2016) 'Nature, Revelation and the State in Pre-Modern Sunnī Theological, Legal and Political Thought'. *The Muslim World*, 106 (2), pp. 271–290. www.doi.org/10.1111/muwo.12141

— and Monette, Connell. (2019) *The English Language Translation of the Muwaṭṭaʾ of Imam Malik b. Anas, Recension of Yahya b. Yahya al-Laythi (Royal Moroccan Edition, 2013)*. Cambridge, MA: Harvard Islamic Legal Studies Program.

Fahd, Toufy. 'Ibn Sīrīn'. (2012) *Encyclopaedia of Islam*, Second Edition. P. Bearman, Th. Bianquis, C.E. Bosworth, E. van Donzel, W.P. Heinrichs. Eds. Consulted online on 12 November 2019. dx.doi.org/10.1163/1573-3912_islam_SIM_3382

Farstad, Mona Helen. (2012) *Chaste, Chosen, and Purified: An Analysis of the Qur'ānic Narratives about Maryam*. PhD thesis. Faculty of Arts, University of Bergen.

Feldman, Noah. (2008) *The Fall and Rise of the Islamic State*. Princeton, NJ: Princeton University Press.

Finnis, John. (2011[1980]) *Natural Law and Natural Rights*, Second Edition. Oxford: Oxford University Press.

— (2012) 'Natural Law Theory: Its Past and Present', *American Journal of Jurisprudence*, 57, pp. 81–101. www.doi.org/10.1093/ajj/57.1.81

Foltz, Bruce V. (2019). Ed. *Medieval Philosophy: A Multicultural Reader*. London: Bloomsbury Academic.

Galadari, Abdulla. (2013) 'The Qibla: An Allusion to the *Shema*?' *Comparative Islamic Studies*, 9:2, pp. 165–194.

Gilliot, Claude. (2013) 'A Schoolmaster, Storyteller, Exegete and Warrior at Work in Khurāsān: al-Ḍaḥḥāk b. Muzāḥim al-Hilālī'. In Bauer, Karen. Ed. *Aims, Methods and Contexts of Qur'anic Exegesis (2nd/8th – 9th/15th C.)*. Oxford: Oxford University Press/The Institute of Ismaili Studies, pp. 311–392.

— (1990) *Exégèse, langue et théologie en islam: l'exégèse coranique de Tabari*. Pris: J. Vrin.

— (1985) 'Portrait "mythique" d'Ibn ʿAbbās'. *Arabica*, 32:2, pp. 127–184. www.doi.org/10.1163/157005885X00010

Goldberg, Ellis. (1986) *Tinker, Tailor, and Texile Worker: Class and Politics in Egypt, 1930–1952*. Berkeley: University of California Press.

Goldfeld, Yeshayahu. (1988) 'The development of theory of qurʾānic exegesis in Islamic scholarship'. *Studia Islamica*, 67, pp. 5–27. www.doi.org/10.2307/1595972

— (1981) 'The *Tafsīr* of Abdallah b. ʿAbbās', *Der Islam*, 58, pp. 125–135.

Goodman, Lenn E. (2007/1992) 'Time in Islam'. In Netton, Ian R. Ed. *Islamic Philosophy and Theology: Critical Concepts in Islamic Thought*. Vol. III: Aristotelianism and Neoplatonism. London: Routledge, pp. 5–26. (Original publication: *Asian Philosophy*, 2:1 (1992), pp. 3–19)

Gramlich, Richard. (1983) 'Der Urvertrag in der Koranauslegung (zu Sure 7, 172–173)'. *Der Islam*. 60, pp. 205–230. www.doi.org/10.1515/islm.1983.60.2.205

Graves, Michael Wesley. (2015) 'The Upraised Mountain and Israel's Election in the Qur'an and Talmud'. *Comparative Islamic Studies*, 11:2, pp. 144–177.

Gwynne, Rosalind Ward. (2004) *Logic, Rhetoric, and Legal Reasoning in the Qurʾān: God's Arguments*. London: Routledge.

Görke, Andreas and Pink, Johanna. (2014) 'Introduction'. In Görke and Pink. Eds. *Tafsīr and Islamic Intellectual History: Exploring the Boundaries of a Genre*. Oxford: Oxford University Press/Institute of Ismaili Studies, pp. 1–23. www.doi.org/10.1007/978-1-137-35001-5_1

Hallaq, Wael B. (1984) 'Considerations on the Function and Character of Sunnī Legal Theory.' *Journal of the American Oriental Society*, 104, pp. 679–689. www.doi.org/10.2307/601899

— (1987) 'The Development of Logical Structure in Sunnī Legal Theory.' *Der Islam*. 64, pp. 42–67. www.doi.org/10.1515/islm.1987.64.1.42

Halldén, Philip. (2005) 'What is Arab Islamic Rhetoric? Rethinking the History of Muslim Oratory Art and Homiletics'. *International Journal of Middle East Studies*, 37, pp. 19–38.

Hamzah, Dyala. (2013) 'From *ʿilm* to *Ṣiḥāfa* or the politics of the public interest (*maṣlaḥa*): Muḥammad Rashīd Riḍā and his journal *al-Manār*'. Hamzah, Dyala.

Ed. *The Making of the Arab Intellectual: Empire, public sphere and the colonial coordinates of selfhood*. London: Routledge, pp. 90–127.

Hamidullah, Muhammad. (1987) *Majmūʿat al-wathāʾiq al-siyāsiyya liʾl-ʿahd al-nabawiyy wa al-khilāfa al-rāshida*. Sixth edition. Beirut: Dār al-Nafāʾis.

— (1937) ʻʾAqdam Dustūr Musajjal fī-l-ʿĀlam'. *Islamic Scholars Conference*, 1, pp. 98–123.

— (1968) *The First Written Constitution in the World*. Second edition. Lahore: Sh. Muhammad Ashraf.

Hanafi, Sari. (2016) ʻ*ʾAslamat wa taʾṣīl al-ʿulūm al-ijtimāʿiyya: dirāsat baʿḍ al-ishkāliyyāt*. *Al-Mustaqbal al-ʿArabī*, 46, pp. 45–64.

Haque, S. (1966) 'Ibn Taimīyyah'. In M.M. Sharif. Ed. *A history of Muslim philosophy. With short accounts of other disciplines and the modern renaissance in Muslim lands*. Vol. 2. Wiesbaden: Harrassowitz, pp.796–819.

Haque, Ziaul. (1977) *Landlord and Peasant in Early Islam*. Islamabad: Islamic Research Institute.

Harvey, Ramon. (2018) *The Qur'an and the Just Society*. Edinburgh: Edinburgh University Press.

— (2020) 'The *sabab-khāṣṣ-ʿāmm* Process as an Instructional Technique within Qur'anic Rhetoric'. *Journal of Qur'anic Studies*, 22. 1, pp. 78–91. www.doi.org/10.3366/jqs.2020.0412

Hatina, Meir. (2010) 'An Earlier Version of Khomeini's Rule of the Jurist: Muṣṭafā l-Sibāʿī on *ʿUlamāʾ* and Politics'. *Arabica*, 57, pp. 455–476. www.doi.org/10.1163/157005810X519107

Hawting, Gerald. (1994) *The Idea of Idolatry and the Emergence of Islam: From Polemic to History*. Cambridge: Cambridge University Press.

— (2000) *The First Dynasty of Islam: The Umayyad Caliphate 661–750*. 2nd edition. London: Routledge.

Heck, Paul. (2016) 'Māwardī and Augustine on Governance: How to Restrain the Restrainer?' *Studies in Christian Ethics*, 29 (2), pp. 158–168. www.doi.org/10.1177/0953946815623129

— (2004) 'Law in Abbasid Political Thought From Ibn al-Muqaffaʿ (d. 139/756) to Qudāma b. Jaʿfar (d. 337/948)'. Montgomery, James E. Ed. *ʿAbbasid Studies: Occasional Papers of the School of ʿAbbasid Studies, Cambridge 6–10 July 2002*. Orientalia Lovaniensia Analecta, 135, pp. 83–109.

— (2002) *The Construction of Knowledge in Islamic Civilization: Qudāma ibn Jaʿfar and His 'Kitāb al-kharāj wa ṣināʿat al-kitāba'*. Leiden: Brill.

Hilali, Asma. (2017) *The Sanaa Palimpsest: The Transmission of the Qur'an in the First Centuries AH*. Oxford: Oxford University Press/The Institute of Ismaili Studies.

Himma, Kenneth Einar. 'Natural Law'. www.www.iep.utm.edu/natlaw/, accessed 5 December, 2019.

Hobsbawm, Eric. (1983) 'Mass-Producing Traditions: Europe, 1870–1914'. Hobsbawm, Eric & Ranger, Terence. Eds. *The Invention of Tradition.*

Cambridge: Cambridge University Press, pp. 263–307. www.doi.org/10.1017/CBO9781107295636.007

Hodgson, Marshal G. S. (1974/I) *The Venture of Islam: Conscience and History in a World Civilization. The Classical Age of Islam*. Chicago: The University of Chicago Press.

Hoffmann, Thomas. (2018) 'Qur'anic Studies between University Theology and the Humanities: A Field Worth Cultivating?' *Islam and Christian-Muslim Relations*. 29:4, pp. 429–443. www.doi.org/10.1080/09596410.2018.1521562

Hooglund, Eric. (2009) 'Thirty Years of Islamic Revolution in Rural Iran'. *Middle East Report*. The Islamic Revolution at 30. 250, pp. 34–39.

Hoover, John. (2006) 'Ibn Taymiyya as an Avicennan theologian'. *Theological Review*. 27, pp. 34–46.

Hoyland, Robert G. (2001) *Arabia and the Arabs: From the Bronze Age to the Coming of Islam*. New York: Routledge. www.doi.org/10.4324/9780203455685

Humphreys, R. Stephen. (1989) 'Qur'ānic Myth and Narrative Structure in Early Islamic Historiography'. In Clover, F.M. and Humphreys, R.S. Eds. *Tradition and Innovation in Late Antiquity*. Madison: University of Wisconsin Press, pp. 271–290.

— (1991) *Islamic History: A Framework for Inquiry*. Revised edition. Princeton, N.J.: Princeton University Press.

Ihsanoglu, Ekmeleddin. (2010) *The Islamic World in the New Century: The Organisation of the Islamic Conference, 1969–2009*. London: Hurst & Company.

Irwin, Robert. (2006) *For Lust of Knowing: The Orientalists and their Enemies*. London: Allen Lane.

Ishaq, Bushra. (2017) *Hvem snakker for oss? Muslimer i dagens Norge – hvem er de og hva mener de?* Oslo: Cappelen Damm.

Iványi, Támas. (1995) 'The Term *ḥadd* at Sībawayhi: A List and Contextual Analysis'. *The Arabist*, 15–16, pp. 57–68.

Jackson, Pamela I. and Doerschler, Peter. (2012) *Benchmarking Muslim well-being in Europe: Reducing disparities and polarizations*. Bristol: The Policy Press. www.doi.org/10.2307/j.ctt9qgm77

Johansen, Baber. (1988) *The Islamic Law on Land Tax and Rent. The Peasants' Loss of Property Rights as Interpreted in the Hanafite Legal Literature of the Mamluk and Ottoman Periods*. London: Routledge.

Jokisch, Benjamin. (2007) *Islamic Imperial Law: Harun-Al-Rashid's Codification Project*. Berlin: Walter de Gruyter. www.doi.org/10.1515/9783110924343

Kadi, Wadad. (2003) 'The Primordial Covenant and Human History in the Qur'ān'. *Proceedings of the American Philosophical Society*. 147 (4), pp. 332–338.

Kamali, Mohammad Hashim. (2009) 'Diversity and Pluralism: A Qur'ānic Perspective'. *Islam and Civilizational Renewal*, 1:1, pp. 27–54.

— (2016) 'Caliphate and Political Jurisprudence in Islam: Historical and Contemporary Perspectives'. *The Muslim World*, 106 (2), pp. 384–403. www.doi.org/10.1111/muwo.12145

Kara, Seyfeddin. (2018) *In Search of ʿAlī b. Abī Ṭālib's Codex: History and Traditions of the Earliest Copy of the Qurʾān*. Berlin: Gerlach Press. www.doi.org/10.2307/j.ctv4ncp48

Karamustafa, Ahmet T. (2007) *Sufism: The Formative Period*. Edinburgh: Edinburgh University Press.

Khalidi, Tarif. (1994) *Arabic historical thought in the classical period*. Cambridge: Cambridge University Press. www.doi.org/10.1017/CBO9780511583650

Keddie, Nikki R. (1981) *Roots of Revolution: An Interpretive History of Modern Iran*. New Haven: Yale University Press.

King, David. (2004) *In Synchrony with the Heavens: Studies in Astronomical Timekeeping and Instrumentation in Medieval Islamic Civilization. Volume One: The Call of the Muezzin*. Leiden: Brill.

Klein-Franke, Felix. (1982) 'Al-Kindi's "On definitions and descriptions of things"'. *Le Muséon: revue d'études orientales*, 95, pp. 191–216.

Knauf, Ernst Axel. (2010) 'Arabo-Aramaic and ʿArabiyya: From Ancient Arabic to Early Standard Arabic, 200 CE–600 CE', in Neuwirth, Angelika, Sinai, Nicolai, and Marx, Michael. Eds. *The Qurʾān in Context: Historical and Literary Investigations into the Qurʾānic Milieu*. Leiden: Brill, pp. 197–254. www.doi.org/10.1163/ej.9789004176881.i-864.53

Knysh, Alexander D. (1999) *Ibn ʿArabi in the later Islamic tradition: the making of a polemical image in medieval Islam*. Albany: State University of New York Press.

Koc, Mehmet Akif. (2008) 'A Comparison of the References to Muqātil b. Sulaymān (150/767) in the Exegesis of al-Thaʿlabī (427/1036) with Muqātil's Own Exegesis', *Journal of Semitic Studies*, LIII/1, pp. 69–101. www.doi.org/10.1093/jss/fgm045

Kraemer, Joel L. (1986) *Humanism in the Renaissance of Islam: the Cultural Revival during the Buyid Age*. Leiden: Brill.

Lambert, David A. (2016) *How Repentance Became Biblical: Judaism, Christianity, & the Interpretation of Scripture*. Oxford: Oxford University Press. www.doi.org/10.1093/acprof:oso/9780190212247.001.0001

Landau, Rom. (1957) 'The Philosophy of Ibn ʿArabī'. *The Muslim World*, 47:1, pp. 46–61.

Lapidus, Ira M. (1988) *A History of Islamic Societies*. Cambridge: Cambridge University Press.

Leirvik, Oddbjørn and Flaskerud, Ingvild. Eds. (2018) 'The Study of Islam between University Theology and Lived Religion'. *Islam and Christian-Muslim Relations*. 29:4. www.doi.org/10.1080/09596410.2018.1521561

Levey, Martin. (1975) 'Methodology and the History of Science'. Hourani, George F. Ed. *Essays on Islamic Philosophy and Science*. Albany: State University of New York Press, pp. 136–146.

Little, John T. (2007/1987) '*Al-Insān al-kāmil*: The Perfect Man according to Ibn al-ʿArabī'. Netton, Ian R. Ed. *Islamic Philosophy and Theology. IV: Eclecticism, Illumination and Reform*. London: Routledge, pp. 151–163.

Lowin, Shari L. (2006) *The Making of a Forefather: Abraham in Islamic and Jewish Exegetical Narratives*. Leiden: Brill.

Lowry, Joseph. (2008) 'The First Islamic Legal Theory: Ibn al-Muqaffaʿ on Interpretation, Authority and the Structure of the Law'. *Journal of the American Oriental Society*, 128:1, pp. 25–40.

Lumbard, Joseph. (2015) 'Covenant and Covenants in the Qur'an'. *Journal of Qur'anic Studies*. 17 (2), pp. 1–23. www.doi.org/10.3366/jqs.2015.0193

Løkkegaard, Frede. (1950) *Islamic taxation in the classical period: with special reference to circumstances in Iraq*. Copenhagen: Branner & Korch.

Madigan, Daniel. (2001) *The Qur'ân's Self-Image: Writing and Authority in Islam's Scripture*. Princeton, NJ: Princeton University Press. www.doi.org/10.1515/9780691188454

Makdisi, George. (1981) *The Rise of Colleges: Institutions of Learning in Islam and the West*. Edinburgh: Edinburgh University Press.

— (1990) *The Rise of Humanism in Classical Islam and the Christian West, With Special Reference to Scholasticism*. Edinburgh: Edinburgh University Press.

— (1991) *Religion, Law and Learning in Classical Islam*. Farnham: Ashgate Variorum.

Malamud, Margaret. (1994) 'Ṣūfī Organizations and Structures of Authority in Medieval Nīshāpūr'. *International Journal of Middle East Studies*, 26 (3), pp. 427–442. www.doi.org/10.1017/S0020743800060724

al-Marʿashlī, Hoda. (1988) Ed. Makkī b. Abī Ṭālib. *Tafsīr al-mushkil min gharīb al-Qurʾān*. Beirut: Dār al-Nūr al-Islāmī.

Margolis, Eric and Laurence, Stephen. (2014) 'Concepts'. *The Stanford Encyclopedia of Philosophy* (Spring 2014 Edition), Edward N. Zalta. Ed. plato.stanford.edu/archives/spr2014/entries/concepts/

Marogy, Amal E. (2010) *Kitāb Sībawayhi: Syntax and Pragmatics*. Leiden: Brill. www.doi.org/10.1163/9789047440529

Marsham, Andrew. (2009) *Rituals of Islamic Monarchy: Accession and Succession in the First Muslim Empire*. Edinburgh: Edinburgh University Press. www.doi.org/10.3366/edinburgh/9780748625123.001.0001

Metcalf, Barbara. (1982) *Islamic Revival in British India: Deoband, 1860–1900*. Princeton, NJ: Princeton University Press. www.doi.org/10.1515/9781400856107

Michel, Thomas F. (1983) 'Ibn Taymiyya's critique of Falsafa'. *Hamdard Islamicus*. 6: 1, pp. 3–14.

Michot, Yahya. (2007) 'Ibn Taymiyya's commentary on the Creed of al-Hallāj'. In Shihadeh, Ayman. Ed. *Sufism and theology*. Edinburgh: Edinburgh University Press, pp. 123–136. www.doi.org/10.3366/edinburgh/9780748626052.003.0008

Millar, Fergus. (2013) *Religion, Language and Community in the Roman Near East: Constantine to Muhammad*. The British Academy: Oxford University Press. www.doi.org/10.5871/bacad/9780197265574.001.0001

Mir, Mustansir. (1993) 'The *sūra* as a unity: A twentieth century development in Qurʾān exegesis'. In Hawting, Gerald R. and Shareef, Abdul-Kader A. Eds. *Approaches to the Qurʾān*. London: Routledge, pp. 211–224.

Mohamed, Yasien. (1995) 'The Ethical Philosophy of al-Rāghib al-Isfahānī', *Journal of Islamic Studies*, 6:1, pp. 51–75. www.doi.org/10.1093/jis/6.1.51

Morgenstein Fuerst, Ilyse R. (2014) 'Locating Religion in South Asia: Islamicate Definitions and Categories'. *Comparative Islamic Studies*, 10:2, pp. 217–241. www.doi.org/10.1558/cis.30937

Mårtensson, Ulrika. (2001/2015) *The True New Testament: Sealing the Heart's Covenant in al-Tabari's History of the Messengers and the Kings*. Saarbrücken, GlobeEdit.

— (2005) 'Discourse and Historical Analysis: The Case of al-Ṭabarī's *History of the Messengers and the Kings*'. *Journal of Islamic Studies*, 16:3, pp. 287–331. www.doi.org/10.1093/jis/eti152

— (2008) '"The persuasive proof": a study of Aristotle's politics and rhetoric in the Qur'ān and in al-Ṭabarī's commentary'. *Jerusalem Studies of Arabic and Islam*, 34, pp. 363–420.

— (2009a) *Tabari*. Nizami, Farhad A. Ed. Makers of Islamic Civilization. Oxford Centre for Islamic Studies: Oxford University Press.

— (2009b) 'Through the Lens of Modern Hermeneutics: Authorial Intention in al-Ṭabarī's and al-Ghazālī's Interpretations of Q. 24:35'. *Journal of Qur'anic Studies*, 11:2, pp. 20–48. www.doi.org/10.3366/jqs.2009.0003

— (2011) '"It's the Economy, Stupid!" Al-Ṭabarī's Analysis of the Free Rider Problem in the ʿAbbāsid Caliphate'. *Journal of the Economic and Social History of the Orient*, 54 (2011), pp. 203–38. www.doi.org/10.1163/156852011X586822

— (2015) '"Islamic Order": Semeiotics and Pragmatism in the Muslim Brotherhood?' *Tidsskrift for Islamforskning/Journal of Islamic Research*, 9:1, pp. 35–57. www.doi.org/10.7146/tifo.v9i1.25344

— (2016) 'Al-Ṭabarī's Concept of the Qur'ān: A Systemic Analysis', in Klar, (ed.), *Exegetical Facets of Muḥammad b. Jarīr al-Ṭabarī*, special issue, *Journal of Qur'anic Studies*, 18:2, pp. 9–57.

— (2020) 'Prophetic Clarity: A Comparative Approach to al-Ṭabarī's Theory of Qur'anic Language, Rhetoric, and Composition', *Journal of Qur'anic Studies*, 22:1, pp. 216–268. www.doi.org/10.3366/jqs.2020.0417

— (2021) 'Through the Lens of the Qur'anic Covenant: Theories of Natural Law and Social Contract in al-Ṭabarī's Exegesis and History", in Weller, R. Charles & Emon, Anver M. Eds. *Reason, Revelation and Law in Islamic and Western Theory and History*, pp. 45–81. Palgrave Macmillan.

Nasr, Seyyed Hossein. (1993) *A Young Muslim's Guide to the Modern World*. Islamic Texts Society.

Nasser, Shady Hekmat. (2013) *The Transmission of the Variant Readings of the Qur'ān: The Problem of Tawātur and the Emergence of Shawādhdh*. Leiden: Brill. www.doi.org/10.1163/9789004241794

Nawas, John. (1996) 'The Miḥna of 218 A.H./833 A.D. Revisited: An Empirical Study'. *Journal of the American Oriental Society*, 116:4, pp. 698–708.

Netton, Ian. (2007/1980) 'Brotherhood Versus Imāmate: Ikhwān al-Ṣafā' and the Ismāʿīlīs'. In Netton, Ian. Ed. *Islamic Philosophy and Theology: Critical*

Concepts in Islamic Thought. Vol. IV: Eclecticism, Illumination and Reform. London: Routledge, pp. 5–15.

— (1996) *Seek Knowledge: Thought and Travel in the House of Islam*. Richmond: Curzon Press.

Neuwirth, Angelika. (2014) *Scripture, Poetry and the Making of a Community: Reading the Qur'an as a Literary Text*. Oxford: Oxford University Press & The Institute of Ismaili Studies.

Newby, Gordon D. (1989) *The Making of the Last Prophet: A Reconstruction of the Earliest Biography of Muhammad*. Columbia, S.C.: University of South Carolina Press.

Newman, Andrew J. (2000) *The Formative Period of Twelver Shīʿism: Ḥadīth as Discourse Between Qum and Baghdad*. London: Routledge.

Nöldeke, Theodor; Schwally, Friedrich; Bergsträsser, Gotthelf; Pretzl, Otto. (2013) *The History of the Qurʾān. Edited and Translated by Wolfgang H. Behn*. Leiden: Brill. www.doi.org/10.1163/9789004228795

O'Connor, Andrew J. (2018) 'Qur'anic Covenants Reconsidered: *mīthāq* and *ʿahd* in Polemical Context'. *Islam and Christian-Muslim Relations*, pp. 1–22. www.doi.org/10.1080/09596410.2018.1546042

Ohlander, Erik S. (2008). *Sufism in an Age of Transition: ʿUmar al-Suhrawardī and the Rise of the Islamic Mystical Brotherhoods*. Leiden: Brill. www.doi.org/10.1163/ej.9789004163553.i-364

Opwis, Felicitas. (2010) *Maṣlaḥa and the Purpose of the Law: Islamic Discourse on Legal Change from the 4th/10th to 8th/14th Century*. Leiden: Brill. www.doi.org/10.1163/ej.9789004184169.i-370

Pals, Daniel. (2014) *Nine Theories of Religion*. Oxford: Oxford University Press.

Park, Peter K. J. (2013) *Africa, Asia, and the History of Philosophy*. Albany: State University of New York Press.

Perho, Irmeli. (1995) *The Prophet's Medicine: A Creation of the Muslim Traditionalist Scholars*. Studia Orientalia 74. Helsinki: The Finnish Oriental Society.

Peters, F. E. (1968) *Aristotle and the Arabs*. New York: New York University Press.

Pinto, Karen. (2016) *Medieval Islamic Maps: An Exploration*. Chicago: The University of Chicago Press. www.doi.org/10.7208/chicago/9780226127019.001.0001

Pirbhai, M. Reza. (2009) *Reconsidering Islam in a South Asian Context*. Leiden: Brill. www.doi.org/10.1163/ej.9789004177581.i-370

Radtke, Bernd, O'Fahey, R. Seán, and O'Kane, John. (1996) 'Two Sufi Treatises of Aḥmad Ibn Idrīs'. *Oriens*. 35, pp. 143–178. www.doi.org/10.2307/1580547

Reinhart, Kevin A. (1983) 'Islamic Law as Islamic Ethics'. *Journal of Religious Ethics*, 11:2, pp. 186–203.

Retsö, Jan. (2003) *The Arabs in Antiquity: Their History from the Assyrians to the Umayyads*. Abingdon: Routledge.

— (2010) 'Arabs and Arabic in the Age of the Prophet', in Neuwirth, Angelika, Sinai, Nicolai, and Marx, Michael. Eds. *The Qurʾān in Context: Historical and Literary Investigations into the Qurʾānic Milieu*. Leiden: Brill, pp. 281–92. www.doi.org/10.1163/ej.9789004176881.i-864.64

Rippin, Andrew. (1988) 'Lexicographical Texts and the Qur'ān', in Rippin, Andrew. Ed. *Approaches to the History of the Interpretation of the Qur'ān*. Oxford: Clarendon Press, pp. 158–74. www.doi.org/10.31826/9781463234898-013

— (1994) '*Tafsīr Ibn ʿAbbās* and Criteria for Dating Early *Tafsīr* Texts', *Jerusalem Studies of Arabic and Islam*, 18, pp. 38–83.

Rock-Singer, Aaron and Brooke, Steven. (2018) 'Reading the ads in al-Daʿwa magazine: commercialism and Islamist activism in al-Sadat's Egypt'. *British Journal of Middle Eastern Studies*, pp. 1–18. www.doi.org/10.1080/13530194.2018.1500272

Robin, Christian Julien. (2015) 'Before Ḥimyar: Epigraphic Evidence for the Kingdoms of South Arabia', in Greg Fisher. Ed. *Arabs and Empires before Islam*. Oxford: Oxford University Press, pp. 90–126. www.doi.org/10.1093/acprof:oso/9780199654529.003.0003

Robinson, Chase. (2003) *Islamic Historiography*. Cambridge: Cambridge University Press.

Rosenthal, Franz. (1968) *A History of Muslim Historiography*. Leiden: Brill.

— (1989) 'General Introduction'. *The History of al-Ṭabarī. Volume I: General Introduction and From the Creation to the Flood*. New York: SUNY Press, pp. 5–154.

— (2007/1970) *Knowledge Triumphant: The Concept of Knowledge in Medieval Islam*. With an Introduction by Dimitri Gutas. Leiden: Brill.

Rubin, Uri. (1985) 'The "Constitution" of Medina: Some Notes'. *Studia Islamica*, 62, pp. 5–23. www.doi.org/10.2307/1595521

Rubin, Zeev. (1995) 'The Reforms of Khosro Anūshirwān'. Cameron, Averil. Ed. *The Byzantine and Early Islamic Near East. Volume III: States, Resources and Armies*. Princeton, NJ: The Darwin Press, Inc., pp. 227–297. www.doi.org/10.2307/j.ctv1b9f5rq.11

Sadeghi, Behnam and Bergmann, Uwe. (2010) 'The Codex of a Companion of the Prophet and the Qur'ān of the Prophet'. *Arabica*. 57:4, pp. 343–436. www.doi.org/10.1163/157005810X504518

Sadowsky, Yahya. (1997) 'The New Orientalism and the Democracy Debate'. Beinin, Joel and Stork, Joe. Eds. *Political Islam. Essays from Middle East Report*. London: I.B. Tauris, pp. 33–50. www.doi.org/10.1525/9780520917583-004

Saleh, Walid. (2008) 'A Fifteenth Century Muslim Hebraist: Al-Biqāʿī and His Defense of Using the Bible to Interpret the Qur'ān'. *Speculum*, 83, pp. 629–54. www.doi.org/10.1017/S0038713400014615

Salem, Maryam and Kheradmand, Maryam. (2016) 'A Survey of the Active Intellect in Transcendent Theosophy', *Comparative Islamic Studies*, 12:1–2, pp. 139–163. www.doi.org/10.1558/cis.35585

Saliba, George. (2007) *Islamic Science and the Making of the European Renaissance*. Cambridge, Massachusetts: MIT Press. www.doi.org/10.7551/mitpress/3981.001.0001

Sands, Kristin Zahra. (2006) *Ṣūfī Commentaries on the Qur'ān in Classical Islam*. London: Routledge. www.doi.org/10.4324/9780203019566

Sarrio, Diego R. (2011) 'Spiritual anti-elitism: Ibn Taymiyya's doctrine of sainthood (*walāya*)'. *Islam and Christian–Muslim Relations*, 22:3, pp. 275–291. www.doi.org/10.1080/09596410.2011.568812

Schoeler, Gregor. (2011[1996]) *The Biography of Muḥammad: Nature and authenticity*. London: Routledge. (*Charakter und Authentie der muslimischen Überlieferung über des Leben Mohammeds*. Berlin: Walter de Gruyter.)

— (2010) 'The Constitution of the Koran as a Codified Work: Paradigm for Codifying Hadīth and the Islamic Sciences?' *Oral Tradition*, vol. 25, no. 1, pp. 199–210.

— (2010b) 'The Codification of the Qur'an: A Comment on the Hypotheses of Burton and Wansbrough'. Neuwirth, Angelika, Sinai, Nicolai and Marx, Michael. Eds. *The Qur'ān in Context: Historical and Literary Investigations into the Qur'ānic Milieu*. Leiden: Brill, pp. 779–792.

— (1997) 'Writing and Publishing: On the Use and Function of Writing in the First Centuries of Islam'. *Arabica*, vol. 44, no. 3, pp. 423–435. www.doi.org/10.1163/1570058972582371

— (1992) 'Schreiben und Veröffentlichen: Zu Verwendung und Funktion der Schrift in den ersten islamischen Jahrhunderten'. *Der Islam*, 69, pp. 1–43. www.doi.org/10.1515/islm.1992.69.1.1

— (1989) 'Weiteres zur Frage der schriftlichen oder mündlichen Überlieferung der Wissenschaften im Islam'. *Der Islam*, 66, pp. 38–67.

— (1985) 'Die Frage der schriftlichen oder mündlichen Überlieferung der Wissenschaften im frühen Islam'. *Der Islam*, 62, pp. 201–230. www.doi.org/10.1515/islm.1985.62.2.201

Sedgwick, Mark. (2004) *Against the Modern World: Traditionalism and the Secret Intellectual History of the Twentieth Century*. Oxford: Oxford University Press.

— (2017) *Western Sufism: From the Abbasids to the New Age*. Oxford: Oxford University Press.

Shah, Mustafa. (2003a) 'Exploring the Genesis of Early Arabic Linguistic Thought: Qur'ānic Readers and Grammarians of the Kufan Tradition (Part I)', *Journal of Qur'ānic Studies*, 5:1, pp. 47–78. www.doi.org/10.3366/jqs.2003.5.1.47

— (2003b) 'Exploring the Genesis of Early Arabic Linguistic Thought: Qur'ānic Readers and Grammarians of the Basran Tradition (Part II)', *Journal of Qur'ānic Studies*, 5:2, pp. 1–47. www.doi.org/10.3366/jqs.2003.5.2.1

— (2004) 'The Early Arabic Grammarians' Contributions to the Collection and Authentication of Qur'ānic Readings: The Prelude to Mujāhid's *Kitāb al-Sab'a*', *Journal of Qur'ānic Studies*, 6:1, pp. 72–102. www.doi.org/10.3366/jqs.2004.6.1.72

— (2011) 'Classical Islamic Discourse on the Origins of Language: Cultural Memory and the Defense of Orthodoxy'. *Numen*, 58, pp. 314–343. www.doi.org/10.1163/156852711X562335

— (2013a) 'Introduction'. Shah, Mustafa. Ed. *Tafsīr: Interpreting the Qur'ān*, Vol. I: *Tafsīr*: Gestation and Synthesis, London: Routledge, pp. 1–157.

— (2013b) ‘Al-Ṭabarī and the Dynamics of *tafsīr*: Theological Dimensions of a Legacy’. *Journal of Qur’anic Studies*, 15:2, pp. 83–139. www.doi.org/10.3366/jqs.2013.0097
— (2016) ‘The Case of *variae lectiones* in Classical Jurisprudence: Grammar and the Interpretation of Law’. *International Journal of the Semiotics of Law*, 29, pp. 285–311. www.doi.org/10.1007/s11196-016-9461-1
— (2020) ‘Vocabulary of the Qur’an: Meaning in Context’. Shah, Mustafa and Abdel Haleem, Muhammad. Eds. *The Oxford Handbook of Qur’anic Studies*. Oxford: Oxford University Press, pp. 294–314.
Shalabī, Hind. (1980) Ed. ‘Introduction’. Ibn Sallām, Yaḥyā. *al-Taṣārīf li-tafsīr al-Qur ʾān mimmā ishtabahat asmāʾuhu wataṣarrafat maʿānīhi*. Tunis: al-Sharika al-Tūnisiyya li’l-Tawzīʿ.
Smith, Anthony D. (2003) *Chosen Peoples: Sacred Sources of National Identity*. Oxford: Oxford University Press.
Smith, Christian. (2003a) Ed. *The Secular Revolution: Power, Interests, and Conflict in the Secularization of American Public Life*. Berkeley: University of California Press
— (2003b) ‘Secularizing American higher education: the case of early American sociology’. In Smith (2003a), pp. 97–159. www.doi.org/10.1525/california/9780520230002.003.0002
Smith, Jonathan Z. (1998) ‘Religion, Religions, Religious’, in Taylor, Mark C. Ed. *Critical Terms for Religious Studies*. Chicago: The University of Chicago Press, pp. 269–284.
Sourdel, Dominique. (1959–1960) *Le vizirat ‘Abbāside de 749 à 936 (132 à 324 de l’Hégire)*. Damascus: Institut francais de Damas.
Spellberg, Denise A. (2013) *Thomas Jefferson’s Qur’an: Islam and the Founders*. New York: Alfred A. Knopf.
Springborg, Robert. (1991) ‘State-Society Relations in Egypt: The Debate over Owner-Tenant Relations’. *Middle East Journal*. 45:2, pp. 232–249.
Stenberg, Leif. (1996) *The Islamization of Science: Four Muslim Positions Developing an Islamic Modernity*. Stockholm: Almqvist & Wiksell International.
Stern, S. M. (1959) ‘Notes on Al-Kindī’s Treatise on Definitions’. *The Journal of the Royal Asiatic Society of Great Britain and Ireland*, No. 1–2, pp. 32–43. www.doi.org/10.1017/S0035869X00117666
Stewart, Devin. (2016) ‘Consensus, Authority, and the Interpretive Community in the Thought of Muḥammad b. Jarīr al-Ṭabarī’, Klar, Marianna. Ed. *Exegetical Facets of Muḥammad b. Jarīr al-Ṭabarī*. Special Issue. *Journal of Qur’anic Studies*, 18:2, pp. 130–179. www.doi.org/10.3366/jqs.2016.0241
— (2013) ‘Al-Ṭabarī’s *Kitāb Marātib al-ʿUlamāʾ* and the Significance of Biographical Works Devoted to “the Classes of Jurists”. *Der Islam*, 90 (2), pp. 347–375. www.doi.org/10.1515/islam-2013-0011
— (2004) ‘Muḥammad b. Jarīr al-Ṭabarī’s *al-Bayān ʿan uṣūl al-aḥkām* and the Genre of *uṣūl al-fiqh* in Ninth Century Baghdad‘. In Montgomery, James E.

Ed. *'Abbasid Studies: Occasional Papers of the School of 'Abbasid Studies, Cambridge 6–10 July 2002*. Leuven: Orientalia Lovaniensia Analecta 135, pp. 321–349.

Stolcke, Verena. (1995) 'Talking Culture: New Boundaries, New Rhetorics of Exclusion in Europe'. *Current Anthropology*, 36 (1), pp. 1–24. www.doi.org/10.1086/204339

Strobino, Riccardo. (2010) 'Avicenna on the Indemonstrability of Definition'. *Documenti e studi sulla tradizione filosofica medieval*, 21, pp. 113–163.

Sukidi. (2009) 'Naṣr Ḥāmid Abū Zayd and the Quest for a Humanistic Hermeneutics of the Qur'ān'. *Die Welt des Islams*, 49:2, pp. 181–211. www.doi.org/10.1163/157006009X458393

Sultany, Nimer. (2017) *Law and Revolution: Legitimacy and Constitutionalism After the Arab Spring*. Oxford: Oxford University Press. www.doi.org/10.1093/oso/9780198768890.001.0001

Syeed, Muhammad Sayyid. (1986) 'Islamization of Linguistics', *American Journal of Islamic Social Sciences*, 3:1, pp. 77–87. www.doi.org/10.35632/ajis.v3i1.2904

Taji-Farouki, Suha. (2004) Ed. *Modern Muslim Intellectuals and the Qur'an*. Oxford: Oxford University Press.

Thomas, David. (2007/1997) 'Abū Manṣūr al-Māturīdī on the Divinity of Jesus Christ'. In Netton, Ian R. Ed. *Islamic Philosophy and Theology: Critical Concepts in Islamic Thought*. Vol. III: Aristotelianism and Neoplatonism. London: Routledge, pp. 68–90. (Originally in *Islamochristiana*, 23 (1997), pp. 43–64.

Tottoli, Roberto. (2002) *Biblical Prophets in the Qur'ān and Muslim Literature*. New York: Routledge.

Toorawa, Shawkat. (2011) '*Sūrat Maryam* (Q. 19): Lexicon, Lexical Echoes, English Translation'. *Journal of Qur'anic Studies*. 13:1, pp. 25–78. www.doi.org/10.3366/jqs.2011.0004

Troupeau, Gérard. (1985) 'Les livres des définitions grammaticales dans la lexicographie arabe'. *Zeitschrift für arabische Linguistik*, 15: Studies in the History of Arabic Grammar – Proceedings of the First Symposium on the History of Arabic Grammar, Nijmegen, 16–19th April 1984, pp. 146–151.

— (1983) 'Le second chapître du "Livre des définitions d'al-Rummānī"'. *Al-Abḥath*, 31, pp. 121–138.

Tuncer, Ali Coskun. (2015) *Sovereign Debt and International Financial Control: The Middle East and the Balkans, 1870–1914*. Basingstoke: Palgrave Macmillan.

Vali, Abbas. (1993) *Pre-capitalist Iran: A Theoretical History*. London: I.B. Tauris. www.doi.org/10.5040/9780755612499

Van Ess, Joseph. (2017/1991) *Theology and Society in the Second and Third Centuries of the Hijra*. Vol. 1. Leiden: Brill. (German original: *Theologie und Gesellschaft im 2. und 3. Jahrhundert Hidschra: eine Geschichte des religiösen Denkens im frühen Islam*. 6 vols. Berlin: De Gruyter.)

— (1996) 'Verbal Inspiration? Language and Revelation in Classical Islamic Theology'. Wild, Stefan. Ed. *The Qur'ān as Text*. Leiden: Brill, pp. 177–194.

Vasalou, Sophia. (2009) 'Their Intention Was Shown by Their Bodily Movements": The Baṣran Muʿtazilites on the Institution of Language'. *Journal of the History of Philosophy*, 47:2, pp. 201–221. www.doi.org/10.1353/hph.0.0109
Verkaaik, Oscar. (2010) 'The cachet dilemma: Ritual and agency in new Dutch nationalism'. *American Ethnologist*. 37 (1), pp. 69–82. www.doi.org/10.1111/j.1548-1425.2010.01242.x
Van der Toorn, Karel and van der Horst, P. W. (1990) 'Nimrod before and after the Bible'. *The Harvard Theological Review*, 83:1, pp. 1–29. www.doi.org/10.1017/S0017816000005502
Versteegh, Kees. (1997) 'The Arabic Tradition' Van Bekkum, Wout; Houben, Jan; Sluiter, Ineke and Versteegh, Kees. *The Emergence of Semantics in Four Linguistic Traditions*. Amsterdam: John Benjamins Publishing Co., pp. 227–284.
— (1993) *Arabic Grammar and Qur'ānic Exegesis in Early Islam.* Leiden: Brill. www.doi.org/10.1515/islm.1990.67.2.206
— (1990) 'Grammar and Exegesis: The Origins of Kufan Grammar and the *Tafsīr Muqātil*'. *Der Islam*, 67:2, pp. 206–242.
Vishanoff, David R. (2011) *The Formation of Islamic Hermeneutics: How Sunnī Legal Theorists Imagined a Revealed Law*. Connecticut, New Haven: American Oriental Society.
Waldron, Jeremy. (2016) 'The Rule of Law'. *Stanford Encyclopaedia of Philosophy*, published June 22, 2016, https://plato.stanford.edu/entries/rule-of-law/, accessed December 3, 2016.
Wansbrough, John. (1977) *Qur'anic Studies: Sources and Methods of Scriptural Interpretation*. Oxford: Oxford University Press.
Watson, Andrew M. (2008/1983) *Agricultural innovation in the early Islamic world.* Cambridge: Cambridge University Press.
Watt, Montgomery W. (2007/1963) 'The Political Attitudes of the Muʿtazilah'. Netton, Ian (ed.). *Islamic Philosophy and Theology*. Vol. II: Revelation and Reason. London: Routledge, pp. 205–221.
Weismann, Itzchak. (2001) *Taste of Modernity: Sufism, Salafism and Arabism in Late Ottoman Damascus*. Leiden: Brill.
Weiss, Bernard G. (2010) *The Search for God's Law: Islamic Jurisprudence in the Writings of Sayf al-Din Al-Amidi*. Salt Lake City: The University of Utah Press.
— (1998) *The Spirit of Islamic Law*. Athens, GA: The University of Georgia Press.
— (1990) 'Covenant and Law in Islam'. Firmage, Edwin B., Weiss, Bernard G. and Welch, John W. Eds. *Religion and Law: Biblical-Judaic and Islamic Perspectives*. Winona Lake: Eisenbrauns, pp. 49–83.
Wild, Stefan. (2003) 'The Self-Referentiality of the Qur'ān: Sūra 3:7 as an Exegetical Challenge'. In McAuliffe, Jane D., Walfish, Barry D., and Goering, Joseph W. Eds. *With Reverence for the Word: Medieval Scriptural Exegesis in Judaism, Christianity, and Islam*. Oxford: Oxford University Press, pp. 422–436.
— ed. (2006) *Self-referentiality in the Qur'ān*. Weisbaden: Harrassowitz.

Wisnovsky, Robert. (2004) 'One Aspect of the Avicennian Turn in Sunnī Theology'. *Arabic Sciences and Philosophy*, 14:1, pp. 65–100. www.doi.org/10.1017/S0957423904000013

— (2003) *Avicenna's Metaphysics in Context*. London/New York: Ithaca.

— (2000) 'Notes on Avicenna's Concept of Thingness (*shay'iyya*)'. *Arabic Sciences and Philosophy*, 10, pp. 181–221. www.doi.org/10.1017/S0957423900000084

Zadeh, Travis. (2011) *Mapping Frontiers across Medieval Islam: Geography, Translation, and the ʿAbbasid Empire*. London: I.B. Tauris. www.doi.org/10.5040/9780755692859

Ziai, Hossein. (2007/1996) 'Shihāb al-Dīn Suhrawardī: founder of the Illuminationist school'. Netton, Ian R. Ed. *Islamic Philosophy and Theology. IV: Eclecticism, Illumination and Reform*. London: Routledge, pp. 36–64.

Zubaida, Sami. (2003) *Law and Power in the Islamic World*. London: I.B. Tauris. www.doi.org/10.5040/9780755612208

INDEX

A

Abī al-Najūd, ʿĀsim b., 60
Abaza, Mona, 2, 311, 312
Abbasid Caliphate, 140, 143, 154–161, 169, 185, 200–205, 223, 270, 308, 328
Abbasids, 154, 158, 159
Abbott of Cluny, 301
ʿAbd Allāh b. ʿĀmir, 60
ʿAbd al-Dār (family), 143, 150
ʿAbd al-Malik, Sulaymān b., 203
Abd al-Nasser, Gamal, 295, 296
Abdel Haleem, Muhammad, 25, 29, 37, 42, 45, 46, 65, 71, 72, 86, 139, 215, 268, 322, 323
ʿAbduh, Muḥammad, 292–294, 304
Abī Bakr, ʿĀʾisha bint, 184, 190
Abī Ṭālib, ʿAlī b., 56, 61, 141, 158, 162, 222, 256, 275
Abbott, Nabia, 140, 141
Abraham, 35, 48, 71, 72, 77, 90, 110, 111, 132, 135, 136, 139, 141, 142, 146, 153, 160, 172–175, 217–219, 230, 231, 247, 258, 265, 266, 269, 270, 284, 302, 326, 329, 330
al-abrār, 90
Abū Bakr, 56, 140, 149, 156, 191, 223, see also al-Ṣiddīq
Abū al-Dardāʾ, 59
Abū Dāwūd, 186
Abū Ḥanīfa, 158, 248, 249, see also Ḥanafī
Abū Zayd, 59, 307–309
Abu-Odeh, Lama, 296
ʿĀd (city), 88, 212
Adab, 211, see also Literature
Adam, 33–35, 39, 43, 46, 48, 64, 87, 88, 101, 107, 108, 114, 139, 141, 165, 173, 192, 217, 278, 308, 313, 323, 324, 330
administration, 4, 9, 10, 23, 24, 55, 106, 107, 120, 121, 124, 159, 160, 167, 178, 180, 181, 194, 200–213, 221, 222, 227, 237, 238, 239, 243, 253, 254, 286–288, 291–296, 237–331, 336, 348, see also tadbīr
ʿAdwān, 143
ʿAffān, Uthmān b., 6
al-Afghānī, Jamāl al-Dīn, 292–294, 347
Afghanistan, 298
Afsaruddin, Asma, 256, 299
Agger, Ben, 12, 13, 14, 344
ʿahd, 24, 25, 59, 64, 68, 73, 77, 98, 101, 109, 144, 151, 156, 196, 200, 203, 209, 220, 230, 235
ahl al-ʿaqd wa al-ḥall, 203, 241
ahl al-ḥadīth, 156, 169, 224, 227
ahl al-kitāb, 23, 74, 136, 137, 237, 265
ahl al-ṣiḥḥa wa al-salāma, 192
Aijub, Palmer, 161–164, 167
al-aʿjam, 206
Akbar (Moghul sultan), 160, 168, 285
akhbār, 2, 140
Akhbār al-ṭiwāl (history), 211
Akhtar, Shabbir, 309
Algeria, 290, 307
Alhassen, Leyla Ozgur, 5, 268
Alī al-Riḍā, 156, 223
ʿAlī, al-Ḥasan b., 281
ʿAlī, al-Ḥusayn b., 144, 145, 158, 193, 281
ʿAlid, 88, 158, 169, 223, 224
alms, 72, 75, 123, 132–134, 149, 204, 205, 214, 208, 214, 216, 240, 268, 288, see also ṣadaqāt
Altaie, Mohammad Basil, 315
ʿamal, 3, 85, 184, 274
amāna, 11, 24, 25, 27–28, 55, 126, 132, 146, 242, see also security
amārāt, 222
American Journal of Islamic Social Sciences, 311, 313

American University of Beirut, 314
Americanization, 312
al-Āmidī, Sayf al-Dīn, 264
al-Amīn, 156
amīr al-muʾminīna, 197, 198, see also Commander of Those who enact Security
amn, 11, 27, 28, 55, 118, 131, 152, 193, 278, 320, 322, see also security, and amāna
amthāl (examples), 2, 195, 222, see also mathal
analogical reasoning, 251, 253, 254, see also qiyās
analogy, 253, 254, see also qiyās
Anas', Mālik b., 158, 185, 186, 251, see also Mālikī
Anatolia, 159, 168, 290, 292
al-Andalus, 122, 158, 252
Andalusia, 122, 158, 252, 254, 301
Anglo-American, 20, 127
ansāb, 211
al-anṣār, 76, 77, 151, 152, see also Helpers to Victory
Antiquity, 19, 23, 52, 68, 232, 319
ʿAqaba, 150
al-ʿAqāʾid (treatise), 263, 296, see also creeds
ʿaqd, 24, 25, 124, 202, 203
ʿaql, 81, 170, 193, 202, 254
aqsām, 84, 91, see also oaths
Aquinas, Thomas, 103, 104, 118
Arabian Peninsula, 53, 55, 141, 211
Arabic (language), 2, 3, 8, 22, 24, 34, 39, 41, 43, 46, 49, 52–56, 62, 70, 78–80, 82, 84, 86, 117, 159, 170, 178, 181, 205, 216, 249, 251, 287, 301, 304, 305, 313–315, 319, 321, 322, 326, 327, 331, 342–344
Arabs, 3, 53–55, 58, 76, 80, 82, 116, 140, 143, 155, 191, 206, 211, 216, 217, 230, 285, 305, 321, 325, 326
Aramaic, 49, 50, 55, 148, 321
arbitrariness, 287
Aristotelian, 5, 35, 39, 102, 103, 252, 282
Aristotelianism, 35
Aristotle, 39, 40, 100, 104, 118, 127, 179, 201, 202, 252, 274
Arkoun, Mohamed, 307, 309
Aron (prophet), 172, 269
artisanship, 209
Asad b. ʿAbd al-ʿUzza, 144
Asad, Talal, 20, 21
aṣḥāb al-mashʾama, 81, 223
aṣḥāb al-maymana, 81, 223
aṣḥāb al-yamīn, 223
Ashʿarī, 113, 157, 186, 187, 235, 253, 271, 315, 332, 334, 337, see also Ashʿarism, and Ashʿarite
al-Ashʿarī, Abū Mūsa, 157, 187
Ashʿarism, 315, see also Ashʿarite
Ashʿarite, 106, 224, 276, 315, see also Ashʿarism, and Ashʿarī
Ashurbanipal, 53
Āṣim via Ḥafṣ (Reading), 6, 61
Aslam, Zayd b., 219, 231
Association of Muslim Social Scientists, 311
Assyria, 52, 53, 54, 230, 231
astronomy, 42, 180, 205, 206, 208
ʿAwf, ʿAbd al-Raḥmān b., 156
awliyāʾ, 139, 161, 162, 165, 165, 257, see also protective governors
awqāf, 160, see also waqf
āyāt muḥkamāt, 69, 175, 250, 251
āyāt mutashābihāt, 250
ʿAylān, Qays b., 223
Ayoub, Samy A, 160, 291
Ayyūbid dynasty, 168
al-Azhar university, 292, 293

B

Baalbaki, Ramzi, 44
Babylonian Exile, 53
El-Badawi, Emran, 49, 50
badīʿ, 46, 65, 84, 85, 86, 87, 322
Baghdad, 22, 23, 140, 156, 158, 159, 167, 185, 186, 228, 253
al-Bakkāʾī, Zayd b. ʿAbd Allāh, 141, 147, 150
balāgha, 2, 46, 65, 66, 68, 78, 79, 84, 86, 87, 97, 117, 179, 198, 322, 323, see also rhetoric
al-Bannā, Ḥasan, 294–297, 303–307, 315, 317, 337
Bannister, Andrew, 62
al-barr, 202
Basra, 59, 231, 233
al-Baṣrī, al-Ḥasan, 45
Bat-Sheva, 195

ba'th, 259
bāṭil (false), 108, 209
bay'a (pledged allegiance), 150, 235, 236
bayān, 45, 46, 55, 65, 66, 70, 72, 48, 79, 80, 84, 86, 87, 118, 170, 178, 234, 246, 251, 287, 321, 322, see also clear distinctions
Bedouin, 53, 191, 192, 212
Believers, 25, 63, 71, 270, 317
Bhaskar, Roy, 13
Bigliardi, Stefano, 2, 312, 315, 316
Blair, Eric, 32
Bourdieu, Pierre, 12, 15
Brahmins, 263
Britain, 292, 297, 298, 301
Brock, Fiona, 57
Brown, Jonathan, 186, 271
al-Bukhārī, 46, 185–187, 190, 191, 271, 304
al-burda, 280
burhān, 81, 172, see also Evidence
Butterworth, Charles, 179
Buyid (dynasty), 22, 157, 158, 185, 186, 200, 202, 256

C

Cadbury Research Library, 57
Caesar, 285
Cairo (city), 6, 45, 50, 60, 61, 158, 159, 254, 292, 293, 300, 305, 307, see also al-Qāhira
calculation, 91, 198, 207–210, 213, 234, 329
Caliphate, 9, 56, 100, 140, 143, 154, 155–159, 169, 185, 195, 210, 213, 217, 222, 223, 239, 270, 273, 285, 286, 290, 293, 294, 300, 308, 326, 328, 329, 336
Caliphs, 6, 56, 83, 100, 101, 140, 141, 154–159, 160, 169, 194, 197, 201–204, 211, 212, 216, 221, 223, 225, 227, 228, 237, 258, 270, 272, 291, 309, 317, 326, 331
Canon, 1, 7, 8, 49, 52–97, 117, 184, 186, 207, 253, 267, 270, 271, 303, 308, 321–323
canonization, 8, 186
Cantwell Smith, Wilfred, 20, 21, 24–26
Carter, Michael, 38, 44, 181, 224, 225
Caspian Sea, 157
chain of transmission, 58, 141, 184, 256, 257, 281, see also isnād
China, 122, 160
Christianity, 12, 17, 24, 49, 140, 148, 228, 270, 302, 317
clear distinctions, 34, 39, 44, 45, 51, 53, 55, 56, 66, 68, 70, 72, 79, 80, 94, 112, 125, 137, 171, 172, 174, 196, 216, 228, 229, 246, 249, 251, 277, 287, 313, see also bayān
College of Cardinals, 298
Commander of Those who enact Security, 193, 225, see also amīr al-mu'minīna
common good, 67, 68, 88, 105–112, 123, 133, 134, 165, 173, 193, 196–204, 210, 214–216, 237–243, 252–256, 274, 277, 280, 285, 287, 283, 296, 297, 325, 328, 329
Companions (the Prophet's), 47, 56, 57, 58, 70, 149, 150, 151, 154, 156, 157, 159, 164, 176, 189, 191, 193, 203, 211, 212, 216, 233, 258, 259, 285, 326, 333
Comparative Religion, 1, 20
Constantine, 21
Constantinople (city), 159
constitution, 8–10, 23, 25, 29, 100–111, 120, 121, 127–139, 150–157, 175–178, 181, 194, 197, 201, 210, 217, 233, 239, 243, 248, 262, 283–287, 291–299, 303, 308, 324
Córdoba, 158, 159
correct in speech and action, 73, 109, 174, 265, 266, 304, see also istaqim
correct path, 183, 184, 328, see also al-ṣirāṭ al-mustaqīm
correctness, 184, 220, 221, see also istiqāma
Cragg, Kenneth, 309
Creation, 5, 23, 24, 32, 34, 85, 88, 91, 94, 99–101, 106–108, 112–117, 131, 141, 173, 190, 207–213, 217–228, 234, 260–264, 272, 275, 276, 278, 282, 283, 295, 313, 322–330, 334, 335
creeds, 23, 50, 70–72, 92–94, 130, 153, 224, 241, 257, 263, 267, 270, 271, 282, 283, 296, 309, 320, 325, 331, 333, 334
Crone, Patricia, 106, 107, 161
Crusades, 252, 301

D
D'Agostino, Fred, 128, 129
al-dahr, 262
dahriyya, 262
Damascus, 59, 206, 254, 294
ḍarūriyyāt (necessities), 255
David (prophet), 49, 172, 195, 196, 198, 204, 208, 214, 215, 216, 244, 250, 330
Day of Judgement, 85, 183, 245, 325
Day of Standing, 89, 108, 137, 173, 174, 190, 249, 260, 275, 303
Day of the Account, 196
Day of the trial, 89
Daylam (region), 157, 158
de Certeau, Michel, 5–22, 25, 41, 51, 62, 120, 127, 176, 287, 289, 290, 305, 317, 319, 324, 337, 339
de Saussure, Ferdinand, 43, 313
debate, 3, 7, 8, 10, 20, 22, 31–33, 49, 56, 57, 58, 61, 64, 103, 154, 161, 185, 224, 254, 262, 264, 265, 270, 303, 306, 319, 333, see also munāẓara
definition, 2, 4, 18, 20, 21, 22, 35–42, 48, 61, 82, 86, 98, 103–105, 111, 117, 128, 129, 161, 182, 203, 222, 235, 238, 252, 267, 269, 286, 290, 294, 303, 305, 310, 318, 320, 321, 323, 339
Defoe, Daniel, 301
Delhi (city), 159, 261, 273, 279, 334
Déroche, Francois, 42, 56, 178
Derrida, Jacques, 12, 13
dhikr, 90, 100, 101, 163, 167
Dhū al-Marwā, 144
dīn, see judicial order
al-Dīnawarī, 211
disputation, 83, 87, 264, 265
diversity, 17, 22–25, 55, 99, 154, 155, 158, 169, 170, 176, 303, 311, 316, 317, 319
Divine writing, 5, 57, 70, 74, 83–89, 94, 108, 125, 131, 135–139, 147, 165, 169–175, 183, 192, 197, 207, 215, 218, 223, 228, 237, 255, 258, 259, 265, 268–270
divorce, 37, 184, 185, see also ṭalāq
dīwān (registry), 205
Donner, Fred, 25, 26, 49, 270, 347
Dummett, Michael, 32
al-dunyā, 67, 165, 237, 238, 253, see also nearest life
Duri, Abd al-Aziz, 54, 205, 211, 213
al-Durr al-manthūr (commentary), 116, 235, 236, 238, 241, 242
Dutton, Yasin, 6, 59

E
Early Mecca (period), 6, 7, 61, 71, 80, 81, 84, 89, 92–95, 110, 149, 267
Early Standard Arabic, 55, see also Arabic (language)
Egypt, 4, 47, 53, 68, 140, 230, 292, 294–297, 303, 304, 307, 308, 311, 316, 337
Egyptian, 1, 140, 193, 230, 292, 294–297, 304, 307, 308, 316
Elazar, Daniel, 127–129, 325
Elmarsafy, Ziad, 301, 302
Emon, Anver, 106, 107, 113
Enlightenment, 15, 17, 21, 168, 192, 302, 303, 316, 339
Epicurus, 128
epistemology, 13, 35, 102, 103, 232, 252, 26, 271, 272, 274, 312, 314
Ethiopia, 141
ethnicity, 290, 310
Europe, 9, 14, 19, 20, 25, 106, 291, 292, 301–303, 308, 309, 310, 311, 316, 336–340
Evans, John H., 16, 17, 306, 307, 312
Evans, Michael S., 16, 17, 306, 307, 312
Eve, 115
Evidence, 29, 56, 81, 111, 171, 172, 189, 236, 243, 258, 262, 263, 301, 315, 317
Exegesis, 9, 26, 33, 35, 42, 44, 47–49, 60, 63, 65, 70, 80, 82, 89, 98, 101, 113, 115, 118, 162, 178, 181, 232, 233, 242–244, 253, 256, 260, 286, 294, 319, 327, 328, 331, 332, 339, see also tafsīr
Exodus, 68
externalisation, 224

F
faḍl, 141, 180
faith, 3, 20, 21, 25, 63, 225, 307, 320, see also īmān
Fanon, Frantz, 299
al-Fārābī, 179, 180, 181, 184, 194, 200–202, 210, 244, 261, 269, 327, 329
al-Faruqi, Ismail Raji, 311, 312, 314
al-fāsiqūna, 27, 73, 74, 75, 76, 256, 263, see also The rebellious

fatāwā, 160
Fatimid dynasty, 158, 159
Fatimid Ismāʿīlī, 292
faylasūf, 194, see also philosopher
fayʾ, 204
Fedeli, Alba, 57
Fertile Crescent, 290
Ficino, Marsilio, 20
Finnis, John, 104, 105, 107, 111, 118
fiqh, 1, 4, 9, 42, 48, 93, 98, 102, 103, 161, 168, 175, 177, 178, 180, 181, 185, 232, 237, 241, 244, 245, 246, 247, 248, 249, 250–253, 261, 262, 264, 267, 271, 280, 312, 314, 317, 331–335, 339, see also jurisprudence
fitna, 69, 175, 251, see also internal strife
forms for conveying meaning, 46, 65, 82, 83, see also maʿānī
Foucault, Michel, 12
frame of government, 127, 129, 130, 135
France, 5, 293, 301, 302, 315
Frankfurt school, 12, 14
Friday prayer, 285
funūn (arts), 2
fuqahāʾ, 154, 249, 298, 342, see also legal scholars
al-Furqān bayna awliyāʾ al-Raḥmān wa awliyāʾ al-Shayṭān (treatise), 257
Furthest Day, 74, 108, 239, 263
al-Futūḥāt al-makkiyya (treatise), 257

G

Gabriel (angel), 148
Gadamer, Hans-Georg, 308
Garden, 58, 77, 82, 90, 91, 92, 122, 123, 136, 150, 163, 164, 187, 188, 191, 199, 207, 208, 223, 261, 263, 325, 329, see also paradise, and Janna
Gaus, Gerald, 128, 129
Geertz, Clifford, 41
genealogical records, 172, 194, 213–216, see also zabūr
geography, 205, 206, 211
al-ghayb, 282
ghayba, 185
al-Ghazzālī, 106, 161, 167, 168, 252–256, 271, 272, 279–282, 315, 332
ghāʾib (occult), 158
God
  amr (divine command), 4, 45, 82, 87, 89, 259, 274, 275
  amr wa nahy, 82, 87, 89
  attributes, 83, 84, 94, 263, 264, 271, 272, 286, 333, 334, see also ṣifāt
  as Creator, 36, 85, 92, 115, 171, 209, 214, 219, 220, 228, 257, 267, 282, 305
  decree, 259, 282, 283, 285, see also qaḍāʾ
  oneness, 4, 35, 45, 70, 71, 130, 150, 186, 187, 193, 224, 227, 241, 257, 262, 267, 270–274, 296, 302, 312, 320, 325, 333–335
  ḥuqūq Allāh, 106, 107, 108
  irāda (will), 257, 259
  khalīfa (successor), 33, 196, 204
  mashīʾa (will), 259
  his material blessings, 85, 88, 109, 183, 219, 220, 322
  names, 84, 94, 171
  al-nūr, 161, 162, 274, see also God's light
  qaḍāʾ, 259, see also decree
  sacred ḥadīth, 186, 187
  his Speech, 35, 45, 50, 86, 102, 109, 118, 244, 246, 259, 261, 265, 275, 276, 309, 332
  as The Light, 162, 187, 281
  his Throne (ʿarsh), 78, 170, 171, 207, 275, 282
Golshani, Mehdi, 315
Gospel, 26, 27, 49, 50, 69, 72, 77, 84, 135, 138, 148, 237, 249, 255, 256, 262, 269
governors, 74–78, 88, 101, 130, 131, 139, 142, 144, 159, 161–168, 176, 192, 202, 209, 219, 229, 238, 241–243, 257, 270, 271, 274, 279, 283, 324, 326, 331
Graeco-Islamic, 206
Gramlich, Richard, 101, 103, 323
Granada, 254
Greece, 18, 210, 289
Greek, 18, 22, 35, 39, 46, 53, 54, 118, 148, 205, 206, 230, 289, 319
Guardian Council, 298, 299
Guessoum, Nidhal, 315
Guiderdoni, Bruno Abd al-Haqq, 315
Gwynne, Rosalind Ward, 66, 81, 86, 89, 102, 146, 322, 323

H

ḥadd, 37–42, 182, 258, 259
ḥājiyyāt, 255
ḥajj, 184, 265, see also pilgrimage
ḥakama, 246, see also legal rulings
al-Hamdānī, 213
al-Hanafi, Sari, 314–316, 339
Ḥanafī, 124, 158–161, 221, 248, 251–253, 261, 271, 273, 279, 292, 334, see also Abū Ḥanīfa
Ḥanbal, Aḥmad b., 158, 185, 186, 227, see aso Ḥanbalī
Ḥanbalī, 158, 206, 227, 251, 254, 257, 258, see also Ḥanbal, Aḥmad b,
ḥanīf, 136, 269
al-ḥaqq, 28, 102, 103, 108, 114, 116, 138, 144, 164, 166, 167, 186, 187, 192, 202, 207, 209, 220, 323–325, see also True right
ḥaraka, 274
Hard Naturalism, 106, see also Muʿtazila
al-Ḥasafiyya, 294
ḥasan (good), 4, 182, 236, 265
al-Ḥasan b. Yaḥyā, 219, 231
Hāshim (family), 142, 144, 145, 147, 154, 159
Hashimite Abbasids, 194
Hatina, Meir, 241, 297, 298
Hawting, Gerald, 270
Ḥayyān, Jābir b., 42
Hebrew Bible, 21, 23, 49, 50, 53, 62, 68, 99, 102, 121, 127, 146, 149, 214, 231, 266, 321, see also Old Testament
Hell, 30, 67, 91, 209, 214
Helpers to Victory, 151, 152
Hermansen, Marcia K, 194, 261, 267, 279–286
hermeneutics, 4, 36, 93, 106, 178, 181, 224, 232, 241, 249, 250, 251, 287, 332, 333, see also uṣūl al-fiqh
Hermes, 35
Herodotus, 54
Ḥijāz, 53, 159
Hijrī (calendar), 212, 213
al-ḥikma, 86, 133, 161, 170, 191, 194–196, 199, 201, 210, 211, 226, 237, 274, 289, 328, 329, see also Just judgement
Ḥikmat al-ʿarsh (treatise), 275
Hilali, Asma, 57, 61
Ḥilf al-fuḍūl (Pact of Graciousness), 143, 144, 153
Himma, Kenneth Einar, 103, 104, 105, 107, 204
al-Ḥīra (city), 140, 141, 231
al-ḥisāb, 26, see also Reckoning
historicity, 230, 340
History, 1, 2, 5, 6, 9, 10–29, 39, 42, 46, 49, 52, 53, 62, 64, 98–101, 104, 118, 128, 140, 141, 144, 146, 152, 155, 157, 172, 178, 181, 205, 210–224, 230, 231, 270, 286, 290, 291, 298, 302, 304, 307–310, 316, 319, 324, 327, 330–332, 337
Hobbes, Thomas, 106, 128
Hobsbawm, Eric, 18, 19, 289, 319, 320
Hodgson, Marshal, 121, 142, 155, 156
Hūd, 48, 88, 151, 152
ḥudūd, 37, 38, 39, 44, 197, 210
ḥujja (authoritative proof), 60, 81, 86, 109, 172, 192, 265–267, 277
humility, 26, 84, see also al-tadhallul
Humphreys, Stephen, 98, 99, 100, 123, 217
Ḥusayn, Ṭāhā, 304, 305
hypocrites, 75, see also munāfiqūna

I

ʿibādāt, 247
Ibn ʿAbbās, 89, 157, 189, 222, 223, 232, 233, 234, 244, 284
Ibn al-ʿArabī, 35, 161, 162, 168, 257, see also Muḥyī al-Dīn
Ibn Fūrak, 42
Ibn Hishām, 140–153, 211, 217, 218, 325, 330
Ibn Māja, 186, 189
Ibn Manẓūr, 3, 4, 11, 26–28, 34, 36, 38, 46, 54, 55, 66, 108, 117, 155, 161, 221, 321
Ibn Masʿūd, 59
Ibn Mujāhid, 59, 60, 61
Ibn al-Muqaffaʿ, 154, 155, 194–200, 203, 204, 210, 253, 264, 269, 328, 329, 332
Ibn Qutayba, 206, 207, 210
Ibn Rushd Chair of Humanism and Islam, 308, 309
Ibn Saʿd, 58, 59, 156, 157, 176, 232, 326
Ibn Sīnā, 35, 39, 40, 162, 252
Ibn Taymiyya, 254, 257–261, 279, 333

Ibn Ṭufayl, 301
Ibn ʿUmar, 189, 191
Ibrāhīm, Isḥāq b., 225–228
ʿibratan, 229
idolatry, 29, 91, 219, 231, 267, 270
Idrīs, Aḥmad b., 100, 101
Iḥṣāʾ al-ʿulūm (treatise), 179, 200
Iḥyāʾ ʿulūm al-dīn (treatise), 168, 256
ijāra fāsida, 125, 200, see also voidable contract
ijmāʿ (consensus), 248, 252
ijrāʾ mijāh, 206
ijtihād (independent interpretation), 203, 204, 254
ikhlāṣ, 130, 238, 287, 325, see also Sincerity
ikhtilāf, 82, 163, 168, 170, 174, 248, 249, see also legal disagreement
ikhtilāf al-fuqahāʾ (treatise), 249
Ikhwān al-Ṣafā (movement), 169, 170
ʿilm, 2, 3, 4, 5, 22, 31–33, 41, 42, 46–48, 52, 129, 136, 156, 161, 166, 167, 168, 172, 174, 178, 180, 184, 185, 211, 244, 249, 264, 269, 270, 274, 275, 277, 289, 314, 318, 326, 335
al-ʿilm al-ilāhī (divine science), 180
al-ʿilm al-madanī, 180, 200, see also political science
al-ʿilm al-ṭabīʿī, 180, see also natural science
iltifāt, 65, 66
imāma, 202, 203, 263, see legitimate leadership
imams, 61, 156, 158, 161, 162, 169, 185, 186, 192, 193, 224, 240, 241, 242, 252, 256, 273, 274, 275, 281, 285, 326
īmān, 24, 25, 27, 28, 29, 31, 45, 74, 241, 242, 287, 320, 325, see also faith
immorality, 189
India, 122, 279, 290
Indonesia, 160
insān, 89
internal strife, 69, 175, 247, 251, 284, see also fitna
International Institute of Islamic Thought (IIIT), 311
International Islamic University, 311
Internet Encyclopaedia of Philosophy, 103
inzāl, 276, see also sending down
iqnāʿ, 180
Iran, 159, 164, 297, 298
Iranian, 290, 292, 298, 299
Iraq, 60, 140, 158, 205, 228, 231
Iraqi, 44, 140, 231, 233
Isaac, 172
Isḥāq, Muḥammad b., 140, 141, 143, 147, 150, 184, 211
Islamabad, 311
Islamisation, 2, 295, 297, 311–315, 316
Islamism, 296
Islamists, 308, 316
Islamization of Linguistics (article), 313
Islamization of science, 2, 311
Ismail, 110, 132, 141, 142, 172
Ismāʿīlī, 158, 159, 169, 170, 176, 252, 273, 292, 336
Ismailite merchants, 53
isnād, 184, see also chain of transmission
istaqim, 174, 265, see also correct in speech and action
al-Istibṣār fīmā ukhtulifa fīhi min al-akhbār (ḥadīth compilation), 185
istiḥsān, 161
istiqāma, 181, 182, 184, 220, 221, 265, see also correctness
istiṣlāḥ, 253
al-Itqān fī ʿulūm al-Qurʾān (treatise), 1, 61, 113
Izutsu, Toshihiko, 43, 308, 313

J

Jabal, Muʿādh b., 59, 156, 157, 186
Jacob, 172
Jacobites, 50
jadal, 83, 87, 89, 180, 264
Jaʿfarī (madhhab), 273
jahannam, see Hell
Jamāʿat-ī Islāmī, 295, 312
Jāmiʿ al-bayān ʿan taʾwīl āy al-Qurʾān (commentary), 26, 78, 234
jarīrī (madhhab), 60, 249, 251
Jāriya, Mujammiʿ b., 59
al-Jaṣṣāṣ, 253
al-Jawāhir fī tafsīr al-Qurʾān (commentary), 305
Jesus, 27, 48, 50, 51, 60, 137, 138, 153, 172, 174, 196, 226, 228, 237, 238, 247, 255, 258, 265–270, 273, 284, 308, 317,

321, 331, see also ʿĪsā b, Maryam, and Messiah
as ʿĪsā b. Maryam, 50, 60
as Messiah, 74, 137, 238
as son of mary, 27, 60, 137, 138, 226, 228, 237, 255, 273
as Word of God, 226–228, 273
Jewish, 1, 16, 19, 23, 26, 49, 55, 64, 65, 68, 144, 151–153, 230, 231, 240, 242, 249, 252, 255, 262, 330
Jews, 23, 25, 26, 55, 63, 64, 65, 72, 74, 93, 99, 102, 135–139, 152, 153, 160, 230, 238, 255, 257, 263, 265, 270, 309, 320, 333, 338, 339
jihād, 249
jizya, 26, 74, 160, 249, see also tax
Job, 172
Johansen, Baber, 124, 125, 127, 129, 177, 200, 231, 252, 325
Joseph, 4, 47, 48, 121, 258
Judaism, 24
judicial order, 23, 29, 34, 45, 73, 74, 79, 112, 130, 131, 132, 143, 150, 152, 166, 168, 174, 192, 193, 198, 202–204, 225–227, 237, 238, 247, 253–259, 262, 268, 278, 284, 285, 293, 320, see also dīn
judiciary, 8, 154, 155, 168, 173, 227, 237, 291, 326
junūd (soldiers), 275
Jurhum, 142, 145
jurisprudence, 1, 2, 4, 9, 42, 47, 48, 93, 98, 103, 104, 120, 121, 168, 178, 180, 185, 237, 238, 244, 271, 286, 319, 324, 327, 331 see also fiqh
Just judgement, 86, 133, 136, 147, 161, 170, 191, 194–196, 199, 210, 218, 226, 237, 243, 274, 275, 277, 289, 328
al-Juwaynī, 253, 271

K

Kaʿb, Ubayy b., 58, 59, 82, 156, 157
Kaʿba, 123, 141, 142, 144, 145, 146, 176, 192, 193, 217, 218, 239, 240, 241, 242, 326, 330
kabāʾir al-fisāq, 263
Kadi, Wadad, 99
kafara, 11, 25, 236
al-Kāfī fī ʿilm al-dīn (ḥadīth compilation), 185
kāfir, 25, 27, 28
al-Kāfirūna, 27, 74–76, 85, 87, 90, 229, 225, see also Rejecters of security
kāfirūna, 25, 27, 28, 74, 75, 76, 85, 87, 90, 229, 255
kalām, 9, 32, 34, 37, 42, 43, 80, 156, 168, 178, 180–182, 232, 259–264, 267–273, 308, 315, 333–335
al-Kalbī, Hishām b., 231
Kalīla wa Dimna (treatise), 194–196
Kamali, Mohammad Hashim, 24, 155, 303, 309
Kant, Immanuel, 128
Kara, Seyfeddin, 56, 58
Kern, Friedrich, 249
khabar (report), 81, 140
Khadīja, 148
Khalafallāh, Muḥammad Aḥmad, 305, 307, 308
Khalidi, Tarif, 140, 141, 211
khalq al-Qurʾān, 156, 224, 225, 272, 308
Khalwatiyya (ṭarīqa), 101
kharāj, 42, 121, 198, 204, 220, see also land tax
khaṭāba (oratory), 84, 180
al-Khaṭṭāb, ʿUmar b., 56, 155, 156, 157, 189, 191, 203, 205, 213, 216, 221, 222, 223, 258, 259
khiṭāb (divine address), 102, 240, 244, 257, 287, 294
khiṭāb ʿāmm, 241
Khomeini, Ayatollah, 298, 299
khulʿ, 184
khulaʿ (friendship), 271
Khurāsān (city), 156, 161, 164, 233
Khusraw Anūshirwān, 194, 212, 221
al-Khwārizmī, 42, 253, 262, 267
Kiel, 62
Kilāb, Zuhra b., 144
al-Kindī, 39, 42, 269
King Fuʾād I University, 305
Kitāb al-ʿaql wa al-jahl (chapter, ḥadīth compilation), 193
Kitāb al-burhān (treatise), 39
Kitāb al-masālik wa al-mamālik (treatise), 205
Kitāb al-tawḥīd (chapter, ḥadīth compilation), 186, 193
Kitāb al-tawḥīd (treatise), 271
Knauf, Ernst Axel, 55, 59

Kolkata (city), 279
Kraemer, Joel, 22, 23, 158, 179, 206
Kuala Lumpur (city), 311
Kufa (city), 59, 61, 233
kufr, 25, 73, 74, 137, 287, see also rejection of security
al-Kulaynī, Muḥammad b. Yaʿqūb b. Isḥāq, 185, 192–194, 298
al-Kutub al-arbaʿa, 185
al-Kutub al-sitta, 186

L
Lactantius, 21
Lakhm (dynasty), 140, 141, 231
Lambert, David, 21
land tax, 9, 23, 100, 121, 124, 197–200, 204–207, 210, 212, 219–222, 228, 249, 253, 283, 292, 324, 327, 329, 330, see also kharāj
language, 1, 2, 3, 8, 10, 16, 22–24, 31–66, 70, 78–82, 86, 103, 117, 159–162, 170, 171, 178–181, 184, 190, 194, 195, 202, 205, 216, 224, 232, 246, 251, 259, 272, 275, 278, 282, 283, 286, 287, 290, 298, 301–305, 307, 308, 313, 314, 319–322, 327, 328, 332, 334
Late Mecca (period), 6, 7, 62, 87, 94, 96, 110, 235, 263, 267
Laurence, Stephen, 31, 32, 37, 40, 41, 47
al-Lawḥ, 282
lawmaker, 157, 158, 169, 176, 194, 203, 287, 291, 336
lawmaking, 106, 168, 197, 204, 244, 253, 296, 327, 332
legal disagreement, 163, 164, 168, 169, 170, 174, 175, 177, 196, 248, 249, 280, 332, see also ikhtilāf
legal rulings, 4, 26, 156, 172, 246
legal scholars, 154–156, 160, 167, 170, 176, 177, 185, 201, 203, 205, 208, 223–225, 244, 250, 252, 253, 259, 280, 291, 292, 294, 298, 299, 326, 329, 331, 336, see also fuqahāʾ
legitimate leadership, 202, 263, 329, see also imāma
lingua franca, 55, 159
Linguistics, 2, 31, 38, 42–49, 73, 85, 178–181, 184, 232, 252, 265, 269, 286, 313, 314, 317, 321, 322, 324, 327, 328, 331, 339
Lisān al-ʿArab (dictionary), 3, 4, 11, 26, 28, 29, 34, 36, 38, 46, 54, 81, 91, 108, 155, 161, 166, 221
Literature, 1, 24, 25, 42, 49, 51, 62, 68, 93, 159, 205, 211, 230, 231, 262, 270, 303, 304, 305, 307, 316, 337
Locke, John, 32, 106, 128, 142, 301, 302, 310, 337
Logic, 9, 48, 79, 80, 81, 156, 180, 181, 227, 252, 271, 332
Lowin, Shari, 230, 231
Lowry, Joseph, 154, 155, 197, 326
Lumbard, Joseph, 99

M
maʿānī, 46, 65, 82, 83, 84, 86, 87, 322, see also forms for conveying meaning
mabādiʾ (principles), 180
madhāhib, 155, 158, 167, 248, 250, 251, 254, see also schools of law
madhhab, 60, 113, 227, 248–250, 253, 273
al-madhhab al-jarīrī, 249
madhkūr, 90
al-Madīna al-fāḍila, 201
Mafātīḥ al-ghayb (commentary), 235
Mafātiḥ al-ʿulūm (treatise), 42
maḥabba (affection), 271
al-Maḥallī, Jalāl al-Dīn, 116, 235
al-Mahdī, Muḥammad, 140, 158, 169
Mahdi, Muhsin, 201
Majmūʿ fī al-siyāsa (treatise), 201
al-mājūs, 262, see also Zoroastrians
māl, 27, 92, 144, 215, 254, 258
Malaysia, 160, 311, 312
Mālikī, 158, 251, 254, see also Anas', Mālik b
Mamlūk, 3, 50, 159, 206
Man lā yaḥḍuruhu al-faqīh (ḥadīth compilation), 185
al-Manār (magazine), 294
maqāṣid, 107, 254, 314, 332, 333
Maqāṣid al-Qurʾān al-karīm (treatise), 296, 303
Margolis, Eric, 31, 32, 37, 40, 41, 47
maʿrifa, 45, 161, 162, 167, 225
Marogy, Amal E, 44, 181, 182
Marriage contract, 38, 127, 249, see also nikāḥ
Marsham, Andrew, 54, 55, 100

Mårtensson, Ulrika, 4, 23, 26, 28, 42, 49, 51, 53, 60, 63, 86, 100–103, 116, 144, 149, 171, 212, 222, 228, 232, 249, 296, 315
Marwān (family), 154
Marxism, 13, 14
Marxist, 11, 13, 14, 18, 41, 122, 295, 312
Mary (Maryam), 27, 50, 60, 137, 138, 215, 226, 228, 237, 255, 268, 269, 273
masjid, 73, 77, 144, 145, see also mosque
maṣlaḥa, 106, 237, 240, 252–257, 261, 274, 280, 283, 284, 294, 299, 332, 335, see also common good
al-Masʿūdī, 99
maʿṣūm, 240
mathal, 82, 83, 87, 89, 162, 165, 196, see also amthāl
mathematics, 179, 206
al-Māturīdī, ʻAbū Manṣūr, 34, 271, 334, 359
mawāʿiẓ (warnings), 2
mawālī, 140, 147, 162
al-Māwardī, 155, 202, 203, 204, 210, 237, 239, 329
maẓlūm, 144
al-Maʾmūn (caliph), 156, 169, 223, 224, 225, 227, 228, 270, 272, 309, 317, 331
Mecca (city), 6, 7, 59, 61–64, 68, 71, 74, 80, 81, 84, 87, 89, 92, 93, 94, 95, 110, 116, 123, 141–151, 159, 160, 193, 218, 235, 239, 253, 255, 257, 263, 267, 268, 281, 311
medicine, 200, 206, see also al-ṭibb
Medina (city), 6, 7, 26, 58, 59, 61–65, 68, 71, 76, 92, 94, 96, 110, 140, 144, 150, 151–155, 159, 184, 192, 193, 203, 221, 231, 234, 237, 239, 242, 247, 253, 255, 268
Melkite, 153
mercy, 65, 148, 261, 268, 280, see also al-raḥma
Mesopotamia, 218, 230, 231
metaphysics, 42, 179, 180, 262, 271, 272, 274, 279, 280, 286, 312
methods, 1, 6, 12, 14, 41, 49, 50, 57, 208, 243, 252, 253, 256, 284, 295, 304, 305, see also minhāj, and ṭuruq
Middle Mecca, 6, 61, 64, 68, 71, 95, 268
Midyan (city), 88
Migrants, 76, 151, 152, 189, see also al-muhājirūna
al-miḥna, 156, 224
al-milal, 201
minhāj, 27, 175, 249, 250, see also methods, and ṭuruq
mīthāq, 24, 25, 28, 31, 98, 136, 147, 166, 20, 217
Mongol, 159
monks, 72, 74
monotheism, 70, 71, 72
monotheists, 25, 72
Moses, 43, 48, 64, 66–68, 88, 90, 125, 147, 148, 149, 171, 174, 215, 247, 258, 265, 276, 284, 302
mosque, 144, 160, see also masjid
Mossadegh, Mohammad, 298
movement, 12, 17, 18, 155, 156, 169, 227, 274, 290, 295, 298, 303, 340
muʿāmalāt (interactions), 247
Muʿāwiya, 144, 191
al-mufliḥūna, 76, 166
Mughal (dynasty), 24, 159, 160, 273, 279, 290, 293, 327
al-muhājirūna, 74, 76, 77, 151, 152, see also Migrants
muḥāl (impossible), 181, 182
Muḥyī al-Dīn, 168, see also Ibn al-ʿArabī
mujaddidiyya, 279, 280, 281, 294, 334
mujrim (enactor of offence), 66, 75
mujtahid, 160, 168
mukhāṭab, 244, 246, 258, 259
mukhāṭib, 244
munāfiqūna, 75, 76, see also hypocrites
munāẓara, 264, see also debate
al-Munqidh min al-ḍalāl (treatise), 256
Murra b. ʿAwf (family), 143, 152
Murra, Taym b., 143, 144
muṣannafāt, 184
mushabbiha, 263
mushāhada (observation), 200
al-mushrikūna, 71–74, 77, 87, 233, see also Unbelievers
Ṣaḥīḥ Muslim (ḥadīth compilation), 186, 261
Muslim Brotherhood, 294, 295, 296, 297, 303, 308, 312, 336, 337
Muslim Social Scientists, 311
Muslims, 26, 50, 99, 102, 160, 191, 197, 205, 216, 235, 236, 239, 240, 263, 279,

284, 285, 293, 295, 300, 304, 309, 310, 311, 316
Musnad (ḥadīth compilation), 186
mustaqīm, 85, 181, 182, 183, 184, 265, 328, see also istiqāma
mutakallimūna, 262, see also theologians
Muʿtazila, 106, 224, 263, 272, 308, 309, 315, 334, 337, see also Hard Naturalism
Muʿtazilī, 113, 235, 253, 272, 334, see also Muʿtazila
al-Muṭṭalib (family), 140, 144, 147
al-muttaqīna, 27, 73–75, 77, 78, 87, 256, see also those who fulfil their obligations
al-Muwaṭṭaʾ (ḥadīth compilation), 185, 186
al-muzāraʿa, 124, see also sharecropping
muʾmin, 24, 27, 28, 66, 73, 74, 75, 76, 77, 78, 85, 87, 131, 152, 197, 198, 214, 215, 230

N

nabaʾ (announcement), 212
nabī malik (Prophet-King), 258
nafs, 27, 39, 89, 114, 131, 254, 260, 276
al-nafs al-lawwāma (blameworthy person), 89
Najrān (city), 153, 238
Nāmūs, 148
Naqshbandī, 261, 273, 279, 294, 334, 335
narrative accounts, 61, 82, 83, 142, 267, see also qiṣaṣ
al-Nasāʾī, 186, 188
nasl (progeny), 254
Naṣr Ḥāmid Abū Zayd, 307
Nasr, Seyyed Hossein, 311, 312
Nasser, Shady Hekmat, 56, 58, 59
al-Nasʾa (family), 143
nationalism, 18, 289, 290, 294, 295, 312, 319, 339
natural law theory, 8, 9, 23, 98–107, 111–120, 127, 129, 130, 139, 217, 287–300, 305, 323–325, 329, 330, 333, 339
natural science, 180, 181, 305, 315, 317, 337, see also al-ʿilm al-ṭabīʿī
Nawas, John, 156, 224, 227
naẓīr, 45, 82
nearest life, 67, 90, 139, 165, 238
neo-Assyrian (empire), 231
neo-Muʿtazilite, 308
Neoplatonism, 35, 36, 39, 43, 162, 168, 256, 257, 273, 274, 276, 279, 280, 286, 312, 334, 335
Nestorians, 50
Netherlands, 301, 308
Netton, Ian, 170
Neuwirth, Angelika, 62–66, 70, 71
New Testament, 23, 49, 50, 53, 68, 99, 321
nikāḥ, 249, see also Marriage contract
Nimrod, 218, 219, 231, 330
Nimrud (city), 231
Nineveh (city), 231
Niẓāmiyya college, 167
Noah, 48, 88, 99, 172, 174, 212, 218, 245, 247, 265, 284, 291
Nöldeke thesis, 62, 65, 97, 322
non-Muslim, 26, 160, 254, 284, 316, 329, 333
North Africa, 45, 158, 159, 160, 290, 309
North America, 127, 301

O

O'Connor, Andrew, 98, 99
O'Fahey, R. Séan, 100
O'Kane, John, 100
Oath of Allegiance, 100, 235, 236, 296
oaths, 54, 55, 61, 66, 80, 81, 84, 91, 94, 100, 101, 188, 189, 193, 223, 230, 235, 236, 323, see also aqsām
obedience, 24, 26, 84, 88, 99, 218, 220, 240, 241, 243, 258, 263, 280, 331, 333
Old Testament, 21, 62, see also Hebrew Bible
ontology, 13, 31, 35, 36, 102, 162, 232, 252, 262, 271, 273, 274, 312, 334
Opwis, Felicitas, 252, 253, 255, 263, 333
Organisation of the Islamic Conference, 300
Orientalism (book), 289, 301
Orthodox, 19, 49, 153
Orwell, George, 32
Ottoman, 159, 160, 168, 273, 290, 291, 292, 293, 302, 327, 336
Ottoman Empire, 160, 168, 273, 290–293, 302, 327, 336
Ottomans, 159
Oxford University, 62, 301

P

Pagan, 55, 71, 140, 149, 193, 273
Pahlavi (dynasty), 194, 297, 298
Paradise, 58, see also Garden
Paris (city), 12, 14, 26, 27, 28, 46, 49, 61, 63, 79, 81, 89, 104, 115, 118, 128, 149, 192, 228, 237, 243, 256, 292, 308, 329
peasants, 9, 121, 122, 124, 125, 127, 177, 191, 208, 221, 231, 283, 287, 296, 299, 325, 327, 336
Pegasus, 32
people of the divine writing, 74, 135, 137, 138, 269, see also ahl al-kitāb
Pharaoh, 66, 67, 69, 88, 91, 124, 125, 126, 299
Philippines, 160
philosopher, 12, 13, 18, 20, 22, 23, 35, 39, 42, 118, 162, 179, 193–195, 201, 206, 252, 272, 273, 316, 334, 336
philosophy, 2, 9, 18, 19, 22, 23, 31, 35, 37, 42–48, 103, 128, 160, 178179, 201, 205, 210, 252, 262, 271, 289, 301, 303, 308, 314, 315, 324, 332, 333
Physics, 42, 179, 180, 206, 262, 271, 272, 274, 279, 280, 286, 312, 315, 317
pilgrimage, 123, 141–146, 160, 184, 192, 247, 265, 280, 326, see also ḥajj
pístis (persuasion), 54
place of prostration, 73, 144, 145, see also masjid
Plato, 118, 179, 274
Platonism, 20, 257, 273
Pococke, Edward, 301, 302
political community, 99, 100, 152, 201, 202, 259, see also al-umma
political science, 9, 178, 180, 181, 194, 200, 243, 244, 259, 261, 286, 310, 319, 328, 329, 332, 333, 339, see also al-ʿilm al-madanī, and siyāsa
polity, 23, 27, 48, 56, 63, 81, 102, 105, 106, 117, 127, 129, 132–139, 141, 152, 153, 163, 174, 176, 180, 202, 210, 212, 215, 268, 284, 288, 320, 333
polysemy, 84, 251
polytheism, 71, 270, see also shirk
polytheists, 72, 230, 270
Pope, 298
positivism, 13, 14, 106, 311, 312, 314, 316, see also Soft Naturalism
postmodernism, 12, 13
poststructuralist (movement), 12, 13, 16, 18, 19, 22
prophecy, 2, 4, 5, 7, 22, 35, 46, 48, 50, 51–53, 57, 79, 129, 135, 139, 141, 147, 149, 153, 154, 176, 201, 202, 211, 217, 218, 222, 223, 230, 237, 263, 319, 321, 326, 330
Prophet's Biography, 6, 9, 42, 62, 120, 129, 140–154, 160, 175, 176, 160, 175, 176, 202, 211, 212, 217, 218, 270, 325, 327, 330, see also Sīra
Prophetic tradition, 2, 9, 42, 178, 185, 206, 233, 242
prosperity, 76, 133, 166, 179, 180, 202, 210, 286, 287, 288, 300, 327, 332
protective governors, 74, 78, 88, 131, 139, 161, 164–167, 176, 192, 202, 209, 257, 258, 271, 274, 279, see also walāya
protective governorship, 74, 78, 88, 164, 166, 176, 192, 257, 271, 279, see also walāya
Protestants, 17, 21, 301, 303
Psalms, 214, 215, 216, see also zabūr, and Psalter
Psalter, 84, see also Psalms
public welfare, 106, 253, 295, 296, see also maṣlaḥa

Q

Qādiriyya ṭarīqa, 257
al-Qāḍī al-Nuʿmān, 169
al-Qāhira (city), 158, see also Cairo
Qajar (dynasty), 279, 293, 297, 298
al-Qarāfī, 254
Qaṭʿ al-sāriq, 249
Qatāda, 45, 50, 157, 233
qawāʿid, 254
qawānīn (laws), 180, 200
al-qawānīn al-kulliyya, 200
qawm, 23, 38, 54, 81, 88, 126, 268
qirāʾāt, 6, 58, 59
qiṣaṣ, 2, 82, 83, 89, 195, 201, 267, see also narrative accounts
al-qitāl, 116, 151
qiyās, 251, 253, 254, see also analogy
al-Qummī, Ibn Bābawayh, 185
Quraysh, 110, 131, 142–150, 152, 154, 159, 192, 203, 326, 330
qurba (closeness), 161
qurrāʾ (Qurʾān readers), 60, 156

Quṣayy, 142, 143, 146, 150

R
rabbāniyyīn, 5, 57, 237–239, 277
Rabbinate, 16
rabbis, 72, 74
Radtke, Bernd, 100, 101
raḥma, 222, 228, 261
al-raḥma, 261, see also mercy
al-ra'iyya (the flock), 197
al-Rashīd, Hārūn, 156, 203
Rāshid, Ma'mar b., 188, 219, 231, 233
rasūl, 34, 43, 44, 46, 73, 74, 112, 145, 152, 156, 246, 258, 277
rasūl 'abd (Messenger-Servant), 258
rationalism, 106, 205
al-Rāzī, Muḥammad Fakhr al-Dīn, 113, 115, 117, 235–238, 241–243, 252, 297, 331
Reckoning, 26, 84, see also al-ḥisāb
Rejecters of security, 27, 90, 134, 138, 229, 225
rejection of security, 73, 137, 218, see also kufr
Retsö, Jan, 49, 52–55, 66, 68, 82, 117, 191, 230, 231, 321, 325
rhetoric, 1, 2, 5, 22, 23, 29, 35, 44, 46, 48, 52, 65, 66, 72, 79, 83, 84, 86, 94, 98, 101, 102, 113, 117, 129, 178, 179, 180, 196, 212, 228, 233, 266, 285, 287, 319, 321, 322, 324, 333
ribā, 133, see also usury
Riḍā, Rashīd, 293, 294
rifāda (food supply), 143
risāla, 35, 43, 194, 197, 251, 253, 274
al-Risāla (treatise), 251
Risāla fī al-ḥudūth (treatise), 274
Risāla fī ḥudūth al-'ālam (treatise), 35
Risāla fī al-ṣaḥāba (treatise), 194, 197
rizq, 67, 85, 111, 126, 167, 220, 223, 229, 272, 277, see also sustenance
Rizvi, Sajjad, 35, 36
Robert of Ketton, 301
Robinson Crusoe (novel), 301
Roman, 21, 35, 46, 153, 211, 230, 289, 293, 319
Rome (city), 18, 210, 289, 292
Rosenthal, Franz, 3, 5, 211, 212, 213, 217, 249
Rousseau, Jean-Jacques, 128
al-rūḥ al-a'ẓam, 275

S
sab'at aḥruf, 58, 59, 61, 70, 82, 83
sabīl, 74, 77, 89, 90, 133, 166, 196, 201, 230, 246, 274
Sacred Enclave, 282
ṣadaqāt, 75, 132, 133, 149, see also alms
Sadeghi, Behnam, 56
al-Ṣādiq, Ja'far, 156, 158, 162, 256
Ṣadra, Mullā, 162
Safavid (dynasty), 35, 159, 273, 279, 297, 334
Ṣafwān (family), 143
Ṣaḥīḥ (ḥadīth compilation), 46, 261
Said, Edward, 289, 301
salaf, 259, 293, 294
al-salaf al-ṣāliḥ, 293
salafiyya, 294
ṣalāḥ, 195, 197, 253
Saliba, George, 205-207, 308, 309, 317, 329
Ṣāliḥ, 48, 88, 125, 126
Saljuq dynasty, 158, 167
Sallām, Yaḥyā b., 45
al-Sāmirī, 68
Sanaa (city), 56, 57
al-Ṣan'ānī, 'Abd al-Razzāq, 50, 219, 234, 235, 237, 240
al-Sarī, 216, 222
Sassanians, 141, 155, 205, 216
Sassanid (empire), 121, 124, 140, 155, 194, 205, 206, 210, 212, 221, 231, 284, 308, 328, 329
Satan, 64, 88, 133, 134, 214, 239, 242, 257
Saudi Arabia, 291, 312
Schacht, Joseph, 248, 249
Schoeler, Gregor, 42, 59, 140, 184, 185, 232
schools of law, 158, 176, 248, 250, 251, 252, 258, 332, see also madhāhib
security, 11, 27–29, 45, 54–56, 66–69, 77, 80, 81, 90, 94, 108–112, 115, 123–126, 131–142, 147, 152, 166, 167, 172, 174, 175, 183, 187, 193–202, 207, 208, 217–219, 226, 228–230, 239, 247, 251, 255, 259, 260, 263, 265, 266, 270, 275, 277, 278, 286, 287, 293, 300, 303, 320, 322, 326, 330, see also amn, and amāna

sēmeîon (sign), 102
Semitic language, 49, 56, 62, 301, 303
sending down, 83, 276
Seth, 35
seven aḥruf, 82, 83, see also readings
Seven Earths, 190
al-sha'b (constituents), 59
Shāf'ī school of law, 186
al-Shāfi'ī, Muḥammad b. Idrīs, 158, 248, 249, 251
Shāh Walī Allāh of Delhi, 261
shar', 202, 259, 264, 278
sharecropping, 9, 124, 191, 200, 249, see also al-muzāra'a
Sharḥ futūḥ al-ghayb (commentary), 257
al-shāri' (legislators), 238
Sharī'a, 1, 2, 102, 174, 180, 239, 246–249, 253, 261, 264, 281, 293–298, 299, 304, 308, 332, 333, 335, 336
al-Shāṭibī, Ibrāhīm b. Mūsā, 254, 255, 263
shaykh, 100, 101, 113, 160, 279, 281, 297
Shī'a, 158, 159, 185, 256, 273, 279
Shī'ī, 35, 56, 58, 61, 113, 161, 162, 169, 170, 176, 185, 186, 192, 235, 242, 252, 256, 273, 275, 277, 278, 292, 299, 307, 323, 326, 328, 334, 336
Shiraz (city), 273, 334
shirk, 267, 270, 287, 334
Shu'ayb, 48, 88, 200
shūrā, 203, 259, 295
shu'ūbiyya (movement), 155
al-Sibā'ī, Muṣṭafā, 297
Sībawayhi, 38, 44, 181–184, 265, 322, 328
al-Ṣiddīq, 149
ṣifāt, 264, 271, 272, see also God's attributes
ṣifāt al-dhāt, 272, see also God's attributes
signs, 7, 27, 40, 43, 44, 53–56, 63, 69, 81, 88, 102, 103, 107, 109, 123–125, 129, 138, 162, 166, 171, 173, 175, 207, 208, 234, 245, 250, 251, 255, 266, 267, 276, 283, 300, 313
Sikh, 160
silsila, 281
Sinai, Nicolai, 7, 56, 57, 62, 65, 68, 69, 70, 71, 72, 267
Sincerity, 36, 130, 131, 132, 238, 267, 272, 287, 300, 325, see also ikhlāṣ
Sind (region), 159, 195
Sīra, 6, 42, 62, 140, 211, see also Prophet's Biography
al-Sīra al-nabawiyya (manuscript), 140
Ṣirār, 222
ṣirāṭ mustaqīm, 265, see also correct speech and action
al-ṣirāṭ al-mustaqīm, 85, 183, 184, 328, see also correct path
Sirhindī, Aḥmad, 279
siyar, 211
siyāsa, 9, 178, 181, 201, 210, 219, 234, 244, 253, 259, 283, 328, see also political science
Smith, Jonathan Z, 20, 21
social contract, 5, 8, 9, 10, 23, 29, 98, 100–107, 111, 112, 120, 121, 128–131, 135, 139, 141, 146, 153, 175, 178, 181, 189–194, 203, 210, 217, 233, 243, 244, 262, 271, 285–287, 294, 301, 302, 310, 324–336
Soft Naturalism, 106, see also positivism
Solomon, 48, 172, 258
soothsayer-oracle, 240
Spanish Reconquista, 301
Spellberg, Denise, 301
Stanford Encyclopedia of Philosophy, 31, 35, 128
statecraft, 2, 201, 283, 284, 286, 289, 308
Stenberg, Leif, 2, 311, 312
Strasbourg, 62
Stubbe, Henry, 301, 302
Sufi, 35, 99, 100, 101, 160–163, 167, 168, 176, 252, 256–261, 273, 274, 279–281, 286, 292, 294, 295, 312, 326, 328, 333–335
Sufism, 160, 161, 167, 256, 257, 312, 335
Sulaymān, Muqātil b., 33, 34, 36, 45, 50, 113, 233
sultan, 158, 159, 160, 168, 169, 285, 291, 292, 326, 334, 336
sunan, 200, 261
Sunnī, 33, 56, 58, 61, 158, 159, 162, 167, 169, 176, 185, 186, 192, 241, 242, 248, 251, 252, 256, 271–279, 292, 293, 297, 299, 307, 323, 328
Sunnī Mamlūk, 159
sustenance, 9, 67, 85, 88, 90, 91, 109–112, 117, 123, 126, 131, 164, 174, 187,

208, 219–223, 226, 229, 259, 266–268, 277, 286, 325, 335
al-Suyūṭī, Jalāl al-Dīn, 1, 2, 5, 9, 22, 58, 61, 113, 116, 233, 235, 236, 238, 241, 242
Syeed, Sayyid Muhammad, 313
syllogism, 102
Syria, 158, 168, 252

T

ṭabaqāt, 211
al-Ṭabarī, Muḥammad b. Jarīr, 8, 26, 42, 50, 52, 60, 66, 79–89, 93, 94, 99–101, 113–118, 141, 144, 149, 155, 170, 183, 184, 210–213, 216, 217–225, 227, 230, 231, 235–249, 251, 253–265, 267, 272, 284, 317, 321–324, 328, 330–332
tabāshīr, 222
tadbīr, 9, 178, 181, 328, see also administration
al-tadhallul, 26, see also humility
tadhkira (recollection), 90
tafsīr, 9, 33, 42, 78, 98, 116, 178, 181, 232, 233, 244, 277, 304, 305, 331, see also tafsīr
Tafsīr al-Jalālayn (commentary), 116, 235, 236, 238
ṭāghī (tyrant), 195
ṭāghūt (tyrant), 142, 239, 240, 242
Tahdhīb al-aḥkām (treatise), 185
taḥrīm, 185, 259
taḥsīniyyāt, 255
tajriba, 200
takālīf (obligations), 115
ṭalāq, 184, see also divorce
Talmud, 49, 230
ṭarīqa, 100, 101, 167, 257, 274, 281
taṣawwuf, 167, 256, see also Sufism
taṣdīq (inducing truthfulness), 149
al-tawḥīd, 45, 241, 274, see also divine Oneness
taxes, 9, 23, 26, 42, 72, 74, 100, 108, 116, 121–124, 132–136, 143, 145, 151, 153, 155, 160–163, 189, 197–212, 216, 219–222, 228, 247, 249, 253, 267, 279, 280, 283, 291, 292, 296, 324, 327, 329, 330
taʾdīb, 201
taʾrīkh, 9, 172, 178, 181, 212, 213, 217, 330, see also History
Thābit, Zayd b., 6, 59, 83, 156, 157, 232
Thamūd, 45, 88, 212
The History of the Qurʾān (book), 62
The Meaning and End of Religion (book), 20
The Practice of Everyday Life (book), 12, 15
The rebellious, 73, 74, 196, 263
The Seven: Concerning the Readings (book), 59
The spirit, 245, 275, 281, 282
The Wretched of the Earth (book), 299
theologians, 102, 206, 262, 264, 272, 319, 335, see also mutakallimūna
those possessing knowledge, 3, 4, 22, 46, 192, see also al-ʿulamā
those who fulfil their obligations, 27, 73, 77, 83, 138, 162, 173, 201, 256, see also al-muttaqīna
Thrasher, John, 128, 129
al-ṭibb, 200, see also medicine
al-Tibyān fī tafsīr al-Qurʾān (commentary), 235
al-Tirmidhī, 186, 188, 261
al-Tirmidhī, al-Ḥakīm, 161, 162, 164, 257
Torah, 26, 27, 45, 69, 72, 77, 84, 135, 138, 148, 237, 249, 255, 256, 262, 269
traditionalists, 205, 206
tribes, 26, 141, 143, 150, 151, 152, 153, 172, 213, 216, 217, 242
Trinitarian, 153, 262, 267, 270
Trinity, 49, 153, 270, 271, 334
True right, 27, 69, 108, 124, 125, 131, 138, 166, 167, 171, 175, 187, 192, 196, 199, 202, 204, 207, 209, 216, 250, 256, 274, 285, 322, 324, 325
al-Ṭūfī, 254
ṭuruq, 100, 167, 176, 186, 286, see also methods
al-Ṭūsī, Muḥammad b. al-Ḥasan, 113, 115, 117, 185, 235, 236, 238, 240, 242
Twelver Shīʿa, 158, 159, 185, 256, 273
Twelver Shīʿīsm, 186, 224, 273, 297, see also Twelver Shīʿa

U

al-ʿulamā, 3, 4, 22, 46, 161, 170, 192, 238, see also those possessing knowledge
ʿUmayr, Muṣʿab b., 150

Umayyad (dynasty), 25, 52, 56, 144, 154, 158, 159, 176, 195, 203, 212, 270, 308, 329
al-umma, 202, 259, see also political community
Unbelievers, 71, 72, see also al-mushrikūna
Unity of Being, 276
Universal Declaration of Human Rights (UDHR), 104, 105, 107, 117, 118, 120, 300, 306, 323
Uriya, 195
al-ʿUrwa al-wuthqā (magazine), 25, 29, 112
USA, 18
uṣūl al-fiqh, 4, 161, 178, 181, 232, 241, 244, 248, 250, 251, 253, 331, see also hermeneutics
usury, 133, 134
ʿUtba, al-Walīd b., 144, 145
ʿUthmānic script, 6, 56, 58, 59, 60, 83
Utrecht University, 308

V
Vali, Abbas, 121, 122
Vatican (city), 298
velāyat-e faqīh, 298
Versteegh, Kees, 33, 38, 44, 181, 182, 232, 233, 269
Vishanoff, David R, 4, 250, 251
voidable contracts, 125, 139, 197, 200, see also ijāra fāsida
Voltaire, 302, 310

W
waʿd wa waʿīd, 87, 89
waḥy, 43, 201, 245, 308
walāya, 74, 100, 139, 160–169, 176, 186, 192, 256, 257, 270, 271, 279, 326, 333, see also Protective governorship
Waldron, Jeremy, 168, 170, 173
al-Walīd, Khālid b., 239
walīs, 136, 161, 167, 170, 270, 333, 334, see also governors
waqf, 122, 257, 292
Waraqa, 148
Washington (city), 311
waterways, 124, 136, 208, 209
Watson, Andrew, 122–124, 127, 129, 177, 208, 231, 325
Weber, Max, 41
Weiss, Bernard, 81, 93, 102, 103, 136, 146, 244, 264, 332, 333
welfare tax, 132–136, 151, 162, 189, 247, see also al-zakāt
Wittgenstein, Ludwig, 40
written promise, 88
written tablets, 88
al-wulāt, 241, see also governors

Y
al-yahūd, 151, 152, see also Jews
al-Yaʿqūbī, 98, 99
Yathrib (city), 144, 150, 151, 152, see also Medina
al-yawm al-ākhir, 263, see also Furthest Day
yawm al-ḥisāb, 196, see also Day of the Account
Yemen, 56, 141, 213, 231, 233
YHWH, 21

Z
zabūr, 172, 213–216, 330, see also Psalms, and genealogical records
Ẓāhirī, 251
zakāt, 108, 132, 133, 134, 163, 249, see also welfare tax
al-Zamakhsharī, 61, 113, 115, 235, 236, 238, 241, 242
zamān, 212, 274
Zamzam (well), 142
Zanādiqa, 193, 262
Zoroastrians, 26, 160, 262, see also al-mājūs
Zubaida, Sami, 291
al-Zubayr, ʿUrwa b., 58, 140, 151, 184
zuhd (renunciation), 222
al-Zuhrī, Ibn Shihāb, 58, 140
ẓulm, 164, 190, 287, 295
ẓulumāt, 44, 171

www.ingramcontent.com/pod-product-compliance
Lightning Source LLC
Chambersburg PA
CBHW050834230426
43667CB00012B/1998
9781781791714